TODAY'S
BEST
NONFICTION

TODAY'S
BEST
NONFICTION

THE READER'S DIGEST ASSOCIATION, INC.
PLEASANTVILLE, NEW YORK

TODAY'S BEST NONFICTION

Editor-in-Chief: Barbara J. Morgan
Executive Editor: Tanis H. Erdmann
Senior Managing Editor: Marjorie Palmer
Managing Editors: Jean E. Aptakin, Thomas Froncek,
Herbert H. Lieberman, Joseph P. McGrath, James J. Menick
Senior Staff Editors: Anne H. Atwater, Thomas S. Clemmons,
Maureen A. Mackey, Angela H. Plowden-Wardlaw, John R. Roberson,
Ray Sipherd
Senior Editors: Dana Adkins, M. Tracy Brigden, Catherine T. Brown,
Linn Carl
Senior Associate Editors: Christopher W. Davis, Catharine L. Edmonds,
Ainslie Gilligan
Associate Editors: Julie S. Beaman, James R. Gullickson, Barbara M. Harrington,
Paula Marchese
Senior Staff Copy Editors: Maxine Bartow, Jeane Garment, Jane F. Neighbors
Senior Copy Editors: Claire A. Bedolis, Rosalind H. Campbell,
Marilyn J. Knowlton
Senior Associate Copy Editors: Jean S. Friedman, Jeanette Gingold,
Daphne Hougham, Tatiana Ivanow, Charles Pendergast, Miriam Schneir
Associate Copy Editors: Fay H. Ahuja, Barbara Booth, Peter E. Murphy
Editorial Administrator: Ann M. Dougher
Art Director: Angelo Perrone
Executive Art Editors: William Gregory, Soren Noring
Art Editor: George Calas, Jr.
Senior Associate Art Editor: Katherine Kelleher
Assistant Art Editors: Marcelline Lowery, Todd D. Victor
Director, Book Rights: Virginia Rice

INTERNATIONAL EDITIONS

Executive Editor: Gary Q. Arpin
Associate Editors: Bonnie Grande, Eva C. Jaunzems, Antonius L. Koster

The condensations in this volume have been created by The Reader's Digest Association, Inc., by special arrangement with the publishers, authors, or other holders of copyrights. Letters, documents, court testimony, etc. may have been edited for space.

The original editions of the books in this volume are published and copyrighted as follows:

The Commanders, published at $24.95 by Simon and Schuster
© 1991 by Bob Woodward

Inside Out: An Insider's Account of Wall Street, published at $22.95 by
G. P. Putnam's Sons
© 1991 by Dennis B. Levine

Henry and Clare: An Intimate Portrait of the Luces, published at $24.95 by
G. P. Putnam's Sons
© 1991 by Bandwagon, Inc.

There Are No Children Here, published at $21.95 by Doubleday, a division of
Bantam Doubleday Dell Publishing Group, Inc.
© 1991 by Alex Kotlowitz

Contents

The COMMANDERS
BOB WOODWARD

. . . Bush returned from Camp David and stepped off his helicopter onto the White House lawn.

"Are you going to move militarily?" he was asked by one reporter.

"I will not discuss what my options are or might be, but they're wide open, I can assure you." Bush was clearly angered. "Iraq lied once again." Waving his finger, growing visibly hot, he said, "I view very seriously our determination to reverse out this aggression. This will not stand, this aggression against Kuwait."

Powell marveled at the distance Bush had traveled in three days. To Powell it was almost as if the President had six-shooters in both hands and he was blazing away.

—*The Commanders*

Overleaf, the commanders (left to right): General Maxwell R. Thurman, commander of the U.S. Southern Command; Lieutenant General Thomas W. Kelly, operations director for the Joint Chiefs of Staff; General H. Norman Schwarzkopf, commander of the U.S. Central Command; Admiral William J. Crowe, Jr., former Chairman of the Joint Chiefs of Staff; Dick Cheney, Secretary of Defense; Brent Scowcroft, national security adviser; General Colin L. Powell, Chairman of the Joint Chiefs of Staff; James A. Baker III, Secretary of State; (bottom) President George Bush

A NOTE TO THE READER

THIS is an account of U.S. military decision making during the 800 days from November 8, 1988, when George Bush was elected President, through January 16, 1991, the beginning of the Persian Gulf War.

I initially planned to focus on the military and civilian leadership of the Pentagon, headquarters for one of the world's largest enterprises—the modern American defense establishment. I had worked in the Pentagon for a year in 1969–70 as a 26-year-old navy lieutenant. Few can serve in that unique five-sided structure, with its 23,000 employees, its maze of floors, corridors, rings, and offices—or even visit as a tourist—and not wonder how it all fits together.

Eighteen years later I was still curious.

My initial research emphasized the Pentagon under Bush, but I also did extensive interviewing with former Secretaries of Defense and other former senior officials going back as far as the Kennedy administration. The fast-approaching end of the cold war suggested it could be a quiet time for the military, an opportunity for me to try to understand the Defense Department's subtle intricacies.

The December 1989 Panama invasion and, more important, the 1990 Gulf crisis changed all that. The military was not going to play a smaller role in the new world, as some had expected. It was moving to center stage. After the brief Panama operation I spent months piecing together the meetings and decision points leading up to it. From the time of the Iraqi invasion of Kuwait, in August 1990, I concentrated on the evolution of the Persian Gulf crisis and the decision to go to war against Saddam Hussein.

Nearly all the information comes from interviews with people directly involved in the decisions. More than 400 people were interviewed over the course of 27 months. The key sources were administration and Pentagon officials, both civilian and military. President Bush was not interviewed. Many key participants were interviewed repeatedly, some on a regular basis as events unfolded. Several were interviewed two dozen to three dozen times. I interviewed one important source 40 times, sometimes in a rushed four-minute phone call during a crisis, at other times in freewheeling one-hour conversations.

Direct quotations from meetings or conversations come from at least one participant who specifically recalled or took notes on what was said. Quotation marks are not used when the sources were unsure about the exact wording.

Thoughts, beliefs, and conclusions attributed to a participant come from that individual or from a source who gained knowledge of them directly from that person. I've tried wherever possible to preserve the language the participants themselves used to describe meetings, attitudes, and emotions. Nearly all the interviews were conducted under journalistic ground rules of deep background, meaning the sources provided the information with the understanding that they would not be identified by name or title.

The more I learned about the military through this project, the more it was apparent that the Pentagon is not always the center of military decision making. The building's top civilian and military officials can have a great, even dominant, role in the process when the attention of the White House is turned elsewhere. This was largely the case in the months prior to the Panama operation, though the President, as Commander in Chief, ultimately made the decision to invade.

The Persian Gulf crisis was different. President Bush and his White House staff devoted great attention to it from the outset, managing the crisis from Pennsylvania Avenue. When the President and his advisers are engaged, they run the show.

So this is not a book about the Pentagon; it is not about most of the things the military does. It is about how the United States decides to fight its wars before shots are fired. The main setting is Washington; the main action, the tug-and-pull among the players in the process.

Over the first two years of his administration President Bush and his close advisers made a series of important, at times momentous, choices about the military. The choices and the process deserve scrupulous examination even at this early date. The decision to go to war is one that defines a nation, both to the world and, perhaps more important, to itself. There is no more serious business for a national government, no more accurate measure of national leadership.

—Bob Woodward, March 14, 1991

PROLOGUE

THE retired Chairman of the Joint Chiefs of Staff, Admiral William J. Crowe, Jr., hurried through security at the Pentagon's River Entrance in the early afternoon of Tuesday, November 27, 1990. He was late for a private 1:00 p.m. lunch with his successor, army general Colin L. Powell. As soon as he entered the building, Crowe felt the Pentagon's familiar, oppressive atmosphere—the colonels, bursting with self-importance, rushing around the E-Ring, the outermost corridor. It was a building dedicated to appearing busy, he thought.

Wheeling to the right, he slipped into the first doorway, room 2E878, the office of the Chairman. He passed through a reception area and entered the room where he'd worked for four years until Powell had taken over from him, 14 months earlier.

At 53, Powell was the youngest Chairman in history, and the first black to hold the post. He usually conveyed a sense of energy and stamina, but today he looked tired.

The general had redecorated. New windows offered a magnificent view across the Potomac River to the monuments. There was a rich blue carpet and a comfortable couch and matching upholstered chair.

As they sat down at a small antique table set for lunch Powell joked that he wished he'd never accepted the job. Why didn't you warn me? he asked.

Crowe knew he didn't mean it for a minute. It was the classic, transparent lament of a man who loves being at the top.

A steward from the Chairman's mess, in a bright yellow jacket, took their orders. Both chose light lunches.

In the previous four months Powell had overseen the largest American military deployment since Vietnam. Some 230,000 U.S. military men and women had already been sent to the Persian Gulf as part of Operation Desert Shield, following Iraq's invasion and takeover of Kuwait. Three weeks earlier President Bush had announced his decision to nearly double the troop strength, to give himself the option of using offensive force to expel Iraq from Kuwait. The decision had set off a fierce debate, and the national consensus that had been supporting Bush now seemed to be unraveling.

"I hear you're going to testify," Powell had said when he called Crowe the previous week to invite him to lunch. Crowe had agreed to give public testimony on the Gulf crisis before the Senate Armed Services Committee, chaired by Sam Nunn, the Georgia Democrat.

Although he had supported Bush's initial deployment of forces to defend Saudi Arabia from Iraq, Nunn had publicly criticized the decision to create an offensive military capability. He was demanding to know how Bush had determined that it was in the vital interest of the United States to liberate Kuwait. What was the hurry? Why not give the unprecedented United Nations economic sanctions, which had shut down trade between Iraq and most of the world, time to work?

Crowe now recounted how he had been traveling around the country and had heard serious doubts raised about whether the liberation of Kuwait was worth a war. There was great concern in the country about the prospect, duration, objectives, and necessity of war.

Yeah, I have detected the same thing, Powell confided.

Crowe's guard went up. Over the years he'd watched Powell operate up close, especially in 1988, when Powell was Reagan's national security adviser. Powell had a tendency to read people and then tell them in a very general and circumspect way what he thought they wanted to hear, Crowe thought.

Despite the President's statements that he did not want war, Crowe felt that Bush was too anxious to throw thousands of troops into combat. One was Crowe's son, Blake, a marine captain commanding a company of 200 in the Saudi Arabian desert.

"Everyone is so *impatient*." Crowe said some seemed to think the U.S. military had trained its soldiers for combat and hostile fire, but not to be patient and wait. Patience had paid off handsomely in the cold war. Waiting out the Soviet Union for 40 years would be marked as one of the great victories of all time. Why can't we think in the long term? he asked. A war in the Middle East—killing thousands of Arabs for whatever noble purpose—would set back the United States in the region for a long time. And that was to say nothing of the Americans who might die. War is messy and uncertain, he said.

Powell neither agreed nor disagreed. He listened, nodded, and seemed to encourage Crowe to go on.

Where is Cheney on this? Crowe asked. Secretary of Defense Dick Cheney was Powell's immediate boss.

"Beats me," Powell replied.

What does that mean? Crowe asked, lowering his voice.

"He holds his cards pretty close, as you know," Powell replied.

Crowe knew that, indeed. His last six months as Chairman had coincided with Cheney's first six as Secretary. He'd seen how unrevealing Cheney usually was.

Cheney comes back from the White House, from meetings with Bush, and tells nothing, Powell said.

Imagine, Crowe reflected to himself, the Chairman of the Joint Chiefs of Staff not knowing where the Secretary of Defense stands on the most important military and foreign policy decision of the day.

Where are you on the Gulf deployment? Crowe inquired.

"I've been for a containment strategy," Powell replied, "but it hasn't been selling around here or over there." He pointed out the window, north across the river toward the White House.

To a military man like Crowe, containment had a definite meaning—standing firm to resist further advances by an opponent. In this case it would mean keeping the economic sanctions and the diplomatic pressure on Iraqi President Saddam Hussein without attacking him, with the hope of eventually forcing him to withdraw from Kuwait. It was something very different from President Bush's decision to double the forces to provide an offensive option.

Powell said he had been trying to keep the administration tamped down, attempting to dampen any enthusiasm for war.

Crowe grasped the problem. The Bush administration was presenting itself publicly as one happy team marching in unison. If Powell was being honest, he disagreed with Bush to some degree and might have a genuine moral dilemma on his hands. The law designated the Chairman as the "principal military adviser" to the President, Secretary of Defense, and National Security Council. It directed him to give "the range of military advice and opinion." Had Powell told Bush what he thought about containment? Would Bush tolerate a Chairman who had a fundamental disagreement with administration policy? From his nine months in the Bush administration Crowe knew its obsession with consensus and with loyalty to the President and his positions.

Crowe believed that the Chairman had to give more than military advice. For a presidential adviser—the principal military adviser—to talk only about the military at White House meetings was a sterile exercise. Those who disagreed with him would tell the President, That's just military advice, but when you factor in the political, diplomatic, and economic recommendations, here's what you ought to do.

No. Powell had to give his overall policy advice. If it was rejected, he could choose to resign or stay on and accept the decision. There was no way around giving advice direct and undiluted.

Crowe had no notion what Powell had done. But God, he wanted to believe that he had presented his thoughts fully. He had never felt more empathy for Powell or put so much hope in him.

"I've been thinking," Crowe said. "It takes two things to be a great President, and I ought to tell you, because you may be President someday."

"No, no," Powell said insistently, dismissing the reference to his political prospects—a subject of endless media forecasting.

"Yes, you may, and I want to tell you. First, to be a great President, you have to have a war. All the great Presidents have had their wars."

Laughing, Powell acknowledged the truth of the statement.

"Two, you have to find a war where you are attacked."

Powell nodded in agreement.

Crowe could see Powell understood him.

When they finished their meal, Crowe thanked Powell for lunch, and left.

AFTER the lunch Powell concluded that the Bush administration was probably in for a mild blast from Crowe's testimony the next day. He generally found Crowe's musings thoughtful but often somewhat abstract. Crowe had taken an intellectual's approach to the chairmanship. He had bequeathed Powell a Joint Staff that operated as a think tank—hesitant, inclined to debate. Powell had remade it in his own image, transforming it into an action staff that got things done.

As far as the Gulf operation was concerned, Powell had given up pushing containment. He had his orders now. Bush had decided unequivocally to build the offensive option. Powell had thrown himself into preparing as effective an offensive force as possible.

He recalled vividly his efforts to present all the options in the Gulf—including containment of Iraq—to the President, to make sure all possibilities had been considered. It had been hard.

The previous month Powell had written himself some notes laying out the arguments for containment. Several times he had used the term strangulation, a more active word than containment. It referred to the U.N.-mandated blockade of Iraq and all the other allied measures that were putting the squeeze on Saddam. He'd taken these notes and the argument to Cheney—twice. Then to the national security adviser, Brent Scowcroft, and to Secretary of State James A. Baker III.

One Friday afternoon in early October, 1990, Cheney finally had said to Powell, "Why don't you come over with me, and we'll see what the man thinks about your idea." Cheney had a private Oval Office meeting scheduled that day with the President. This was time reserved for the key Cabinet members—the big guys, as Powell called them. Normally he was not included.

Cheney and Powell had gone to the Oval Office to see Bush and Scowcroft. The sun was streaming in. For some reason the atmosphere wasn't right. There were interruptions; the mood was too relaxed, too convivial. Feet were up on the table, cowboy boots gleaming. Powell preferred the formality of the Situation Room, where Bush could stay focused. Still, he plunged ahead.

To achieve the policy of forcing Saddam out of Kuwait, Powell told Bush, there are two courses of action. One, build up the forces for an offensive option. Two, containment, which would take longer.

"There is a case for the containment, or strangulation, policy," he told the President, "if you do not want to make more military investment." The force level associated with containment was what they would reach by December 1—about 230,000 troops. Saddam would be fully boxed in. Containment would grind him down.

"It may take a year—it may take two years—but it will work someday." Powell tried to adopt the tone of an advocate. His hands were in the air, emphasizing his points; he spoke with conviction. But he did not say that containment was his personal recommendation.

In military terms, Powell said, he could live with either containment or an offensive option.

The others, Cheney and Scowcroft, had a few questions. No one, including the President, embraced containment. If only one of them had, Powell was prepared to say that he favored it. But no one tried to pin him down. No one asked him for his overall opinion.

"Where do you want to go, Mr. President?" Powell finally asked. "As each week goes by, there are more and more troops going in."

"I don't think there's time politically for that strategy," Bush said, referring to containment.

Powell took this to mean the President hadn't made his mind up completely. He felt that Bush had not yet fully shot down containment.

Afterward Powell's conscience was clear. He'd presented the military implications of each choice. There was only so much he could do.

PART ONE

1

WEDNESDAY, November 9, 1988. Powell, then a three-star general and the national security adviser to President Reagan, stepped briskly along one of the narrow carpeted hallways in the West Wing of the White House. He was heading toward his spacious corner office, perhaps the second most prestigious in the White House and a nerve center formerly inhabited by the likes of Henry Kissinger.

It was about 4:00 p.m. Vice President George Bush was in the hall outside his own small West Wing office. The day before, Bush had been elected President. A Rose Garden ceremony welcoming him back to the White House had just ended, and he was saying hello and shaking hands, all jittery enthusiasm. He spotted Powell.

"Come on in here," Bush said. "Tell me what's going on." He drew Powell into the vice-presidential office. By both title and temperament Powell was information central on world events, often the first within the upper ranks of the White House to know the latest, whether it was a developing crisis or the freshest high-grade foreign affairs gossip.

Congratulating Bush, Powell flashed a broad, confident smile.

The Bush administration-to-be was already taking shape. That morning Bush had announced his first Cabinet appointment, naming his campaign manager and old Texas friend Jim Baker as

Secretary of State. Baker was seen as the Bush insider to watch.

Bush asked about Powell. What were his plans? Where might he fit?

"Mr. Vice President," Powell said, "you have got a lot more on your hands and on your mind than me."

Bush had three specific suggestions. Would Powell like to stay on as national security adviser for, say, six months while he figured out what he wanted to do next? Or would he like a different, permanent position in the Bush administration? Bush suggested director of the Central Intelligence Agency. Or how about becoming Baker's number two at the State Department, a key post in foreign affairs? Exciting and important times are coming, Bush said.

Powell noted that the army was his chosen career and that he had the opportunity to stay in. Also he was considering some offers to leave government to make some money. He was flattered by Bush's offers and would consider them. As Bush would understand, he was at an important crossroads.

Bush, who had changed jobs more than most, indicated he understood completely.

Powell said he would get back to him. Congratulations again.

ONE thing was clear to Powell. The offer to stay on in his current post for a few months was merely a courtesy. It meant, I don't want you to be my permanent national security adviser.

Powell later took out a piece of paper and listed the reasons to stay in government and the reasons to get out. The only argument favoring departure from public service was money, and money didn't interest him particularly. The offers to head the CIA or to be number two at State had to be weighed. It would be a demotion to go from the security adviser's post, coordinating all foreign and defense policy issues, to the number two slot at State, responsible for managing the bureaucracy. And in most respects the security adviser was more powerful than the CIA director.

Powell had another problem. He felt uneasy about the man who was about to become President.

Unlike Powell himself, who had been the consummate administration insider, Bush was a stepchild in the Reagan White House. Though more in the loop than most Vice Presidents, he was nevertheless not a player. Bush and Powell had built no bond of loyalty, and as Powell knew, personal alliances were everything with Bush.

Powell was also troubled by the way the Bush presidential campaign had been run. The race-baiting Willie Horton television commercial especially bothered him. Horton, a black first-degree murderer, had been given a weekend pass from a Massachusetts prison when Bush's Democratic opponent, Michael Dukakis, was governor. While on furlough Horton stabbed a white man and raped a white woman. Did the people around Bush believe that stuff belonged in the campaign?

Powell sought out his good friend Richard L. Armitage, the outgoing assistant secretary of defense for international security affairs. Burly and intense, Armitage knew that Powell's charm and offhandedness hid his competitiveness and ambition. Don't go to the State Department as number two, Armitage advised. You should be the Secretary. The CIA is not your image. It is demoralized and run down.

Let things shake out, Armitage recommended.

Powell had taken care to ensure that he could return to the army. Before the election he'd gone to see his friend and mentor General Carl Vuono, the army Chief of Staff. Vuono, who controlled army promotions and assignments, was a meaty, happy-go-lucky West Point graduate, with dark Mediterranean eyes, who had known Powell since they'd worked together as junior officers in the Pentagon.

Vuono urged Powell to do what would make him and his wife, Alma, happy. If Powell wanted to come back, there would be a slot open: promotion to a fourth star to head the Forces Command. This was the nation's strategic reserve of some 1 million land forces—most in the National Guard and reserves. While it was not a glamorous assignment, it would make Powell one of the ten commanders in chief (C in Cs, pronounced "sinks") of U.S. military forces and war-fighting units worldwide. It was an important ticket to punch, and it would put him in line to succeed Vuono as army chief.

Powell considered himself a soldier first. Beginning in 1958, he had spent 14 years as a garden-variety infantry officer, without a West Point ring or any other reason to think he was on a fast track. As a young officer he wasn't particularly dedicated to the army. His plan was to stick it out for 20 years and retire with a 50 percent pension.

His introduction to the upper reaches of government came in 1972. That year he was chosen for the prestigious White House Fellows program, which gives young military officers and other professionals a taste of the executive branch for one year. In 1977 he went to the Pentagon as military assistant to the deputy secretary of defense.

His four years in that job, and then three as military assistant to Secretary of Defense Caspar Weinberger, were a chance to see the top military leadership up close. He had a notion that a new, more worldly brand of senior officer could be more useful to the Secretary and the President. The Joint Chiefs of Staff, the top uniformed echelon, were too insulated from the outside world, not sufficiently able or inclined to assess the political aspects of defense decisions. They also tended to be inept at public relations. Yet politics and public relations were the arenas in which the Secretary flourished or failed.

Now, in November 1988, Powell decided he had better stay in the army. It was home, and the prospect of four stars had a certain mystique. He went to see Bush, thanked him for the offers, and said he wanted to move on. "Out with the old and in with the new," Powell said. He knew the rules. The President picked his own team.

The President-elect accepted his decision without argument.

Powell knew he was in for a different kind of life down in Atlanta, where Forces Command had its headquarters. As security adviser he'd felt a constant sense of risk. President Reagan had delegated an enormous part of his responsibility to his staff. Powell found that if he told Reagan he didn't have to worry about something, the President would soon be happily gazing out the window into the Rose Garden. Although Powell was on two medications for high blood pressure, he had enjoyed that risky, stressful existence.

His fourth-star promotion went through without delay.

On November 23, 1988, Bush made the surprise announcement that retired air force lieutenant general Brent Scowcroft would be his national security adviser, replacing Powell.

Brent Scowcroft had been a low-profile presence in top national security circles for two decades. He'd started as Henry Kissinger's deputy national security adviser, moved up to the security adviser's post under President Ford (when Bush was CIA director), and then worked on various presidential commissions and as a highly paid international consultant at Kissinger Associates. He tended to stay in the background as a mirror and implementer of the President's views.

Balding and slight, the 63-year-old Scowcroft was a Mormon who avoided the Washington social scene and had a priestlike dedication to his work. His idea of recreation was attending seminars on arms control, a subject he loved in all its obscure detail. He had once spent an hour and a half refereeing a debate over a single phrase proposed for a blue-ribbon commission report on strategic missiles.

Although he'd had many close ties to the Reagan administration, in private Scowcroft had been a scathing critic of its foreign and military policy. He thought that under Reagan the United States had first taken a naïve and foolish hard-line approach to the Soviet Union, then rushed blindly into Mikhail Gorbachev's arms. And he believed that the Reagan national security team had failed to compensate for their boss's inadequacy and romanticism in the realm of foreign affairs.

Scowcroft's differences with the Reagan line were well known. His return as national security adviser was a clear signal that Bush intended to cut a new path in defense and foreign policy.

In a press conference on the morning of December 16, 1988, Bush announced his selection of John Tower, the former Texas Senator, as his nominee to be Secretary of Defense.

Craig Fuller, Bush's vice-presidential chief of staff, watched in dismay. Along with Treasury Secretary Nicholas Brady, a longtime Bush friend, and Bush pollster Robert Teeter he had run an unsuccessful behind-the-scenes campaign to derail the Tower nomination. Fuller and Teeter were worried about Tower's reputation as a heavy drinker and womanizer. Brady disliked Tower personally. The three had failed to come up with a consensus alternative.

During one discussion with Fuller, Bush had said that Tower had been there "in good times and bad times." He had come to Houston in 1968, when Congressman Bush was in reelection trouble because of a vote for fair-housing legislation, and had defended Bush to important conservatives. He had been one of the first senior Republicans to come out for Bush's 1988 presidential bid. Fuller knew loyalty was a core value for Bush, and there was no budging him.

But by early February, 1989, just weeks into the Bush administration, the Tower nomination was in serious trouble. Rumors about Tower's drinking habits and personal life were popping up everywhere. There were stories of alcohol abuse during his Senate years.

On February 23 Senator Sam Nunn's Armed Services Committee

voted 11–9, along straight party lines, to recommend that the Senate reject the nomination.

Across town at his official residence, high up on Observatory Hill, Bush's Vice President, Dan Quayle, had two visitors that night—his friends and fellow Republican conservatives Ken Adelman and Dick Cheney. Adelman, a cocky 42-year-old Shakespeare scholar, had headed the Arms Control and Disarmament Agency under Reagan and now wrote a nationally syndicated newspaper column. Cheney had been President Ford's White House chief of staff and was now Wyoming's sole member of the House of Representatives.

Soft-spoken and serious, Cheney had an impeccably conservative voting record. Though he was only 48, his eyeglasses, thinning hair, and calm and reasonable demeanor gave him an older, wiser look. He had risen from freshman Congressman to House Republican whip, the second-ranking party leader, in only ten years.

Quayle blamed conservatives for abandoning the good fight on Tower. "God damn, we have got to get this man confirmed," he said.

"Don't put me on the team to do it," said Adelman.

"Tower's down the tubes," Cheney said flatly. "You've got to get someone to work with Congress."

On March 9 the Senate rejected the Tower nomination, 53–47.

THAT afternoon Dick Cheney received a call from John Sununu, the 50-year-old former New Hampshire governor whom Bush had chosen to be his chief of staff. Could Cheney come to the White House at 4:00 p.m.? Sununu wanted to talk about what to do now that Tower was going down in flames. Cheney said he could be there at five.

Based on his own experience 14 years earlier as White House chief of staff, Cheney knew it was unlikely that the current chief of staff would be merely soliciting the opinion of the second-ranking House Republican in the heat of a nomination decision controlled by Senate Democrats. Something was up.

At 5:00 p.m. Cheney arrived at his old corner White House chief of staff's office, now Sununu's. Scowcroft was also there. The three talked about Tower's defeat and about what should be done next.

"If the President offered you the Secretary of Defense post, would you consider it?" Sununu asked.

Cheney said he would.

Scowcroft asked Cheney about his health.

Cheney had had three heart attacks. The previous August he had undergone a quadruple coronary bypass. Cheney said he had had the operation not because it was medically necessary but because he wanted to continue backpacking and skiing. His doctor had given him a clean bill of health and would supply records and a statement.

They all agreed that Cheney should have a night to sleep on this. He needed to consult with his family.

Scowcroft had been Gerald Ford's national security adviser when Cheney was chief of staff. Running the daily obstacle course of White House business together, they had become close. Now Scowcroft was pushing hard for Cheney for Defense. He wanted a known commodity in the Pentagon.

Jim Baker had already given his support to Cheney. He and Cheney had weathered the 1976 Ford campaign together, with Cheney supervising from the White House end as Baker managed the campaign itself. At the time both had been new to national politics. Their friendship had survived Ford's defeat.

Back at his House office, in the old Cannon office building, Cheney ran into his press secretary, Pete Williams. Williams, 37, a tall, outgoing former Wyoming television reporter, asked how it had gone at the White House. He did not know the purpose of the meeting.

Okay, Cheney said. They were concerned about replacing Tower.

Cheney's administrative assistant Patricia Howe later stuck her head into Cheney's office. "Anything we should know about?"

No.

Cheney and his wife, Lynne, a Ph.D. in English literature who was chairman of the National Endowment for the Humanities, went out for dinner that evening with friends from Wyoming. Walking in the door of their McLean, Virginia, house after dinner, the Cheneys were greeted by their 19-year-old daughter, Mary, home from college on spring break, who said that Jim Baker had called.

Cheney called Baker at once, and they had a long conversation. Baker urged him to take the job as Defense Secretary. Afterward Cheney sat down with Lynne, and they talked it over.

Cheney liked the House of Representatives. After the White House staff years, when his job and future had depended entirely on someone else's political success, he enjoyed being his own man. Cheney also loved the personality of the House—its rough-and-tumble atmosphere and its history and traditions. In 1983 he and Lynne had co-authored an affectionate book about House Speakers from Henry Clay to Sam Rayburn, entitled *Kings of the Hill.*

In his mind he ran through the advantages of the Defense job. He had decided previously that he would not go back to the executive branch unless one of two or three slots opened up. This was one. The Secretary of Defense mattered. And the idea of working with Baker and Scowcroft carried great weight. In the Ford years Cheney had seen how the national security process could get mired down in useless infighting and power plays. Here was a chance to work with people he knew, and possibly to get it right.

Cheney decided if the job was offered, he would accept.

The next morning Cheney discussed with his staff the usual array of subjects important to Wyoming's sole Congressman—irrigation, weeds, pests, and the fires in Yellowstone National Park that summer. A call then came in from Sununu. The staff left the room so Cheney could talk in private.

Cheney told the chief of staff he wanted to go to the next step. Sununu said, Come to the White House about noon.

When it was time, Cheney had the driver of his official whip's car go to the East Wing—the social and First Lady's entrance—so he would not be noticed by the media people on the alert for a new Defense play by the President. He entered an office the President had set up in the second-floor residence. He and Bush talked about Defense and the reforms that Bush thought were needed.

After half an hour Sununu joined them. "If the President asked you to be Secretary of Defense," Sununu asked, "would you accept?" This conditional offer protected the President from a turndown.

"Yes, sir, I would," Cheney replied.

The three talked some more. The job was not formally offered.

When Cheney arrived back at his office, the FBI had been there for a background investigation. A few minutes later Bush called.

Let's do it, Bush said.

Okay, Mr. President.

Bush said he wanted to announce it right away. At 4:00 p.m. Bush and Cheney appeared before reporters. It seemed to Cheney that Bush took great delight in springing his unexpected nominee on the press.

PETE WILLIAMS HAD BEEN AT A briefing on acid rain, a big issue in Wyoming. Since it was a nice Friday afternoon, he hoped to sneak out of work early. Arriving back at his office, however, he was amazed to find a large stack of phone messages. Odd, he thought. What could be happening? The other staffers had to tell him three times before it sank in. He glanced up at his television set, tuned to CNN. There was Bush with Cheney, the new Secretary of Defense–designate.

At about 5:30 Cheney returned to the office. Congratulations were barely out when FBI agents entered, a few paces behind. Cheney took them into his office and closed the door.

Williams finally got hold of Cheney, and the two of them sat down in a quiet corner. "Why have you done this?" Williams asked, his voice full of bafflement. But Williams knew it was classic Cheney—he had been told not to mention it to anyone, so he hadn't.

"When the President of the United States looks at you . . ." Cheney began.

Williams thought to himself, Oh, come on, don't give me this crap.

Cheney continued on about the power of a presidential request, the honor of presidential service. He said he wanted the administration to succeed and was looking forward to working again with Scowcroft and Baker, who had said, "We need you."

Williams realized it was those two, the old ties, that had been decisive, much more than Bush.

Even to his closest aides Cheney was something of an enigma. If they asked him something specific, he generally would give an answer, but he was not one to relax and unburden himself to others. Talking about himself and his feelings did not come naturally.

One subject Cheney didn't talk much about was his time at Yale. In the first or second year he had taken six months off to be a laborer and power-line worker in Wyoming. He returned to New Haven, but by the end of sophomore year he was gone for good. Cheney would joke with his staff about his academic problems, but he had never shared the full story of his lackluster academic career at Yale.

He received a bachelor's degree in 1965 from the University of Wyoming, followed the next year by a master's in political science. He and Lynne, whom he married in 1964, were both Ph.D. candidates at the University of Wisconsin in 1968, when Cheney won a one-year fellowship that brought him to Washington to work as a Capitol Hill staffer. While on the Hill he was noticed by Donald Rumsfeld, director of President Richard Nixon's Office of Economic Opportunity, who had given him a job. When Ford named Rumsfeld his chief of staff, in 1974, he brought Cheney to the White House as deputy, and Cheney's career took off.

Cheney's staffer and former Yale classmate Alan Kranowitz was going to pilot the Defense nomination through the Senate. A long-time Cheney watcher, he knew all about his boss's conservative voting record and pet issues. And Cheney's past seemed easy. He had few financial assets. He had lived in the same house for years and had been married only once. But after a large staff meeting on March 11 Cheney privately told Kranowitz that there were some "youthful indiscretions" that might come up. He had been arrested twice, he said, for drunk driving—both times more than 25 years ago, when he was in his early twenties. And he had been caught fishing out of season once and been fined.

"The twenty-five-dollar fine was not the worst part," Cheney said. "They took my f_____ fish."

ON MARCH 14, 1989, at 2:00 p.m., Cheney, wearing cowboy boots and a business suit, walked across a light green carpet to his seat in a packed Senate hearing room before Sam Nunn's Armed Services Committee. In three hours of questioning, Cheney referred frequently to his past work on intelligence and defense issues, but also admitted that he had to get up to speed in many areas. He explained his military deferments during the Vietnam War: a 2-S student deferment and, after his first daughter was born, a 3-A deferment for parents.

The next day Nunn and Senator John Warner, the ranking committee Republican, reviewed the FBI's background investigation of Cheney and briefed the committee in closed executive session.

"He got fined for fishing out of season," Nunn said. The charges of driving while intoxicated were ancient. Nunn and Warner did not see them as impediments to confirmation. The members agreed.

The next morning the full committee's conclusion was that there was nothing in Cheney's background that "would render him unfit to serve," Nunn said. The few Senators who spoke were enthusiastic. The sense of relief was palpable. The vote to confirm was 20–0.

At 10:50 a.m. March 17, Saint Patrick's Day, Nunn took to the

Senate floor. He said the committee had approved Cheney unanimously "after careful and thorough consideration." The final tally of Senators was 92–0 to confirm.

Cheney had asked his press secretary, Pete Williams, to be the new Pentagon spokesman, and Williams had accepted. After the vote Cheney went over to the Pentagon. Williams and three other aides all piled into the Secretary's limousine, with the red light on top. On the third floor a nameplate emblazoned RICHARD B. CHENEY was already on the door of the Secretary's suite. Williams thought, Now, there's one thing we're going to have to change. He's not a Richard B. kind of guy. He made a mental note to have it changed to DICK.

Inside the office, photos were taken, and Cheney looked pleased.

On Tuesday afternoon, March 21, thousands of civilians and military men and women streamed into the Pentagon's internal courtyard for Cheney's formal swearing-in as the seventeenth Secretary of Defense. President Bush spoke first, delivering a stock speech about peace through strength, reform, teamwork, and opportunity. Cheney was then sworn in by a federal appeals judge.

"It is a humbling experience to assume office," Cheney read from a prepared text, his voice bouncing off the walls. "To the men and women of America's armed forces: I am honored to serve with you in the defense of freedom." Then, departing from the text, he added, "You, our uniformed men and women, are my number one priority."

Later that day Cheney went to the White House to see Sununu and the President's personnel chief, Chase Untermeyer. Sununu—in public a strong opponent of racial and gender quotas—told Cheney the White House wanted 30 percent of the remaining top 42 jobs in the Defense Department to be filled by women or minorities.

CHENEY went to work filling key posts. To run the talent hunt, he brought in Steve Herbits, a 47-year-old Republican political operator. Herbits presented a one-page diagnosis of each of the services and the kinds of civilians Cheney should appoint to run them.

The army, he'd written, was in deep trouble. It was going to take the biggest budget cuts over the next eight years. For secretary of the army Cheney should choose someone who could plan the cuts logically, then beat the s--- out of the generals to implement them.

Herbits said the navy was run by tradition-bound admirals who were defiant of civilian authority and spoke a language outsiders didn't understand. They had to find a secretary who understood the tradition and language, but would not be captured by the admirals.

The air force is totally out of control, Herbits' diagnosis said. The Chief of Staff, General Larry Welch, was disdainful of civilians, and the whole service was cliquish. There was only one way to beat them: brains. They had to find a civilian secretary who knew the air force culture, weapons systems, and habits.

Cheney already knew enough to be wary of the air force.

AIR force chief Larry Welch had a chilly reputation, not just inside the Pentagon but all around Washington. He seemed to emerge with reluctance from the absolute order of his fourth-floor office, where papers, pens, and folders were arranged in perfect stacks and rows.

Welch's manner at congressional hearings left no doubt about his low view of the messy legislative-media arena. But Welch realized he had to accept the congressional role in military issues. One such issue that he thought it was time to resolve was the decade-long debate over how to upgrade the air force's land-based intercontinental ballistic missiles (ICBMs). The Bush White House had put off a decision for the time being, but in Congress a debate had been raging over whether the air force should go with the small missile known as the Midgetman or the larger one called the MX.

Before Cheney's confirmation Welch had gone to acting Secretary William Howard Taft IV. The air force couldn't be silent on this, he told Taft. Congressmen were asking for the air force's position, yet there was no clear administration policy for the service to push. Should we fall off the wagon? Welch had asked. There was no telling what decision the Congress might reach without air force input. He would like to talk to the key members in the House and Senate.

Taft told Welch he was right and that he should go do it. Welch began visiting Hill offices.

George Wilson, the Pentagon correspondent for the Washington *Post,* heard that Welch was making the rounds with a compromise ICBM proposal. The night of March 23 Wilson called Welch, who confirmed that he had been "pulsing the system." A front-page story in the next morning's *Post,* headlined AIR FORCE ACTS TO END ICBM DEADLOCK, reported that Welch had suggested a compromise plan.

Cheney read the story. It was his eighth day in office. He had heard several days earlier that Welch had been trying to make a deal with Les Aspin, chairman of the House Armed Services Committee.

Ever since his time as White House chief of staff Cheney believed that strategic missiles were the President's turf. It wasn't so much the Secretary's business that Welch was trying to do, it was the President's.

Cheney was scheduled that day to give his maiden press conference as Secretary. Dan Howard, the holdover Pentagon spokesman, came in to go over potential questions. Howard said that Cheney was sure to get a question on the *Post* story.

"You've got two choices," Howard said. "You can slide off it or come out swinging."

"My instinct is to cut him off at the knees," Cheney responded.

Howard said that normally he would not agree, but this situation called for strong action. Welch will be pissed off, Howard said, but the damage can be repaired later.

Cheney understood the symbolic importance of first impressions. In the earliest days of his presidency, in 1974, Gerald Ford had been photographed toasting his own English muffin for breakfast. Widely publicized, the photo had set a tone of nonimperial simplicity that endured and boosted Ford's popularity. Now Cheney knew he would be setting his own tone, not just publicly, but in the Pentagon itself.

At noon Welch settled down to watch the first public performance by the new Secretary, a press conference televised live.

The first question was about talk of an ICBM compromise.

"To say that a compromise is near, I think, would be premature," Cheney replied.

The second question was specifically about Welch. "Mr. Secretary," a reporter asked, "General Welch, the Chief of Staff of the air force, apparently has been up on the Hill working this program himself. Is that a change of policy for the Defense Department to have a service chief negotiate his own strategic system?"

"General Welch was free-lancing. He was not speaking for the department. He was obviously up there on his own hook, so to speak."

Cheney was asked if he accepted that sort of action.

"No. I'm not happy with it, frankly," Cheney said, his voice steady. "I think it's inappropriate for a uniformed officer to be in a position where he's in fact negotiating an arrangement. I have not had an opportunity yet to talk to him about it. I've been over at the White House all morning. I will discuss it with him. I'll make known to him my displeasure. Everybody's entitled to one mistake."

Wilson, the *Post* reporter, said now to Cheney that Welch had "made very clear he was not preempting you or the President."

"Good," Cheney replied. "Well, I'm sure he'll make that clear when he talks to me about it." There was laughter in the pressroom.

Welch was stunned. One of the first rules they taught in any beginning military leadership course was that you praised subordinates in public and rebuked them in private. Nothing could be more humiliating or demoralizing than a public scolding. This reprimand had been broadcast to the entire world.

The general took several minutes to compose himself, then walked out of his office and down a flight of stairs to the Secretary's suite.

"I am not a free-lancer," Welch said, standing before Cheney. "I have never been a free-lancer. I support the administration's position and have worked harder than anybody in this town to make it come out the way the administration wants it to."

Cheney said the issue was closed.

Welch saw that he was not going to get an apology. Cheney seemed to want to smooth the issue over. Maybe, Welch thought, Cheney could not afford to backtrack.

Welch tried to convince Cheney that the greatest support he would get in the building would come from the military leadership. Cheney did not want to discuss it further.

Within the military the public dressing-down was known as the shot heard round the world.

2

By THE time Cheney had been in office about a month, Chairman of the Joint Chiefs Admiral Crowe was beginning to see how the inner councils of decision making were going to work under Bush, and he wasn't happy. Much of the discussion at National Security Council (NSC) meetings was political. Decisions were made based on their likely impact on the Congress, the media, and public opinion, and the focus was on managing the reaction.

For all the impressiveness of his title Crowe knew he occupied a tenuous position in the government, and it frustrated him. By law he was the principal military adviser to the President, Secretary of Defense, and NSC—but only an adviser. He commanded no military forces, and technically neither the Chairman nor the four service chiefs of staff were even in the chain of command, which ran from the President to the Secretary of Defense to the C in Cs of the ten major war-fighting commands. The Chairman directly oversaw only the 1600 deskbound officers, drawn from all four services, of the Pentagon-based Joint Staff.

Advice and communications could be pretty thin gruel in a business where real command is the name of the game. And the specific day-to-day demands of the job were feeling more burdensome than ever. Capitol Hill was sometimes a downright ordeal.

Crowe's second two-year term was due to expire at the end of September, 1989, though Bush had asked him to remain for another term. At the end of one of the budget hearings on the Hill, Crowe whispered to an aide, "I'm not going through this one more time." The next day he went to Cheney and said he had decided to retire. Then he went to the White House and sat down with Bush.

Crowe had to finish out the spring and summer, and there were more than a few problems demanding his attention. General Manuel Antonio Noriega, the strongman who ran Panama, was a major irritant. Suspected of involvement in illegal drug trafficking, Noriega ran a notoriously corrupt regime and was viewed as an outlaw and an enemy of U.S. interests. With the strategically important Panama Canal scheduled to pass from U.S. to Panamanian control at the end of the century, and with 12,000 American military personnel and many of their families living in Panama, the Bush administration wanted Noriega out. But Crowe knew that the C in C responsible for Panama (known as C in C South), army general Frederick F. Woerner, Jr., of the Southern Command, had a reputation as a wimp. He was opposed to aggressive U.S. military intervention in Latin America.

On Wednesday, May 10, Crowe was watching the evening television reports on election troubles in Panama. Three days earlier Noriega's handpicked candidates had been soundly defeated, but the general had nullified the election. The opposition candidates, who'd had victory stolen out from under them, had taken to the Via España in

Panama City in a demonstration of honking cars that drew thousands.

In response the so-called Dignity Battalions (or Digbats, as they were known in the Pentagon), paramilitary pro-Noriega units, attacked the opposition candidates. Presidential candidate Guillermo Endara, 52, a 240-pound man with a benign face, was hit in the forehead with an iron bar. The bodyguard of Guillermo "Billy" Ford, a vice-presidential candidate, was shot dead. Ford himself was shown on television as he was struck by a fist. As he staggered out of his car another man swiped at him with a pipe.

This film, and one of Endara in the hospital, ran again and again on American television. The coverage of the chaos in Panama jolted Crowe, who went to the Pentagon that evening. Five inconclusive reports of harassment of U.S. servicemen in Panama had already been received. The Chairman soon received word that he was to be at the White House later that night for a meeting with President Bush and the rest of the national security team.

Crowe was fed up with Panama. Nothing had worked with Noriega—not drug indictments, negotiation, economic sanctions, or CIA covert action. Crowe had balked at using the military to throw Noriega out, and favored limited applications of force in pursuit of well-defined, achievable goals. The goals in Panama were obvious: protection of U.S. citizens and interests, and installation of a friendly democratic government. The question was by what means.

In April 1988 Crowe had General Woerner develop a series of secret contingency plans in case the military had to be used in Panama. They were given the overall code name Prayer Book, though each plan had its own secret name, and included a plan to defend the Panama Canal, a massive plan to take control of Panama City, and a plan to assist the Panamanians in setting up a new government. There was also a plan for offensive operations against Noriega's Panamanian Defense Forces (PDF), which was called Blue Spoon.

At the White House meeting the night of May 10, Crowe saw that Noriega's decision to nullify the opposition victory was perceived as a big setback to U.S. policy. President Bush was eager to solve the Noriega problem. But the United States could not run the risk of making him an overnight martyr. The tenor of the meeting was that the administration should find some measured, symbolic step.

Over the next 24 hours Crowe and Cheney attempted to formulate a military recommendation to the President. Crowe suggested to Cheney that they propose augmenting the U.S. forces in Panama with a brigade-size reinforcement of 2000 to 3000 troops. This would send an important psychological message to Noriega. Cheney agreed.

Crowe called Woerner on the secure line. He proposed sending the reinforcement, but Woerner said he did not need it. He said an influx of thousands of troops could be an unneeded burden.

Things were moving pretty fast, Crowe said, and Woerner might have to accept some kind of force package for political reasons.

CROWE decided there was one more step that could be taken. A secret deployment of a small, superelite special operations task force could be ordered. After the failed Iranian hostage rescue operation of 1980 the Department of Defense had created the Joint Special Operations Command (JSOC, pronounced "J-sock") to conduct counterterrorist operations. Based at Fort Bragg, North Carolina, JSOC had several tiers of operators. The top tier consisted of three elite army Delta squadrons and the navy's sea-air-land (SEAL) teams.

Dispatching these special forces would give the President considerable flexibility. Cheney approved Crowe's suggestion to recommend to the President the dispatch of a Delta team and part of SEAL Team 6, the best of the best, to Panama.

Crowe then called Fred Woerner, in Panama. Once again the general said he did not desire the new deployment. It was one of the few times in his career that Crowe had encountered a commander who resisted additional forces.

Woerner was troubled by the push from Washington. The Blue Spoon contingency plan called for a Delta unit to capture Noriega, and now a Delta unit was coming down. Woerner felt a snatch operation was too risky. If it failed, it would represent a major escalation, putting all the U.S. citizens in Panama in jeopardy.

Although Crowe doubted the wisdom of abducting Noriega, he needed to get a better idea of what would be acceptable to Cheney. Crowe felt he had not closed the loop with Cheney, had not come to know the man beneath the unrevealing surface. One day during a private discussion Cheney had dropped his guard. "You know," he said, "the President has got a long history of vindictive political actions." Cross Bush and you pay, he said, supplying a few victims' names and adding, Bush remembers, and you have to be careful.

What an important notion, Crowe reflected. *Bush remembers, and you have to be careful.* Cheney's mask had momentarily slipped. Was it a warning to Crowe? Or a reminder for Cheney himself? Crowe was not at all sure. But apparently Cheney was afraid of Bush.

The new Secretary did not appear to be squeamish about the kinds of aggressive actions now under consideration for Panama. In one session Crowe had mentioned the possibility of a Noriega snatch to Cheney, saying it would be very risky and not necessarily wise. Cheney explored the details of this option and said he favored it if an opportunity arose—if there was good intelligence on Noriega's whereabouts or if he did something openly provocative. But not, Cheney said, if such a snatch was going to have any political negatives.

On Thursday, May 11, Cheney and Crowe finished work on their recommendation to Bush: an announced troop deployment, plus a secret dispatch of a Delta squadron and part of SEAL Team 6. Bush agreed. The President later appeared in the White House pressroom to announce that over the next several days he was sending an additional 1881 American troops to Panama. Asked if the United States would look favorably on a coup attempt against Noriega, Bush sidestepped. "I've asserted what my interest is at this point. It is democracy in Panama; it is protection of the life of Americans in Panama."

Most people cleared for access to details of the operation were told the special units were being sent for possible rescue of American hostages. But there was another mission for the Delta squadron.

A month before, a CIA operative named Kurt Muse had been arrested for running a clandestine radio network, which was part of the Agency's covert operation to unseat Noriega. Muse was being held in Modelo Prison, across from Noriega's headquarters, known as the Comandancia. Intelligence reports said that a guard with a submachine gun was stationed outside his cell with orders to kill him at any sign of hostilities by the Americans. The CIA was deeply concerned about Muse. Director William H. Webster pressed Cheney to have the military draw up a rescue plan ready for execution on short notice.

A special plan was developed for a Delta team to rescue Muse, in an operation that would take only nine minutes.

Crowe saw that the President—former CIA director Bush—was very worried about the Agency's captured operative. Bush also had made it clear that he wanted the military to be able to seize Noriega and bring him back to the United States for trial.

On May 13 Bush made his strongest public comments so far, calling on the Panamanian people and military to overthrow Noriega. "They ought to do everything they can to get Mr. Noriega out of there," he said. It was highly unusual for a President to call publicly for a coup.

ON MAY 17, in a secure phone conversation, Crowe told General Woerner that Bush had decided to authorize new exercises in Panama that would aggressively assert U.S. rights under the Canal treaties. "But understand you are to do nothing provocative," Crowe added.

Woerner had grown accustomed to executing a Panama policy that amounted to a sequence of subtleties and innuendos. He interpreted Crowe's new instructions to mean that the command should be intimidating, show resolve, and act tough, but not pick a fight that would draw an armed response from the PDF. It seemed a thin distinction.

In the following days Noriega drew back. According to one intelligence report, he warned his forces, "Don't piss off the Americans."

But the Secretary of Defense did not like the subtext of the Southern Command's reactions to events. When anything aggressive was proposed, Woerner argued against it. The general's heart didn't seem to be in a timely solution to the Noriega problem.

Cheney concluded that Woerner had gone native.

Outgoing army secretary Jack Marsh had heard that there was going to be a game of musical chairs in the upper ranks of the military. So on May 30, when Cheney came over to join Marsh for one of the army mess's famous catfish lunches, Marsh spoke in glowing terms about one of his favorite army generals, Maxwell Reid Thurman.

ON JUNE 13 a small-framed man with a large head and thick glasses rushed down the Pentagon's third-floor E-Ring corridor. If it hadn't been for his army-green uniform and the four stars on each shoulder, he might have been taken for a Pentagon budget analyst. A bachelor workaholic, he spoke with piercing directness, and he did not accept excuses. Known variously within the army as Mad Max, Maxatollah, and Emperor Maximilian, General Maxwell Thurman, 58, was stopping by for a private lunch with Jack Marsh and Dick Cheney. Marsh had arranged it.

It was a rare opportunity for Thurman, scheduled to retire in two months, to speak with the Secretary of Defense. Commanding general of the Training and Doctrine Command—the army's brain—since 1987, he had spent his life as an army officer, the last six years as a four-star general. Like most four-star officers, he was going to leave without having risen to a high-visibility post.

The army secretary's office was as large as Cheney's. In the center was the giant Lincoln Desk, built for Abraham Lincoln's son Robert when he served as Secretary of War, from 1881 to 1885. Cheney took his seat at the small dining table. Marsh sat at the head, looking out the window to Arlington National Cemetery. He had always thought it appropriate that the army secretary and the navy secretary—whose office was one floor above—had this view of seemingly endless rows of white tombstones, a reminder of the true, measurable price of war.

As they began lunch Thurman described how he had organized the army's modern recruiting drive, building up the all-volunteer force and changing a dispirited army to a proud one. Knowing Cheney was under pressure to get the military more actively involved in the war on drugs, Thurman said this was a case where the military was dragging its feet. The Defense Department could be more aggressive.

Thurman got worked up as he delivered his monologue. Cheney thought Marsh was right about him. Here was a no-bulls___, straight-ahead guy. Things clearly happened when Max was in charge. Where many senior officers saw obstacles, Thurman saw possibilities. Cheney was pretty sure a C in C position would open up earlier than expected.

ON JULY 6 Woerner received a call from army chief Carl Vuono, who said he wanted to come down to Panama to see him. Why? Woerner asked. Vuono, a good friend of Woerner's, wouldn't elaborate. He said only that he would be staying about an hour.

At the Southern Command headquarters, Vuono took Woerner into a small room. "Fred," Vuono said, looking Woerner straight in the eye, "the President has decided to make a change."

Woerner felt ill, as if he had been kicked hard in the stomach. His 34 years in the army, his whole life . . . "Why, Carl?"

"I don't know," Vuono replied. "The secretary of the army came and told me and said I couldn't tell you." Vuono explained that he had told Marsh that Woerner had given years of loyal service.

Woerner pressed. Why was he being fired?

"I don't know why," Vuono repeated. "All I know is it is an irrevocable decision." He proposed that they develop a reason—health, family, a job offer, anything.

Woerner would not hear of a cover story. He understood the rules: he served at the pleasure of the President and needed the support of the Chairman and the army chief. Vuono left 45 minutes later for his flight back to Washington.

The decision had been reached while Crowe was out of the country, in the Soviet Union. When he learned of it, he said to Cheney, "I wish you wouldn't do something like that without involving me."

"The White House did it," Cheney replied.

The decision had been made. That was the way. But Crowe felt bitter. Most chilling to him was the indifference that the Secretary of Defense seemed to have about the career of a four-star officer.

On July 17 President Bush approved a plan proposed by Crowe and Cheney to have the Southern Command conduct new intensive exercises asserting Panama Canal treaty rights. These Category Three and Four exercises would involve hundreds of U.S. troops.

Three days later, on July 20, Cheney announced that General Woerner was retiring. He would be replaced by General Max Thurman.

IN A comfortable, brightly lit office suite behind a security checkpoint in the Joint Staff's inner sanctum in the Pentagon, Lieutenant General Thomas W. Kelly roared into a telephone behind his desk. Kelly, 56, a barrel-chested, take-few-prisoners three-star, was chief operational traffic cop for Crowe and the Joint Staff. As director of the operations staff, or J-3, Kelly lived in the world of the immediate. If Qaddafi was stirring or Gorbachev had not been seen for a week or there was a coup in the Caribbean, the problem landed on Kelly's plate. He was responsible for positioning the U.S. military with the proper forces, plans, and approvals to respond to just about anything.

A tank commander by training and temperament, Kelly would insist on beer in a can and display his wisecracking "so's your mother" style at the most formal cocktail party. But he also had a sophisticated side. A Philadelphian with a journalism degree from Temple University, he was a smooth writer. And as a one-star, he had worked for Crowe in Italy when the admiral was the C in C for southern Europe.

Aware that the Category Three and Four exercises in Panama could flare up instantly into a confrontation that might require presidential decisions, Kelly had all his lines out. He knew that the plans for Panama were his most important contingencies for the moment, and he hoped to minimize surprises for everyone.

ON AUGUST 5 army lieutenant general Carl W. Stiner took his seat among the dignitaries at Fort Monroe, Virginia, headquarters of General Thurman's army Training and Doctrine Command. Thurman's long-awaited retirement ceremony had turned into a mere change of command, since he was going to be C in C South. Stiner, commander of the army's XVIII Airborne Corps, based at Fort Bragg, wanted to be on hand nevertheless. Thurman was an old friend.

Stiner, 52, a taut Tennessean, had one of the army's premier commands, charged with responding to a short-notice crisis anywhere in the world. Any of the C in Cs could call on the 41,000 troops of his corps for help in carrying out contingency plans. The modern airlift capability of the air force gave Stiner's outfit a tremendous edge over most other U.S. forces. There was probably no general in the U.S. Army with more experience in quick-response warfare.

After the ceremony Thurman stepped off the reviewing stand and approached Stiner. "Carlos," he said, poking his finger gently into the three-star general's chest, "you are my man for Panama. I hold you responsible for all contingency planning and any combat operations."

Stiner did not seem to fully understand.

"I need a man to plan and to execute contingency operations down there if they have to be executed," Thurman went on. "And I want you to go down there and take a look at this thing. Look at the staff."

"But you've already got a JTF down there," replied Stiner, referring to the Joint Task Force in Panama. General Woerner had designated an army two-star in Panama to have command of the task force, which would mainly use the forces permanently stationed there.

"You absorb it," Thurman said. "I'm gonna hold you responsible."

"I understand that. Yes, sir."

As the C in C, Thurman knew he was going to be an administrator and supervisor. He needed a war fighter, and Stiner was the essence of the hard-nosed battle commander. Just as important, Stiner had all the best equipment, an operations staff three times the size of his own, a big intelligence shop, and the best communications.

Stiner put his staff to work at once. Like Thurman, Kelly, and Powell, Stiner had not gone to West Point; he held a degree in agriculture from Tennessee Polytechnical Institute. Known for his aggressiveness and enterprise, he was a very controversial figure. In 1985 he had been the special operations ground commander when the Italian cruise ship *Achille Lauro* was hijacked. In Sicily with the Delta team sent to seize the hijackers, he wouldn't take no for an answer when the Italians refused to surrender them. He had nearly fired on Italian forces, and then shadowed the plane carrying the hijackers to Rome. This set back U.S.-Italian relations for some time.

Kelly thought Stiner was a great soldier, though too outspoken. As long as he was not made ambassador to France, he could be handled.

FROM his vantage point Kelly watched Thurman's arrival with some wonder and much pleasure. "You don't have to do nothing to mobilize Max Thurman," Kelly said. "He is mobilized when he gets up in the morning, which is in the middle of the night."

Both men realized that Bush's order to conduct exercises could set something off in a second. Thurman wanted to know more about the Prayer Book contingency plans and what General Stiner could really do. But when he was briefed, Thurman was appalled. The plans were built around the forces in place, and the reinforcement—if things really got bad—was expected to take five days! Operational security would be blown; Noriega would surely know that the Yankees were coming. It was contrary to two of the basic requirements of successful warfare: surprise and speed.

The five-day buildup was all part of Woerner's strategic plan. But it wasn't good enough for Thurman.

3

IN THE months since he left the White House, Colin Powell had seen his life transformed. After living two years at the center of the policy storm, he was floating in calm, uneventful waters in Atlanta, where Forces Command had its headquarters. When he relinquished the national security job to his successor, Brent Scowcroft, he had observed an old army tradition—when relieved, you salute, leave the post, and *never* call back. He had not spoken with Scowcroft since.

There were occasional reminders he hadn't been forgotten. At the end of March, 1989, he'd received a handwritten note from the President. Addressed simply to "Colin," it was a one-sentence congratulation for pinning on the "4th bright one," referring to Powell's fourth star. This was pure Bush: to recognize an important personal event by dashing off a line or two. Powell set it aside for his scrapbook.

He was spending much of his time crisscrossing the country, visiting the various units in Forces Command, an umbrella organization comprising the service's strategic reserve of 1 million active-duty, reserve, and National Guard troops. Powell was shocked to see it was business as usual, as if nothing in the world had changed. Communism was collapsing in Eastern Europe, and the army's freezers were still making ice for the cold war. Planning and training were still centered on the scenario of a massive Soviet invasion of Europe. For his part, Powell thought the Soviet Union was changed almost beyond recognition.

On Sunday, August 6, 1989, he arrived at Belmont House, a conference center outside Baltimore, for a three-day meeting of top army generals called annually by army chief Vuono. The second morning, Powell read with distress a story in *The New York Times* headlined SCRAMBLE ON TO SUCCEED CHAIRMAN OF JOINT CHIEFS. It reported that Powell and the JCS vice-chairman, General Robert Herres, were the leading candidates for the job. "General Powell," the story stated, "has been keeping in touch with Mr. Cheney through frequent letters." The implication was obvious—Powell was campaigning.

He had written only one letter to Cheney, and that was a routine quarterly report required of each C in C. Not only was he not lobbying for himself, he wasn't encouraging anyone else to push him either, though he knew that former Secretary of Defense Frank Carlucci was promoting him all over Washington as the ideal candidate.

Powell's personal assessment was that he had lost out to Herres, who was backed by Admiral Crowe. Further, Powell assumed Scowcroft would be uncomfortable with a former national security adviser coming in as Chairman and maybe second-guessing him. Nor was Powell sure Cheney had the most favorable view of him. The two had worked together in 1987 and 1988 during the various congressional debates on the Nicaraguan contras, Cheney's pet cause. Representing the

Reagan White House, Powell had concluded that the contras were of no military significance, and he had worked out a compromise with the Democrats. He suspected that Cheney thought he had not been sufficiently stalwart. Since he had heard nothing from Cheney himself or from his numerous Washington contacts—there was not a single tom-tom sounding in the distance—he concluded it was over.

Yet even before Cheney had been confirmed as Secretary, he had been thinking about Powell for Chairman. The new Chairman would be the fifth player in the national security team of Bush, Baker, Scowcroft, and Cheney. They had to get the right person.

Cheney had twice talked at length with Frank Carlucci, who argued essentially that Powell was one of Washington's best problem solvers. No matter what the task, Powell was a right-hand man who delivered results, generally without ruffling feathers. For the last six years, as Weinberger's military assistant, Carlucci's deputy at the NSC, and Reagan's national security adviser, he had probably not made a single major misstep. No one was more steeped in foreign policy, defense, and military issues. Powell had strong views, Carlucci said, but he knew when to follow orders and fall in line with the boss.

Carlucci also said that Powell seemed never to tire or lose his enthusiasm. He had remarkable endurance and could handle vast amounts of work.

Like nearly everyone, Cheney found Powell charming and likable. Over the summer Cheney had arranged a short-notice stopover in Atlanta. Powell had put on an impressive briefing, which showed he was fully absorbed in the job at hand. His people seemed to love him, and he was tending to the nuts and bolts of being the Forces Command C in C—spending time with the troops, worrying about the National Guard and the reserves. Over lunch at Powell's antebellum official residence, the two discussed the army's future and their overall defense philosophies. Cheney saw that Powell was feeling good to be back in the army and had none of the post-Washington hang-ups, like unhealthy curiosity about power plays in the administration.

They hadn't discussed the Chairman's job.

Mulling it over, Cheney weighed Powell's drawbacks. One was that he was not only the junior C in C but also the most junior of all the fifteen eligible four-stars. Cheney knew there would be some resistance in the military to the idea of choosing someone whose senior posts had mostly been in staff and political assignments. So Cheney had looked hard at Bob Herres, the vice-chairman, as another possible candidate. But Crowe had recommended Herres, and Cheney did not like the idea of Crowe's effectively naming his successor. Civilian control would be enhanced if the civilian leaders—the President and the Secretary of Defense—picked their own Chairman.

Cheney finally made his decision in favor of Powell. In early August he quietly went over to the White House and talked to the President. He'd looked at the entire pool of candidates—the C in Cs, the four chiefs, and the vice-chairman, he said. Both Herres and Powell were on the shortlist. His recommendation was Powell.

Bush was also high on Powell, but he wanted to be certain not to offend the upper ranks of the military. He asked Cheney to talk to Powell specifically about the seniority question.

On the third day of the army commanders' conference at Belmont House, Powell was asked to a meeting with Secretary Cheney. The Secretary went right to the point. You are on the shortlist for Chairman, he said. Are you interested? Is this a job you want?

Powell said he was, but added, "I do not seek the job. I'm happy where I am. If you pick someone else off the shortlist, I would not be upset at all. If you and the President want me, I'll do it."

Cheney ticked off Powell's qualifications for the post: (1) you know the Pentagon; (2) you know the White House; (3) you have punched the proper tickets in the army and have the credentials; (4) you know arms control—a topic that will be important in the coming years; (5) I know you and worked well with you when I was in the House.

The one problem was that Powell was the most junior of the eligible four-stars. Will you have problems being jumped over so many senior officers? Cheney asked directly.

Powell had the impression that the question came from the President. He replied that this was a fair question, but he thought he would have no problem dealing with the chiefs and C in Cs. He knew most of them well and had worked with them.

Cheney agreed, and said he wanted Powell for the job.

Cheney then went back to the White House and reported Powell's answers to Bush. On August 9 Cheney called Powell to say that he had talked with the President and they both wanted Powell as Chairman. Cheney then formally offered him the job. Powell accepted.

POWELL HAD 40 DAYS BEFORE HIS Senate confirmation hearings. He had no secret plan for change, and he did not want to come crashing through the gate with new ideas. But he did want to look at the major operations that might have to be executed after he took over.

Recognizing that Panama was a military crisis waiting to happen, he flew to Fort Bragg to examine the Panama plans. While he was there a terrible storm hit, keeping him at Bragg for two days. Carl Stiner took advantage of the delay to brief Powell in extensive detail. They went over the Prayer Book plans, including the individual Blue Spoon plan for offensive operations against the PDF. Powell was surprised that it took so many days for the force buildup. Within a day, or even hours, the entire landscape of a crisis could change. Night-vision goggles and other technology gave U.S. forces unmatched ability to launch a large operation at night. Hey, what gives? Powell asked.

He decided they should see if it was possible to come up with a new concept that emphasized surprise, speed, and the *night*. Soon Stiner had five of his best officers down in Panama reworking the plans.

On September 20, 1989, Powell went to Capitol Hill for his confirmation hearing at the Senate Armed Services Committee.

The committee voted unanimously to confirm him, and within a day the full Senate approved his nomination on a voice vote, a procedure reserved for the most uncontroversial questions.

ON SATURDAY, September 30, at a ceremony in Panama City, Max Thurman took over the Southern Command. Thurman went right to work, receiving extensive briefings—the dump, as he called it—on each country in his new area of responsibility. At about 9:30 p.m. on Sunday an assistant called. The CIA station had received information from the wife of a fairly senior PDF officer—the name was unclear—that her husband was planning a coup against Noriega the next morning and wanted the U.S. military to block some roads.

"Okay," Thurman said. "Find out what the hell's going on."

Thurman went to his headquarters at the Tunnel, his secure complex in the side of a hill at Quarry Heights, in Panama City. At about 2:00 a.m. two CIA men arrived.

"I've got bad news," one of them said. "We don't like the guy that's running it." They identified him as Major Moises Giroldi, a quiet 38-year-old member of Noriega's PDF leadership. As a major, Giroldi was in a position to carry out a successful coup. But he had helped Noriega crush a coup only 18 months earlier, in March 1988, and Noriega had had the coup participants jailed and tortured. Now this same guy was requesting U.S. military roadblocks at two key routes into Panama City to block Noriega's troops.

Thurman suspected immediately that this was an attempt to drag him personally into some crazy sting operation, destroying his credibility in his first days of command. So what is the Giroldi plan? he asked. What do the plotters plan to do with Noriega?

"They're going to talk him into retirement," the men explained.

"Say what?" Thurman exploded.

"They hope he's not in the Comandancia when the coup gets going." Giroldi planned to seize Noriega's headquarters, cutting him off from his communications and staff, and then convince him his rule was over and that he ought to retire peaceably to the countryside.

"It's preposterous," Thurman said. "Why wouldn't they grab him and do something with him? That's cockamamy."

Just over 24 hours in command, and now this. Thurman concluded he had better report to Washington. He reached General Tom Kelly at home at 2:30 a.m. on his secure phone.

"Got a report for you," Thurman said. "There's a coup going down." He summarized what the CIA men had said, adding that the coup was scheduled for 9:00 a.m.—about six hours away.

"What's your recommendation, sir?" asked Kelly, who had three stars to Thurman's four.

"Simple," Thurman said. "This is an ill-motivated, ill-conceived, ill-led plan. I'd recommend you stay out of it. Stay out of it big time."

Powell, who had just taken over the chairmanship of the JCS at midnight, without fanfare, had spent the day at home waiting for his first duty day, on Monday. He was asleep when Kelly called.

"We have some indications in Panama there's going to be a coup," Kelly told his new boss.

Powell agreed to meet Kelly at the Pentagon within the hour, but first he woke up Cheney to tell him. Then he headed out into the rainy predawn to start his first day four hours early. Arriving at the National Military Command Center, in the Pentagon, he ribbed Kelly for getting him out of bed so early.

It sounds goofy, Powell said after he saw a summary on the coup.

There seemed no reason for the United States to sign on. Getting rid of Noriega was something to do on a U.S. timetable—not a half-baked coup with a half-baked coup leader, he said.

The specific requests presented problems. A normal exercise could be staged by U.S. troops on one of the roads the coup plotters wanted blocked. This was recommended and approved by Cheney. The second request, to secure the Bridge of the Americas—which traverses the Canal into Panama City—would take U.S. forces close to the Comandancia and could not be masqueraded as a routine exercise. Powell did not recommend it.

Rear Admiral Edward D. "Ted" Sheafer, 48, Powell's intelligence officer, put together an assessment. In intelligence language Major Giroldi could easily be a "dangle"—a decoy sent out to mislead or trick—Sheafer said. Giroldi seemed to be planning a coup against the Comandancia, not against Noriega. If it was genuine, it was based on the mistaken idea that seizing a building constituted seizing power. It was absurd, flaky—right down to the notion of retiring Noriega to the countryside with a full pension.

Powell took Kelly and Sheafer up to Cheney's office. The White House was trying to set up a secure video conference with the Pentagon so President Bush could be briefed, but the equipment wasn't working properly. Scowcroft suggested that Cheney, Powell, Kelly, and Sheafer all come to the White House to meet with Bush.

Once in the Oval Office, Powell summarized the situation: neither the leader of the coup nor the plan was reliable. He recommended the President await further information. The President agreed.

When the coup did not go off that day, Giroldi's wife passed word that it would start the next morning.

AT 7:40 THE next morning there was shooting at the Comandancia, about a mile from Thurman's headquarters. Thurman called Powell. "Allegedly Noriega's in there, but I haven't heard his voice." Thurman liked to listen in himself to the electronic eavesdropping devices.

By 9:00 a.m. it was clear to Powell that an attempted coup was under way, but there was still no definitive intelligence about whether Noriega was in the Comandancia. Powell phoned Cheney.

Just after noon U.S. forces blocked the road outside Fort Amador—the PDF base closest to the Comandancia—under the guise of a routine exercise. Ten minutes later local radio announced the coup.

At 12:18 p.m. Thurman was notified that two Panamanian lieutenants identifying themselves as coup liaison negotiators were at the front gate of Fort Clayton, a U.S. base nearby. They said that Noriega and his staff were inside the Comandancia under the control of the coup leaders, who were looking for an honorable way for Noriega to remain in Panama. The head of the U.S. Southern Command's army forces told them that the United States would take Noriega into custody if he was brought to Fort Clayton. The lieutenants said they had no intention of turning him over to the United States.

Thurman got on the secure line with Powell at 1:30 p.m. For the moment, he said, he was following standing Bush policy to avoid conflict. Since it was not a U.S.-sponsored coup, Thurman wondered what he could do. Could he apprehend Noriega?

"If they bring him to you," Powell said, "you can do it, but you don't have authority to go in and get him." Still, if Thurman thought there was an opportunity to get Noriega overtly with just a very small U.S. force, he could go ahead and plan that. But that would clearly be an escalation, requiring a new administration policy. This small-force option would have to be approved by President Bush.

Powell cleared all this with Cheney, who briefed Bush, Scowcroft, and Baker at the White House and obtained presidential clearance. Both Cheney and Powell now felt that it might be time to act, and they wanted to make sure Thurman was ready.

At about 2:30 p.m. Thurman passed up word that the coup had failed. It was over, Powell realized, and so were the opportunities, however inexact or fleeting they may have been. Noriega was soon on Panamanian television condemning the United States for an attempt to "install a government of sellouts."

The White House moved quickly to distance itself from the coup, insisting that it was neither an American nor an American-sponsored operation. Press secretary Marlin Fitzwater said that administration officials had only heard "rumbling" about the planned coup; they had not been directly informed.

CHENEY arrived back at the Pentagon as employees were streaming out to the parade ground, overlooking the Potomac. They were gathering to witness Powell's full-honor arrival, the military equivalent of an inauguration, scheduled for 3:00 p.m. It had turned into a fine Indian-summer day.

The crowd cheered as Cheney escorted Powell to the reviewing stand. Cheney told the assembled group that over the next four years he would spend more time with this new Chairman than with his family. Powell appeared relaxed as he sat with his legs crossed. The only suggestion that he might have something on his mind was the folding and unfolding of his large hands.

When it was his turn to speak, Powell told the crowd that the period the United States was entering "may be the most historic period of the postwar era." Afterward Marybel Batjer, Powell's former White House executive assistant, went up to him. She had heard about the Panama coup and could tell that Powell was jittery.

How's it going with Cheney? she asked. She knew that Powell had had his worries about Cheney during the Iran-contra investigations.

Powell smiled. The coup was precisely what he and Cheney needed to break down the barriers, he told her. "The bonding process is working," he said. "There is nothing like a crisis for good bonding."

PETE Williams spent lots of time in Cheney's office that day as Powell—usually accompanied by his operations chief, Kelly, and his intelligence officer, Sheafer—came in repeatedly to provide new information and updates for the Secretary. Williams was struck by how on-point Powell's summaries were. If a stranger had come into the room and been told that one person there was new to his job, he would never guess it was Powell. The new Chairman was utterly confident. He absolutely filled the room. There was a quality about him that announced, Hi, get the hell out of the way. I'm Chairman.

Over the next two days both Republicans and Democrats in Congress attacked the administration for failing to exploit the coup attempt. Editorials compared the incident to Carter's Iran hostage rescue mission and Kennedy's Bay of Pigs fiasco.

At a White House meeting at the end of the week, deputy national security adviser Robert Gates gave a spirited defense of the CIA and the intelligence on the coup. But the missed opportunity prompted a reconsideration of the administration's objectives in Panama. Was the goal to overthrow Noriega? To arrest him and bring him to trial? To help establish a new government?

It was pretty clear that Bush's hard-line anti-Noriega rhetoric was not matched by specific plans or contingencies, either by the CIA or the military, Powell realized.

John Sununu was very agitated. This was a coordination issue—his primary task as White House chief of staff—and there had not been much to coordinate. He put his spurs into people very hard.

"Amateur hour is over," Bush declared. He told the National Security Council that Noriega would overstep someday and he wanted them to be ready. Nothing should be left to chance. "I want some follow-through planning," the President said.

ON THE afternoon of Friday, October 6, Bush went into Walter Reed Army Medical Center for removal of a benign cyst from one of his fingers. After the operation a reporter asked, "Sir, how about Panama? Simply put, a lot of critics say you blew it."

"Well," Bush said, "what some people seemed to have wanted me to do is to unleash the full military and go in and, quote, get Noriega. But that's not prudent. I would not rule out any option. But you have to look at the facts at the time. And you've got to keep in mind the lives of American citizens, lives of your own troops, and what you're trying to do."

At a morning news conference on October 13, in answer to the question "Has anybody been fired lately?" Bush replied, "No, and they're not going to be over this, because they all did a good job. And I haven't lost any confidence in our top people handling these matters, including—and I want to repeat it here—our military officers in Panama. None at all. And certainly not General Powell."

Powell, who followed every presidential statement closely, could have done without the "I haven't lost any confidence" endorsement. He knew well that such a sentiment was articulated when it was in question. My God, what has happened to this town? he thought to himself. It was as if there were a lynch mob out there. He had been away from Washington only six months, but something had changed.

He thought he saw several reasons for the frenzy. First, it had been a slow news week. Second, whenever there was a simple contradiction between rhetoric and action, reporters jumped hard. Third, frustration with Noriega was at a fever pitch. Fourth and most important, perhaps, was the question of presidential image—lingering doubts about Bush as wimp. Nine months into his presidency Bush still had not defined himself, and this failure left open a basic question: Was the essential Bush indecisive and hesitant?

Powell felt that this was the wrong case on which to judge the Bush presidency.

Cheney and Powell got together for one final scrub. They asked, If this *had* been the right coup, one the United States could and should have supported, would they have been ready? The answer was no.

If things were so bad that officers like Giroldi, a former close Noriega ally, had tried to overthrow him, Cheney thought, others would try again. It was time to go back to the drawing board.

IN PANAMA City, Thurman put his feet up, looked out his window, and identified a first step. If there was going to be a major fracas with Noriega, Thurman had to get the U.S. dependents out of Panama. So he began requesting authorization to send the dependents home or move them onto U.S. military bases in Panama.

He was summoned to testify at closed-door sessions of the Senate and House Armed Services committees. In separate sessions of three hours each he was faced essentially with a single question: Did we miss a golden opportunity? His answer was no.

"I'm going back to Panama and get me a good contingency plan," Thurman told the Senators. He had read the papers. It was clear that nobody—not President Bush, Cheney, Powell, nor he himself—could withstand another failure or perceived failure.

Thurman went to see Powell. Is the planning on track with a new intensity? Powell asked.

"Sure. We get paid for doing that," Thurman said. He returned to Panama and intensified the Category Three and Four exercises.

One night during the week after the failed coup, Lieutenant General Stiner arrived at Howard Air Force Base, in Panama, aboard a C-20 transport airplane. He and his key planners were all wearing civilian clothes so they might slip in unbeknownst to the PDF.

Thurman met with Stiner and said he wanted the Blue Spoon contingency plan refined down to the finest details, "to a cat's eye." Then you and the XVIII Corps will rehearse it every two months.

Yes, sir, Stiner replied.

Soon 24-hour-a-day police patrols were set up along sensitive routes.

Thurman ordered his helicopters to fly exercises to the headquarters of the PDF's Battalion 2000—an 800-man force considered Noriega's most potent and lethal—at Fort Cimarron, east of Panama City.

POWELL was already intimately familiar with the PDF leadership. As Reagan's national security adviser he had spent hours examining the intelligence files of PDF officers, looking for alternatives to Noriega. He'd concluded there was no one the United States could support.

With the prestige of President Bush and the United States on the line, Powell concluded, there was only one answer: the Blue Spoon plan had to be made more ambitious. Any offensive operation against the PDF must capture or drive out the entire leadership. Then legitimate civilian political leaders could take charge.

Powell directed Thurman to be ready to respond to a contingency on two hours' notice with the forces already in place. And for a full offensive operation against the PDF, Thurman would be given only 48 hours instead of the previous mobilization time of five days.

During the week after the coup Powell had ordered Kelly and Sheafer to set up a small secret planning cell in the Pentagon. This cell was to work closely with Thurman and Stiner and their people to make sure that every detail was shared and coordinated.

Traditionally operations and intelligence worked separately. Powell now wanted them in each other's back pockets. One key to a lightning offensive operation was making sure the U.S. forces knew everything possible about what they were attacking, down to which squad would go through which door in which building.

ON SUNDAY, October 15, Carl Stiner flew to Washington. He arrived at the Pentagon accompanied by Major General Gary Luck, 52, the commanding general of the Joint Special Operations Command (JSOC). Stiner told Powell that substantial modifications of Blue Spoon were in the works. If he got the full 48 hours' notice, Stiner planned to bring in perhaps 11,000 additional troops to supplement the 13,000 at the Southern Command. He felt it was important to go with the full force to strike targets simultaneously and ensure that the PDF leadership was dislodged.

The plan was set to be executed at night, Stiner said, and his instructions from Thurman were to rehearse so much that the

Panamanians would grow numb watching ground and air exercises.

But Stiner emphasized that the in-country troops would not be enough to do all that was required. My recommendation, Stiner told Powell again, would be to go with the total Blue Spoon plan.

Powell agreed.

On Monday, October 30, Thurman signed a quarter-inch-thick document designated Commander in Chief Southern Command Operations Order 1-90 (Blue Spoon). The plan was built around three principles—maximum surprise, minimum collateral damage (damage to nonmilitary targets), and minimum force.

A few days later, on November 3, Thurman, Stiner, and Luck gave the Blue Spoon briefing to the chiefs in the Tank, the second-floor Pentagon conference room where the Joint Chiefs of Staff hold their regular meetings.

Luck said that a plan to rescue CIA agent Kurt Muse from Modelo Prison by helicopter with Delta forces was going to be incorporated into Blue Spoon, as Muse would be in danger at the very instant of any offensive operations.

An intelligence directive from the President also was issued around this time, authorizing the CIA to spend up to $3 million on a covert plan to recruit Panamanian military officers and exiles to topple Noriega. In effect the CIA and the Pentagon were in competition to see who could first rid Bush of the Noriega problem.

THE November individual-unit rehearsals under Blue Spoon went well, but Thurman decided that during December he would conduct a joint-readiness exercise that would amount to a full rehearsal of the plan. Special operations forces, the in-country forces, and some other units could rehearse in Panama, but most of the reinforcement units would rehearse in the United States.

In addition, night-readiness exercises were conducted at regular intervals in Panama, a practice Thurman felt would help mask any large force movement if an actual operation were to take place.

Back in Washington, Tom Kelly pondered the radical transformation of the Southern Command that had taken place over just two months. The departed General Woerner had seemed unable to imagine the use of military force in Panama. Maxwell Thurman seemed to see a war coming.

4

LATE in the day on Thursday, November 30, reliable reports came into the Pentagon that a 1000-man rebel force had seized two air bases in the Philippines. Powell, who'd spent the day in budget sessions, was alarmed. There were constant rumors that someone was plotting a coup to end Philippine President Corazon Aquino's shaky three-and-a-half-year rule, but now the rebels had aircraft.

Powell went up to Cheney's office with maps and intelligence reports. The situation was murky, he told the Secretary.

Afterward an interagency deputies' committee meeting began at the White House, with Powell's vice-chairman, General Robert Herres, representing the JCS. The deputies monitored the crisis as the evening wore on. At one point a request came in from the Philippine defense minister for U.S intervention. Herres said that U.S. bases in the Philippines should not be used to intervene in civil strife, and Robert Gates, Scowcroft's deputy, was also reluctant.

Shortly after 11:00 p.m. a formal NSC meeting was conducted by video. Vice President Dan Quayle was going to chair the NSC because the President, accompanied by Baker and Scowcroft, was airborne, on the way to Malta for a summit meeting with Gorbachev.

As reports of rebel bombing started coming in, Powell took his seat in the Crisis Situation Room, at the Pentagon's National Military Command Center. Herres sat at his right. The C in C responsible for the Pacific region, Admiral Huntington Hardisty, in town for the budget discussions, was at Powell's left. Cheney was at home with a flu, but a phone link to his home was set up.

Back in the White House Situation Room, Quayle was at the head of the table. Robert Gates sat to Quayle's right, and the Vice President's chief of staff, William Kristol, was to the left. The large video screen in front of them was broken up into sections, one each for Powell; a CIA representative; a Justice Department lawyer; Henry S. Rowen, the assistant secretary of defense for international security affairs; and deputy secretary of state Lawrence Eagleburger.

"Look, we have no choice," Eagleburger said. "We have to go in, in some form." Given the major role the United States had played in ousting the dictator Ferdinand Marcos, it had an obligation to stand behind Aquino. Eagleburger proposed that the Defense Department should figure out how to intervene.

After half an hour of discussion Powell received reports that Aquino's presidential palace, in Manila, was being bombed and strafed. These were followed quickly by requests from the Philippine government that U.S. Air Force F-4 fighter-bomber jets at Clark Air Base bomb the two captured airfields the rebels were using to launch the attacks. The requests were accompanied by claims that intervention was required at once and that it could tip the balance and save Aquino.

Powell was concerned that the requests lacked precision and crispness. They were all coming secondhand through the U.S. ambassador in Manila, but attributed to Mrs. Aquino or her defense secretary, Fidel Ramos. Powell smelled panic on the Philippine end.

At around midnight Quayle received confirmation that the request for intervention was coming directly from Aquino.

Quayle said they had to give President Bush a recommendation and indicated that he thought Mrs. Aquino's request was legitimate and that the United States should comply. State and the CIA agreed.

Powell stressed the uncertainty of the situation. What is our purpose? he asked. I've got to tell my guys what the mission is.

State and the White House responded that it was to support Mrs. Aquino and keep her in power.

What is the immediate objective we seek in bombing the airfields? Powell asked. He answered his own question: to keep the rebel aircraft from taking off. But these Philippine aircraft were T-28s, old World War II trainers with propellers. Without dropping any bombs, F-4 jets could scare any T-28 pilot into thinking twice before taking off. "I think we can do this without getting ourselves into more trouble," he added. Bombs are terrible things, he said.

Powell had an army officer's natural distrust of air power. Big bombs promised great achievement, but he had seen them fail too often—in Vietnam, for example. But he kept these thoughts to himself.

He could not guarantee whose side bombing would help, he said. These were captured Philippine air bases, so there would be both rebels and loyalists all around. The United States would wind up killing some Filipinos. If we kill Filipinos, Powell said, no one in the Philippines will forgive us.

"Let's try something short of bombing," Powell proposed. "We can't stick our nose too far into a family fight."

After he had expressed his views, Powell called Cheney to explain that something stupid was about to happen that could cause big political and public relations problems for the United States. People who had never dropped bombs before were about to make a decision to do just that. Powell said he could come up with an alternative.

Cheney said, Do it fast. He called Air Force One and urged that they wait for Powell's recommendation before making a decision.

Powell began dictating new rules of engagement. First, the U.S. pilots were to fly over the captured air bases and demonstrate extreme hostile intent—in other words, to buzz the rebel T-28s on the ground. Second, if the T-28s began to taxi on the runway, the U.S. pilots were to shoot in front of them—the classic warning shot across the bow. And third, if at any point the rebels broke ground in a takeoff, the U.S. pilots were to shoot the planes down.

General Herres and Admiral Hardisty both agreed with his proposal. Powell had no time to ask for any other advice. Instead he immediately passed the suggested new rules to both Cheney and Quayle.

Quayle had asked that a call be placed to Air Force One so he could talk to the President and forward a recommendation. The NSC discussion resumed, and the group agreed to recommend Powell's plan.

When Quayle got through to Air Force One, there was some tension. Scowcroft seemed reluctant to delegate management of this crisis to Quayle. The Vice President said there was no point in recreating the tactical picture for those who were with the President somewhere over the Atlantic, because he had it fully in hand in the White House Situation Room.

Quayle asked to speak with the President. Scowcroft said he didn't want to wake Bush, who was getting a few precious hours of sleep before the Malta meetings with Gorbachev. But Quayle insisted, and Scowcroft finally relented and roused the President.

Quayle told Bush, We're giving you the unanimous recommendation that we intervene, but in this way—and he proceeded to lay out Powell's three rules of engagement. Bush approved.

By 1:30 a.m. Washington, D.C., time, the air force had launched the F-4s. Once the sorties began, there were no reports of any T-28s in the air or any new rebel bombing.

At about 2:30 a.m. Quayle called Aquino. He wanted her to restate her request for assistance so that it would appear that the United States was providing what she had asked for, although in fact it had rejected her initial plea for bombing. This would allow her to save face and the administration to say it had complied with her request.

Mrs. Aquino came on the phone to the Situation Room.

"Hello, Mr. Vice President," she said in a booming, confident voice.

Quayle asked if Aquino had wanted the United States to keep the rebel aircraft on the ground.

She said yes, that was what she wanted, and she reported that the F-4s had been successful so far.

"We're with you," Quayle told her.

White House counsel Boyden Gray, who'd been called in to handle the legal implications of any decision to intervene, thought Aquino sounded more in charge than Quayle. But to Gray the most important performance during those early morning hours was Powell's. Not only was the Chairman backstopping Quayle but his had been the only voice to challenge the growing consensus that Mrs. Aquino's initial request for bombing should be approved. Gray felt that Bush would be interested to hear what had occurred that evening and who had minded the store in the President's absence.

By 3:00 a.m. everything seemed to be on track. The discussion turned to what to tell the press and Congress. Powell proposed they focus on the reformulated request that Quayle had prompted President Aquino to make. It was decided that this story would be put out.

Quayle and his chief of staff, Bill Kristol, left the White House with a few major impressions of the evening's decision making. It had been Quayle's first chance to act as a crisis manager for the administration, but they were both well aware that Bush had made the final decision. They noted how well the JCS had performed, and particularly Powell.

Pete Williams arrived at the Pentagon at about 6:00 a.m. to see what the media fallout was going to be. Soon calls began coming in from reporters, who were trying to piece together the story. Some already had versions emphasizing that Dan Quayle had turned in a solid, steady performance filling in for Bush as crisis manager.

Powell thought the episode confirmed a few of his own notions about the use of military power. The first was that there is no legitimate use of military force without a clear political objective. The second was an idea Powell felt had been best expressed by the Athenian historian Thucydides: "Of all manifestations of power, restraint impresses men most." Third was that a demonstrated willingness to use force often did the job as well as, or even more effectively than, direct force itself. A neat, surgical application of a threat could work wonders.

POWELL was feeling very good after two months in the job. The pieces were falling into place as he worked his way through the daily run of problems and crises. More than anything, he was the action officer connecting the military forces to the political system and the political system back to the forces.

And the forces were trained and ready. Powell wanted to be sure there was never a repeat of the post-Vietnam years. He himself had served two tours in Vietnam, where he'd seen some action, but had worked mostly as an adviser and staff officer. In the early 1970s, after he returned to the States, he'd felt a deep sense of rejection and inferiority as a professional army officer.

The embattled army turned inward in the 1970s to try to solve its problems. In Powell's view Lieutenant General William E. DePuy, U.S. assistant vice chief of staff, was the brain of the army, the man who succeeded in repairing it after Vietnam. Late in the 1970s DePuy had overseen the drafting of a new how-to-fight doctrine. Training standards were established on everything—from the minimum number of push-ups a soldier should be able to do, to marksmanship scores. DePuy saw that an army had to perform thousands of discrete tasks, many of them boring and repetitive, but they added up to overall success or failure. The key was making sure they were performed well under the pressure of battle conditions.

To Powell the most important result of the DePuy legacy was the creation of the National Training Center, on 1000 square miles in the Mojave Desert, south of Death Valley. Beginning in 1981, army combat units had been going there to spend two weeks straight, day and night, fighting an opposing force specially trained in Soviet tactics. The battle realism and live fire brought the soldiers and their officers as close to real war as possible.

Powell felt another key to the army's—and the entire military's—success was a mature understanding of public relations and politics, and how to use them. On December 13 he addressed the officers at

the National Defense University, in Washington, where he had studied 13 years earlier. He spoke at length about the responsibility of
modern military officers to understand the political and media components of their jobs.

The Chairman told how he worked on his relationships with reporters, so they trusted him and accepted his explanations of events. "Once
you've got the forces moving and everything's being taken care of by
the commanders, turn your attention to television. You can win the
battle or lose the war if you don't handle the story right."

Politics, he said, is fundamental. "People sometimes say, Well, Powell, he's a political general anyway. The fact of the matter is, there isn't
a general in Washington who isn't political—not if he's going to be
successful—because that's the nature of our system. It's the way the
Department of Defense works. It's the way in which we formulate
foreign policy. It's the way in which we get approval for our policy."

LIEUTENANT General Kelly was at home on Saturday evening, December 16, when the phone rang at 9:25. It was the Southern Command's operations director, Brigadier General William Hertzog, calling from Panama City. He sounded agitated.

"We just had a guy shot," Hertzog said. "He might be dead."

Kelly asked for more information.

Hertzog said it was an off-duty marine lieutenant. "We don't know
what's happening right now. We're still working on it."

Fine, Kelly said. He hung up and began dialing.

Powell was at home, at Quarters 6—the Chairman's official residence, at Fort Myer, Virginia—up in the second-floor living area. The
Powells spent most of their time there, away from the spacious, formal
first floor, used for official entertaining. All indications from intelligence were that it was going to be a quiet weekend around the world.
Alma Powell was reading. The Chairman's private phone rang.

"General Powell," he answered.

Kelly reported the Panama shooting.

"S___," Powell said. He asked Kelly to report further developments.
Soon Powell received a confirmed report that the marine, Lieutenant
Robert Paz, had died at Gorgas Army Hospital.

Powell called Cheney at home. "It is starting to build," Powell said.

Kelly went to his Pentagon office and was joined by his deputy for current operations, Rear Admiral Joe Lopez. They formed a crisis action team of a handful of Joint Staff specialists and began work.

There were more details on the shooting. Paz had been one of four off-duty officers, unarmed and in civilian clothes, who had gone into Panama City for dinner and had apparently made a wrong turn onto a street near PDF headquarters. Their car had been stopped at a PDF roadblock. They said PDF soldiers had tried to pull them from the car and aimed weapons at them, so the driver had tried to speed away. The PDF had opened fire. Besides Paz's fatal wounding, another of the officers had been grazed on the ankle by a bullet.

Kelly was still personally tracking all the major incidents of Americans being abused or harassed in Panama. Until now no American serviceman had been killed by the PDF. As he read through the reports Kelly saw that the Paz incident wasn't a clear-cut incident of unprovoked PDF aggression—the car had sped away from a legitimate roadblock, lending an element of ambiguity.

Earlier that evening General Thurman had arrived at Andrews Air Force Base for a planned two-day blitz around Washington—the Pentagon, the State Department, Congress. From Andrews he had gone to his brother's house in town, had dinner, and gone to bed. At 11:00 p.m. he was awakened and told about the shooting. He went right to the Pentagon, where he called Panama to talk with Hertzog. Intelligence now was showing that Noriega himself was managing the aftermath of the shooting incident.

Something always happens when I leave that goddamn joint, Thurman thought to himself. He could see events coming to a head. "It's time for me to go back," he announced. By 1:00 a.m., now December 17, he was headed back on the five-hour flight to Panama.

By 6:00 A.M. more reports were coming in from Panama. Another, related incident had occurred at the same PDF checkpoint about half an hour before the shooting. Navy lieutenant Adam J. Curtis and his wife, Bonnie, had been stopped and told to wait for a check on their identification. While waiting, they had witnessed the shooting. Blindfolded with masking tape, both were taken to a nearby PDF office, then to another building, which turned out to be the Comandancia.

A senior PDF officer, at least a major, had overseen a four-hour interrogation of the Curtises, during which they were beaten and verbally abused. Lieutenant Curtis was kicked in the groin repeatedly and hit in the mouth. A gun was put to Curtis' head. The Panamanians fondled Bonnie Curtis' neck and the back of her legs. At several points she was sexually threatened. She was interrogated about her husband's job, which the PDF claimed was with the CIA.

After four hours the Curtises were abruptly released. They returned to the U.S. Naval Station and reported what had happened.

Kelly wondered if the PDF was coming apart. Had the situation in Panama reached a point of dangerous instability? Noriega had been meticulous about not having a direct face-off showing senior PDF involvement and a lack of discipline. This was a regime out of control.

The detention and harassment of the Curtises was reported in detail to Powell and Cheney. Cheney said that he wanted to have a meeting in his Pentagon office at ten o'clock Sunday morning to review the options. He called Scowcroft and said that he thought there would have to be a meeting with the President later that day.

At 8:30 a.m. Powell went to the Pentagon and sat down with Kelly and the crisis action team. Kelly reported that Noriega was really scrambling on this one. Noriega had issued a communiqué blaming the shooting incident on the four U.S. officers, alleging that the men had broken through a PDF checkpoint in their car and shot at Noriega's Comandancia, wounding three Panamanians, including a soldier and a one-year-old girl. U.S. intelligence listeners had heard Noriega himself on the telephone and radio working out false stories.

Powell talked with Thurman, now back in Panama, on the secure line. Thurman already had his more than 13,000 troops on so-called Delta Alert, the second-highest state of readiness. Thurman said that Noriega's actions were just about as inflammatory as could be. He reminded Powell that just two days earlier Noriega's appointed legislature had named him "maximum leader for national liberation" and declared that Panama was "in a state of war" with the United States. Thurman said that the PDF bullies had soaked up all the rhetoric and were giving Noriega what he wanted.

Thurman said he saw three options: (1) do nothing militarily—just protest; (2) execute some portion of the Blue Spoon offensive operations against the PDF and try to snatch Noriega; (3) execute the full Blue Spoon plan.

"Do nothing, and we'll pay a horrendous price," Thurman said.

"Because all that will do is elevate his stature in the minds of his major thugs." The killing of Paz in cold blood required an answer.

The snatch job on Noriega puts you in harm's way, Thurman said, rejecting option two. They were tracking Noriega and knew his whereabouts perhaps 80 percent of the time. If the U.S. military went after him and missed him and he still had his PDF, no American in Panama would be safe.

Thurman recommended option three—do it all, demolish the PDF, and get it over with. We are rehearsed, he said.

After about ten minutes Powell said, "Okay, fine, got your pitch on it. I've got to go brief Cheney." Powell was clearly reserving his opinion. "I'll get back to you later."

Powell went up to Cheney's office, where the two sat down alone just before 10:00 a.m. As usual, Cheney seemed mainly to want to listen.

There was a lot of premeditation in what the PDF was doing to Americans, Powell said. "It was not a snap judgment by the PDF." The Chairman said that the Blue Spoon plan was good. They had rehearsed; they might never be more ready. He was for recommending to the President the execution of the full Blue Spoon plan.

Cheney did not disagree. He seemed open to all possibilities, but said he wanted to hear what the others had to say.

At this point they were joined by Henry Rowen, assistant secretary of defense; Richard C. Brown, the deputy assistant secretary for inter-American affairs; spokesman Pete Williams; Rear Admiral William Owens, Cheney's military assistant; Dave Addington, Cheney's civilian special assistant; and Kelly and Sheafer of the Joint Staff.

After the latest reports were summarized, Cheney wanted assessments and recommendations. He asked each man for his opinion.

Several of the civilians asked if the killing of Lieutenant Paz, apparently the main issue, constituted a sufficient smoking gun to justify military action. Would the facts as now presented hold up under the scrutiny that would inevitably come? Did Noriega's claim that the U.S. officers had fired first have any merit? Did speeding away from the checkpoint give the PDF justification for shooting?

Powell and the others said they were checking everything, but it looked as if the Noriega claim were provably untrue.

When it seemed each man had had his full say, Cheney thanked them all politely and asked Powell to stay behind so the two could talk alone again. He realized now that Americans—military and civilian—were seriously at risk in Panama. That changed the entire situation.

Powell agreed.

They talked about the mess in Panama. It had been that way for a long time, but frankly, Cheney said, they now had an obligation if they were going to have their guys there.

They could not allow this kind of thing to happen, Powell said. It was probably time to act.

Yes, Cheney said. And not just against Noriega. The whole PDF. They had finally reached a point where they could justify U.S. military intervention.

Powell said that he would very quietly call the Joint Chiefs together, get their views, and make sure they were on board.

POWELL did not want to call the chiefs into the Pentagon, where a Sunday meeting would be noticed by the press. Instead he sent word that he wanted them for coffee at his quarters at 11:30 a.m. Army chief Carl Vuono lived just down the street, at Quarters 1; Chief of Naval Operations Carl Trost was contacted at chapel at the Navy Yard, in Washington; marine commandant Al Gray was standing by, and air force chief Larry Welch was also anticipating trouble.

The four chiefs gathered in the first-floor study, at the back of Quarters 6. Powell greeted each man warmly—Al, Larry, Carl, and Carl. They all took seats, and coffee was served. Kelly briefed them for about ten minutes, providing the latest on the killing of Paz and the harassment of the Curtises. He could see from the chiefs' looks and questions that the plight of the Curtises had caught everybody's attention more than the shooting. Here were Noriega's men mistreating a family, a woman, a noncombatant. Kelly very quickly summarized the Blue Spoon plan, which all the chiefs had been briefed on the previous month.

Powell told them he had met with Cheney and Cheney's staff earlier that morning. Both the Secretary and he were inclined to recommend to President Bush later that afternoon that Blue Spoon be executed. But he and Cheney wanted their views and advice.

Carl Vuono said that Blue Spoon was a good plan—complex, yes, but it would achieve the objective of wiping out the PDF. Any attempt to dilute the plan with lesser options had to be resisted. The operation was fully supportable and sufficient to achieve the assigned task.

Marine general Al Gray was fidgety. "My world is divided into acceptable and unacceptable acts," he said. "This is unacceptable." The situation would not get better. He was totally in favor of military action, and he was sure the Panamanian people wanted Noriega out.

Kelly silently observed that Gray spoke with bittersweet enthusiasm. Panama was a classic candidate for a marine landing; it was a small country, virtually all coastline. But Blue Spoon was almost exclusively an army operation. Surprise and speed dictated an airborne operation. Everyone in the room knew that it would take the marines too long to get there on ships. Still, Gray said that if the fight in Panama got mired down, his marines would be handy.

The navy had ships in the Caribbean and the Pacific, Admiral Carl Trost knew. There was some symbolic appeal to showing the force of a carrier battle group, but he didn't think it would be needed or could have much of an impact. Trost was willing to concede it was predominantly an army–air force operation. He told the others he strongly supported Blue Spoon.

Characteristically, air force general Larry Welch listened quietly, not saying a great deal, coming to his own conclusions. This was a very important meeting, he thought. For good reason the chiefs were traditionally conservative on the use of military force. They did not typically support hasty or primarily political interventions. He thought the execution of Blue Spoon would be both.

Welch said they had to consider the downsides of a massive invasion. First, they had to expect that the other Latin American nations would, at the least, posture against what the United States was doing. U.S. policies in the region could be set back years. Second, the PDF might be far more resistant than expected. He hoped a quick fix had not been promised. Third, some critics would say that the Department of Defense was running out of enemies and had seized on this opportunity to demonstrate the need for military force. Fourth, Welch said, was the real possibility that popular feeling would see Noriega as the little guy, unfairly overwhelmed. And fifth, the American military had to be certain that the provocation was genuine.

It was a long list of negatives. Welch finally summarized his argument: As long as they went in with their eyes open to these downsides and were committed enough to overcome them as events unfolded, he supported the operation. There was no other solution, he said.

Powell took the floor. He and Kelly were going over to see the President, he said. My recommendation is going to be that we execute Blue Spoon. "I want to make sure that we're all agreeing." He went around the room once again, asking for final recommendations.

All four chiefs said they were with him.

Powell and Kelly climbed into the Chairman's car and were driven to the White House. That Sunday was a beautiful wintry day. The city streets were decked out for Christmas. It was a time for family and peace, perhaps the most difficult season in which to recommend an offensive military operation to the President, Powell reflected.

Kelly and Powell, wearing casual civilian clothes, trooped through the White House up to the second-floor residence for a 2:00 p.m. meeting with Bush. One of the Bushes' many Christmas parties was winding down on the first floor. Carolers in eighteenth-century costume were singing, off to one side, and a few hangers-on lingered.

Cheney arrived. Baker, Scowcroft, Bob Gates, and press secretary Marlin Fitzwater also came in. Bush was wearing a white shirt, blue blazer, gray slacks, brown shoes, and a pair of bright red socks, one emblazoned with the word "Merry," the other with "Christmas." Kelly thought they were the most god-awful socks he'd ever seen.

Powell noted to himself that the only key players missing were Vice President Quayle and Chief of Staff Sununu.

Kelly gave a seven-minute summary of the facts gathered about Lieutenant Paz's death and the harassment of the Curtises. Kelly, who favored an invasion, laid it on as heavily as he could. He said these two actions were unprecedented, even in Noriega's Panama.

Powell presented only one option to the President: Blue Spoon.

Why don't we just go get Noriega? Bush asked. Take me through why we shouldn't do this with a smaller force.

Reeling off all his arguments about the need to destroy the PDF, Powell said that the massive use of force was in fact less risky than a smaller effort. The choice was pay now or pay later. You go down there to take Noriega out, and you haven't accomplished that much, because he would be replaced by another corrupt PDF thug.

Powell said he would need at least 48 hours' notice to prepare and marshal the forces and air transportation for Blue Spoon. The ideal

H-hour was 1:00 a.m., late enough to surprise the PDF, but leaving five hours before daybreak to decapitate them. Also 1:00 a.m. would be close to high tide, a real benefit for the navy SEALs.

Blue Spoon would be a complete takedown of the PDF and the Panamanian government. "We are going to own the country for several weeks," Powell said, underscoring that this plan was not a surgical strike or a simple in-and-out operation. Bad things will happen, the Chairman said. There will be casualties—ours and theirs, military and civilian. "We will do all we can to keep them at a minimum."

Scowcroft inquired about casualty levels.

"We are going to hurt people," Powell responded. He avoided naming a specific number. He said he could guarantee rapid success, but could not tell how long it would take.

Bush probed. He had all kinds of questions that challenged the plan, some of them very specific; for example, how long it would take to get from one road to another. "Well, I don't know," the President said at one point.

Powell feared that the meeting was drifting, like a sailboat tacking back and forth across a bay, and he didn't know where it would end up. After answering the questions put to him, he concluded, "My recommendation is that we go with the full plan. I can tell you that the chiefs agree with me to a man."

When Powell was finished, Cheney spoke up. "I support what the Chairman just recommended to you," he told Bush.

Kelly had the impression that Cheney's relative silence meant he'd talked with the President privately and felt that since his position was already on the table, he didn't have to say a lot. But in fact Cheney had not spoken with Bush. It was simply that after the failed coup it had become clear to him that the President wanted this problem solved. It had been up to Powell, he felt, to carry the ball by outlining the military plan.

"I think we ought to go," Baker said. "As you know, the State Department has been for this for a long time, but these are the downsides of doing it." He then made a tour of the world, predicting the negative responses the U.S. invasion would prompt. But over all, Baker said, he did not think that any nation's heart would be in the criticism, and he anticipated that privately most of these governments would send back-channel word that they were neutral or even pleased.

What about the casualty levels? Scowcroft asked again, raising his voice. As Powell saw it, Scowcroft was doing Bush's sharpshooting.

Powell said no number could be given.

Damage levels?

Again it was hard to say, but each of the 28 targeted assault points was there for a reason.

Would Noriega be captured?

The best special operations people would be on his trail.

One of the President's stated goals in Panama was to bring about democracy, Scowcroft noted. Would this do it? And how?

The plan was to secretly swear in Guillermo Endara, the winner of the May election, as President, just before the invasion.

Soon they turned to the aftermath of Blue Spoon. At this moment Powell thought it finally looked as if Bush would approve. The sailboat had finished its tacking and was heading directly to its destination.

Someone asked about the public and press reaction.

Marlin Fitzwater, who had said very little, now remarked that he thought both would generally be positive. "Of course, you're going to have that element in the press that will criticize you," he told Bush. But he did not think that would be a major problem.

After an hour and 40 minutes Bush said, as if to summarize the view of Noriega that had emerged, "This guy is not going to lay off. It will only get worse." He looked at Powell and said very quietly, "We're going to go."

"Roger, sir."

Kelly felt an immediate rush to his gut, the first time in his two years as director of operations. They were committing young Americans to combat, and some of them were going to die.

Because Blue Spoon required a 48-hour minimum advance notice, H-hour was set for 1:00 a.m. Wednesday, December 20.

POWELL and Kelly were quiet in the car going back to the Pentagon. "I want you to get this information out," Powell said, referring to the key operations people in the commands involved. "I don't want an order published. Just call people on the [secure] telephone."

Both pondered how long the secret could be kept. They hoped to make it through the Monday evening news without some direct information leaking. Something would get out on Tuesday for sure, but perhaps the leak would be late enough or unclear enough that they would still have a chance for some kind of surprise at H-hour.

Back at the Pentagon, Powell called the four C in Cs who would be immediately involved. One was Max Thurman. Powell also called the C in C of the Special Operations Command, General James J. Lindsay; the Forces Command C in C, General Edwin H. Burba, Jr.; and the Transportation Command C in C, General Hansford T. Johnson. Finally Powell called each of the chiefs to inform them of Bush's approval. He apologized to Vuono for failing to show up at his Christmas party that afternoon. Cheney also had been a no-show.

Kelly went to his own office and summoned his deputy for current operations, Joe Lopez, and four junior officers on his Latin American team. "We're going to execute Blue Spoon," Kelly said, swearing each to maximum secrecy and instructing that every step was to be carried out with opsec—operational security—foremost in their minds.

Kelly received a call from General Lindsay, commander in chief of the Special Operations Command. Lindsay said he thought it was a terrible name for an operation. "Do you want your grandchildren to say you were in Blue Spoon?" he asked Kelly.

It could have been worse, Kelly thought. One Panama contingency plan was named Blind Logic. Other operations had been given equally strange names over the years. One general had executed a Stumbling Block and a Lima Bean. Kelly tossed around ideas for a new name with Joe Lopez. "How about Just Action?" Kelly proposed.

"How about Just Cause?" Lopez countered.

They agreed that would be much better. The name was sent up the chain of command and approved.

Powell went back to Quarters 6. There were a few more calls, to make sure that each of the key people knew what the others were doing. After the calls, suddenly with time on his hands, he let the enormity of the decision sink in. They were going to war.

He'd personally known, but heard and read more, about the self-doubt the commander feels on the eve of battle. Now such misgivings struck him hard, and thinking through the plans again did not make the doubts yield or go away. Blue Spoon was an incredibly complex plan, requiring precision. One miscue could set off a string of others, like a pileup on the freeway.

And where was Noriega? Did he know? Would he find out?

5

WHEN Powell returned to the Pentagon very early Monday, December 18, he felt uneasy. He went upstairs to bring Cheney up to speed.

Cheney himself did not feel much in the way of jitters. He knew when he accepted the job as Secretary that it might entail using force and sending men to die. He had been in the Ford White House and had seen firsthand the tendency of the people at the top—the President, the national security adviser, the Secretary of Defense—to meddle needlessly and counterproductively in military operations. The one remedy, he had decided, was a clean, clear-cut chain of command—as short as possible. And no meddling from the top.

As the chief intermediary between the uniformed military and the White House, Cheney felt he could do as much as anyone to reduce interference. But he would also make sure he understood the plan so he could answer questions that might come from the White House.

That morning Cheney asked a lot of questions. It seemed to Powell that he wanted to know all the details, right down to the squad level.

Later Powell called in Kelly and began his own interrogation. He wanted to review each element, every single event of the plan. Kelly gave the best answers he could.

After preaching the importance of sufficient force, Powell now spoke of reducing risks and damage. In Kelly's opinion it was as if Powell had reached into his desk and brought out a wire brush—and he was now scrubbing everything and everyone, including himself. Necessary and inevitable, Kelly concluded; there was a lot at stake. The leader's great fear before battle was not just a personal fear or fear of failure, but a larger, moral kind of fear. Powell was afraid that he was going to get a bunch of people killed because of stupidity.

Powell wanted to know more about the F-117A Stealth fighters and their planned use at the Río Hato PDF barracks.

Two 2000-pound bombs were going to be dropped about 50 yards from the barracks, Kelly said. This offset bombing might break a few windows, stun the troops in the barracks, and cause some electrical fires, but not do a great deal more.

Who says? Powell wanted to know.

That's what the weapons effects experts claimed anyhow, Kelly said.

Powell realized that the United States had to put Panama back together as quickly as possible after the invasion. This would require popular support from the Panamanians, which meant killing as few as possible of the kinds of people—PDF privates—who would be asleep in the barracks and who, Powell hoped, would surrender. He ordered that the offset distance be increased dramatically, to 250 yards.

As Powell went through this process he felt more comfortable. He was just following the lessons of his military experience. As a new major, in 1966, he had taught precisely this subject—operations and planning—at the Army Infantry School, Fort Benning, Georgia.

By that evening Powell felt a momentary sense of contentment.

STINER had arrived in Panama that Monday night dressed, as usual, in civilian clothes. At 10:00 p.m. he gathered all his commanders down to the battalion level—30 officers in all—and said, "This is it. This is a go." Security, he said, is of the greatest importance. They could now tell only those officers with top secret clearance.

He was worried about leaks. U.S. servicemen and servicewomen lived all over the place in Panama; some even lived at the same installations as PDF troops. It was agreed that not until the next night would the troops be brought in, briefed, and then sequestered, so they could load ammunition and get ready to go. There was to be no increased level of activity, no signal of any kind.

CHENEY was also worried about leaks. He decided that he would not have Pete Williams notify the media pool—the small group of reporters who would cover the invasion for all the news organizations—until after the evening television news shows the next night. This would be less than six hours before H-hour, making it impossible for reporters to make it to Panama in time for the start of Just Cause.

The Secretary raised his worries with Powell. What happens if the cover is blown, if it becomes public? Does Max Thurman have, on the ground in Panama, the capability to go ahead and start the operation early with what he's already got on hand?

Powell checked and then assured Cheney they could go early.

Later that night, after the Monday evening news shows, Tom Kelly sat at his large desk in his windowless office. Too quiet, he concluded. H-hour was still some 30 hours away. It was too silky. Things weren't going wrong. With each minute passing he felt a sense of foreboding.

AT 7:00 A.M. the next day—Tuesday, December 19—Powell called in his chief public affairs aide, army colonel Bill Smullen, told him the operation was going to occur, and pledged him to secrecy.

"I want to maintain as much normalcy as possible," Powell said. Looking at his schedule for the day, he saw he had a noon lunch with Naval Academy midshipman Tom Daily. At the Army-Navy football game several weeks before, Powell had accepted Daily's friendly wager on the outcome, and Navy had won. Daily's prize was lunch with the Chairman at the Pentagon, set for this worst of all possible days, just before the largest U.S. military operation in years. Okay, Powell said, I'm going through with the lunch. It lasted 45 minutes.

The day was otherwise filled with preinvasion meetings and briefings. Cheney and Powell went to the White House to update Bush.

Around 5:00 p.m. Powell had the chiefs into his office for a final run-through. Cheney came down to join them. For Cheney it was a satisfying symbolic moment. It showed he was keeping the chiefs involved. He felt that the chain of command was just right, running as it did from him to Powell, rather than to the chiefs as a committee.

Powell watched the evening news on television. CBS and NBC had stories that some kind of operation was about to happen, but neither had any idea of its dimensions. On CBS, Dan Rather led off the news, saying, "U.S. military transport planes have left Fort Bragg, North Carolina. The Pentagon declines to say whether or not they are bound for Panama. It will say only that the Eighteenth Airborne Corps has been conducting an airborne readiness exercise."

NBC reporter Ed Rabel said, "United States C-141 Starlifters flew into Panama this afternoon, one landing every ten minutes. No one here could confirm that these aircraft were part of a U.S. invasion group. But tensions on both sides are high this evening."

Mighty close, but no compromise. Powell realized he would wind up having to thank some reporters.

Kelly was still astonished that it had not leaked. There was already a lot of aluminum flying through the air to Panama.

Powell, home for dinner, told Alma he was going back to the

Pentagon and didn't know when he would return. He knew she had noticed all the movement and the phone calls, but he hadn't told her what was happening; he never did. The Powell family policy was to keep their home life as separate from military business as possible.

Powell returned to the Pentagon after dinner and took a nap.

The building was eerily quiet. In the Crisis Situation Room, 15 people were working in an atmosphere of hushed excitement and tension. Secure phone lines to the Southern Command had been activated. The television was tuned to the three networks and CNN. On a wall screen were the latest data on the status of Just Cause.

Kelly and intelligence specialist Ted Sheafer sat at the center of the room's long table. Kelly was running things, checking periodically with Thurman, whose twangy voice would issue from a loudspeaker so everyone in the room could hear. Kelly was pounding hard on the key question of Noriega's whereabouts. They had lost him at around 6:00 p.m. Goddamnit, we want him, Kelly was saying. Where is he? There were three dozen to four dozen people in Panama specifically designated as the Noriega tracking team. And yet he'd slipped away.

At 11:30 Thurman reported that Noriega was possibly in the city of Colón, the last place he'd been spotted by his trackers.

Powell arrived at the Crisis Situation Room at 11:52, wearing a black sweater, with four stars sewn on each shoulder, and green army pants. His shirt was open at the neck, where his white T-shirt showed.

DOWN in Panama, two U.S. soldiers who had somehow found their way outside Stiner's lockup were overheard mentioning H-hour by a PDF eavesdropper, who reported up the chain to Noriega.

"The Americans aren't coming," Noriega said. "They wouldn't do a thing like that." He arranged to have a meeting at the Comandancia the next morning at eight o'clock to review the situation.

U.S. listeners picked up part of a conversation in which someone from the PDF said, "The ball game starts at one."

Stiner was convinced that this referred to H-hour and that the operation had been compromised. He picked up the direct line to Thurman. "We need to advance the timing," he said, and explained.

"How much advance do you want?" Thurman asked.

"How about thirty minutes?"

"Okay. Do it," Thurman said.

But there were complications. The Muse rescue and the attack on the Comandancia had to be precisely coordinated. A swing bridge had to be placed over the Canal so four Sheridan tanks could be moved onto a hill, where they could hit the Comandancia with direct fire. A ship in one of the Canal locks had to be cleared out first.

Stiner picked up the phone again to Thurman. "I can't do it in thirty minutes. How about fifteen?"

"Fifteen's okay too," Thurman said.

At 12:07 a.m. Thurman officially sent out the order to JSOC to execute the Muse rescue mission at H minus 15, or 12:45. At 12:18 he directed the same execution time for the attack on the Comandancia and for the navy SEALs' mission at Puenta Paitilla Airport, where they were to come ashore and disable Noriega's private jet.

A report of a female U.S. dependent wounded by the PDF at Albrook Air Force Station, in Panama City, came in over the speaker at 12:29. For five minutes Thurman reported gunfire at Fort Amador and the Bridge of the Americas, as well as Albrook.

President Bush had informed Cheney and Powell that the point of no return would be achieved once Endara agreed to be sworn in as President of Panama and to request U.S. intervention. If Endara would not play, they had to check with him personally, Bush said.

Thurman was heard from again at 12:39. The swearing-in of Endara as the new President of Panama had been completed.

Although some units had moved into place in advance, official execution of Just Cause took place at H minus 15. At exactly the moment of execution Thurman's voice came over the speaker, reporting gunfire in the vicinity of the Comandancia. The PDF was firing at the helicopters coming in for Muse at Modelo Prison.

Divided into task forces, the troops so carefully prepared by Thurman and Stiner were swinging into action all around Panama.

Around this time President Bush arrived in the Oval Office wearing a dark blue sweater over his shirt and tie. He signed a short order authorizing the armed forces to apprehend and arrest Noriega and others in Panama currently under indictment in the United States for drug-related offenses.

At 12:57 gunfire was reported on the Atlantic side of Panama.

At 1:00 a.m. the military officially moved up to the highest defense-readiness condition, called DefCon 1. Hostilities were under way.

FROM HIS EXPERIENCE IN THE FORD White House, Cheney knew the human reaction to this kind of crisis. The situation would build, and everyone would stay up all night to hear the latest news on events they could do nothing about. Then when the moment of action or decision arrived, they would all be exhausted and in the worst possible shape to make judgments. So Cheney had gone up to his Pentagon office after dinner and fallen asleep in a small bunk room there. After several hours he rose. For the first time he used his office shower.

He then went down to the Crisis Situation Room. It was 1:02. He moved in next to Powell, at the center of the long table.

Almost immediately great news came in: the PDF Zone 3 commander had ordered his unit to stand down. This was significant, as it meant several companies were out of action on the PDF side.

At 1:07 there was a report that U.S. troops, using a loudspeaker to order the PDF troops in the Comandancia to lay down their arms, had been met instead with return fire. Just two minutes later CNN reported that U.S. troops had attacked Noriega's headquarters.

At 1:11 Powell and Cheney listened as the news came over the loudspeaker that the Delta team was on the roof of the Modelo Prison. Two minutes later word came that Muse was out.

At 1:14 the PDF was retreating at Albrook Air Force Station.

At 1:17 the Southern Command—SouthCom—reported that the Comandancia was calling for reinforcements.

The PDF commander of the 5th Company at Balboa had shut down his operation, Thurman reported at 1:23.

The next report said the marines at the U.S. embassy were taking fire from rocket-propelled grenades.

Just before 1:30 SouthCom reported that army Rangers had parachuted into Río Hato, and the Bridge of the Americas was secure.

There was a report that the helicopter carrying Muse had crashed. The crew and Muse might be dead. Disappointment was written all over Powell's face. Muse was the guy they were going to rescue for the President. At about the same time, word came that U.S. troops had broken into Noriega's likely hideout, a beach house, and found it empty. This intensified the pessimism in the room.

Powell knew there was an apartment near Colón that was another Noriega hangout. He called Thurman.

"When are we going to take down the apartment?" Powell snapped.

"We're working on it," Thurman replied.

Soon Thurman was back with the news that the apartment too was a blank. A third downer in a very short period.

OVER at the White House, Bush turned on the television set in his study. At 1:40 Marlin Fitzwater appeared on the screen. "The President has directed United States forces to execute at one a.m. this morning preplanned missions in Panama to protect American lives, restore the democratic process, preserve the integrity of the Panama Canal treaties, and apprehend Manuel Noriega," he told reporters.

JUST before 2:00 a.m. Powell and Cheney received word that all was quiet at the U.S. embassy and that the mission to neutralize a PDF company at Tocumen Airport was going okay. Minutes later there was a report that the commander of the PDF's Zone 6 had ordered his troops to abandon posts before the Americans arrived.

At 2:20 a.m. word came that Muse had survived the crash and was safe. Instantly the atmosphere became buoyant, almost joyful.

Powell called CIA director William Webster. Cheney, who had been calling the President about every half hour, told Bush that Muse was out and safe. And the Delta team had done the job in record time.

At 2:40 SouthCom reported the Comandancia was in flames.

A sour note was struck at 2:49, when Thurman reported that Noriega was still at large. Except for this large problem, the operation seemed to be going well. Shortly after 3:00 they learned that PDF forces at Colón, Tocumen Airport, and near the Costa Rican border had fallen. The PDF was surrendering left and right without a fight.

Powell listened, made notes, and talked quietly to Cheney. Neither was trying personally to manage the operation. Both felt they had to let Thurman and the others do their jobs. Although Powell was glad about all the reports of success, he knew that war—particularly war fought in darkness—is a funny thing. Bad news, especially really bad news, would likely be the slowest to work its way up the chain.

More bad news did come. The navy SEALs had succeeded in disabling Noriega's private jet, but had met heavy PDF resistance. Of 15 men, four had been killed and seven wounded.

The Noriega question tugged at Powell throughout the night. At 3:39 they received a report that he had fled and was still safe.

Cheney continued to give the President half-hour updates. The Comandancia had been reduced to rubble. The key military targets had been overrun, and much of the organized PDF resistance had been eliminated. At 4:00 a.m. Bush went to bed.

About 4:30 a.m. Powell started to prepare for a public briefing that he and Cheney would be giving in a few hours. He went into a little room off to the side of the Crisis Situation Room that had a map of Panama on the wall. The Chairman sat there for 15 or 20 minutes in a kind of trance, alternately making notes and studying the map. He remarked to an aide that the American public's opinion of the operation would start its rise or fall on the basis of his and Cheney's presentation. When Powell was done, he went down to his office bathroom, took off his sweater, and put on a tie and army jacket.

At 6:30 a.m. Bush returned to the Oval Office. An 11-paragraph speech to the nation had been prepared. There was not enough time to put it on the TelePrompTer. He would have to read from a typed version with his own notes in the margin. By 7:20 Bush was before the cameras. He gave a very broad overview of the situation.

Immediately afterward Cheney and Powell appeared at the Pentagon pressroom to brief reporters and answer questions. Cheney delivered a seven-paragraph statement that echoed the President's.

Powell took the podium as Kelly stood by the maps. Speaking without notes and taking more time than Cheney had, Powell moved confidently over the geography of Panama, matching units to missions and locations. He began with a report of success. A PDF infantry company had been neutralized. The Bridge of the Americas had been taken, and the area around Howard Air Force Base was secure. The same with Río Hato, the Comandancia, and the Torrijos airport.

"We have not yet located the general," Powell said, tight-jawed. "But as a practical matter we have decapitated him from the dictatorship, and he is now a fugitive and will be treated as such."

So far, he said, preliminary information indicated that nine Americans had been killed in action and 39 wounded.

At the end of the session, when the questioning was over, Powell stepped to the microphone and said, "Could I just say that I hope you recognize how complicated an operation this was and how competently it was carried out by the armed forces of the United States. We all—the Secretary and I, all of our associates—deeply regret the loss of American life. But that's sometimes necessary in pursuit of our national interests and in the fight for democracy."

ALMA Powell had not known her husband was going to be on television that morning, but a family member had called to alert her. Normally very critical of his performances, she called him later that day at the Pentagon. "That was good," she said.

BY DECEMBER 21—D-day plus 1, as it was called in Pentagonese— almost all the goals of the operation had been achieved. The task forces had secured the key target sites. The Canal, closed down during the battle, was reopened for daylight operations. A snag, the PDF's holding of U.S. hostages—among them some journalists—at the Marriott Hotel, was resolved when the hotel was taken by U.S. soldiers.

The elusive Noriega, still at large, was the most serious stain on the operation. The United States announced that it had put a $1 million bounty on him, hoping that a PDF member or some other Panamanian anxious to end the Noriega era would step forward. Powell began referring to the capture of Noriega as "this last little irritant." Just finding him was turning into an obsession.

On Sunday, December 24, at about 3:30 p.m., a car drove up to the residence of the Vatican's representative in Panama, the papal nuncio. General Noriega, wearing a T-shirt and carrying two AK-47 semiautomatic rifles over his shoulder, emerged from the car, went inside the nunciature building, and requested political asylum.

Powell knew this did not solve the problem. Noriega could stay in the residence indefinitely, creating a diplomatic standoff. The Chairman expected that Thurman and Stiner would come up with some ideas. Stiner would have to respect the double sanctity of the papal nuncio's residence as both embassy and church property.

But there were ways to put pressure on the church. A visiting archbishop was taken on a tour of Noriega's former house and office. He was shown witchcraft materials, a library of books on Hitler, albums of pornographic and torture photos, and a large poster that suggested all the Catholic priests in Panama and other high Catholic officials in Central America were on a hit list.

The nuncio, the Reverend Sebastian Laboa, met with Thurman and

Stiner. He gave them a handwritten note that said if shooting started inside the nunciature, they were authorized to conduct an emergency assault to rescue as many people as possible.

On Wednesday, December 27, Thurman and Stiner ordered the troops to blast the nunciature with earsplitting rock music, to prevent anyone from eavesdropping on SouthCom's negotiations with the nuncio. It could be heard for several blocks.

Other troops acted as if they were preparing for an assault. Brush in the neighborhood was cut down; streetlights were shot out; barbed wire was laid; an army Black Hawk helicopter unloaded troops and equipment; tanks and armored personnel carriers blocked the streets.

At 8:44 P.M. on Wednesday, January 3, 1990, Noriega walked out of the nunciature in his military uniform and surrendered to members of Delta forces. When he was handcuffed, he shouted and cursed at the nuncio, who was standing nearby. Apparently Noriega had expected to be treated as a head of state or a prisoner of war. The nuncio blessed Noriega, who was taken to Howard Air Force Base, where a U.S. Drug Enforcement Administration agent arrested him.

At 9:00 p.m. Cheney called Bush. Forty minutes later Bush walked into the White House briefing room to announce the arrest.

"The United States used its resources in a manner consistent with political, diplomatic, and moral principle," he said.

The smoke eventually cleared concerning Noriega's movements before he gave himself up. At the start of Just Cause, Powell learned, the general had been at a brothel at Tocumen. When Noriega heard gunshots, he climbed into his trousers and jumped into an escape vehicle. Taking a well-traveled highway, he disappeared into Panama City, where he moved from one hiding place to another.

On January 5 Powell flew down to Panama to visit the commanders and the troops. In a meeting there with reporters he emphasized the political result of the operation. "The most important mission we accomplished is that we gave the country back to its people."

Why such a large force? he was asked.

"I'm always a great believer in making sure you get there with what you need and don't go in on the cheap side."

What do you think the impact of the operation will be on the debate on the cuts in the defense budget?

"Thank you for the question," Powell boomed. "I hope it has enormous effect. And as we start to go down in dollars and as we see the world changing, don't bust this apart. Don't think that this is the time to demobilize the armed force of the United States, because it isn't. There are still dangers in the world."

He knew this statement would attract little or no attention. Nonetheless, he felt that Panama was truly manna from heaven.

He flew home glad that the operation didn't look any different on the ground than it had from the Pentagon. There was no sign of buried secrets. The politicians and the media would have little alternative but to declare it a success.

The next day, Saturday, Powell was out in the garage behind Quarters 6, immersed in a favorite pastime: fixing up an old Volvo.

AFTER the operation Powell settled back into a peacetime rhythm. Panama was behind him. Now the focus was back on the military needs of the post–cold war era. He spent many hours in his office, being briefed, working the phones, trying to come up with a strategy for change. He was sure that the best way to proceed was to trust his gut instincts, but he also had a collection of rules and maxims he used as a practical road map for each day of decisions. Many were on a list he kept on display beneath the glass cover on his desk top:

COLIN POWELL'S RULES
1. It ain't as bad as you think. It will look better in the morning.
2. Get mad, then get over it.
3. Avoid having your ego so close to your position that when your position falls, your ego goes with it.
4. It can be done!
5. Be careful what you choose. You may get it.
6. Don't let adverse facts stand in the way of a good decision.
7. You can't make someone else's choices. You shouldn't let some one else make yours.
8. Check small things.
9. Share credit.
10. Remain calm. Be kind.
11. Have a vision. Be demanding.
12. Don't take counsel of your fears or naysayers.
13. Perpetual optimism is a force multiplier.

To the left of that list was an aphorism not for public consumption that the Chairman had written out by hand on a piece of paper: Sometimes being responsible means pissing people off.

There was yet another axiom Powell tried to live by, especially in his professional life. He occasionally confided it, but it wasn't written down. Powell didn't need to remind himself of that one: You never know what you can get away with unless you try.

PART TWO

6

IN EARLY April, 1990, the Saudi Arabian ambassador to the United States, Prince Bandar bin Sultan, received a call from his uncle, Fahd ibn Abdul Aziz, King of his country.

Fahd reported that Iraqi President Saddam Hussein had just phoned to say that he wanted someone to come to Iraq to see him personally and discuss an urgent matter relating to America. Fahd wanted Bandar to undertake the mission. Bandar had been directly involved in the 1988 U.N. negotiations arranging a cease-fire in the eight-year Iran-Iraq War, and Saddam Hussein had agreed to receive him now as the emissary.

Bandar, 41, had an absolutely unique position in Washington. Most ambassadors spent their time on the fringes of real power. Bandar had long-term friendships with Bush, Baker, Cheney, Scowcroft, and Powell, having plied his backslapping irreverence and directness with all of them. This gave the Saudi royal family a channel into the upper reaches of the U.S. government. Until Bandar had become ambassador, in 1983, the Saudis had worked through obscure State Department officials. Bandar insisted on dealing with the top.

During the Reagan administration Bandar had taken Vice President Bush seriously, even when Bush was dismissed as a weak number two to Reagan. Bandar felt that Bush had a balanced view of the Middle East and was not emotionally or exclusively attached to the interests of Israel. The two men had had lunch together several times a year, and Bandar even went fishing with Bush.

A Saudi fighter pilot for 17 years and a favorite of King Fahd's, Bandar still walked with a fighter jock's swagger. He spoke perfect English and was steeped in American habits. Working political and media circles with cigars, gifts, invitations, information, off-color stories, and practical jokes, the prince was smooth and attentive. He could be both boyish and ruthless.

Now Fahd's request suggested that Bandar could act as intermediary between Saddam and the United States—just the kind of task he enjoyed. He left immediately for Iraq in his private jet.

At the airport on April 5 Saddam's personal secretary pointed the way. When Bandar sat down with Saddam, the Iraqi President said he had requested the meeting because officials in the United States were grossly overreacting to his April 1 speech. In the widely publicized talk Saddam had discussed his chemical weapons capability. The West, he had said, "will be deluded if they imagine that they can give Israel the cover to come and strike. By God, we will make the fire eat up half of Israel if it tries to do anything against Iraq."

On April 3 the White House had issued a statement calling the remarks "particularly deplorable and irresponsible." President Bush had publicly said, "This is no time to be talking about using chemical or biological weapons. This is no time to be escalating tensions in the Middle East. I would suggest that those statements be withdrawn."

Saddam told Bandar that his words had been misunderstood to mean he intended an offensive strike against Israel. His speech had been delivered to members of his armed forces at a public forum, where emotions ran high. As they both knew, it never hurt in the Arab world to threaten Israel, and so he had done it. Nonetheless, he had threatened to attack only if attacked. A surprise strike by Israel was always possible. In 1981 Israel had launched a preemptive air strike, destroying the nuclear research reactor south of Baghdad, and the memory lingered. He did not want to provoke another attack.

"I want to assure President Bush and His Majesty King Fahd that I will not attack Israel," Saddam stressed. In return the Americans would have to work to ensure that Israel would not attack Iraq.

Bandar said he would carry the message back to the United States.

There was a pause in the conversation. Then almost out of the blue Saddam referred to what he called the imperialist-Zionist conspiracy. "We have to be very careful about this conspiracy because the imperialist-Zionist forces keep pushing this theory that I have designs over my neighbors. I don't have designs over my neighbors."

Saddam did not name these neighbors, but Bandar interpreted him to mean the small Arab Gulf states, such as Kuwait, which held 10 percent of the world's oil reserves, and the United Arab Emirates.

"Well, Mr. President," Bandar said, "your brothers, your neighbors don't suspect you. And if you tell me now that you don't have designs, then there is no reason for either of us to worry about it at all."

"No, no," Saddam said. "But it's important that we don't allow the imperialist-Zionist rumor mill or forces to get between us."

Saddam then turned to justifying his verbal assault on Israel, though he continued giving assurances he would not attack the Jewish state. Israel was the natural lightning rod for creating a crisis atmosphere, he said. Two years after the Iran-Iraq cease-fire the Iraqi people were getting relaxed. "I must whip them into a sort of frenzy so they will be ready for whatever may happen."

Bandar left after four hours. He prepared an 18-page memo for his records, summarizing his discussion with Saddam. Bandar also reported to King Fahd, who told him to pass the message directly to Bush.

Saudi Arabia shared more than 500 miles of its northern border with Iraq. A friendly, stable Iraq was very much in Fahd's interest. For years he had been vouching for Saddam, who shunned the moderate Arab camp. Iraq, like Syria and Libya, was an outlaw state often tied to terrorist groups and accused of flagrant human rights abuses.

The Iran-Iraq War had provided an opportunity for the Saudis to bring Iraq closer. Bandar had acted as middleman between Iraq and CIA director William Casey so Iraq could obtain highly classified satellite information about Iranian troop movements. The Saudis had also signed a contract with the French for Mirage jets delivered to Iraq and done countless other large and small favors for Saddam.

Bandar felt that Saddam appreciated the assistance, but he also sensed that Saddam hated the dependence.

Four days after his meeting with Saddam, Bandar was in the Oval Office to see Bush. "His Majesty sent me here," Bandar began, "to give you a message that I got from President Saddam to you, which is, he assures you he has no intention of attacking Israel."

Bush seemed flabbergasted. "Well, if he doesn't intend it, why on earth does he have to say it?"

Bandar reminded Bush of the 1981 Israeli attack on the Iraqi reactor. Some Israelis were saying a newly built Iraqi reactor would have to be hit sooner or later. There were grounds for nervousness.

Bush was skeptical.

Saddam is suspicious there is a conspiracy against him, Bandar said.

Bull, Bush said. There is no conspiracy against him. It's his behavior that worries people.

Saddam is paranoid, Bandar said, like most military, security-conscious dictators. Little things mount up. In Bandar's view Saddam had been shaken by the reaction in the West and by Bush's own statements and now was just trying to do the right thing.

Bush said he would think about it all, but the bottom line was, Saddam should not have made the verbal attacks he did.

Two days later Saddam contacted King Fahd and the Iraqi ambassador to the United States, asking if there was any response from Bush. Having given his assurances that he would not attack Israel, Saddam wanted explicit assurances that Israel would not strike Iraq.

It was mid-April when King Fahd told Bandar to go back to Bush again. Bandar requested an immediate meeting that day. Bush was very busy, but he could always give Bandar a few minutes. Between meetings at the White House the two stood off to the side.

"You know, Mr. President," Bandar said, "they really are serious about this, and they want to assure you." Saddam and the Iraqis would not attack Israel. "And they would like to have assurance that Israel will not attack them."

"I don't want anybody to attack anybody," Bush said. He just wanted people to settle down. "We will talk to the Israelis, and I will get back to you. But everybody must just cool it."

Bush also indicated he was baffled by Saddam. "If this guy really doesn't mean it, why the heck does he go around saying these things?"

The White House contacted the Israelis, who said if Iraq did not launch anything against them, they would not launch anything against Iraq. The United States then passed that Israeli assurance directly to Saddam. Bandar also passed along his understanding of these assurances to King Fahd, who called Saddam with the report.

THREE months later, early in the week of July 16, 1990, in a second-floor office in the innermost ring of the Pentagon, a stocky, balding, well-dressed man was working the phones like a bookie. The red, gray, and green secure phones allowed him to discuss top secret code-word material with the National Security Agency, CIA, National

Photographic Intelligence Center, and other U.S. intelligence units in and out of the Pentagon.

Walter P. "Pat" Lang, Jr., a 50-year-old retired army colonel, was the Defense Intelligence Agency's national intelligence officer for the Middle East and South Asia, the senior Pentagon intelligence civilian for the region. He reported to the head of the DIA, a three-star general overseeing about 5000 civilian and military personnel who coordinate intelligence for the army, navy, air force, and marines. Lang evaluated raw intelligence, then relayed it in digested form to the highest level in the Pentagon, including Cheney and Powell. Lang not only had hands-on knowledge of satellite photos and communications intercepts but was a Middle East expert fluent in Arabic.

This morning Lang was hunched over the satellite photos of his region. Where there had been empty desert in southeastern Iraq, north of Kuwait, the day before, he now saw T-72 tanks—the top-of-the-line heavy tanks supplied to Iraq by the Soviet Union. The photos also showed all kinds of equipment being loaded on rail lines, equipment that could only belong to the Republican Guard, the most elite units of President Saddam Hussein. These units existed primarily to protect the regime in the capital of Baghdad and normally stayed in central Iraq. Why had the tanks been moved hundreds of miles? The satellite photos were so detailed that Lang could identify the tanks as belonging to the Hammurabi Division, named after the Babylonian King who devised the first formal legal system. Lang knew that there was no more potent division in all of Iraq.

Iraq had been complaining bitterly that Kuwait was exceeding its oil production quotas, set by the Organization of Petroleum Exporting Countries (OPEC), driving the prices down. Though Kuwait had once been part of Iraq, it had been granted independence in 1961 by the British. For practical purposes Iraq had acquiesced to Kuwait's status as a nation by permitting its admission to the Arab League in 1963.

To Lang the military logic was overwhelming: the movement meant Saddam intended to use force somehow. But Lang needed to see more. One day's photos were not enough to start raising alarms.

The next morning's photographs were even more disconcerting. The whole of the Hammurabi Division, all 300 tanks and more than 10,000 men, was in place near the Kuwaiti border. A second division—another crack armored unit of the Republican Guard—was showing up on the border. The third day a third division could be seen.

By July 19 more than 35,000 men from the three divisions were within 10 to 30 miles of the Kuwaiti border.

Over the years Lang had closely followed Iraq. In 1986, during the Iran-Iraq War, he had seen Iraq turn a major corner militarily. The sprawling nation of nearly 18 million people, in an area larger than the state of California, was no longer a Third World military power. Its 1-million-man army was the fourth largest in the world.

The sudden placement of three divisions on the Kuwaiti border was perplexing to Lang. In the fall of 1989 a secret assessment by all the U.S. intelligence agencies concluded that although Saddam wished to dominate the Gulf region, he was unlikely to try to do so, because the eight-year war had so severely strained the country's economy. And Lang could find no rehearsal indicating Saddam would take the three divisions to battle. So the intelligence summaries forwarded up the chain of command stressed the extraordinary nature of the troop movements, but did not forecast they would be used.

Powell read the intelligence summaries. Troubling but not alarming, he concluded. General Kelly and the JCS intelligence analysts were saying it looked as if Saddam were using the deployment as a threatening lever in the ongoing negotiations over oil. Earlier in the month Powell had visited Morocco, Egypt, Jordan, and Israel and felt reassured of continuing stability in the region.

But he still had some concerns about Iraq. Saddam had just had himself declared President for life by the powerless legislature. It was reminiscent of Noriega's having himself named maximum leader. Powell wanted to take some preliminary planning steps.

He called army general H. Norman Schwarzkopf, 55, the commander of the U.S. Central Command, the C in C responsible for the Middle East and Southwest Asia. Because the Gulf countries did not wish a visible U.S. presence in the region, Schwarzkopf's headquarters was at MacDill Air Force Base, in Florida. CentCom was largely a paper command. Its commander had a staff of 700, but in a crisis, fighting units would be assigned to him from all over the world.

A burly, aggressive, and outspoken former West Point football player, Schwarzkopf was known as the Bear and Stormin' Norman. At 6 foot 3, he was a terror as a boss, often furious when unhappy or dissatisfied. Schwarzkopf sometimes exploded when Pentagon civilians

Secretary of Defense Dick Cheney in a private moment, left, with President Bush at the White House. Below, an Oval Office meeting in December 1990. From left to right, Robert Gates—then deputy national security adviser—Dick Cheney, President Bush, Colin Powell, John Sununu, and Brent Scowcroft.

Above, Admiral William J. Crowe, Jr., Chairman of the Joint Chiefs of Staff from October 1, 1985, to October 1, 1989. Left, Lieutenant General Carl W. Stiner, war-fighting commander of the 1989 Panama invasion. Below, General Maxwell R. Thurman, commander in chief of the U.S. Southern Command, on December 22, 1989, two days into the Panama operation.

Secretary of State James Baker,
left, voting at the United Nations
on November 29, 1990, for the
resolution authorizing the use of force
against Iraq. Below, Prince Bandar
bin Sultan, Saudi Arabian ambassador
to the United States, with Dick Cheney.
Bottom, President Bush meets with
the Emir of Kuwait in the Oval Office.

The Bush inner circle conferring at Camp David. Below, General Colin Powell addresses the troops on the battleship U.S.S. *Wisconsin,* in the Persian Gulf.

An Oval Office meeting at the height of the
Persian Gulf War. Below, generals Colin Powell
and Norman Schwarzkopf.

with little or no military experience made proposals he found militarily unsound. When an army under secretary had proposed robot infantrymen and radio-controlled armored cars, Schwarzkopf had launched into a desk-thumping tirade.

He was familiar with the Middle East, having spent two years as a teenager living in Tehran. His father, a two-star army general, had been sent there to set up an Iranian national police force.

Powell had come to know Schwarzkopf about five years earlier, when they both had quarters at Fort Myer, Virginia. They had grown close two years later, when Powell was the national security adviser and Schwarzkopf was the army's operations deputy, or "little chief." Schwarzkopf was one of the dozens of four-stars Powell had leapfrogged to become Chairman, but since then he had become one of Powell's favorite C in Cs because he had adjusted to the twin realities of a diminished Soviet threat and a smaller U.S. force. Also, when he felt Powell was wrong or had pissed someone off, he said so.

Now Powell asked Schwarzkopf for an evaluation of the Iraqi buildup, and the general said it looked at most as if Iraq were poised to launch a punitive but limited strike into Kuwait. Powell said that he wanted Schwarzkopf to draft a two-tiered plan for possible U.S. responses to any Iraqi move against Kuwait. The first tier was what U.S. forces could do to retaliate against Iraq; the second was what the United States might do defensively to stop any Iraqi move.

Meanwhile, Pat Lang continued to monitor Iraq. Within 11 days eight divisions had been amassed to positions north of Kuwait. Each had moved 300 to 400 miles. Giant heavy-equipment transport trucks carried the tanks, protecting their delicate tracks for use in battle. In all, Saddam had 100,000 troops on the border.

WITH one hour's notice, on July 25, Saddam summoned April Glaspie, the U.S. ambassador to Iraq, to his office. Glaspie, 48, a career diplomat who had been ambassador since 1988, did not have time to obtain any new instructions from the State Department. She was suspicious of Saddam and told colleagues that she intended to keep the "thug" in place.

U.S. policy toward Iraq was muddled. Bush administration officials had been talking tough about Saddam's threats against Israel, the movement of Iraqi Scud missile launchers closer to Israel, and Iraq's illegal efforts to import components for nuclear weapons. At the same time, the administration had blocked congressional efforts to impose economic sanctions on Iraq or cut U.S. food assistance.

"What can it mean when America says it will now protect its friends?" Saddam asked Glaspie, in an apparent reference to a statement by Cheney that the United States would stick by its friends in the Gulf. "It can only mean prejudice against Iraq. This stance, plus maneuvers and statements which have been made, has encouraged Kuwait. The United States must have a better understanding of the situation and declare who it wants to have relations with and who its enemies are."

Glaspie said, "I have direct instruction from the President to seek better relations with Iraq." More talks and meetings would help. "I am pleased that you add your voice to the diplomats who stand up to the media, because your appearance in the media, even for five minutes, would help us to make the American people understand Iraq."

Later in the meeting Glaspie told Saddam, "We have no opinion on the Arab-Arab conflicts like your border disagreement with Kuwait." She said the United States would insist on a nonviolent settlement. "I received an instruction to ask you, in the spirit of friendship—not in the spirit of confrontation—regarding your intentions."

Saddam said that through the intervention of Egyptian President Hosni Mubarak he had agreed to talks with the Kuwaitis.

"This is good news," Glaspie said. "Congratulations." She had planned to postpone a trip to the United States the following week, but with this good news she would leave on Monday.

Powell was relieved when he saw Glaspie's cable on her meeting with Saddam. It suggested there was room for negotiations between Iraq and Kuwait. Powell remained cool about the prospects for trouble. He knew how a field army prepared for combat, and the Iraqi army was not acting as if it were going to attack. Four things were missing: communications networks, artillery stocks, other needed munitions, and supply lines for armored tank forces.

SAUDI ambassador Prince Bandar asked to stop by and see Powell at the Pentagon at 4:00 p.m. on Friday, July 27. Powell and Bandar had known each other for more than a decade. They had played racquetball when Bandar was a major in the Saudi air force assigned to Washington in his preambassadorial days.

Powell was somewhat wary of Bandar, a specialist in out-of-channel solutions and relationships. His fingerprints were all over the Iran-contra affair, as well as several other covert operations.

Bandar worked hard to keep in touch with the five key people in the administration—Bush, Baker, Scowcroft, Cheney, and Powell. No more politically oriented group could be running the U.S. government, he felt. To a certain extent he found the five interchangeable—each half statesman, half warrior, half politician, half of everything. A very lethal inner circle, capable of playing at the highest level of political gamesmanship, he had once remarked. Of the five he judged Powell probably the most cautious.

This Friday afternoon Bandar told Powell that Saudi King Fahd was being assured by everyone in the Middle East that Saddam was not going to invade Kuwait. Saddam had given personal assurances to Mubarak and King Hussein of Jordan. It isn't going to happen, Bandar said confidently. Saddam was saying it was only a military exercise of his crack divisions. His summons to U.S. ambassador Glaspie was a positive sign, Bandar said.

Powell agreed that Saddam was saber-rattling. His information supported that view.

The crisis has peaked and will be resolved peacefully, at least for the moment, Bandar said.

Like Bandar, Powell said he too expected August to be quiet and was planning to take some leave.

"Well, Colin," Bandar said, "it looks good. Everything looks on track. Of course, if he escalates this, you may have to come help us all."

"Let's pray he doesn't escalate it," Powell said.

"Well, what would you do if he did?"

Powell waved him off. His eyes were very careful. "I have no view," Powell said. "That would be up to the President."

Bandar, probing and testing, pushed. As a former national security adviser, as the Chairman, how would you look at it? Come on, Colin.

"In the hypothetical," Powell said, "if I was asked, Should we go? I would say no. If I was told, I'd go, but I'd go to win. I don't want to go to lose."

Bandar said that he hoped it didn't come to that.

"I hope too."

Robert Kimmitt, the under secretary for political affairs at State, called a deputies' committee meeting that same Friday, July 27.

A general feeling of optimism characterized the meeting. President Mubarak had sent a personal message to Bush, repeating his forecast of no imminent trouble. Let the Arabs handle it, Mubarak said.

A direct message from Baker to Iraq was drafted. Restrained in tone, it assured Saddam the United States was trying to get along with Iraq and establish a way to work with him, and Iraq must reciprocate.

Paul Wolfowitz, policy under secretary in the Department of Defense, objected. If a stiffer message could not be sent, he said, it would be better to send nothing. But the general feeling was that Saddam was not going to cross Mubarak, a fellow Arab. And it would be unprecedented for one Arab state to attack another.

Kuwait had not requested any help, Powell noted. The Kuwaiti ambassador had come to see Wolfowitz in the Pentagon earlier that week and said how worried he was. Wolfowitz had given the ambassador every opening to ask for assistance, but he had not done so. Kuwait had not moved any of its small army of 20,000 to meet the Iraqis at the border.

On Monday, July 30, Pat Lang sat down to write a top secret electronic-mail message to his boss, the director of the Defense Intelligence Agency, Lieutenant General Harry E. Soyster, and to division heads within the agency. Lang typed on his computer:

> I have been looking at the pattern of reinforcement along the Kuwaiti border. There is some artillery and logistics moving; aircraft are moving. There is absolutely no reason for Saddam Hussein to do this. He has created the capability to overrun all of Kuwait and all of Eastern Saudi Arabia. If he attacks, given his disposition, we will have no warning.
>
> I do not believe he is bluffing. He doesn't know how to bluff. In short, Saddam Hussein has moved a force disproportionate to the task at hand, if it is to bluff. Then there is only one answer: he intends to use it.

Lang wanted his new analysis to serve as a thunderclap.

Soyster told Lang he did not believe his assessment. The DIA director just did not find it conceivable that Saddam would do something so anachronistic as an old-fashioned land grab. But Soyster knew the message from Lang could not be ignored. He ordered copies hand-carried to Cheney and Powell.

Powell considered Lang's interpretation a mere personal assessment. Iraqi communications and munitions were still at insufficient levels. No Iraqi air power was in place to support a ground attack.

After Lang sent his message, he was dispatched to give the Kuwaiti ambassador in Washington a briefing. He described the situation in great detail and asked him, "Are you going to do anything?"

"What can we do?" the ambassador replied.

WHEN Lang arrived at his office, about 6:00 a.m. on Wednesday, August 1, some of his staff were waiting for him. They directed him to the latest pictures of the Kuwait-Iraq border, which had arrived moments before. All three Iraqi armored divisions had moved dramatically forward to within three miles of the Kuwaiti border. It was breathtaking—a beautiful military maneuver. Hundreds of tanks were facing Kuwait, spaced 50 to 75 yards apart, in a genuine line of death, miles long. Artillery had moved in behind the tanks.

He had been wrong about there being no advance warning, Lang realized. Here it was. Saddam was being very deliberate. As Lang's eyes raced over the images he realized that armored units could not more vividly advertise their intent. It was as if a gun had been loaded and aimed and a finger put on the trigger. Now he was watching the muscle in the finger tighten before his eyes.

The photographs also showed that the Iraqis had moved some 80 helicopters closer to the border, in a classic air-land assault posture.

Lang drafted a highest-priority flash warning message describing the situation and forecasting an attack that night or the next morning. A special top secret bulletin was put out to senior Pentagon officials. The whisper raced through the building among those who were cleared: it was going to be a long night for the Middle East staffs.

That morning Powell read a CIA assessment that said all indicators showed that Saddam was going to invade. Powell knew that this assignment of intent was a big deal. The CIA tried to avoid crying wolf too often. Now the DIA warnings also landed on his desk. Not only had Saddam moved his tanks on line overnight but the communications, artillery, munitions, logistics, and air power were in place. A field army of great capacity had sprung to life. My God, Powell thought.

Schwarzkopf briefed the Joint Chiefs and Cheney in the Tank that afternoon. Giving a status report on the 100,000 Iraqi forces, he said they were positioned in a way to give Saddam lots of options—not just an attack. He did not predict an invasion or a border crossing.

Cheney agreed that everything Saddam had to do to prepare for an invasion was exactly what he also had to do simply to scare the Kuwaitis. There was no way to distinguish between the two.

Schwarzkopf said that there was little or nothing he could do. There were only 10,000 U.S. military personnel in the region, almost all naval forces. Briefly he referred to CentCom's Operations Plan 90-1002, a top secret contingency plan for moving in about 100,000 ground troops over three to four months. There was one big hitch: the plan assumed 30 days' advance warning before the actual commencement of the deployment.

Powell found the field commander's perspective sobering. But there was also an air of incredulity in the Tank. It was difficult to believe that Saddam would use or need 100,000 troops to invade Kuwait, a country that could be taken over with much less force.

But Powell himself now no longer believed that Saddam was bluffing. He suggested that Cheney sound the alarm at the White House. This was the moment to mobilize the President, perhaps get him to issue a presidential warning to Saddam through secret diplomatic channels. We've got to do something, Powell told Cheney.

They pushed the White House. As far as Powell could tell, either the White House had another idea about how to handle the problem or the suggestion just fell through the cracks.

7

ABOUT 9:00 p.m., August 1, 1990, Cheney received a phone call at home from his military assistant Rear Admiral Bill Owens. The Iraqi forces had crossed the border. Hundreds of tanks were racing south and east, toward Kuwait City.

Cheney wasn't entirely shocked. He told Owens to keep him informed.

Powell also received a call at home. The Chairman decided to stay home and get updates. Vice-chairman Admiral David Jeremiah went to the Pentagon for the night. General Kelly was in the Crisis Situation Room by about 9:30 p.m., overseeing a team of operations specialists and intelligence analysts. He sat in the center of the long table in the front. Before him were three large projection screens. One screen had a time log that scrolled up, marking key events, communications, and intelligence. Another was tuned to CNN's 24-hour news coverage. If what was going out publicly wasn't correct, Kelly knew Powell would want to take steps to fix the impression.

The DIA had sent an intelligence specialist to Kuwait City several days earlier. He was able to funnel out intelligence describing the virtual sacking of the city. The small Kuwaiti army was putting up a fight, but it was hopelessly outnumbered.

Scowcroft received his call at his home, in suburban Maryland. He was astonished—he had been sure it was all bluster. He returned to the White House and informed Bush of the invasion.

The President said he wanted something done right away. Scowcroft called an emergency meeting of the deputies' committee by secure video link, and a public statement was drafted. Scowcroft gave it to Bush for approval. At 11:20 p.m. a statement was issued that strongly condemned the invasion and called for "the immediate and unconditional withdrawal of all Iraqi forces."

With legal counsel Boyden Gray and Treasury officials, Scowcroft went to work on a plan to freeze Iraqi assets in the United States and prohibit any transactions with the aggressor. Since it was clear that Kuwait was being overrun, a second plan was drafted to freeze Kuwaiti assets so that Saddam could not get at any portion of the estimated $100 billion in investments held abroad.

Scowcroft pressed for more actions that would demonstrate that the United States was taking the invasion seriously. He proposed that a squadron of air force F-15 fighters—about 24 planes—be offered to Saudi Arabia if the kingdom would accept them. He also called a National Security Council meeting for first thing in the morning. The Pentagon reported that General Schwarzkopf was in town and might be a good resource at the meeting.

Schwarzkopf, however, had gone back to his headquarters, in Florida. About 2:30 a.m. Powell called Kelly in the Crisis Situation Room. Call Schwarzkopf, Powell directed, and tell him I want him back in my office at 7:00 a.m. because there's an 8:00 a.m. NSC meeting at the White House I want him to attend.

Kelly picked up his secure line to Schwarzkopf.

"Sir," he said, "Tom Kelly. The Chairman just called and said he would like you in his office at seven a.m."

Long pause.

"Yes, sir, this morning."

Long pause.

"Yes, in four and one half hours."

AT ABOUT 4:00 a.m. Scowcroft went to sleep in his office. He awoke about 45 minutes later and by 5:00 a.m. was at Bush's bedroom door so the executive orders on freezing the assets could be signed.

Powell arrived at the Pentagon at 6:00 a.m. At about 6:50 Schwarzkopf also appeared, and the two had a closed-door meeting until 7:30, when they left for the White House.

The full National Security Council gathered at 8:00 a.m. in the Cabinet Room. In addition to Powell and Schwarzkopf, Cheney and Wolfowitz, from the Pentagon, were there. Kimmitt, from State, was sitting in for Baker, who was in Siberia, meeting with Soviet foreign minister Eduard Shevardnadze.

Before the meeting Bush answered a few questions from a media pool so he could be seen on television stating his concern about the invasion. "We're not discussing intervention," Bush told reporters.

"You're not contemplating any intervention or sending troops?" one reporter asked.

"I'm not contemplating such action," he said.

Scowcroft believed that Bush didn't mean what that sentence said. He was talking off the cuff. Clearly, it was too early to rule out anything; the statement would have to be corrected later.

Bush said there was no evidence that any other countries in the Middle East were threatened, but he said that he wanted to "have this invasion be reversed and have them get out of Kuwait." He also said, "I'm sure there will be a lot of frenzied diplomatic activity. I plan to participate in some of that myself."

Powell noticed yet again the sharp contrast between Bush and Reagan. Bush had spent eight years watching Reagan operate, and delegate. Unlike Reagan, Bush wanted the details, all the details. He wanted to be the player, the guy who made as many calls as possible. It was not a matter of one style being good and one being bad. It was just different. On occasion Powell had to remind himself that the people had elected Bush, not his advisers. The net result was that principal military adviser Powell had a much smaller role under Bush than national security adviser Powell had had under Reagan.

When the reporters left, the President immediately took charge of the meeting. CIA director William Webster opened with an intelligence briefing. The Iraqi forces in Kuwait were being resupplied and reorganized. The 100,000 troops could easily continue their march and punch through meager Saudi defenses. Saudi Arabia had a military of less than 70,000, and only one small unit stood between the Iraqi units and the vast Saudi oil fields.

Next Bob Kimmitt summarized the diplomacy: the U.N. Security Council had met most of the night and had condemned the invasion; the Arab League was being convened; but no one had yet joined the United States in freezing Iraqi and Kuwaiti assets.

The President said they needed to think about additional economic sanctions. He had acted quickly to freeze the assets, and he wanted to make sure the United Nations was moving forward on additional measures. U.N. ambassador Thomas Pickering, who had arrived from New York City on a 6:30 a.m. flight, said they were.

Bush said that he wanted the diplomatic effort to be massive, and he ordered that nothing be left undone that might add to the pressure and help organize world opinion against Iraq.

Treasury Secretary Nicholas Brady next explained that Iraq would get potential oil profits of about $20 million a day from Kuwaiti production. Iraq held 20 percent of the world's known oil reserves. If Saddam were to take over Saudi Arabia, he would have 40 percent.

Bush seemed horrified that Saddam might get Saudi Arabia. He engaged in an extended analysis of the impact on world oil availability and price. Could the United States and others slap an embargo on Iraqi oil? With just 20 percent of the world's oil Saddam would be able to manipulate world prices and hold the United States and its allies at his mercy. Higher oil prices would fuel inflation, worsening the already gloomy condition of the U.S. economy.

An air attack package, Powell said—referring to the squadron of F-15s—was on alert to go to Saudi Arabia if the Saudis gave their approval. Energy Secretary James Watkins, the former navy chief, pointed out that Iraq moved its oil in pipelines through Turkey and Saudi Arabia. Could they be hit with air strikes? Powell said they could, though he didn't know how permanent their shutdown would be. They could be too easily repaired and put back into action.

A question was raised about the possibility of shutting down Iraq's entire oil export business, not just the pipelines, but the refineries and terminals and pumping stations. Cheney said that wouldn't make a lot of sense. Saddam's move on Kuwait was among other things an attempt to meddle with the world's oil supply. The United States could not respond by bombing the world's oil supply.

Scowcroft worried that the debate was wandering and unfocused. "We don't have the option to *appear* not to be acting," he said.

Cheney said that the marriage of Iraq's military of 1 million men with 20 percent of the world's oil presented a significant threat. They ought to distinguish between defending Saudi Arabia and expelling Iraq from Kuwait, he said, suggesting he favored protection.

Scowcroft mentioned the U.S. protection of Kuwaiti tankers in the Gulf in 1987–88.

"The military requirement would be much greater," Cheney said.

Powell said that the Iraqi military had conducted a very professional operation. The Chairman then introduced General Schwarzkopf, who put up maps and charts showing the Iraqi attack routes.

Two tiers of responses were possible, the general said. The first tier could be single retaliatory strikes carried out by U.S. naval aircraft based on carriers in the region. Tier Two, the execution of Operations Plan 90-1002 for the defense of the Saudi peninsula, would take months and involve 100,000 to 200,000 military personnel from all the services. This could not be executed unless Saudi Arabia or some other country allowed the United States to set up bases.

John Sununu, also present at the meeting, pressed the possibility of some kind of economic move. Isn't there some way to organize to prevent Iraq from selling not only Kuwaiti oil but its own? he asked.

Economic embargoes historically haven't worked, Richard G. Darman, the budget director, said. In an embargo the price goes up and the incentive to violate the embargo increases.

Right, Bush said. Where there was a buck to be made, someone would buy and sell the oil. "Like my Texas friends."

Darman said an embargo needed an enforcement mechanism. He knew this implied a military operation, such as using the navy for a blockade—a bigger step, perhaps, than the President wanted to take.

"But we just can't accept what's happened in Kuwait just because it's too hard to do anything about it," Bush said. He did not indicate he was eager to use the military for that or for any purpose.

Powell posed a question. "Don't we want just to draw a firm line with Saudi Arabia?" That country was the real U.S. interest.

Pickering remarked that such a firm line would leave Kuwait in the hands of Iraq. The meeting ended on this very inconclusive note.

Legal counsel Boyden Gray left feeling that the military now had a real opportunity. It seemed to him that Bush was certainly going to do something. Over the years Gray had seen Bush charged up many times—in some respects it was a natural state for him—but rarely this much. Bush was now betraying the traits of a cornered man. Gray thought this was when the President was at his best, as he was in a tennis match when he was down 4–1 in the final set.

Powell had also watched Bush carefully, yet he did not think it was at all clear what the President was going to do or whether he would accept the loss of Kuwait. Cheney too was puzzled about what Bush might do. The Secretary felt a little unprepared. He didn't have any practical military options to lay before the President.

Scowcroft was alarmed. Iraq was a major threat to the vital interests of the United States. And the national security adviser saw another principle at stake. The Vietnam syndrome was alive and well—the military didn't want to use force unless everyone approved. Scowcroft believed the United States could choke on such strictures. For Scowcroft, war was an instrument of foreign policy, pure and simple.

Afterward, in the Oval Office, Scowcroft indicated to Bush that the meeting had seemed to miss the point about the larger foreign policy questions. Mr. President, Scowcroft said, I think you and I are the only ones who really are exercised about this.

Before rushing off to Aspen, Colorado, for a speech, the President had a private meeting with his counsel, Boyden Gray. Bush wanted to be sure about his legal authority to deploy or use military air power—Tier One options.

In the afternoon, at a press conference in Colorado, Bush shifted some ground from the early morning. "We're not ruling any options in, but we're not ruling any options out."

Two hours later Bush talked with King Fahd of Saudi Arabia. The immensely wealthy Fahd, 69, was known as a supercautious, pro-Western monarch who tended to pursue his foreign policy goals through financial diplomacy—in short, payoffs. The two spoke for nearly half an hour. They agreed that the attack on Kuwait was unacceptable, but did not settle on a course of action.

Returning to Washington on Air Force One, Bush also spoke with King Hussein of Jordan and President Mubarak of Egypt, who were together meeting in Alexandria. The two Middle East leaders passed the phone back and forth as each spoke with Bush. Their message was, Give us more time, and let the Arabs try to handle this.

That afternoon Cheney called a meeting, in his office, of his top civilian and military advisers. About 15 people gathered, an unusually large meeting for Cheney, who liked groups of two, three, or four.

General Kelly started out. Here is the story of how Iraq took Kuwait, he said. His tone of voice reflected professional admiration for the rapid, precise, massive and technically brilliant operation.

Okay, guys, Cheney said. What do we do?

Powell told him the chiefs and Schwarzkopf were working on options. Cheney seemed incredulous there were so few. It's hard, Powell said. They were dealing with a huge instant invasion that was now over and complete. Saddam's initial mission had been accomplished.

There was a growing tension in the crowded office.

"I need some options I can show the President," Cheney said.

Powell reiterated that they were working on it. Both he and Kelly wanted it made clear they were not going to come up with some half-baked proposals. Powell didn't want the U.S. military to deliver a few pinprick surgical strikes. What would they do after that? There wasn't much that could be done from this distance, and the Pentagon would look impotent and weak.

Spokesman Pete Williams and Dave Addington, Cheney's special assistant, left the meeting before it ended, signaling to the other backbenchers that it was time to depart. When Cheney and Powell were finally alone, the Secretary said he felt blocked. The President did not need political advice. Both he and Bush needed military options, and they did not seem to be forthcoming.

Mr. Secretary, Powell said, it's 6000 miles plus away. We don't have any ground forces. An air strike would be pissing into the wind and might provoke what we don't want—an assault on Saudi Arabia.

It was one of the tensest exchanges the two had ever had.

Privately Cheney was stewing.

THE next day, Friday, August 3, the National Security Council met again at the White House. Clasping his notes, Scowcroft began, "We have got to examine what the long-term interests are for this country and for the Middle East if the invasion and taking of Kuwait become an accomplished fact. We have to begin our deliberations with the fact that this is unacceptable. Yes, it's hard to do much. There are lots of reasons why we can't do things, but it's our job."

Darman felt that Scowcroft's introduction was a plea for the Cabinet to unify, to fall in line.

The President indicated that he agreed with his national security adviser. The participants discussed economic sanctions and the ways the administration might work with the allies and the United Nations to isolate Saddam. They discussed a CIA report arguing that the invasion posed a threat to the current world order and that the long-run impact on the world economy could be devastating.

Scowcroft said there had to be two tracks. First, the United States had to be willing to use force to stop Saddam and had to make that clear to the world. Second, Saddam had to be toppled. That had to be done covertly through the CIA and be unclear to the world.

Bush ordered the CIA to begin planning such a covert operation. He wanted an all-fronts effort to strangle the Iraqi economy, support anti-Saddam resistance groups, and look for alternative leaders in Iraqi society. He knew Saddam ran a police state and brutally repressed any dissent or opposition. Still, he wanted to see what could be done.

He also wanted Cheney, Powell, and Schwarzkopf to brief him on the military options.

THAT afternoon Scowcroft arranged for Prince Bandar to come to the White House.

Bandar had been in London when he received word of the invasion of Kuwait. He immediately ordered his private jet to take him back to the United States, and tried to digest what had happened.

Back in Washington, Bandar had his staff retrieve the 18-page memo of his meeting with Saddam four months earlier. As he read the words he said to himself, My God, this guy was setting the stage to attack. Saddam had sought and received American and Israeli assurances he would not be attacked. He had protected his western flank with Israel, freeing him to do what he wanted on the east with Kuwait. Bandar's conclusion was that he and the Bush administration had been set up.

At the White House, Scowcroft told Bandar he was speaking for the President. The Saudis had not given an answer on the U.S. offer of a squadron of F-15s, and Scowcroft knew that such a nonanswer was, for the moment at least, a Saudi no. He said that Bush was willing to up the ante.

Bandar reminded Scowcroft that only a decade before, when the Shah of Iran had fallen from power, President Carter had told the Saudis, Let me send over a couple of squadrons of F-15s. His Majesty had agreed. When the planes were halfway over, Carter had announced they were unarmed. The consequences had been devastating, and lived on. Frankly, Bandar said, we're worried. Do you guys have the guts, or don't you? "We don't want you to put out a hand and then pull it back," the ambassador said, "and leave us with this guy on our border twice as mad as he is now."

"We're serious," Scowcroft said. "And we'll do what is necessary to protect you." But he added that the Saudis would have to demonstrate that they too were serious and would accept U.S. forces.

At that moment President Bush dropped in to Scowcroft's office.

"This is your friend?" Bush said to Bandar, clearly referring to Bandar's earlier pleas for assurances for Saddam.

Bandar chuckled.

"This is the guy you came to me telling me he's okay."

"Water over a dam, Mr. President," Bandar said. He acknowledged that both the Saudis and the United States had been used.

Bush turned to the problem at hand. He said he was upset that Kuwait had not asked for help from the United States until apparently half an hour or a few minutes before Iraq invaded. He was scared the Saudis, who might be next on Saddam's list, would ask too late.

What sort of help can be provided? Bandar asked. How many aircraft? What sort of weapons? King Fahd would have to know.

Bush and Scowcroft said they didn't have those answers. Cheney and Powell would have to provide them.

Bandar pressed and alluded sarcastically to Jimmy Carter's un-armed F-15s. Bush seemed almost hurt, as if the Saudis suspected his resolve. He seemed to be taking the questioning personally.

"I give my word of honor," Bush finally told Bandar. "I will see this through with you."

Bandar felt his hair stand up. The President of the United States had just put his personal honor on the line.

SCOWCROFT called Cheney and said that the President wanted to help the Saudis. Show him the best we have—Tier Two, the massive operations plan. "Get Bandar in and brief him on what we can do for him." The President did not want any half measures. He had given his word. To convince the Saudis, he wanted Cheney to show Bandar the top secret satellite photos. They would demonstrate the peril as Saddam massed his forces in the direction of Saudi Arabia.

Cheney made arrangements to brief Bandar that afternoon. But first Cheney had to have a come-to-Jesus meeting with Powell.

The Secretary and the Chairman sat down alone. There could be no more stalling, foot-dragging, or the appearance of either, Cheney said. Serious talk was coming out of the White House. The President would be better served if there was more military advice commensurate with the seriousness of the situation. The Pentagon had to stick to its knitting, Cheney said firmly.

"I can't do it unless I know what the pattern is," Powell replied.

Cheney explained they now had it. Scowcroft had just called. Bush wanted them to brief Bandar on Operations Plan 90-1002.

BEFORE the Bandar briefing, Cheney called Lang to his office. The DIA's Middle East specialist had written another of his electronic messages that day reviewing the possible outcomes of the crisis. Chief among them was the high likelihood that the Saudis would turn inward and refuse assistance. They were turning down requests for overflights of U.S. military planes and had also denied a U.S. request to augment radar coverage of the region.

Lang seemed to be the only analyst who had taken the Iraqi troop buildup with the seriousness it deserved. Cheney wanted to talk about the Iraqis. He had one question: "What are these people really like?"

"They are formidable," Lang said. "They have a very capable military and a developed industrial base. They are modern for a Third World country. They are nationalistic. They are dangerous." He backed up his analysis with statistics and anecdotes.

CHENEY had known Prince Bandar for years and liked him. He was intrigued that a mere ambassador was able to have such a wide impact in Washington and the world. But Cheney worried that the prince had his own agenda. He considered Bandar a little bit off the wall and not necessarily a clear channel to King Fahd. Messages might get distorted for purposes that Cheney might not even be able to imagine.

When Bandar arrived in Cheney's office in the afternoon of August 3, he took a seat at the small, round conference table with Cheney and Powell. Policy under secretary Paul Wolfowitz and NSC Middle East expert Richard Haass joined them.

Cheney said that if the United States was invited in to defend the kingdom, it would be a very very serious commitment. To emphasize the problem the Saudis were facing, Cheney and Powell produced copies of the satellite photographs and pointed out the three Iraqi armored divisions that had been the initial thrust into Kuwait. One was moving to the Saudi border; the others could follow. Still more divisions were taking places behind the armored units. The kingdom appeared to be in grave danger.

It took Powell about ten minutes to summarize Operations Plan 90-1002, noting that it included more than four U.S. divisions, three aircraft carriers, and many attack squadrons. He allowed Bandar a peek at the top secret plan and charts showing the movement of forces over the months. "That's a rather large force," Powell said.

"How many are you talking about?" Bandar asked.

Powell said 100,000 to 200,000 in the theater.

Bandar let his breath out audibly. "Well, at least this shows you're serious."

This is serious, Powell insisted.

Bandar agreed with the plan and promised to convey to the King and to his father, Saudi defense minister Prince Sultan, what could be done. He described a controlled state of panic back home—controlled, he said, because as everyone knew, royalty never panics. He once remarked, "Composure is very important in our culture, even if it doesn't make sense."

As Bandar rose to leave, Cheney said that if the Saudis invited the U.S. forces and President Bush approved, they could send General Schwarzkopf, or somebody, to coordinate, making sure that, for example, the U.S. Air Force jets landed where the Saudis wanted.

Bandar assured them that he would be an advocate for an immediate U.S. deployment. He then left.

Cheney told Powell he wanted Schwarzkopf to bring the key commanders from each of the services up to Camp David. He knew that personal contacts were essential for the President. People didn't exist for Bush until he had met them. It was important that the President be given eyes-on personal knowledge of the men who might be running such an operation, Cheney said. He asked Bill Owens, his military aide, to arrange for one of the large White House helicopters to take them all to Camp David the next morning.

Later in the day Cheney was getting a haircut in the Pentagon barbershop when Owens tracked him down. John Sununu's office had said no to the helicopter request, Owens reported.

Typical crap out of Sununu's office, Cheney thought. He felt that Sununu had adopted an imperial role for himself as White House chief of staff. When Cheney held the job, under Gerald Ford, he had worked assiduously to stay in the background and avoid the mantle of assistant president. Sununu had donned it. Once Bush had been late for a Cabinet meeting, and Sununu had plunked himself down in the President's chair—a small impropriety, but to Cheney it symbolized the self-importance Sununu brought to his post.

As Secretary of Defense, Cheney had control of more helicopters than anyone. He ordered Owens to use their own choppers for the flight.

Bandar called King Fahd to report. Fahd wanted to be assured the threat from Iraq was real. The satellite photos supported the case that the kingdom was in serious trouble, Bandar said. "Have you seen—with your own eyes—have you seen the overheads?" Fahd asked.

"Yes, sir."

"Then tell them to come and bring the overheads."

On an overcast Saturday morning, August 4, Cheney, Powell, Wolfowitz, Schwarzkopf and several of his top commanders flew up to Camp David.

Cheney was comfortable with Operations Plan 90-1002. It was the only one they had, and he did not want to reinvent the wheel in the midst of a crisis.

They all went into the retreat's big lodge, with its modern conference room. Bush, Quayle, Cheney, Sununu, CIA director Webster, and Wolfowitz sat on one side of the 25-foot table. On the other side were Baker, Scowcroft, Powell, Schwarzkopf, Fitzwater, and Haass. Five model airplanes were arranged down the middle of the table.

Webster opened with an intelligence update. Iraqi soldiers were approaching and massing near the Saudi border. The only thing standing between Saddam and the vast Saudi oil fields was a battalion of the Saudi national guard, fewer than 1000 men.

Cheney called on Powell, who said that General Schwarzkopf would give an expanded version of Operations Plan 90-1002. "The plan is doable," Powell said. "It will achieve the mission of defending or repelling an attack. There's a deterrence piece and a war-fighting piece. The sooner we put something in place to deter, the better we are. What we can get there most quickly is air power. The navy's in position. There's more moving. Within a month we could have a large field army in Saudi Arabia."

What about the Iraqi air force? asked Sununu.

Iraq has 1127 aircraft, Schwarzkopf replied. Limited quantities of good ones. The Iraqi air force is predominantly used for defense.

He then began his presentation by saying that although the Iraqis had a large army, "they're not ten feet tall." Their forces included:

- A total land force of 900,000, consisting of 63 divisions; but only 8 of them, the Republican Guard, are really the focus of our concern.
- In all, 5,747 tanks, of which 1,072 are the Soviet-supplied T-72s. Most of the T-72s are in Kuwait now.
- About 10,000 lightly armored vehicles, of which only 1,600 are the advanced type.
- Some 3,500 pieces of artillery, but only 330 are self-propelled.
- A total of 3,000 heavy-equipment transporters for moving tanks, a remarkable number. The whole U.S. Army has only 500.

"We would not have to worry about the air force after a fairly short period," the general said. "The navy's not a problem." The Iraqi strengths were the size of their land force—and their chemical weapons, which they had used in the Iran-Iraq War and in 1988 against some of their own citizens, Kurdish rebels in northern Iraq. Their weaknesses included centralized command and control, dependence on foreign countries for spare parts, and lack of experience in deep operations away from the front in battle. They were accustomed mainly to frontal attacks, like those used by Iran in the Iran-Iraq War.

Schwarzkopf said it would take 17 weeks to get the full deterrence piece of Plan 90-1002—totaling some 200,000 to 250,000 army, navy, air force, and marine personnel—into the region.

The offensive capability, he warned, was something very different. In an offensive mode the plan called for six and two-thirds divisions on the ground—about 150,000 on the U.S. side—against the Iraqi force of 100,000. This wouldn't yield the desired attacker-to-defender ratio of 3 to 1 or 4 to 1, but better U.S. equipment, better tactics, control of the air and sea, and many other factors would make an attack possible.

On this war-fighting piece Schwarzkopf said it would take 8 to 12 months to put in place the U.S. force needed to kick Saddam out of Kuwait. He underscored the U.S. limitations. Sixty percent of the army's logistics support personnel are in the reserves. The force would be dependent on supplies of fuel from the nations in the Middle East. Munitions shortfalls could be expected if shooting started.

Discussion briefly turned to a possible air campaign—going in with nothing but air power, the obvious U.S. advantage. Cheney and Powell made it clear they were not at all comfortable with air power only. To Cheney's mind, defensive or offensive U.S. air superiority might do what was needed right off the bat, but no one could be sure.

Cheney turned to Iraq's chemical weapons. What would it be like to operate in the chemical protective gear U.S. forces would have to wear in the Saudi desert during the month of August? he asked.

Schwarzkopf said that the units that might be deployed had all trained in summer at the National Training Center in the California desert. "The equipment is very uncomfortable," he said. "It degrades fighting ability. But we have practiced with it a lot."

Bush then entered the discussion. "My worry about the Saudis is that they're going to bug out at the last minute and accept a puppet regime in Kuwait. We should be asking them how committed they are."

"It's a chicken-and-egg problem," Scowcroft said. "They can't go out front until they know whether we can be counted on."

"But this is like if your homeland is about to be invaded," the President replied, "you grab a pitchfork and go to the border."

"But this is the Middle East," Scowcroft said. He reminded them that the Kuwaitis hadn't mobilized when they were threatened.

"What about this withdrawal announcement?" the President asked, referring to a statement issued by the Iraqis the day before, claiming their forces were going to begin leaving Kuwait in two days.

Everyone at the table seemed to agree this announcement might be enough to get the Arab states circling the wagons, saying everything is going to be fine and insisting that the United States butt out.

This led the discussion back to the unanswered questions: What did Saddam really want? What were his ultimate objectives?

Schwarzkopf said that the conditions before the invasion boiled down to adjustments of the Iraq-Kuwait border in favor of Iraq, debt forgiveness, payment of $4 billion, and control of two tiny Kuwaiti-controlled islands that blocked Iraqi access to the Gulf.

"Even if the Iraqis go all the way back," Powell said, "it's going to be a different Emir and a different situation." Powell's point was that the head of the Kuwaiti state would be a changed man, and the status quo in Kuwait and elsewhere in the region had been forever altered.

"This is all designed to be attractive to the Arab League," Scowcroft said. "Kuwait is not popular among the Arabs."

"That's why our defense of Saudi Arabia has to be our focus," Bush finally said.

The meeting was adjourned, but the top officials—Bush, Quayle, Sununu, Baker, Scowcroft, Cheney, Powell, Webster—were asked to stay for a principals-only get-together. Some very sensitive intelligence was then presented, showing that the Saudi leaders were getting cold feet and giving some consideration to buying their way out of the threat by offering billions of dollars from their oil revenue to Saddam. The Saudis had been willing to pay blackmail before.

Among those gathered there was a pessimism about the Arabs in general. Everyone heaped blame on them. They could not be relied on; they would pay off the thief at their throat.

Despite this negative note, it was decided that the President would call King Fahd to take a sounding and make a pitch.

Scowcroft stayed on with the President while he called the Saudi King. It was time for some pressure. Bush told the King that Saddam was piling up forces near the King's border. The Saudis had to act.

Fahd said that Saudi Arabia did not need ground troops to defend itself. The Saudis only needed help with air power and perhaps some equipment. He also said that Prince Bandar had reported to him on the previous day's Pentagon meeting. I understand you are going to send a team to brief me on the latest overheads and on what your capabilities are to help us defend ourselves, the King told Bush.

Bush hadn't the foggiest idea what Fahd was talking about. Such a plan had not been discussed with any of his advisers.

"I did not know you were expecting one, but we'll put one together," the President told Fahd.

Fahd said yes. He wanted a low-level technical or management team.

Afterward Bush and Scowcroft realized that the team idea was all the King and Bush had agreed on, and it was not clear what kind of team was best. Who should be sent? For precisely what purpose? When?

A round of telephone calls followed. Bandar thought that he had mentioned a team to Scowcroft. Scowcroft didn't recall.

"I want to do this," Bush told Scowcroft. "I want to do it big time." And later he added, "I want to send somebody personally. It has to be with the understanding they will not come back with no decisions having been made." They decided they had to send an offer King Fahd could not refuse.

Bush continued his personal diplomatic activity. He spoke with President Turgut Ozal of Turkey and Prime Minister Brian Mulroney of Canada, two leaders who had already voiced strong opposition to Saddam's invasion. He also spoke with the Kuwaiti Emir, Sheik Jabir al Ahmed al Sabah, head of Kuwait's large ruling family since 1978.

With the Emir, Bush was sympathetic and emotional. He made a vow to the exiled Kuwaiti leader: the United States would help win back his country and would ensure that he was restored to power.

WHEN Powell heard about the Bush-Fahd conversation concerning a team, he immediately saw Bandar's hand. The prince had been working overtime. Bush's inclination to help and Cheney's suggestion that Schwarzkopf coordinate a possible operation had been transformed into a team to make a presentation to the King. Powell called it "convenient confusion" on Bandar's part. Bandar had once again cleverly moved the two nations into each other's arms.

Scowcroft, worried that the team might be doomed to failure, had a series of conversations with Bandar. He wanted to know if it was possible for the King to agree to accept U.S. forces beforehand.

Bandar said the King was not yet ready. Intense discussions were going on within the royal family.

Meanwhile, Bush decided that Cheney should head the team if the Saudis would accept him. At about 3:00 p.m. Scowcroft called Cheney and explained. The President wants you to head the team, he said. There was, however, some doubt about whether the King would accept someone as highly placed as Cheney, because it would make it almost impossible to say no. Stand by, Scowcroft told the Secretary of Defense.

About an hour later Cheney called his spokesman, Pete Williams, who was at home waxing his car. He told Williams to pack his bags; they were going to Saudi Arabia the next day. "I'm not certain we're going, but it looks like it," Cheney said.

8

WILLIAMS packed and went to the Pentagon on Sunday morning. Schwarzkopf, summoned from Florida again, arrived in the Secretary's office. As they were awaiting word from the Saudis, Scowcroft came over to the Pentagon. Cheney, continuing his education on Iraq, had invited a group of experts up for a briefing. They included Pat Lang, former U.S. ambassador to Iraq David G. Newton, and two other experts. "I want to know how this looks from the Iraqi side," Cheney said.

Ambassador Newton had served in Iraq from 1984 to 1988. He told Cheney that Saddam was "a tough, ruthless, hard-nosed, intelligent, and sometimes brutal leader who is used to getting his own way." Saddam's political history emphasized physical survival. He would not tolerate political opposition, and had killed opponents.

Saddam was indifferent to the suffering of others and justified his actions as serving the higher purpose of the Iraqi state, Newton added. The Iraqi army was no pushover. Saddam thought he was tougher than the United States and did not respect democracies.

The experts also told Cheney and Scowcroft that Saddam's objective was power and he had the flexibility and manipulative skills of a person who tries to maximize power.

BANDAR, who was now back in Saudi Arabia, was told the King had ordered scouts to cross into Kuwait to see if they could see the Iraqi troops that Bandar had reported. The scouts had come back reporting nothing. There was no trace of the troops.

Bandar explained again to the King that he had seen the overheads. Much doubt was expressed among the King's advisers. Bandar said the King ought to see for himself. All the more reason to give the okay for the American team to come make their presentation. And they might as well accept Cheney, not some lower-level representative.

King Fahd finally agreed.

Bandar called Scowcroft. The Cheney mission was approved.

Departure time was set for 2:30 that afternoon. Cheney was taking Gates, General Schwarzkopf, and half a dozen others.

Before he left, Cheney spoke to Bush, who was still at Camp David. The President outlined the mission. Get the King to agree to accept U.S. forces, he said; get that invitation. Prove that the administration will commit fully to a defense and will not back down. If King Fahd invited the U.S. forces in, Bush would send them en masse, and they would stay as long as necessary, but not longer than the Saudis wanted.

POWELL didn't get word that Cheney was off to Saudi Arabia until Cheney was almost in the air. As Powell ran over the events of the past several days in his mind, one thing was clear: the President was deeply, even emotionally, concerned about the fate of Saudi Arabia.

That afternoon Powell was watching CNN as Bush returned from Camp David and stepped off his helicopter onto the White House lawn. Bush went to the microphones to comment on the diplomatic activity. "What's emerging is, nobody seems to be showing up as willing to accept anything less than total withdrawal from Kuwait of Iraqi forces, and no puppet regime," the President said.

"Are you going to move militarily?" he was asked by one reporter.

"I will not discuss with you what my options are or might be, but they're wide open, I can assure you of that." Bush was clearly angered. "Iraq lied once again. They said they were going to start moving out today, and we have no evidence of their moving out."

When pressed by the reporters, Bush snapped, "Just wait. Watch and learn." Waving his finger, growing visibly hot, he said, "I view very seriously our determination to reverse out this aggression. This will not stand. This will not stand, this aggression against Kuwait."

Uh-oh! Powell said to himself. The President had now clearly, categorically, set a new goal—not only to deter an attack on Saudi Arabia but also to reverse the invasion of Kuwait. Powell was stunned. He had not been consulted. He had not spoken with Bush since the Camp David meeting the previous morning.

The Chairman could not understand why the President had radically changed the definition of success. It was one thing to stop Saddam from going into other countries, like Saudi Arabia; it was very much another thing to reverse an invasion that was accomplished. In military terms it was night and day. And Powell, the number one military man, had been given no opportunity to offer his assessment.

Powell marveled at the distance Bush had traveled in three days. It was almost as if he had six-shooters in both hands and he was blazing away.

Powell went to the White House that evening for an NSC meeting. Bush, he saw, was still one determined President. He was worked up, his mind made up.

Baker, like Powell, realized there had been no debate on whether to make the deployment. Later he worried to several of his closest aides that the White House was speeding, not thinking through what it was doing. Saudi Arabia was a vital national security interest, and the intelligence showed it was threatened. But Baker knew about moving troops. The first arrivals would be only several thousand. He had grave reservations. "These young men could be slaughtered if Saddam Hussein attacked," he said.

ACCOMPANYING Cheney on a comfortable modern jetliner very like the Vice President's Air Force Two were General Schwarzkopf, Bob Gates of the NSC, Paul Wolfowitz, Pete Williams, Charles W. Freeman, Jr.—the U.S. ambassador to Saudi Arabia, who spoke Arabic—and a CIA expert, with the latest top secret satellite photographs.

At about 1:00 p.m. local time on Monday, August 6, the Americans arrived in Jidda. They were taken to elaborate quarters. Their meeting with the King had been scheduled for two hours later, but word came that His Majesty, a night person, preferred to delay it six to eight hours. Unbeknownst to Cheney, Fahd was checking with Muslim religious leaders to see if they would tolerate a U.S. deployment.

Fahd's realm was very secretive and conservative, consisting of an area one quarter the size of the United States, with only 14 million people. That evening Cheney, Gates, Schwarzkopf, Wolfowitz, and Ambassador Freeman were conducted to the royal family's private council room in the summer palace. Fahd and half a dozen key members of his government and the royal family, including the foreign minister, the deputy defense minister, and Crown Prince Abdullah, were there. Prince Bandar was to translate for both sides.

The meeting began with small talk about Fahd's long relationship with Bush. When Bush had been CIA director in 1976, Fahd, who'd run Saudi intelligence for 13 years as interior minister, was overseeing Saudi foreign policy as crown prince. Ordinarily at royal meetings the King would open with a lengthy statement. This evening he turned to Cheney rather quickly.

The Secretary began by reminding his hosts that the United States had come to the assistance of Saudi Arabia in 1962 against Yemen and Egypt. He cited U.S. protection of Gulf tanker shipments in 1987–88. "It's not a commitment that we take lightly," Cheney said. "Saudi Arabia faces what may be the greatest threat in its history. The President stands personally behind the American security guarantee. Saddam Hussein has used lies, deceit, and naked aggression to already change the balance of power. He will only become more dangerous if he goes unchallenged."

France, the Soviet Union, and China had all agreed to take action, Cheney said. President Bush had spoken personally with the leaders of Great Britain, France, Germany, Turkey, Japan, and Italy.

"We all have to cooperate to see that this man does not succeed," Cheney said. He proposed a two-part strategy: first, cooperation to defend Saudi Arabia against a future attack; second, the strangulation of Iraq. "Economic measures are important, but as Saddam Hussein begins to feel the pressure he could lash out and attack."

Schwarzkopf then showed King Fahd the satellite pictures of Iraqi tanks on the way to the Saudi border. The pictures clearly explained why Saudi scouts sent into Kuwait had not been able to find the Iraqi forces. As was their style, the Iraqis were moving their command, control, and communications units ahead of the mass of troops. The pictures also showed the menacing Scud launchers. And Schwarzkopf mentioned 22 Iraqi aircraft loaded for combat at one base.

Fahd seemed disgusted. "We used to think Saddam Hussein tells the truth. He told us he wouldn't attack Kuwait, but the opposite happened. So we know his bad intentions are there. As long as the right preparations for the right response at the right time are done, that is the best way to roll back these Iraqi actions. And I am grateful."

It seemed that Fahd was moving in the direction Cheney wanted to take him.

Bringing U.S. forces, Schwarzkopf explained, would entail a 7000-mile journey for those coming by air, and 12,000 miles by sea. Fighter air squadrons would come first, followed by light ground troops. Schwarzkopf then went through a week-by-week description of the buildup. By week 17 it would be a very large force—many air force planes, navy ships, two tank divisions, and two other divisions.

No one asked for the total number of personnel, so Schwarzkopf did not have to give the 250,000 figure. He did not offer the estimate of 8 to 12 months for a full offensive option. He did say that after the 17 weeks the force could defeat anything that came against it.

"The President asked me to emphasize four things," Cheney now said. "The United States can put in enough force so that Saddam Hussein will be deterred. Should deterrence fail, our forces together will suffice to defeat him. Second, to be successful, we have to have forces in place. We can't wait until Iraq crosses the border. Time is of the essence. Third, after the danger is over, our forces will go home."

Under his breath in Arabic, Crown Prince Abdullah interjected, "I would hope so." Bandar did not translate this.

"Because of our cooperation," Cheney continued on the third point, "your forces will be better able to defend your country after we leave. And we will be able to return more quickly if we're needed."

Fahd said, Yes, almost like a joint training exercise when the United States leaves equipment behind—a standard U.S. practice.

Schwarzkopf joked, "I might want to think about that a little bit."

Fahd seemed to be looking for a long-run, concrete benefit from such a deployment. Cheney picked up on it. "Our position would be much easier now if equipment were in place." He continued with his message. "Fourth, if we fail to deal with Saddam Hussein now, he will only grow stronger. I'd like to receive your approval to proceed."

Fahd turned to his entourage. "Does anybody have any comments?"

A lively exchange in Arabic ensued between the King and the crown prince. Bandar did not translate. On the U.S. side only Ambassador Freeman understood what was said.

"We have to do this," Fahd said. "The Kuwaitis waited too long, and now there no longer is a Kuwait."

"Oh, yes, there is," Crown Prince Abdullah shot back.

"Yes," Fahd replied, "and all the Kuwaitis are living in our hotel rooms."

After this the King turned to Cheney. Bandar resumed translation. "Mr. Secretary, we approve of the principle. Let's believe in God and do what has to be done. We will proceed with the details. The most important thing is to proceed to protect our country together with the Americans, also bringing some people from other Arab countries that are friendly to you and us, like Egypt and Morocco."

"I think that would be excellent," Cheney said. "I'm very pleased."

"The United States has no ulterior motive," Fahd said. "We have taken this country from bushes and stones and built it to a nation equal to few. I wish you could see where the billions of dollars of oil income go. Twenty-two years ago, where you sit was formed a desert. Who would have believed? From nothing to twenty-two hundred factories."

Why such success? the King asked. Because, he answered, "we're not afraid to learn from people who are better than we are. The Saudi people have no complexes. We want to cooperate with other people. I want to thank the President, the Vice President, his administration, both houses of Congress, you personally," he said to Cheney. "You've come here with one objective, which is to help Saudi Arabia. [I] hope that these problems in our part of the world can subside, and I still owe you a visit to the United States, and I am holding to it."

Cheney said that President Bush was eager for the King to visit. "This has been a truly historic meeting," Cheney added.

"No doubt it is," Fahd replied.

The Secretary said, "I will give word to the President. He will start moving forces right away."

Back in his room, Cheney phoned the President and said King Fahd had approved the deployment. Bush sounded quite happy. Cheney formally asked for approval to begin moving the forces.

"You got it. Go," Bush said.

CHENEY called Powell to tell him.

General Kelly and his operations staff had spent much of the weekend working to prepare for a deployment, and then waiting. About 4:00 p.m. the order came to execute Operations Plan 90-1002.

The first unit sent would be 48 advanced F-15 jets from the 1st Tactical Fighter Wing, at Langley Air Force Base, Virginia. The Division Ready Brigade of 2300 men from the army's 82nd Airborne Division—the troops in the highest state of readiness—would be next.

Powell was concerned. The Division Ready Brigade was an extremely light force. The brigade, the 48 jet fighters, the naval air power in the region, and the small Saudi army were no match for Saddam's six divisions. It was naked vulnerability—prime time for Saddam to strike.

AT 9:00 A.M. on Wednesday, August 8, President Bush appeared on national television from the Oval Office to announce the troop deployment. He looked tired and drawn. His voice was a bit scratchy and his rhythm off as he spoke words of high purpose. Holding to his "this will not stand" position, the President called for "the immediate, unconditional, and complete withdrawal of all Iraqi forces from Kuwait."

But, he explained, "the mission of our troops is wholly defensive. Hopefully they will not be needed long. They will not initiate hostilities, but they will defend themselves, the Kingdom of Saudi Arabia, and other friends in the Persian Gulf."

A nervous smile flashed at several inappropriate moments. Bush stuck his fist in the air as he spoke of "unity of purpose."

At 1:00 p.m. Cheney and Powell appeared at a Pentagon press conference. Cheney had arrived back in Washington just three hours before the President's speech. Because this was an ongoing operation, Cheney said, he couldn't answer many questions about what units were going, when they were going, and their strength. He outlined his trip to Saudi Arabia, then turned the conference over to Powell.

Powell made an unusually direct appeal to the media. "I would ask for restraint on your part as you find out information—if you would always measure it against the need for operational security to protect our troops. That should be uppermost, I think, in all our minds."

To a question concerning the vulnerability of the initial troops, Powell stretched the point. "I think they are pretty secure," he said. But privately he was still concerned. Many in the world, apparently including Saddam, thought somehow that the United States could deploy tens or hundreds of thousands of troops instantaneously. Of course, it wasn't true. In the first three or four weeks Powell's troops would be excruciatingly vulnerable. It was a secret that needed to be guarded at almost any cost. Lives depended on it.

DIA officer Pat Lang briefed Prince Bandar at his elegant, sprawling residence in Virginia. The former British commandos who acted as Bandar's security guards had escorted Lang into an ornately decorated room, where he put up a map. For an hour he went over in detail what had happened during the Kuwait invasion and how Saddam was massing the same eight elite divisions on the Saudi border.

Lang crisply described how nearly 800 T-72 tanks were on the battle line and could move unimpeded into eastern Saudi Arabia and duplicate the Kuwait success. "We are powerless to stop them," he said.

"Oh, God," Bandar said. "Oh, God. Do *they* know this?" Does Saddam realize he can overrun Saudi Arabia this easily?

"I think they suspect it," Lang replied, "but they don't know it." He added that reading Saddam's mind had become the question of the day, and that so far everyone had flunked the test.

PETE Williams, who had top security clearances and was as trusted a Cheney aide as any, did not know exactly how many troops were scheduled for deployment. Whenever he asked Powell, the Chairman was vague. He seemed almost paranoid about the numbers and the locations of the troops.

From the White House, Sununu put out the figure 50,000, which was published Thursday, August 9, and attributed to an unnamed senior administration official.

When army chief Carl Vuono saw the lowball figure, he was distressed. The operation, now dubbed Desert Shield, could sour on the question of expectations and credibility. With the White House and political leadership concealing facts and risks, creating false hopes for a small, short-lived operation, he heard echoes of Vietnam. Vuono recognized that the military was in for the long haul—months and months, if not longer. Such a massive deployment could not be concealed; orders were going to units in dozens of states. A Vuono aide soon leaked the real number of up to 250,000 to the press.

BUSH decided to go to the Pentagon. On Tuesday, August 14, Cheney and Powell held a one-hour rehearsal in the Tank of a briefing for the President. The next day, Wednesday, Bush visited the Tank.

Powell was alarmed about all the troops and military force he was beginning to pour into the Gulf without any clear notion of where the buildup would end. Where was it all leading? If the invasion of Kuwait was going to be reversed, what did that mean in practical military terms? How much force was needed?

After the Tank session Bush, Cheney, and Powell went to Cheney's office. Powell showed the President a chart that illustrated graphically, week by week, the U.S. forces going into the Gulf. The chart ended on December 1, the closure point for the mission, when 250,000 troops would be there. "If you want me to do more, the curve goes up," Powell said. "If you want more, I need to know whether it's two miles or three miles down the road that I get off and exit here."

Powell wasn't pushing for a decision, just inquiring whether they had—or were going to get—a new military mission. There was no response from Bush, but Powell felt that he had at least put the President on notice that a decision would have to be made soon.

Later Bush spoke to Pentagon employees at the River Entrance, overlooking the Potomac. He said, "Saddam has claimed this is a holy war of Arab against infidel—this from the man who has used poison gas against his own country; who invaded Iran in a war that cost the lives of more than half a million Moslems; and who now plunders Kuwait. Atrocities have been committed by Saddam's soldiers and henchmen. Reports out of Kuwait tell a sordid tale of brutality." It was a fiery attack on Saddam. "It is Saddam who lied to his Arab neighbors. It is Saddam who invaded an Arab state. And it is he who now threatens the Arab nation," Bush said, his voice rising.

Standing near Bush, before the crowd, Cheney thought to himself that it was far too personal an attack—harsh and overdone, ratcheting up the rhetoric way too much. The text of the speech had come over from the White House only an hour before, and there had been no chance for anyone in the Pentagon to suggest changes.

Cheney later mentioned his concern directly to Scowcroft. Saddam now had roughly 200,000 troops in Kuwait to the 20,000 of the United States—a 10 to 1 advantage. The possibility of a slaughter still could not be ruled out, and Cheney did not want some debate-team flourish by the President to provoke Saddam.

Though Bush had gone to Kennebunkport to take his summer vacation, Cheney had canceled two weeks of fishing, scheduled to begin that day. He did not see how the Secretary of Defense could order hundreds of thousands to the Saudi desert, then go fishing.

ON FRIDAY, August 17, Cheney left for Saudi Arabia and a four-day swing through Bahrain, Oman, the United Arab Emirates, and Egypt. He was seeking landing and staging rights for U.S. forces.

Visiting the U.S. units already in Saudi Arabia, Cheney was dramatically reminded of their precarious situation. Everyone seemed consumed with logistics, transportation, and just getting settled. Suppose there was a fight before all the U.S. forces were in place?

Cheney called Powell on the secure line. Is Schwarzkopf making certain that we are ready for any short-term contingency? he asked.

Powell agreed they were vulnerable. But if Saddam was going to move into Saudi Arabia, why hadn't he done it earlier? Powell said that each day the United States is better off.

When Cheney returned to Washington, he and Powell flew to Kennebunkport, on Wednesday, August 22, to brief the President and discuss the next steps.

It was a bright, sunny day at Walker's Point, a beautiful piece of oceanfront real estate on the craggy Maine coast. Cheney and Powell sought Bush's final approval to call up some 50,000 reservists. Certain critical military specialties, such as logistics, transportation, medical services, construction, and intelligence, were concentrated in the reserves. Frustrated by President Johnson's refusal to fully mobilize the military in the Vietnam War by calling up the reserves, the Pentagon had intentionally organized the services so that the specialists required in a large deployment were in the reserves. This would force a President to use the reserves for any major military action, making it difficult to slide slowly into war without the public's participation.

Bush, Powell, and Cheney knew the reserve call-up was inevitable. Bush now authorized it.

The United Nations, which already had approved economic sanctions against Iraq, was now considering a blockade. The navy had stopped some Iraqi tankers, but had not yet boarded any. Bush was skeptical the United Nations would come through. When he was U.N. ambassador, in 1971–72, the Soviets had blocked everything the United States tried to do. But this was a new era. He decided he would wait for a ruling from the U.N. Security Council.

Powell informed the President that for the first time since the deployment began, the situation was not dicey. There were some 35,000 troops in Saudi Arabia or on the way and another 20,000 U.S. sailors on ships in the region. General Schwarzkopf, of course, was not satisfied, but Powell never expected a commander to be satisfied. Saddam probably would not attack now, Powell said, because he had not taken the chance during the first two weeks, when he really had the upper hand.

Yet, Powell said, the Iraqi military was still capable of inflicting tremendous damage. One big factor was the Iraqi ground-to-ground missile force, including large quantities of Scud-B, modified to have a range of 615 kilometers. Saddam's forces in Kuwait were also digging in. As the United States brought in heavy armored forces, two of the world's large armies would be facing off. If there was conflict, it would be major land warfare.

Bush asked Powell for his view—not just his military advice, Bush added—on what course of action to take. He wanted an overall assessment. Powell said they were doing fine defending Saudi Arabia.

By the end of the meeting Powell saw that Bush was somewhat sobered. Talk of liberating Kuwait was no longer on the front burner. In the following days he toned down his public attacks on Saddam.

On Saturday, August 25, the U.N. Security Council voted to give the navies of the United States and other countries the right to use force to stop trade with Iraq. It was the first time in the United Nations' 45-year history that individual countries outside an umbrella U.N. command were authorized to enforce an international blockade—an extraordinary diplomatic victory for the administration.

Bush, who had sweated out the U.N. vote, was euphoric.

9

O N September 21, 1990, the sixth week into the U.S. deployment, Saddam's Revolutionary Command Council issued a bellicose statement, saying, "There is not a single chance for any retreat. Let everybody understand that this battle is going to become the mother of all battles."

Satellite photos and other intelligence presented to President Bush showed that Iraq was systematically dismantling Kuwait, looting the entire nation. Everything of value was being carried back to Iraq. The populace was being terrorized, starved, beaten, murdered. Kuwait would soon become a perpetual no-man's-land, Bush was told.

U.S. intelligence claimed Saddam now had 430,000 troops in Kuwait and southern Iraq. His forces were digging in, moving into even more defensive positions. This made an offensive attack into Saudi Arabia less likely; the Iraqis would have to dig out and move into the open desert, where the United States could obliterate troops and tanks with superior air power and Schwarzkopf's own ground forces. Though the United States had less than half as many troops in the theater as Iraq, Cheney and Powell told Bush they now felt quite sure the U.S. and allied forces could defend Saudi Arabia.

Friday, September 28, was the day of the Emir. Bush had the exiled Emir of Kuwait, who was visiting the United States for the first time, into the Oval Office. Scowcroft joined them for the hour-long meeting. Though the Emir did not directly ask for military intervention to liberate his country, Scowcroft could see that was his subliminal message. That afternoon Cheney and Powell met with the Emir privately.

Afterward Bush said that Kuwait was running out of time. It certainly wasn't going to be around as a country if they waited for sanctions to work. The Emir himself and the stories of destruction supported by intelligence reports left an indelible mark on the President. Iraq will fail, and Kuwait will endure, Bush said.

At the same time, Powell realized that Schwarzkopf, in Saudi Arabia, was growing increasingly nervous about the scale of the Iraqi buildup and about U.S. objectives and force levels. In his daily secure phone conversations with Powell, in the Pentagon, Schwarzkopf was regularly looking for clues or asking directly about the next step.

"Norm, I'm working on it," Powell was telling him.

Cheney and Powell spent much time on these questions.

"You know," Powell told Cheney in early October, "we're going to have to get a decision." The President had to tell them—well before the defensive mission's cutoff date of December 1—whether to continue deploying forces or to stop. "When I put the last thing in the funnel, two weeks later it will come out in Saudi Arabia. We need to know when to stop putting things in the funnel," Powell said.

Cheney didn't give much of a response.

Powell started jotting down some notes. He felt that containment, or strangulation, was working. An extraordinary political-diplomatic coalition had been assembled, leaving Iraq without substantial allies. Intelligence showed that economic sanctions were cutting off up to 95 percent of Saddam's imports and nearly all his exports. The impact could take months. There would come a point, a month or six weeks before Saddam was down to the last pound of rice, when the sanctions would trigger some kind of response.

POWELL went to Cheney to outline the case for containment. All he had were his handwritten notes. Until they were sure sanctions and strangulation had failed, it would be very difficult to go to war, Powell said. If there was a chance that sanctions would work, there might be an obligation to continue waiting—at least to a certain point.

"I don't know," Cheney responded. "I don't think the President will buy it." Bush was committed to policy success. Containment could leave Kuwait in Saddam's hands. That would constitute policy failure.

Powell wanted another dog in the fight. He was concerned that no one was laying out the alternatives to the President. A full slate of options should be presented. Several days later Powell went back to Cheney with an expanded presentation on containment.

"Uh-hmm," Cheney said, noncommittal. "It certainly is another way to look at it."

Powell next went to see Baker about containment. The Secretary of State was Powell's chief ally in the upper ranks of the administration. They thought alike on many issues. Both preferred deal making to conflict. And both worked the news media assiduously to get their points of view across. Baker was very unhappy about talk of an offensive military option. He wanted diplomacy—meaning the State Department—to achieve the policy success. He told Powell he had some of his staff working on an analysis of the advantages of containment. This should force a discussion of containment within the Bush inner circle, Baker indicated, or at least it would get out publicly.

But no White House meetings or discussion followed. Powell felt that he'd sent the idea up the flagpole, but no one had saluted or even commented. Plainly the President was dug in, insisting that Kuwait be freed. Bush had not blinked, and frustrations were obviously mounting in the White House. Powell decided to go see Scowcroft.

Scowcroft indicated he was having a difficult time trying to manage and control an incredibly active President. Bush was out making statements, giving press conferences almost daily, up at dawn making calls—on the phone with one world leader after another. On a supposedly relaxing weekend Bush talked with or saw more people related to his job than most people did in a normal workweek.

Powell listened sympathetically. Turning to the question of the Gulf, he said he wondered about the advantages of economic sanctions.

Scowcroft knew Powell's attitude because Cheney had hinted at it. But now Powell was indirect. He did not say, This is my position.

"The President is more and more convinced sanctions are not going to work," Scowcroft said. He made it clear that he had a solid read on the President. Bush's determination was undisguised, and he had virtually foreclosed any possibility that his views could be changed.

Powell could see that Scowcroft agreed with Bush and was strongly reinforcing his inclinations. As national security adviser, it was his job to mirror the President. But the security adviser also had a responsibility to make sure the range of alternatives was presented.

Scowcroft was substantially more willing to go to war than Powell was. War was an instrument of foreign policy, in Scowcroft's view. Powell did not disagree; he just saw that instrument much closer, less a disembodied abstraction than real men and women—faces, many of them kids' faces, that he looked into on his visits to the troops.

Powell told Scowcroft that if there was an alternative to war, he wanted to make sure it was fully considered. Scowcroft became impatient. The President was doing everything imaginable, he said.

Powell left. He had become increasingly disenchanted with the National Security Council procedures and meetings. Scowcroft seemed unable, or unwilling, to coordinate all the components of the Gulf policy—military, diplomatic, public affairs, economic, the United Nations. When the principals met, Bush liked to keep everyone around the table smiling—jokes, camaraderie, the conviviality of old friends. Clear decisions rarely emerged.

The operation needed a field marshal—someone of the highest rank who was the day-to-day manager, Powell felt. The President, given his other domestic and political responsibilities, couldn't be chief coordinator. It should be the national security adviser. Instead, Scowcroft had become the First Companion and all-purpose playmate to the President on golf, fishing, and weekend outings. He was regularly failing in his larger duty to ensure that policy was carefully debated and formulated.

Sununu only added to the problem, exerting little or no control over the process as White House chief of staff.

As a result the President was left painted into a corner by his own repeated declarations. His obvious emotional attachment to them was converting presidential remarks into hard policy. The goal now, more than ever, was the liberation of Kuwait at almost any cost.

POWELL thought that containment had not been fully shot down by Bush, but he was soon corrected. Within days Scowcroft told Cheney that Bush wanted a briefing right away on what an offensive operation against Saddam's forces in Kuwait might look like.

Over the Columbus Day weekend of October 6–8, army chief Carl Vuono flew to Saudi Arabia to see General Schwarzkopf. They'd been friends since they were teenage cadets together at West Point in the 1950s, and on three occasions during their careers Schwarzkopf had worked for Vuono. Vuono considered Schwarzkopf one of the most difficult, stubborn, and talented men in the army.

When they went off for a private talk, Vuono could see Schwarzkopf was upset. The C in C—all 240 pounds of him—seemed about to explode out of his desert fatigues. He was precisely halfway through the 17 weeks he'd said he would need to put the defensive force in place. Now Washington was beginning to talk offense. Worse, Powell had just phoned Schwarzkopf to tell him that Bush wanted a briefing right away on what an offensive operation would look like.

Schwarzkopf was furious. They had to be kidding. He was not

ready to present such a plan, and he didn't want to be pushed prematurely into offensive operations. Now he was afraid some son of a bitch was going to wake up some morning and say, Let's get the offense rolling. In about 48 hours he had to get someone to Washington to offer a preliminary plan.

After listening to Schwarzkopf for four hours, Vuono felt as if he'd been through a psychotherapy session. He could see his old friend felt very lonely and vulnerable. Vuono promised to do what he could.

On Wednesday morning, October 10, Powell received Schwarzkopf's chief of staff, marine major general Robert B. Johnston, at the Pentagon. Johnston, a stiff, deferential, buttoned-down marine with extensive briefing experience, began by reminding the chiefs and Cheney that the Central Command had deployed its forces in accordance with the President's deter-and-defend mission. But if the President tells us to go on the offense tomorrow, he said, here's what we would do. Right now, this is our best shot at it.

The plan was broken into four phases, he explained. Phase one, an air attack on Iraqi command, control, and communications, would be an attempt to sever Saddam, in Baghdad, from his forces in Kuwait and southern Iraq. Simultaneously air power would destroy the Iraqi air force and air defense system. An additional attack would destroy chemical, biological, and nuclear weapons facilities.

Phase two would be a massive, continuous air bombardment of Iraqi supply and munitions bases, transportation facilities, and roads, designed to cut off the Iraqi forces from their supplies.

Phase three would be an air attack on the entrenched Iraqi ground forces of 430,000 men and on the Republican Guard.

The three phases would overlap somewhat. As early as a week after the beginning of the first air phase, the ground assault, phase four, would be launched on the Iraqi forces in Kuwait. There would be an amphibious assault from the Gulf by U.S. marines while the U.S. Army and an Egyptian ground division attacked directly into enemy lines.

Cheney, Powell, and several others asked question after question.

Cheney felt good about the three phases of the air campaign. The planning looked detailed and complete. The phase four ground plan, however, looked inadequate. The offensive U.S. units would be sent against a potentially larger defensive Iraqi force, depending on what remained of Saddam's troops after the bombing. It looked unwise.

Cheney remarked that many of the U.S. forces were lightly armed and might have to fight heavily armored tanks. There were no reserve forces for backup. Also, the ground plan called for an assault straight into the Iraqi entrenchments. Why go right up the middle? he asked.

Johnston deflected most of the questions. The plan was preliminary, he reminded them, and the questions reflected caveats from Schwarzkopf. "We do not have the capability on the ground to guarantee success," Johnston said. Schwarzkopf would need an additional three heavy armored divisions for a proper offensive option.

Cheney concluded that an attack with the U.S. forces now in place and based on this plan would be a risk of a high order.

Johnston said there was a window of opportunity, from about January 1 to February 15, 1991, when offensive action would be most desirable. After that the weather and Muslim religious holidays would conspire to make combat more difficult. Heavy rains would begin in March, and the temperatures could rise to 100 degrees Fahrenheit or more. On March 17 the Muslims would start the observation of Ramadan, one month of fasting from sunrise to sunset, and in June would be the annual pilgrimage to Mecca, presenting complications for Arab states in the anti-Saddam coalition.

Cheney recognized that he had an obligation to present this brief to the President. The next day, October 11, Johnston made the presentation in the Situation Room at the White House. The meeting took nearly two hours. Bush's reaction was similar to Cheney's, particularly on the phase four ground plan. The military was not ready for an offensive operation; they didn't have enough strength.

After the Johnston briefing, Cheney leaned hard on the system. He wanted the planners to move away from throwing all the forces straight through the Iraqis' frontline barriers. He asked Powell to think about making a ground assault into Iraq somewhere far west along the Saudi-Iraq border, 300 to 400 miles from Kuwait, out toward the Jordanian border. Such an unexpected attack on the western approaches to Baghdad would put a ground force in a location where there would be no Iraqi resistance, would cut the lines of communication between Baghdad and Jordan, and would allow a direct ground attack on the fixed Scud missile sites threatening Israel.

Powell quickly came back with an answer: No. It was way too far to take U.S. forces.

ON SUNDAY, OCTOBER 21, POWELL left Washington for Saudi Arabia. Arriving in Riyadh late the next day, he went right to Schwarzkopf.

Powell immediately saw that everyone in the command, including Schwarzkopf, was pretty raggedy. They had been deterring and defending for nearly three months. The uncertainties, risks, and discomforts had been building on one another.

Whatever the case, Powell said, they now had to come up with a fully scrubbed offensive plan. More important, Schwarzkopf had to specify what additional forces he would need for that mission. Powell needed his wish list and pledged to back him up.

Schwarzkopf had said in a recent *Life* magazine article that he was no fan of war:

> In a lot of ways I am a pacifist—though that might be too strong a word. But I know what war is. I am certainly anti-war. But I also believe there are things worth fighting for.

Frankly, he told Powell now, he was not sold on an offensive operation as the solution. Pushing Saddam out of Kuwait at this point would be dirty and bloody. Schwarzkopf estimated that it would take about twice the force level he had. Double the air force presence; double the navy carriers, from three to six; double the marine and army ground forces. "I want the Seventh Corps," he said finally.

The VII Corps was the centerpiece of the U.S. ground defense in Europe—three of the best-trained, best-equipped divisions—two heavy tank and one mechanized. It was a stunning request, inconceivable even a year ago, but Gorbachev and the collapse of the Warsaw Pact made it feasible. If the President was serious about offense, Schwarzkopf said, he was going to have to send the VII Corps.

Powell wanted to go even further. He was determined to make the buildup as massive as possible. The Big Red One, the 1st Mechanized Infantry Division, would fit in nicely. Schwarzkopf agreed.

ON WEDNESDAY, October 24, Cheney was summoned to the White House. The President said he was leaning toward adding the offensive forces. Nothing could be announced for two weeks, because any move would be assumed to be an attempt to influence the November 6 elections. Cheney said that he was waiting for Powell's report from Saudi Arabia, and they should wait.

It was apparent to Cheney that Bush would be happy with some public hint. Cheney was already scheduled the next day to go on the early morning shows of the three major networks and CNN. He felt that the White House's inept handling of the recent budget talks with Congress had cast a pall over the entire administration, even eroding confidence in the Gulf operation. Cheney also felt it was best to prepare the public for the likely decision.

Later that day Cheney joined Baker in giving a classified briefing to legislators in the Capitol. Neither dropped a hint that a reinforcement was being considered. But in the television interviews the next morning, October 25, Cheney intentionally laid the seed. "We are not at the point yet where we want to stop adding forces," he said on ABC. On CBS he was asked if the Pentagon was getting ready to send another 100,000 troops. Cheney replied, "It's conceivable that we'll end up with that big of an increase." He repeated this point on NBC.

The big news of Cheney's statements reached Powell, who was on a stopover in Europe. "What is going on?" he asked an aide. When it sank in, he told one person, "Goddammit, I'll never travel again. I haven't seen the President on this." There had been discussions, but no decision as far as he knew. But there it was, in clear language from Cheney, a man who chose his words carefully.

Bush, Scowcroft, and Sununu were making decisions again without a full airing of views. Powell was tired of learning of major administration decisions after the fact. Sununu had been advising and urging the President to speak out strongly and to back up his words with a military threat. He or someone else apparently had won.

In Saudi Arabia, Schwarzkopf also heard Cheney's remarks. Before his own surprise and distress could fully register, the Saudis were on the phone pounding him with questions: What is this? What's going on? Where were the consultations before making such a decision or announcement? Schwarzkopf tried to stumble through with some answers. He was fuming. Not only did he have to learn about something this important from the media but he had to explain it to the Saudis without any guidance from Washington.

Soon after he returned to Washington, Powell was watching NBC's Saturday *Nightly News* broadcast, with Mary Alice Williams. She introduced a report on troop morale from Saudi Arabia.

Reporter Arthur Kent came on, saying that "nerves are being

severely strained in Saudi Arabia. U.S. troops here spend most of their energy just killing time. The days drag on. There are still no clear military objectives to go after. Perhaps half of the troops we spoke to said they were very unhappy with the way things are going."

What the hell are they talking about? Powell asked himself. The report had offered nothing hard. It was foolish, but it reminded him that if war came, it would be on television instantly, bringing home the action, death, consequences, and emotions even more graphically than during Vietnam. The reporters and the cameras would be there to record each step, vastly complicating all military tasks. Powell was sure of one thing: a prolonged war on television could become impossible, unsupportable at home.

SEVERAL times in October, Robert Teeter, Bush's chief pollster, talked with the President about the Gulf policy. Teeter said he thought the administration had too many messages flying around. He suggested that the two with the strongest appeal were fighting aggression and protecting the lives of Americans, including the more than 900 Americans being held hostage in Iraq and Kuwait. More than 100 had been moved to Iraqi military and industrial installations to serve as human shields to deter a U.S. attack.

Bush acknowledged the points, but nonetheless seemed confident. He said he felt he knew more than anyone about the region, and also about the diplomacy, the military, the economics, and the oil. I have been dealing with these issues for 25 years, he said. One night he told Teeter it was important that he had served as U.N. ambassador, U.S. envoy to China, CIA director, and Vice President. Those experiences allowed him to see all the pieces. Now he could put them together.

There might be some rough times, some down times, Bush conceded, but he felt good. "This will be successful," he assured Teeter.

FOR months Scowcroft had been concerned that Baker was not a supporter of the Gulf policy. In the inner-circle discussions he seemed to oppose the large deployment of troops, favoring a diplomatic solution almost to the exclusion of the military pressure. But Baker was coming around. Cheney was going fishing with him over the weekend, and they would have time to talk.

The polls showed that the public's greatest concern was the American hostages in Iraq and Kuwait. Baker had argued that the focus of the Gulf policy should be shifted to the hostage issue. It was the one issue that would unite Americans and the international community, because most nations, including the Soviet Union, had hostages held in Iraq. It was the one issue that might justify a war.

Baker wanted to play the hostage card himself in a strong speech. Scowcroft was willing to go along. The national security adviser also realized that Baker saw the handwriting on the wall. The Bush presidency was likely to rise or fall on the outcome of the Gulf policy. Baker—Bush's friend of 35 years, his campaign manager, and the senior Cabinet officer—had no other choice than to become an aggressive supporter of the policy.

On Monday, October 29, Baker addressed the Los Angeles World Affairs Council, describing the terrible ordeal of the more than 100 American human shields. "We will not rule out a possible use of force if Iraq continues to occupy Kuwait," the Secretary of State said.

The next day Bush had 15 congressional leaders from both houses and both parties to the White House. He opened the meeting with a status report—Iraq had released the French hostages, but more reports of maltreatment of American and British hostages were coming in.

Visibly riled, Bush said that the treatment of the hostages was horrible and barbarous. Baker then made some supporting points.

Speaker Thomas Foley said, Mr. President, we're with you on this.

AT 3:30 P.M. that same day Bush met with Baker, Cheney, Scowcroft, and Powell in the Situation Room of the White House.

"We are at a Y in the road," Scowcroft began. The policy could continue to be deter and defend, or it could switch to developing the offensive option.

Powell was struck once again by the informality of the rolling discussion among these few men, who had been friends for years. There was no real organization to the proceedings as they weighed the options. Ideas bounced back and forth. Bush and Scowcroft seemed primed to go ahead with the offensive option. Baker, less anxious and more cautious, was measured, inquiring about the attitudes in Congress and of the public, but he was no longer reluctant.

Cheney said he had a growing conviction that they had to develop the offensive option. The international coalition was too fragile to hold out indefinitely. To outsiders it might look different, but they knew, from the inside, that the arrangements were delicate.

Powell saw that patience was not the order of the day. He had found that the others previously tolerated his broad political advice, but now he sensed that he had less permission to speak up, having already made the case for containment to the President.

The meeting had been billed in advance as a chance for the Chairman to report on his discussions with Schwarzkopf. "Okay, okay, okay," the President finally said. "Let's hear what he has to say."

"Mr. President," Powell began, "we have accomplished the mission assigned." The defense of Saudi Arabia had been achieved earlier than expected. He then unveiled the Schwarzkopf request to double the force if the President wanted an offensive option.

Scowcroft was amazed Schwarzkopf wanted so much more. Several oohs and aahs were heard around the table, but not from Bush.

Powell said he supported Schwarzkopf's recommendations. He turned to the President. "If you give me more time, say three months, I'll move more troops. It's that important. You can take me to the savings and loan bailout account, and we'll all go broke together." Powell's message: it was going to be expensive.

Cheney said he supported Schwarzkopf and Powell without conditions. He went even further. It was not a question *if* the President wanted the offensive option; the President should want it and should go ahead and order it. This would guarantee success if they had to fight. Saddam was fully capable of responding with more of his own forces. Cheney did not want to be back in the Situation Room, come January or February, saying, We still can't do it.

Finally Bush said, "If that's what you need, we'll do it."

The President gave the final approval the next day.

On Thursday, November 8, Cheney called the major congressional chairmen to inform them that Bush was going to announce a troop reinforcement that afternoon. He reached Les Aspin, chairman of the House Armed Services Committee, in Kenosha, Wisconsin.

Aspin had pretty much given up on trying to communicate with Dick Cheney and had taken to calling him the Sphinx. Instead, Aspin's channel into the administration was Scowcroft.

After telling Aspin about the reinforcement package, Cheney listed some of the units, but didn't provide an overall number of troops.

"That's a lot bigger than I expected," Aspin said. He did the arithmetic in his head and realized it meant another 200,000 men.

Cheney tracked down Sam Nunn in a restaurant. The Senator was unhappy that he was being informed rather than consulted. Why the hurry? Were they sure the economic sanctions would not work?

Cheney sensed a real change in Nunn. Ever the political calculator, Cheney concluded that Nunn was planning a long-shot run for the Democratic presidential nomination in 1992 and wanted to get in the good graces of his party by taking on President Bush.

Cheney monitored the public debate. The administration was trying to keep the American people behind the policy, explaining to the troops what was being done and why, while attending to the Congress, the United Nations, and the Arabs. It was also trying to manage the Israeli problem. Saddam was attempting to link resolution of the Kuwait question with resolution of the Palestinians' grievances against Israel. It was difficult to come up with one single message to speak with equal credibility and force to all those groups.

Bush and Cheney appeared at a 4:00 p.m. news briefing. "I have today directed the Secretary of Defense to increase the size of the U.S. forces committed to Desert Shield," Bush said, "to ensure that the coalition has an adequate offensive military option should that be necessary to achieve our common goals." He mentioned no numbers.

The next afternoon, Friday, November 9, Prince Bandar stopped by the Pentagon to see Powell.

"If we don't have to fight, it will be better," Powell told the prince. "If we have to, I'll do it, but we're going to do it with everything we have." Powell said that the President had ordered that this not turn into another Vietnam.

Later Cheney told Bandar, "The military is finished in this society if we screw this up."

The White House had made no arrangements for administration officials to appear on that Sunday's television talk shows or the morning shows on Monday. The Democrats were out in force. The Veterans Day–weekend newspapers were filled with stories about discord among coalition members, the difficulties Bush would have in selling a war, and the problems of fighting a distant war on the ground.

Scowcroft and his staff began referring to the three-day weekend as the Veterans Day Massacre. A poll published in *USA Today* said 51 percent approved of Bush's handling of the Gulf crisis, down from 82 percent approval three months before.

Powell found the stories exaggerated, alarmist, and speculative.

The political uproar continued over the next several days. Bush and Scowcroft were astounded at the speed with which the support for the Gulf operation seemed to be unraveling. Bush recalled that during the Vietnam War his fellow Texan, President Lyndon Johnson, had made a mistake by not officially getting Congress to vote on the war, beyond the controversial Gulf of Tonkin resolution.

Scowcroft was not confident the votes were there. It would be a disaster to go to Congress and lose.

Some top Republicans were calling for a special session of Congress to debate the Gulf buildup. They argued that Bush would win.

On November 14 Bush met with the congressional leaders of both parties and made a plea for unity. He insisted that he had not yet decided on war. "I have not crossed any Rubicon," he said. He pulled out a report of Iraqi news coverage and read aloud headlines showing a picture of disunity in the United States. The President's implication was obvious: this was the precise message that would make Saddam think he could stay in Kuwait. Bush also pulled out a pocket-size copy of the U.S. Constitution and read from Article II, section 2: " 'The President shall be Commander in Chief. . . .' "

Bush said he wanted the leaders to call a special session on the Gulf, but only if he was going to receive a substantial vote in his favor.

The Democratic leaders said at this time they would not call an emergency session. Instead, they would hold hearings.

10

POWELL now had his own crucial choices to make about the war plan. He had directed General Tom Kelly to set up a special planning cell of half a dozen of his best officers. Working in a special-access room within the Joint Staff, they were coordinating every step with Schwarzkopf's planners to address all needs—from supplies and ammunition to medical teams, rules of engagement, and procedures for dealing with potential prisoners of war.

The first commandment for a U.S. military leader is Take care of your men. Though the overall offensive mission would be to expel the Iraqi army from Kuwait, the best way to take care of the men was to destroy the Iraqi military. As in Panama, the military capability in Iraq would have to be eliminated or disabled—this time a monumental task.

But the United States had some very secret advantages.

After the decision had been made to deploy for the offensive option, Cheney and Powell had made several visits to perhaps the most secret part of the Pentagon—2C865, the Special Technical Operations Center (STOC). Here a group of about 30 men ran the only unit in the building where regular lie-detector tests ensured they were not security risks. The center was often called the Starship Enterprise because of the high-tech displays, the computers, and the communications to key intelligence agencies and the unified commands.

The STOC was the command-and-communications center for operations involving the sensitive "black" programs. Included were special operations units, intelligence-gathering capabilities, and advanced weapons systems and equipment—everything from the navy SEAL teams to the Stealth jet fighters to special spy satellites. Most of the supersecret black weapons had been developed primarily with one scenario in mind: war with the Soviet Union. But since Iraq had purchased many of its key weapons from the Soviets, the U.S. weapons were tailor made to fight the new adversary.

The United States would be able to capitalize on decades of work.

Powell was skeptical of miraculous whiz-bang solutions. He wasn't thrilled with the STOC's cost of approximately $100 million. The center reminded him of room 208, the high-tech command center in the Old Executive Office Building, next to the White House, that Ollie North had used for some of his far-flung, ill-fated operations during the Reagan administration.

Like the Chairman, Cheney was taking all the high tech with a grain of salt. He expected the people who ran the black programs to be enthusiastic advocates, but he also knew that systems often didn't perform as advertised. He had learned the value of questioning everything, and he was not taking anything on faith in the Gulf operation. He knew the military was confident about what its weapons and men could deliver. But he had taken three steps.

First, he had been very careful not to paint too rosy a picture to the

President, the public, or the Congress. Second, he had insisted on redundancy in the war plan. He wanted to make sure there was the capability to go to particular key targets several times. Third, he personally was digging into the plan and the concepts behind it.

Most mornings Cheney was given an operations and intelligence briefing by the Joint Staff. Fidgety, he wanted to know more. He requested highly classified presentations on offensive war planning and peppered the experts with questions. In less than a month he received 15 briefings. At the last one Tom Kelly presented him with a framed diploma stating that Dick Cheney had completed a course in war planning and was now designated a "Joint Planner." "This will be my most treasured possession," Cheney said with evident sarcasm.

ONE of Powell's primary tasks in planning for an offensive war was developing lists of key strategic targets in Iraq for the three air phases. Schwarzkopf's planners were working with a series of matrixes and computer models to match the targets with the available weapons over a time line of 20 to 30 days of bombing. The ground campaign would hinge on the levels of damage done in the air war and finding a way to engage the Iraqi army on terms favorable to the allies.

ON NOVEMBER 28 former JCS Chairman Admiral Crowe testified before Senator Nunn's Armed Services Committee. It was the day before that he'd told Powell, over lunch at the Pentagon, that he thought it was time for patience in the Gulf crisis. Crowe now told the Senators, "Our dislike for Hussein seems to have crowded out many other considerations. We should give sanctions a fair chance."

Without directly criticizing Bush, Crowe hinted at his fear that the President was leaning toward war. "In my judgment, we are selling our country short by jumping to the conclusion that we can't stare down our opponent. It is worth remembering that in the 1950s and '60s, individuals were similarly advising an attack on the U.S.S.R."

The testimony of Crowe and another retired JCS Chairman, General David C. Jones, was the main news event that night.

Scowcroft was irked at Crowe. The national security adviser felt that someone who had been in such a senior role in the administration should try to find common ground, not undercut the policy. And Bush told Scowcroft that he was personally disappointed in Crowe.

Crowe heard about Bush's distress and wrestled with a letter to the President. But he was too angry, and too convinced that Bush was making a terrible mistake. The letter went unfinished.

Crowe did, however, compose a letter to his son, marine captain Blake Crowe, who was stationed in Saudi Arabia. He told his son not to be guided by his father's testimony:

> You have a strong sense of duty and I know you'll perform it. When it comes time to fight, you fight. The American people are behind you, you can count on that no matter what they or I say about the policy or the administration.

Crowe's son phoned and told his parents that the bravado, the talk of kicking ass, was gone. It now looked serious, and his men and the others there just wanted to be used properly by their leaders.

Later Crowe received a holiday card from Bush. The President had written a personal note: "May God bless your son."

THE day after Crowe's testimony, November 29, the U.N. Security Council met to vote on an authorization to use force to expel Iraqi forces from Kuwait. If it passed, the resolution would be the broadest authority for war the council had granted since Korea, in 1950.

Baker had touched down in various world capitals to bring key heads of state on board and iron out the language of the resolution. He had spent ten weeks traveling 100,000 miles and had held more than 200 meetings with foreign ministers and heads of state. His strategy had been to obtain ironclad assurances of support from the key U.N. countries before publicly acknowledging that the administration was even seeking a resolution on the use of force.

Of the five permanent members of the Security Council, the Soviets were the big question mark. From the beginning of the crisis Gorbachev had opposed the possibility of military force, but he had finally come around. In a series of conversations and meetings in the weeks and days leading up to the U.N. vote, Baker and Soviet foreign minister Shevardnadze had hashed out the final wording.

In one of their conversations Shevardnadze said he wanted some language that would allow force but also encompass all other possible measures—diplomacy, sanctions, anything that might work. The broader the better.

How about "all necessary means"? Baker proposed. In Russian the same word could be used for "means" and "measures."

They went back and forth. Soon Shevardnadze was favoring "all necessary means." It was the broadest phrase they had found.

Now Baker backed off his own phrase. It was too indefinite.

"The United States knows what 'all necessary means' is," Shevardnadze said. "Don't push us. Don't push us." The Soviet Union could not be seen voting for war. At home, war still meant Afghanistan.

Baker said the United States wanted to avoid ambiguity. But Shevardnadze was immovable. Finally Baker gave in. The coalition would be authorized to use "all necessary means" to eject Saddam's forces from Kuwait if he had not pulled them out by the resolution's deadline, January 15, 1991.

The resolution passed in the Security Council, 12–2, with Yemen and Cuba against and China abstaining.

PRINCE Bandar, delighted by the U.N. resolution, received word that night that the Iraqi ambassador to the United Nations wanted to see him. It was an emergency. At last, Bandar thought, Saddam was scared. Bandar agreed to set up a meeting for the next day.

The following morning, November 30, Bandar sat down to watch President Bush on television. Bush went through a 20-paragraph statement about his Gulf policy, listing all the steps he had taken. "However, to go the extra mile for peace," he said, he would receive Iraqi foreign minister Tariq Aziz in Washington. "In addition I'm asking Secretary Jim Baker to go to see Saddam Hussein at a mutually convenient time between December fifteenth and January fifteenth."

Bandar nearly shot out of his chair in disbelief and surprise. How stupid, he thought. Americans would never understand Arabs. A peace offering 24 hours after the U.N. victory would send precisely the wrong message to Saddam: a message of weakness.

Bandar complained to the White House. Why did you not consult with us? he asked Scowcroft. The offer to meet right up to the deadline would be an invitation for Saddam to stall. To you, Bandar said, sending Baker is goodwill; to Saddam it suggests you're chicken.

Scowcroft replied that it had been a last-minute decision—but a needed step to prove to Congress and the American public that the President was willing to exhaust all diplomatic alternatives before war.

Maybe it was the right domestic message, Bandar conceded, but it was the wrong telegram to Saddam. King Fahd was extremely displeased at the failure to consult with him. What is going to happen if there is a war? Bandar asked. Are we going to get a call saying, Oh, by the way, we just started?

Bandar also spoke with the Iraqi mission at the United Nations, inquiring about the emergency meeting Saddam's ambassador had requested the night before. The staff said the Iraqi ambassador just wanted to chat and certainly there was no emergency.

Bandar concluded that Bush and Baker had given Saddam great comfort at what should have been his moment of greatest distress.

BAKER had recommended the Baghdad mission to Bush. He had been thinking of it for weeks. He had never been to Iraq and never met Saddam. By every available account, Saddam was pathological. And he was totally isolated. The Soviets had told Baker that the only way to get a message to this guy was to sit before him and state it.

The domestic political considerations were as important to Baker as the diplomatic possibilities. Now that the United Nations had authorized force, people were scared. The President had to stop the political bleeding, Baker had argued. When a Washington *Post* poll showed that 90 percent of Americans approved of the Baker-to-Baghdad offer, Prince Bandar received three separate calls noting the wide support. The calls were from Scowcroft, Baker, and Cheney.

LATER on November 30 Bush met with the congressional leadership in the Cabinet Room of the White House. The announcement of the Baker mission had nearly all the two dozen men in a jocular, even boisterous mood. The atmosphere was like a men's clubhouse, with much backslapping and joking. It calmed down only when Bush took his seat. Quayle, Baker, Scowcroft, Cheney, and Sununu also sat down.

"The Secretary of State has been engaged in a marathon to get the United Nations on board," Bush said. "He knows of the difficulty concerning the issue of force. It's a combination of [our increased] deployment and the United Nations resolution which gives us the best chance to get a peaceful resolution of the issue."

The President added, "I know there are differences around the table, and with former chiefs. But I want to show you I have no second thoughts at all." The Iraqi nuclear weapons potential is a real danger, he said. He mentioned his concern about the effects of increased energy costs worldwide and became very emotional about the brutality in Kuwait. "We really ought to care." He said he hoped Saddam got the message that the United States was serious.

"If the Congress wants to come back and endorse the U.N. resolution, let's go," Bush continued. "But let's not have a hung jury. If you can't support, frankly I'd be wary. So I'd welcome your support."

Then Bush turned the meeting over to Baker. "In this forty-five-day period, let us use the threat of force to solve this peacefully," the Secretary of State urged. In a beseeching tone he added, "You've got to give us the threat as a diplomatic tool."

House Speaker Thomas Foley praised the administration for being open and forthcoming. He said that Bush should consult the new Congress in January. "If after January fifteenth you decide to go to war, you'll have to come to Congress," Foley added.

Senate majority leader George Mitchell was emphatic on the same point: a vote was constitutionally required. As he spoke, Bush stared coldly in the other direction.

Baker, looking for consensus, asked if Congress might approve offensive operations limited to the use of superior allied air power.

"No," Mitchell said.

Senator Richard G. Lugar of Indiana, a top Republican, told the group that he had counted seven times in the meeting when the President had appealed for the support of the Congress, yet the congressional leaders were saying they weren't going to give it. "It just seems inconceivable that we are going to leave it at this," Lugar said.

"We don't need another Vietnam War," Bush said. The logistics would be different. "World unity is there. No hands are going to be tied behind backs. This is not a Vietnam. I know whose backside's at stake and rightfully so. It will not be a long-drawn-out mess. As Mubarak says, we trained the Iraqi pilots. They stink."

The room filled with laughter again.

CHENEY thought the U.N. resolution on the use of force was a watershed for the President. If Saddam did not withdraw during this 45-day pause, Cheney did not doubt that Bush would use the military to drive Iraq out.

The Secretary had been asked to be the first witness at Nunn's committee hearings on the Gulf operation, but he had declined. The White House, less confident it would have its way in Congress than in the United Nations, did not want anyone from the administration testifying during the debate. Cheney agreed to appear in the second week of the hearings. He and Powell would testify together.

Make the opening statement long, Cheney had instructed his staff. Make it very long. Not only did he want to lay out all his reasoning, he wanted the Senators to be exhausted by the time the question period began so he would have an easier time.

At the December 3 hearing Cheney read aloud a lengthy statement reviewing the entire history of the Gulf operation. He said that since Saddam would probably be able to ride out sanctions, force was the only way to guarantee that Iraq got out of Kuwait.

Powell was the only other witness. He did not come down on either side of the key question before the committee: how long they should wait to see if economic sanctions would work. "In the final analysis, how long to wait is a political, not a military, judgment," he said.

At the conclusion of Powell's statement Nunn asked him about a recent interview given by General Schwarzkopf. He had said that time was on the side of the United States and the coalition, as long as the sanctions remained in place. Nunn quoted Schwarzkopf: "If the alternative to dying is sitting out in the sun for another summer, that's not a bad alternative." What do you think? Nunn asked Powell.

"I wouldn't criticize General Schwarzkopf or in any way disagree with him. I would say that we don't know if the sanctions will work."

"If we have a war," Nunn said sharply, "we're never going to know whether they would have worked, are we? I mean, the way you find out whether sanctions work is to give them enough time to work."

Later in the hearing Senator William Cohen of Maine quoted former Secretary of State Henry Kissinger: "High military officers have an innate awe of their Commander in Chief. Contrary to some of the public mythology, they rarely challenge him." What did Powell think of this? Cohen asked.

Powell replied, "I am not afraid to give either the Secretary of Defense, the President, or any other members of the National Security Council my best, most honest, most candid advice, whether they like it or not. And on—on some occasions, they do not like it." Turning to Cheney, who was by his side, Powell asked, "Isn't that right?"

"I will confirm that," Cheney answered. There was laughter.

"Which part, sir?" Powell asked.

"All of it, Colin," Cheney replied.

ON SUNDAY, December 16, Bush left Camp David for the White House, where he was to do a taping of a public television interview with David Frost. In the helicopter on the way down, he read a 79-page report by Amnesty International on human rights violations carried out by the Iraqis in Kuwait since the invasion.

"Oh, David," he told Frost later, "it was so terrible, it's hard to describe." Bush explained how his wife, Barbara, had read two pages and could not read any more. "The torturing of a handicapped child. The shooting of young boys in front of their parents. The rape of women. Electric shocks to the private parts. I mean, it—it is primeval."

The President said that a more peaceful world was possible if the United States and the coalition stood up to Saddam. "It won't happen if we compromise. We have such a clear moral case. It's that big. It's that important. Nothing like this since World War Two. Nothing of this moral importance since World War Two."

POWELL was determined not to be crushed or even nagged by ambivalence. If there was a war, the United States had to win it. A spectacular victory was required. At stake was not only the nation's foreign policy but also the reputation and morale of the military for years, even decades, to come.

On December 17 President Bush spoke twice to reporters. At the first session he was asked what he was going to do after the expiration of the deadline, on January 15.

"You just wait and see," he said.

At the second session that afternoon, a reporter asked why he had not come right out and said he would attack.

"Because I'm not in a threatening mode," Bush answered.

That day Powell and Defense policy under secretary Wolfowitz discussed Bush's method of getting his message out. Powell was in real agony. Although he didn't intend to, the President was sending mixed signals. He had blown hot, then cold. Explaining the policy and managing the message were very close to the single most important thing the President did, and Powell hated to see it botched.

This period before the January 15 deadline was particularly critical. It was a war of nerves, and the President's words were very important. First, Saddam had to be intimidated. Second, the Congress had to be kept on board. And third, if force had to be used, reasonably strong public support had to be maintained. Powell did not want to be forced into a war because of a monumental lapse in communication.

That week of December 17 Les Aspin went to the White House for a session with Scowcroft. Aspin's House Armed Services Committee had just completed its own hearings on the Gulf policy.

It was obvious to Aspin that Scowcroft had lost his patience with diplomacy. Saddam had said that he could only receive Baker in Baghdad on January 12, three days before the deadline. Bush had rejected this. Saddam was jerking everyone around. There was no reason to deal with him, Scowcroft said. The four months of diplomacy and economic sanctions had failed. Scowcroft said he was now convinced that war would be a two-to-three-week solution.

Prince Bandar also stopped by to see Scowcroft that week. The Saudi ambassador knew Scowcroft was a nearly perfect mirror of Bush.

"Basically the President has made up his mind," Scowcroft confided. The diplomatic efforts, he told Bandar, "are all exercises."

ON DECEMBER 19 Cheney, Powell, and Wolfowitz arrived in Saudi Arabia for a detailed examination of Schwarzkopf's war plan. As far as Cheney was concerned, if Saddam was not out of Kuwait, they were going to have to begin the air war right after January 15, and the air force and navy air would be ready then.

During this trip Powell, Cheney, and Wolfowitz had time to talk in a more relaxed atmosphere. Powell said that looking at the whole situation, he thought Saddam would pull his forces out of Kuwait at the last minute, that Saddam was a ruthless survivor who would do anything to hold power. They had seen it time and time again.

Cheney didn't buy any of this. Look at the evidence, he said. Saddam was still moving reinforcements into Kuwait, not taking troops out. There was not one concrete piece of evidence to support this optimism. It could become dangerous. That was why he wanted to make sure that Schwarzkopf was ready for war and had made the plan sufficiently bold and imaginative.

The three men spent a day and a half with Schwarzkopf. After briefings on intelligence, the readiness of the forces, and logistics, Schwarzkopf laid out the overall war plan. Like the earlier plan, it included three air phases followed by a ground campaign.

Schwarzkopf said he feared that the political apparatus—the President, the Secretary, or the Congress—would call a halt before he could achieve his objectives in either the air or ground phases.

The President has said he does not want another Vietnam, Cheney reminded Schwarzkopf. The administration was committed. The military commanders would not have their hands tied. The President, Cheney, and Powell had to sign off on the plan, but once it was approved, it would for the most part be in Schwarzkopf's hands. The President would make the final decisions, such as when to launch the phase four ground campaign.

Key portions of the ground campaign had been developed by half a dozen junior officers in their second year at the Army Command and General Staff College, at Fort Leavenworth, Kansas. These majors and lieutenant colonels, nicknamed the Jedi Knights, had been sent to Saudi Arabia to apply elements of advanced maneuver warfare— probing, flanking, surprise, initiative, audacity—to the war plan.

Working in a small, top secret corner of Schwarzkopf's headquarters, they had applied the principles of the army's unclassified 200-page operations manual. Chapters 6 and 7, on offensive operations, were built around concepts established in General Ulysses S. Grant's 1863 Civil War campaign at Vicksburg, Mississippi. Instead of attacking directly into enemy fortifications, Grant had sent his troops in a wide maneuver around the Confederate front line and then attacked from the side and rear. This indirect approach was deemed the best way to beat Saddam.

The initial terrain analysis had concluded that the ground was too soft. But reconnaissance proved this wrong. The Iraqi desert was in fact adequate to support a tank attack. A maneuver plan would work.

Since Saddam had most of his forces in southern Kuwait and along the Gulf coast, to the east, the ground plan called for moving the VII Corps several hundred miles in a wide arc to the west and attacking through Iraq to hit the Republican Guard. It would amount to a gigantic left hook. Massive tank attacks were central to the plan.

Meanwhile, in a helicopter air assault, other U.S. forces would be dropped behind the Iraqi lines, where they would be unopposed.

The idea was to force Saddam to move his hundreds of thousands of troops from dug-in positions so they could be picked off with superior U.S. air and ground fire.

Marines would carry out a frontal ground attack at the Saudi-Kuwait border, attempting to breach Iraqi lines there. Other marine forces offshore would do everything they could to make it appear as if they were going to launch a major amphibious landing on the Kuwaiti Gulf coast, where the Iraqis had built extensive defenses. But it would be a feint, designed to keep the Iraqis pinned down.

Cheney had many questions about the ground plan. There was also much discussion of chemical weapons. It was a virtual certainty that Saddam would use them. When? How? No one knew exactly what supplies he had, but they were surely vast. The military and psychological impact of a chemical attack was hard to measure.

Cheney and Powell told Schwarzkopf to expect execution of the air phases soon after January 15.

The Secretary and the Chairman received a highly classified medical briefing on anticipated casualties. The senior medical officer said they were planning on 20,000, including about 7000 killed in action.

The room fell silent.

Then Schwarzkopf spoke up. "That's a worst-case planning model," he said. "It isn't a prediction. I don't make predictions."

The Pentagon leaders also had a chance to visit troops in forward positions. Powell was treated like a pope returning to the village where he had been the parish priest. Mobbed for autographs, he scribbled his name on anything available—magazines, Saudi currency, a skateboard. He posed for photographs. He told the soldiers that he knew and understood the uncertainty of their assignment—the waiting, the long nights, the churning in the stomach.

To all those who made inquiries about their future—and to many who did not—Powell repeated four words: "Be ready for war."

ON FRIDAY, December 21, Bush invited the ambassadors from each of the countries in the 28-member coalition to the White House. After the meeting he took them for a tour of the Christmas decorations.

Prince Bandar was the last to leave.

"Are you in a hurry?" Bush said. "Come say hello to Barbara."

Bandar wished the First Lady a merry Christmas, then went with Bush to the Oval Office, where the two men stepped outdoors to talk.

Bush asked about Saddam. "Does he know what he is up against?"

For several months Bandar had privately been saying to Bush and others that the quality of the Iraqi military was greatly exaggerated. He still felt that Saddam could be defeated in two weeks.

Bandar noticed that Bush was stiff. None of the loose, flappy awkwardness. There was no smile. Though Bush's eyes were cool and calm, he seemed to be carrying some inner weight. For months Bandar had seen both the public and private anger building, resulting in an eerie accumulation of willfulness.

"If he does not comply," Bush said of Saddam, "we'll just have to implement the resolutions."

Bandar nodded. He thought, This is serious. He's going to do it.

On Christmas Eve, Cheney and Powell returned from the Gulf and flew up to Camp David to brief the President. Scowcroft and Gates were also there.

The ground forces would not be ready until February, Cheney reported. In fact, he was not yet fully satisfied with the ground plan. But the air campaign was ready, and he and Powell said that it could be started before the ground forces were in place.

Bush said they should think seriously about starting the air campaign at the best and soonest point after January 15, if Saddam had not withdrawn.

Operating on the secure telephone, Powell asked Schwarzkopf for his recommended date and time. Schwarzkopf said 3:00 a.m. Saudi time on January 17. That would be 7:00 p.m. Washington, D.C., time on January 16, just 19 hours after the U.N. deadline. It would be a moonless night. Indications were that the weather would be clear.

Stormin' Norman said that when the offensive began, he would change the name of the operation from Desert Shield to Desert Storm.

On New Year's Day, Tuesday, January 1, Bush returned from his Camp David holiday. That evening he met in the White House residence with Quayle, Baker, Cheney, Powell, and Sununu.

Bush directed that the NSC staff begin drafting a formal presidential order, called a National Security Directive, that would lay out the policy reasoning for going to war. Since this would be a historic document, he wanted it given the attention it deserved.

Since Baker's Baghdad meeting had never come off, Bush decided to propose that Baker meet Iraqi foreign minister Tariq Aziz in Switzerland during the period January 7–9, when Baker would be in Europe anyway. But there would be no negotiations, no compromises.

On Thursday morning, January 3, Bush met with the congressional leaders. He announced that he was making one last diplomatic effort: the Baker-Aziz meeting. The President also made two strong references to the Amnesty International report he had read before the holidays, and he urged the Congressmen to read it.

The leaders told Bush that he still could not be assured of a majority vote authorizing the use of force after January 15.

As they discussed the possible war Bush said, "There is no Vietnam parallel."

Cheney reported that there were 325,000 troops in the Middle East now and another 12,000 were moving into Saudi Arabia each day.

Bush convened his inner circle in the residential quarters again on Sunday night, January 6. Baker was already in Europe. Saddam had agreed to a Baker-Aziz meeting in Switzerland on Wednesday.

The President said he wanted to get the Congress to authorize the use of force if possible. It was the one final box that had not been checked, the one piece missing from his overall strategy.

Cheney was dubious. Congress was never a sure thing. The administration, the coalition, the troops in the field could not afford a negative vote, he said. He saw no gain and lots of risk.

No one else said he shared Cheney's deep reservations. The meeting was adjourned, with the issue unresolved.

The next day, January 7, Speaker Thomas Foley announced that the House would begin debate later in the week on a resolution authorizing the use of force. Senate majority leader George Mitchell said the Senate would probably also begin debate on a resolution.

Bush began calling Senate and House Republicans that night to obtain a head count. He personally typed out the draft of a letter he could send to the Congress requesting that both houses endorse the "all necessary means" language of the U.N. resolution.

Powell was fearful of sending the troops to war without the explicit backing of Congress. A nation at war had to say it was at war and had to speak with one voice. Knowing Cheney's view, he didn't want to attend a large White House meeting the next morning where he would differ with the Secretary. So he told his legal counsel, army colonel Fred K. Green, to attend the meeting and report back.

At 11:00 a.m. on January 8, Bush went to the Cabinet Room. Present were Cheney, Scowcroft, and Sununu. Deputy secretary of state Lawrence Eagleburger was sitting in for Baker. Boyden Gray and the senior lawyers from the departments were also present.

Bush had a copy of his draft letter. He said that he was inclined to send it. The question was whether to remain passive or attempt to control the outcome with a specific administration proposal. Would he win? he asked the legislative directors for the White House, NSC, State, and Defense.

The consensus was that he would. But it was not 100 percent sure.

Bush asked for another evaluation of his legal authority.

William P. Barr, the deputy attorney general, said that in his opinion and that of the senior department lawyers, the President had full authority to conduct military operations as the Commander in Chief, regardless of whether Congress voted a resolution of support.

"Is your advice solely political?" one of Bush's advisers asked.

No, Barr said. War is in the gray zone. The war power is a shared power with Congress; the Constitution intends it to be shared. Congress has the power to declare war, but it usually has voted after the war has started.

Bush then asked each of the government lawyers present to speak.

Though not immune from legal challenge, the lawyers said, the President was on solid constitutional ground.

Scowcroft spoke in favor of going to Congress and of submitting a proposed resolution. Even if he had constitutional authority, the President's political authority would be vastly enhanced with congressional backing, Scowcroft said.

Cheney cautioned about sending the letter. No matter how it was phrased, it would be interpreted to mean that the President thought he needed a vote. To go with it and lose would be devastating.

Bush said he had to try. After sending the letter, they would mount a full-scale lobbying campaign. He said that he just could not believe that the Congress would leave the troops in the Gulf hanging.

"We've got to," Sununu said. "We've got to try to shape it."

Within the hour the letter was on its way to the Hill.

11

Iɴ Gᴇɴᴇᴠᴀ, the next day, January 9, Baker held a six-and-a-half-hour
meeting with Tariq Aziz. The Secretary of State presented an
eight-paragraph letter from the President as a final declaration and
ultimatum. The letter said, "We stand today at the brink of war
between Iraq and the world." Aziz read it and left it on the table. He
declined to accept it or to carry it to Saddam. Back at the White
House, Scowcroft knew that negotiations were now really over.

The Secretary of State flew on to Saudi Arabia to meet with King
Fahd. Under secret agreement with the United States, Fahd had to
give his permission for any offensive military operation that might be
staged from his country. Baker now asked for that permission. Fahd
quickly gave it. Baker promised that he would personally pass the
word to Prince Bandar in Washington before any attack.

On Saturday, January 12, after three days of sober debate, the
Congress granted Bush the authority to go to war. The resolution it
passed included the "all necessary means" language of the U.N. resolution but also specifically authorized "use of military force." The vote
was close in the Senate, 52–47. The House approved it, 250–183.

Bush told reporters, "This clear expression of the Congress represents the last, best chance for peace." Asked if this made war inevitable,
Bush said no. He said Saddam's "instant commencement of a large-
scale removal of troops with no conditions" could still "avert war."

Eagleburger and Wolfowitz had been dispatched to Israel that
weekend. Israel was still the wild card. No one on the U.S. side was
sure what Israel would do when it was attacked by Saddam, as was
now certain to happen. Prime Minister Yitzhak Shamir said that he
naturally could make no promises about what Israel would do. But he
agreed to consult with the United States before acting.

Eagleburger and Wolfowitz offered to improve Israel's defenses
through an expansion of a deployment of U.S. Patriot missiles already
under way. These ground-to-air antimissile missiles could be used
against Iraqi Scuds. It was not a proven system, but it was the best
available. The Israelis were skeptical, but they accepted the offer, which
would later include U.S. operation and maintenance crews.

Bush had also authorized a special top secret, secure voice communications link between the Pentagon operations center and the Israeli Defense Force headquarters, in Tel Aviv. Code-named Hammer Rick, it would give the Israelis advance notice before any offensive operation was commenced. The system became operational on January 13.

ON MONDAY morning, January 14, Cheney and Powell spent an hour going over the targets for the air campaign one final time. They needed to make sure that a crippling blow would be dealt to Saddam's communications and air defenses in the first 24 hours. Thereafter the air campaign would be a systematic juggernaut that would reduce the Iraqi war machine more each day.

Congressional leaders were summoned later in the day to an urgent meeting at the White House. Asked when the United States would attack, Bush replied, "Sooner rather than later."

Late in the afternoon Baker went to the Pentagon and spent an hour reviewing the targets. Cheney wanted Baker to apply his political eye to the air campaign to see if he spotted any unforeseen consequence. No changes were made in the target lists.

Bush spoke with Baker by phone at 6:30 a.m. on Tuesday, January 15, then went for a solitary walk around the White House South Lawn.

The President called two clergymen that morning. One was the head of Bush's own church, Bishop Edmond Browning, the presiding bishop of the Episcopal Church. Bush also phoned the Senate chaplain, the Reverend Richard C. Halverson, who joined him in a prayer for the nation.

At 10:30 a.m. Bush met in the Oval Office with his inner council: Quayle, Baker, Cheney, Scowcroft, Powell, Sununu, and Gates. Bush had the two-page draft of the top secret National Security Directive (NSD) before him. It had been modified to include two conditions. It now authorized the execution of Operation Desert Storm, provided that: (1) there was no last-minute diplomatic breakthrough, and (2) Congress had been properly notified.

The President signed it. The NSD was intentionally not dated. The date and time would be added when and if the conditions were met.

Bush authorized Cheney to sign a formal execute order and send it to Schwarzkopf that day. At 5:00 p.m. Powell arrived in Cheney's office with a top secret folder containing the execute order. The

Chairman had written it out himself. He went over it with Cheney. This was a historic document. Both men signed their full names.

Powell had a copy faxed "eyes-only" to Schwarzkopf. Operation Desert Shield was about to become Desert Storm.

Until now Powell had kept the decision secret from his staff. Now he called Tom Kelly in. The war begins tomorrow night, Powell said.

AFTER many meetings and consultations with the news media, Pete Williams that day released the ground rules for reporters in the event of hostilities in the Persian Gulf. The 12 rules banned publication or broadcast of specific information the department wanted kept secret, including numbers of troops, aircraft, weapons, equipment, and supplies; future plans and operations; locations of forces; and tactics. All combat reporting would be done by groups of reporters in pools, whose work would be subject to security review. No reporters would be allowed to rove freely in combat zones as they had in Vietnam.

THE next morning, January 16, Cheney packed a suitcase. He expected to spend several nights in his office. So as not to tip off his driver and security people, he decided to leave the packed bag at home. He could dispatch his driver for it as H-hour approached.

By the time Cheney arrived at the Pentagon, B-52 bombers had been launched from Barksdale Air Force Base, in Louisiana, flying 18 hours to the Gulf. These planes could be recalled. The decision had not yet reached the point of no return.

Cheney had cleared his schedule. He picked up the hand-held remote-control unit for the television in his office and clicked it to CNN. He thought the first leak or hint that the air operation was under way would most likely come from the 24-hour news service.

That morning Baker summoned Bandar to the State Department to say it was a go that night: 7:00 p.m. here, 3:00 a.m. in Saudi Arabia.

Bandar called King Fahd.

At 4:50 p.m. the first F-15 Eagles were taking off for their targets. More and more of the air war was moving toward the brink. Cheney saw that no one in the press was picking up on it. The news reporters were so bottled up by the rules, and there had been so much air activity over the previous months, that it all looked routine.

The White House had assigned Cheney the responsibility of keeping the Israelis plugged in. At around 5:00 p.m. Cheney picked up the Hammer Rick line to notify Israeli defense minister Moshe Arens.

At precisely 5:30 the U.S.S. *Bunker Hill,* an Aegis-class cruiser in the Persian Gulf, fired a Tomahawk missile to its designated target inside Iraq. This unmanned cruise missile could not be recalled. There was no turning back now.

About 20 Tomahawks were preprogrammed to hit Saddam's presidential palace, the main telephone exchange, and Baghdad's electrical power–generating stations at H-hour. The air campaign would involve more than 1000 sorties in the first 24 hours.

Cheney continued to watch CNN. Anchorman Bernard Shaw was in Baghdad interviewing former CBS anchorman Walter Cronkite, in New York, about covering wars. Shaw explained that he had gone to Baghdad to interview Saddam, but the interview had not worked out and therefore he was leaving on a flight the next afternoon.

There weren't going to be any flights out the next afternoon, Cheney knew. He felt a strange sensation watching this conversation, knowing that hundreds of attack missions were heading for Kuwait and Iraq unbeknownst to the media and almost all Americans.

POWELL did not want to keep a deathwatch down in the operations center. For the hour or so before 7:00 p.m. he sat alone in his office in his large maroon leather executive chair. In his last conversation with Schwarzkopf, earlier that day, he had said, "Good luck, Norm."

The minutes ticked by. Powell expected this would be the most important day of his life. More than 32 years in the army, and he was the top military man on the eve of a big war. But the day was falling short. The old Robert E. Lee quote went through his head: "It is well that war is so terrible, or we should grow too fond of it." How the military loved the preparation for war. From the Pentagon, war at times looked like a great game. If people were not going to die, it would be great fun, Powell thought. He had to remind himself constantly that this was real, not a game. The public and the world were going to see an incredibly limited and antiseptic version of the war. The media were going to be kept away. Even the videos from the gun cameras in the bombers were going to be distortions when they were made public. The audio would be edited out in most cases so the pilots' nervous yells of "Holy s___!" or whatever would be excised. The distinctive rapid-fire hyperventilation of the pilots, feeling the pressure of their G-suits and the terror of combat, would not be heard.

Powell was still alone. On this most important day of his life he had one overriding thought. There was no cheering, no thrill, no eagerness, no battle fever. None of the emotions of war raged. He thought only one thing: How many will not come back?

Over the border, inside Iraq, it was nearly 3:00 a.m. A U.S. Army Apache helicopter was 12 kilometers from the electrical power–generating station at an Iraqi air defense radar site protecting Baghdad. This was going to be the first target of the war. The pilot could see the building on his Forward-Looking Infrared Sensor, a tiny, dancing square on the horizon. He launched his Hellfire missile. "This one's for you, Saddam," he said. He could see the Hellfire come in over the building and descend like a rock. The tiny square became an explosion, suddenly and quietly filling his radar screen.

In the White House, Bush, Quayle, Scowcroft, and Sununu gathered in the small private study adjacent to the Oval Office to watch television. When the sounds of bombing could be heard behind the voices of the reporters still in their Baghdad hotel rooms, Bush, visibly relieved, said, "Just the way it was scheduled."

The Gulf war lasted 42 days. The three air phases took 38 days. The ground war took four days, before Bush declared a cease-fire. The U.S. and coalition forces overran Kuwait and southern Iraq, destroyed Saddam's army, routed the Republican Guard, dictated the terms of peace, and killed tens of thousands of Iraqis. Kuwait was liberated. American casualties were seven missing in action and 137 killed in action.

Inside Out

AN INSIDER'S ACCOUNT
OF WALL STREET

Dennis B. Levine with William Hoffer

. . . Insider trading is a difficult crime to prove. What could they do to me? Relax, Dennis, I counseled myself. Tough it out.

Then I heard unbelievable words: "Mr. Levine, we are placing you under arrest. You have the right to remain silent, and if you give up that right, anything you say can and will be used against you. If you can't afford counsel, counsel will be appointed for you."

I felt light-headed, barely hearing the words. Wall Street executives don't get placed in custody, I thought. They may be subpoenaed, indicted, even arrested, but they are not thrown into jail.

Dennis, I lectured myself, you aren't as smart as you thought you were.

—Inside Out

Part One: Panic on Park Avenue
CHAPTER ONE

I woke with numbers in my head, a one followed by seven zeros. That was ten million.

More precisely, it was ten million six hundred thousand.

As in *dollars*.

The nagging question was, Where was it?

If it had been transferred according to my instructions, it was safely lodged in my new account at Morgan Grenfell Ltd., in the Cayman Islands, and everything was all right.

But if it was still at Bank Leu International Ltd., in Nassau, there was trouble ahead.

Laurie, waking slowly at my side, fought off a bout of morning sickness; we had just learned that she was pregnant with our second child. She knew nothing about the secret hoard and thus could not realize my turmoil. Money was not a worry to Laurie. Long ago I had proclaimed to her, with youthful exuberance, that I would be a millionaire before I was thirty, and she believed me. I had achieved that goal with room to spare, and if I had told her about the secret $10.6 million that preoccupied my thoughts this morning, she would have asked—after expressing her initial shock at learning of its existence—Why in the world do we need it?

I would have had no coherent answer.

Sometimes, in those scarce moments when I allowed myself time to reflect, it all sent me reeling. When I started in the business world, in 1977, I earned $19,000 a year. Now, a mere magical nine years later, as a managing director of the investment banking house of Drexel Burnham Lambert, my annual salary, bonus and investment income had skyrocketed to more than $2 million. Laurie and I had more than $1 million socked away in legitimate investments. We lived in a beautiful Park Avenue co-op in Manhattan. In a garage was a 1983 BMW 633CSI and a fire-engine-red Ferrari Testarossa, my fantasy embodied in steel, so fresh that it still had only about 3000 miles on it.

I had worked my way into a position of power within the firm now universally acknowledged as the hottest player in the most volatile game on Wall Street, the specialty known as mergers and acquisitions, or M&A for short. Drexel was more than an investment banking house; it was an iconoclastic cult that attracted and held employees with an incredible sense of esprit de corps. Drexel people relished catchy slogans, and one of them was One hundred percent market share. We wanted it all, and in the current milieu that goal seemed altogether reasonable.

Working from his Beverly Hills office, superfinancier Michael Milken had made Drexel famous for its ability to raise astonishing sums through the technique of issuing high-risk, high-interest financial instruments. Those who were jealous of Milken and Drexel referred to these derisively as junk bonds, but those who were interested in becoming major players in the M&A field called them high-yield securities and lined up at Milken's door to join the network that bought and sold the bonds, passing billions of dollars back and forth.

Here in New York I had moved into the role of one of Drexel's key deal makers. I was one of the privileged few who put together the transactions that Milken financed. Only last month I had been a featured speaker at Drexel's annual Bond Conference. Beyond all this I was considering a new job offer—a sweetheart of a proposition from Wall Street's most famous risk arbitrageur (from the French word *arbitrer*, "to judge"), Ivan Boesky. Boesky's specialty was trading in the stocks of companies involved in takeover situations, playing the odds that the values of those companies would jump dramatically.

Boesky was acknowledged to be the best arb in the business, but he longed to take the next step up and become a corporate raider and bask in the public glory now enjoyed by Drexel's largest clients—men such as Carl Icahn, T. Boone Pickens and Ronald Perelman. To do that, he needed help, and he was determined to lure me away from

Drexel. He had offered me a $5 million premium just for coming on board. On top of that, he promised what he called a "seven-figure" salary, plus bonuses, that would bring my total annual income to more than $5 million. And on top of *that*, he offered me a $20 million ownership position in the company.

We had a phenomenal enterprise going on Wall Street, and it was easy to forget that the billions of dollars we threw around had a material impact upon the jobs and, thus, the daily lives of millions of Americans. All too often the Street seemed to be a giant Monopoly board, and this gamelike attitude was clearly evident in our terminology. When a company was identified as an acquisition target, we declared that it was in play. We designated the playing pieces and strategies in whimsical terms: white knight, shark repellent, poison pill, greenmail, the golden parachute. The winner was the one who finalized the most deals and took home the most money.

The principal players, men and women just like me, were the young superstars of the financial world. We were perhaps a less patrician breed than Wall Street had ever seen before, but we were no less enthused and awed by the task of making money. Ours was a space-age world that brooked no waiting. We were in a hurry because we had to be. If you did not rush to grab a deal, your competitor would take it from you. If you did not engineer a string of transactions that grew ever larger and showier, others would eclipse you. There was no time to think about all this; there was only time to do it. Every waking moment and many a sleeping hour was devoted to *the deal.*

Thus it was not unusual for me to awaken with money on my mind.

If I had been able, at the moment, to ponder the issue dispassionately, I would have realized that it was true: we did not need the money in my secret bank account. But making money was my passion, more than ever, and the $10.6 million represented not so much buying power, but points on the scoreboard. If it had arrived in the Cayman Islands, I was a winner. If it was still in Nassau, I was a loser.

That, in my naïveté, seemed to be the key issue.

Laurie and I were more in love than ever. Our son was the joy of our lives, and we had a new baby on the way. That was all I needed, but I was not yet sophisticated enough to realize such a basic truth. Only on this day, Monday, May 12, 1986, in the thirty-third year of this crazy life, would I begin to learn.

SUNLIGHT WAS BEGINNING TO FILTER in through the windows when I finished dressing in my basic investment banker's uniform—a navy-blue suit, a white shirt and a yellow tie. I slipped into a pair of shiny black loafers. I kissed Laurie good-bye and patted her tummy. "I'll be home early," I said, and Laurie nodded. A function was on for the evening, a black-tie charity dinner at the Waldorf-Astoria for the benefit of Mount Sinai Hospital. It was the sort of gala where it was important to see and be seen. Although it was not the type of occasion that Laurie often relished, she was looking forward to this one. For the first time in her life she had gone to Givenchy's, on Madison Avenue, and ordered a beautiful evening gown with a long black skirt and a shimmering gold top. I knew she would look stunning in it.

I traded a few mock blows with our four-year-old son, Adam, then headed out the door and off to the job that consumed me.

A car and driver awaited me, provided by my employer. It was an acknowledged fact that those of us who had reached the high echelons of power at Drexel were far too busy to drive ourselves.

As the car headed down Park Avenue I studied *The Wall Street Journal,* but the text blurred in front of my eyes. Where's the money? I wondered. Where's the money?

I arrived at the office at eight a.m. Before I could settle my mind for the upcoming meeting with my staff, I had to answer the burning question. Normally I shied away from using the office phones for clandestine calls, but the moment was too intense, the issue too extraordinary, for normalcy. I found an out-of-the-way telephone in the conference room and called Bank Leu, in Nassau.

It was early, but I reached a young bank executive named Andrew Sweeting, who knew me only by my code name. "Mr. Sweeting," I said, "this is Mr. Wheat. I'm confirming the transfer of my money."

There was silence for a few moments. Where's the money? I asked myself in agony. Where's the money?

Sweeting announced, "Mr. Wheat, everything is taken care of pursuant to the instructions from your attorneys."

"The wire transfer has been made?"

"Everything is being taken care of, sir."

I hung up the phone and whistled a victory tune. The money was safe and so, I believed, was I.

I was in a bubbly mood when I met with my staff to review the day's agenda, which centered around a meeting with Ronald Perelman. Only months ago I had been a driving force behind the deal that transformed Perelman from a middle-level entrepreneur to the corporate raider who had wrested control of the giant cosmetics conglomerate Revlon. His task now was to revitalize Revlon's flagging business.

He was also ready to consider an encore. This morning in his Manhattan town house we would discuss two possible deals. One was the multibillion-dollar acquisition of a major consumer-products company; the other was the buyout of a major entertainment corporation.

Something of note happened at that meeting. Perelman listened intently as I addressed my attention to the larger target, the consumer-products company. After studying the projections carefully, on paper and in my head, I had come to believe that the risk level was too great. I showed Perelman the spreadsheets that my staff had assembled. Sure, he could probably pull off the takeover, but the target company had plenty of resources and tough management. It would defend itself with vigor, meaning that the final price was likely to be stiff. Beyond that, there were complex regulatory issues involved that could add delays and legal costs. I pointed out that this was not a recession-proof buyout. If the cash flow stalled, the company might spin down the drain, sucking Perelman along with it.

It is always easy to say, Let's do the deal. Wall Street lives on deals. Without a deal you don't have anything. But it is incumbent upon an adviser to look at the whole picture and, when the circumstances demand it, say, as I did now to Perelman, "Don't do it."

Perelman is a good listener and, unlike many corporate raiders, is not in the business of making critical decisions on an emotional basis. In terms of savvy he is up there with the best of them, as evidenced by the fact that the Revlon deal vaulted him to the upper reaches of the *Forbes'* 400 list of wealthiest Americans (as of this writing, he is third). He puffed on his cigar and stared at the smoke for a moment, watching it curl toward the ceiling. Then he announced that he agreed with my assessment. If I did not think that the deal was safe over the long-term, he was not interested.

WHEN I returned to the office, my secretary, Marilyn Stewart, announced, "There were two gentlemen here looking for you."

"Yes?"

"They didn't look like clients."

Process servers again, I thought. It was routine for Drexel partners and associates to be ordered to give depositions regarding shareholders' suits; it was just as routine for us to try to avoid subpoenas. "Let me know if they return," I said.

On my desk was a message slip noting that Ivan Boesky had called. Obviously he wanted to see if I had made a decision on his job offer. I called him back, but he was out.

Fifteen minutes passed. I was busy preparing for a meeting with Marty Davis, C.E.O. of Gulf + Western, when Marilyn buzzed on the intercom and said, "The two gentlemen who were here earlier are back to see you."

"Tell them I'm not here. Refer them to legal and compliance." I thought, I don't have time to play around with these guys.

"Okay," Marilyn said. Then she added, "Oh, by the way, they're from the Department of Justice."

The Justice Department? Not the Securities Exchange Commission? I saw my fist pound upon my desk. My stomach cramped. I've got to get the hell out of here, I said to myself. But somehow I found the composure to say to Marilyn, "No problem. I'll take care of this."

Grabbing my briefcase, I slipped out of my office from a side exit and edged toward the reception area to get a good look at these men. One of them was huge, perhaps six feet nine inches tall, with shoulders that seemed to span the width of the room. His partner was of average height, but the giant's commanding presence made the pair appear like Mutt and Jeff. They were incredibly out of place—their baggy off-the-rack suits glaring in contrast to the tailored pinstripes of the men who whirled about them.

Think, Dennis, I commanded myself. Do something. I ducked into the back stairwell. Holding my wire-rimmed glasses in place with one hand, I scurried down two flights of stairs to the sixth floor and punched the DOWN button on the elevator. Nothing happened. No light illuminated. The elevators were not working, due to a fire alarm, but I was too upset to realize that. Instantly I conjectured that the feds had sealed off the building and surrounded it. I was trapped!

I needed time to think. Get out of here, Dennis, I told myself. Call in. Get the facts. Assess the situation. Preserve your options. Get help.

I headed back down the staircase, the echo of my footsteps now competing for attention with the thud of my heartbeat. My muddled brain tried to formulate a plan. I knew that I could not exit the stairwell on the first floor or I would trip the fire alarm.

When I reached the second floor, I decided that I had no choice but to try the elevator again. Emerging from the stairwell into the lobby of the operations department, I bumped into one of the women who worked there, nearly knocking her down.

"Mr. Levine, what are you doing here with the little people?" she asked good-naturedly.

I mumbled something about the elevators being out of order. But I jabbed at the button, and to my relief it illuminated. On the brief ride to the ground floor I donned sunglasses, the only disguise available. When the door opened, I glanced toward the front exit. I saw nothing untoward, but I headed to my right, to the service exit.

Suddenly I was out on the street. I hailed a taxi and commanded, "Ninety-third Street and Park Avenue."

My mind now weaved in and out of a traffic jam of ideas with greater skill than the cabbie. What is going on? I asked myself. It has to have something to do with the Bank Leu investigation. But what could it be? All the SEC had was a trail of suspicions. I could only be one of hundreds of suspects who were privy to the inside information upon which the Swiss bankers had traded. At worst, I conjectured, the Justice Department men only wanted to question me.

But if that was the worst, why did they come looking for me at the office? The Justice Department never got involved in SEC investigations. The SEC concerned itself with civil violations. The Justice Department was a *criminal* unit!

The conclusion was inevitable: the worst-case scenario was worse than I thought.

CHAPTER TWO

LAURIE's morning had been comfortably routine. She had confirmed arrangements with the baby-sitter for the evening. Then she had tried on her Givenchy gown, thankful that she had asked the saleswoman for something that was not too tight across her newly pregnant stomach. It fit comfortably, and Laurie, pleased that she did not feel fat, could not wait to model it for me. After an early lunch she had pampered herself with a nap.

Now she awoke to find me standing over her. It was only noon. I was *never* home during the day. She had known me since I was twenty years old, and I had always appeared to be in control. Until now.

Her face paled. "What's the matter?" she asked.

"I might be in a lot of trouble," I stammered. "I don't know. But if anybody comes here to see me or calls for me, you don't know anything. You haven't seen me. Say nothing to anybody."

"Dennis, what are you talking about?" Her face registered total confusion. It was inconceivable to her that I had done anything wrong. She reached out toward me, but I squirmed away. "What's happening?" she asked. "What's wrong?"

"I can't tell you now," I said. "I have to get the car." My thoughts were jumbled, my words incoherent. I raced to my desk, and as Laurie followed, I issued directions. "Call for the car," I said. "No, tell them— No, call for the car." I wanted the BMW because it had a cellular phone and because it was far less conspicuous than the Ferrari.

I began stuffing papers into a large manila envelope. The more Laurie begged for an explanation, the more adamant I became. "I can't discuss it now," I said. "Just do as I ask, please!"

She called the garage. Then she asked, "Where are you going?"

"To Dad's. Just wait for me to call."

The car almost guided itself north toward the Triborough Bridge and Queens, toward Dad's house, an instinctive haven. I forced my mind to concentrate upon damage control. My family, my friends, my entire world would learn about the double life I had led for these few frantic years. There was no time for self-pity or moralizing; that would come later. Now I had to minimize the effects upon those I loved.

From the car I called my brother at his office. "Robert," I said, "I want you to meet me at Dad's house. I'm in serious trouble. I don't know what is going on yet, but we have to talk. Get hold of Daddy. He's probably playing racquetball."

"I'll be there before you," Robert pledged. He asked no questions. I was his brother and I was in trouble, and that was all he needed to know at the moment.

I called the office of Laurie's obstetrician and badgered the nurse into putting him on the line. I asked if a severe emotional trauma might jeopardize Laurie's pregnancy. He said he did not think so. She was a strong, healthy woman, and he believed that even a severe stress would cause no overt problems. That calmed my worst fears.

Then I called my office. I could tell that Marilyn was crying as she asked, "Have you seen the Dow Jones tape?"

"No," I answered. "I really don't know what is happening."

Marilyn tried to tell me, but the words would not come. In frustration she transferred my call to my old friend David Kay, head of Drexel's M&A department. He said with genuine concern in his voice, "How are you?"

"I'm trying to find out what's going on here."

"Dennis, I don't think I should talk to you too much, but I can tell you that the SEC is after you. If I were you, I would get a lawyer."

I heartily agreed.

Kay switched me to Cathy, a new arrival at Drexel. I had given her my old job of breaking-news coordinator. Part of that task was to monitor the heartbeat of Wall Street—the Dow Jones news ticker.

"I understand there is something on the tape regarding me," I said. "Marilyn is too choked up to read it. Could you please read it to me?"

Cathy intoned:

"The SEC charged Dennis Levine, a managing director of Drexel Burnham Lambert, Inc., with insider trading in connection with an alleged scheme to buy and sell securities based on non-public information gained through his employment as an investment banker.

"Drexel Burnham said it will 'cooperate fully with the SEC' in the investigation.

" 'The SEC allegation, if true, would be a most serious breach of Drexel Burnham Lambert's standards,' Drexel said. The company said this is the first such allegation made against a Drexel employee in its fifty-one-year history. The SEC's allegation covers the period of 1980 to the present. Levine joined Drexel in 1985.

"The SEC alleges that Levine used non-public inside information to trade in the securities of 'at least fifty-four companies since May 1980.' The SEC also charged Levine's Bahamian broker, Bernhard Meier, in the insider trading scheme.

"A source close to the SEC said that the agency also expects to file soon another major insider trading case.

"Levine is widely known and well-liked in the closely knit frater-

nity of Wall Street lawyers and investment bankers who dominate
the takeover business. Many said they were stunned by the SEC
charges against him."

As HE had promised, Robert was waiting for me when I reached
Dad's home, but he had been unable to track down our father. I
answered the questions in his eyes just as I had to Laurie. "The
government is after me," I said. "I don't want to tell you more."

I then called Arthur Fleischer, Jr., the senior partner in the New
York law office of Fried, Frank, Harris, Shriver & Jacobson. I knew
that Harvey Pitt of Fried, Frank's Washington, D.C., office was representing Bank Leu. I wanted to see if the same law firm could take my
case or whether that would place it in an adversary position with Bank
Leu. Fleischer was not available at the moment, so I spoke with
another partner, Steve Fraidin. Only days earlier Fraidin had initiated
the job offer to me from his client Ivan Boesky.

"Dennis, I'm aware of what's going on," he said. "What can I do
for you?"

"Steve, I need a lawyer. I'd like to hire Fried, Frank."

"Let me see if we have a conflict," he said.

I held the phone. Minutes passed before he returned to report,
"Dennis, we have a very serious conflict. We can't represent you."

So there it was. Somehow the SEC had cajoled or threatened Bank
Leu officials into giving me up. Somehow the U.S. government had
managed to circumvent the heretofore airtight Bahamian bank-
secrecy laws. This—and nothing else—was the logical conclusion.

Next I called Joe Flom of Skadden, Arps, Slate, Meagher & Flom.
He had been an ally in numerous transactions, including Revlon.
When I asked if he could help me, Flom replied, "That's not what we
do. You need Arthur Liman."

I knew him also; this was an exclusive fraternity. Liman and I had
labored together on Carl Icahn's successful proxy fight against Phillips Petroleum. I had a great deal of respect for Liman. In my
judgment he was technically without peer as a securities attorney, and
I knew that he had also achieved national renown as a trial lawyer.

Liman, a fifty-three-year-old senior partner of Paul, Weiss, Rifkind,
Wharton & Garrison, had headed Mayor Ed Koch's investigation of
allegations against New York City's medical examiner, Elliot Gross.

His list of former clients included John Zaccaro, the real estate developer and husband of former vice-presidential candidate Geraldine Ferraro; Steven J. Ross, chairman of Warner Communications; and fugitive financier Robert L. Vesco. "I have a call in to him," Flom said. "We'll call you back."

The moments ticked away. I had to do something, but what? With shaking fingers I dialed my home number and asked, "Laurie, has anything happened?"

"Two people from the Justice Department were here looking for you," she reported.

Life had exploded upon her, yet she still had to take care of business. She told me that as she had readied herself to pick up Adam at nursery school the intercom had buzzed. "Mrs. Levine," the receptionist said, "two men from the government are here to see your husband."

"Well, he's not here," Laurie replied. "There are two other Levines in the building. They must have us mixed up with someone else."

Just as she was ready to leave, the doorbell rang. She opened the door and found herself face to face with two serious-looking men.

"Are you Mrs. Dennis Levine?" one of them asked.

"Yes."

"Is your husband at home?"

"No," she said. "What is this all about?"

The reply was a curt and uninformative, "Obstruction of justice."

"Could you be more specific?"

"No. Is he here?"

It made no sense. Laurie asked to see the men's credentials and was satisfied that they were legitimate. But why would federal agents be looking for her husband? She gazed up at one of the men and was so taken aback by his size that she stammered, "How tall are you?"

"Six foot nine," he answered, seeming accustomed to the question.

Laurie suggested that the men try to reach me at the office. "My son is expecting me at nursery school," she said. "I've really got to go."

"When will you be back?" one of the men asked.

"About an hour."

"Does it always take an hour to pick up a child at nursery school?"

These men are grilling me! Laurie realized. She replied, "Well, I do a little shopping." The men waited for her to continue, so she said, "If

I speak to my husband, I'll tell him you were here. Look, I've got to
go now. My son is expecting me."

The agents left. Laurie shut the door behind them and took several
deep breaths in an attempt to stop her body from shaking. Adam, she
thought. I've got to get Adam!

She rushed downstairs and outside to Park Avenue, where the
doorman flagged her a taxi. During the short ride she tried to reason
out an explanation for this sudden attack of madness. But of course,
too many of the jigsaw pieces were missing. She worried, irrationally,
about an expensive pair of earrings that she had charged on our
American Express card, her private celebration present upon learning that she was pregnant. Did I put too much on the card? she
wondered. Did Dennis forget to pay the bill?

She purposely took her time returning with Adam, walking, stopping at several shops along the way. When she arrived home, she sent
Adam into his room to play a video game. She sat on the sofa shaking.

She reported all of this to me in a tone that was a strange combination of panic, concern and icy aloofness. One of the men had left his
card, she said. He was Thomas Doonan, a criminal investigator with
the U.S. Attorney's Office for the Southern District of New York.
"Dennis," Laurie demanded, "what is going on?"

What could I say? This was the woman whom I loved so dearly, and
she was in agony. How could I ease her pain when my own was so
intense? "Don't worry. Everything is under control," I said, forcing a
calm tone. "There is nothing to worry about. I'm dealing with this."

"We're starting to get a lot of calls from the press."

"Don't take any of those calls."

"Dennis, I—"

"Laurie, I have to go," I interrupted. "Try to stay calm." I hung up
the phone, but my mind was making a thousand connections.

If the men had come looking for me at home, I reasoned, perhaps
they would look for me here at Dad's house, too. I decided to get back
into my car, to remain on the move. "Robert," I asked, "please just
stay available. I want you and Daddy to come to the city tonight."
Robert nodded, and I hopped into the car.

A short time later, while driving toward the city, I was on a conference call with Joe Flom and Arthur Liman. Liman agreed to represent
me and asked what was happening at the moment.

"The Justice Department wants to serve me a subpoena. They are looking all over the city for me."

"All right. Who is trying to serve you a subpoena?"

I relayed the information Laurie had given me. Liman said, "Here's what you do. First thing, you call this Doonan and arrange to meet him. Get the subpoena, and then we'll know what we're dealing with."

That seemed reasonable. Until we saw the formal charges, we were in the dark. We needed information.

"This is very important," he added. "Don't make any statements. Don't talk about the case to anybody."

"Okay."

I dialed Doonan's number and said, "My name is Dennis Levine. I understand you are looking for me."

"Yes, we are."

"I also understand you'd like to serve me with a subpoena. I am prepared to meet with you and take care of that."

"Okay," Doonan replied. "When is a good time and place to meet?"

"Why don't we meet at my apartment at seven thirty this evening? I'm in my car right now, returning to New York."

Doonan agreed to the plan, so I called Laurie back. I had to wait frustrating seconds for the answering machine to play and beep. I knew that she was screening what must be an onslaught of incoming messages. Finally I heard the beep, and I said, "It's me." She picked up immediately. "I'm on my way back," I said. "I'm meeting Mr. Doonan at the apartment at seven thirty."

"I don't think you want to do that," Laurie replied.

"Why?"

"The building is surrounded by reporters. CNN, all the networks, all the newspapers. They have vans and cables all over the place. It's a zoo." She made no attempt to keep the fury out of her voice.

"Okay," I said. "I'll call Doonan back and meet him someplace else."

Doonan understood the situation. "Would you like to come here?"

"I have no problem with that. Where are you?"

"The U.S. Attorney's office, right behind the federal courthouse."

DAD and Robert arrived at the co-op about six p.m., prepared to give support to Laurie and Adam. Robert had a cigarette in his mouth as he stepped inside. A few weeks earlier Laurie had decided to give up smoking for the duration of the pregnancy. But now she ripped the cigarette out of Robert's mouth and took a deep draft.

Adam was still in his room playing. As Dad, Robert and Laurie sat down to discuss the events of this unfathomable day, their thoughts were interrupted by a report on CNN announcing that I had been accused of insider trading.

"This is a mistake," Laurie decreed. "Dennis never did anything wrong. What's insider trading?"

IT WAS seven fifteen in the evening when I pulled up at the designated address, but no legal parking spaces were available. Reasoning that it should take only a few minutes to have a subpoena slapped into my palm, I parked illegally. I passed through a metal detector, signed into the building and was directed to the sixth floor.

The elevator opened onto a reception area. I pushed a buzzer and announced to the inquiring voice, "Dennis Levine to see Thomas Doonan." I glanced at my reflection in a glass partition. There I was, still dressed for my daytime role, briefcase in hand. I was the picture of a successful investment banker, and the image suddenly brought a sense of calm. I remembered Ivan Boesky telling me about the dozens of times he had been questioned by SEC officials. Insider trading is a most difficult crime to prove. What could they do to me?

Relax, Dennis, I counseled myself. Tough it out.

A firm, well-modulated voice asked, "Are you Dennis Levine?" I turned to see a rugged, physically fit blond man who introduced himself as Thomas Doonan. He led me about thirty feet down a corridor, to the office of Assistant U.S. Attorney Charles Carberry.

The room was hot and stuffy, and I was hit in the face by the overpowering odor of onions. On Carberry's desk, amid a clutter of paperwork, was an array of carryout hamburgers, french fries and Cokes. Obviously I had interrupted dinner.

Pudgy and prematurely balding, Carberry was chief of the securities and fraud unit and a seven-year veteran of the federal prosecutor's office. He introduced a third man in the room, a postal inspector, but I did not catch his name.

Doonan stood behind me as Carberry repeated the question for the record: "Are you Dennis Levine?"

"Yes, I am."

"Please have a seat."

I sat. Then I heard unbelievable words. "Mr. Levine, we are placing you under arrest. I would like to inform you that you have the right to remain silent, and if you give up that right, anything you say can and will be used against you. If you can't afford counsel, counsel will be appointed for you."

I felt light-headed, barely hearing the words.

"Mr. Levine?" Carberry said. "Do you understand your rights?"

"Yes, I do."

"There is a fear that you will flee," Carberry explained. "So we are arresting you, and we are going to place you in custody tonight."

Wall Street executives don't get placed in custody, I thought. They may be subpoenaed, indicted, even arrested, but they are not thrown into jail. Dennis, I lectured myself, you aren't as smart as you thought you were. Aloud I said, "You're going to put me in jail? I came in here on my own. If I had any intention of fleeing, why would I be here?" Then I added, "Is this like the movies, where I only get one phone call?"

The meeting was interrupted by a man who introduced himself as Peter Sonnenthal, an attorney with the SEC. His eyes carried a look of disdain. "Are you Dennis Levine?" he asked.

"Yes." I was weary of the question.

He tossed a voluminous lawsuit onto my lap. Its cover declared that it was a civil complaint against me. But the weight of the papers informed me that I was the object of a double-pronged attack. There were both criminal and civil charges to deal with here.

Carberry said, "We have a very strong case against you."

He slipped across the desk the form I had used when I opened my account at Bank Leu, my signature clearly legible. From some unknown reserve I mustered the ability to keep my face impassive.

"Would you like to make a statement?" Carberry asked. "It will go a lot easier on you."

"No," I replied. "I'd like to call my attorney."

"Who is your lawyer?"

"Arthur Liman."

His reputation obviously preceded him, for behind my back I heard Doonan mutter, "Oh, s___!"

I reached Liman at home. "Arthur," I said, "they're arresting me!

I'm going to jail. I didn't think this was going to happen. Arthur, what is going on?"

Liman was in shock. He said that he never would have advised me to meet Doonan if he thought I would be arrested. He asked, "Who is arresting you?"

"Mr. Carberry."

"Okay. Let me speak with him."

The two men conversed for a few minutes out of my earshot before Carberry called me over and handed me the phone.

Liman said, "You're going to spend the night in jail. We can't find a magistrate to bail you out at this late hour. I will talk to your wife. We will get you out first thing tomorrow. I'm sorry."

Doonan said, "We're going to take your jewelry, your cuff links, your watch, your money, your briefcase, your wallet."

Suddenly I remembered the BMW. "I have another problem," I said. "My car is outside in a no-parking zone. Can I please move it?"

Doonan and the postal investigator shared a glance and a shrug. "Sure," Doonan said.

The three of us rode the elevator downstairs and stepped out onto the street. I indicated the spot where I had parked the car. A ticket decorated the windshield. "Sorry about that," Doonan said.

"That's the least of my problems right now," I pointed out.

When I pulled the car keys out of my pocket, Doonan extended his hand and declared, "I'll drive."

I sat in the back and watched him fumble with the keys. Obviously he had never driven a BMW before, and I had to tutor him. Soon he was babying the car into a multilevel municipal parking garage.

The two men took me into the courthouse and led me across an enclosed walkway to the federally operated Metropolitan Correctional Center. It seemed like the longest walk I had ever taken. We rode an elevator to the bottom floor and stepped out to confront a barred door. A guard sat behind a glass booth.

Doonan said, "Dennis Levine for processing."

The guard pressed a button. The barred door slid open, and we stepped into a small security area. Doonan handed over a batch of paperwork and left me in the custody of the jail guards.

One of the guards grasped my arm and led me toward a waiting room where a half dozen other men lingered. I was the only white man and the only one dressed in a suit. "Stay here," the guard said.

I was petrified. This was all so alien, something that never happened in real life. My head ached with worry: What would happen to my family, my career, my life? Everything was shattered.

A pay phone in the corner caught my eye immediately, and I asked, "May I use that?"

"Yes."

Once more I had to wait for the answering machine to cycle before Laurie heard my voice and picked up the phone. "Where are you?" she cried. "What is happening?"

"Honey, I've been arrested. I'm going to be spending the night in jail. I can't talk." I assumed the phone was tapped. "Arthur will call you. He wants you to come to court tomorrow. He's arranging bail."

"He's already called," she said. It was obvious from the clipped, cool tone of her voice that Laurie was operating on a crisis footing. Later, when I was out of jail and back home, she knew there would be plenty of time to give in to hysteria. I winced when I realized the amount of explaining I had to do.

I offered a bald-faced lie. "Don't worry about me. This place is fine."

"Your name is all over the news," she reported. "You're a big story." There was quiet anger in those words. Laurie is a very private person. It was not on her wish list to be a media star. Nor did she appreciate learning the details of her husband's private life from a TV anchorman. "Your dad's here," she added. "Robert, too."

"Let me speak to Dad."

He reassured me. "Everything is okay here. Laurie is fine. Adam is fine. We'll be in court tomorrow. I'll bring Laurie down. There's nothing for you to worry about—on our end."

We said good-bye, and I heard the phone line go dead. The silence reminded me of how totally removed I was at the moment from everyone and everything I loved. I turned away from the phone.

I paced a few steps, moving toward solitude, wondering what I should do. After a while a guard led me to a corner office, where I stood in front of a desk and waited as a lieutenant reviewed my papers. He slid his chair back and stared at me. "How're you feelin'?"

How do you answer such a question? Can you say that you feel as if a brick wall has fallen on top of you? I tried to answer in a firm voice, "Just fine," but the words sounded a bit shaky to my ears.

Once I had filled out numerous forms and received a perfunctory physical examination, a guard brought me a fluorescent orange jumpsuit. When I was attired in prison garb, he announced, "We have no cells for now. We'll have to place you in the holding tank."

Zzzzzzz . . . clank! The electronic metal doors slammed shut behind me, locking me in with the rest of the night's haul. A toilet occupied one corner. The smell of urine and feces was overpowering. Somebody had taken wads of damp toilet paper and thrown them against the walls. The air was cold and somehow foreboding. Here I was, fallen to the very bottom of the heap.

I tried to lie down on a folding cot, but it was broken and collapsed to the floor.

I sat alone on a bench in a corner of the room. My head pounded. My eyes blurred. I was ill with worry over Laurie and Adam. Oh, I wanted to see Laurie! I wanted to throw my arms around her and tell her I loved her. And yet I did not want to tell her what I had been doing all these years behind her back. I had no idea how she would react to the story of my years of deceit.

A thousand times since that day I have been asked, "If you were making two million dollars a year, why did you risk everything by trading on inside information?"

There is no easy answer. To comprehend such a story, one must study its evolution.

Part Two: Money in the Bank
CHAPTER THREE

WE ASSUMED a collective air of reverence on that morning in early March, 1977, as we assembled in the vice presidents' cafeteria in the Citibank headquarters, at 399 Park Avenue. There I was, one of scores of young but otherwise nondescript management trainees, at once expectant and apprehensive over the prospect of rubbing elbows with the elite. No one quite knew what to do. Should we disguise our anxiety with the façade of normal conversation? Should we open our mouths at all?

The decision was made for most of us when Walter Wriston, the chairman of the board, strode in accompanied by a retinue of attendants. As if by signal, the other trainees sorted themselves into a line that wound its way up to the eminent ruler of one of the world's largest financial empires. I stood silently off to one side, observing. It was not that I was above kowtowing—it just seemed to me to be a colossal waste of time. Why would he remember one name, one face, one handshake offered from the bottom of the corporate ladder?

I was twenty-three years old and in my first week on the job in Citibank's corporate counseling department. The salary was $19,000 a year, and it seemed like a great deal of money. It was enough of a start to solidify my plans to marry my college sweetheart, Laurie Skolnik. My task would be to help advise large U.S. firms on how to avoid foreign-currency losses, and I wondered whether I was equipped to handle it. What educational credentials I had came from the mass market of Queens public schools and tuition-free college classes. I possessed the obligatory M.B.A. degree, but to obtain it, I had commuted by bus and subway for three hours a day to attend the Baruch School of Business. I supposed that I knew as much as or more about the real world than many of the others in this room, but the inner workings of the corporate suites were a total mystery to me. What I needed from Wriston was the opportunity to pick his brain.

Suddenly a man approached and interrupted my thoughts with a disparaging remark about the gamesmanship being practiced by the other management trainees. He introduced himself as Robert Wilkis, a lending officer in the bank's chemicals division. He was somewhat balding, tall and slender, and there was something in his eyes, or perhaps in the tone of his voice, that communicated an affinity.

It took only a few minutes of conversation to seed a friendship. We were both the products of middle-class families, and we both had an ardent desire to succeed in the business world, but Bob had a head start on me. He was four years older than I and boasted more impressive academic credentials. He had a degree from Harvard and an M.B.A. from Stanford. He was also fluent in five languages and had already developed contacts throughout the global investment community. I, on the other hand, was a raw beginner—a baby. What bound us to one another, almost immediately, was an intuitive realization that we were both mavericks.

SOME KIDS WANT TO BE PRO football players or cowboys or soldiers of fortune; to me all of those roles were encompassed by the field of investment banking. My father, Philip, had shown me how to read *The Wall Street Journal* at a young age, and it was love at first sight.

As a kid, I always worked. I shoveled snow. I delivered newspapers. I mowed lawns. By my early teens I was making money playing keyboards in bands that performed at parties and school dances. Eventually one band achieved modest success; we opened local concerts for touring groups, including the Association, the Turtles, and Jay and the Americans. We even cut some records.

Dad had forged his own successful home-improvement business, Armstrong Aluminum Company, in Queens, and during my high school and college years I worked for him, cold-canvassing door to door. It was exhausting work that taught me valuable lessons. I learned to overcome rejection. When a door slammed in my face, I had to move on to the next opportunity. Success was directly related to tenacity; the more doorbells I rang, the better were my chances of realizing a sale.

Dad made a good, honest living at this business, and the key to his prosperity was the satisfied customer. He taught me that a business is built upon referrals. Do one job well, and others will come.

But of course, you have to get your foot in the door first, and this was the difficult part. Wall Street was an unlikely environment for a middle-class boy from Queens, and I charted my course with care. I watched in fascination during the go-go '60s as American business entered the conglomerate age. Megafirms such as Gulf + Western, ITT and LTV were fashioned by what was, to me, the creative use of paper. Repeatedly I saw money conjured from thin air. A firm would authorize a new preferred stock issue and—as long as it could persuade investors that there was value behind it—simply swap the freshly printed paper for the stock of smaller companies.

To me the geniuses in these transactions were the people behind the scenes, and I read whatever I could find about them. In a simplistic sense the traditional role of an investment banker was to buy a new issue of corporate securities wholesale, directly from the issuing company, and retail them to the public, taking a profit in the markup. But my perception grew that the investment banker was the one who quietly orchestrated complex transactions, performed important functions for the business community and, at the same time, earned significant amounts of money. What's more, the investment banker of the '70s was taking on a new role. No longer was he a mere purveyor of securities. Increasingly he was the creator of new financial instruments and new tools for the wise use of business resources.

For me there was a distinct downside. Investment banking jobs were often parceled out on the basis of social connections, old school ties and breeding. Some said that Morgan Stanley was a Princeton firm and First Boston was a Yale firm. There seemed to be no place in the industry's higher echelons for a kid from Queens. I reasoned that I could possibly find a spot on the fringes, but the top jobs in the prestigious companies were limited to those with impeccable credentials. Numbers alone dictated my chances. A large investment firm might receive 4000 applications to fill a mere twenty positions a year. When I finally had my M.B.A. in hand, full of hope and ambition, I made the rounds of the major firms. No offers resulted.

All right, I thought, if an investment bank won't hire me, I'll start my own. I approached Professor Jack Francis at Baruch College. He was a well-known authority in the field and had inspired me through his teaching. He liked my idea. I would be the front man, selling our services more or less door to door, as I had done for Dad; he would be the behind-the-scenes technician. In a matter of weeks Levine, Francis & Co., Ltd., was born. After considerable legwork and much study we almost pulled off a small-scale leveraged buyout, but at the last moment one of the principals backed off. And by then I had landed my first job on the fringes of Wall Street.

The Citibank job was a compromise, an entrée into the financial world, where from my small desk in the bull pen on the fourth floor I could at least observe the promised land.

I plunged into the training program, learning what I could about foreign-currency markets. Despite an A in my obligatory graduate school course on international finance, I was far from an expert. If you are a U.S. corporation and you sell your products for Swiss francs, what do you do with them? What are the tax considerations? What are the conversion restrictions? How and when do you move the francs into dollars or deutsche marks or yen? It was fascinating to realize the intricacies of the worldwide cash flow, and it was exhilarating to realize that I could play a role in these global economic transactions.

One day my cousin Stuart came into the city to meet me for lunch. I retained a warm feeling for Stuart, for it was at his wedding reception, a few years earlier, that I had first set eyes on Laurie, who was the cousin of the bride. Now we spoke of my upcoming wedding as we walked through the Citibank lobby. We were two young men only a generation removed from immigration. Stuart was from Brooklyn and I grew up in Bayside, Queens, but either place might as well have been the wheat fields of Kansas. Stuart glanced about at the lunchtime mob of men in blue pin-striped suits and wingtip shoes, and commented, "Dennis, this is a strange world you're living in."

Strange and overwhelming.

Several times each business day I found myself wandering toward the Quotron at one end of the floor. Here I could push a button and get up-to-the-moment information on world currency prices. This was good cover for my visits, but it was not my primary interest. As a would-be investment banker, I was fascinated by the manner in which stock price fluctuations mirrored real-world activities. For instance, the moment that a potential merger was announced, it was generally reflected by a spurt in the stock price of the target company. The rationale was simple: In order to acquire a company on the open market, in order to induce a sufficient number of shareholders to sell, you had to offer a price that was higher than the prevailing stock price. Therefore the level of the offer set a new, higher market rate.

The stock ticker reflected the beginnings of the next major trend in American business: consolidation. History had seen three such waves already. The first came at the turn of the century and resulted in the formation of U.S. Steel, Standard Oil, General Electric and Eastman Kodak. The second wave, in the latter half of the 1920s, brought giant banks and utilities into existence. The third wave, in the late 1960s, spawned the conglomerate age, largely through friendly acquisitions. And the signs were in place for the fourth wave to hit, in the approaching '80s. The stock of thousands of companies was undervalued, and that made them very good acquisition prospects.

It was almost routine for Bob Wilkis and me to encounter one another at the stock terminal. Unlike me, he was an active trader, and he always had a few particular stocks to check.

Before long we were frequent lunch partners. Sometimes after work we had a drink together. On one of these occasions, between puffs on his cigar, he mentioned in an offhand manner that he had recently earned an easy profit on a stock deal. By keeping his eyes and ears open on the job, he had learned the supposedly secret information that Airco, a New Jersey–based producer of gases and related products, was to be acquired by a British firm. Acting upon this news, he had bought Airco stock. When the merger deal was announced, Airco's stock rose quickly in price, and Wilkis sold out.

I knew without being told that this was a violation of both SEC regulations and Citibank rules. Profiting in the stock market as a result of "material information" unavailable to others has long been officially prohibited.

Wilkis contended that it was not only easy to deal in stocks this way but also safe. Shortly after the transaction Citibank investigated reports of insider trading activity, but could prove nothing. Citibank, of course, had no way of knowing that Wilkis had traded in his mother's name, through her brokerage account in Baltimore.

I listened to this story with interest. I sat at the small cocktail table trying to determine whether Wilkis was more jaded than I or more realistic. He had just confessed to me that he had shaded the rules. Did this make me feel uneasy? Or did I now view my friend as more sophisticated than I had realized? I was unsure.

LAURIE is slim and lithe, with long, dark blond hair and blue-green eyes. She is the most exquisite and captivating woman I have ever known, but beneath the beauty is a warm, sensitive and intelligent individual. Her personality complements my gregariousness.

From the outset we shared the same dreams—a successful business career for me and a family for both of us. Laurie has a degree in education from C. W. Post College. She worked for a time in advertising and then as a teacher, but her vision is inward. Her primary goals were, and are, to be the best wife and mother she can be. She has always desired a quiet, warm life, with family as the core.

We were married on December 17, 1977, at Congregation Beth Shalom in Lawrence, New York. We leased a $379-a-month apartment in Queens, on Yellowstone Boulevard in Forest Hills.

Almost immediately Bob and Elsa Wilkis became our close friends. They drew us into their world, introducing us to a wide range of new friends and business contacts, and we often went to dinner together.

Meanwhile, on the job I watched. I learned. I grew uneasy. From my entry-level perspective I found myself amazed at the enormous inefficiency I witnessed. This isn't how Dad does it, I thought. When a decision had to be made, he made it on the spot. Too many people at or near the top in big business seemed to be obsessed with a cover-your-ass mentality. All important decisions were made by boards and committees. The results were predictably ponderous—write a memo not to any person, but simply "to the files."

This was distressing, for big business was where I wanted to be. Yet I had only placed my foot upon the bottom rung of the ladder. Was I just being a smart-ass kid? I wondered. Did they know something I did not? Perhaps. I reminded myself to keep my mouth shut and study the available data.

ONE day early in 1978 Wilkis drew me aside from the Quotron to share a stock tip. Citibank was involved in financing the takeover of a major U.S. chemical company. To protect the identity of the companies involved in any merger proposal, code names are assigned, accessible only to a few key individuals. But Wilkis had seen an overseas Telex relating to the deal, and he had cracked the code.

Almost idly he disclosed that he had bought a position in the company, as much as he could afford, once again trading through his mother's account. "It's easy," he said. "Everybody does it."

Only in retrospect would I realize that something snapped at this very moment, something that caused me to cross the clear lines of morality delineated by my father and my late mother, Selma. Somewhere between Queens and Wall Street I was losing track of those values. Throughout my college and graduate studies I do not believe I even heard the word ethics. In the big-business environment of the late '70s, morality was not an issue. The liberal, radical, humanistic '60s were gone, and society was veering toward materialism.

My response to Wilkis' words should have been, Trading on the basis of inside information is wrong. Instead, I thought, Here's a way I can make some extra money.

I was a big boy. It was my decision. Wilkis did not twist my arm.

I thanked my friend for the tip and headed for the Citibank library to research the stock. If Wilkis' information happened to be wrong, I did not want to take a bath. The basic public information convinced me that the company was sound, and therefore there was no reason to believe that its stock would plunge too drastically in any eventuality. I raided my savings account of its $2000 balance and took a check over to the brokerage firm where I maintained a minuscule account. Exploiting my margin privileges to the limit, I bought about $4000 worth of shares in the chemical company. Laurie did not know the reason for my investment, but she trusted my judgment. She knew that I took a conservative approach to the stock market.

In the nearly half a century of its existence the SEC had brought only seventy-seven actions against inside traders, and the penalties, if any, were limited to fines and other civil sanctions. There had never been a single criminal prosecution for insider trading. In trading the chemical company stock, Wilkis and I had committed what we believed to be no more than a minor civil infraction, if indeed it was a crime at all. It felt loosely analogous to jaywalking.

In the spring a young man's fancy returns to investment banking. This is when the houses recruit, and in 1978, with a year at Citibank under my belt, I enhanced my résumé and tried my luck once more.

Smith Barney, Harris Upham & Co. responded quickly, with an invitation for a lunch meeting with Leslie Hannify and Norman Brown, associates in the M&A department. Prior to the appointment I researched Smith Barney in the Citibank library. Historically Smith Barney was a conservative, old-line "white shoe" firm. By now Jewish-founded houses such as Salomon Brothers, Goldman Sachs & Co., Kuhn, Loeb & Co. and Lehman Brothers had assumed their own established positions in the business, but as best I could tell, Smith Barney had never hired a Jewish associate before. (It was a well-kept secret that a past president, Nelson Schaenen, was Jewish.) The lunch invitation was prima facie evidence of the fundamental, substantial changes taking place within the investment banking industry.

The upheaval had commenced in July 1974, when International Nickel Company of Canada (INCO) announced that one of its subsidiaries was issuing a $157 million tender offer for the stock of the Philadelphia-based Electric Storage Battery Company (ESB). The price worked out to $28 per share, which was about 40 percent above the current market. Nonetheless, the ESB board of directors declared the offer to be too low. The board's recommendation that shareholders not tender their stock to INCO placed the proposed transaction into the hostile category and touched off a round of lawsuits. By August, INCO had raised its offer to $41 per share and corralled 95 percent of ESB's stock.

Prior to this a hostile takeover was considered more or less unethical, and the large investment banking firms generally did not lower themselves to become active participants. But this time the venerable firm of Morgan Stanley took the role of adviser to INCO, and when the hostile takeover succeeded, such activity was legitimatized.

This development took on greater significance after "May Day," May 1, 1975, when the SEC deregulated the heretofore fixed-rate commissions on stock transactions. Suddenly scurrying for customers, brokers slashed their commission scales, and basic revenues dropped accordingly—by about 40 percent. Numerous firms folded; others merged, and Smith Barney was one of them, joining forces with Harris, Upham & Co. in 1976.

Jacob Schiff, who headed Kuhn, Loeb & Company in the early part of the century, had once remarked that competition between investment banking firms was "not good form." But suddenly it was the only form. Everyone on the Street was desperate for new business and naturally looked with favor upon the fertile field opened up by Morgan Stanley's participation in the INCO-ESB deal. As the decade of the '80s approached, it was obvious that American business was on the brink of a boom in mergers and acquisitions, whether friendly or hostile. The economy was emerging from a recessionary cycle. The market was loaded with companies whose stock was trading significantly below book value; each was a bargain ready to be snatched.

The personality of the Street changed radically in response to this more competitive environment. Genteel, patrician relationships gave way to more creative and aggressive deal making. Old school ties now mattered far less than the ability to get the job done. The question was not, Who are you? It was, Can you generate fees? In this environment a boy from Bayside could make it if he was willing to work hard.

I wanted in on this trend. At lunch Hannify and Brown seemed impressed with my knowledge of Smith Barney and informed me on the spot that they were inviting me back to meet some of the senior people. After a second round of interviews a job proposal materialized from the corporate finance department, and I was ecstatic. I called Laurie and said, "We're going out to dinner." Wilkis joined us at the "21" Club and treated us to cocktails.

Before the change became official, I cleaned out my closet. I knew I would have to inform Smith Barney's legal and compliance department of all stocks I owned, and I did not want anyone to have a record of my chemical company transaction. By now I knew that Wilkis' tip had either been wrong or the plans had stalled, for no merger announcement had been made. I sold the stock for about the same price I had paid and considered myself lucky that I had not lost my savings.

ORIENTATION sessions at Smith Barney explained the security procedures that are basic to any brokerage firm or investment bank. They are designed to guard against the premature release of information: Transactions are given code names. Access to documents is restricted, and those documents are shredded rather than trashed. Offices and telephones are swept routinely for bugs. New employees are fingerprinted and checked for criminal backgrounds.

The message of my orientation was that if I wanted to trade stocks, I had two choices. I could open a Smith Barney account, which would be monitored by the legal and compliance department, or I could provide a compliance officer with confirmation of each transaction handled by an outside broker. On balance, I decided, it would be easier to remain out of the market altogether. My career dream was assuming reality—my $23,000 annual salary felt like big time—and there was no need for me to risk it by dabbling in stocks.

My new title was corporate finance associate, which, I discovered immediately, translated to "grunt." I was assigned to an open, hustling, humming bull-pen area, on the forty-eighth floor of the headquarters building. More than thirty associates labored here in what seemed to be the modern-day equivalent of indentured slavery. An investment banking firm operates on the binary system—a partner is a one and everyone else is a zero. A zero is expected to do whatever a one tells him to do, without question.

You never want to be the last associate to arrive at work in the morning or the first to leave in the evening. In this ultracompetitive environment, aware that you are constantly being watched, you search for some positive way to distinguish yourself, and you pray that you will not screw up.

I rolled up my sleeves. Most of the work involved rudimentary tasks such as comparisons of the values of common stocks, bonds and/or indentures of similar but different companies. For example, if I was given the task of analyzing the common stock of Ford Motor Company, I would compare it to the stocks of Chrysler and General Motors. I would hustle to the library and pull all the publicly available information concerning the three automakers, array the data and try to make some sense of it. What are the recent stock price ranges, what are the dividends, what are the performance ratios?

I found work on fairness opinions to be the most interesting. In a fairness opinion an analysis of a given transaction is provided at the request of a company's board of directors. It was our job, as an independent outside expert, to comment on the fairness of the transaction from the shareholder's point of view. Is the price too high or too low? What effect will the acquisition have on the stock price? In sum, is this the right thing for the company to be doing?

This is all known as crunching numbers, and it was the constant activity of the bull pen. In this precomputer era we pulled most of our recent stock performance information directly from old copies of *The Wall Street Journal*. Associates waited in the library with varying degrees of impatience for their chance at the stacks of newspapers. Often the lights of the library blazed throughout the night as we huddled over the pages, rubbing our eyes with ink-stained hands.

There was art to this work as well as science. Our numbers were necessarily based on the publicly available data provided by the corporations and audited by independent accountants. In theory the numbers all related to one another. In practice there was considerable variability. Companies can play with the numbers by deciding, for example, when to credit certain revenues, when to take various deductions or how to treat tax considerations. As long as everything remains within the realm of "generally accepted accounting principles," it is all quite legal. Many corporations have a tendency to skew these numbers so as to show consistent growth. That is what keeps shareholders happy and corporate officers employed. To an associate it meant that one sometimes had to compare apples and oranges.

Whatever the task, it resulted in a potpourri of raw data that had to be organized into legible form. I would produce a large spreadsheet that compared the figures in various categories. There was no margin for error; big decisions would be made on the basis of these numbers. The bull pen was clearly a winnowing area, and the winners and losers became obvious at end-of-the-year bonus time. If you received a good bonus, you could look forward to moving up in the investment banking world. If you received no bonus, you went job hunting. It was extremely tedious work, but I did it because that was my task. What kept me going was the realization that it was the only way to advance. Every vice president and partner above me had crunched numbers at some stage of his career.

A simple mathematical slip could be equivalent to professional suicide, so I triple-checked the numbers before rushing my data to a statistical typist. When the typed version was ready, I triple-checked the numbers again.

With the final version of the spreadsheet prepared, some associates considered the job finished. They passed the work on to the appropriate partner, sat back and sipped a cup of coffee. But I wanted to try to make some sense of all the data. What did the numbers really tell us? Often I included a bit of analysis along with my numbers. Some of the partners received such work with a cold "You're not paid to think" stare, but others appreciated it and took the time to show me where and why I might be mistaken. On occasion some actually accepted my interpretations and acted upon them.

The reward for work well done was when an astute partner took an associate along to participate in a client meeting. The first time I was accorded such a privilege I came to understand that there was method to this madness. My numbers actually figured prominently in key decisions surrounding the deal. And it was fascinating to watch the partner work this particular client. There was art to this, too. The more you understood about a client's personality and motivations, the better your chance of bringing him around to your point of view.

I was thinking about this when the partner put me to the test. "Dennis, you did all the numbers. Why don't you answer that?" I breathed a sigh of relief that I had thought to bring the raw data with me. The client leaned close as I reviewed the numbers with him, and when I was finished, he accepted the package we were presenting. It was an exhilarating feeling, and I believed that I had found my future niche in the business. Crunching numbers was fine for the time being, but I was an outside man, a contact man. I could sell, and I knew it.

The workweek required of the associate was obscene. If you wanted to stick around, you stayed at your tasks for as much as 100 hours a week. Pulling an all-nighter was a common phenomenon. Laurie, Dad and Robert jokingly referred to me as a wage slave.

But I thought, I'm doing what I want to do, and I'm doing it well.

WILKIS was a genuine friend, who was delighted that I had landed my fantasy job. Beyond that, slowly, quietly, we started to explore the avenues of opportunity opened by my new position. Whenever we spoke, he asked, "What are you working on? What's going on?" and I responded by sharing with him stories of the incredible amounts of information that now flowed through my daily life. I understood, without his directly admitting it, that he was trading on the basis of my news. It produced a delicious tingling sensation to realize that Bob was beating the system, but it was not for me. I saw no reason to jeopardize my good fortune.

Two months after joining Smith Barney, I was laboring over a spreadsheet at eight thirty on a Friday night. The bull pen was empty, save for me, when David Faber, the man charged with the special responsibility of supervising the associates, approached. In a southern drawl he asked, "Dennis, do y'all speak French?"

"No," I replied, unable to hide the curiosity in my voice.

Without explanation he walked away. Then curiosity got the better of me. I set down my spreadsheet and walked over to his office. "Dave," I asked, "what's going on?"

Each year, he explained, Smith Barney sent one of its associates to its Paris office to crunch the numbers for a multinational group of partners who worked the European markets. "Based on your fine work and your international experience at Citibank, you'd probably be a natural," Faber said. I would be the only associate there, so I would be involved in every aspect of the business. When I returned after a year, I would have a unique experience on my résumé, and I could choose my next assignment.

"M and A department," I said without hesitation.

He nodded.

I was flabbergasted. I called Laurie and said, "You're not going to believe this. I'll tell you when I get home. I've got a great proposition for you."

I cleaned up my paperwork and hopped a subway train for Forest Hills. When I arrived, Laurie met me at the door.

"I was asked to move to Paris for a year," I told her. "I don't know how you feel about just picking up and—"

"Let's go," Laurie interrupted.

CHAPTER FOUR

WE TOOK a crash Berlitz course in French. Before we realized what was happening, we found ourselves off the North American continent for the first time, living in a spacious two-bedroom penthouse on Avenue Foch. The terrace offered a distant view of the Eiffel Tower.

Unable to secure a work permit, Laurie busied herself with activities conducted by the American Women's Group. She immersed herself in French culture as I, at the tender age of twenty-five, sat at an antique desk in an office on the Place Vendôme and studied market data by the light of a Louis XVI chandelier. When I was not working late, Laurie and I spent time in Left Bank clubs listening to jazz.

At my new office I plunged into the task of preparing a $25 million Eurobond convertible issue for Texas International Air Corporation, Frank Lorenzo's holding company. The son of a Spanish immigrant, Lorenzo and his partner, Robert Carney, had purchased Texas International in 1972 and turned it around with an innovative offering of off-time, cut-rate fares. Now they had their sights on other acquisitions, and they planned to use European money in their attempts to strengthen their hold on the airline business.

Smith Barney was co-manager of the issue with Kidder Peabody. My job was to make the numbers meaningful from a European perspective, prepare a prospectus and arrange for the "road show" Lorenzo would take to Europe to familiarize analysts and institutional purchasers with the details concerning the bond issue.

I was low man, but here, in Paris, the totem pole was not that tall, so I had a chance to observe closely. I was amazed at Lorenzo's energy, vitality and grasp of the human elements of business. He had a little-boy look about him and a zeal in his eyes. He was one of the first to raise publicly the themes that would fuel the fires of a coming business revolution: Big business had grown fat and lazy; overpaid executives act as if they, and not the shareholders, own the corporations; an isolated management is insensitive to employees; productivity is sacrificed in favor of policy; mountains of paperwork stifle efficiency; long-term planning is lost in the rush for short-term results; creativity is dead. These were to become rallying cries of a new populist movement in the American business world. The have-nots looked at the haves and declared, We can do a better job.

Change could not occur, of course, as long as the haves controlled the purse strings, and this was why Lorenzo was in Europe seeking $25 million. With the money we helped raise for him, Lorenzo set about implementing his own lean management style.

LAURIE relished the role of playing hostess to a continual stream of family members and friends who took advantage of our temporary address as a jumping-off spot for seeing the Continent. One of these was Bob Wilkis. From time to time during this busy year he phoned from New York to ask how things were going. Once he called with the news that he had landed a position as an investment banker for Blyth Eastman Dillon & Co. I was as pleased for him as he had been for me.

I had been in Paris for nearly a year when Wilkis came over on a business trip. It was a warm feeling to see him. He came to our apartment for dinner, and I had the opportunity to see him several other times during his stay. Quite naturally and easily we spoke about private stock trading. Wilkis said, "We have all this information that we could trade on. We could make a lot of money."

Almost immediately I realized that I had changed. Life in Europe opened my eyes. Here was laissez faire practiced to the extreme. It was the norm, not the exception, for European executives to maintain bank accounts in Switzerland, Liechtenstein and Luxembourg. International bank accounts were often perceived as necessary tax havens. In industrialized nations other than the United States the major shareholders are institutions, and thus insider trading is not seen as an abuse but as a part of the normal course of business. It seemed natural to respond to Wilkis' words with the acknowledgment, "Everybody's doing it," followed by the question, "Why not us?"

We spoke at length about how best to proceed. "How do you open a secret account?" I asked.

"I don't know," he admitted, "but it can't be that difficult."

I trudged off to the American Book Store and bought copies of *How to Open a Swiss Bank Account* and *Everything You Wanted to Know About Swiss Banking*.

Wilkis and I studied carefully. It did seem easy.

"But if we are serious about doing this," I declared, "we have to set careful ground rules and follow them." We hammered out a strategy that if we had dared commit it to paper, would have looked like this:

1. *Each of us will only trade on the other's information.* Since neither of us would exploit our own information, how could anyone prove inside knowledge?

2. *We will never share tips with other family members or with friends, and we will keep our activities secret even from our wives.* In what we considered to be the most unlikely event that we got into trouble, our wives would thus be protected. Beyond that, of course, I knew that Laurie would disapprove strongly.

3. *We will trade stocks only through secret foreign accounts.*

4. *We will share information only in person, and when we speak to each other by phone, we will refer to one another by a code name so that no one will notice our association.* We chose Alan Darby. If either of us had to leave a message for the other, that is the name we would dictate.

5. *We will use common sense.*

"Dennis," Laurie said. "You've been tossing and turning in your sleep. What's wrong?"

"Nothing," I replied. "Everything's great."

"Something's bothering you," she continued. "Is the job that stressful?"

"No. I love my job."

"What's wrong?" she asked again.

"Nothing," I repeated.

Early in July I bought an airline ticket—paying cash so as not to leave a paper trail—and flew to Geneva. Somewhere in the back of my brain I knew that what I was about to do was wrong, but it simply did not feel that way. No one would get hurt. I did not believe that I would in any way undermine the ability of my clients to do business. All I would do was take advantage of my position on the inside of the industry, and this by now appeared to be a normal course of action. The benefits outweighed what I perceived to be a minuscule chance of getting caught.

In Geneva, I made my way to the financial district, and I soon found Pictet et Cie, one of Switzerland's most prestigious financial houses. An account officer said that he needed a reference.

"I work for Smith Barney in the Paris office," I said.

"You must know Mark de Frishing!" the banker exclaimed.

De Frishing, I remembered, was a Swiss citizen as well as an Englishman. I replied, "I work very closely with Mark."

"There will be no problem in opening your account."

The banker was very pleased with the prospect of my business and openly discussed my special requirements. I explained that I would be returning to the United States soon and wanted to handle long-distance transactions with ease and discretion. Secrecy was my top priority. To maintain it, the banker suggested I utilize a code name.

"How about Mr. Gold?" I asked. That seemed in character with my fantasies.

He furrowed his brow. "No. We already have a Mr. Gold."

I chuckled at this confirmation of my suspicions that others were doing this, too.

After a moment the banker suggested the alias Milky Way. "When you call," he said, "why don't you just say it's Mr. Way?"

"Fine. Now there's another thing. I want to make my deposits in cash because I don't want any instrument being traced back to me, but I don't want to come over here every time. What do you suggest?"

Without any sign of reticence the banker declared that I might find it convenient to deal through Pictet Bank & Trust, Ltd., the firm's subsidiary in the Bahamas. This sounded perfect. Nassau is less than a three-hour flight from New York, close enough for me to visit and return in a single day without anyone, particularly Laurie, knowing that I had been out of the country. I could come and go without a visa and its telltale trail. Since Nassau is in the same time zone as New York, telephone communications would be easy.

Beyond that, this Swiss banker explained, the Bahamas are blessed with bank-secrecy laws that are, if anything, more stringent than the Swiss codes. My Bahamian bank would be prohibited from disclosing any account information without my prior written consent.

I told the banker that within a matter of weeks I would visit the Bahamian branch and make an earnest deposit.

We shook hands. It was as easy as the books said it would be—so easy that the full import of what I had just done did not hit me until I was in a cab headed back to the airport.

I had flown to Geneva to open a secret bank account.

I was positioned to cash in on whatever information Wilkis could supply concerning deals at Blyth Eastman.

Who knew how much money I could make? What were the limits? Suddenly I felt like a character in a James Bond novel.

LATE in the summer of 1979 Laurie and I returned to New York. After a three-week stay at The Plaza Hotel, we moved into a one-bedroom apartment in Manhattan, at 225 East Fifty-seventh Street.

As soon as I checked in at Smith Barney, I reminded my superiors that they had promised me an opportunity to join the M&A department, and they set up a meeting for me with the new department head, J. Tomilson Hill III. Until recently he had called himself Jim, but having lost a power struggle at First Boston Corporation's pioneering M&A department, he had joined our firm and introduced himself to everyone as Tom Hill. We could only suppose he had decided to change his image.

Hill took me out to lunch to find out why I was so interested in his line of business. He seemed suitably impressed with my enthusiasm and knowledge, and agreed to take me on at a salary of $31,000.

He decreed that my time would be divided between two specific tasks. The first was to assist on any and all tender offers: crunch the numbers, deal with the lawyers and company officials, proofread the documents. I knew instantly that this would be far more interesting than anything I had yet done. The M&A boys were the hired guns, brought in for specific transactions. They hit, then ran on to the next deal. It promised to be fast, furious and fun. Within the firm, M&A business was beginning to bring high fees and, it followed, high recognition. It was a unique opportunity for a young associate.

My second task was even more intriguing. The best way for an investment banking firm to land a hot client, Hill lectured over lunch, is to identify it before it is publicly in play. "At First Boston," he said, "we had a function called breaking-news coordinator. I'd like you to handle that here. You'll have to watch the tape to see what companies suddenly become active. You've got to study the news of the entire business world and bring important events to our attention."

This was fascinating. Hill wanted me to train myself to ferret out the evidence of aberrant trading!

Hill also wanted me to stay in close contact with the new in-house rumor mill, otherwise known as Smith Barney's arbitrage department. Arbs had become critical players in M&A transactions. Hill spelled it out: Suppose a company announces that it is involved in merger discussions, and the announced or rumored price that it will offer for the stock of the target company is $50 per share, perhaps $20 higher than the current market price. Typically the price of the target company stock will jump up almost immediately to a level slightly below that speculative price, say $47 per share. There are likely to be thousands of investors quite happy to sell immediately for $47. In such a market environment an arb will buy a significant position in the stock at $47 if he believes the deal will close at $50 or if he suspects that another bid will surface at an even higher level. As the process continues, more players may enter the game, stimulating news or rumors of still higher prices, bringing fresh waves of buying. At each stage the arbs will calculate whether or not to plunge more deeply. Performed skillfully, risk arbitrage is lucrative.

In sum, Hill said, it would be my job to listen to the distant tom-toms of the trading world and report the messages to the partners.

Hill asked, "Would you like to do that?"

"Yes," I responded immediately. "I'll need a Quotron." No one in the M&A department had one of these little screens on his desk. But how else could you follow the pulse of the market?

"You'll have one," Hill promised.

EVEN as I settled into my new job I hustled about to plan my financial future. Wilkis and I had a good system outlined, but I needed to fund it. I approached family members with a quiet request to borrow cash in order to finance a nebulous business proposition. To them I was the sophisticated banker, just back from Europe. They trusted me, asked no questions and handed over the money.

In addition, I took my credit cards to their limits. It all added up to a $40,000 fund. Seed money, I thought. The start of my fortune.

One Friday I found a pay phone and placed a collect call to Pictet Bank & Trust, Ltd., identified myself as Mr. Way and arranged an appointment for the following day.

That evening I told Laurie in a nonchalant voice, "I'm going on a business trip tomorrow."

"Oh, where?"

"Florida." This did not really feel like a lie. It *was* business. And Nassau was close to Florida. The trip did not surprise Laurie, for such journeys were now a fact of my life as an investment banker.

I had the entire $40,000 on me—stashed in a briefcase under a pile of papers—when I arrived at La Guardia Airport. Once more I purchased my ticket in cash so that there would be no paperwork trail. But as I sat in the terminal before boarding, sudden dark thoughts gnawed at me. What was I doing? I had put Laurie and myself into debt to our family as well as to the credit card companies. It was not scruples that bothered me, but a pragmatic question. What if the plane went down in flames, incinerating not only me but the money as well? Forgetting my precaution concerning paperwork, I rushed to the flight-insurance counter and bought $40,000 worth of coverage.

Once in Nassau, I made my way to Bay Street, a boulevard of banks. The names read like a roll call of financial giants: the Bank of America, Citibank, Chase Manhattan, Bankers Trust, Crédit Suisse.

"I have been expecting you," the Pictet manager said as he pumped my hand. "I received a Telex from Geneva regarding your account. We are happy to accommodate your business. . . ."

The conversation satisfied me completely. In a half hour I was on a return flight to New York, muttering to myself, "This was so easy."

Soon after I arrived home, Wilkis announced that he was ready, too, with his own account at the Nassau branch of Crédit Suisse.

IN THE office, at a desk near the back of the M&A bull pen, I conducted a pro forma analysis on one proposed merger after another. This was the M&A version of number-crunching. If a merger was proposed or even fantasized, we needed a statistical picture of the results. I analyzed the two companies separately, and then attempted to forecast what would happen if they merged into a single entity. How much capitalization would they have? What were the tax considerations? Would we have antitrust problems? What would the combined earnings ratio be? What would be the best form of financing to consummate the deal? Bonds? A new stock offering? Straight cash? The bottom-line question was, What is the proper price to offer for the target stock—the price that will persuade shareholders to sell and yet will still make the deal profitable for the acquirer?

Meanwhile, I kept one eye on the Quotron, watching zillions of numbers fly by. The market tells us on a second-by-second basis what is going on out there in the real world, but it is sometimes very difficult to interpret the messages. A stock shoots up three points in a week on twenty-five times its normal volume. Why? The answer is obvious in its broad parameters: somebody is accumulating it because he thinks he knows something that others do not.

If I spotted anything of interest concerning a specific company, I ran for the brokerage library. One of the first things to check was who, if anyone, had filed a Schedule 13D. SEC rules dictated that when any single investor achieved a 5 percent ownership position in the stock of a given company, he had to file notice declaring the size of his ownership position within ten days, and he also had to disclose whether or not he was planning to attempt a takeover.

One day during lunch we previewed Smith Barney's ambitious new ad campaign. The TV screens showed the sagacious, no-nonsense face of actor John Houseman proclaiming, "Smith Barney makes money the old-fashioned way. They *earn* it!" That was the hallmark of this firm, traditionally oriented toward long-term relationships. Of course we all realized that the message was aimed at the retail market. In investment banking the old-fashioned ways appeared to be dying.

Undervalued corporations were running scared and increasingly exhibited an acquire-or-be-acquired mentality. They were creating their own strategic development departments to consider their proper roles: what companies to buy and what divisions to sell in order to make themselves less desirable targets. They now had men and women whose sole jobs were to ponder defensive strategies in the event of unfriendly attack. Armies of advisers were kept on retainer so as to be ready to swing into action at a moment's notice.

Investment banks had beefed up their own intelligence-gathering capabilities. We all maintained extensive files on corporate America. Who owned what? Who owed what? What was the corporate history? What was the stock performance history?

Whenever an official offer to purchase and a letter of transmittal were sent out to the shareholders of a target company, my phone rang off the hook. In its simplest form the offer detailed: if you, the shareholder, tender your stock by such-and-such a date, you will receive X number of dollars per share. But there were always far more intricate conditions involved, many of which were naturally confusing to the layman. Because I was the grunt working behind the scenes, calls came to me. I spent a great deal of my time explaining the details of a sophisticated merger to neophytes. And to arbs.

As part of their nonstop information-gathering task, arbs spoke to anyone they could find who had some knowledge of a pending deal. That included me, and they, in turn, developed into natural resources of information for a breaking-news coordinator. Soon I had built contacts with various men in numerous arbitrage firms, and we shared public information with one another freely. If in the course of general conversation one arb referred to a deal that neither I nor anyone else at Smith Barney was working on, it was quite ethical for me to pass that rumor along to others.

The smart arbs never tried to put me into a compromising position, but they could impart great knowledge, aware that information flows in two directions. They would do anything to stimulate the market, to drive up the price of the target stock. The bigger the deal, the greater the barrage of information and innuendo that came my way. It was a constant task to separate the real information from the self-serving gossip. I kept a logbook of information to achieve a better understanding of what was really happening.

To my delight the effort translated into fees. One day I heard a rumor that a large block of stock in Koehring Company, a heavy-machinery manufacturer, might be up for sale by its owner, U.S. Filter. I knew that if a new buyer gained control of that key block, he would be positioned to initiate a takeover action. I rushed to the Smith Barney library and pulled whatever information I could on Koehring. Then I identified several companies that might be interested in it.

I delivered this information to Hill, and he passed it on to officials at Koehring. For weeks I watched the Koehring stock carefully. Its price rise seemed to indicate that the rumor had substance. Finally the public announcement came: a Canadian firm, Dominion Bridge, had bought the block and would initiate merger discussions with

Koehring. Because we had exhibited such foreknowledge of the deal, Koehring hired us to render a fairness opinion, for a $250,000 fee.

It was found money. Hill and I shared a knowledgeable grin and basked in the compliments of those about us. We had generated significant revenues and that, in the current environment of the investment banking world, was becoming the one and only reason you came to work in the morning.

Here was a paradox: Information was the lifeblood of my job. Using it within the confines of my office resulted in millions of dollars in gains and losses; using it outside the office could be illegal.

As COGS in our respective investment banking machines, Wilkis and I were now both perfectly positioned to benefit from each other's information. One day I found a message that Alan Darby had called. I called Wilkis back, and he suggested we meet.

Between the Smith Barney office in the Burlington building, at Fifty-third and Sixth, and Blyth's offices, two blocks south, lay the labyrinth of pedestrian tunnels beneath Rockefeller Center. Amid the bustle of the lunch traffic Wilkis and I met. As we munched on slices of pizza he told me that one of Blyth's new clients was ERC, a reinsurance company that was about to become the target of a take-over bid by Connecticut General. I thanked him for this news, wiped the tomato sauce from my face and ran back to the Smith Barney library to do some quick research. Having reassured myself that ERC was basically sound, I returned to the underground maze, found a pay telephone and, as Mr. Way, placed a collect call to Pictet. I instructed my Nassau banker to purchase stock in ERC—as much as I could afford.

Only a few days later, when the merger announcement was made, the stock shot up and I sold out quickly, realizing my first tangible insider profit. I grew uneasy when I learned that Smith Barney had represented the acquirer, since this was contrary to the guidelines Wilkis and I had established, but there were no repercussions.

Another time, as Wilkis and I spent our lunch break punching the buttons on pinball machines, he disclosed that Blyth was working on an acquisition of Furr's Cafeteria. "It's a done deal," he assured me. I headed to the pay phones and made my second profitable deal.

This was almost too easy to believe.

GIFFORD HILL, A DALLAS-BASED cement manufacturing firm, wanted to acquire a similar company, in California, known as Amcord, and hired Smith Barney to represent its interests. One October day Tom Hill and I, with a briefcase full of documents, walked a few blocks to Forty-eighth Street and Park Avenue, to the offices of the powerhouse law firm of Wachtell, Lipton, Rosen & Katz, the legal reps for Gifford Hill. Our task was to review the paperwork with a team headed by Marty Lipton, the patriarch of the firm and—along with Joe Flom of Skadden, Arps—one of the two foremost legal experts in the M&A world. Hill and I were ushered into a conference room where more than twenty men were assembled. The meeting began at ten a.m., but soon Lipton drew the principals off for private talks.

Those of us who remained behind gravitated into those small cliques where so much real business is done. After a time I approached a tall, slender, good-looking and somewhat timid appearing young man. A bit of premature gray was mixed in with his dark hair.

"Hi," I said, offering my hand. "I'm Dennis Levine from Smith Barney."

"I'm Ilan Reich," he replied. He was twenty-five years old and had graduated from Columbia Law School less than six months earlier. Now he was working as Marty Lipton's associate. There was a quickness in his eyes that broadcast enormous intelligence.

As the Gifford Hill deal progressed over the course of several weeks, Reich and I spent long, late hours together, preparing documents, proofreading them and even hand-carrying them to the printer. Reich was less gregarious than I, but affable and extremely capable. The more I got to know him, the more my sixth sense told me that he might be willing to bend the rules. This could be important, I thought. It would be nice to have another source of information.

Meanwhile, Wilkis had moved to Lazard Frères, taking a job in the international department. This was an exciting development for both of us. Wilkis' move meant that more information would come our way. Lazard had been the first investment banking firm to downplay the traditional role of underwriting securities.

One day I said to Wilkis, "I met a guy at Wachtell. He's about our age, very capable. He doesn't appear to have the typical corporate-soldier mentality."

We both knew that a contact at Wachtell would give us a line on perhaps half of all pending merger deals. Furthermore, our trading would have a much less discernible pattern if some of the leads came from outside either of our firms. Wilkis readily agreed that I should try a discreet approach. There was no need for Wilkis to know the other man's name, so we decided to refer to him as Wally.

Reich and I met for lunch in early March, and after we shared small talk about our families and our jobs, I carefully brought up the subject of trading on nonpublic information. In the proper quiet tone I said, "You know, a lot of people do this."

"I know," he replied.

"We're the guys at the bottom, killing ourselves so that our clients and our partners make money. Everybody's getting rich but us."

Reich nodded.

"If you do things right, it's pretty foolproof," I said. "There is virtually no chance of getting caught."

I told him about some of the executives I had met in Europe who maintained hidden trading accounts. It was a simple matter, I said, to set up a foreign bank account and handle transactions over the phone anonymously. Reich's silence was tacit agreement, and it emboldened me. "We already have a lot of sources on the Street," I added. "Nobody has to know your name. I would trade securities for you and even give you a nest egg to start. You could make a lot of money."

Reich was cautious but interested. "How much of a nest egg?"

"Twenty-five thousand. On a margin account you'd be able to buy fifty thousand dollars' worth of securities just by talking to me."

Reich was clearly intrigued, but not yet convinced. "Maybe," he said. "But you have to prove to me that you have other sources."

"Fair enough."

I reported this conversation to Wilkis, who scurried about his office to see what he could learn.

A deal came up shortly. Wilkis learned that the big French energy company Elf Aquitaine was planning a hostile takeover attempt of Kerr-McGee Corporation, a major oil and gas producer based in Oklahoma City. This could be the first hostile takeover in history with a price tag of more than $1 billion. It was a *big* secret.

As it happened, Wachtell, Lipton was handling the legal end. Wilkis managed to copy drafts of working documents composed by Marty Lipton himself, complete with a key to the confidential code names of the principal companies. He supplied the package of information to me, and I called Reich, announcing, "I think we should meet."

Our rendezvous took place in front of The Plaza Hotel on Saturday morning, March 22, 1980. It was the first day of spring, and the weather was satisfyingly mild. Both of us wore blue jeans. We strolled into Central Park and sat on a large rock. Reich glanced around nervously. "Are you sure we weren't followed?" he asked.

I told him not to worry, but I thought a bit of paranoia was a healthy defense mechanism. Then I disclosed that I was aware that his firm was working on a deal for Elf Aquitaine to acquire Kerr-McGee.

"You're unbelievable!" he exclaimed.

"Here are the documents," I added, handing over the packet of information that Wilkis had purloined.

Reich's eyes grew wide as he studied the secret file. He was both flabbergasted and convinced, and he was in, enthusiastically.

We planned to do as much of our business as possible in person, but in case we had to transmit information over the phone, we set up a code, using various editions of Standard & Poor's *Stock Guide*. Reich could phone me, identify himself as Mr. Davis, and say simply, "One, one hundred ten, fourteen." I would grab the first edition of the stock guide, turn to page 110, count down to line fourteen—and know that this company was about to come into play.

On Monday I was ready to plunge headfirst into the market. This latest deal, with its potential to reach historic proportions, was a grand temptation, and I threw caution to the wind, multiplying the power of my money by purchasing call options on Kerr-McGee rather than settling for a mere stock position.

The deal proved to be volatile, and I was able to play it both on the upside and the downside. Before long, Kerr-McGee became a rumored target of Elf Aquitaine, and when the stock rose in price, I sold out. Then when Reich informed me that the deal was about to fizzle, I sold Kerr-McGee short and profited from the drop in price when the merger failure became public information.

Late one night, when Laurie was asleep, I sat at my desk and pondered the delicious feeling of success. Through only a few transactions I now had more than four times my annual salary stashed secretly in the Bahamas. It was a comforting, intoxicating feeling.

CHAPTER FIVE

W HEN I phoned Pictet to verify my account balance, I was surprised to receive a lecture. My account manager said that his boss in Geneva was concerned about the timing of my Kerr-McGee trades. The transactions were too suspicious, and he suggested that I might do well to modify my trading tactics.

This was more confusing than disturbing. Why, I wondered, should the bank care what I did so long as it reaped lucrative commissions?

I called the man's superior in Geneva. He acknowledged that yes, both Swiss and Bahamian law guarded the secrecy of my transactions, but some banks were more cautious than others. Pictet, he said, tended toward the conservative view. He intimated that it might be best for me to take my business elsewhere.

"Get another account," Wilkis agreed when I reported this to him.

UNBEKNOWNST to my father or my brother, I sneaked their passports out of their desk drawers and made photocopies.

Then I took advantage of the Memorial Day holiday to fly to Nassau on May 27, 1980. When I arrived, dressed like a tourist in blue jeans and a sport shirt, I simply looked up banks in the local version of the yellow pages. The first ad to catch my eye was that of Bank Leu International Ltd., a subsidiary of Bank Leu Ltd. in Zurich. Among its listed services was "International Portfolio Management." I located the office in Rosen Square and walked in.

I did not know how to pronounce the name of this institution. "Loy," the receptionist said. "Like toy." She directed me to the third-floor desk of General Manager Jean-Pierre Fraysse. He appeared to be in his mid-forties and carried himself with a Continental air.

I announced, "I'm interested in opening an account to trade U.S. securities."

"Yes," he replied.

"I am currently dealing with another Swiss bank," I said. "But I'm not pleased with the way it is handling my affairs, and I am seeking an alternative. My first requirement is absolute security."

"Yes."

"You never call me. I call you, collect. I need to have my transactions executed promptly, immediately. I want you to deal through different brokers. Break up the transactions so that no large deals are going through any one broker."

"Yes."

"You have someone who understands U.S. markets?"

"Yes." He brought in Bruno Pletscher, assistant vice president, an unassuming man, surprisingly young for having such a pronounced beer belly. All business, Pletscher explained that Bank Leu handled many trusts and "discretionary" accounts for U.S.-based clients.

I asked, "What do you require from me?"

Fraysse answered, "A letter of reference from your existing institution. Can you tell us who that is?"

"I am currently banking with Pictet."

Fraysse said, "You will have no problem with us."

That very day my banker at Pictet provided the necessary recommendation, and Pletscher processed the paperwork for my interest-bearing account. I filled in my name and address on the signature card. I provided a power of attorney, which could be used by either my father or my brother, and I also handed over signature samples as well as copies of their passport pictures. All of the background paperwork was placed into a special vault. Fraysse and Pletscher pledged that my identity would be known only to them.

I settled upon the code name Mr. Diamond.

To these sophisticated international financiers it was all business as usual. They were happy to accept the transfer of my account balance of $128,900. Fraysse told Pletscher that my account was good for the bank and to do everything possible to provide outstanding service.

Back home, I entrusted my father with a sealed envelope containing the power of attorney and instructions on how to deal with Bank Leu. "In case something ever happens to me," I said, "open this." Dad looked perplexed. I had a fleeting vision of him grieving for me, opening the envelope and pondering its curious contents.

THROUGHOUT the course of the summer I developed a friendship with Ira Sokolow, a husky, mustachioed six-footer, who, like Wilkis, was addicted to cigars. At twenty-six, Sokolow came with the proper credentials—an undergraduate degree from the Wharton School of

Business and a master's degree in taxation from Bentley College. He was a CPA, who had previously worked for the respected accounting firm of Arthur Anderson. He had completed the first of his two years of M.B.A. studies at Harvard and was interning at Smith Barney. He was on the fast track, and Smith Barney wanted to hire him full time after he completed his coursework. Since Sokolow was such a good catch, I was assigned the task of wooing him.

Sokolow was a hardworking man, a good number-cruncher and analyst. Beyond these basic skills, he possessed the proper personality for the Street. He was efficient at employing the social graces, but he was not overly effusive. There was a chemistry between us, the same spark of irreverence that had passed between Ilan Reich and me.

"I have this kid working for me this summer," I said to Wilkis. "He's very discreet. I think he wants to play."

"Okay," Wilkis said.

At what I felt was an appropriate moment I broached the subject of insider trading to Sokolow, making the same offer to him that I had made to Reich, a $25,000 stake in my secret account.

"I would love to do it," he responded without hesitation. We reached the clear understanding that after he finished his M.B.A. studies, wherever he went to work, he would join our network.

On September 24 I was sitting at my desk in the back of the M&A bull pen when the phone rang.

"This is Mr. Davis," said a curt voice that I recognized immediately as belonging to Ilan Reich. "I'm out of town."

Referring to my *Stock Guide*, I replied, "Give me the number."

"I don't have one." He paused to think, then suggested, "Get *The Wall Street Journal*. Turn to the OTC [over the counter] page. . . . Okay, look in the fourth column, count ten down."

My finger rested on the name of Jefferson National Insurance.

"Buy it," Reich said. "Now."

I glanced at the clock. It was almost three p.m., one hour before the market closed. "Okay," I said. "Bye."

I hustled down to the first floor of the building, found a pay phone, called Nassau and ordered Pletscher to sink the entire balance of my account into shares of Jefferson National. Then, as Alan Darby, I called Wilkis and advised, "Shoot the load."

One hour later I was back at my desk when Reich called again. "The deal's dead," he told me.

My body went limp. I felt my pulse flutter. I had my *entire* account riding on this one deal. My eyes shot to the clock, and I grimaced with the realization that the market had just closed. I hung up with Reich and rushed back downstairs to grab a phone and report to Wilkis. He was as stunned as I was, but there was nothing we could do until the morning. Nothing but hope. I had no idea what had gone wrong.

After a sleepless night I was at my desk early, waiting for the market to open so that I could sell out and eat whatever loss I had to digest. But Reich called again: "Everything is okay. The deal is all right." With a lightened heart I relayed the news to Wilkis.

That morning, trading in Jefferson National was suspended pending an announcement, and later Zurich Insurance Company disclosed that it was buying Jefferson National. The target's stock soared.

"There was a breakdown in the discussions," Reich explained later. "The deal died and then it came back." He asked, "How did we do?"

I reported that we had sold our 8000 shares for a whopping profit of $155,734. Reich's share of that was about $20,000.

Jefferson National was the first big hit, and it changed the parameters of the game. Now we would be able to take larger positions, just as the M&A boom was picking up steam. It was a time of unprecedented opportunity.

The winter months were a blur of activity as Reich threw deals my way. Though I only made about one investment a month—with most of my business being handled by Christian Schlatter, Bank Leu's new securities trader—life screamed along at an incredible pace.

There was no time for reflection, no time to worry about where all this might lead. If I had stopped to analyze it, I would have seen that there were now two Dennis Levines. One was a conservative investment banker, busier than ever at his office, working his way up the ladder as quickly as he could. Laurie was very proud of this persona, but she knew nothing of the ethereal Dennis Levine, who had hundreds of thousands of dollars stashed in a secret bank account.

JOHN R. Shad, a balding, bespectacled gentleman, had recently left his post as vice-chairman and head of corporate finance at E. F. Hutton to become chairman of the SEC. Upon taking the post, he announced that policing the crime of insider trading would be his top priority. In fact, he declared to one reporter that the SEC was going to come down on insider trading "with hobnail boots." Rallying to his cry for justice, SEC staffers bought him an actual pair of hobnail boots, which he displayed in his office.

Now those boots trod upon what the SEC described as "certain unknown purchasers" of stock and options in St. Joseph Minerals Corporation, who had bought immediately prior to the public announcement of the Joseph E. Seagram & Company takeover bid. Federal Judge Milton Pollack froze certain suspected insider trading profits in the New York branch of Banca della Svizzera Italiana. Then he threatened to slap the Swiss bank with a $50,000-per-day fine until it identified the purchasers. The government soon learned the identities of a principal trader and three affiliated offshore corporations.

By sheer luck I had missed on that deal, placing an order too late. The close call scared the daylights out of me. I resolved to curtail my trading in options. It was too obvious. From now on, if a deal was not yet publicly announced, I would trade only in standard stock shares.

What I did not know at the time was that Fraysse, at Bank Leu, was also very concerned. He wrote a memorandum to Schlatter—with a copy to Pletscher—dated April 10, 1981, noting that the SEC was cracking down on inside traders. "We have one," Fraysse said.

But in fact, Bank Leu continued to process my trades willingly. Only much later would I learn how much attention Fraysse and the others were paying to my business.

My BROTHERS and I booked a banquet room at the Waldorf-Astoria, hired a band and threw a surprise black-tie sixtieth birthday party for Dad. My brother Larry and his wife flew in from California as a special surprise.

Dad was overwhelmed by emotion, and the grin on his face was ample evidence of the pride he felt for his sons. Robert was moving the family contracting business into bigger and better things. Larry was successful in the tough world of California real estate. And although I was a very small cog in the financial markets, my proud father was convinced that I had taken Wall Street by storm.

Laurie was especially radiant that night. One evening not long after the party she informed me that she suspected she was pregnant.

This was long-term good news and short-term disaster. We both very much wanted to start a family, but as far as Laurie knew, we were still living from paycheck to paycheck. I was accustomed to methodical strategic planning, and I did not feel prepared for the unexpected onset of fatherhood.

On the afternoon of Laurie's pregnancy test I phoned her at home and asked, "What did they say?" The eyes of my co-workers showed interest. Several of them grinned. I felt my face redden.

Laurie had not yet heard the results. "Give me the number of the lab," I suggested. "I'll set up a conference call, and we can hear the news together."

Soon we were on the line with a receptionist at the medical laboratory, who announced, "Mrs. Levine, your test results are positive."

"Positive she is pregnant, or positive she is not pregnant?" I asked.

"Mr. Levine, your wife is pregnant."

It was one of the few moments in my life when I could think of nothing to say. I caught the eye of a colleague, working at the desk next to mine. He grinned and waved his checkbook at me.

Incredible conflicting emotions ran through my heart. I loved the idea of being a father, and I shuddered at the responsibility. My mind boggled at blurred visions of baby food, diapers, school clothes, a car on his sixteenth birthday—it would be a boy, wouldn't it?—college tuition. That was a father's job, wasn't it, to pay for all this? But how could I be a good father when I was working eighty hours a week?

When the shock wore off, I found myself enchanted by the growing bulge in Laurie's tummy. She was determined to deliver naturally, so we enrolled in a course of Lamaze classes, but my attention was diverted by another business deal. Amfac Corporation, based in Honolulu, was contemplating a major investment in the Fairmont Hotel Corporation, and I found myself traveling for extended periods of time. I was only able to attend the first Lamaze class. Many of Laurie's fellow students were convinced that she was a single mother.

THERE it was in front of me. Tyler Corporation, a manufacturer of explosives and cast-iron pipes, was in the process of acquiring the specialty chemical manufacturer Reliance Universal. Smith Barney represented Tyler, and it was my job to coordinate the preparation of the tender offer. It was only a small, $72 million deal, and the companies involved were decidedly boring, but it was business. I shared the information with Wilkis, and I knew that he would profit from it, but why, I wondered, shouldn't I go ahead and do the same thing?

The ground rules that we had sketched in Paris—it seemed like a century ago—prohibited this. But I had developed enormous confidence in the veils that I had set in place. My bankers assured me that everything was safe, and I even made sure that I switched the locations of the pay phones that I used whenever I called the Bahamas, on the off-chance that the bank's line was tapped. There was not a piece of paper anywhere in the United States that could link me with the trades, and by law Bank Leu could not provide any outsider with information regarding my account. What could be more safe?

Our machine was humming. Wilkis and Reich were enthusiastic. Ira Sokolow, finished with his Harvard studies, had joined Lehman Brothers, Kuhn, Loeb and was ready to play.

My God, this is so easy, I said to myself, and I ran for a pay phone to call in a buy order for Reliance Universal.

SEVERAL transactions competed for my time. I was performing advisory tasks for Penn Central Corporation and doing work for J. Ray McDermott, a New Orleans–based offshore-drilling-platform manufacturer, while I helped service Smith Barney's largest account, Dow Chemical. On top of all this, I got my first chance to work on a leveraged buyout (LBO) when I helped Olin Corporation divest itself of its subsidiary Winchester Firearms Company.

The LBO was an old idea that was back in vogue, a fiendishly simple device that paid off handsomely. The word leveraged is a euphemism for OPM, or other people's money; the term buyout is self-explanatory. On a relatively small scale those concepts are the basis for the spate of get-rich-quick investment strategies proposed by real estate gurus. The ideal is for an investor to purchase a home or apartment building or office complex for little or no money down. The purchase price—or the bulk of it—is financed by one or more mortgages. If the deal is a good one, the monthly rents generated by the tenants will be enough to cover the mortgage payments, and the investor will eventually reap his profit from the appreciation of the property—all without putting up a cent of his or her own money.

Multiply that concept by $100 million, add refinements tailored to the specific deal, and you have an LBO as it applies to corporate business. The LBO specialist sniffs out a company that he can buy with borrowed money, secured not by his own assets but by those of the target company. Once he acquires the target, he will repay that money in one of two ways. Perhaps the company will generate enough cash through its normal operations to service the debt, or perhaps the entrepreneur can sell off enough assets to pay his creditors. The goal is to wind up with at least a portion of a viable, ongoing business.

As the M&A boom picked up steam, the LBO—fair or foul—was becoming a major feature of the business landscape. Before the '80s most LBOs had been small potatoes, generally involving less than $100,000. They began to gain momentum, however, as corporate executives watched the success of a few pioneering deals. The archetypical example occurred during this year, 1981, when a group called Wesray, headed by former Secretary of the Treasury William E. Simon and his partner, Ray Chambers, pulled off an LBO of Gibson Greeting Cards, purchasing it from RCA in a transaction that appeared to hold lucrative potential for the principals.

By now there were investment firms formed specifically to pull off LBOs, hold the companies private for a time and then take them public or sell them. The average profit on such a deal was reported to be about 40 percent but was often much higher. Ultimately one of the SEC commissioners would characterize an LBO as "little more than a charade," and a financial officer of Goodyear Tire and Rubber would call it "an idea that was created in hell by the devil himself." It was, nonetheless, effective and lucrative.

IN THE past the path to success in investment banking was slow and steady. If you managed to land an entry-level job with a respected firm, you stayed put for the rest of your working life, climbing slowly up the ladder. Today's world was different. Du Pont Corporation had just spent $9 billion to take control of Conoco, and the transaction was a clear indication that absolutely no company was immune. The M&A business was on the move and so, in turn, were its practitioners. Three of Smith Barney's most senior partners were leaving to launch their own M&A "boutique." I knew the volume of our business would drop dramatically. It was time to hunt for a better paycheck.

Ira Sokolow was not the only person I knew at Lehman Brothers.

Another friend had moved there recently, and I reasoned that this gave me a foot in the door. That venerable firm, launched as a cotton brokerage in the mid-nineteenth century by Henry, Emanuel and Mayer Lehman, had passed through several incarnations and nearly gone bankrupt in 1968. But now—under the management of Peter G. Peterson, who at age thirty-four had been president of Bell & Howell and then served as Secretary of Commerce under President Nixon—Lehman Brothers was challenging First Boston for the role of the most active and respected M&A deal maker on Wall Street. For the past three years it had earned record profits.

I asked my friend if he could arrange an introduction for me with Eric Gleacher, the head of Lehman Brothers' M&A department. That feeler resulted in an appointment for a breakfast meeting downtown at 55 Water Street. In my usual manner I studied everything I could find concerning Lehman Brothers and Gleacher. He was a former marine who had reached a status in business where he was frequently quoted in newspaper reports.

On the appointed morning I stepped off the elevator into the Lehman Brothers' offices and gaped. Original works of impressionist painters graced the deep-grained wood-paneled walls. Here and there a sculpture stood on a pedestal. Gleacher greeted me warmly and took me to an exclusive dining room. This was only breakfast, but we feasted on exquisitely prepared omelets and croissants.

Gleacher and I got along well. He was suitably impressed by my work and was aware that Smith Barney, despite its ad campaign, was not doing things "the old-fashioned way." He was interested in bringing fresh enthusiasm to his own firm. At one point he cast a conspiratorial glance about the opulent dining room and declared that he had always viewed himself as a maverick, not one of the typical Ivy League kids, but a scrapper.

"A marine," I pronounced.

"Yes." He laughed.

During the conversation I quoted several of the statements he had made recently to financial reporters. "You've done your homework," Gleacher acknowledged. Like me, he believed that the successful deal maker transcended number-crunching. He knew that a client would pay for shrewdness, for instinct, for a carefully timed smile. "I want you to see some of my partners today," he said.

Within days Lehman Brothers made me an offer that, as a prospective father, I could not refuse. On November 3, 1981, I would join the firm as a vice president, at a base salary of $50,000 per year plus, of course, an annual bonus that would be a multiple of my salary.

As THE starting date of my new job neared, Wilkis, knowing that my position would bring me more prominence on the Street and concerned over the SEC's increased vigilance, suggested that I take further steps to shield my other life. He had already insulated his position by setting up a dummy corporation to stand between him and his account. He gave me the name of his Bahamian lawyer, Hartis Pinder, and urged me to set up the same sort of arrangement.

I arrived in Nassau the day before Halloween with a mission to fulfill. First, I met with Pinder and explained that I wanted to establish a corporation and transfer the assets of my personal account at Bank Leu to the new business entity. Pinder suggested, since I was especially concerned with secrecy, that I base the corporation in Panama, because Panamanian law would not require that my name be disclosed on any documents. For appropriate fees, certain individuals in Pinder's law firm would act as directors. All I had to do, Pinder said, was arrange for Bank Leu to transfer the fees to his law firm.

When I explained the corporate arrangement to Bank Leu officials, they jumped onto the bandwagon. There were fees to be earned here, and everyone wanted them. "You're a valued customer," Fraysse acknowledged quietly. In fact, I was by now Bank Leu's *most* valued customer. They suggested a mutual fund acting only on my orders, but I declined. In truth, I wanted to spread the business around.

Back home, I retrieved from Dad the envelope containing the power of attorney. I replaced it with an envelope containing new instructions and bearer shares of Diamond Holdings. Whoever walked into the bank with those shares controlled the company and its account.

Thus was born Diamond Holdings, consisting of a few legal papers in a file folder. Pinder was listed as the president. His law partner was vice president, and one of his employees was secretary.

ON SATURDAY, December 5, not long after I joined Lehman Brothers, Laurie went into labor. I rushed her to New York Hospital and, with my mind in a fog, arranged the details.

My child was in no hurry to be born. Laurie did the hard work as I held her hand, tried to help and, paradoxically, tried to stay out of the way. Lamaze or not, Laurie had been in labor for eighteen hours when she begged for an epidural. The doctor moved her into a delivery room, and I donned a gown and mask to accompany her.

All of a sudden the baby was *there.*

The doctor said, "You have a son."

Laurie shrieked, "I can't believe it." Tears poured from her eyes. Pain and anxiety drained away in an instant, replaced by pure joy.

Now we heard from the principal character. He emitted a wondrous, joyful, incredible cry.

Scrubbed and polished, wrapped in white linen, the boy was placed in Laurie's arms. She clutched him eagerly and cried, "It's a baby!"

I laughed and asked, "You expected a watermelon?"

I found my hands quivering as I reached for my son. He felt so fragile in my arms. I could barely see his tiny features through my own tears. I leaned close and said, "Hello, Adam. I'm your daddy."

Through fuzzy eyes he tried to gaze back. I knew then that Laurie and I were partners in a deal that made anything on the Street fade into insignificance. If I had been able to hold that concept in the forefront of my mind, perhaps everything would have been so different.

But I was a baby myself in so many ways. And I was, unknowingly, already too addicted to the elixir of success.

CHAPTER SIX

IN THE past, deals simply came to Lehman Brothers, but now the partners sensed that some business was passing them by, corralled by more aggressive firms.

I brought them an innovation, suggesting the position of breaking-news coordinator. "I can't believe you guys don't do this," I said to Gleacher. The competition had grown too fierce to be passive, I argued. Morgan Stanley, for example, had established a group whose job was to study every announced merger and search for a white knight—a more friendly would-be acquirer—that it could persuade to come in with a better offer. We had to seek out targets and then propose them to other companies. I explained how the job of breaking-news coordinator had paid off for us at Smith Barney, and I volunteered for the task. "I'll need a Quotron on my desk," I said.

Lehman Brothers was in the process of computerizing its operations, and I spent considerable time establishing an ambitious electronic spreadsheet file containing data of major U.S. and multinational corporations. I categorized them by industry, size and location. Special files showed me at a glance a company's M&A history, whether as an acquirer or target. After a time I had at my fingertips the basic data necessary for evaluating almost any deal.

One day Ira Sokolow mentioned that Motorola was preparing to acquire Four Phase Systems and he was working on the target's end of the deal. He asked quietly, "Are we doing this?"

"I don't know anything about it," I replied. "Tell me."

He explained what was afoot and declared, "We should do it."

I relayed the information to Wilkis, and we plunged ahead, making more than $60,000.

Deals came and went. In August 1982 Reich passed on a tip that Dyson-Kissner-Moran Corporation was considering an offer for Criton Corporation, an aerospace firm near Seattle. I bought a position in the company and at the same time saw a chance to demonstrate to Gleacher the value of a breaking-news coordinator. I told him that I had picked up rumors that Criton might become a target. Gleacher called a Criton official, who claimed we were out of our minds. After the deal was announced, he called back and asked us to huddle with him to map out defensive strategies.

While Sokolow and I were out at Criton's headquarters, in Bellevue, Washington, it became obvious that the price was going up. Over lunch at a Mexican restaurant we quietly debated what we should do.

"I don't want to make a collect call from here," I said. "How many people are in Bellevue, Washington? I don't know if it's traceable."

But it seemed like very easy money—after all, the deal was announced—and we could not resist the temptation. Before returning to Criton, I called Nassau and increased my position to 27,000 shares of the company's stock. I sold within a week, after Dyson-Kissner-Moran announced its increased tender price, for a profit of $212,628. The money was nice, but in addition, Gleacher's confidence in me increased; obviously I had impeccable sources of information.

On a July trip to Nassau I had met a new employee at Bank Leu, Bernhard Meier, an investment expert transferred from Zurich to replace Chris Schlatter. He was a small, sophisticated man, about my age, outgoing and gregarious. His wife, Helene, was a member of one of Switzerland's most prominent banking families, the Sarasins. Meier had studied at the Wharton School of Business. He chain-smoked throughout our conversation.

Only much later would I learn that Meier, after viewing the success of my market activities, concluded that I was on to something big. Mr. Diamond was making big bucks with his fast turnaround buying and selling, and Meier decided that he, too, could participate in what seemed to be as close as possible to a sure thing. He determined to copy at least some of my trades.

This is a tactic known as piggybacking. It is not illegal in the Bahamas, nor is it illegal under U.S. law, per se, unless the piggy-backer has knowledge—or ignores strong evidence—that the trader he is copying is acting upon illegal information. However, piggyback-ing was very much contrary to the rules that governed the actions of officers and employees of Bank Leu. To cover his tracks, Meier set up a private account for himself at Bank Leu, code-named Ascona.

True to Shad's vow, the SEC appeared to be taking more vigorous action against inside traders. Wilkis and I paid careful attention when-ever anything hit the press and compared the details to our own situation. There was, for instance, the case of Carlo Florentino, an associate of Ilan Reich's at Wachtell, Lipton. I had worked with him on a couple of deals, but no hint of impropriety had passed between us. When he was arrested, I was amazed to learn that he had traded, through his personal brokerage account at E. F. Hutton, in the securi-ties of companies that he was personally advising. Wilkis and I said to one another, "Can you believe how stupid he was?"

Florentino's lawyer managed to get him off with a sentence of two years' probation, but his career, of course, was finished. The incident stunned Reich into caution. By now his share of my account was more than $100,000. I asked him if he wanted any money, but he said he wanted to stop.

"Fine," I told him. "No problem. But your money is there, anytime you want it."

The clandestine portion of my life took relatively little time and energy. What really preoccupied me were legitimate endeavors. I was at my desk one day in May, 1983, when word came over the wire that Maryland Cup Corporation was in merger discussions with an undisclosed acquirer. Scuttlebutt held that the potential buyer was a European firm. My fingers spun across the computer keyboard, and my eyes scanned the CRT to discern what our data bank could tell me.

Based in Owings Mills, Maryland, the target company was an important manufacturer of disposable paper and plastic products, and it happened to be the single largest producer of ice-cream cones. Its most recognizable brand names were Sweetheart paper plates and Eat-it-All ice-cream cones. It had $400 million in assets.

The most interesting tidbit I learned was that Maryland Cup was a previous client of Lehman Brothers'. Back in 1980 and 1981 we had represented the company in merger discussions with Fort Howard Paper Company. No deal had been consummated, but I wondered, Was Fort Howard still interested? Were they interested enough to assume the role of a white knight? I ran to the appropriate partner and asked, "Are we doing the Maryland Cup deal?"

He replied, "What are you talking about?"

Within a half hour we had tracked down Merrill L. Bank, chairman of the board and C.E.O. of Maryland Cup. We spoke to him via a golf course telephone and persuaded him to give us a chance to find another buyer, a higher bidder. Through Fort Howard's investment banker, Morgan Stanley, we opened negotiations. Fort Howard was a natural buyer. The deal made sense.

Early in June I phoned Meier, in Nassau, and ordered him to purchase about $600,000 worth of Maryland Cup shares for my account. I did not know that after buying 15,200 shares for me, Meier then bought 300 shares for his own account.

After a furious few weeks of clandestine meetings, where we brought together the principals at airport hotels, we cut a deal. The shareholders voted their approval, and Maryland Cup became a wholly owned subsidiary of Fort Howard Paper. We kept the business under U.S. ownership and generated a commission of $2,732,000 that otherwise would have gone elsewhere!

I sold out my private holdings of Maryland Cup on July 7 for a profit of $121,807. Meier earned $1,769.

WITH AN EVER GROWING NETWORK of contacts and a track record of successful transactions, I gained the reputation of being a rainmaker, someone who could bring in new clients. My career was on the move, and for the first time I really began to believe I could make it to the big time—legitimately. This realization helped Laurie and me decide to go house hunting. Adam had reached the toddling stage, and we felt cramped in our one-bedroom Manhattan apartment.

A broker had shown us a co-op at 1199 Park Avenue within our price range, but my father came to look at it and found several flaws. When he and I left the building, we walked south, past a magnificent structure dripping with old-world charm. "Boy, I'd like to live in that building," I said to Dad.

A short time later a six-room apartment became available in that very building through an estate sale. If we financed to the hilt, we could afford it, so we took a look. Laurie admired the ornate entrance gate and the vaulted ceilings in the hallways, but the unit itself was a disaster. It had been built in 1929 and showed its age. Nevertheless, it was spacious, with 2200 square feet to work with, and priced well below market. We made an offer, putting down 10 percent in earnest money, which was accepted pending approval by the co-op board.

We submitted our application, along with a letter of reference from Lehman Brothers' chairman, Pete Peterson, who declared that I was "extremely well regarded" and respected within business circles. My integrity, he said, was "of the highest order."

The board ultimately granted its approval. Then we contracted to have the apartment gutted and remodeled before we moved in. The entire process would encompass more than a year.

EVER since the February death of Gulf + Western's chairman, Charles Bluhdorn, the conglomerate had been liquidating its holdings in subsidiary companies such as J. P. Stevens, Brunswick, Hammermill Paper, and the Bank of New York. One of its last remaining holdings was the educational book publisher Esquire, Inc. Rather than sell its 30 percent interest, Gulf + Western decided to buy a majority share. In October, Esquire engaged Lehman Brothers to work on the transaction, and I was assigned to it. In the process I bought and sold 15,200 shares of Esquire's stock, netting $121,728. Once again, without my knowledge, Meier piggybacked 300 shares.

Sometime after that, Ira Sokolow informed me that he had recruited an associate at Goldman Sachs who had agreed to pass on information. He did not tell me the man's name, and we referred to him merely as Goldie. Sokolow's share of my account was now worth several hundred thousand dollars. He asked for some of it in cash, and I made plans to have Bank Leu supply it.

Ilan Reich suddenly reappeared. In November 1983 he and I were both present at a "21" Club lunch celebrating the closing of a deal in which both of our firms had participated. This renewed our friendship, and once more we began to meet for lunch. He did not provide any additional tips, but I sensed he was merely biding his time.

How, I wondered, could he afford to ignore the opportunities? The M&A boom had accelerated beyond anyone's wildest predictions. Prior to 1980, U.S. business history recorded only seven acquisitions capitalized at $1 billion or more. Already, little more than three years into the decade, there had been more than thirty such deals. Not only were these transactions bigger and more numerous than before but they were also tougher. Hostile deals now accounted for about one third of all mergers and acquisitions.

I was promoted to senior vice president. I scrambled toward a future that seemed rosy indeed, although there was never any time to stop and think about it.

These days I never saw a product. If I was in a supermarket and I saw a brand name of anything, I thought of the company behind it. I saw a balance sheet, a takeover candidate, a possible acquirer. I saw a deal. Sometimes Laurie would interrupt herself in midsentence to ask, "Are you with me, Dennis? Am I talking to the wall?"

SEC chairman John Shad kept his "hobnail boots" promise. In three years' time he brought more than forty cases of insider trading to the courts. Shad was joined in his crusade by Representative Timothy Wirth, who sponsored the Insider Trading Sanctions Act, enabling the SEC not only to demand that an inside trader return his profits but that he pay treble damages as well. And on top of *that,* Shad developed good relations with the U.S. Attorney's office in Manhattan, paving the way for more vigorous prosecution on criminal charges. All of this seemed a bit watered down to President Reagan, who when he signed Wirth's bill into law, commented that there was still no definition of insider trading and that such a definition "might be appropriate."

But in truth, the definition was evolving right under the President's eye. On January 4, 1984, deputy secretary of defense Paul Thayer resigned in the aftermath of SEC and Justice Department charges that he had illegally provided confidential stock information to acquaintances. And in March came the story of dapper, avowedly gay R. Foster Winans, one of the two authors of *The Wall Street Journal's* "Heard on the Street" column. The column was so widely read that if a rumored deal appeared there, the publicity alone might be enough to move the market. Winans admitted that he had accepted, in concert with his roommate, David Carpenter, $31,000 for providing advance notice of the news contained in his upcoming columns to two Kidder Peabody stockbrokers. Winans contended that the activity did not fall into the category of insider trading. Nevertheless, he was convicted and sentenced to eighteen months in prison.

Perhaps these cases should have caused Wilkis and me to temper our activities. Instead, we scoffed, noting with disdain that Winans and his buddies had made no attempt to hide their transactions. We agreed with the conclusion reached in the March 12 issue of *Forbes* magazine: "Most people who get caught are dumb or naive or careless." The magazine openly offered this advice: "It helps to hide your trail if you deal only with foreign banks that have no presence in the U.S., which leaves the U.S. courts with little leverage."

Wilkis, having experienced a falling-out with his Crédit Suisse bankers, had moved his business to the Bank of Nova Scotia Trust Company in the Cayman Islands, and my private corporation traded under Bahamian secrecy laws. We saw no reason to stop.

MY 1984 base salary at Lehman Brothers was $75,000, and I was guaranteed a minimum annual bonus of $100,000. The senior management of the firm also made me a "profit participant." As one deal after another flew across my desk, as I saw my efforts turn into mountains of cash for my clients and the firm, it became obvious that I was positioned to earn more than some of the partners. Indeed, I believed that this year I was going to become a partner myself.

But suddenly I became a victim of the M&A trend. For 134 years Lehman Brothers had been a privately owned firm, its stock held by the partners. Thus it was invulnerable to a hostile takeover bid; it could be acquired only if enough partners chose to sell. But the resolve of those partners had been sapped by the bitter battle between Peterson and Lewis Glucksman. In May, Shearson/American Express acquired Lehman Brothers at a cost of $360 million and immediately set about to put its imprint on the Lehman mystique. The new entity was called Shearson Lehman/American Express—later shortened to Shearson/Lehman Brothers.

Wall Street's oldest investment banking partnership was gone. The unique flavor of the small firm disappeared overnight. Now I was a cog in the machine of a financial conglomerate. *Business Week* quoted me as saying, "A lot of the spirit, a lot of the drive was gone."

I searched for a new position. Updating my résumé, I was able to report that I had generated $10 million in fees for Lehman Brothers in 1982 and $15 million in 1983. My projection for the current year was $20 million.

It was gratifying to realize that the headhunters were after me, trying to lure me to any of several firms. I was wooed by Merrill Lynch, Pierce, Fenner & Smith; E. F. Hutton; Kidder Peabody; and Morgan Stanley. The New York offices of several foreign banks were after me. A partner in Hadley Lockwood was trying to persuade me to join Drexel Burnham Lambert. A preliminary report to Drexel declared that I enjoyed two things—doing deals and making money.

I took a hard look at Drexel. Long entrenched in the second tier of investment banking firms, it finally seemed to be on the move. During the past year it had drawn the Street's attention with its role in a pair of high-profile dramas. Early in 1984 Texas financier T. Boone Pickens, Jr., through his company, Mesa Petroleum, set his sights on the acquisition of Gulf Oil. Pickens came to us at Lehman Brothers for tactical advice, but he went to Drexel for financing. In short order Drexel obtained commitments to raise a whopping $1.7 billion for Pickens' war chest. He bought up more than 13 percent of Gulf's stock but lost a proxy fight that would have given him the authority to restructure the company. The ultimate winner, Standard Oil of California, paid $13.2 billion for Gulf. When Pickens sold out, Mesa Petroleum earned a pretax profit of about $500 million, but Drexel had missed out on financing the largest takeover deal in history.

The second notable event occurred in midyear, when Saul P. Steinberg, through his Reliance Group Holdings, Inc., launched an attempt to take over Walt Disney Productions Corporation. Steinberg, a baby-faced, roly-poly fellow who favored bright red bow ties, had been regarded as the *enfant terrible* of the takeover world ever since he launched a hostile takeover bid for the giant Chemical Bank. The traditional business powers had ganged up on him, dumping his company's stock by the truckload, sending its price into a downward spiral and causing him to abort his attack.

Now the swashbuckling Steinberg was attempting to take control of Disney, an American institution. Steinberg set up a new corporate shell to handle the bid, dubbed MM Acquisition Corporation—unabashedly named after Mickey Mouse. Some suspected, however, that the name was a tip of the hat to Michael Milken, Drexel's by now legendary financial wizard, who arranged $1.5 billion worth of financing for the proposed transaction. MM purchased 11.1 percent of Disney's stock and announced a $970 million tender offer for an additional 37.9 percent of the shares.

Disney squirmed out of the tight corner by agreeing to buy back the stock, paying a premium over the market price that resulted in a profit for Steinberg in excess of $30 million. Disney also agreed to reimburse MM for some $28 million in "out-of-pocket" expenses; the money was, in fact, out of Disney's pocket and mainly into Drexel's.

It was a classic example of what had come to be known as greenmail. The incident demonstrated the muscle that Drexel could flex and the fees it could generate, but it also exhibited a lack of finesse. Observers wondered, Could Drexel ever finish what it had started?

In sum, Drexel had Pickens, Steinberg and a horde of other wheeling, dealing entrepreneurs ready to become major figures on the American business scene, but it still lacked the deal-closing ability.

Drexel's mistake in the Gulf Oil and Disney deals, I thought, was in offering shareholders a mixed bag—half cash and half equity and/or debt instruments that were difficult to evaluate. It would be better to offer all cash; then the shareholder would know what he was getting and would be more likely to surrender his stock. I said to myself, If these guys at Drexel ever get their act together, they will be unbeatable.

I checked with my acquaintance Jay Bloom, who had recently left Lehman Brothers to join Drexel as a vice president. "It's the greatest place to be," he enthused. "We need people like you."

ILAN REICH WAS BACK IN THE game. A tip on Warburg, Pincus & Company paid off in August when the firm announced its plan to acquire SFN Companies. The SFN stock shot up, and I sold out the 20,000 shares that I had acquired for a profit of $129,316.

Reich came right at me with another deal, disclosing that Wachtell, Lipton was representing the Searle family, owners of G. D. Searle & Company, the maker of NutraSweet. The family had decided to sell much of its closely held stock, and Reich and I knew that once that stock arrived on the market, Searle would be an appealing takeover target. I shared the tip with Wilkis, bought 60,000 shares and waited for something to happen. For a time, nothing did.

Searle is based in Chicago. Near the end of September, Wilkis and I, our patience growing thin, placed a call to Herb Greenberg of the Chicago *Tribune*. Wilkis had spoken with this reporter previously, using the alias Mr. Freeze, and had provided a news tip that ultimately proved correct. So now, once he identified himself as Mr. Freeze, Greenberg expressed immediate interest. Wilkis reported, "The Searle family is selling its stock. The company will be a target."

"How do you know?" Greenberg asked.

"Because we're in the business of knowing," Wilkis replied.

Greenberg checked around, verified the tip and published his latest scoop. When the story broke, I netted $834,743. I was thrilled to hear Meier report the results. The high was still there, but it was not as tingly as before, and I wondered if I was growing jaded. By now, taking down nearly a million dollars almost seemed routine.

OFTEN I groaned when I realized that I had to blow an evening at a function. Sometimes these obligatory social occasions led to important contacts, however, and I was excited about attending the 1984 annual dinner of the United Jewish Appeal, for it would provide an opportunity to meet the UJA's man of the year. He also happened to be Wall Street's most renowned arb. The son of a Russian-born Detroit delicatessen owner, he was known by some in the business as Ivan the Terrible. Some others called him Piggy.

An attorney by training, Ivan Boesky had become a Wall Street legend during the past decade by building a personal fortune of about $200 million, qualifying him for a spot on *Forbes'* list of the 400 richest Americans. For a minimum of $10 million you could buy a piece of the action of his Ivan F. Boesky Corporation, which now had nearly $1 billion at its disposal for use in arbitrage deals. Through a subsidiary, Seemala Corporation—named after his wife, Seema—Boesky owned a seat on the New York Stock Exchange (NYSE). He also controlled a British investment trust, in which he held about $50 million. He and his wife owned 53 percent of the Beverly Hills Hotel.

Boesky was so successful that Wall Street flattered him by emulating him. If word leaked out that Boesky had plunged into a stock position, that alone was enough to bring a horde of copycat investors in after him. He could move the market all by himself. His reputation was so secure that an investor who wanted to pour money into his arbitrage fund had to agree to give him 40 percent of all profits— while absorbing 90 percent of all losses.

One of my investment banking colleagues once remarked, "Ivan has the ability to coin money." Another said, "Boesky's up to his ass in inside information."

Over the years he had used some of his fortune to buy respect. After he contributed hundreds of thousands of dollars to Harvard University, he was appointed to an advisory panel at the school and thus qualified for membership at New York's Harvard Club, a location he preferred for business meetings as well as squash matches. After he donated $2 million to the Jewish Theological Seminary of America, the school named a library for him and his wife. Now he was the UJA's man of the year, which implied another large contribution.

I wondered if he ran his business endeavors on a similar theory of quid pro quo.

Photos I had seen showed a handsome, polished man, and I had a mind-picture of him as tall and stately, a person with presence. "He's not at all what I pictured," I said to Laurie as we inched along in a receiving line. He was lean and trim; however, he stood only about five feet six inches tall. The eyes were dark and seedy. The nose was far too big. A crooked, somewhat sardonic grin played upon his forty-seven-year-old face. His hair was dishpan gray. The man was a giant in business but in person resembled a gnome. As we moved closer I thought, It may be unkind, but he's just plain unimpressive.

He was glib and smooth as he pumped hands. He did not know me, but as our eyes met briefly his seemed to say, What can I do for you and what can you do for me?

CHAPTER SEVEN

I MET with David Kay, the debonair, extroverted head of the M&A department at Drexel Burnham Lambert, to discuss the possibility of coming on board. He began with the brash proclamation that Drexel was about to revolutionize the industry. Drexel alone, he said, could now provide enormous amounts of financing to companies that normally would not qualify. This activity emanated not from New York, but from California, from the high-yield and convertible bond department, known informally as the Drexel Bank.

The Beverly Hills office was run by Michael Milken, whose title as a mere senior vice president obscured his importance to the firm; in fact, he owned 8 percent of the company, making him the largest individual shareholder. Milken had maneuvered Drexel into a position unique in the history of investment banking. For the first time, he could offer gargantuan sums of fast cash to medium-sized and even smaller companies and to individual entrepreneurs. All told, the Drexel Bank had as much as $200 billion at its disposal.

But there was a hitch. Kay bemoaned the fact that Drexel, as yet, had very little effective deal-making ability. Drexel's goal was to couple tactical expertise with Milken's financial muscle. I would be the strategist and tactician, the man whose assignment was to figure out how best to bring a deal to completion. Kay was also aware of my rainmaker reputation, and he proclaimed that Drexel needed me to help create deals as well as to close them.

It sounded appealing, but I wondered if this new kid on the block could realize his ambitious dreams. Drexel was poised to leap over the old-line companies and become the new power in investment banking, but would it succeed? Should I cast my lot with the upstart or with the venerable powers that be? It was a tough call, and I wavered.

Kay introduced me to Frederick H. Joseph, Drexel's head of corporate finance. The son of a cabdriver from the tough Roxbury section of Boston, he had risen from those humble beginnings to study Shakespeare at Harvard. He was a sandy-haired man, forty-seven years old, with a straightforward, self-assured style. Despite his high-level position, he maintained his desk in the middle of the corporate finance bull pen; he wanted to be out with the troops. Joseph casually propped one leg over an arm of his chair and told me that his slogan was Ready, fire, aim! I liked him immediately.

"Excuse me," Joseph said, responding to a buzz from his phone only a few minutes into our discussion. "Michael's on the phone."

I backed off, idly watching the activity in the bull pen as Joseph conversed with Milken, in California. A deal was obviously pending, but Joseph kept his end of the discussion discreet.

When we resumed our talk, Joseph extricated a page of paper from his wallet and unfolded it meticulously, displaying it. It was a typed summary of Drexel's revenues and profits for the past five years, and it revealed exponential growth. The M&A craze continued to accelerate: Standard Oil of California paid $13.4 billion for Gulf; Texaco acquired Getty Oil for $10.1 billion. The numbers were growing ever larger, and who, Joseph asked rhetorically, had the money? Drexel was increasing its market share by dramatic proportions each year, cutting into the profits of the old-line firms. The bare numbers proved that this was an awesome financial machine, fueled by Milken's fund-raising abilities. "With people like you coming in," Joseph declared, "we're going to be able to continue this trend."

After Joseph and I concluded our conversation, I met several other senior bankers in the firm. I found myself impressed with their knowledge and ambition; the atmosphere here was supercharged. We had several additional meetings. I was close to making a decision, but I wanted to wait until the end of the year, when I received my annual bonus from Lehman Brothers. Absolutely no one on the Street announces a career move until his bonus check has cleared the bank.

Bob Wilkis told me that he had cultivated a new source, "a kid," working as an M&A analyst at Lazard Frères. Wilkis had seen hunger in the young man's eyes and had quietly and carefully offered him the same sort of deal that I had struck with Ilan Reich and Ira Sokolow. All that the "kid" had to do was provide information; Wilkis would stake him to a share in his own private account.

At Lehman Brothers, the powers that be were increasingly impressed with my string of successful transactions. I wondered whether they had also gained inside information concerning my round of job interviews. Whatever the reasons, someone had realized that the firm was going to have to resort to extraordinary means to stem an exodus of key personnel. Lehman Brothers informed me that my annual bonus check would be in excess of $500,000, more than five times the amount they had guaranteed me. They also promised to promote me from senior vice president to managing director.

But it was not enough. I had seen the future, and it was Drexel.

OVER lunch the mercurial Ilan Reich told me that he was now in line to become a partner, and I, in turn, told him that I was seriously considering moving over to Drexel. After lunch, as we walked along the sidewalk, Reich announced that he was once again going to withdraw from participation in our clandestine activities.

"Okay," I said. "Do what you have to do. You've got about four hundred thousand dollars in the account now. Do you want any of it?"

"No," Reich said.

I repeated what I had said the first time he pulled back: "Anytime you want it, it's yours."

I was now sure that Reich was out for good, but that was all right. In the back of my mind I believed I would stop someday also. I considered Reich to be a superb attorney, and I wished him well.

FINALLY the work was completed on our new home. Contractors had smashed down the old walls and restructured the rooms to our specifications; some of the walls included decorative archways. A glass-block wall separated the dining room from a bedroom, and the marble-walled master bath included a Jacuzzi. The living-room and dining-room floors were covered with bleached oak.

We moved into our Park Avenue apartment in December 1984.

BEFORE making a final decision on whether or not to jump to Drexel, there was one thing I had to do. I said to Fred Joseph, "I'm interested, and I might come on board. But I want to meet Milken."

"Well, that's a little unusual," Joseph replied.

"Unusual or not, I don't come to Drexel until I talk to him."

"He's very busy. Maybe we can get you fifteen minutes with him."

"Okay," I agreed. "I'll go out to Beverly Hills to meet him, and while I'm there, I'd like to meet the corporate finance people."

Laurie and I flew to California for an extended New Year's weekend, coupling my Drexel interview with a visit to my brother Larry in Orange County and a brief vacation at La Costa spa. When we arrived in Beverly Hills, we checked into the Bel-Air Hotel and rented a car.

Drexel's office was located at the corner of Rodeo Drive and Wilshire Boulevard, which is about as good an address as you can get. I knew that Milken himself owned the four-story glass-and-polished-granite office building and leased most of it back to Drexel. Here, in the predawn hours of Friday, January 4, I met with John Kissick, who headed corporate finance. "We need people like you," he said.

Kissick took me around to shake the hands of various individuals, who greeted me effusively, with comments such as "What can we do for you?" and "Is everything okay?" All were bent on selling Drexel to me, and I was pleased and flattered by the attention.

Kissick then ushered me into an elevator, and we rode down. When the door opened, we stepped into a foyer and faced a tough-looking security guard who resembled a New York Giants linebacker. He nodded when he saw Kissick and passed us through into the inner sanctum of the trading area. Kissick explained that over the years Milken had grown ever more security conscious. He was making waves in the business world, facing down the big boys. Who knew what measures a desperate foe might take? During business hours Milken never went anywhere, Kissick said, without his guards.

Kissick took me to a small conference room and told me that Milken would meet with me in a few minutes. There was an air of anticipation.

MANY people in the business referred to him simply as the king. No one had ever seen anybody like him.

Michael Robert Milken was a curious and unique combination of a '60s flower child and a modern-day business hotshot—he was politically and financially liberal, yet conservative in his personal life. Rumor held that Milken's income was the highest on Wall Street. He had been married for seventeen years to his wife, Lori; images of his children—twelve-year-old Gregory, nine-year-old Lance and four-year-old Bari—decorated his desk. He disdained alcohol, tobacco, caffeine, carbonated beverages and profanity.

Milken had enrolled at the University of California at Berkeley in 1964, when that school was the philosophical launchpad of the anti-Establishment generation. While there he declared that he had chosen Wall Street as "my battleground" for improving society. His theories of finance were particularly influenced by an esoteric multi-volume study of bond performance from 1900 to 1943, W. Braddock Hickman's *Corporate Bond Quality and Investor Experience.* Hickman concluded that a portfolio of low-rated, high-yield bonds, if held over a long period of time, generated greater revenues than a comparable portfolio of highly rated bonds, although the low-rated bonds did, indeed, exhibit a greater default rate.

After graduation from Berkeley (where he was elected to Phi Beta Kappa), in 1968, Milken married Lori and headed for Philadelphia and the Wharton School of Business. He began his own analysis of low-rated bonds and concluded, contrary to traditional wisdom, that many of the issuing corporations were better credit risks than perceived.

He joined the Philadelphia office of Drexel in 1970, and in 1973 he was assigned to head Drexel's New York Wall Street department that specialized in non-investment-grade securities, also known as high-yield bonds, or junk bonds. His compensation agreement, providing that as much as 35 percent of the department's annual profits be placed into a year-end bonus pool, remained in force over the years as Milken turned the high-yield and convertible bond department into a booming concern. The ever growing bonuses tied employees to Drexel, and Milken cemented the relationships further by bringing employees in as partners in lucrative sideline investments and partnership arrangements, known as golden handcuffs.

Through the early years of the '70s, stock prices had been in an extended slide; all told, the equity value of American corporations was eroded by about 40 percent. Banks became ever more selective in their lending practices. Only a handful of America's elite companies had access to large-scale financing on the most favorable terms, and this ruffled Milken's innate sense of fair play. He counted less than 800 U.S. corporations that received an investment-grade rating for their bonds. Any bond classified lower than BBB by Standard & Poor or Ba by Moody was lumped into a category known as speculative grade.

Milken saw basic inequities. It was the old binary concept. A bond was good or bad, and there was no gray area in between. What's more, the bond-rating companies factored a company's size into the equation, as if big meant good and small meant bad. The predictable result was that only the largest and oldest firms, more or less the *Fortune* 500, qualified for an investment-grade rating and were "allowed" to raise billions of dollars via the sale of new bonds. Portfolio managers were prevented by their own criteria from investing in speculative-grade bonds.

Where did that leave the well-run but smaller companies? What about the 22,000 U.S. corporations that did not belong to the club?

Milken concentrated on selling bonds that paid 3 percent to 5 percent above the prevailing U.S. Treasury bond rate. Over time his customers came to the happy realization that these high-yield bonds exhibited a surprisingly low default ratio. These were not junk bonds, Milken argued, but bargain bonds. High-yield bonds brought about twice the profits available from AAA corporate bonds, and yet the default rate was less than 2 percent.

In the past no bond began life with a low rating. New bonds were issued almost exclusively by the elite companies and became speculative grade only when those companies ran into financial difficulty. But in 1977 Lehman Brothers and Goldman Sachs underwrote the first new bond issue *conceived* as junk; it produced $75 million for LTV Corporation.

Now the way was clear for an investment banking firm to underwrite issues of high-risk, high-yield bonds. If a medium-sized firm or even a new venture was confident enough in its business projections, it would be willing to offer investors a premium rate of interest, if it had to, in order to gain access to capital.

Thousands of companies were so eager for cash that they readily agreed to pay a premium not only to investors but to the investment banker. The sale of investment-grade bonds generally brought a commission of 0.875 percent of face value. But when Milken discovered that he could get 2 percent, 3 percent, or even 4 percent commission, the onslaught began. He established a trading floor where anyone could buy or sell high-yield bonds via a quick phone call or Telex. He promoted the establishment of mutual funds dedicated to these new investment vehicles, to tap into the money of the masses.

The high-yield bond, a Drexel publication proclaimed, was "a financial instrument whose time has come." Drexel's client list soon included corporate names associated with fiscal integrity—Prudential, Equitable, Fidelity, Kemper.

In the summer of 1978, when Milken learned that his father was stricken with terminal cancer, he had persuaded Drexel to allow him to move the entire department to California so that he could be close to his family. It was an unprecedented decision to forsake Wall Street, and Drexel's approval was a clear measure of Milken's value to the firm; about twenty of the department's professional staff members relocated. Milken hired his younger brother, Lowell, an attorney, to manage corporate and personal assets, with an eye toward tax savings.

In 1978 a total of $1.5 billion worth of junk bonds were issued, and the beginnings of a trend were apparent. The next ingredient was supplied in 1981 by Leon Black, of Drexel's corporate finance department, who hit upon using junk-bond issues to finance LBOs and other acquisitions. Thus emerged the corporate raider, who no longer had to wrestle with the often slow, always finicky bankers. If he needed big cash fast, he could come to the Drexel Bank.

In 1982 the U.S. Congress deregulated the savings and loan industry and allowed thrifts to invest in corporate-debt securities. Suddenly there was $1 trillion worth of S&L money ripe for the picking. By the end of 1983 the total sale of new junk-bond issues had risen to $7.3 billion, and Drexel was responsible for nearly 65 percent of it. Drexel's July offering of $1 billion worth of high-yield bonds for MCI Communications enabled the upstart firm to carry on its epic struggle with AT&T for control of the nation's long-distance telephone lines. Milken was able, like no one before him, to arm David for a battle with Goliath.

Milken's success had snowballed to the point where he was not only the greatest marketer of junk bonds, he was also one of the largest customers. His personal trading account held more than $100 million, and he had woven a complex web of partnerships, not only with key associates but also with outside entrepreneurs.

He and his brother, Lowell, had established the Milken Family Foundation, which had grown into a cluster of charitable organizations. He was reported to have donated more than $350 million to these foundations, which, in turn, passed the money on to worldwide social service agencies, with emphasis on programs in education, health, medical research, human welfare and community services.

But it was business for which he was known, and he had transformed Drexel into something special. At Drexel, Milken's high-yield and convertible bond department was the engine that drove the train. Its power could easily be measured in one simple statistic. In 1978 there were twenty-five employees in Drexel's Beverly Hills office. Now there were more than 200.

SHORTLY before seven a.m. Milken strode into the conference room and greeted me cordially. He was jacketless and thus appeared to be in an all-business mode, which was a true picture. He was just shy of his fortieth birthday, slim built, and the sharp features of his elongated, steel-jawed face were reminiscent of actor Ted Danson's.

He made direct eye contact as he pumped my hand.

Milken knew what I—and any other job candidate—would want to see first, so he drew me forward, toward the trading floor, and waved his hand to display the setup. Computer screens, keyboards and phone lines littered the floor space. Market makers sat at small stations along four long rows of desks shaped into a huge letter X. They held phones in either hand, shouting out buy and sell orders, quoting prices, tossing wads of paper at other traders to get their attention. In the midst of this barely controlled mayhem was Milken's chair, offering a view of everyone. This was a war room. Every trader here would be judged on the basis of his or her sales figures. There was no room here for the laid-back easy sell.

Milken introduced me to Jim Dahl, one of his top salesmen, but there was no time for anything but a brief amenity. In an instant Dahl was back on the phone dealing, dealing, dealing! On any given day the department's trading position approached $4 billion.

Someone ran up chattering, "Michael, what do I do about this?"

He turned from me and devoted his full attention to the task of the instant. Do this, do this, do *that,* he commanded with cool confidence.

Then he glanced briefly at his desk and surveyed a gargantuan sheaf of telephone messages—he took more than 200 calls every day—before he returned his attention to me. Despite the sense of urgency that enveloped us, he took a few moments to straighten the stack of message slips and otherwise place his desk in order.

After he ushered me back into the conference room, he said earnestly, "Fred wants you at Drexel. We've heard wonderful things—"

Suddenly the conference room door flew open, and a young wild-eyed man screamed, "Michael, Occidental just announced!"

"Get me bodies!" Milken shouted, and through the open door I could see the electricity level of the trading room skyrocket.

Milken turned back to me. He was obviously stunned and trying to think of a thousand strategies at once. He said quickly but quietly, "Excuse me. I have to get on top of this."

"I understand," I replied. The Dow Jones tape had just broken the news that Diamond Shamrock was in merger discussions with Occidental Petroleum; a $3 billion deal was in the offing, and naturally teams from First Boston, Morgan Stanley, Kidder Peabody, Salomon Brothers and other investment banking houses were marshaling their forces. Everyone wanted in on the deal. I already knew that Lehman Brothers had the Diamond Shamrock account.

"I hope we can have a few minutes to speak later this afternoon," Milken said.

"It would be my pleasure," I replied.

Then he was gone. Within minutes he had Armand Hammer on the phone, and within a few more minutes he had piled his "bodies" into a special chauffeured van loaded with deal-maker's paraphernalia.

As the van headed for Hammer's office at Occidental, Peter Ackerman, executive vice president of the division, resumed the task of selling Drexel to me. Smooth, confident, articulate, he explained that Drexel was a cult of relative youngsters with a "we try harder" attitude. I simply would not find a higher level of esprit de corps anywhere in the business. The firm had assembled a cadre of talented, aggressive individuals and kept them loyal by paying them well and treating them as important parts of a whole. This was a firm of rebels, shaking Wall Street and all of corporate America.

Others spoke with me and preached that the offer of a high-level Drexel job was akin to stumbling upon a pot of gold. Quite apart from the salary and the annual bonus, they said, was the matrix of private investment partnerships that would be offered along the way.

"Within two or three years," John Kissick predicted, "you will have personal investments worth at least ten million dollars."

It was two p.m. when Milken reappeared and declared that he had fifteen minutes for me.

The promised quarter hour turned into a three-hour discussion as Milken spoke with fervor about the rosy future of the takeover business. We discussed the Pickens versus Gulf deal and how he had raised nearly $2 billion and changed the rules of the M&A game. He flashed evidence of an incredible memory for detail. He possessed an almost clairvoyant grasp of the broad strokes of the business. His comprehension of the intricacies and possibilities of financing was on an intellectually higher plane—far higher—than anyone I had ever met. Even so, I could see that he did not possess a strong sense of the technical and political aspects of handling a merger. That was not his field; he needed me, or others like me, for that.

I pointed out that despite his success in securing money for Pickens, the deal had fizzled.

"It's your type of skill we need," Milken acknowledged. "We need people who know how to do good deals and how to close them."

I spoke at length about my own developing philosophies. The ability to close deals, I said, is the essence of modern high-level investment banking, requiring equal doses of financial acumen and psychoanalytic finesse. The other players in these high-stakes games have *enormous* egos, and it is the investment banker's job to subordinate his own feelings. Only then can you balance the interests of the managers, the directors, the shareholders, the banks, the lawyers and the other investment bankers—and still manage to stay three jumps ahead of them all. "That's what clients pay for," I said. "They pay for negotiating skill and judgment that transcends anything that the business schools teach. They pay for instinct."

Milken grinned when I confessed that at night, visions of white knights rode through my brain, often precluding sleep.

"If I come on board," I said, "I'm going to take a firm position. We've got to make sure that our clients actually merge and acquire."

Milken again nodded his agreement, and then he spoke, with fire in his eyes, of how Drexel had already transformed the world of finance and how it would, in the future, alter the existence of perhaps every man, woman and child on the face of the earth. The world needed capital. Money could feed the hungry, clothe the naked, house the homeless. Milken was determined to carry his gospel to Japan, Germany, the other industrialized nations and, ultimately, to where it was needed most, the Third World.

It could happen, he said. It will happen.

When I left that day, I knew I was going to Drexel. I *had* to.

CHAPTER EIGHT

O N FEBRUARY 4, 1985, at the age of thirty-two, I joined Drexel
Burnham Lambert as a managing director—the equivalent
of partner. My annual salary was $140,000, but that was only
the tip of the iceberg. Almost immediately Drexel authorized a
$200,000 advance to me from the corporate finance bonus pool. I
was, in fact, guaranteed a minimum annual bonus of $750,000.
Drexel operated on the assumption that owner-employees were the
most loyal, and they issued me 1000 shares of Drexel common stock,
worth about $100,000. I purchased another 2000 shares. Fred Joseph
told me that I would be invited to participate in various co-investment
programs available to senior executives; they were putting on the
golden handcuffs right from the start.

This all went far beyond my early fantasies of a career on Wall
Street, and it sent my head spinning.

My new office was on the eighth floor of 55 Broad Street, across
from company headquarters and a football field away from the New
York Stock Exchange. There was little time to acclimate myself, however. On my second morning Joseph said to me, "I'd like you to get
involved in this deal—see how we operate." It was Carl Icahn's attempt to take control of Phillips Petroleum Company. I had to pick
up the history of the deal very quickly.

The drama had begun the previous year. Having failed to acquire
Gulf Oil, T. Boone Pickens had trained his attention upon Phillips
and its $13 billion in corporate assets. When word of the possible
assault hit the Street, speculators naturally plunged, buying up Phillips stock in enormous chunks. The arb who accumulated the strongest position was Ivan Boesky.

Over the past few years Boesky had developed a working relationship with Milken. In September 1983, for example, Drexel, through
Milken's office, underwrote a $100 million public offering of high-
yield debt to capitalize Boesky's subsidiary, Vagabond Hotels. In
January 1984 Milken purchased a block of nonvoting shares in
Boesky's Seemala Corporation. But their latest deal had run into
snags. Boesky wanted to arrange a financial restructuring of his

company that would provide him with $660 million worth of fresh capital. The closing had been delayed, partly because of objections from Drexel's underwriting assistance committee, which balked at the idea of putting fresh capital into the hands of the notorious arb. Some raised a conflict-of-interest objection; as part of its fee for conjuring the capital, Drexel was to receive an equity interest in Boesky's arbitrage firm. Normally Boesky would in turn use that capital to bet on the outcome of Drexel's deals. If he guessed correctly, Drexel would gain a percentage of the profits. It was incestuous at best.

On the surface there was little reason for the two men to become business allies. On the whole, Boesky traded stocks; Milken traded bonds. But each was the major player in his field. It was undoubtedly galling to Milken and his competitive drive that Boesky took much of his business elsewhere. Milken wanted it all, and that included the significant chunk in Boesky's pocket.

Having accumulated 3.7 million shares of Phillips for about $49 per share, Boesky was one of the most interested spectators in the Pickens-Phillips negotiations. Everything looked good for him when Pickens' firm, Mesa Petroleum, commenced a tender offer for Phillips; the price of $60 per share would allow Boesky to turn a profit of more than $40 million. Feeling confident, Boesky increased his holdings to a total of 5.87 million shares, paying ever higher prices.

Boesky, I learned, happened to be vacationing in Barbados on the evening of December 23, 1984, when an aide informed him by phone that Pickens had reached an agreement with the Phillips board and its chairman, William C. Douce, turning a potentially hostile takeover into a friendly restructuring. Phillips proposed a recapitalization plan, and Pickens agreed to call off his tender offer. If the plan was approved at an upcoming special shareholders' meeting, Pickens would receive a minimum of $53 per share for his holdings in Phillips.

Boesky, who had continued to buy near the $60 level, was understandably upset. He flew to New York, but the market was already open by the time he arrived, and Phillips stock was down ten points. If Boesky sold now he stood to realize a loss of about $25 million. Instead, he decided to hang tough. He descended upon his friends at Drexel, raging that the price was too low, demanding that they hunt for another buyer who would pay more.

Drexel obligingly hounded its list of clients and found one who was willing to play. He was Carl Icahn, who through his Icahn Group, Inc. authorized Drexel to buy blocks of Phillips stock at the current, somewhat depressed, price.

Late in January, 1985, Icahn decided to make a takeover bid for Phillips. To strengthen his position, he bought 2.74 million shares from Boesky at a price of about $47 per share. It may have been an interesting gambit on Boesky's part, selling a portion of his stock low to aid a takeover bid that would enable him to sell the remainder high.

The very day I came on board, Icahn wrote to Phillips announcing his interest in acquiring 100 percent of the company's stock at $55 per share, payable half in cash and half in the form of a subordinated note. It was my job to help follow through on the details.

I teamed with my new colleagues Leon Black, head of the leveraged buyout department, and John Sorte, who headed the petroleum department. They introduced me to the incredibly intense Icahn. He was a former options trader whose private passion was gambling; it was said that he enjoyed playing Monopoly for real money. But it was also said that he was tightfisted and known for a hot temper.

Almost before I could take a breath, things turned ugly between Icahn and his target. The Phillips board issued a public statement on February 6 rejecting Icahn's friendly proposal. It was to be war.

Both Black and Sorte were good men, but they reflected Drexel's lack of experience in mergers. I argued that we had to persuade Icahn to shift toward an all-cash offer. To my relief, Icahn understood how important this would be to shareholders. He exhibited a pillow inscribed with the motto Happiness is a positive cash flow.

All of us were willing learners. Black and Sorte had much to teach me about raising capital at Drexel, and I, making delicate suggestions, showed them how to handle a thousand details, how to work with Icahn's staff, how to draft the language of press releases, how to coordinate with Icahn's special counsel, Arthur Liman.

Having come from Lehman Brothers, where the M&A people almost never spoke with the traders, I was taken aback by the volume of calls I got from people in Beverly Hills seeking details on the progress of the deal. These were people who had no "need to know," and I tried to give only routine information. My concerns were compounded as I received calls from arbs and other information seekers saying, "I heard this from your Beverly Hills office."

One day my secretary buzzed and announced that Ivan Boesky was on the phone. I picked up and heard a voice say, "Mr. Levine, this is Ivan Boesky calling. I understand from one of your partners that you are handling the Phillips thing for Carl."

"Yes."

"What can you tell me?"

Wall Street's most famous arb, I knew, still held a huge position in Phillips and was extremely nervous. I provided him with routine, public-record details. Boesky thanked me and hung up. I knew that he would immediately dial another number, seeking yet more data.

On February 13 we commenced the tender offer to buy 70 million shares—about 45 percent—of Phillips common stock at $60 per share, to be paid in cash. It was conditional upon the shareholders rejecting the recapitalization program already proposed, but Icahn was confident that they would see things his way, since they stood to gain about $7 per share. To cover the costs and expenses associated with the deal, Icahn estimated that he needed to raise $4.05 billion.

Now Drexel unleashed its secret weapon, an idea that evolved from the collective consciousness of all of us who were involved in the planning. Over the past two years Drexel had polished its abilities to obtain blind financing commitments. A borrower would agree to purchase perhaps $10 million worth of an upcoming junk-bond issue simply because Milken advised that it would be a good investment.

In the traditional deal a corporate raider had to have his money in hand before he could initiate a tender offer, but Milken realized that it did not have to be so. If the deal fell through, the raider did not need the money, so why not make the financing contingent upon the consummation of the deal? There was no law that said the money had to be assembled; the only issue was whether or not the shareholders believed that the money could and would be there. And in the current market the words money and Milken were becoming synonymous. The money could be there at the wave of Milken's hand.

Realizing this, Drexel now unilaterally made a fundamental change in the procedures of the M&A business. Milken devised a simple letter, which he unveiled in the Phillips tender offer. "Based on current conditions," Milken wrote, "[Drexel] . . . is highly confident that it can arrange the necessary financing commitments." That was it—a simple pledge offered by the wizard of Beverly Hills. It was the first-ever tender offer for which the financing was not yet in place.

When Phillips' management questioned this unheard-of tactic, Icahn responded, "Drexel's ability to raise financing is well established." If Milken was highly confident, so was everyone else on the Street.

Nobody could quite believe the simple, clever solution. In all, we proposed to raise $2 billion in floating-rate senior notes, $2 billion in senior subordinated debentures, and $600 million in preferred stock— and everyone was willing to take Milken at his word. We did not even have to enlist the aid of a bank to swing the senior financing. For starters, Icahn paid Drexel a $1 million fee. He further agreed to pay a 2 percent commission on the financing package of $4.6 billion.

The "highly confident" letter set Wall Street on its ear.

THE Phillips board launched a desperate media campaign against Icahn, but the campaign did not fly with the vast majority of share-holders. The board had no choice but to meet us at the negotiating table. On March 4, with the company's investment bankers from Morgan Stanley and a bevy of lawyers, we hammered out a revised plan. Icahn agreed to withdraw his tender offer. Phillips agreed to pay $25 million to "cover his expenses," and also to offer all share-holders the chance to redeem their stock for a package of securities worth $62 a share. Icahn had raised the value of the stock by $9 per share, assuring himself and Boesky of astronomical profits.

Other winners were those investors upon whom Milken was "highly confident," to whom Ichan paid $5,625,000 in commitment fees.

The newsletter *Corporate Control Alert* concluded that Drexel's per-formance for Icahn "has given credibility to its claims that it can finance almost anything."

ANOTHER big deal occurred simultaneously.

I was in John Sorte's office when he took a phone call from David Arledge, senior vice president for finance of Coastal Corporation, a major oil and gas exploration company, in Houston. Coastal was ready to go ahead with plans for a tender offer for American Natural Resources Company. Coastal had a market value of about $450 mil-lion, whereas ANR's market value was four times larger. Yet Arledge wanted Drexel to arrange $600 million of financing. Sorte, picking up quickly on Milken's new catchphrase, responded that he was "highly confident" that the Beverly Hills boys could raise the money both quickly and quietly. He added that Drexel had a new man on board, a specialist in deal-making details. Me.

Sorte briefed me. If the deal flew, it would exceed $2 billion and would bring us much attention.

I studied carefully and was pleased to realize that the numbers crunched in Coastal's favor. Both Coastal and ANR were pipeline companies, and when I mapped out the geographical patterns of their operations, it was obvious that the two systems would mesh perfectly into one larger, far more efficient system. This meant Coastal could afford to offer more for ANR than any other possible buyer.

Together, Milken and I decided that $60 per share was the critical point. If the price approached that level, we believed that the ANR directors would be unable to defend. If we had to, Milken said, we could go $5 per share higher.

Once I had satisfied myself that the deal was viable, I arranged a meeting with Bob Wilkis at lunchtime on a Thursday. As we stood out on the sidewalk after lunch, not far from the New York Stock Exchange, I disclosed, "We're working on a deal for ANR. It looks like it's gonna go."

We parted, and I sought out a pay phone, placed a collect call to Bernhard Meier, at Bank Leu, and instructed him to begin buying stock in ANR, as much as he could without moving the market. I reminded him that I wanted him to spread the purchases among several brokers.

Meier set about executing the trades for me. In the meantime, without telling me, he bought 2000 shares for his own account and persuaded the previously skittish Bruno Pletscher to join him. Pletscher was in for 500 shares.

Twenty-four hours later I was even more confident of the deal. I called Meier again and told him to sink the entire balance of my account, now more than $7 million, into ANR stock.

On Sunday night I met with Arledge and two of Coastal's other senior management officials. We prepared for war. The chairman and C.E.O. of Coastal was Oscar S. Wyatt, Jr., a Texas rancher and oilman. He was one of the more feared takeover artists in the business, but he had compiled a less-than-distinguished track record. When Arledge told me that Wyatt's plan was to announce a tender offer in the mid-50s, I protested that this would be a critical mistake.

"If you want to win, you don't lowball," I argued. "You go in with a winning bid. You go in in the fifties, and you're going to get overbid at sixty—either by a white knight or in an LBO attempt led by ANR management. I've already talked to people on the Street." I disclosed that I had learned that arbs were already buying up ANR stock.

I concluded, "We strongly recommend that you go in at sixty dollars per share. That tells the world you can go higher. But I've talked with our West Coast people, and they don't believe that ANR can put together an LBO at the sixty-dollar level without Drexel to finance it." I also pointed out the need to make the offer an all-cash deal.

Figuratively I kept my fingers crossed throughout this entire lecture. I knew that it was going to take considerable persuasion to get Wyatt to budge from his lowball offer.

FROM Nassau, Meier reported to me that he had acquired a total of 145,000 shares of ANR for my account at an average price of just under $50. All told, I had a whopping $7.2 million at risk. It was virtually my entire portfolio, but it was more than money that I gambled. For the first time, I had made an insider trade based on a deal where I was the senior banker intimately involved in the transaction.

In my consciousness everything was nicely compartmentalized. I saw no conflict between my $60-per-share recommendation and my $50-per-share purchases. My advice to Coastal, I rationalized, was based upon sound business reasoning and would have been the same whether or not I had a personal stake in the matter.

Nonetheless, I was ecstatic when Wyatt finally agreed to my pricing structure. On Friday, March 1, after the market closed, we announced the offer at $60 per share, all cash. On Monday morning ANR stock opened near that price, and I sold out for a profit of $1,370,610. Wilkis, playing more conservatively, made $300,000. Unbeknownst to me, Meier profited nearly $25,000.

The news brought a delicious sense of giddiness, of invulnerability, despite reports from Washington, where the day after I instructed Bank Leu to sell my ANR stock, former deputy defense secretary Paul Thayer and Dallas stockbroker Billy Bob Harris pleaded guilty to charges of giving false testimony and obstructing justice in connection with insider trading activities.

ANR's MANAGEMENT FOUGHT BACK even harder than I had anticipated. Its boys from First Boston tried to fashion a modified LBO, but
as I had predicted, Coastal's bid was just high enough to discourage
serious competition. ANR's only viable choice was to get the most it
could out of Coastal's offer.

Realizing this, my counterpart at Goldman Sachs, ANR's traditional
investment banking firm, reached me by phone and asked, "What's
your number?"

"I think the principals should negotiate," I replied.

Much happened within a matter of days. On March 13 Boesky
disclosed to the SEC that he owned 3.74 million shares of ANR, about
9.9 percent of the company. I found it interesting to learn that he had
begun his buying two weeks prior to the public announcement of our
offer. Obviously he made a lucky guess or he had very good sources
of information. Who, I wondered, might have tipped him?

Also on March 13 the SEC opened an inquiry into the possibility of
insider trading on ANR stock. The NYSE's computerized monitoring
equipment had picked up a pattern of heavy trading before the official
announcement. I was not concerned about the scrutiny, for I knew my
activity paled in comparison to that of Boesky and other arbs.

AFTER a late night of negotiations that Wyatt termed "sincere and
businesslike," he announced that Coastal and ANR had hammered
out a compromise. By raising his price to $65 per share, Wyatt turned
the hostile tender offer into a friendly deal and saved himself considerable headaches, not to mention legal expenses. At $2.46 billion it
stood as the largest successful unsolicited takeover in history wherein
the initial bidder prevailed. I calculated Boesky's profit at about $15
million. Drexel earned a $20 million commission.

SEC investigators made initial checks but discovered insufficient
evidence to pursue charges of insider trading in ANR stock. How can
you prove a contention based upon rumor and innuendo? My confidence in the safeguards Wilkis and I had in place escalated.

THE Regent Air jet, a private Boeing 727, carried me and an army
of Drexel operatives to California in high style. Our destination was
Drexel's seventh annual Institutional Research Conference, known
informally as the Bond Conference or the Predators' Ball. The stated

purpose of the gathering was for bond buyers to mingle with bond issuers. Attendance was by invitation only—Drexel spouses were conspicuously excluded—and if you were there, you knew that you had achieved status in the M&A world.

The four-day affair was timed to occur the week after the Academy Awards. Drexel had booked virtually every room in the pink-and-green Beverly Hills Hotel. When I checked in, one of the clerks remarked, "Gee, we thought the movie people put on a show, but you guys take the cake!" It was an exciting, ironic moment, for I knew that our host, who owned 53 percent of this hotel, was Ivan Boesky.

By five thirty the next morning what seemed like an endless loop of stretch limos (each with a well-stocked bar) began shuttling the movers and shakers of the business world from various hotels to the Beverly Hilton, only a few blocks from Milken's office. In a ballroom of the hotel about 2000 people awaited the opening session of the conference with a high sense of expectation. Here were the money managers and the world's best-known corporate raiders.

At about six thirty a.m. the lights dimmed, and Milken walked on stage. He greeted everyone effusively and presented the first of countless Drexel sales pitches, augmented by slick videos shown on floor-to-ceiling screens. He then presented Dr. Armand Hammer, who responded with brief remarks extolling the virtues of Drexel and Milken.

The keynote speaker was Oscar Wyatt, who detailed the Coastal-ANR deal to an audience that had envy dripping from its collective eye. Every corporate raider in attendance wanted to pull off such a coup, and we all wondered who would be standing up there next year as the man who had just concluded a deal of historic size and significance.

A break followed Wyatt's speech. I was chatting with a few new acquaintances when Milken's voice penetrated my consciousness: "Dennis, come over here." I turned to see him wave. "Come over."

I joined Milken, who was surrounded by an assortment of businessmen, groupies and security guards. "I'd like you to meet Dennis Levine," he said to the crowd. "Dennis just joined us from Lehman Brothers. He was the man who orchestrated the Coastal-ANR deal."

I shook hands with T. Boone Pickens, whose slim, deep-lined face had recently graced the cover of *Time;* Carl Lindner of Cincinnati, one of the richest men in America, whose American Financial Corporation was among Drexel's biggest purchasers of junk bonds; Saul Steinberg, who with Disney's greenmail cash in his pockets was an ever more highly valued Drexel client; Nelson Peltz, relatively unknown until the previous week, when his tiny vending machine company bid $456 million for National Can, backed by Drexel-issued junk bonds; Irwin Jacobs, the tall, dark, broadly built Minneapolis-based raider known as the Liquidator; and Dort Cameron, a former Milken assistant, who managed the Bass Investment Limited Partnership for the Bass brothers of Fort Worth.

"How do you do? How do you do?" I said as I pumped hands. It was heady wine. Here was Milken certifying to the other members of the club that I was "good people." In this milieu Milken was clearly the king of finance, indicating to others that I was to be trusted.

THURSDAY night found me at a champagne function in a pink three-bedroom cottage at the Beverly Hills Hotel. By now this was a famous—or infamous—annual event, the bungalow 8 party. The rank and file among the conference attendees had been shuttled off to a special show at a movie lot; this party, at a remote, private corner of the hotel grounds, was reserved for the one hundred heaviest hitters among Drexel's clientele. Some brought their spouses; others preferred to tap the resources of the multitude of social climbers, parasites and beautiful, elegant young women who seemed to make themselves visibly available.

This conference, this night, this world was unlike anything I had ever witnessed at Smith Barney or Lehman Brothers. I accepted some of the excesses as a necessary evil of the business world. I enjoyed swigging a drink with the best of them, but the overt philandering disgusted and even bored me. If Drexel was going to gain respect as a first-tier firm, I thought, it was going to have to clean up the environment.

The next morning, shortly before the corporate finance breakfast in the Beverly Hills Hotel, I stood at the back of the room surveying the scene. Suddenly I recognized the man next to me. The dreariness of his appearance startled me, as it had during our brief introduction the previous year. Although we had spoken by phone several times, this was only our second personal encounter.

I offered my hand and said, "Hi, Ivan. I'm Dennis Levine."

"Ahhh, how are you?" Boesky asked, pumping my hand effusively, flashing a toothy Cheshire-cat grin.

"Good," I said. "I've enjoyed the meeting." I waved my hand at our elegant surroundings and added, "And I've enjoyed your hotel."

"Let's chat," he suggested. He drew me behind a curtain and congratulated me on both the Phillips Petroleum deal and the Coastal-ANR deal. "I'd like to get together with you in New York," he said. "We've got a lot of things to discuss."

"I'll look forward to it," I replied.

THE Bond Conference traditionally culminated on Friday night, when Drexel booked a major entertainer into the ballroom of the Century Plaza, and the identity of the star was guarded more closely than any stock market secret. Last year's guest was Frank Sinatra.

Inside the ballroom was an atmosphere of tension, as the wealthiest businessmen and businesswomen in the world, attired in their finest, tried not to show what was the primary concern of the evening: Where am I sitting? America's most powerful business tycoons, as evaluated by Milken, sat at the center of the ballroom floor. Those of lesser rank were scattered throughout the remaining space. During dinner I watched in fascination as the deal makers worked the room.

Suddenly, without any introduction, the band struck up a fanfare. Artificial fog billowed across the stage. A slim woman in a glittery evening gown appeared in the haze, microphone in hand, and began to sing, "Ain't No Mountain High Enough." The room burst into applause as an unmistakable voice filled the air.

Diana Ross sang for about forty minutes, interrupting her performance with occasional patter keyed to this unique audience. At one point she exclaimed, "I can't believe how much money is in this room, how much power is here!" The audience erupted with self-congratulatory applause. Then she brought her act into the audience, where she finally settled onto the lap of Carl Lindner and sang to him.

I was one of the last to leave that evening, lingering to prolong the euphoria. The ballroom was nearly deserted by the time Diana Ross emerged from the wings. She was flanked by a bodyguard and by Milken himself. At the moment it was difficult to decide who was the bigger star. Milken escorted her into a limo, and they rode off.

AT DREXEL I WAS IN A FAR BETTER spot than ever to know what was going on inside Wall Street. The same was even more true of Wilkis, who had landed a new job as a first vice president in the M&A department of E. F. Hutton. When Hutton spoke, Wilkis listened— and passed the news on to me.

After Drexel turned down a chance to finance Ted Turner on his plan to raid CBS, Turner scurried to E. F. Hutton. CBS hired Drexel to look at possible defenses. For a time I was perhaps the best-informed spectator on the Street. On the one hand, CBS chief financial officer Fred Meyer called me every day to ask, "What do you hear?" On the other hand, Wilkis kept me apprised of developments at Hutton.

THE April issue of *Business Week* carried a cover story entitled "The Epidemic of Insider Trading." The magazine reported the results of a commissioned study of fluctuations in stock prices prior to public notice of a takeover attempt. It discovered that in the month before an announcement 72 percent of the target stocks rose in price. The magazine declared, "Insider trading is running rampant, despite a major law-enforcement crackdown and toughened penalties."

On the day after that article was published, Wilkis reported to me that his "kid" at Lazard Frères had tipped him that InterNorth, Inc. was set to approve an offer to acquire Houston Natural Gas. Wilkis said, "They're meeting tonight."

I phoned the Bahamas and made my buy quickly, routinely. Meier bought 74,800 shares for my account.

By now Boesky was after me relentlessly, pressing for information on deal after deal. If I brought him in on the deal of the day, his trades would make mine seem comparatively modest. When he called, I found an appropriate moment to drop the tip. "I hear good things about Houston Natural Gas," I said. "If I were you, I'd own that stock."

"How did you get your information?" Boesky asked.

I did not respond. I merely repeated, "I would own the stock."

In the six trading days before the public announcement of the deal, the price of Houston Natural Gas rose by $13.25 per share. I profited $907,655. Boesky, who bought more than 300,000 shares, made more than $4 million.

ON MAY 6 IRA SOKOLOW PHONED ME and suggested lunch. We met at the Palm Too restaurant, at Forty-fifth Street and Second Avenue. Over sirloin steak he alerted me to a big one: RJR, the tobacco company, was in friendly but secret negotiations with Nabisco Brands, Inc. Nabisco had hired Sokolow's firm, Shearson Lehman, as its financial adviser, and it looked like a good deal. That afternoon I bought small holdings in Nabisco, and alerted Wilkis.

CHAPTER NINE

LATE one afternoon Ivan Boesky and I met for cocktails at the Harvard Club. We sat at a corner table in the dimly lit lounge. He took the chair next to the wall so that he could see who else was there. We both ordered Perrier.

During an otherwise forgettable conversation he dropped a bombshell. He said, "You have excellent information, Dennis. You always seem to know what's going on. You are also very discreet. This could all be very useful to me, very helpful, and I feel that you should be compensated for this information."

It was difficult to maintain the veneer of gentility. Inside I was flabbergasted that he would so expose himself to a relative stranger.

I already had one secret life going, and I did not need another. The purpose of my relationship with Boesky was information and not money. "That's completely unnecessary," I replied, "and I'm shocked that you would make such an offer. We have a wonderful relationship. I'm already well paid. I'm just not interested."

For a few moments we stared into one another's eyes, and I wondered how many of my secrets he could discern. He suggested, "Let's think about it logically."

"First of all," I countered, "I would never want any record of you paying me any money for anything. Second, I would never give you information about Drexel deals—any deals that I'm involved with."

"Yes," Boesky said, "but you have knowledge about many things beyond Drexel deals, and I'd be willing to pay you for that other knowledge. As to *how* I could pay you, well, that could be done through foreign bank accounts or through the transfer of shares in foreign companies. It could be done in cash."

I asked an obvious question. "You've done this before?"

"I can't talk about what I do and don't do. Ours would be a very special relationship that no one else would know about. We could work out a formula for me to pay you."

It was clear that Boesky had thought through this entire proposal, but I wanted no part of it. I waved my hand and said, "Ivan, I don't think this is worth exploring." He changed the subject, and within a few moments it was as if the conversation had never occurred. Yet with his proposal Boesky had crossed the line.

My brain was bombarded with stimuli. At the office, deals and potential deals flew about at the speed of light. If I dared arrive at my desk a few minutes past eight a.m., there was likely to be a small stack of messages from Milken and his Beverly Hills crew.

I loved it. This is where I had always wanted to be. This is what I had always wanted to do.

Two, three or four times a day Boesky called. On each occasion he had a specific query, but the larger question remained unspoken.

It was difficult to find time to slip away, but when I could, I checked with Wilkis and Sokolow. Drexel accorded me the privilege of a private phone line, and I gave the number to Wilkis and Sokolow, but not to Boesky—not even to Milken—not even to Laurie. When I heard that phone ring, it sounded like the ding of a cash register.

Throughout the month, as Sokolow briefed me on the Nabisco negotiations, I called the Bahamas to increase my position. By mid-May I owned 150,000 shares, with a whopping $9.2 million tied up.

By now it was routine for Meier and Pletscher, too, to piggyback my trades without my knowledge.

The more I pondered, the more I wondered why I had been so reluctant to accept Boesky's offer. If he was going to make a fortune off my information, why shouldn't I enjoy a slice of his pie? After all, I would never disclose Drexel deals to him. I was more receptive when during a meeting in his office he again raised the subject.

Displaying confidence that I would come to my senses, he described his formula: "If the information you give me is new, I will pay you five percent of any profits from the transaction. If I make a hundred million dollars on the deal, you make five million dollars. No risk to you. No questions asked." If I gave him information that merely corroborated his previous knowledge, he would pay me 1 percent. On the scale on which he dealt, that could still be considerable money.

The plan did not seem to entail any additional exposure on my part, but I laid down specific ground rules: we would use foreign bank accounts to exchange money, and no third party was to be involved, ever. He readily agreed to this and also said he would provide me with access to his trading records whenever I wanted to see them. This was acceptable; he could not skim profits on me.

He grinned and offered his hand. "We have a deal."

It was only a few days later that we put the new arrangement to its first test. I called Boesky to arrange a meeting, and he suggested that we rendezvous in the lobby of the Waldorf-Astoria.

There, as we walked a plush-carpeted hallway, I disclosed, "Nabisco would be an interesting stock to start accumulating a position in." His eyes lit up. I did not reveal the source of my information nor did he bother to ask. That afternoon he began to buy Nabisco.

At the end of a week Boesky had amassed 377,000 shares, at a cost of more than $25 million. But he went beyond that, employing a crafty strategy—purchasing positions in General Foods and Kraft as well. It was insurance. Boesky explained to me that if he was ever questioned as to why he had bought Nabisco before the deal was announced, he could simply say that it was one of many acquisitions he made because he believed in foods as a group.

On May 29 RJR and Nabisco announced merger talks. Throughout the morning, as I attempted to concentrate on other business, I kept one eye glued to the Quotron. Suddenly the stock popped. Nabisco opened a full $18 per share higher than its previous close.

Within seconds Boesky was on the phone, laughing as he said, "We did very well." He saw the potential for a third-party bidder and an even greater run-up, and he announced that he was going to buy more. I had just hung up when my private line rang. It was Wilkis, exhibiting the same exultant glee. Sokolow called, too, barely able, in his excitement, to speak.

Keep the grin off your face, Dennis, I said. Anybody might pop into your office.

What should I do now? I wondered. Should I hold the stock and bank on Boesky's being right? Or should I take my profits and be satisfied? Suddenly I slapped myself on the brow. Boesky and the other arbs were buying. It was the perfect time to sell!

"Back in a few minutes," I said to Marilyn, my secretary.

I raced onto the street, hunted up a phone booth, called Meier and sold out for $2,694,421—my largest trading profit ever. I was on an adrenaline high. This is beautiful, I thought. This could go on forever.

TROUBLE suddenly erupted in my private life. Laurie's mother called from Miami with the news that Laurie's dad, Leonard Skolnik, had been diagnosed with cancer of the esophagus. Doctors gave him six months to live.

I was crushed. Laurie's dad and I had grown very close. He was a man of tremendous energy, with a ribald sense of humor.

Laurie sobbed and said, "Dad always promised me he would live to be a hundred."

I sprang into action. I called my in-laws back and said, "Come up here and see some real doctors. I'll get you set up with the best in New York. We'll get other opinions. Don't give up."

Laurie and I scurried about getting her father to the top specialists. Ultimately we heard the bittersweet prognosis that a team of surgeons at Mount Sinai Hospital believed they could extend his life with radical surgery. They removed half of his esophagus and portions of his stomach, and he remained in intensive care for a prolonged period. We all pulled for Dad, but it was a difficult, wrenching time. My business activities should have paled in importance. Still, if I worked less than eighty hours a week, I felt as if I were stealing time.

The drama with Laurie's dad made me think of my own father more and appreciate all that he had done for me. As Father's Day approached, I decided to do something special for him. I asked him what his fantasy car was. Without hesitation he replied, "A Jaguar XJ six." I bought him a spanking-new one, shiny black.

OFTEN now our home phone rang before six a.m. Laurie, rubbing sleep from her eyes, would answer, hand me the receiver and grimace as she said, "It's Ivan."

More and more Boesky became an unrelenting intruder, calling me a dozen times a day—from his office, from his home, from a phone in his limo, from a private rented plane—tracking me down. He was an indefatigable and pesky spider whose web grew ever stickier, and once I had crossed the line, I was hopelessly entangled.

Everything intensified when my superiors at Drexel asked me to handle Boesky's corporate finance business. Boesky was ready to take the next step on the ladder. Instead of merely speculating on takeovers, he wanted to become a takeover artist himself. He felt that he was in position to become the new entrepreneur on the block.

This was also in line with my own burgeoning fantasies. I, too, could acquire a corporation and use that as a start to mold my very own, and very substantial, business empire. Why not? I was earning multimillions of dollars for my clients. I knew how to create wealth and value. Why shouldn't I have a chance at the really big money?

Boesky surprised me one day with a copy of his book, *Merger Mania*, hot off the presses. It was inscribed: "To one of the most creative investment bankers I know. I.B."

THE billion-dollar-per-year conglomerate Revlon Cosmetics was run by its president and C.E.O., Michel C. Bergerac, an imperious, urbane businessman of French descent. Although Bergerac had been successful with the firm in its early years, many observers felt that now Revlon had stagnated. By making acquisitions and focusing its attention on subsidiaries, Revlon had lost dominance in its primary business—consumer cosmetics. The malaise had caused Revlon's stock to languish in the mid-30s, considerably below its breakup value.

This fact, in the milieu of the '80s, was of considerable interest to anyone in the M&A business. The presence of the subsidiary businesses was intriguing; each was a distinct entity likely to be of interest to another purchaser. They included Ethical Pharmaceuticals, Diagnostic, Vision Care, and International Beauty. Anyone who bought Revlon could probably sell off many of these subsidiaries in order to pay back all or most of the purchase price. The situation was ripe for someone to step in and acquire Revlon through an LBO.

Drexel first identified Revlon as a takeover target for the Frates Group, but the deal fizzled. A similar probe by another investor also fell flat. Part of the problem was that Revlon had set up certain safeguards—known as shark repellents—to protect itself against a hostile bid. If an outside entity took control, Bergerac was guaranteed a $20 million golden parachute. The board had denied shareholders the right to call special meetings. Directors could be removed only if 80 percent of shareholder votes approved.

All in all, Revlon had been shopped to death by us and others. Still, it had an unusual mix of businesses that were attractive. One day David Kay came to me and said, "Why don't you go with the team that's going to talk to Ron Perelman about Revlon?"

Ronald Owen Perelman was a forty-two-year-old raider operating perhaps in the high minor leagues. He had parlayed a $2 million investment in the jewelry distribution firm of Cohen-Hatfield Industries into an ever growing empire. Through Cohen-Hatfield he bought MacAndrews & Forbes Holdings, Inc., whose primary business was licorice. Now he was chairman of the board, C.E.O. and, in fact, the sole shareholder of MacAndrews & Forbes, which in turn owned Consolidated Cigar Company, Video Corporation of America and Technicolor. Some of my associates at Lehman Brothers had become acquainted with him when they represented the Pantry Pride supermarket chain, Perelman's most recent acquisition. Perhaps now he dreamed of what he would do with the $750 million that Milken was in the process of raising for Pantry Pride, Inc. through an issue of debt securities and preferred stock. The cash would constitute a sort of pocket-money fund for the ambitious entrepreneur.

I had only an hour or so to study the data prior to the scheduled meeting. In the company of others from Drexel who already knew him, I visited Perelman at his luxurious town house on East Sixty-third Street. We met in the second-floor "war room," and Perelman greeted me with a firm right hand. His left hand held a cigar, which, I soon learned, was a constant companion. Perelman looked me directly in the eye and suggested that we get down to business. Save for the cigar smoke, I liked him immediately.

In the early stages of the discussion I sat back listening. Perelman seemed determined to move forward, but the odds were very much against us; Pantry Pride was only one eighth the size of Revlon. Even more intriguing was the potential personality clash. What we contemplated was a war that would pit the upstart Perelman against the patrician Bergerac. It would be the anti-Establishment Drexel against the toughest traditional opponents that Revlon's money could buy.

This was a challenge not to be underestimated, and yet all about me I heard the rosiest of predictions. Finally I opened my mouth, declaring, "I don't think that the type of transaction you are proposing works. Your breakup values are a little on the high side."

Several of the men in the room leveled stares at me, and the most scornful look came from Perelman himself, whose eyes asked, Who the hell do you think you are?

I answered the unspoken question: "I'm the person who is going to fine-tune the numbers. I'm the person who will tell Milken whether this transaction makes any sense."

Everyone in the room tensed. Perelman, like anyone else—especially an entrepreneur—does not relish being told that he might be wrong. The remainder of the meeting was strained.

By the time I arrived back at my desk, a message waited: Perelman wanted me to call. When I reached him, I attempted to be congenial but firm. "Look," I said, "my first reaction is very negative. I don't think there is a strong command of the values, on the part of both your people and my people. I don't think enough thought has gone into the analysis. I want to get more comfortable with the numbers."

Perelman said nothing.

"What good does it do if you make an offer for Revlon and fall flat on your face?" I asked. "We don't want to tee them up and lose. We have to win. And if we're going to win, we have to look at all the variables. Who are the other players? How are they likely to respond to our offer? How do we structure the deal? Most importantly, what is the price that will work?" I vowed to myself that this would not be a Ready, fire, aim! deal. The stakes were far too high.

Perelman responded with a grudging agreement to give me time to study the numbers. He had visions of glory, but he was not stupid.

I tried to look at the deal from a realistic perspective. If you took a snapshot of the deal, it looked atrocious. Perelman would have to borrow so much money that on day one it would appear that he could never hope to meet the interest payments on his gargantuan debt. But if you looked at it like a motion picture, you saw something different. *If* Perelman could sell off the subsidiaries profitably, he could retire significant portions of the debt and eventually own a financially healthy cosmetics company. It was a big if.

"What is Revlon going to do?" I kept muttering to myself. I needed a handle on Bergerac, as well as his board members.

A sudden idea came to me. I called Don Engel, a former managing director of Drexel, now a consultant. Engel was involved in a deal with Harold Geneen, the legendary former C.E.O. of ITT. Bergerac had been Geneen's protégé. "Don," I requested, "see if hypothetically you can find out from Geneen how he thinks Bergerac will react."

Engel called back some time later and reported that according to Geneen, "Bergerac will fight you to the death."

Okay, so be it, I thought. At least we knew what to expect.

WE DECIDED to start by proposing a friendly acquisition. Bergerac knew Revlon was vulnerable, and perhaps he would surrender easily in order to cut the best terms for himself. Arthur Liman, who had worked as counsel for both Revlon and Perelman, set up a meeting.

On June 17 Perelman met with Bergerac in the latter's apartment and delivered the message that Revlon was one of a number of companies that he was looking at as acquisition candidates. The price, he said, would be somewhere in the 40s. Bergerac responded that Revlon's investment adviser would only approve "a price which began with a five," meaning $50 or more per share. After an hour and a half of fruitless discussion Bergerac suggested that the two men meet again the following week, over dinner, to continue. Although many on the team viewed Bergerac's willingness to have another meeting as a positive sign, neither Perelman nor I trusted him.

As it turned out, at the last moment Bergerac canceled the meeting. When I learned that Marty Lipton, the patriarch of Wachtell, Lipton, had been retained by Revlon, I called him to find out what had happened. Lipton said cryptically, "Don't waste your time. Pantry Pride will *never* get Revlon." My biggest fear was that Revlon would now adopt Lipton's hallmark poison pill defense. This is the strategy whereby a company sets into place procedures to dilute the value of its stock if a would-be acquirer appears on the horizon.

I told neither Wilkis nor Boesky about Revlon; yet in the second week of August the NYSE volume of trading in Revlon stock quadrupled. It was fresh evidence that other inside traders were at work. One arb after another phoned me trying to unearth information.

We laid plans to announce a hostile takeover attempt. To raise the cash for Perelman to buy Revlon, we would offer junk bonds directly to the public. They had been marketed to the public before, but never for the express purpose of financing a hostile takeover. On top of this,

Chemical Bank, which had never before participated in a hostile deal involving junk bonds, agreed to handle the senior financing. This development gave enormous credibility to Perelman's position.

On August 14 at nine a.m. Perelman's board authorized a tender offer for the purpose of acquiring Revlon.

Before that offer was announced, the target company issued a press release headlined REVLON NOT FOR SALE. It revealed that Revlon had adopted a poison pill defense. In the event a single entity gained control of 20 percent or more of Revlon's common stock, each shareholder would have the right to exchange one share of common stock for a Revlon note with a face value of $65, paying 12 percent interest, maturing in one year. In plain English, Bergerac had just upped his asking price by 30 percent over his original demand.

At a press conference Bergerac declared, "People have inquired. The message we have given to them is, The company is not for sale."

A pressure-filled week followed. There was little time for sleep. Talking over strategy, we crunched the numbers again and again.

On August 23 Pantry Pride commenced a tender offer for Revlon at $47.50 per share, conditional upon the ability to raise $900 million in cash and on the removal of the poison pill provisions.

Now, of course, came the lawsuits. For me this was the dull part of any battle, but the attorneys were in their glory. Perelman filed suit in a Delaware chancery court—where both MacAndrews & Forbes and Revlon were officially incorporated—charging that Revlon's poison pill provisions "have transferred from the stockholders of Revlon to the board the power to consider any takeover proposals." Revlon filed a countersuit.

I continued working day and night on the deal, finding it to be the most exhilarating time of my career. Several times a day I shuttled between meetings at Perelman's town house and other meetings at Drexel. Once Perelman went public with his tender offer, I was able to do more precise work on evaluating the subsidiaries. We opened quiet discussions with, among others, Bruce Wasserstein at First Boston to see what offers might surface. To our surprise he reported considerable interest in some of the subsidiaries—at higher prices than we originally estimated. The deal was beginning to look better.

On August 29 Revlon commenced an offer to exchange 10 million shares of its common stock for a package of notes and preferred stock valued at $57.50—$10 per share higher than our offer. With that one stroke Revlon turned 25 percent of its equity into debt, increased its long-term debt from $480 million to nearly $1 billion and reduced shareholders' equity from $1 billion to $460 million, making an acquisition—by anyone—far less attractive. In addition, the company's new paper included highly restrictive covenants, making it virtually impossible for anyone to take over the company without board approval.

Bergerac reportedly declared to his board, "We have just cut off Perelman's balls and nailed them to the wall."

ALTHOUGH I was not to become aware of it for months, the trouble had begun back on May 22—the very day I had tipped Boesky to the Nabisco deal. On that day an anonymous source in Caracas, Venezuela, wrote a strange letter full of errors in spelling and grammar to the compliance unit at the headquarters of Merrill Lynch in New York. It arrived in a plain white envelope. The letter read:

> Dear Sir: pleased be informed that two of your executives from the Caracas office are trading with inside information. A copie with description of ther trades so far has been submitet to the S.E.C. As is mantion on that letter if us customers do not benefit from their knoleg, we wonder who surveils the trades done by account executives. Upon you investigating to the last consequencies we will provide with the names of the insider on their owne hand writing.

The letter identified the two suspected Merrill Lynch employees as Carlos Zubillaga and Max Hofer.

Steve Snyder, a senior analyst at Merrill Lynch, was assigned to look into the charges. He studied the trading records of Zubillaga and Hofer over the past year and discovered that both men exhibited the same curious pattern of buying takeover stocks immediately prior to public announcements. How in the world, Snyder wondered, could Zubillaga and Hofer have unearthed takeover information while operating in far-off Caracas?

He checked the records of their Merrill Lynch personal cash-management accounts and learned that Zubillaga had written two checks, totaling $8000, to a Brian S. Campbell, a young Merrill Lynch broker in New York City. A quick check disclosed that

Campbell had left the firm a few months earlier to join Smith Barney. Digging into Campbell's personnel records, Snyder discovered that he and Zubillaga had attended the same Merrill Lynch training class in 1982.

The next step was to look at Campbell's trading records. In deals for both his personal account and his client accounts Campbell's activity showed the same pattern of successful investments in takeover stocks. Where, Snyder wondered, did Campbell's information come from? Rather quickly Snyder zeroed in on Campbell's biggest commercial customer—Bank Leu International, located in Nassau.

The Bank Leu trading record sent a shiver of electricity up Snyder's spine. The Bahamian bank had traded in the same takeover stocks as Campbell, Zubillaga and Hofer but on a far larger scale—5000 or even 10,000 shares at a time. Snyder concluded that Campbell had spotted a pattern of success in the buy-and-sell orders coming from Bank Leu and had copied some of the transactions. In addition, he must have passed on information to his friend Zubillaga, in Caracas, who shared it with another friend, Hofer. As Snyder probed, he discovered that Campbell had also provided takeover tips to his girlfriend, to his former college roommate and to a business partner.

Unfortunately, as far as Snyder was concerned, the trail reached a dead end at Bank Leu, given the Bahamian bank-secrecy laws.

In mid-June, Zubillaga and Hofer were summoned to New York and questioned by the Merrill Lynch compliance officers. Both admitted that they had received their tips from Campbell, but they denied wrongdoing, claiming that so far as they knew, Campbell was merely riding the coattails of a hot client.

Because Campbell was no longer a Merrill Lynch employee, his former employers could not question him. So they called Gary Lynch, the SEC enforcement director. Lynch put together a team to begin a federal inquiry into the Bank Leu trades.

It was early in July when the compliance department at Campbell's new firm, Smith Barney, informed him that he was under investigation by the SEC on suspicion of insider trading. For three days in August, Campbell was questioned by SEC investigators about his relationship with Bank Leu. The government then trained its guns on the bank. On August 28 an SEC lawyer telephoned Bernhard Meier to ask him about the suspicious pattern of trading in twenty-seven specific stocks. Meier, not knowing how to respond, said he would get back to the caller shortly.

Somewhat shaken, Meier discussed the call with Bruno Pletscher. It was an awkward situation, Meier said, but the SEC would expect a response and so would their own superiors at the parent firm, in Zurich. But problems with their superiors seemed more formidable because—as I would soon find out—Meier and Pletscher had violated certain bank guidelines, and they knew it. Meier observed that they were in the "s___." He moaned, "What are we going to do?"

Pletscher suggested that they get legal advice from their Zurich office. Together the two men went to Meier's office and placed a call back to the SEC lawyer. Their message was that they would seek legal advice in order to respond appropriately to the SEC's request.

WHEN I placed a collect call to the Bahamas to make a routine check on the status of my account, Meier said, "There's a problem. We should get together soon."

"What kind of problem?" I asked.

He responded with the three letters I did not want to hear: SEC.

"I'll be down on the weekend," I said immediately.

I hung up and called Wilkis. Within minutes we were together, out on the hot, summery streets of New York. We reminded one another that the Bahamian bank-secrecy laws were strict. There was no way that my bank could release any information to the SEC without my prior approval. Whatever the problem, it was clearly manageable.

I went back to work. Nevertheless, the image of U.S. government agents snooping around the Bahamas plagued me.

When the course of business took me to Boesky's office, I asked him a probing question. After all, he had been investigated—and cleared—by the SEC on numerous occasions. "Ivan," I said, "you get called down to the SEC all the time. What do you tell them?"

He took me into his file room and exhibited one thick folder after another. Each contained background information, such as press clippings and analysts' reports. He showed me how it was possible to justify nearly any trade—in retrospect—on the basis of publicly available information. "I tell them that I buy stocks in broad industry groups, and I have all this research to back me up," he said. "They can't prove otherwise, so they buy it."

Boesky suggested that if I needed a lawyer, I might try his man in Washington, Harvey Pitt. He was no Perry Mason, but he was the former general counsel of the SEC and thus had connections. He was now in private practice with the firm of Fried, Frank, Harris, Shriver & Jacobson. Pitt, Boesky said, "does all this crap for me."

I ARRIVED at Bank Leu on the Saturday of Labor Day weekend, 1985, to meet with Meier and Pletscher. General Manager Jean-Pierre Fraysse was at this meeting, although Bank Leu would later deny it.

The bankers showed me the formal Telex that had arrived from the SEC affirming the oral request for information. The worst part of this, as far as they were concerned, was that the SEC had sent a copy of the Telex to the bank's home office, in Zurich.

I told them that under no circumstances could they provide information about my account to the SEC or to anyone else. Such an action, I said in a firm voice, would be a violation of Bahamian law.

That was true, Meier acknowledged, but he noted that the situation was delicate; the SEC had already identified so many of the trades.

"How?" I asked.

Somewhat sheepishly Meier said, "The SEC is investigating one of the brokers with whom we have been executing trades."

"What are you talking about?"

"We have executed a lot of our trades through one brokerage firm. . . ."

"Weren't you instructed to always break up the orders?"

"Yes." But, Meier explained, he had steered much of his business to Brian Campbell at Merrill Lynch because Campbell knew when to buy quickly, but he also knew when to slow his pace lest the SEC become suspicious. Furthermore, Campbell gave Bank Leu the best available break of brokerage commissions—which, I realized, Bank Leu had not bothered to pass on to me.

I still did not understand. "Why is this a problem?" I asked.

Meier was clearly uncomfortable as he explained, "It appears as though—this disappoints me a great deal—Campbell was also buying the same stocks you were. Now the SEC wants to talk to us."

In frustration I said, "But you can't tell the SEC anything. *What's the problem?*"

Meier whispered, "We also bought the stocks here."

"Who?"

"I did," Fraysse admitted. Meier said he had, too, making a profit of more than $150,000 in his Ascona account. Pletscher said he had invested also, under the code names Yellow Bird and Grouper.

After an uncomfortable silence Meier added enigmatically, "Other clients of the bank." Meier was responsible for numerous managed investment accounts, and he had brought them into this busy arena, satisfying his customers with handsome trading profits, and fattening his own commission and service-fee income.

They had a cottage industry going here! They had piggybacked my trades and magnified the effects in markets around the world. I gulped and asked, "Well, how many of your so-called managed accounts did you make these trades in?"

"Twenty-five or thirty."

"Oh, my God! And you did most of this through one broker?"

Meier nodded.

"You know that it was in direct defiance of my specific orders?"

"I know," Fraysse said, "but we have to deal with this problem. Our home office is going to be made aware of this, and if they find out we were piggybacking, well, it's going to be a very serious problem for us."

Typical middle-management mentality, I thought. There is no real problem here, because the simple fact of the matter is that they cannot give the SEC my records. But the first instinct, of course, is to cover your ass, and that was what each of these men was trying to do.

The dimensions of their problem were staggering. The SEC was looking at possible insider trading profits in excess of $10 million. If it could prove the contention, the SEC could demand that the bank return the $10 million, plus pay treble damages.

It's not my problem, I thought, with a mixture of relief and anger. It's their problem.

As the others went about their business Meier privately suggested a solution. "We are proposing to say that yours was a managed account just like the others, that you played no role in the investment decisions. I will say that I picked all these stocks." He added, "I would like you to come up with reasons why I bought the stocks."

It was viable. As Boesky had learned, in retrospect you can generally find public material to support the contention that you were an astute market analyst rather than a privileged insider. I was red with anger that I had to help these men cover for their stupidity, but I did not see a choice. I agreed to put together a package of information.

Fraysse rejoined us and suggested "that the files be updated to reflect the current situation." He placed a form in front of me authorizing the Bank Leu officers to make investment decisions for my account at their own discretion. He asked me to sign it and backdate it. I signed, and both Fraysse and Meier sighed with relief.

Fraysse then said, "We do not have any connection with counsel that would be appropriate to deal in SEC matters. Can you recommend somebody?"

I suggested Harvey Pitt, the lawyer whom Boesky said handled the SEC "crap" for him. I told them that Pitt was formerly the general counsel for the SEC, and I was sure that he could use Bahamian banking laws to quash the investigation on the U.S. end.

Fraysse asked if I would help to defray the legal expenses.

Now, finally, I exploded. "This is not my problem!" I raged. "You guys have made millions on me. You have the nerve to ask me to pay for your lawyer? For a problem you created?"

Fraysse dropped the issue, giving me time to cool off. Stop it, Dennis, I told myself. Keep your wits about you. There is no reason to overreact.

At any rate, I volunteered, I would suspend my trading activities until this was all cleared up.

BACK in New York, Wilkis listened to my story with controlled concern and immediately volunteered to help me assemble the necessary paperwork that would, in retrospect, justify my trades. After all, he was my friend. We were in this together.

Whenever I could steal a spare moment from the Revlon deal or one of the many other transactions competing for my attention, I punched instructions into a computer, calling up research materials that predated my transactions. It was a pleasant, calming surprise to realize that much justification existed.

For each deal, I attempted to create a convincing paper trail, and I spent considerable time with long computer printout sheets. Many of the junior associates in the office were impressed with how much time I, as a managing director, devoted to research.

When I next spoke with Meier by phone, he informed me that the bank had followed up on my recommendation and hired Pitt. Meier told me that he was coming to New York on September 18 to clean up his affairs with Brian Campbell and that Pitt was flying up from Washington to consult with him then.

I told Meier that I would contact him when he was here, to see how things were going. "Where are you staying?" I asked.

"The Waldorf-Astoria."

"I'll call."

CHAPTER TEN

L AURIE'S father took a turn for the worse. Both she and I were preoccupied with this personal pain. We spent much time on the phone with Laurie's mother in Florida.

On top of this, I labored as best I could to assemble the defense package for Bank Leu. And amid everything else, I found myself at the center point of Perelman's epic battle. The new Revlon barriers seemed insurmountable, but Perelman was determined not to capitulate. I admired his tenacity. We all donned our thinking caps.

The most important point to emerge from our fresh analysis came as we pondered the implications of Revlon's move to dilute its stock value. Collectively, those of us who sat in Perelman's war room came to attention as a great truth dawned: We had offered $47.50 per share. In response, Revlon had found ways to cheapen the stock, reasoning that neither Perelman nor anyone else could persuade his lenders to fund him, because the offer was now unrealistically complex.

As we met regularly to discuss our options the solution evolved. Was the offer of $47.50 written in stone? Of course not. If Revlon devalued the stock, why could we not devalue our offer?

We crunched the numbers one more time and decided that if we *lowered* our offer from $47.50 to $42 per share, we not only were paying a fair price to the shareholders but we could move our junk bonds back to the private market and avoid the delay caused by SEC regulations of public issues.

Conventional market wisdom had never encountered the tenacity of Drexel. The investment world was flabbergasted when we rescinded our previous tender offer and commenced our lower offer on

September 16. All the shareholders had to do was total up the values to see we were still giving a good deal—perhaps better than before.

In the new offer Pantry Pride detailed that it had $750 million in available cash (the bulk raised by Drexel, in July), plus $340 million in bank credit. The remaining $500 million was to be raised in Pantry Pride notes marketed by Drexel, which was "highly confident" that it could do so. Pantry Pride paid Drexel a half million dollars for the use of those two simple words in the tender offer and agreed to other fees and commissions that would bring Drexel's total income to $60 million on this single transaction—if it closed.

On September 18 I located a pay phone a few blocks from my apartment. My paranoia was on the rise, and I made sure I found a phone I had never used before. The operator at the Waldorf-Astoria connected me with Meier, and I asked, "How did it go?"

"Everything is fine," he reported. He said that he had told Pitt that the bank should take a tough stand and refuse to provide the SEC with information, and in addition, he said, there was no case, because he had picked all the stocks himself and executed the trades.

I was pleased. It sounded good to me, and I told Meier so.

"Excuse me," he said. "Someone is at the door."

He returned to the phone in a few moments and announced in a shaky voice, "I have just been served with a subpoena." Actually there were two. One demanded Bank Leu's business records from October 1, 1983, forward; the other sought access to Meier's personal records. He had until October 1 to deliver the package to SEC investigators.

"It's bulls___," he said, attempting a cavalier pose, but his voice betrayed tension. "They have no right to do this to me. I'm a Swiss citizen." With regard to the subpoenas, he declared flatly that the bank would not and could not provide any information. Furthermore, he added, he would "alter the files to protect the bank's interests."

After we hung up, Meier's final statement haunted me. If the bank was not going to turn over any records, why did it have to alter them?

My stomach was in turmoil.

This was all so crazy! So much was happening on so many fronts that I could not keep track.

On one front, we were suddenly confronted by a pair of white knights on the horizon, riding headlong toward Revlon's rescue. The private investment partnership of Adler & Shaykin agreed to buy the cosmetics portion of Revlon's business, and set to work negotiating a price. The LBO firm of Forstmann Little was prepared to purchase the remainder of the company in a sweetheart deal that would allow Revlon's top management to come along for the ride.

Perelman, fighting mad, wanted to raise his tender offer from $42 to $50 per share. Dozens of calls were placed to Beverly Hills. Could we finance the deal at a historic level? The answer, after much consultation, appeared to be yes.

On October 1 we heard a rumor that the private deal between Revlon, Adler & Shaykin, and Forstmann Little would result in a combined bid of $52 per share. It was a world-class poker game now, and Perelman refused to fold. He called the two dollars and raised another dollar, offering $53 per share. I rode off in a chauffeured Rolls-Royce to personally deliver this latest bid to Revlon's headquarters.

On that same day, Harvey Pitt met with members of the SEC staff and informed them that their subpoenas raised certain considerations regarding Bahamian law. He contended that the subpoenas delivered to Meier related only to Meier's activities and not to the bank's records as a whole. They hashed out a compromise whereby Meier would provide his own trading records, along with a copy of his background research records. He would also submit to a deposition. In addition, Bank Leu agreed to provide records of the managed accounts, though all materials that might identify the traders would be edited out. The bank apparently had set up a strategy whereby it was about to break Bahamian law.

BERGERAC, continuing to spurn Perelman, announced on October 3 that he would sell to his cronies. Adler & Shaykin was going to buy the cosmetics end of the conglomerate for $900 million, and the rest would be sold to Forstmann Little for $1.4 billion, with Bergerac as one of the principal new owners. It was a carefully crafted LBO. It smelled very fishy, but it also smelled successful, because this new proposal would net the shareholders $56 per share. Outside observers now seemed confident that the pot was too rich for Perelman.

There was, however, a kicker here, which we believed Revlon had overlooked. In order to make the company worth $56 per share, the board had voted to remove the restrictive covenants it had previously created. The poison pill defense had been abandoned. Now suddenly the company was worth more than ever!

Again we crunched the numbers, calculating ways to minimize the tax consequences via creative accounting. Perelman finally offered $56.25 per share, and Milken backed that with an announcement that we had already raised most of the cash and were "highly confident" that we could place the remaining $350 million in junk bonds.

But Bergerac's behavior was in line with all of our intelligence estimates, which painted him as arrogant and intractable. He would not back down. Within days Forstmann Little raised its bid to $57.25 per share, and the Revlon board announced plans to grant Forstmann a lockup option—the automatic right to buy two of the health-care subsidiaries at a cut-rate price of $525 million if anyone else acquired 40 percent of the stock. It was another new showstopper, and it would effectively preclude any other bidder from coming in.

That's illegal, we responded. It was a Thursday when we asked Justice Joseph Walsh of the Delaware Chancery Court to grant a temporary injunction to stop the plan.

Two weeks passed, and the waiting was excruciating. Finally Justice Walsh formally declared that by granting the lockup option the Revlon board had "failed in its fiduciary duty to the stockholders." Once it became apparent that Revlon would be sold to somebody, the judge declared, the only proper role for a director was as "an auction-eer attempting to secure the highest price for the pieces of the Revlon enterprise." He directed the board to sell to the highest bidder.

Perelman's response was to raise his offer to $58 per share.

Revlon and Forstmann were unwilling—or unable—to top the bid. Instead, they appealed the ruling, which kept everything in limbo.

The Street followed every nuance of the deal. If the appeals court upheld the ruling, it would place an official seal of approval on the principle that anyone could buy any company—so long as he could come up with the most money.

As we waited for the dust to settle we learned that some of the Revlon board members had hired their own lawyers to guide them through the maze, making sure they discharged their duties in the interests of the shareholders rather than management. It was an unprecedented move, and it was further confirmation of the value of our psychological intelligence gathering. This was exactly how we had expected certain directors to react.

We had them now. I knew it!

THE Delaware Supreme Court was scheduled to rule on Revlon's appeal on November 1, and everyone on the Street knew that this was the final battle. Billions of dollars were staked on the outcome.

The arbs were in up to their eyeballs, and the market had developed to the point where a single moment could make a huge difference in profit-and-loss figures. Every major arb in the country had a representative on the scene in Delaware. They had commandeered every pay phone in sight, determined to outrace even the Dow Jones ticker.

As a group of us sat in Perelman's office—our stomachs rumbling in protest over the sumptuous breakfast that we were too nervous to digest—I kept a phone pressed to my ear. On the other end of the line was an arb from a major brokerage firm, doing me a favor.

Perelman's secretary, Sue, anticipating victory, set exquisite goblets upon a silver tray. In her hand was an ice-cold bottle of Cristal, Perelman's favorite Champagne.

Minutes passed in quiet, nervous small talk, but as the time dragged, the room grew silent. Perelman puffed on a cigar. His eyes issued a silent scream: What do you hear?

"Yes?" I said into the phone.

The room came to attention.

I dropped the phone, turned to stare Perelman directly in the eye and said softly, "We won."

Suddenly everyone was on his feet, engulfed in a collective embrace. Sue popped the cork on the Champagne bottle.

When I returned to my office later that morning, I felt like a general returning home from a victorious battle. We had just won the most fiercely contested takeover in history. There were dozens of congratulatory phone messages awaiting me. Several magnums of Champagne were sent over by arbs and even by competitors.

Drexel's $60 million in fees set a record as the highest investment banking commission in history, and I knew that my end-of-the-year bonus would make personal history, amounting to more than $1 million in cash. I treated my colleagues to a case of Champagne.

Right, Laurie and I in Maui for her birthday in 1982. I had just made my first million, at the age of twenty-nine. Below, working at home as a Smith Barney associate. I could never leave my work at the office.

Celebrating the hotly contested takeover of Revlon by Ron Perelman's Pantry Pride, Inc. From left, Don Engel, David Kay, Ron Perelman and I. My dual life was yet to be exposed. I thought the world held no limits. Little did I know.

ABOUT A WEEK LATER I walked into a showroom just off First Avenue and announced to a salesman, "I would like to buy a Ferrari
Testarossa."

"There's a long wait," he replied.

"I would like the car tomorrow," I said.

He quoted me a price $15,000 higher than the sticker.

"You're trying to be cute with me," I said. I listed the equipment I
wanted and told him what the price *should* be: $125,000.

"You know what you're talking about."

"I've done my homework," I said. "Here's a check for ten thousand
dollars. I want to finance half of the price, and I'll pay you the
balance."

Laurie and I were planning to take Adam out into the country for
the weekend, so I left the office early on Friday to pick up the car. It
was an awesome fire-engine-red dream with a beige interior, and
when I pulled it through the arched gateway of the entrance to my
building and into the circular drive, the doormen went berserk.

I brought Laurie down to see my surprise. Her mouth dropped
open in amazement at the incredible beauty of this machine. She said,
"Dennis, I'm so happy for you. I know it's what you always wanted."
She hesitated, then asked, "How much did it cost?"

When I told her, I had to remind her about the bonus check.

We headed over to pick up Adam from his school. Proudly I inched
my new Ferrari into the line of black limos waiting for the children
of New York's elite. Adam bounced out of school, saw us and
squealed. He and his friends gathered around to take a closer look.

Then we were off for the weekend. Confident that the Revlon deal
would solidify my position in the most compelling business Wall Street
had ever invented, I drove off into the sunset.

AS THE airliner maneuvered on its landing approach to Nassau, I
pondered my particular set of problems. Already the press was
characterizing Revlon as perhaps the pivotal deal of the '80s. Reporters from the financial press dubbed me the new star of the M&A
business, and after the adrenaline faded, I found this surprisingly
unsettling. I always envisioned a good investment banker as a sort of
invisible man, working discreetly to accomplish his client's goals. Yet
only a few days earlier Tom Cassidy, a CNN business reporter, called

me. He wanted to profile a rising star in the M&A field. "You're the hottest new guy on the Street."

"I'm flattered," I said. "But no way." I did not need any kind of high profile at the moment.

Once on Bahamian soil, I headed for the all-too-familiar offices of Bank Leu armed with additional paperwork that Wilkis and I had assembled. We had thus far succeeded in putting together a reasonably comprehensive portfolio. Meier was pleased.

Back home, I calculated our profits. In six years we had transformed an initial investment of $40,000 into an account balance of more than $10 million. Reich's share amounted to about $480,000 (although he had never taken a dime), and Sokolow's profits were approximately $540,000; Sokolow had taken several cash payments and passed a portion of the money on to Goldie, his informer at Goldman Sachs. What struck me as the most amazing aspect of it all was that I had accumulated this fortune with very little time or effort.

Perhaps it's enough, I thought. Maybe now I'll just deposit the money and let it amass interest.

The day after Thanksgiving I returned to Nassau to find that everyone at Bank Leu seemed confident that our defenses were strong. Pletscher suggested that it was all right to resume trading. He was, in fact, anxious to do so.

Despite my previous resolve, I found the temptation irresistible. Almost every day on the job there was a new tip floating around. There was money to be made. We created a new company called International Gold, and a new account in that name at Bank Leu. Meier and Pletscher were the new signatories. My name no longer appeared on any bank records. The bankers were now very relaxed and eager to resume earning commissions.

We settled on a new telephone code name. When I left the bank that day, Mr. Diamond was dead; Mr. Wheat had risen in his stead.

On December 3, I called Bank Leu and instructed Pletscher to buy 100,000 shares of Union Carbide, which was about to be taken over by GAF Corporation. Drexel was arranging the financing. I checked back later in the day for a report. On my behalf Pletscher had bought the stock at a cost of $6.3 million. What he did not tell me was that—even in the midst of his own set of problems—he had also bought 300 shares for his own account.

ON DECEMBER 5 BANK LEU violated Bahamian law by providing Harvey Pitt with the actual statements of approximately twenty-five managed accounts. Pitt made a rough total of the accounts, compared it to the omnibus records Meier had presented, and realized that a large gap remained. Rather quickly he called the bankers' bluff.

Where, Pitt asked, were the missing records? No one knew how to respond. The only records missing were mine. One of the bankers said, "There are certain sensitive accounts that we are unable to tell you about."

This was perhaps Pitt's first real indication that the trading activity emanated from a single well-informed source.

He returned to Washington to think things over.

On December 9, I learned that MidCon Corporation, a natural gas pipeline company, was a potential takeover target. Nearly all my capital was tied up—Sokolow had told me that RCA was in merger discussions—but still I called Bank Leu and put the remainder of my cash into MidCon stock. *I simply could not stop.*

Even as Meier placed the stock purchase orders Pitt was meeting with Bank Leu's chief legal counsel, Hans Peter Schaad, who confirmed what Pitt suspected—one account was responsible for the majority of the suspicious trading. Pitt insisted that Bank Leu immediately stop trading in the account, and Schaad apparently agreed. Pitt also suggested that the assets of the account be frozen.

Pitt summoned Pletscher and Meier and questioned them into the night. The bankers flinched, and in one instant everything fell apart. They disclosed that the customer was an investment banker in the New York office of Drexel Burnham Lambert—Mr. X.

Pitt considered the alternatives. He could still wage an all-out battle in the interests of the bank-secrecy laws. Alternately the bank could agree to identify Mr. X to the SEC in return for a pledge of immunity from prosecution for the bank and its employees. He favored this latter strategy for it would shift the emphasis from the bank to its client, despite the fact that it constituted a flagrant violation of both law and tradition. No wonder Pitt had done so well at the SEC.

ON THE following day I checked the Quotron in my office and calculated that I would earn more than $60,000 on a small, quick transaction. I hustled out to a pay phone and called Meier.

Before I could issue the order, he moaned, "It's no good."

"What's no good?" I asked quickly.

"It's no good. It's no good," he said. "They know."

"They know?" I replied. "Do they know my identity?"

Meier would not, or could not, talk further.

I felt a sharp pain in my chest, as if a dagger had pierced my heart. I knew with certainty that someone else was in Meier's office listening to this conversation, perhaps recording it. My body went limp.

"Sell everything," I commanded. "Now!"

Numerous times over the next several days I tried to call Meier back. Whoever answered the phone simply said that he was not in the office. In desperation I tried his apartment number at the posh Lyford Cay Club and was told that the phone was disconnected. I called every hotel in Nassau, but none had a Bernhard Meier registered.

Nevertheless, Meier was still in town, still torn among his options. On the night of Friday the thirteenth, while driving out to the Lyford Cay Club, Pitt played a game with Meier. He knew that Mr. X was in a high position at Drexel, and he tossed out various names, asking, "Is it . . . ? Is it . . . ?" Finally he asked, "Is it Dennis Levine?"

Meier responded quietly, "Yes."

On Tuesday, December 17, Pitt visited SEC headquarters in Washington and met with Gary Lynch, the SEC's enforcement chief. Off the record Pitt said that the individual in question is "a status player on Wall Street." He hinted that the man was a "big fish," and as a result, SEC investigators dubbed their prey Moby Dick.

I stood at the desk in the bank lobby and looked once more at the check in my hand. It was my annual bonus from Drexel, and it amounted to more than $1 million—after taxes. By now I was supposed to be sophisticated in the face of such numbers. But this money was somehow more *real*. Do you just deposit a million-dollar check in your account as if it were a normal event?

I stood in line, like everyone else. When it was my turn, I approached the teller's window and slid my deposit toward her.

She grasped it with a routine, somewhat bored air. Then she did a double take. "Mr. Levine," she squealed, "you're rich!"

Yes, I thought. Yes, I am. This was the quantification of my legitimate success. No more trading, Dennis, I said to myself. No more.

ON MARCH 19, 1986, PITT AND the SEC and Justice Department attorneys finally reached an accord. The U.S. lawyers pledged that Bank Leu would not be sued, nor would any of its assets be frozen. No further subpoenas would be served, and the bank's officers would receive immunity from prosecution if they produced by April 7 the complete records associated with Moby Dick's trading activities. The documents would not reveal the trader's identity. It was the first time in history that a Swiss or Bahamian bank had agreed to such a clear and willful violation of secrecy laws in order to protect itself.

Still, beyond the account records, the government felt it needed a star witness. Nervously Pletscher agreed to testify against me.

Bank Leu agreed to pay all of its piggybacking profits to the U.S. government, which in return pledged not to seek the treble damages that it could have demanded. Finally, the agreement specified that Bank Leu would have to reveal the identity of Mr. X/Moby Dick if a U.S. court ordered it to do so or if it received permission from Bahamian authorities.

A rider to the agreement disclosed that the target of the probe was "an American customer who is presently a managing director of a major investment banking firm in the United States. It is believed that the customer resides and works in the Southern District of New York." This was a reference to the jurisdiction of U.S. Attorney Rudolph Giuliani.

WHEN I arrived on the eve of the 1986 version of Drexel's Bond Conference and checked into the Beverly Hills Hotel, a bottle of expensive Champagne awaited me, courtesy of the hotel owner, Ivan Boesky. Fred Joseph had assigned me an important role at this conference. I was now Drexel's major M&A spokesman, and I was to talk about the highlights of the Revlon deal and paint a glowing picture of future M&A possibilities.

This year, no doubt thanks in part to our distinguished performance, more blue-chip companies were represented than last year. Although it was still early in 1986, we projected that by the end of the year Drexel would be the most profitable securities firm in history. Yet the gut-wrenching and, paradoxically, glorious facet of that prediction was that in the context of the '80s this would be insufficient. Set a record for business volume in 1986, yes, but make sure you eclipse that record in 1987. There was no such thing as enough.

The prevailing theme of it all was presented in a big-screen film clip from the movie *Ghostbusters*, with dubbed voices singing:

> *"When it's money you need,*
> *And you gotta have it fast,*
> *Who ya gonna call? Call Drexel."*

This was the gathering of the anointed. Only a handful of people in the entire world conducted business at our level. We were a small, tight community, able to work on a friendly basis as allies or adversaries, depending upon the needs of the moment. We knew one another's personality and style, and it was fun to mingle in a generalized setting and talk shop.

Still, by the end of the week a morose mood had settled upon me. I realized that I was nearer to a panic attack than I had ever been before. A debate brewed within me. One faction of my mind argued that everything was under control. Pletscher and Meier were leveling with me; they were stonewalling the SEC. The opposition argued that my life was crumbling, that everything I had toiled for was about to go up in a brilliant flame.

IT WAS one of those rare days when I left the office early. Laurie and I had a business dinner to attend that evening, and I knew it would be a late night, yet I was already exhausted.

"I'm going to lie down for a while," I announced as I came through the doorway at four p.m. I headed directly to the bedroom, drew the curtains and turned off the lights. But I had barely closed my eyes when Laurie barged into the room and flipped on the overhead light. I glanced up in pain to see her standing over me, looking somewhat absurd with a headful of rollers in her blond hair.

"Dennis," she said, "I want you to play a game of charades with me."

"What?"

"Charades," she repeated. "Just one."

The woman has lost it, I said to myself. She's gone round the bend. I'm tired and grumpy. Why do I need a game of charades?

Laurie held up three fingers, and reluctantly I muttered, "Three words."

On the nose, she signaled.

First word. She pointed to herself.

"I . . ."

For the second word she inverted three fingers of her hand.

"M," I intoned. "I . . . M. I am."

On the nose.

Now she turned to one side, so that I viewed her in profile. Her hands outlined the silhouette of a bulging tummy.

I sat up in bed and screamed, "I am pregnant?"

"Yes!" she squealed.

I leaped up and hugged her. A nap was out of the question now. I floated through the evening.

EVEN as Harvey Pitt was piecing together the defense for Bank Leu, one of his partners at Fried, Frank was hard at work on a special deal involving Boesky and me. Steve Fraidin, a round-faced gentleman with large oval-framed glasses, was a longtime Boesky adviser.

We met in Boesky's office one day to discuss, I thought, routine matters. Choosing his moment, Boesky walked out of the office on an "errand." It was then that Fraidin "happened" to mention that Boesky's number two man, Steve Conway, was leaving.

"Gee, that's interesting," I said. The implication was obvious. I added, "I think Ivan would like me to take that job."

"It's a great job for you," Fraidin said excitedly. "It makes a lot of sense. It is a match made in heaven."

When Boesky returned, he caught Fraidin's eye and suggested, "Let's resume this conversation over lunch."

Fraidin left us. Along with lunch, Boesky put his offer on the table.

He explained that his long-delayed $660 million financial restructuring deal was about to close. Milken had silenced the more vocal members of Drexel's underwriting assistance committee. What Boesky did not tell me was that on March 21, in order to finalize the deal, he had written out a $5.3 million check for what was described as consulting services, but was more likely compensation covering a variety of proper and/or improper activities.

Now that the capital infusion appeared likely, Boesky had set up an entity, Hudson Funding Corporation, for the single purpose of marketing $660 million worth of notes on the public markets. On his own, Boesky was also selling another $220 million worth of limited partnership interests. All told, he was about to receive almost $900 million worth of fresh money, and he was ready to put me in charge of a large chunk of it, directing takeover operations. "I'd like for you to come in and run the Beverly Hills Hotel, the Vagabond Hotels," he said. "You'll run my operation in London, everything here. But most importantly, I want to set up an LBO firm, which you will handle."

I had always dreamed of becoming a principal, and here was my chance. But I wanted to know the stakes. I countered, "How much money are you going to put into it?"

"One hundred million dollars."

"I want a carried interest. I want twenty percent."

He hesitated, then said, "All right."

All of a sudden my secret bank account almost seemed irrelevant. "I want to bring in my own people," I said.

"Good," Boesky pronounced. That settled, he sweetened the pot. He offered what he called a seven-figure salary, plus bonuses that would bring my total annual income to more than $5 million. And on top of it all, he offered a signing bonus of $5 million.

When I told Laurie about Boesky's job offer, she was totally supportive. She wanted me to do what I thought was best for my career. In my mind I was through with investment banking as well as insider trading; I needed a new mountain to climb.

On April 24 I met with Ilan Reich and told him I had been approached by Boesky to become president of his company. "Would you be interested in coming in?"

"Absolutely," he replied. "I'd be very interested in that."

Sokolow, too, was ready to join the new team.

On May 6 I headed for the Cayman Islands, changing planes in Miami. I met with Wilkis' lawyer, Darryl Myers. He initiated the paperwork to set up a new corporation for me. Then we walked over to the local office of Morgan Grenfell Ltd., where I was introduced to the bank's managing director, Brian Kieran, as Robert Gold. I arranged to open an account under the name of my new business. I deposited $5000 and informed Kieran that I would wire $10 million to the account as soon as the necessary papers were filed.

This was a nontrading account. Once I got my money out of Bank Leu, I vowed, it was really, truly over.

At three p.m. the next day Pitt, along with the American ambassador to the Bahamas and a team of men from the SEC, the U.S. Department of Justice and the U.S. State Department, descended upon the office of Paul Adderly, who had held the posts of justice minister, public prosecutor and minister of education. The visitors disclosed that they were on the trail of an American investor who had made what they suspected were illegal insider trades through a Bahamian bank account, and they wanted Adderly to grant extraordinary permission for the bank to disclose the customer's identity.

To almost everyone's surprise Adderly consented. His rationale was that stock trading was separate from normal banking transactions; therefore, he could make the exception. He said he would formalize his approval in a letter to Bank Leu, to be delivered on Friday, two days hence, whereupon the bank would be free to disclose to the SEC the identity of Moby Dick.

ON THURSDAY I slipped away from my desk and phoned Bank Leu. Mr. Pletscher was unavailable, the receptionist informed me. I demanded to speak to an officer and reached Andrew Sweeting.

I did not know who he was, but I identified myself as Mr. Wheat and told him I wanted all of my money transferred to my new account in the Cayman Islands. Sweeting responded that he could not accept a verbal order to do this; he would need the instructions in writing.

I called my lawyer, Hartis Pinder, in Nassau and instructed him to hand-deliver the required letter.

On Friday, May 9, at five thirty p.m. Justice Minister Adderly's letter arrived at Bank Leu. Pitt telephoned SEC enforcement director Gary Lynch and reported, "We got the letter. Moby Dick is Dennis Levine, a managing director at Drexel Burnham Lambert."

A half hour later the letter arrived from my attorney, Hartis Pinder, instructing Bank Leu to transfer my money. It was too late.

Unaware that my life was now out of control, I went on Friday night to the Gulf + Western building for a buffet dinner and a private screening of their Paramount subsidiary's new release, *Top Gun*.

Boesky and I never had an opportunity to complete our job negotiations, for on the following Monday I was arrested and tossed into jail.

And after that, I faced the formidable task of explaining everything to Laurie.

Part Three: Withdrawal
CHAPTER ELEVEN

BOB Wilkis happened to be on a business trip to Omaha the day of my arrest, but he called on me at home as soon as he could. When we met each other at the door of my co-op, I reported the obvious. "Bob, they arrested me. I spent the night in jail."

"I know," he said softly. "They're gonna get me next."

"How could they do that? There's no way they could trace me to you or vice versa. All of this is coming from the Bahamas. They don't know who my trading partners were."

We spoke briefly, and Wilkis' fears were allayed somewhat.

"Everything is going to be okay," I assured him.

"Everything is going to be okay," he agreed.

THE short-term effects were dramatic. One day soon after my arrest Laurie and I stopped at a bank machine to get some cash, but the computer informed us that our account was empty; federal agents had seized it. I had to borrow cash to feed my family.

As the Street professed its shock, brokers, bankers, arbs, lawyers and financiers of every ilk searched frantically through their own closets trying to clean out the skeletons. Everyone expected a flurry of subpoenas to descend. Government agents padlocked my office at Drexel and allowed access to only their own investigators, who poked and prodded through my personal effects as well as my business files. The worst pressure of all was that the government dragged in the rest of my family, issuing subpoenas to my father and my brothers.

Wall Street heaven was replaced by the hell of reality. Media crews camped around our building; my phone rang incessantly. Almost everyone wanted to talk with me, of course, but Laurie was not spared the unwanted attention. Diane Sawyer, Maria Shriver and Barbara Walters all called her seeking interviews. I took Liman's advice to heart. "Cases are not won or lost in the media," he counseled. "They are won and lost in the courtroom." I refused all interview requests.

I did not know quite what to expect from my Drexel associates. It would be natural for them to distance themselves from me, and some did, but most offered help. Several friends helped me assemble the mountain of paperwork that we needed to verify what I did and—in some cases, more important—did not do on various transactions.

Several days after my arrest I encountered one of my elderly neighbors as we were both leaving the building. "I'm quite upset with you," he said. I expected an angry lecture, but he surprised me by smiling and commenting, "All these years we've been neighbors. How come you never gave me any stock tips?"

MY ATTORNEYS' first priority was to gather information, since we were operating in the dark. A criminal complaint had been filed against me, but I was not indicted, and by law the U.S. Attorney's office was not required to supply us with information concerning the evidence.

However, the SEC moved with unusual speed to file a civil action, and my attorneys used the civil proceedings to discover the government's evidence against me. An assault squad of attorneys and research associates scurried to dig up legal and press records regarding the fifty-four transactions that concerned the SEC, and they went wild, issuing subpoenas to a variety of entities involved with Bank Leu. Within days they had copies of all of the evidence amassed by the SEC.

Arthur Liman's partner Marty Flumenbaum, a Harvard Law School grad, was a veteran of this very same U.S. Attorney's office. "Why don't you go into that room all by yourself," he said to me one morning as he handed over a loose-leaf binder. "Read this."

I had no idea what was in the binder, but I did as he suggested. In a quiet conference room, alone with my memories, I leafed carefully through the material. Flumenbaum and others had compiled the most damaging portions of the evidence against me and placed them here. It was beautifully organized and even indexed.

I studied the printouts of Bank Leu's trading records, which depicted trade after trade occurring prior to a public announcement; it was an unmistakable paper trail leading back to my office at Drexel.

The bank had provided the U.S. government with copies of its telephone bills, indicating the collect calls I had made. Almost all of these were from New York, and the few from other locations were even more damning when correlated with my business travel records.

Here was Pletscher's deposition, describing how I had come to

Bank Leu to trade securities through an offshore account, detailing how I had demanded stringent security procedures.

It was apparent that I had grossly underestimated the capabilities of the government investigators. They had carefully compared my business track record with the accounting of my trades. It was solemn, depressing reading. It was clear that I had few options. Dennis, I thought, all your life you've been a fighter. But this is a fight you can't win. You're guilty. You're caught.

I pushed the chair away from the table and stood up. My hands slapped against my forehead and remained there, trying to hold in the sudden throbbing pain. On wobbly feet I edged toward a window and glanced down upon Manhattan. How high up am I? Thirty-some floors. The people below were ants.

Which was worse—the pain in my head or the ache in my heart? Laurie's face appeared in front of me. My sweet, loving, innocent wife was carrying our child. And Adam, who looked to me as his guide for life. What had I done to them? How could I ever make it up?

Just jump, Dennis, I thought. They'll be better off without you. It'll be easy. Just pull open the window and dive through.

Many moments passed. I did not move.

Finally I said to myself, It's a long way down, Dennis. I reminded myself, You're not a quitter. Somehow we'll get through.

When I finally stepped out of the conference room, my body still shook and I was ghostly pale. Liman tried to ease the tension with a quip. "The only thing I think we have a chance of winning," he declared, "is the parking ticket you got the night they arrested you."

He said that in all his years as a lawyer he had never seen anyone delivered so completely to the government. Bank Leu, he said, had served me "on a silver platter." He informed me solemnly that the government could use the evidence in an attempt to prove an organized criminal conspiracy and thus prosecute me under the harsh terms of RICO—the Racketeer Influenced and Corrupt Organizations Act. That law was intended to be a tool for use against mobsters, but U.S. attorneys had discovered it to be a convenient pressurizing device to use against white-collar criminals. The potential penalty was pretrial forfeiture of all my assets—down to the food in the refrigerator—and as many as twenty years in prison on each count.

Liman spelled out the situation for me. This was America. I had freedom of choice. One, I could plead not guilty and stand trial. But I had no chance of winning. The prosecutors would probably convict me under RICO, throw me into prison for a long time and, quite literally, throw my family onto the street. Two, I could plead guilty and refuse to cooperate, but would have to plead to RICO. The consequences of choice number two, Liman said, were similar to those of choice number one. Three, I could agree to forfeiture of the proceeds of my trading and plead guilty to lesser charges, which the government would allow me to do *if* I agreed to cooperate; we could undoubtedly negotiate a similar settlement of the civil charges.

"You're going to do some time," Liman warned. But choice number three would result in a shorter sentence and—far more important— would allow my family to survive. He recommended that we enter into plea agreement negotiations with the government.

"I need time to think about it," I said. "I have to talk to Laurie."

My attorney nodded his understanding.

I WAS in Flumenbaum's office one day in late May for another in the interminable round of strategy sessions when someone said, "Dennis, the new issue of *Newsweek* is out, and you're the cover story."

"You've got to be kidding," I said. I had never contemplated the notion that all of this would snowball into something so large.

Later that day Wilkis tracked me down by phone to ask how things were going. I said, "We should get together."

We met on a corner and then walked into a parking facility seeking privacy. It was a dark, dirty garage crowded with cars, attended by one old man. The smell of gasoline attacked.

Wilkis announced, "I've hired a lawyer. I've got to protect myself."

The gloomy cast in his eye gave me pause. "Bob, what's going on?"

He admitted in a morose, defeated voice, "Dennis, I bought and sold a good portion of the stocks here in the U.S."

"Through your mother's account?"

"Through hers and others."

My jaw dropped. I thought, but did not say, You stupid son of a bitch. What I said was, "It's all over, Bob."

Government sleuths had tracked some of my sources to Lazard Frères, and Lazard had conducted an internal investigation. Somehow Wilkis had been identified as a suspect. Now I knew the investigators would strike pay dirt. Wilkis had left a paperwork trail that a blind man could follow, and it would lead to the others involved in our conspiracy. All of our care to use code names and cryptic messages was worthless. "Bob, why? How could you do this?" I asked.

"I'm on my way to talk to my lawyer right now," he said.

My friend's face was pale and contorted with inner pain, as if he were heading off toward his execution. His first priority, like mine, would be to protect his family, but unlike me, he had involved them long ago. I knew at this instant that he was going to break.

Shortly after this, Wilkis retained Gary Naftalis to represent him. Naftalis, former chief of the criminal division of the U.S. Attorney's office in New York, advised Wilkis to surrender to the government and tell investigators everything he knew.

"Okay," I said to Liman. I took a deep breath. Through clenched teeth I said, "I'll plead."

"Okay," Liman agreed. His relief was obvious. He assured me that I was doing the right thing.

The attorneys hammered out a plea agreement that was acceptable to all parties, and we were encouraged to reach a rapid settlement with the SEC as well. The government was adamant on one particular: I had to answer the investigators' questions truthfully.

Speaking with the prosecutors would be tough, I knew, but not nearly as difficult as explaining all this to my family. Over time Laurie's initial fury gave way to more deliberate anger. Night after night we stayed up until the wee hours talking, sometimes arguing, often crying. She came to understand and even accept the fact that I had kept everything from her in order to protect her. What was more difficult for her to comprehend was why I had pushed my luck so far for so long. Why was the temptation so strong even after my legitimate income was far more than we needed?

I did not quite understand that myself.

"Dennis," Laurie asked during one of our extended talks, "do you realize how much you changed over the years when you were racing to the top? We—Adam and I—were always your top priority, but you became somewhat aloof. You were too busy and important to find time for people you considered beneath you."

This comment stung. Had I been too blind to see it?

THE GOVERNMENT HAD ME IN A BOX. I had to answer the questions, and I knew the process would be painful. I felt numb.

I hired well-known criminal lawyer Mark Pomerantz, of the firm of Fischetti & Pomerantz, to help me through what I knew was going to be the arduous task of submitting to the government's debriefing. Pomerantz and his associate Warren Feldman were with me in Assistant U.S. Attorney Charles Carberry's office on Monday, June 2, when I gave what is called a proffer—an overview of the scope of my improper activities. I explained that I had maintained over the years a relationship with another investment banker and that we had shared stock tips.

"We know that," Carberry replied. "The guy who went from Lazard to Hutton—Robert Wilkis. Who else?"

I gulped water from a glass in front of me. "An attorney," I stammered, "from Wachtell, Lipton."

Carberry probed for the man's name. Finally I said, "Ilan Reich."

Minutes later Carberry had pulled Ira Sokolow's name from me, too. Then he asked quickly and without preamble, "Who's the arb?"

Everyone in the room leaned forward. My world was very silent. I felt pressure in my temples, as if a vise were being clamped down.

Carberry waited me out.

I shifted in my chair, but this did not break the tension.

My eyes met Carberry's and I whispered, "Ivan Boesky."

Carberry could not hide his reaction. His eyes twitched and seemed brighter. He let out a deep sigh. I realized with sudden force what emotions were surging through him. A prosecutor spends his career waiting for the big one to come along. Here was Carberry's Revlon! With ill-concealed excitement he asked for details.

"The relationship started at arm's length," I said. I felt my voice crack a few times as I detailed how Boesky had drawn me in, eventually proposing a commission scheme, and how I had accepted.

The proffer was exhausting, humbling and very very painful. Several times during the torturous day the prosecutors indicated that they were unhappy with my reticence and were ready to walk out and leave me facing a lengthy prison term. Several other times I was poised to leave and take the full dose of judicial medicine. Pomerantz and Feldman grew exhausted holding together Liman's deal.

I felt weak, and I must have looked it.

It was late in the evening when the government struck below the belt, first suggesting, then demanding that I telephone my trading partners to elicit incriminating statements from them. My mind was clouded and spent. I barely realized what was happening as they led me to a special room adjacent to Giuliani's office, on the eighth floor, but my exhausted brain rebelled when I saw the equipment set up to record both ends of a telephone conversation.

"No way!" I shouted. I pointed out that it would be out of character, after years and years of subterfuge—using code names and all—for me to call my friends and try to get them to make damning admissions.

Pomerantz tried to keep me cool, but I was not a rational man at this moment. A bitter argument ensued for more than a half hour, punctuated by my screams of protest and pain. Finally one of the government men decreed, "That's it. Make the calls or the deal's dead."

Silence followed for several full minutes.

Pomerantz drew me aside and reminded me of the stakes. Under RICO the government could take me away from my family for most of the rest of my life. "Your friends might be walking in right now to cut their own deals. That's what I would advise them to do."

This was, I realized, the most painful, gut-crunching moment I had ever known. On the outside I was sopping with perspiration. On the inside I felt as if I were bleeding. The vise was closing.

Finally I returned to the investigators and announced quietly, "I'll make the calls if I can tell my friends the truth."

Someone asked derisively, "What's the truth?"

"The truth is quite simple," I replied. "I'll say, 'The government has an overwhelming case. It's all over. I'm pleading guilty, and I recommend that you get a lawyer and do the same.' " I felt my voice waver.

Another half hour passed in negotiation before the feds agreed to the compromise plan. By now it was eleven p.m. I was exhausted, hungry, too numb to even realize that I had for the first time in memory given up a fight. The activity around me was a dim cloud.

As if from a distance I realized that someone was dialing Wilkis' number. I recited my prearranged speech, and said no more. Wilkis wished me luck. Then a similar call was placed to Sokolow, and he, too, wished me luck.

I prayed that they would minimize the consequences for themselves and their families.

LAURIE WAS ALREADY ASLEEP WHEN I arrived home.

I lay my troubled head upon a pillow, but comfort eluded me. I felt my body twitch with involuntary spasms, and I knew I was disturbing Laurie. In frustration I rose and paced the living-room floor.

How could it have come to all this? I wondered. It wasn't supposed to end this way. Was I really the mastermind that the government seemed to consider me? Or was I more or less a rather average man, blinded by unrelenting ambition, to be sure, but now facing consequences far beyond my calculations?

It was nearly four a.m. when I threw on some clothes and stepped out onto the nearly deserted Park Avenue sidewalk. I realized that my feet were heading toward the parking garage. I looked down and found the Ferrari keys in my hand.

"Don't drive the Ferrari!" These were Liman's words ringing in my memory as I slipped the protective blue cover off my beautiful red baby. "The government is going to want it. It's a symbol. You must stay low key. Don't touch that car!"

I drowned out the warning words with the explosive, satisfying roar of the 12-cylinder, 48-valve engine. Thunder reverberated through the parking garage and echoed inside my head. I slipped the gear shift into position and heard the tires squeal on the pavement.

I drove for hours, until the sun filtered into my consciousness and the highways were crowded. I looked with envy at the ordinary people driving their ordinary cars to their ordinary jobs.

I WAS allowed to clean out my desk. The task was to be accomplished on the evening of June 4, and Drexel bigwigs spread the word that all employees of the M&A department were to be absent.

Liman's associate Brad Karp was with me. An IRS agent and a Drexel security guard accompanied us. We passed the office of Marty Siegel, Drexel's newest superstar in the M&A department. Siegel had come from Kidder Peabody, and was well known on the Street as a defender of takeover targets. I reflected ruefully upon the news that someone at Drexel had yanked my picture from the 1985 annual report and replaced it with Siegel's image.

The security guard opened the padlock on my office door. Then as the IRS agent watched carefully to make sure that I did not dip into the business files, I began the solemn task.

I went through the desk drawers slowly, carefully, savoring each moment. Here were some letters; there were some photographs. After a time I had several boxes full of material.

There were no more drawers to explore, but still I sat at my desk for many minutes. No one spoke to me. Here was the symbolic end of the most exciting, fascinating portion of my life. I was thirty-three years old. I had been a managing director of the most upbeat, powerful investment banking house of the '80s.

This desk was a throne, and I had toppled from it.

I closed my eyes and wept inner tears.

Why? I asked myself. Why did I do it? Why did I succumb so completely to the lure of excess? It would be easy to blame it all on Wall Street, but the Street, at its most basic level, simply pumps money into the business world. In the '80s it had done so at a crazy pace, supplying a demand that was incredible. It was easy to lose perspective, to forget that there are tangible costs to everything. Too late I totaled them up: my career had evaporated, my financial life lay in ruins, my self-esteem was zero.

My family was suffering intense anguish. I was going to jail.

On June 5, without ever being indicted, I stood before Judge Gerard Goettel in federal court and declared, "To contest the charges against me on technical grounds would serve only to prolong the suffering of my family. It would also convey the wrong message. I have violated the law, and I have remorse for my conduct, not excuses." Then I entered a plea of guilty to four felony charges. Sentencing was deferred until the judge could study all the issues. I faced maximum penalties of twenty years in prison and $610,000 in fines.

That covered the criminal charges, but I still had to deal with the civil penalties. On the same day I agreed to pay restitution to the SEC of $11.6 million in alleged trading profits. The bulk of that was covered by the cash frozen in my Bank Leu account, but that still left about $1 million outstanding, and my assets were fair game. Perhaps the worst of the civil penalties was that I had to agree to accept an injunction barring me from employment in the securities business for the rest of my life. The career I loved was now forbidden to me.

Laurie and I were allowed to keep the Park Avenue co-op, our personal effects, our BMW, and personal savings that would allow my family to survive for a time, but the rest—real estate investments, my retirement account, my Drexel stock and my shares in various Drexel partnerships—vanished from our lives. It was called a global settlement. This theme reached its peak the day the government demanded the Ferrari. Officials refused to pick up the car, because they were unsure they could handle such a high-performance vehicle. They insisted that I deliver it to a designated location.

Laurie and I traded in the BMW for a Ford.

THE very day I entered my guilty plea, Wilkis turned himself in to the U.S. Attorney's office. Very quickly he provided prosecutors with the identity of his "kid" at Lazard Frères. He was Randall Cecola, a junior financial analyst at Lazard from September 1983 to July 1985.

Meanwhile, investigators probed into every nook and cranny of my affairs. I had to supply them with all my personal telephone bills. From Drexel they received copies of my office long-distance logs and my expense account vouchers. They demanded copies of all my bank records, all my correspondence—business and personal—as well as calendars and daily logs. They even demanded my family tree.

The paper trail led inexorably to others.

On July 8 the SEC served a subpoena on Wachtell, Lipton, demanding documents concerning numerous trades. At first, Ilan Reich was assigned to compile the records, but Gary Lynch of the SEC disclosed to Herbert Wachtell that Reich was the target of the inquiry.

As the heat increased, Ira Sokolow turned himself in and implicated "Goldie," who, I discovered, was David Brown, a vice president in the mortgage-securities department of Goldman, Sachs. He and Sokolow had roomed together in college.

It felt as if I spent several lifetimes in my lawyers' offices. I was huddling with Liman when one of Laurie's family members in Florida called with the news that her father, after his long, valiant, painful struggle, had finally left us. Laurie was now seven months pregnant, and I had asked her family to tell me first so that I could break the news to her as gently as possible.

"Go," Liman said. "Leave. Be with your wife."

When I walked into our home, Laurie glanced up, alarmed to see me back so early. She read the message in my eyes. We clung to one another in sorrow, in desperation, in fear.

Liman spoke with Carberry, and the prosecutor arranged to have my bail restrictions relaxed so we could fly to Florida for the funeral.

At the cemetery, as the service neared an end, Laurie clutched at her stomach. I grasped her hand. Then as Leonard Skolnik went to his final rest I felt his unborn grandchild shift and stretch.

DREXEL managed to slough off the negative publicity concerning my arrest in large part by pointing out that my alleged insider trading activities had begun long before I joined the firm. I was cut loose, but Drexel soared ever higher.

Milken was at the very top of his game. *Institutional Investor* quoted an investment banker who dribbled praise: "Mike is the only person in the securities business today who can do it all. He is a master." Estimates of his net worth ran as high as $1 billion. Some spoke openly of him as a candidate for Secretary of the Treasury, but I was dubious; that would be a gigantic step down. In a decade Milken had taken the annual junk-bond market from $15 billion to $125 billion.

I was necessarily preoccupied with my own affairs, but an occasional story from the outside world returned me to my Wall Street life. On November 14, with intense internal pain, I contemplated the news that Perelman had issued a tender offer valued at $4.12 billion for Gillette. The deal would more than double the assets of his corporate empire. I could have been there, I knew. I also knew that I would probably never be there again.

My phone rang. I heard Flumenbaum ask, "Are you sitting down?"

"Yes." I took a deep breath, awaiting yet another blow.

"Ivan Boesky today is pleading guilty in a case related to yours. I don't have details, but I wanted to let you know." I was in shock, like everyone else.

At that moment Marty Siegel, who had had many business dealings with Boesky, was in Marty Lipton's office at Wachtell, Lipton, stunned by the subpoena a federal marshal had slapped into his hand. Other subpoenas were served upon executives at Salomon Brothers, Prudential-Bache, and Goldman, Sachs. As these various Wall Street stars studied the legal papers the SEC announced that Boesky was implicated in the insider trading scandal, as well as other schemes to manipulate securities transactions.

Within minutes a cadre of federal marshals appeared with grand

Left, Arthur Liman, my principal attorney. Right, Ivan Boesky leaving court after being sentenced to three years in prison for his role in the insider trading scandal. Below, the king of finance, Michael Milken, shortly before his fall.

jury and SEC subpoenas for both Michael and Lowell Milken, as well as other employees of the Drexel Bank.

Now it was announced that Boesky, through Harvey Pitt, had carved out an agreement with the U.S. Attorney's office. The SEC agreement charged Boesky with profiting more than $50 million from nonpublic information that I had provided. Despite claiming evidence of an incredible array of crimes, the government agreed to allow Boesky to plead guilty to a single count of conspiring to make a false filing with the SEC. That crime carried a maximum penalty of a five-year prison term and a $250,000 fine. In addition, Boesky consented to a civil injunction and an SEC order requiring him to pay a $50 million penalty and to place another $50 million into an escrow fund to settle claims. He resigned from the bar and agreed to accept a lifetime ban from employment in the securities market.

Boesky was reported to have once said, "I can't predict my demise, but I suspect it will occur abruptly."

As all of this filtered into the collective consciousness of the investment community, it caused tremors. While Boesky's fine was a whopper, it could have been twice as much, based on the treble-damages provision of the law. Why had the government allowed him to get off fairly easily? It could only mean that he was cooperating with an ongoing investigation. It could only mean that others would fall.

These suspicions were summed up by Stanley Kon, a member of the finance faculty of the University of Michigan business school, who was quoted in the Washington *Post:* "Boesky had three hundred buttons on his telephone console. I wonder who else besides Levine he has been talking to."

Speculation on the Street held that Drexel and Milken had been dealt mortal blows. Boesky was intimately associated with both.

CHAPTER TWELVE

THE December issue of *The American Lawyer* carried a story based on an interview with Ilan Reich, depicting the fallen lawyer in a black-and-white photograph that accented his prematurely gray hair and his morose spirit. Here I found myself cast as the seductive mastermind of a diabolical network, the man who preyed upon innocents. Reich, like others, was painting me as the heavy. I understood this, since it reduced his culpability, but it was disturbing to read.

The attack continued later that month when Wilkis pleaded guilty to four felony charges and declared to U.S. District Judge Peter K. Leisure, "I was recruited by Dennis Levine to reveal to him confidential information."

SARAH'S birth, on December 18, 1986, was so different from Adam's. Yes, there was unbelievable joy, but it was tempered with the realization that I would spend the first days, months, years—we still did not know how long—of her life in prison.

Ira Sokolow was the first to be sentenced, and we awaited the action nervously. Clearly his term would serve as a benchmark. When he received a year and a day in prison, followed by three years' probation, I said to myself, Okay, Dennis. That's the minimum you can expect. Sokolow also agreed to pay the SEC $210,000 in illegal profits and fines.

Ilan Reich pleaded guilty to one count of securities fraud and one count of mail fraud, which resulted in his automatic disbarment. He signed a consent agreement to pay the SEC $485,000 in assets. He was allowed to keep his home on West Ninety-fourth Street, $10,000 in cash, $14,000 in an IRA account and a used Oldsmobile. He pleaded guilty to two criminal counts of insider trading, and received a year and a day in prison, plus five years' probation.

Robert Wilkis received a year and a day in prison, plus five years' probation. He settled civil charges with the SEC by agreeing to turn over $3.3 million in assets, including the balance of his Cayman Islands account, as well as $50,000 in cash, which he had kept in a shoe box in his apartment.

Now, of our group, I was the only one awaiting sentencing.

ON FEBRUARY 20, 1987, Laurie and I were driven to the federal courthouse in White Plains, New York. The moment we arrived, the car was surrounded by a gaggle of reporters. They pounded on the windows and climbed on the hood.

"Why are they doing this to us?" Laurie sobbed. "My God! Why are they doing this to us?"

The assault lasted a full fifteen minutes before mounted police officers could restore order and open the door. My brother Robert raced from the courthouse and helped clear a pathway for us. We ran a gauntlet through the freezing cold and into the temporary sanctity of the tiny courthouse, where Judge Goettel had recently been transferred. We entered an elevator and pushed the button for the third floor, where the courtroom was located.

I thought I was prepared for anything, but I was wrong. When the elevator door opened, Laurie and I hustled out and, in our haste, almost ran into Dad.

Our eyes met, and I saw within him the most excruciating pain I could imagine.

"Everything will be okay, Dad," I said.

He mumbled an incoherent response.

Dad took Laurie off to the courtroom as I turned aside to huddle with counsel. I had a full contingent there: Liman, Flumenbaum, Pomerantz and others. By now we all knew one another very well.

"Arthur," I warned Liman, "I'm going to probably be very emotional. I might have great difficulty speaking to the judge."

"Do the best you can," he said.

A standing-room-only crowd spilled into the hallways. Reporters and sketch artists were everywhere. When I entered the courtroom, Laurie was the first sight my eyes spotted. She appeared solemn and sad but very pretty in a gray dress. She was seated in the spectators' section, flanked by Dad and my brother Robert. I moved toward the defendant's table. The attorneys moved in concert to join me.

Liman issued an eloquent plea for leniency, pointing out that I had already endured a form of banishment. Judge Goettel then asked if I had anything to say. I certainly did, but as I rose to my feet I did not know if I could say it. Over the years I had made countless presentations to the richest and most powerful business executives in the world, and stage fright had never been a problem. So why did I now feel as if someone had jammed a huge rock into my throat?

I struggled for breath. "Last June," I said finally, "when I pleaded guilty before Your Honor, I was automatically sentenced to a life of disgrace and humiliation. I have disappointed my wife, my children, my father, my brothers, my family, my friends, my colleagues. I abused the system I believe in, and I will never forgive myself. I'm truly sorry and ashamed, not only for my past criminal behavior but for all the anguish and humiliation and embarrassment I caused my family, mostly because it's been their love and support that has sustained me throughout this very difficult period. Your Honor, I assure you that I have learned my lesson. I swear in this court that I will never violate the law again, and I beg you to allow me a chance to put the pieces of my life back together, to help my family get through this, to try and become a contributing member of the community again. Thank you."

I remained standing alongside Liman as Judge Goettel pronounced, "On count one, two years, fifty thousand dollars." I had the ratios memorized, and the calculator in my mind told me that minus good behavior, the sentence was seventeen months and five days.

The judge said, "On count two, two years, fifty thousand dollars. On count three, two years, sixty-two thousand dollars. On count four, two years, two hundred thousand dollars."

The judge paused. The vital question now was whether the judge decreed that the terms run concurrently or consecutively.

I looked directly into his eyes. His gaze locked upon mine. What he said next would make the difference between seventeen months and five days, and sixty-eight months and twenty days.

He said, "Sentences to run . . ."

I was sure that my heart had stopped.

". . . concurrently."

Although the sentence was twice as long as others in my case, I thought it was fair.

Then the judge said he would delay the imposition of the sentence for two months so that I could spend time with baby Sarah.

Afterward, when I encountered Dad in the courthouse hallway, I saw anguish in his face. Here was his youngest son, of whom he had always been so proud, sentenced to prison. He wanted to cry, but his pain was beyond tears. I repeated what I had told him earlier, "Everything will be okay, Dad."

ONE of our biggest concerns was five-year-old Adam. Until now we had tried to shelter him, making sure he was not around the television whenever a news report came on. But Laurie and I knew that Adam needed to know why Daddy was going away.

I was supposed to be his role model. I was the one who was charged with the responsibility to impart wisdom to him, to help him set his personal standards, to teach him values. I had to admit to my son that I had broken some very important rules.

We were at my brother Robert's house, sitting in the den, when I tried to explain. I drew Adam onto my lap and began, "You know, when little people make mistakes, they have to be punished. Well, it's the same for big people. They get punished by a judge."

I had difficulty continuing, and Laurie picked up the theme. "Daddy made a mistake," she said. "He didn't hurt anybody, but he broke some business rules. He didn't realize it at first, but eventually he did know it was wrong, but he continued to do it. Now he has to be punished."

"I went to see a judge," I said. "A man who punishes big people."

Adam asked fearfully, "What did he do?"

My body went numb. I felt paralyzed.

Laurie tried to explain. "The biggest punishment that an adult can have, especially if he has children, is to be taken away from his family for a time. The judge is probably going to take Daddy away from us for a while."

Through tears Adam asked, "Daddy, did you know what you were doing was wrong?"

Through my own tears I replied, "Yes."

"So then why did you do it?"

The room reeled in front of my eyes. I still had no answer to this.

Next to me, Laurie turned restlessly, as she had all night. Down the hall I knew that Adam was awakening to a frightening and incomprehensible day. Only tiny three-month-old Sarah had slept reasonably well, although I sensed that somehow she also knew the world was awry. Dad and Robert were already on their way into the city, each probably lost in his own gray thoughts. This morning, April 6, 1987, I was heading into the unknown.

I eased out of bed, and Laurie arose, too. We dressed wordlessly. I helped get Adam and Sarah ready for the day. Breakfast stuck in my throat. Suddenly Dad and Robert were at the door. All too soon it was time to go.

I cradled Sarah in my arms and caressed her soft, tiny cheek with my finger. Then I picked up Adam. He hugged me as tightly as he could and planted a slobbery kiss on my cheek. Laurie and I squeezed one another so hard that it hurt. Our tears mingled.

I followed Dad and Robert into the elevator and out the door of our building. We stepped into the courtyard, where my Ford waited. The garage man had left the engine idling. I turned to look back and up. They were there at the window, seven floors above—Laurie with Sarah in her arms, and Adam at her side, waving good-bye.

I'm actually driving off to prison, I thought. It's really happening. I waved back to my family and mouthed the words, "I love you." I stood there for many moments as the picture in front of my eyes blurred. I deserved this punishment, but they did not.

Then I felt the touch of Robert's hand on my arm, and I let him guide me toward the car. "I'll drive," I said. "It's going to be a long time before I can drive again."

"Are you sure you're up to it?" Robert asked.

"Yes."

I sat in the driver's seat and took a moment to compose myself. Then I headed the car out onto Park Avenue and guided it with deliberate slowness up the FDR Drive, across the George Washington Bridge and out through New Jersey. We picked up I-80 and aimed west. Our destination was Lewisburg, a tiny town in north-central Pennsylvania. I was headed for the minimum-security federal prison camp adjacent to the penitentiary. It was about three hours away from home, but in fact, it was in an alien universe.

This was probably the first time in my life that I ever drove the speed limit, but we still arrived more than an hour prior to my one p.m. reporting time. "Let's have some lunch," I suggested. "I want a last meal." We spotted a diner in the center of the drab little town. I parked the car and we got out. As we walked toward the diner we passed a newsstand. I stopped to buy a copy of *USA Today*.

We ordered sandwiches, and as we waited, I opened the newspaper. There, inside, was a photograph of an inmate's cubicle at the Lewisburg federal prison camp and a story about the place where Dennis Levine would be serving his sentence.

The reality really hit after lunch, when I pulled the car down a long, treelined drive and stopped alongside a thirty-foot-high concrete wall surrounding a forbidding complex of brick buildings. Atop the wall was a system of sentry towers. In them I could see armed guards watching us. Then as we neared the front gate I saw a squad of reporters, photographers and videotape crews.

My God, I thought. Will I ever have any privacy? "Drop me off," I said. "Get out of here."

I hugged my father and my brother; then I grabbed my duffel bag and walked toward the prison. I ignored the questions that flew at me, concentrating on keeping dignity intact as best I could.

I WEIGHED in at 241 pounds and was disgusted with the way I had let myself go. The guards handed me a set of surplus army fatigues and a pair of blue sneakers.

"Socks?" I asked.

"No socks."

After I dressed, I was driven to the camp compound and left in the care of a dormitory officer. He told me to find a bed. If the camp had ever been a "country-club prison," it sure was not now. Built to hold 165 inmates, it now had 240, and about 90 percent of them were drug offenders. Two men had to share four- by seven-foot cubicles that were designed originally for one inmate.

The large dorm was relatively empty as I made my way through one cubicle after another, finding myself more and more disgusted by the filth that cluttered the place. Despite my efforts, I could not find a bunk that appeared unused. Finally the dormitory officer assigned me an upper bunk with a a lumpy, soiled mattress. He issued me a pillow and sheets and left me alone.

About 4 p.m. the inmates began to return from their various work assignments. A burly man entered the cubicle and expressed his disapproval at my presence. We regarded each other warily for a moment before I ventured a question. I made a sweeping gesture with my arms and asked, "Do they ever clean this place?"

My cubicle-mate found great delight in this. He roared with laughter and explained that the warden, knowing that the press was about to descend in concert with my arrival, had ordered a massive cleanup. "Everybody here hates you," he said.

The next morning I was put to work scrubbing toilets and urinals, then made to clean various nooks and crannies with a toothbrush. It was harassment, of course, and I simply shut up and swallowed it. I knew I was being tested. Gradually the hazing subsided, and I was assigned to mop floors and mow lawns.

It was no surprise to find myself in the midst of an antisocial crowd, but far too many of these men were strung out. Every evening the guards doled out "hot medicine" to the more overt psychos, who soon drifted into a chemically induced euphoria, allowing the rest of us to get some sleep.

Recreational opportunities were limited. There was a gymnasium with a basketball court, a makeshift track and a baseball field. The social hubs were the dorm's two TV rooms. The sets were tuned to whatever action-adventure programs were on the air, and everyone around me rooted openly for the bad guys.

On October 19, 1987, my tasks were completed when most of the inmates were still out on the grounds. I had the chance to watch CNN, and I was transfixed by the coverage of the stock market crash. The Dow Jones industrial average was in a free-fall, on its way to a record one-day plunge of more than 500 points.

Suddenly two guards were standing behind me.

"Come with us," one of them ordered. They explained that a high-ranking official wanted to see me. I followed them to the prison offices, where they ushered me in to the official.

"Dennis," he said cordially, "please sit down. Cigarette?"

"No, thanks," I replied. "I don't smoke."

He lit up. Then, in a quiet voice that nonetheless belied tension, he asked, "Are you aware of what's going on in the market?"

"Yes. I've been watching CNN."

He leaned forward. His voice grew more intense. "Dennis, can you give me some advice on what to do with my portfolio? Should I sell out and take my losses, or should I hold on?"

I countered in a lighthearted tone, "If I give you advice, is there any way I can go home sooner?"

"Oh, no," he retorted. "No, I can't do anything like that."

"Then I can't help you," I said.

I COULD not remember a time when I had time. At Smith Barney, at Lehman Brothers and, most of all, at Drexel, there was never enough of the commodity. Here the universal goal was to *do* time, to get it out of the way, to kill it. I discovered very quickly that one of

Right, Rudolph Giuliani, who headed the U.S. Attorney's Office for the Southern District of New York. Below, press coverage of the scandal. Not the way one wants to live life, believe me. Bottom, the four- by seven-foot cubicles at the Lewisburg prison camp weren't designed for two. The camp was adjacent to the penitentiary.

the things you do with time is to think. I took long, isolated walks on the prison grounds and asked myself painful questions.

Why was I here? The answer was simple, but admitting it to myself was profoundly therapeutic: I was here because of my own actions. No one led me down the garden path. I was a big boy, and I made the decision to cross the line. *I was to blame.* There was a big part of me that wanted to take the easy emotional out and contend that everything would have been all right if my bankers had been more honorable: if they had played by Bank Leu's rules, they would not have piggybacked my trades; if they had played by Bahamian rules, they would never have sold me out. But this argument was a cop-out. I would have been caught sooner or later. I was to blame.

Once I accepted this truth, other questions gnawed.

Why had I started? This was another easy question. In those early years I had regarded my offshore trading activities as just a method to make fast, easy money. It doesn't hurt anybody, I rationalized. And besides, there was always that delicious delusion that everybody is doing it.

The difficult question was: *Why had I not stopped?* What was the answer to that nagging inquiry, voiced by Laurie and almost everyone else? Why did I continue trading on inside information well after my legitimate income was far greater than my needs? I was earning more than $2 million a year at Drexel. And why, when I already had a considerable bankroll and a comfortable, quiet system in place, did I make perhaps the single stupidest decision of all and agree to Boesky's deal? There was more at work here than simple greed.

But if not greed, what was it?

I reconstructed my reasoning, although it had been vague at the time. It went something like this: So what if you have $10 million in the Bahamas, Dennis? You're helping your clients amass hundreds of millions of dollars. You negotiate billion-dollar deals every day, so where do you get off thinking that $10 million is big time?

Something deep inside forced me to try to catch up to the pack of wheeler-dealers who always raced in front of me. Whatever it was, placed in the context of workweeks that ranged from sixty to 100 hours, leaving little or no time for reflection, it had a narcotic effect.

But it was not money.

To those of us who raced along the Wall Street treadmill of the '80s, money assumed a mystical aura. Once you knew that you had your mortgage and your car payment covered, once you had a full belly, money simply became the way you gauged your level of success. Competitive jealousy is normal in any workplace, but in this microcosm the numbers were so enormous that they threw everything out of scale.

In sum, money became the points on the scoreboard. If I checked the Quotron and discovered I had just earned several hundred thousand dollars on an insider trade, I felt a rush of euphoria that had to be akin to a drug high. But the high always wore off because I soon remembered that there were so many ahead of me on the scoreboard.

In time I came to view myself as an insider trading junkie. I was addicted to the excitement, the sense of victory. Some spouses use drugs; others have extramarital affairs. I secretly traded stocks.

I came to understand it all better when I compared my legitimate success to my illegitimate activities. In the beginning perhaps the insider trading was more intoxicating, but as my career progressed, the excitement of the "deal" eclipsed, by far, the thrill of the private victory. Perelman versus Revlon was a much greater challenge than enhancing the value of my secret bank account.

Looking back, I could see that at each new level of my career I had pushed my goals higher. When I was an associate, I wanted to be a vice president. When I became a vice president, I wanted to be a senior vice president. When I became a senior vice president, I wanted to be a partner or managing director. When I became a managing director, I wanted to become a client. When I was earning $20,000 a year, I thought, I can make $100,000. When I was making $1 million, I thought, I can make $3 million.

Ambition eclipsed rationality. I was unable to find fulfillment in realistic limits. One frenetic meeting followed another. One deal was piled atop the next. The hours grew longer, the numbers grew bigger, the stakes grew more critical, the fire grew ever hotter.

By the time I became a managing director, I was out of control.

So was Boesky.

So was Milken.

So was Drexel.

I thought of Ronald Perelman, ranked number three on *Forbes'* list of the 400 richest Americans. Was he content? Or was he obsessed with catching the two individuals above him? When does it stop?

Sometimes with such thoughts spinning through my mind I looked about in surprise at my environment. Here is where it stopped for me. I was in prison.

Dennis, I said to myself, this is a blessing in disguise. You need this withdrawal. You were hooked; you overdosed on deals. And you were not about to stop until someone caught you or until the irresistible lure of the action on the Street killed you.

I burned with anger at my own blindness. I had to change my priorities. I had to regain control of my own life.

WEEKENDS and holidays were visiting days. The visiting area was furnished with chairs and picnic tables jammed on top of one another, precluding privacy. This was the only place where I could visit with my family. I will be haunted forever by the memory of Sarah taking her first toddling steps toward her daddy in a room crowded with convicted drug dealers and other felons.

Laurie dreaded these days. On the morning of a visit she woke feeling disgusted and angry, wondering why she and her family had to suffer like this. After the exhausting three-hour drive she knew that guards would empty her purse and check Sarah's stroller for contraband. The degradation always rekindled her free-floating anger toward me, and she could not hide it nor feign affection. She looked at the people around us and felt soiled. She came out of duty, but she did not want to be there and made sure I knew it.

Once Adam came in clutching a Mickey Mouse coloring book. The guard was a strict, humorless sort who grabbed the book out of my son's hand and growled, "You aren't allowed to bring that in here."

I was outraged. I could feel my face redden. "Why can't he bring a coloring book into the visiting room?" I asked.

The guard sneered at me and answered, "We wouldn't want to stimulate the inmates' minds too much."

Near the end of that visit Adam asked the same question he always did: "Dad, when can you come home? I hate this stupid place."

I answered as I always did, through a parched throat, counting down the days.

Laurie, dazed and distressed, was too overwrought for tears. No wonder the wives of so many of my fellow prisoners filed for divorce.

SIXTY-SEVEN POUNDS LIGHTER THAN when I went off to prison, I was released from federal custody on September 8, 1988, pondering this question: After skyrocketing to the top of the world and crashing down even faster, what do you do next? I realized that I would face each day with enormous uncertainty, trying to put together the scrambled pieces of the jigsaw puzzle of my life. I vowed to spend the bulk of my time with my family, to help heal their—our—wounds.

One of the first things I did was take Adam to Disney World.

Then I had to come to grips with Laurie's pain.

"Do you know what I did the day you went to prison?" she asked.

"No."

"I went over to your once sacred desk and began to reorganize it."

Ours had always been a traditional marriage. Laurie managed the children and the day-to-day running of the household. I went off to my business of juggling billions of dollars and, at home, took care of the family finances. Now someone else had to assume that task, and the only candidate was Laurie.

"I relabeled folders and arranged things the way I wanted them," she recalled. In addition to the normal household costs, there were extraordinary expenses. Every day brought new bills from the army of attorneys who had worked on my case, and each time she saw an envelope with an attorney's return address, her resentment grew.

In short order Laurie had lost her father to cancer, given birth to Sarah and sent her husband off to prison. For seventeen months she was a single parent. She was the one who had to make the long drives to Lewisburg with two kids squirming in the car. Socially she was a fifth wheel, a woman with two kids and no spouse. It was difficult for her to hold up her head with pride.

Nevertheless, throughout this time she kept the pain inside so as to minimize my own. After a time she found herself enjoying her new independence, and as the months passed, she contemplated my return with a certain scary feeling of ambivalence.

The words cut deeply. There was no choice but to let her vent her accumulated rage. It was time to have it out, and we did so.

She was still angry that I had persisted in my trading long after my legitimate salary had increased exponentially. But she had come to understand the force of the addiction that had controlled me. What bothered her most now was the nagging truth that I had been immoral. "My God!" she said. "It was like you were having an affair. There was a part of you I never saw."

Perhaps what kept us together was her growing understanding that as sophisticated as I had seemed, I was in reality a victim of my own naïveté. She realized that I had been convinced that if I was involved in a crime, it was victimless. In my mind I never hurt anybody.

Months passed before I began to see glimpses of the laughter that used to be endemic in our household. At that point I knew that we could survive anything.

Nevertheless, Laurie still cries whenever she discusses the year and a half when I was gone.

It seemed obvious that the investigators would not stop until they reeled in as many targets as possible, including the largest. My former firm was unquestionably in the hottest water. The government lodged numerous charges that Drexel had abused its position by such actions as parking stocks for other investors and pressuring entrepreneurs to initiate takeover actions against target companies in which Drexel quietly owned large positions. A Drexel spokesman declared, "A financial institution cannot stand up to a RICO indictment."

In January 1989 Drexel Burnham Lambert, Inc. and the Drexel Burnham Lambert Group, Inc. agreed to plead guilty to six felony counts involving securities fraud and market manipulation and to pay a total of $650 million in fines and penalties. Drexel also agreed to cooperate with the ongoing investigation. Although Milken had not been charged with any wrongdoing, part and parcel of the agreement was that Drexel "not be involved with Michael R. Milken directly or indirectly in any business transactions or activities."

The action tore Drexel apart. Employees were told that speaking with Milken was now grounds for dismissal; they were to advise their clients that if they talked to Milken, Drexel could not deal with them.

Milken's departure spelled the end for America's highest-flying investment bank. Fred McCarthy, one of my former partners in the corporate finance department, commented that Drexel had "lost its soul," and subsequent events proved him correct.

Nevertheless, Drexel persisted with its characteristic tenacity. One day I encountered Leon Black on the street. He greeted me cordially and asked the obligatory questions. I brought him up to date and told him that I had just formed the ADASAR Group (named after Adam and Sarah), a financial advisory firm specializing in mergers and acquisitions and capital formation. I asked how he was doing.

"We're working on the Nabisco-RJR thing," he said.

I said to myself, It's history making, and I'm not involved.

"It's a very very tough sell," Black remarked. "We've got everybody in the firm going on it. I think we'll pull it off."

And indeed they did. In the midst of a barrage of adverse publicity Drexel managed to place $4 billion worth of junk bonds to fund the LBO. It was the largest junk-bond issue ever.

Drexel earned fees of more than $200 million on the RJR deal, but it was the last great gasp. In the months that followed, Drexel lowered its standards, financing marginal deals that Milken would never have approved. In several cases the firm was forced to buy heavy positions in new securities issues because it could not sell them on the open market. This tied up its capital and made it difficult to meet short-term obligations.

For the first time some Drexel clients filed for bankruptcy. The end was in sight.

Addressing business students at New York University in 1989.
It's my hope I can steer students away from the mistakes I made.

THERE WAS PERHAPS ONLY ONE FISH bigger than Boesky, and the team of federal investigators pursued Milken relentlessly. Prosecutors contended that Boesky and Milken initiated a "secret arrangement" in early 1984 calling for Boesky to buy and sell stocks at the direction of, and for the benefit of, Milken. This would allow Milken to make clandestine trades of stocks that were on Drexel's restricted list. At other times, the government said, Drexel bought or sold securities for Boesky, hiding the true identity of the dealer so that Boesky could reap certain tax benefits or evade SEC reporting requirements.

On March 29, 1989, Milken was indicted by a federal grand jury on ninety-eight criminal counts. His brother, Lowell, was also indicted on a variety of complaints. The charges alleged insider trading violations concerning securities of a number of firms.

As the details surfaced, I was amazed to learn the astronomical total of Milken's Drexel income. The government said that in 1987 alone he was paid $550 million in salary and bonuses—and that did not count income from his various partnership arrangements. He was the highest paid U.S. executive in history.

IN JANUARY 1990 Robert Campeau's Allied and Federated Department Stores filed for Chapter 11 bankruptcy protection, and the effects were felt economywide. The garment manufacturers were hit, as were the appliance manufacturers. In fact, any industry that sold products through these large department stores had difficulty collecting its accounts, and the ripples washed on to their suppliers.

Left hung out to dry was a string of creditors who had funded Campeau's overambitious acquisitions. The effect on the junk-bond market was chilling.

Drexel frantically sought bank financing to meet $100 million in obligations due on February 13, 1990. The day before the deadline Citibank led a group of lenders into a meeting to consider extending short-term credit. For collateral Drexel offered a portfolio of junk bonds, private placements, and oil and gas limited partnerships. One banker called it "an eclectic collection of illiquid securities." Shortly before midnight the bankers turned thumbs-down.

The following day Drexel's 5300 employees gathered in offices all over the world to listen to Fred Joseph announce in a sober monotone that Drexel was filing for Chapter 11 bankruptcy reorganization.

"I WAS THE FOUNDER AND HEAD of the high-yield and convertible securities department at Drexel," Milken began as he appeared in a Manhattan courtroom before Judge Kimba M. Wood.

It was April 24, 1990. For years now Milken had been recognized as *the* force behind the junk-bond juggernaut and as Drexel's Midas-in-residence. Everyone wanted to know what made him tick.

Still, he remained an enigma.

The private bodyguards were gone, replaced by federal marshals and a phalanx of attorneys. Now he stood symbolically naked, stripped by the government of his job and his glory. But even without those trappings the mystique remained. The largest federal courtroom in Manhattan overflowed with spectators, and hundreds more stood outside in Foley Square.

"I am here today because in connection with some transactions, I transgressed certain of the laws and regulations that govern our industry," Milken said. "I was wrong in doing so and knew that at the time, and I am pleading guilty to these offenses."

One by one he addressed the six violations of securities laws to which he was admitting. With his voice breaking, Milken concluded, "By my acts I have hurt those who are closest to me. I am truly sorry."

Repeatedly Judge Wood asked Milken to assure her that he was, in fact, guilty of the crimes. Repeatedly Milken said yes, he was guilty. In my view, further evidence was unnecessary. Yes, it was true that an important part of Milken's plea agreement called for the government to drop all charges against his brother, Lowell. Yes, it was true that the drama this day would bring an end to four years of hounding by government prosecutors. But—and I knew this fact well—no one pleads guilty to criminal charges unless he is, in fact, guilty.

The judge warned that the six crimes carried a maximum prison term of twenty-eight years. She deferred sentencing until she could study presentencing reports.

In another room of the courthouse, Milken settled the SEC's civil charges by agreeing to pay a fine of $200 million and further agreeing to place an additional $400 million in a restitution fund. It was the largest individual settlement figure in SEC history, exceeded only by Drexel's $650 million fine. Milken's remaining assets, which by all estimates were still considerable, would remain subject to perhaps dozens of civil lawsuits. Both of the Milkens signed consent decrees in which they neither admitted nor denied SEC charges, and both accepted a permanent ban from participation in the securities industry.

On November 21, 1990, Michael Milken again faced Judge Wood, this time to await sentencing. The courtroom was hushed as the judge lectured, "When a man of your power in the financial world repeatedly conspires to violate and violates securities and tax laws in order to achieve more power and wealth for himself and his wealthy clients, and commits financial crimes that are particularly hard to detect, a significant prison term is required in order to deter others."

After a few more remarks she said, "Mr. Milken, please rise."

Milken stood, flanked by his attorneys, for the moment of judgment.

"I sentence you to a total of ten years in prison, consisting of two years each on counts two through six, to be served consecutively, and I also sentence you to three years of probation on count one. A special condition of your probation is that you serve full-time community service, eighteen hundred hours per year for each of the three years, in a program to be determined by the court."

THE week before Milken was due to report to prison, Judge Wood announced an extraordinary finding. Prosecutors had contended that Milken's six crimes bilked the investing public of $4.7 million. Lawyers had backed lawsuits claiming billions of dollars in damages. But based upon all she had learned from the volumes of evidence she had reviewed and the hours of testimony she had witnessed, Judge Wood concluded that her best estimate of total investor losses was $318,082. The judge indicated that she was surprised by the relatively low figure and that she now believed that Milken—pending his cooperation—would serve thirty-six to forty months of his sentence.

I FELT a stab of empathy on Monday, March 4, 1991. This was the day that Milken was to report to the federal minimum-security facility in the ironically named town of Pleasanton, California.

The question of his motivation remained, as Milken was probably a billionaire by the time he allied himself with Boesky and other conspirators. Clearly, he did not have to break the law. When I considered the facts, I was left with only partial answers. In the weeks and months following my downfall, countless psychiatric "authorities" propounded various theories as to my motivation. Many of them proclaimed that my incessant drive for money and success was undoubtedly rooted in my relationship with my parents or siblings. To me it appeared to be so much hokum. My childhood was as normal as they come. And how could I, in turn, attempt to explain Milken's motivation?

Perhaps Milken's success was simply too great to hold. Perhaps he would have fallen eventually under any circumstances. But as far as his criminal conspiracy with Boesky is concerned, I suspect that—like Marty Siegel and me before him—Milken was enticed into the web. Boesky was a serpent in the garden, whispering, "I can do certain things for you. I can be very helpful to you. I can show you how to cut some corners. You want control? I can help you control everything."

Milken spoke with arbs every day, dozens of them. Yet not a single charge of impropriety was raised concerning Milken and any other arb. I had to conclude that Boesky sucked him in.

And now, on this day, I could feel Milken's personal pain perhaps better than anyone else. Getting your comeuppance hurts. The ache lodges in your throat and remains there for a long, long time.

ALTHOUGH the investigation continues, for me, in a real sense, it is over. Laurie and I are extremely grateful for the positive reactions displayed by so many of our friends and business associates. To my surprise, upon my return to society many companies sought out my advice. The luckiest aspect for me is that I am still relatively young, able to start over. This time I will do it right.

My goal, through the ADASAR Group, has been to go back into the business community and apply whatever skills I have with enthusiasm, and it is working. It is an uplifting feeling to realize that there are many fine men and women in the business world who believe that a man should be given a second chance.

HENRY

An Intimate Portrait of the Luces

by Ralph G. Martin

& CLARE

. . . Henry Luce had never met a woman like Clare, and he wanted to see her again. And so [he] did, at a dinner party given by Condé Nast. The party was a prelude to a birthday ball at the Waldorf-Astoria in honor of Cole Porter.

They sat down in a far corner and talked. Long after the entertainment was over and the lights came back on, Clare and Harry still seemed oblivious to everyone and everything, both talking intensely.

As he sat with her—absorbing her, admiring her, fantasizing a life with her—suddenly it was as if something within Harry exploded. His conscience was gone, his family was gone, and he wanted this woman more than he had ever wanted anything.

—*Henry & Clare*

1

OFTEN it is the simplest detail that helps explain the enigma of a man's life. For Henry Robinson Luce that clue lay inside his passport. Most husbands would want their wives or families notified in case of death; Luce, however, listed his next of kin as Time Inc.

Luce's first wife, Lila Ross Hotz, would often say that *Time* magazine was the love of her husband's life. It was his passion and his creation. To call it a next of kin was almost an understatement, for *Time* was part of Luce's very soul. Readers quickly discerned a very powerful presence behind the magazine, and the presence was Luce.

Once, speaking to students in Boston, Luce was asked how he could call *Time* a newsmagazine when it was so filled with opinion. He paused, then said, "I invented the idea, so I guess I can call it anything I like." He also believed he could *do* anything he liked with his magazine. When he felt strongly about an issue or a personality, he had no qualms about twisting the facts to present his version of the truth.

Luce often repeated his contention that the most astonishing thing about a human being was his range of vision, his willingness to suffer grief and frustration for a dream. Luce himself began dreaming about *Time* as a prep school student and later refined his ideas at Yale. With a scant $86,000 in seed money Luce and his school friend Briton Hadden were able to expand their dream into an influential journal of news and opinion. When Hadden suddenly died at age thirty-one, Luce carried on alone, turning a piecemeal news operation into the

most powerful publishing empire in the world. *Time* became a part of
the lives of millions of Americans and prodded people to think about
not only the news but religion, medicine, science, and culture in a way
they never had before. Many critics felt that much of *Time* was predi-
gested pap and very superficial, and some of it was. But the magazine
stirred the mind and made a profound impact on how daily papers
reported the news.

With the creation of *Life* and *Fortune,* Luce grew so influential that
he became the most important advocate—even more than President
Roosevelt—of leading a reluctant United States into World War II.
He was so powerful that he could pluck out a politically naïve general
named Eisenhower and help make him President. Harry, as those
close to him always called Luce, once told his friend William F.
Buckley, Jr., that though he was proud of being an editor, he was
really a promoter. And so he was. Luce promoted not only patriotism
but God. More than anything, he yearned to be a great American and
a true Christian. It was a small secret that he prayed every morning
in the elevator as he rode up to his office. Moreover, when he viewed
a person or a cause as godless, he was a forceful opponent. The major
reason for Luce's lifelong hatred of communism was that it was
godless.

Luce could be wrong and vengeful in his actions, but few questioned
his integrity or his personal honesty. Many hated some of the causes
he stood for, but few hated him. He was an ideological curmudgeon
who could roil the waters, upset political applecarts, and prick the
comfortable conscience of a nation. Yet this was a conservative-minded
man, an avowed Republican. He told his staff that it was the business
of *Time* to make enemies and *Life* to make friends.

Luce was a lonely man, and part of his loneliness came from his
power. He was a man on top of a mountain, with few true peers and
fewer friends. "We looked at him as a god," said a *Time* researcher,
"but he was never godlike."

He was a man of contradictions, seemingly cold and controlled,
with a highly disciplined mind, yet capable of an almost boyish enthusiasm. He had an unceasing, omnivorous curiosity for trivialities, yet
believed in the epic sweep of events. He was a man of conscience, but
he could resort to petty and shortsighted methods.

Basically a shy man, he had married a well-bred, wealthy young woman from Chicago who wanted nothing more than to be his help-mate. Lila adored and admired her husband, and earlier she had satisfied his romantic yearnings, but now he wanted something more. Luce fantasized himself as a swashbuckling lover, a man who could sweep any woman off her feet. His Presbyterian conscience had managed to hold him in check, but his days as a faithful husband were nearing an end. He was a man aching for a great love in his life, aching for an affair.

When he received an invitation to a cocktail party one night, he did not know that the evening would change his life. He hated small talk, but he accepted the invitation from his friends the Hobsons because Thayer Hobson was an old Yale classmate and his wife, Laura, had an intriguingly sharp mind.

It was the fall of 1934, and the President of the United States was Franklin Delano Roosevelt. Americans had just celebrated their first year without Prohibition. And in Hollywood, *It Happened One Night,* starring Clark Gable and Claudette Colbert, won an Academy Award. If the Depression was still dark and deep in many parts of the country, in the upper echelons of New York the parties continued almost as if nothing were wrong. The gaiety was brittle, the women slinky, and the view from the terrace of the seventeenth floor of the Hobsons' Manhattan apartment absolutely spectacular.

IT WAS one of those small moments of magic. A beautiful woman makes a grand entrance at a cocktail party, the noisy chatter stops dead, and the crowd stares.

She wore a striking black dress and exquisite diamond jewelry, and tilted her blond head ever so slightly. She simply stood under the hallway arch, clutching a nosegay of white flowers in her hands. Her extraordinary blue eyes looked demure and slightly expectant as she waited for the hostess to scoop her up and introduce her.

Most women hated Clare Boothe Brokaw because she was so young and beautiful and had such a tart tongue; most men loved her for the same reasons. She had been the celebrated editor of *Vanity Fair* and the author of a deliciously satirical novel that tore apart the high society in which she had lived. Since her divorce from a multimillion-aire drunk who was old enough to be her father, a line of admirers had waited impatiently for her attention.

A long time before, Clare's heart had been broken by her first lover. She promised herself that she would never be hurt again. "She was no vamp, but all she had to do was just smile at a man and the guy would fall down dead," noted a *Time* executive. She was a worldly, sophisticated woman capable of real conversation. When she talked to a man, it often seemed as if she knew the answers before she asked the questions. Her life was full of outstanding men because it took such men to please her. She would seek them out—and excite them. But the passion was theirs, rarely returned.

Clare's careful game plan at a party was to survey the scene as soon as she arrived, target someone worth talking to, and then zoom in. The man she wanted to meet that night was tall and intense-looking, with brooding blue eyes and a strong jaw. Harry Luce wore a preoccupied frown and seemed so aloof as to appear inattentive. Some years before, Clare had tried to interview him, but he had been too busy to see her.

Luce didn't reach out to women, because he was naïve about the opposite sex. He talked to women as he talked to men. He could understand their minds, but he knew nothing of their hearts.

The night Harry met Clare all that changed.

Hostess Laura Hobson watched their first encounter with special interest: "They stood a little apart from everybody, talking by themselves, she leaning back into the curve of the piano, facing the room, and Harry ignoring the room, holding forth intensely, and then listening intensely. Clare was too clever to be impressed with him; she would say something light, and laugh, then change moods and seem totally impressed by what he was saying."

Clare focused on subjects she knew interested him and piqued his curiosity. She also looked Luce straight in the eye, which pleased him. To talk to him, even Clare had to shift her mind into high gear, because his was never in neutral. A friend depicted Harry as "so fierce, so obsessed, so narrow, a man who could operate at a frightening velocity without coming apart."

Confronted with the force of Luce's personality, Clare was careful not to make a point too forcefully, lest she seem strident or caustic. She began with a short, fervent summary of conditions in Europe, then a pointed critique of his magazines. She baited him about his beloved *Fortune*, tossing out little mots about how easily it could be made better.

Finally, she added, "I hear you're getting out a picture magazine."

"No, I don't think it would work."

"But why not?"

She then proceeded to detail her own idea for a picture magazine. Intrigued, Luce asked many questions.

He was so sure of himself and what he wanted, and so little bothered by doubt. The initial attraction for Clare was that this man was even more forceful and domineering than she. This was a man of such terrific power and sheer strength that friends said he might well have been a gangster had he not been so stirred by God. Clare also found Harry physically appealing. She liked his tall, lanky frame and large head, which she called the Gary Cooper look. She was drawn to his dark, bushy eyebrows. Everything about Luce was compelling.

Suddenly, in the middle of their conversation, Luce pulled out his pocket watch and abruptly announced, "Well, got to go!"

Men didn't do that to Clare. But she was intrigued.

Harry was more than intrigued; he was caught. He appreciated intelligent women who could express themselves, but this one also had a scintillating beauty as well as the aura of being a celebrity. Harry now wanted a woman who better meshed with his own exalted status. And the more he thought of Clare, the more he wanted her.

The life they later built together was once described as a mating of eagles. Clare became a celebrated Congresswoman, the first female ambassador to a major country, an internationally known playwright, and the most influential woman in the Republican Party. He would grow into an elder statesman and adviser to Presidents, a man both feared and admired. Secretly he yearned to hold office, but contented himself with behind-the-scenes politics.

To the outside world Harry and Clare were two powerful people living in an idyllically privileged world. They enjoyed many homes and all the money they needed, but happiness eluded them. Their marriage was tarnished by constant competition, sharp cuts, and deep hurt. Most of the cuts came from Clare, and most of the hurt was Harry's. Still, they sparked each other's minds and, in their own way, enriched each other's lives. But in the end they remained lonely people searching for love and excitement.

Theirs is the story of a royal American marriage—fabulous but bitter, and ever fascinating to watch.

2

G OD and country and China: this was the passionate core of the
Luce heritage. God shaped the life of Henry Winters Luce
as he sat in his small study in the old North Hall at Yale University on
Easter Sunday, 1892. It was there that Luce—a tall, freckle-faced
young man with red hair and blue eyes—claimed he had heard the
clear call of evangelism. He felt, he said, "intoxicated with God." He
decided to become a missionary and chose China as the country where
he would work God's will.

Had he needed any further inspiration, Luce could have taken
some from his very name. "Luce" comes from the Latin, meaning
"light." The Luce family crest is actually an eagle holding a sword—
all of which fit the senior Luce and, later, his son.

Before going to China, the senior Luce got his Doctor of Divinity
at Princeton and chose a bride in his hometown of Scranton, Pennsylvania. Elizabeth Middleton Bloodgood Root, born in Utica, New
York, was a social worker in the drab factory section of Scranton. Like
the Luces, many Roots had been prominent public servants in law,
medicine, education, and the military. The couple married in the
Second Presbyterian Church, on June 1, 1897. Pastor Charles E.
Robinson urged them, "Strive to learn the Chinese way of looking at
things." He impressed them both so much that they would give their
first son the middle name Robinson.

THE Luce mission to China was in the northern province of Shantung, 150 miles from Shanghai. When the Luces arrived, they were
taken on a two-day trek to their Presbyterian mission at Tengchow, the
"city of heights," an ancient walled city, steep and rocky, with narrow
dirt streets. The mission compound was built like a fort, surrounded
by a high brick wall. Life for the Luces was spartan. Their house had
no gas, no electricity, no steam heat or plumbing. Light came from
kerosene lamps. Reverend Luce set a strict schedule: up at six, cold
bath, Bible study before breakfast, three hours of Chinese lessons
before lunch, a nap, three more hours of lessons, supper at six, a long
walk, general reading, with more Chinese study. Luce concentrated

on the long-range vision of educating Chinese for Christian leadership. His fellow missionaries quickly assessed him as a man of strong will and vigorous intellect.

The Luces' first child, Henry Robinson Luce (soon called Harry, like his father), was born on April 3, 1898, and baptized. The Chinese gave him their own name: Lu-Shao-i—Small Boy Luce.

Small Boy Luce was born the year President William McKinley voiced the view of many American missionaries that God had given the United States a manifest destiny to spread its goodness elsewhere in the world. After escaping to Korea during the Boxer Rebellion two years later, the family returned to Tengchow, soon moving to another compound, in Weihsien, a bigger city 125 miles to the southeast. At the elder Luce's insistence the Christian college was being moved there and a bigger one built.

Young Harry learned most of his kitchen Chinese from his amah, or nannie. As he grew older his father occasionally took him on expeditions to various little villages. "He had very vivid recollections," said his Presbyterian pastor, Dr. David Read.

Luce had a wistfulness about not having American roots. "How did I come to know about America?" he said. "My father and mother told me about it. They told concrete things—like about uncles and aunts and about the home church back in Scranton, Pennsylvania. My mother read to me a *Child's History of America*. And I cannot remember a time when I did not know about the Declaration of Independence and the American Constitution. I was brought up as an American."

Harry's mother had a hard life, but she was totally committed to their existence in China. In the Luce household there was an emphasis on strictness and rules. But the undercurrent was Harry's intense admiration for his father and love for his mother. His father had merged his patriotism and his religion into a moral force, and so, too, would young Harry.

The mission decided to send Reverend Luce back to the United States to raise money for their new college, at Weihsien—the first united college of a dozen missionary groups. Since the tour would take more than a year, the Luce family went together. There were three children now: Harry and his sisters, Emmavail and Elisabeth (who was called Beth).

It was in Chicago that the Luces met the woman who would be their lifelong benefactor, Mrs. Cyrus Hall McCormick, the kindly matri-arch of the International Harvester Company dynasty.

"I shall never forget my first meeting with Mrs. McCormick," said Reverend Luce. "I had been in China eight years and came home in 1905. We had never been able to buy a book or any apparatus except as we filched it from our all too meager salaries. Coming to Chicago, I of course wanted to see Mrs. McCormick. A mutual friend gave me a letter of introduction. Sitting close to each other, she asked me very earnestly, 'Why do you want money for this college?' In two or three sentences, I told her about our needs. That was all that was ever said. One day a check arrived for twenty thousand dollars, which laid the foundation for the endowment of Shantung Christian University."

Forever after, the Luce family would refer to her as The Dear Lady. Mrs. McCormick was so struck with young Harry that she made the Luce family an offer they found generous and terrible. Harry himself remembers sitting on a couch and listening to Mrs. McCormick's plans. If his father would let her bring Harry up, she'd give so much to the missionaries. Harry felt that his father was selling him. He recalled that discussion as a time of terror, the most awful experience he could remember from his childhood.

After private prayer the Luces gently refused to part with their son. But Mrs. McCormick became his patron, his sympathetic ear, his refuge. He would write her things that he would not tell his parents. Without her ready financial help his rough early school years would have been even more formidable, perhaps even impossible.

Soon after Christmas, Harry, then seven, had to undergo a difficult tonsillectomy. Thereafter his parents blamed that for the difficult stammer he developed. His stuttering made Harry a more private person and more of a reader. Years later he would largely overcome this stuttering. Yet in moments of stress the m's and the s's would again stick in his throat. His words often came out in short, staccato bursts, and his sentences were often unfinished.

The Luces eventually settled on a beautiful country farm outside Scranton. The farm belonged to the family of their sponsor, James Linen. In a sense Dr. Luce now became a missionary in reverse, trying to explain China to Americans. What appalled him most was the minimal concern and knowledge Americans had about China. To them it was "more remote than the moon." It took fifteen months before the Reverend Luce could raise enough money to return to China.

During those days, the Chinese greeted each other by asking, "Have you eaten rice yet?" Hunger was rampant. Disease was everywhere. Missionaries returning from visiting villages were quarantined in rough huts near the compound.

Harry always remembered some stone towers he saw on his hikes. Families would put their children there to die because they couldn't feed them. For the Luces, to simply maintain a sense of normal family life in this stark, brutal land was a major achievement.

"Mother was fierce about every bit of food that came into the house," recalled Harry's sister Beth. "It not only had to be washed but some of it had to be dipped into a disinfectant."

The children's mother also insisted on reading the classics aloud: Shakespeare, the Bible, Dickens. "I think this accounts for Harry's beautiful use of the English language," noted Beth. Their mother taught Harry writing, arithmetic, and discipline as well. In this environment he learned to be resilient and self-sufficient. "He would take over the nursery with his damn forts and soldiers," said Beth, "always marshalling armies. Everything he did was always very intense."

It was said of Dr. Luce that he never gave orders to his children. Instead, he tried to be a counselor, drawing out their thoughts and opinions, stating his own views but leaving the final decisions to them. What he *did* do was set an example of work and dedication.

In 1909 a younger brother was born. Sheldon's later memory of his father and brother was that they were both serious, undemonstrative, "and almost zero on small talk." Yet Harry and his father were always able and ready to talk to each other about substantive issues. In these talks the big word was "balance." Put your life in balance, his father would tell him.

To get this proper balance for young Harry, it was soon time to prepare for Yale, the Luce alma mater. The first step was a British boarding school at Chefoo.

CLARE's grandfather, John William Thomas Boothe, was a man of God. From 1890 to 1898 he served as pastor of the Second Baptist Church in Holyoke, Massachusetts. He preached powerful sermons, without notes, and was known for his very fine mind.

Born in Maryland in 1838, the Reverend Boothe married a woman named Sarah Rebecca Deaver, who bore him four sons and seven daughters. One daughter created a scandal when she married the manager of a theater company and shot herself in a New York hotel room. This news caused the reverend's resignation.

Clare later commented, "All the people of my youth firmly believed in the Ten Commandments, even when they broke them."

Clare's father broke them often. William Franklin Boothe, one of John and Sarah's eleven children, was born in 1861, attended Purdue University for several years, then left to study violin at the Cincinnati Conservatory of Music. A handsome man, strongly built and athletic, Billy Boothe had thick eyebrows, dark hair, and a bushy mustache. He was a brilliant raconteur, "dreamily artistic . . . a man who loved music more than he loved anything or anybody," a newspaper reporter later wrote about Clare's father. His great lack was strength of character.

The woman he loved was Anna Clara Snyder. She was "tiny but perfectly formed—a pocket Venus. She had wonderful eyes like wet violets," an observer would later write. At eighteen she changed her name to Ann Clare and traveled across the Hudson River from Weehawken Heights, New Jersey, to Manhattan to work as a salesgirl, then as a typist. But secretly she yearned to go into show business and finally landed a job as a chorus girl in a musical comedy.

It happened that handsome Billy Boothe had settled in New York and was playing in the orchestra. Six months later, in 1894, they eloped. Both families were shocked by the marriage because of differences in religion. The Snyders were devout Lutherans. To them their daughter was now living in sin.

Abandoned by their families, the newlyweds managed well without them. On April 10, 1902, Ann Clare gave birth to a son, David Franklin. Their second child, Ann Boothe, called Clare, was born March 10, 1903, though for some unknown reason, thereafter she celebrated her birthday in April rather than March.

The Boothes were then living in a three-room apartment on West 124th Street, in one of the poorer parts of New York City—the so-called respectable slums. Billy was a convivial man with many friends, a large number of them in music or the theater. His wife was of a similar spirit. They always seemed to be moving to different places in different jobs.

"We traveled all over the place," said Clare. "Memphis, Racine, Des Moines." But wherever they were, both parents often read aloud to their children, mostly from the ten-cent volumes of the Little Leather Library. "I had no formal education," Clare later said, "but books, books, books." History was a favorite subject, though randomly taught. Her father also taught her a little Latin, French, and German.

In 1911 the Boothe family fortunes changed dramatically. Billy got a job as a concert violinist with a traveling symphony orchestra and took his family with him. When the tour ran out of money in Nashville, Tennessee, the Boothes settled there for a while. Billy went to work in a soft-drink bottling business, and his family was delighted. They lived regular lives with regular hours and saw each other every night at supper. Some time later Billy left the bottling plant to take up an offer to play the violin in the Chicago Grand Opera orchestra. Chicago was a happy time for the Boothes, but only at the beginning.

Suddenly one day in 1911 Billy was gone. Ann Clare simply told the children their father was dead. There was no grief, no funeral, and their mother never again mentioned his name. Many years later Clare and David learned that their father had gone away with another woman. "My mother had to struggle for a bare existence," Clare said. Inevitably Ann Clare grew bitter. Her mother's attitude toward men, Clare said in later years, was, "You shouldn't let none of them out except on a leash."

In 1913 Ann Clare obtained a formal divorce on grounds of desertion. She was still beautiful, bitter, and unbowed.

"I live in my children," Mrs. Boothe told her daughter. Young Clare was convinced of this. "She had persuaded me early that her whole existence would somehow be justified in me," Clare later recalled. "My mother felt she had given up a promising career in the theater to marry. When my father later ran off with another woman, my mother decided she had been a complete failure. She began pressuring me to excel. 'You,' she would say, 'are the real reason I was born'—because I would become all she had ever hoped to be. I believed my mother, and I tried hard to justify her reason."

Mrs. Boothe took her children home to New Jersey, then back to New York City. Clare later described it as "a poor and starving" existence.

"My mind and heart grew so bewildered, I could no longer function intelligently or happily," she recalled. "I grew moody, distracted, restless, fickle, subject to fits of inexplicable depression."

Financially things began to look up for the family. Mrs. Boothe had received a small inheritance from her father, and with a friend's advice she had multiplied it in the stock market. Billy Boothe, who had founded the Boothe Violin School, in Los Angeles, reportedly sent money at irregular intervals for the children's education.

In 1913 Mrs. Boothe felt flush enough to send her son to military school for a year while she took her ten-year-old daughter to Europe. Basically Mrs. Boothe was a romantic—but a pragmatic one. She wanted to give Clare a sophisticated exposure to the world and hence prepare her for the inevitable road to success. Mrs. Boothe's constantly repeated slogan was Up the ladder, up the ladder.

Mother and daughter lived in Paris on the cheap, but they saw everything in style—the theater, the festivals, the museums, all the sights. Clare read about what she didn't see. She listened when she didn't know something. She dreamed about what she didn't have.

By this time, war had come to much of Europe. It was time for the mother and daughter to go home. The trip had consumed most of Mrs. Boothe's savings, and they faced a most uncertain future.

Once they were back, Mrs. Boothe got a job selling costume jewelry. Her salary was enough to maintain her son at military school. Mrs. Boothe's ambitious hopes centered on Clare, not David. She decided that her pretty, curly-haired daughter might catch some producer's eye and become a child star. Hence she took Clare for a screen test to the Biograph Studios in Fort Lee, New Jersey, a film production center. Clare listened to the director explaining the art of expressing the three necessary emotions: fear, abject fear, and stark horror. Her test was terrible.

Since stardom seemed elusive, the undaunted, irrepressible Mrs. Boothe swiftly made other plans for Clare. In 1915 she got her twelve-year-old daughter a scholarship at the Cathedral School of St. Mary in Garden City, Long Island. Clare qualified for a scholarship because her grandfather had been a clergyman.

"My mother was determined I'd never find myself in her situation, depending on physical beauty, which was not enough to protect against the misfortune of an unhappy marriage and no money. I was to have a good education," Clare explained.

At first Clare was deeply homesick living away at St. Mary's. Also, she felt so much older than most of the other girls, who had never known her world of adults. She felt awkward, a stranger among strangers. "I was so lonely I became a compulsive eater," she later said. Twenty pounds overweight, she found solace in reading books, and selected a favorite secret place in an old apple tree. She would climb up there and read. The other girls noticed how withdrawn she was. They were also struck by Clare's poise and compulsive neatness.

One of the few bright spots of Clare's childhood was meeting her St. Mary's classmate Elizabeth Cobb, whom everybody called Buffy. Years later Buffy vividly remembered Clare. "She was fat as butter but she had long golden curls and clear blue eyes and lovely pink and white skin. There was always a terrific drive in her to achieve, to have, to learn." Soon Clare confided to her diary her determination to make Buffy Cobb her "bestest" friend.

Buffy's father was Irvin S. Cobb, a former Kentucky newspaper columnist who wrote for *The Saturday Evening Post*, then the most popular magazine in America. Invited to the Cobb home for Thanksgiving, Clare was quickly accepted as part of the family. Many literary and theatrical celebrities who gathered there were surprised that this little girl talked to them on an adult level and was unawed by them.

For Mrs. Boothe during this period, the picture suddenly brightened. She had acquired a serious suitor, a wealthy Philadelphia man with two children. When things didn't work out, Clare described him as "a nasty little toad, a selfish snob." She remembered her mother crying so hard it seemed as if her body would break. She felt her mother was simply tired of struggling with poverty. Clare wondered why money was so all-important in the world and vowed that she would never be in a position like her mother's.

As a tenth grader, Clare was admitted to the Castle School, in Tarrytown, New York. Castle had huge rooms with beamed ceilings, dark wood, and wonderful views of the Hudson River. Clare was delighted. At St. Mary's the headmistress was stern and dry; at Castle the founder-headmistress, "Cassy" Mason, was gentle and inspiring.

Clare recalled this amazing woman who was years ahead of her time: "She said to me, 'Clare, I think you will go far. You have talent. But always remember only two things you need: confidence in yourself and confidence in God and *She* will protect you.' "

As a student, Clare excelled so that Headmistress Mason offered her a chance to graduate a year early. She was particularly good in history, literature, and French. Clare was also business manager of the yearbook, *The Drawbridge,* and was widely known for her intensity. Dorothy Burns, Clare's close friend at Castle, recalled, "When the other girls were reading a racy, contraband account of their favorite movie star, Clare would have a volume of Racine or Molière. She wasn't stuffy about it. She just didn't have time for trash."

"Clare was always boss," said another of her schoolmates. "She always knew what she wanted."

Clare abruptly decided she wanted to be a writer, and wrote a one-act comedy called *The Lily Maid.* She also wrote articles for her school paper and drew cartoons. The class prophecy for Clare was that she would marry a college professor and dedicate one of her books to the Castle. About this time a palm reader advised her to take up public speaking, journalism, or art. Clare listened and quietly promised herself that she would also have a serious love affair.

AT SIXTEEN Clare was summa cum laude, the youngest graduate in the school's history. The yearbook said of her: "Yes, yes, she is our prodigy and our genius, yet just the same she is as lovable as she is brilliant. You all know her wit."

In her diary Clare wrote what she wanted out of life was to write something memorable, marry a publisher, have three children, and be fluent in four languages. Her class voted her the prettiest, cleverest, and most artistic. But she ranked only second for ambition, which she regarded as a major slight. "Oh God, help me to succeed. Success is not life, but life should be success," Clare said at the time. She described herself as someone with "ten thousand dreams."

3

CHEFOO, the home of the China Inland Mission School, was a squalid, uninteresting town 450 miles north of Shantung, on the Yellow Sea. Most of the 120 students at the Chefoo boarding school were children of Christian missionaries and, like the staff, English or Scottish. The fourteen American boys had second-class status because the British were the foreigners who dominated China, especially in trade.

Luce's memories of the school were vivid and intense: "I hated it and loved it. There were millions of rules. We boys were always in trouble." It was a rough, tough school, and he recalled bloody noses, skinned knees, and swollen hands.

Harry's close friend at Chefoo was Thornton Wilder, whose father had been a newspaper editor, then consul general in Hong Kong and Shanghai. Luce admired Wilder because he was a year older, was born in the United States, had a hometown (Madison, Wisconsin), and was such a good talker. Like Luce, Wilder was a reader. The two also shared a common resolve to go to Yale.

Determined to overcome his stuttering, Harry helped start a debating society. He would not sit there and suffer his embarrassment, but would cope with it and conquer it. He was like an actor with stage fright pushing himself. The remarkable thing was that he somehow managed by sheer willpower and practice to eliminate any stammering during any debate. Then afterward his stutter would return.

The Chinese have an adage: A great man has the heart of a boy. "Harry was never a young boy," said his sister Beth. "We children were always 'old' in those days. We were grown-up much sooner."

Their father had set a pattern of discipline and ambition to achieve that was so overpowering it swept away most childish concerns. But for Harry part of this growing up was his closeness with God. He had his own vision of God, that God would help him get into the fourth form, that God would help him get one hundred percent in algebra.

Harry wrote weekly letters home. They dealt with everything, including the way he traded stamps for picture postcards of the country (he had a large collection), the pros and cons of having white mice as pets, the terrible school food, and the consequences of flood and famine in China. In discussing the attempted revolution of 1911 to replace the Manchu dynasty, Harry wrote that his sympathies were with the rebels as long as they had good and honest leaders. He then saw a revolution as the hope of the future.

For a boy not quite thirteen this was quite a profound dictum.

Few boys had greater intellectual curiosity about absolutely everything—and a phenomenal memory to retain it. He was always near the top of his class but had a secret longing for something more spectacular. There was little fault to find with Harry. He was ready to face the world and conquer it. He was highly serious, highly moral, and highly determined. If he lacked anything then, it was a sense of humor. He had never learned to laugh enough. He almost never would. The largest laugh he had was a chuckle.

IN 1913 FIFTEEN-YEAR-OLD Henry Robinson Luce arrived at the Hotchkiss School, in Lakeville, Connecticut, looking "sandy-shaggy" in his unstylish Chinese-made suit. Of the 250 boys, he was the only one born abroad. The others promptly nicknamed him Chink.

Hotchkiss was one of the most prestigious prep schools in America. The students at Hotchkiss were mostly white, Protestant, Republican, and rich, with the exception of six scholarship students and a few townies given free tuition. As one of the scholarship boys, Luce swept, cleaned rooms, waited on tables, and was generally treated like a second-class citizen.

"I detested [the cleaning]," Luce later said. All this pushed him further to one side and made him seem more aloof. His stammering didn't help.

The school talk was mostly of girls, sports, and clothes, and Harry cared for none of these things. His fellow students saw their young lives in terms of fun and laughter, and Harry couldn't understand why their fun was fun and why they would waste their time like that. Life to him now was serious, serious, serious. He was soon known as The Brain.

Still, he never stopped trying to be good at everything at Hotchkiss. He tried out for the dramatic club, traveled with the football team as a photographer and even played center on the team. He became captain of the soccer team, sang first bass in the glee club, and wrote the words for the school song.

But no matter how he tried, he was not a typical Hotchkiss boy. Few other students made special trips to New York on holidays to hear special sermons, and almost nobody felt free to embarrass the head-master in Bible class by asking, "Why should we have to ask an all-protecting God not to lead us into temptation?" As a friend of Luce's later noted, "In a kind of dour, Presbyterian way, Harry was thinking in ultimate terms, almost as if he were playing chess with God."

"Harry wasn't very popular at Hotchkiss," said one of his few friends, John Hincks, "but one thing we all envied was that he had come there all alone from China by way of India and the Suez Canal and Constantinople and Rome and taken a month to do it. We thought that was wonderful."

Of Harry's few friends one of the most important was Briton Hadden, nicknamed Cat because of the way he grinned and wrinkled his nose. Cat was everything Chink was not—gregarious, full of fun, sports-loving. Son of a wealthy Brooklyn banker, Brit Hadden had come to Hotchkiss determined to outdo his older brother, who had been captain of the baseball team. His one ambition was to become a big-league baseball player. But he was no athlete.

Harry had no such frustrations. His prime aim was literary. What tied these two young men together was a mutual admiration and a love of language. Their competition was keen. Both tried out for staff positions on the school weekly newspaper, *The Record,* and both were accepted. Brit became editor and Harry his assistant.

At graduation time Harry was named Class Poet. He ranked third as the brightest, fourth as the most absentminded, sixth as the most pious, and ninth as the worst woman hater. His scholastic record read, "Honor Roll, Leader of the Class." A class book comment about him read, "All wisdom's armory this man could wield." Brit won the Declamation Award for his rendition of "Casey at the Bat," wrote the lyrics for the class song, and delivered the class oration on the need "for bettering the political conditions of the land we live in."

After Hotchkiss there never had been any doubt that Harry would go to Yale. He scored the highest mark in the College Board Greek exams in the history of Yale. Hotchkiss's headmaster thought this event important enough to declare a school holiday.

That summer, Harry got a job on the Springfield, Massachusetts, *Republican,* working at the front counter of the business office, handling subscriptions, complaints, and local advertisements. He described himself as being at the foot of the newspaper ladder, although he saw it as good training in precision and accuracy. When his editor let him do some reporting, his excitement increased. He wrote home of his fascination with courtroom drama and seeing the inside of a prison cell for the first time. Furthermore, he was now convinced that journalism came closest to the heart of the world. For Harry Luce it was a prophetic comment that his family would soon comprehend.

SEVERAL DAYS AFTER GRADUATION from Castle, Clare took the train to New York, settled down to read a book on Plato, and soon became aware that an older man sitting next to her was examining her very closely. She now knew how pretty she was and expected men to stare at her occasionally. But this man never stopped staring. Finally he spoke up. He asked if she understood what she was reading. "Yes, I do. At least I think I do, and I enjoy it." They discussed Plato for a while, "and he talked wisely and well," Clare recalled. Then as the train approached Grand Central station the man asked, "Is your name, by any chance, Clare Boothe?" Astonished, she said yes. He then asked if her mother was as beautiful as ever and if she was well.

Clare looked more closely at the man. His hair was thick and gray, and he was good-looking but slightly shabby. Mostly he looked somewhat familiar. She told him about her mother, and he then asked about her brother, David. She replied that David was in the Marine Corps. Finally Clare asked him how he knew their family.

"Why, child, I am your father," he told her. "We haven't seen each other for a long, long time, but your mother sent me a snapshot of you and David a few years ago."

Clare was too shocked to say anything or ask anything more. He said he had been visiting his brother who was a professor at Yale, and that he now lived in San Francisco. They parted at the exit.

Clare immediately confronted her mother. Why had she told them ten years ago that their father was dead? Tearfully her mother insisted that she had done so to make it easier for them. The truth, she said, was that their father had run off with the famous opera singer Mary Garden.

Several days later Clare's father called and said he wanted to see her again. Over dinner with the family, Billy Boothe told them he had married three more times after he and Ann divorced. He also made no pretense of apologizing for deserting them. Clare felt forced to admit that he was indeed personable. She marveled at his nerve in coming to face them without any regret or shame after all the years, yet confided to her diary that she wanted to wipe him out of her mind.

IF HAVING an absent father was the major regret of her life, Clare once said, another was that she never went to college. After graduating from Castle, she attended Lee's Business Course, in Connecticut, to study shorthand and typing, but only, she said, to help her at Columbia University. Columbia didn't accept her.

Not long after that, Clare left home, rented a room in New York, and got a job cutting paper flowers and painting paper nut cups for Christmas at Dennison's, on Fifth Avenue, for eighteen dollars a week. All Clare has said of this period was, "I had to get away." But several months later she moved back with her mother.

In many ways Clare and her mother were of the same mold. She had long envied her mother's beauty, but now, finally, she had her own. She had long envied her mother's warmth and easy popularity, yet these were qualities that still eluded her. She envied her mother's ambition, and she knew that this was directed mainly at her. She and her mother were two fierce women fighting the world, and they needed each other to continue the fight.

One of the men Mrs. Boothe knew well at this time was Dr. Albert Elmer Austin, a surgeon whom she had met socially and then again when she suffered a ruptured appendix. Austin, forty-two, was a very proper and conservative man with graying hair. A former Latin teacher, he had served in the World War as a regimental surgeon, then became head of the Greenwich Hospital staff in Greenwich, Connecticut. Austin was then in the midst of a difficult divorce. He could not propose to Ann Clare, but he could court her. Clare called her mother's suitor "the most adorable man on the planet."

While her mother and Austin were courting, Clare, too, enjoyed herself. There were soon a variety of young men calling on her, most of them in the army. But none of them were Mr. Right.

What Clare most wanted was the love of a strong man. He should be sensitive, brave, and a little reckless. She didn't care what his religion was, but she wanted him to love her more than he loved God or honor or country. She wanted a masterful man, and she prayed that he would not be poor—she wanted someone who made at least $12,000 a year. Never would she fall in love with an ordinary man or have an ordinary courtship or an ordinary wedding.

Her brother, David, returned in his marine uniform, and Clare was sad to see that he was the same selfish, complaining boy he had been for some time. She didn't like his companions, who were invariably tough. But despite everything, she was happy he was home, happy to be with him.

For Mrs. Boothe the world brightened when Dr. Austin proposed marriage. This marriage gave her a sparkling new community status.

Clare wasn't concerned about status—she was sixteen and too busy having fun. Her stepfather provided a fresh adventure in 1920, another trip to Europe, only this time first class. Dr. Austin had been awarded a grant to investigate plastic surgery techniques in Berlin, and wanted his new family along. Joining them was her mother's old friend Adele Schmeider, who came mainly as a companion for Clare.

En route to Germany, they stopped in England. Clare found Englishmen very charming. In her letters to friends she poured out how she loved London with all her heart. After a stay in Paris the travelers' next stop was Berlin. Clare studied German, and she and Mrs. Schmeider saw a lot of theater. She also wrote about the chaos of German politics and blamed much of it on France for grinding Germany's face in the mud after the Great War, demanding reparations that it could never pay. She was so stirred by what she saw that she decided to become a journalist so she could "do something about it."

While Dr. Austin was happily at work Clare and Adele went for a week to Vienna, where they learned the tricks of riding over five-foot hurdles in an English saddle. Clare then joined the Austins on a trip south to the Riviera—where she won a beauty contest. She was five feet six and willowy, "with the most beautiful legs of any woman I know," gushed a reporter.

Clare's plan had always been to fall in love, and when it happened, nationality was no barrier. The object of her passion was a war hero, Major Julian Simpson, tall and handsome and an Oxford graduate who planned to go into politics. They met at a party at the Guards' Club, in London, and before the evening was over, Clare was completely entranced.

Here was her romantic fantasy come true. In the four days before her ship sailed, she and Simpson were constantly together. They toured the city, saw the sights, went to the theater. They talked about their future, and he promised to come to Greenwich to continue their courtship. An eager seventeen, she gave him her heart.

Aboard ship, Clare wrote love poems saying how perfect Julian was, how utterly she loved him, and how she would not let him go.

Sighing at the ship's rail, she said, "Everything is love. Love is the most important thing in the world."

WHEN EIGHTEEN-YEAR-OLD HARRY Luce entered Yale, in 1916, he exhibited his usual discipline. He made time for singing bass in the glee club, rowing with the freshman crew, and waiting on tables. He had arrived with $500—the rest was for him to earn.

Harry's class—Yale 1920—included the son of a partner at the prestigious banking house Morgan Brothers, a du Pont, an Adams, and an Auchincloss. Luce developed an awe of social aristocracy that never left him.

During his first year at Yale, Harry told a friend, "I couldn't decide whether to be an anarchist or a great publisher. It was only after much thought that I decided to be a publisher."

With this notion in mind Harry started "heeling" for the Yale *Daily News*. Heeling was a process of points. You earned them by the quantity and quality of the stories you suggested and wrote, the number of ads you sold, and the time you spent running errands for the staff. Harry called the competition "awful, a blind desperateness. It robs you of the mood to do anything like studying or reading or writing letters."

Of the several dozen freshman candidates for the *News*, however, Harry was one of four chosen. So were Brit Hadden and Thayer Hobson. The four winners were at a party celebrating when somebody rushed in with a newspaper headlined U.S. DECLARES WAR.

The departure of senior students for military training intensified competition for top editorial positions on the *News*. Hadden later beat out Harry for chairman of the board by a single vote. "My fondest college ambition is unachieved," Luce wrote home about his disappointment in not being able to follow in his father's footsteps. In *his* letter home Hadden wrote, "Luce is the best competition I ever had."

In the summer of 1918 Luce and Hadden and most of their class went to Camp Jackson, South Carolina. They were part of a cadre of student-officer instructors for the incoming flood of draftees. Eventually they were commissioned second lieutenants and celebrated by smoking big cigars. But the war ended before they could see active duty. "What are we going to tell our grandsons that we did in the war?" Harry asked. "Cleaned a horse's hoof at Camp Jackson!"

One night Brit and Harry walked through the sprawling camp and discussed how the soldiers were enormously ignorant of the war and of the world. Or, as Luce later put it, "Their knowledge didn't equal their interest." He and Brit felt the dire need to produce a newsmagazine so interesting that everybody would want to read it. "Here we were, talking about 'that paper,' about something we would do—cross our hearts—someday. I think it was in that walk that *Time* began."

WITH the end of the war, in November 1918, Luce and Hadden returned to Yale and their college newspaper. But Yale now seemed tame, and Harry had to think of himself and the future. His newspaper dream with Hadden was still nebulous. Now he had to think of more pragmatic possibilities. He spent a summer at law school, but discovered he had no aptitude for law.

Everything about Harry seemed geared up for purpose. At his Yale graduation, in 1920, he was summa cum laude and was regarded, along with Stephen Vincent Benét and Thornton Wilder, as one of the three outstanding poets of his class. Harry later said, "I came to the conclusion that I was never going to be a really good poet, so the hell with it." He also made Phi Beta Kappa. The issue now for him was what to do next.

In July 1920 Harry sailed on the *Olympia* to England with two Yale friends. With a thousand-dollar graduation gift from Mrs. McCormick and $1500 he had earned from his share of the profits from the Yale *News,* he traveled throughout Europe, then took a postgraduate year at Oxford to study history. Life was serene. "Harry considered Oxford a holiday," said Beth. There was research reading, of course, but he always found reading fun. Afternoons meant bicycling and tennis, followed by tea. Evenings meant conversation, literature, and chess.

That Christmas of 1920 Harry journeyed to Rome with an Oxford friend and accidentally bumped into Thornton Wilder, his old classmate. On New Year's Eve they all went to a party at the American Academy. Harry suddenly noticed a tall girl with curly brown hair. Lila Ross Hotz was a lighthearted, spirited young woman who spoke fluent French and Italian and loved music. A student at the fashionable Miss Risser's School, in Rome, Lila came from a wealthy Presbyterian Chicago family. She was just what Harry needed. He was dazzled.

The day after the party Harry left for Florence. "I wasn't sure if I'd ever see him again," Lila recalled. "Two days later, there was a letter from him and he asked me to write. So, we started a correspondence."

On his return to Oxford, Harry continued their correspondence, which became regular and heavy. During spring vacation, when Lila stayed with her aunt in Paris, Harry also came to Paris for a little sight-seeing. He and Lila arranged a meeting. The once awkward young man in ill-kept suits now owned a Savile Row suit and sported a mustache and a cane. Their relationship at this point was totally chaste.

By the summer of 1921 Harry decided it was time to enter the real world, which seemed to be in Chicago. Lila was there, back from finishing school, and so was the Chicago *Daily News*. After several months of courting Lila, Harry applied at the paper and was hired as an assistant to writer Ben Hecht.

Ben Hecht never let facts interfere with his fiction. His daily column, "One Thousand and One Afternoons," featured stories about the city's odd characters. In asking for an assistant, he said he wanted "a very naïve fellow who will notice everything going on and bring me tidbits that I can work into columns." But from the outset Harry did not fit in. With his Yale and Oxford background and society fiancée he never felt at home in the city room. Lila called Harry's stint at the *Daily News* "an annoying, stupid little job, not really a writing job. Very boring. Harry was bored stiff."

Soon afterward, in September 1921, Harry wrote home that his department had been instructed to eliminate five men, and since he was the last one hired, he was the first one fired. The final advice to Harry from an editor, reportedly, was, "Get out of newspapers."

"IF WE'RE ever going to start that paper, this looks like our chance." This message came in a letter from Brit Hadden about their fantasy and their future. Their Yale friend Walter Millis was doing so well at the Baltimore *News* that his editor had asked him, "Do you know any more Yale boys who write as well as you?"

Luce and Hadden were then not quite twenty-four years old. Just as Luce's reporting career on the Chicago *Daily News* had been unremarkable, Hadden's writing experience on the New York *World* was largely confined to animal stories. They moved to Baltimore.

Harry and Brit found Baltimore a pleasant, old-fashioned city where people were even-tempered and tactful. Though Harry had been deeply reluctant to leave Lila and missed her terribly, even she was pushed into the back of his mind as he and Brit began work on their dream—starting a newsmagazine.

The *News* job was perfect for their project. Their newspaper work ended by midafternoon, which gave them the rest of the day and night to work on their magazine. They kept busy cutting stories from *The New York Times,* classifying them by subject and condensing seven days of news on any subject into a single concise story. They made it feisty and provocative, then pasted the finished stories into a dummy layout. They not only wanted their stories bright and tight but opinionated.

Within three months they had assembled a sample issue and a prospectus. The two brash young men also persuaded their editor to give them seven weeks' leave of absence without pay, plus a promise to take them back.

Harry and Brit now wanted to show their magazine dummy layout to some thirty or forty editors, publishers, and businessmen to get their counsel. Then if advisable, they would start raising money. So they took off for New York with their dummy and their dream.

THE grande dame and an undisputed queen of New York society was Mrs. Oliver Hazard Perry Belmont. The granddaughter of a southern general, the former Alva Erskine Smith came from Mobile, Alabama, and had married William K. Vanderbilt, whose wealth could not compensate for his philandering. Alva shocked society by suing for a divorce on grounds of adultery. She later selected another well-heeled spouse, O.H.P. Belmont. When he died and left her his many millions, Mrs. Belmont became a woman of many causes, including the fight for women's suffrage.

By some twist of fortune Mrs. Belmont was traveling on the same ship back to New York as Ann Clare and Clare Boothe. It was perhaps more Clare's mother's manipulation than fate that found Clare and Mrs. Belmont in adjoining deck chairs.

The two women quickly charmed each other. Clare was nineteen, vividly pretty and bright, and the seventy-year-old Mrs. Belmont was captivated. She saw in Clare much of her younger self—the wit, the enthusiasm, the drive. "You stick with me," she told Clare.

In her memoirs socialite Elsa Maxwell confided that she had seldom seen Mrs. Belmont "so animated" when she later told her, "I met a girl on the boat who has all the earmarks of talent and success. Remember her name: Clare Boothe."

For Clare such attention was heady stuff. Still, her heart and thoughts were back in London with Major Julian Simpson, the handsome young Englishman with whom she was so in love. He would surely soon come to America, sweep her off her feet, and marry her.

When Julian finally came, a bewildered Clare found a different young man—his ardor cooled, his manner almost distant. Soon after his arrival he announced suddenly that something unexpected required him to leave. Clare quickly discovered what the "unexpected" was. Julian had thought that the Austins were very wealthy. When he saw the modest Austin home in Connecticut, the romance was over. He could not afford love without money.

The lesson was sharp and deep. It would be a long time before Clare again let her heart rule her mind.

She then went to work for Mrs. Belmont in the women's movement. She put on airplane goggles, got into an open-cockpit World War Jennie, and scattered handbills announcing the seventy-fifth anniversary of the Women's Rights Conference. She helped stage a pageant as well.

Clare also found time for two other shipboard friends, Mr. and Mrs. James Stewart Cushman, who were very social, rich, philanthropic, and religious. When Clare came to visit them in New York one Sunday, they took her to the morning service at the Fifth Avenue Presbyterian Church.

Sitting in the same pew was "a rather distinguished older man," as Clare remembered him. She noticed him keenly observing her. The Cushmans later introduced them. He was George Tuttle Brokaw, forty-three, a multimillionaire lawyer, and one of the most eligible bachelors in New York. He was also a playboy.

The Cushmans, playing matchmaker, invited Clare and George to lunch at their Fifth Avenue home. Clare thought he was nice enough, good-looking, with a courtly charm. It is doubtful that she then had any thoughts of marriage with this man twenty-four years her senior. But George was smitten enough to phone Clare's mother the next day to ask if he could call on them. Mrs. Austin, who read all the society columns, knew all about the wealthy George Brokaw and was delighted. Her husband was not; he knew George's reputation.

Still, George drove up to the Austin cottage in Greenwich in his impressive yellow Locomobile and took the whole family to dinner. He played the perfect, considerate gentleman, and even Dr. Austin was impressed. The man was plainly in love. As the courtship continued, Clare's mother pressed her daughter to give George serious consideration.

Clare dreaded the necessary visit to George's mother. The Brokaw family's Fifth Avenue mansion was gloomy, with jagged gables and protruding turrets. Mrs. Brokaw, a forbidding woman in her eighties, greeted Clare graciously. The tea was uneventful until Mrs. Brokaw suddenly asked Clare to stand near the window, where the light was better. Clare later recalled feeling like a pinned butterfly under a microscope while the old woman stared at her intently, then loudly told George, "She's a good girl and a healthy girl. You marry her."

George hugged his mother, kissed Clare for the first time, and rushed her to Cartier to pick out a seventeen-carat blue-white diamond solitaire engagement ring. George wanted to marry quickly, mainly because his mother was ill and he wanted to give her grandchildren soon. Brokaw also knew his brothers and sisters opposed his marriage. If anything were to happen to him while he was a bachelor, they would inherit his share of the family millions. "I was about as popular as the smallpox," Clare later said.

For once in her life Clare was curiously complacent. She could have said no at any time, but her mother said, "Get married." "So I did what my mother said," explained Clare, who soon busied herself with dressmakers and milliners.

The wedding took place at Christ Episcopal Church in Greenwich, Connecticut, on August 10, 1923. Though the nation was mourning the death of President Warren G. Harding, the wedding was still hailed as "the most important social event of the season." Yet there was an omen of problems ahead when George's siblings used the presidential mourning as their excuse for not coming.

Even in her fantasy Clare had never imagined such a wedding. There were more than 1000 guests. "Not only were the motorcars lined up for several blocks but there were photographers and motion picture men grouped near the entrance to the church," she wrote afterward.

Clare was twenty years old. The thoughts she had that day were surely mixed: the money must have seemed like a fairy tale, but the prince was old enough to be her father. Reflecting on this later, she said that she married the first man who was kind to her.

The Austins gave a wedding reception for 150 friends, in Greenwich. That night the newlyweds stayed at The Plaza Hotel in New York and sailed the next morning for a four-month honeymoon in Europe.

Materially, at least, the honeymoon was everything Clare might have wanted. George was a lavish spender, buying her clothes and jewels, anything that caught her fancy—and many things did. He was also surprisingly tender and much more knowledgeable than she had supposed, particularly about art. George filled in many gaps in her education. But writing of the honeymoon later, Clare noted that it was not a great success.

Though her mother had assured her that love would come, it never really did—not with George. Soon enough Clare learned that he was one of the better-known drunks in New York. Worse, because he didn't need to work, he stayed home most of the time except when he was busy touring the country's top golf courses, winning more golf trophies, in which he hid his gin.

Clare tried to turn her back at first. Of course she had married this man for his money, but she was determined to make him a proper wife. She had an intuitive sense of what made society move, and she was determined to shine in it and make him proud of her.

The newlyweds stayed with George's mother and her seventeen servants for almost a year. Finally, ready for her own home, Clare picked a palatial colonial house set on six acres, fronting Long Island Sound in socially correct Sands Point, where her good friend Mrs. Belmont was a neighbor. For the moment all was relatively serene. George behaved himself, and bought Clare plenty of beautiful frocks, splendid jewels, and a luxurious motorcar.

That December, Clare gave George the news he most wanted—she was pregnant. The idea of a possible son and heir made George ecstatic. The baby was a girl, born August 25, 1924, at Greenwich Hospital, and was christened Ann Clare Brokaw, just like Clare's mother.

As much as she had wanted a child, Clare quickly learned that she was not a natural or giving mother. In one of the short stories she would write years later, one of the characters asked another, "Do you like children?"

"Other people's" was the telling reply.

Like most women of her social class, Clare delegated most of Ann's care to nannies. "Rich women are not too put upon by their children," she later said. "You don't have to do all those things for a child that those women who had to stay at home did."

When Clare's mother-in-law died, in June 1925, the Manhattan mansion passed on to George to live in for his lifetime but was held in trust for all the children.

"It was a frightfully difficult house," Clare said of her new home. "It took at least fourteen servants to run it. There was a huge stairway with the most horrible yellow marble I had ever seen." She also complained about the imitation tapestries, the clutter of soiled Japanese screens, the bad plumbing, and the "execrable carvings. After a year, I tried to re-decorate the thing, but it was impossible. Really, the ugliness of the house was just appalling."

Meanwhile, Clare was generous with her family. Not only did she promote her mother's entry into society, she persuaded her husband to find David a job as a stockbroker after he got out of the marines. Clare also helped her father by sending him money. Billy Boothe needed it. He was then sixty-eight and seriously ill and had lost his music school.

Around this time Clare's mother moved in with her. They badly needed each other. Ann Clare had separated from her husband because the doctor had taken up with a nurse. And Clare needed to talk about her disintegrating relationship with George.

Sober, he was generally kind and thoughtful, pleasant and charming. Drunk, he was jealous, even vicious. He beat Clare—sometimes badly. During this period, Clare had at least three miscarriages. After her last, doctors told Clare she could no longer have children.

"I know all about violence and physical abuse," Clare later confided.

The situation grew intolerable. All the money, all the mansions, all the jewels, all the clothes were not worth the terror of a beating by a vicious drunk who even raped her on the night she returned from the hospital after a miscarriage. When George drank too much, he was simply out of control. Clare confided this to several of her friends.

Clare's mother, always pragmatic, urged her to play for time:

Left, the close-knit Luce family during Henry's boyhood. Emmavail, Henry, and their father, Henry Winters Luce, stand behind Beth and mother Elizabeth Root Luce.

Above, as a young woman, Clare went to Europe with her mother and stepfather, Dr. Albert Austin. Left, with her first husband, George Tuttle Brokaw, Clare struggled to be a good society wife, but she soon tired of the role.

George could not live too long this way. When he died, Clare would still be a very young, very rich widow with her whole life ahead of her.

But Clare could not and would not wait until her husband drank himself to death. She refused to allow her life to grow bitter and fearful. She would leave him. She moved into a hotel, hired a top lawyer, then left for Reno, Nevada, taking her four-year-old daughter with her.

Clare had chosen Reno because there she would not have to re-count the story of the drunken beatings. In Reno mental cruelty was sufficient grounds for divorce for some 2000 women every year.

For most of the women awaiting their decrees, Reno was a frustrat-ing, deadly place. To get a divorce there, it was necessary to stay six weeks. But to her surprise Clare found she enjoyed this time of togetherness with her daughter. She and Ann rode horseback to-gether and visited old gold mines, ghost towns, and lovely blue lakes. It was an interlude that would not soon be duplicated.

When it came time for the final divorce arrangements, Clare tried to be fair. "I may have married for money," she said, "but I certainly didn't divorce for it." She settled for a lifetime yearly income of $26,000, plus a trust fund of $425,000, to revert to Ann after her death. George agreed to pay for Ann's education. Clare would have custody from January 1 to June 30, and George would have Ann for the rest of the year.

That same year, 1929, twenty-six-year-old Clare not only lost a husband, she lost a father. Billy Boothe died. He was nearly seventy. Clare was not named in his obituary, and she was not present at his funeral.

4

HARRY Luce called 1922 "the hardest year of my life." It was also his best.

That year he and Brit settled into a dilapidated brownstone office in the basement of Nine East Seventeenth Street in Manhattan. They furnished it with a filing cabinet and four secondhand desks, up against the walls. Two young ladies sat in the back room clipping newspaper articles for possible rewrite. They would later be replaced by researchers who would check the correctness of every statement that appeared in the magazine.

Around the office the atmosphere was that of a college newspaper. Smoking end on end, Harry and Brit managed to feed off each other's strengths and weaknesses. "I think Harry cared more about the substance of stories than Hadden," said Harry's sister Beth. "Hadden was more the decorator; he liked the language."

Harry worried about everything, and a major concern was raising money. "Part of the advantage of going to Yale was to get to know rich people. We thought the fund-raising would be just easy arithmetic—but it turned out differently," Harry told the Yale *Daily News*. "Our classmates weren't rich, their fathers were, and they wouldn't put up money for such crazy schemes."

Somehow Harry and Brit managed to get to see the famed magazine editor and critic H. L. Mencken, who listened to them quietly, then said, "It will never work. Nobody will read it."

Their former professor William Lyon Phelps told them they had a wonderful idea, "but it would be impossible to make it financially successful." The consensus of most people was a firm "Don't do it!"

Over the next year, consorting with golfing friends and their fathers, they raised some $86,000 from seventy-two investors. Their biggest contributor was a Yalie's mother, Mrs. William L. Harkness of Cleveland, whose hearing was so poor that she could not understand the fervent pitch delivered by Luce and Hadden. Still, she said, "That will do, boys. You may put me down for $20,000."

When she later lost her money in the Wall Street crash, her investment in *Time* helped support her in her old age.

Luce and Hadden now had enough to set up shop. The search was on for a name. They had considered *Facts*, but discarded it. *Time* finally came to Luce one night while coming home from work.

"On the subway, my half-glazed stare fell on an advertisement with the headline, TIME TO RETIRE, or TIME FOR A CHANGE. I remember the name *Time* occurring to me. It stayed with me overnight. The next morning, I suggested it to Hadden and he accepted it immediately."

The style Luce and Hadden eventually developed discarded the news lead. Since the news was four to ten days old, the editors tried to enliven it. They used the most vivid adjectives and verbs possible, and relied on bold, teasing headlines. They aimed for a facetious tone mixed with an underlying seriousness: thought and meaning with a light touch. They also felt that since the average American had no time to form his own opinions, the magazine must do it for him.

The next months were frenzied. In February 1923 the entire staff piled in three taxis that would take them from their new office on East Fortieth Street to the printing plant in lower Manhattan. They all watched as the first issue of *Time* magazine went to press.

Luce later reminisced about working until dawn in the composing room, rewriting to cut and fit. "It was daylight when I got home and went to sleep," he said. "That afternoon, I found an uncut copy of the little magazine in my room. I picked it up and began to turn through its meager thirty-two pages. Half an hour later, I woke up to a surprise: what I had been reading wasn't bad at all. In fact, it was quite good. Somehow, it all held together, it was interesting."

Now came the matter of circulating the issue. Roy Larsen, then circulation manager, sat on the floor of the office, hopelessly mixed up. He was trying to sort the wrappers by states. They were still mailing out the first issue when the third went to press.

Volume I, Number I of *Time*, The Weekly Newsmagazine, was dated March 3, 1923. Sales price: fifteen cents. Reading time: one hour. It compartmentalized the weekly news into twenty-two departments, with only a meager four pages of advertising. It sold about 8500 copies.

On the cover of the first issue was eighty-six-year-old Speaker of the House James G. "Uncle Joe" Cannon, who was retiring after twenty-three years. The national affairs section dealt with the controversy over U.S. membership in the World Court. In the foreign affairs section the main article discussed the big sale of Soviet wheat to Western Europe. The aeronautics section described a possible dirigible service between Chicago and New York.

The style for everything was saucy, with an air of omnipotence. "Let all stories make sharp sense. Omit flowers. Remember you can't be too obvious. People talk too much about things they don't know," Luce said at the time. The basic belief was that busy, influential people preferred a digested substitute to the long, original stories.

Every story had its slant. Asked once why *Time* did not present two sides of a story, Luce answered, "Are there not more likely to be three sides or thirty sides?" His idea was that the American press had a mission that could influence the fate of American civilization. "Give the public the truth we think it must have." As one writer said, "We went in every week to remake the world." The editors got the facts, then rearranged them according to the truth they wanted to tell.

Sales zigzagged up and down that first year, then up again because the audience was there, and it kept growing. People seemed to like their news tasty, snappy, short, and in gulps.

About once a week Lila would come by train from Chicago. "I would spend three or four days in New York," she said. "Sometimes [Harry] could get away for an hour a day to come and see me. He'd arrive in the evening, and we'd read some books aloud together. And mind you, nobody would believe this, but no embraces! It's incredible because we were terribly in love."

Within four months things were going well enough for *Time* to take half a floor in an old brewery building on East Thirty-ninth Street between Second and Third avenues. By this time even Lila's stepfather, who had once described Luce as "a person of no position, worthless," now agreed that this young man was bright with promise and gave permission for the young couple's marriage.

For Lila and Harry this was an enormous relief. On December 22, 1923, the long wait was over. The discreet announcement in *Time*'s Milestones simply said, "Married, Miss Lila Ross Hotz, 23, of Chicago, to Harry Robinson Luce, editor of *Time*, The Weekly Newsmagazine."

After a honeymoon in Virginia, Harry and Lila found a four-room flat on Fifth Avenue and Ninety-seventh Street, overlooking Central Park but "very much at the edge of nothing," as Lila noted. Rent was cheap, and they filled the apartment with Lila's mother's expensive antiques. Her mother also quietly supplemented their income so that Lila could afford regular help.

HARRY and Brit's original agreement was that they would alternate as editor and business manager. "Brit won the toss of the coin and got to edit first," said Beth. "Harry concentrated on the advertising and the money. He was thrilled the next year when they switched jobs, but then Brit floundered on the financial end. And so Harry reluctantly had to take over the business end again to make it work." Brit later referred to Harry as a "financial genius."

Hadden, meanwhile, put his firm imprint on *Time* style. A true wordsmith, he liked to make everything flip and feisty, so tightly edited that everything seemed compressed, even encapsulated. He invented words like "tycoon" and used foreign words like "pundit"— from the Hindu meaning a learned man. "Kudos" was another Hadden word that received wide acceptability.

Hadden also urged the use of words that packaged two meanings into one, such as "uprighteous," which combined upright and righteous, or "sarcastigator" (sarcastic and instigator). The most successful blended word was "socialite" (a combination of social and light). And then there was "smog," a blend of smoke and fog.

Though Harry and Brit basically agreed about style, they differed about many other matters. The careful, businesslike Luce and the flippant, disorganized Hadden were an odd, mismatched team. The breach between them kept widening. In almost every way they were opposites. Yet each man had parts of the other and envied the rest. This was part of their bond, and the birth of *Time* needed them both.

In 1928 Harry Luce was thirty years old. He told his wife that he expected to be a millionaire before the year was out, and indeed he was. What made 1928 *more* important for him was that Hadden had promised to stay on the business management side all that year and let Harry be the editor.

Luce took his role as editor very seriously. Instead of too frequent use of the heavy black pencil, he concentrated on steering the story line straight, keeping the main idea clear and concise. "He'd galvanize a page by putting two pencil marks on it," recalled a consultant.

Luce was a man of ideas, and there were those who felt he cared more for ideas than for people. With people he never seemed completely comfortable. Partly it came from shyness. He couldn't seem to navigate through human relationships. He had no natural intuition about it. An associate once explained that he never meant to hurt or snub people; it was just that he was impatient. He couldn't stand things getting in the way, and got testy if he was kept waiting. On the other hand, if you caught his interest in something, he would want to know all about it.

Here was a man who was never afraid of seeming stupid. His curiosity was insatiable. "After you had been with Luce for a day, you felt as if a suction pump had been applied to your brains and pulled every bit of information out," said one of his secretaries.

He was basically a loner. Almost nobody came into Luce's office uninvited. Later even his sons had to make appointments to see him.

If Luce was truly passionate about anything, it was *Time*. He believed anything important could be made understandable and popular, that there was no such thing as a dull important subject.

"He really loved Time Inc., the company and the people," said his secretary, Gloria Mariano. "He didn't care if people had odd hours, as long as they worked hard, did their work, and cared about Time Inc. In those days, you'd have gone to work without being paid. It was just a joy; it was fun."

In the winter months of 1928 Brit Hadden seemed listless and called in frequently to say, "I'm not well. I don't know what's wrong with me."

At his mother's insistence he moved back home to Brooklyn, where she could care for him. But Hadden got worse. He came down with influenza, and an infection in his bloodstream that affected his heart. He was swiftly hospitalized and in need of blood. Harry, the first to donate blood, was a daily visitor. But Hadden quickly deteriorated. He died on February 27, 1929, at the age of thirty-one.

They had had differences in the past, but those who knew Harry and Brit well felt they had resolved them on Brit's deathbed. Harry missed his friend deeply. "I don't know what I'll do without Hadden," he said.

He soon found out.

CLARE had expected to feel happy and free after her divorce from Brokaw, but instead she drifted through her days in a miserable, lonely daze. She had neither direction nor goal. She felt, she said, "like a useless member of the world."

She tried to understand her own angst, and was puzzled. "I did not lack for money or health, or the affection of friends or attention from the opposite sex. But some vast uneasiness, restlessness, spoiled every pleasure and heightened every pain, and poisoned every relationship. I was just not at peace with God." In search of a cure, she turned to psychoanalysis, but quit it soon after. She admitted, "Of all the things I have done in my life, my abrupt retreat from [my analyst's] office has given me the most pleasure and the least regrets. I demonstrated that I possessed a free will: I could choose my own path to doom!"

Afterward her impulse was to meet men—interesting men, important men. Gossip columnists soon associated her with some of the most celebrated men in the city, including Condé Nast, who bought *Vogue* magazine in 1909 and made it one of the first modern illustrated magazines. His *Vogue* patterns became famous and made him a fortune. Four years later he transformed a magazine called *Dress and Vanity Fair* into *Vanity Fair*. Nast was a patriarch in his fifties who always seemed to be in between marriages and always in the company of the world's most beautiful women. At his twenty-room Park Avenue penthouse he was a lavish host. Nast's guests might include everybody from the young pilot Charles Lindbergh, to George Gershwin, playing the music of a future show.

At one of his midnight parties Clare cornered him. Knowing she needed the discipline of a job, she asked him for a position on one of his magazines. Nast later recalled, "I didn't think she was serious. I told her, 'I'm off to Europe. See Edna Chase.' I was counting on Edna to get me off the hook." Edna Woolman Chase was the editor of *Vogue*.

"Edna gave me the same runaround," said Clare, "the same talk. She too was off to Europe and when she got back, well, maybe."

Clare, persistent, returned to the *Vogue* office sometime later, but Mrs. Chase was still not back. "By this time I knew the set-up. I walked along the corridor peering into offices until I came to one in which there was a dear old lady writing a social letter. It was the office of the caption writers. There was one empty desk. I kind of oozed in."

"Whose desk is that?" Clare asked the woman.

"No one's at present."

"Then it's mine," said Clare.

"What are you doing?"

"Writing captions."

"Well, here are some to write."

She promptly began writing captions for pictures of what the well-dressed woman will wear. "I worked there every day," said Clare, "scared to death somebody would find out I hadn't been hired. But nobody noticed me. Nobody knew anything about me. It was three weeks before I got a pay envelope." (Her salary was twenty-one dollars a month.)

The halls of Condé Nast publishing company were set up in such a way that anyone bound for the *Vogue* offices had to pass by the door of *Vanity Fair*. The *Vanity Fair* staffers got a jolt the first morning Mrs. Brokaw arrived to report for work at *Vogue*. She was slim and pretty in a simple gray frock with touches of white at the throat and wrists, and the light from a window at the end of the hall celestially illumined her face and hair. "Geez, what was that?" a *Vanity Fair* editor murmured as she passed.

Still, no one quite knew how she got there. "Condé and I were on one of our transatlantic shuffle routines," said Mrs. Chase, "and each assumed that somewhere—Paris, London, New York, or the high seas—the other had engaged her. Her status was vague, but after a bit she began to prove herself."

Condé Nast promptly invited her to dinner. "Those were still the days when at the end of a dinner, the ladies left the room while the men remained for brandy and cigars," he said. "Clare, however, blandly stayed on with the men, while the other women, banished into the drawing room, fumed helplessly." Edna Chase recalled, "When Clare came into the office, all the editors' backs would stiffen like cats watching a confident dog stroll by."

She seemed to fluster everyone around her. "Clare had a hypnotic effect on me when she came to my studio," said a woman photographer who was taking pictures of Clare. As an acknowledged beauty of the era, Clare was often asked to pose. "I could hear myself saying idiotic things that I wasn't conscious of thinking."

Clare's ambition was to move to Nast's other publication, *Vanity Fair*. She described her work at *Vogue* as "monkey jobs," while *Vanity Fair* was a showcase for some of the best, wittiest writing in the country. Contributors included Dorothy Parker, Robert Benchley, P. G. Wodehouse, Edna St. Vincent Millay, Colette, Aldous Huxley, Edmund Wilson, Robert Sherwood, and Gertrude Stein, with art by Picasso and Matisse.

Nast called *Vanity Fair* an intellectual exercise for nice people. Its credo was to chronicle the progress of American life cheerfully, truthfully, and entertainingly. As an organ of the elite, it tried to define much of the taste of the time.

The celebrated editor in chief of *Vanity Fair* was Frank Crowninshield, a New York legend. Crownie, as he was called, was dapper, with curly hair and a curly mustache, a constant twinkle, and a complex, remarkable mind. When Clare came for her interview, Crownie told her to come back in a week with a hundred suggestions suitable for publication. When she delivered them, he read them, patted her arm, then said with a twinkle, "Well, well, you've done a lot of work. Now confess, who was the bright young man under your bed who thought up all these ideas for you?"

Clare was so angry she almost cried. Crownie quieted her, warned her never to take him—or life—too seriously, then hired her.

Crowninshield was the editor and unique spirit of the magazine, but twenty-nine-year-old Donald Freeman, managing editor since 1924, was its working genius. Short, balding, and slightly fat, Freeman was one of the best editorial minds in the country.

Clare used "Julian Jerome" as a byline on her first article, "Talking Up and Thinking Down," which poked fun at café society, and enclosed it with a group of other manuscripts she passed on to managing editor Freeman.

"These first three pieces are useless," he told her, "but find this fellow Jerome. I'd like to print more of his stuff." When she confessed she was the author, Freeman said, "You're really a first-class writer. Stick with it. Write what you know best and you will go a long way."

Freeman was hooked. He was delighted to discuss Clare's ideas and problems, and she was even more delighted to have gained his interest. But his major contribution to her welfare was keeping her mind in focus, her work disciplined. Clare was soon doing everything at *Vanity Fair*. She read unsolicited manuscripts, helped photographers make appointments with celebrities, and translated French writers.

Behind the scenes Freeman fell hopelessly in love with Clare. He was willing to give what he had and get what he could. And she needed everything he had. "He encouraged me at a critical time in my life to believe in myself and my talents," she later said. "I loved him for that, but not in the same way he loved me." He was shaping her style, her habits, her personality, her life—and she loved it.

Before long, Clare was made associate editor. She knew she could write, edit, think, and organize. She could produce ideas filled with imagination. Finally she had a function and an excitement in her life.

In her new position Clare busily set about creating new features. One of the most popular was called "Ike and Mike—They Look Alike." Clare would sit in her office searching hundreds of photographs, pairing pictures of mismatched people who looked like each other. Another department she created was called "We Nominate for Oblivion," to counterpoint the magazine's well-known "Hall of Fame." And she dreamed up an idea of putting Roosevelt's New Deal Cabinet on playing cards.

Not everyone admired her at *Vanity Fair.* In a letter to a Vassar friend, Helen Brown wrote:

> Mrs. Brokaw is twenty-eight. She comes sweeping into the office around ten in the morning, looking blond, beautiful, expensive, her perfume leaving people practically in an olfactory swoon. She lives in a penthouse with four servants, including a personal lady's maid to draw her bath and help her dress, just like a movie star.

Yet gradually Clare won her over. Brown described Clare as encouraging and scrupulously fair, and added, "She's clever and quick-witted. If we need a title, a caption, a word, an idea, she can think of one right off the bat. She's not a profound thinker, but she's one of the fastest, trigger-quick." Summing Clare up, she called her "so ambitious that it hurt."

Another friend, the actress Arlene Francis, put Clare's aspiration more pointedly. "She wanted to be queen, and why the hell not?"

The queen kept enlarging her court. Her contacts expanded with her horizons. Men were crazy about her. As Clare's power and prestige grew, her relationship with Donald Freeman changed.

"She treats him like a faithful old dog that gets on her nerves," Helen reported to a friend.

But Freeman persisted. He knew he still held great sway as her mentor and intellectual guide. He sent a manuscript of Clare's collection of stories, entitled *Stuffed Shirts,* to noted critic H. L. Mencken for possible review. Mencken replied, "It looks immensely interesting." When it was published, it became a social sensation.

Clare's dreams of being a successful author were smashed when she got her first accounting from her publisher. *Stuffed Shirts* sold only 2600 copies, netting Clare $600. She ruefully announced that she would concentrate on writing plays "for cash and kudos."

Meanwhile, she put aside any pretense of fidelity to Freeman. Her name was romantically connected with a great many men, from millionaire Jock Whitney to noted author John O'Hara. She had moved on. There were worlds to conquer, and conquering them called for a hard heart, sharp mind, and cool head. She had them all.

Soon she would find a man she had subconsciously been waiting for.

WITH Hadden's death Luce became "the spark plug as well as the transmission of the machine" and started remaking *Time* in his own image. As it blossomed, so did Harry and Lila.

Lila then was "very likable, very gay, very talkative." But what mattered to Harry at this point in his life was his concept for a new magazine, a business monthly that would simplify and illuminate finance the way *Time* had illuminated the news. He felt that the great businessmen were the new supermen of civilization and that their lives represented a romantic adventure, a story of high drama and excitement. He saw all this as a challenge, an untold story.

Luce selected Parker Lloyd-Smith, a calm, almost languid young man with a Mona Lisa smile, to explore his notion of a business magazine. The tentative title was *Power*, but Harry wasn't happy and asked Lila to jot down some other names. "I put four down; at the top was *Fortune*," she recalled. "He read that and said, 'That's it!' "

Fortune seemed a very poor idea all of a sudden when the stock market crashed in 1929. As some of his wealthy cronies plunged from windows Luce grew nervous and tight with his money. He wrote a memo to his staff cautioning them against extravagance, including extravagant ideas. Above all, he told them, "Don't waste time!"

But nothing would stop him from publishing *Fortune*. Volume I, Number 1, appeared in February 1930. Priced at a dollar, handsome with handsewn binding, *Fortune*, said Luce, was "designed to be the most beautiful magazine in America." The first issue featured magnificent color photographs by Margaret Bourke-White, who found poetry in big hulking machines and the people who worked them. The same issue featured a profile of the Radio Corporation of America. There was also a family album on the Rothschilds, an article on how to live on $25,000 a year, and a personality profile of Mr. Gamble of Procter and Gamble.

To create stories with sufficient punch and depth, Luce argued that writers, not editors, should be the heart of the magazine. What was remarkable about the early staff of *Fortune* was that the strongly

Republican Luce had hired mostly ardent liberals. He once told a friend that the reason most of his writers were not Republicans was because "I guess Republicans don't write so good."

Luce supplemented his liberals with a collection of poets to help give *Fortune* prestige. The best of them was Archibald MacLeish, who had done part-time writing for *Time* in Paris. Luce now offered him a full-time job as a *Fortune* editor. When MacLeish replied that he knew nothing about business, Luce thundered, "That is exactly why I want you! The men who read balance sheets cannot write. It is easier to turn poets into business journalists than to turn bookkeepers into writers." His goal, he later explained, was to find "writers who could see beyond the balance sheets and describe the lights and shadows of factories and the men who ruled them."

Luce's editors admitted he was a critical gadfly who kept them on their toes. According to one, "It was not so much that we were afraid of Harry (although we were a little) as that we busted our guts trying to keep pace with him and please him. We didn't love him in those days. He wouldn't permit it. He was too preoccupied, intense, hard driven. He was a generous, just, inspiring boss, but also a rigorous perfectionist."

While *Fortune* was busy winning an audience the Luce empire now began growing in different directions. Time Inc. was branching into radio with *The March of Time,* a program in which a small cast of actors reenacted and dramatized the news of the week.

National reaction to the first network radio show, in February 1931, was mixed. Some felt it was too sensational, too much editorializing of the news. But Luce was confident that *The March of Time* would eventually find a large audience, and again he was right. He left the details of the show to others and focused on creating the right leadership at his magazines.

In 1933 *Time* celebrated its tenth anniversary; the magazine now boasted one million readers. Luce was feeling both proud and magnanimous. He decided the time had come to give not only to his magazines but to his family. He and Lila now had two young children, young Henry and Peter Paul. He knew that Lila loved the world of the seventeenth century and that what she wanted most was a Norman castle. One day a real estate agent told him that a fifty-acre estate had come up for sale in New Jersey.

"So Harry rushed out," remembered Lila, "and we bought it."

The house and the working farm on the property would be their home until they built their stone castle. Harry enjoyed the feeling of a farm and wanted his two sons to share it.

For Lila this was a wonderful time. She had spent many of the previous years confined by a succession of pregnancies. Between Henry and Peter Paul another son, Christopher, had died at birth. Building her dream house was a much needed diversion for her.

Still, there were those friends who felt a growing distance between Harry and Lila. Harry's work dominated everything they did. If he was expanding his horizons, some felt she was not. If there was a change in his feelings for Lila, a change in their relationship, she did not sense it then. Perhaps Harry didn't either.

5

A T A dinner party at the Colony Restaurant in New York, in the early 1930s, financier Bernard Baruch met Clare Boothe. Immediately they were engrossed in conversation. Clare was entranced and later described Baruch as "a king, or some gangster chieftain, always surrounded by an impressive entourage whose duty it was to protect and promote the Baruch cause of the moment."

An adviser to Presidents and a global statesman, Bernard Mannes Baruch grew up a "poor boy," as he told the writer John Hersey. After attending City College, in New York, young Bernie discovered Wall Street when he delivered some papers to financier J. P. Morgan. He was so impressed with the scene that he promptly quit his three-dollar-a-week job with a glassware company and never looked back. Before he was thirty, Baruch was one of the richest men in the country and one of the most powerful. Eventually he quit fortune making to dedicate the rest of his life to public service.

Clare fell for Baruch hard. He was a miracle for her, one of the great influences on her life. "She was passionate about Baruch," said her longtime friend writer Wilfrid Sheed, who became Clare's confidant. "You could tell by the intensity with which she talked about him."

Baruch was similarly entranced. "I remember little wispy curls on her forehead, but under that was a matter-of-fact, thoughtful person," he said. "Character, work, courage. When courage was given out, she was sitting in the front bench. Clare has the spirit only generals have, and it shines in her eyes. She reacts automatically against injustice, against anything that is wrong."

For Clare the attraction was not only Baruch's reputation but his personality. He was charming, courtly, and impressive. The fact that he was sixty-one when they met—more than twice her age—mattered little to her. Baruch was vital and vibrant, and Clare, after all, always preferred the mature man and the mature mind—not to mention power. Baruch often swept the willing Clare away to his great estate, Hobcaw, near Georgetown, South Carolina. On that huge plantation it was a life of walking, sitting around the fire, riding, and shooting. "He really was the great love of her life," reminisced Shirley Clurman, an intimate of Clare's later years.

For his part Baruch seemed to put Clare first among his various women. Constantly traveling, he always brought back gifts for his women friends, and Clare always had first pick. "Poor little rich kid," Baruch commented. "It's hard to refuse her anything."

Baruch began introducing Clare to the leading lights in the Democratic Party. She attended the 1932 Democratic National Convention, in Chicago, where Franklin D. Roosevelt, the governor of New York, received the nomination. Clare described the convention as "a great eye-opener—a significant event in my life."

By this point in her career Clare had recognized the power of politics. Through Baruch she defined her political sensibilities, and her liberalism extended to many facets of her life. Her ideas about men and relationships indeed seemed far more liberal than the times. She loved Baruch deeply, but was pragmatic enough to know that he had other women and that he could never commit himself to her. The major difficulty, of course, was that his wife was mentally ill, and he would not leave her. Clare proceeded to fill her life with an admiring coterie of other men, most of whom were useful to her in one way or another.

Men gravitated to Clare almost automatically, and she had become a shrewd judge of them—and a good actress. Each of her lovers thought he knew a different Clare. And of course, they were jealous of each other. Yet she was able to juggle many men in her life largely because these lovers were terribly busy, as she was, and mostly married.

As a young divorcée, above, Clare took her daughter, Ann, to the beach; later she would shunt Ann off to boarding schools. Left, Luce's first wife, Lila Ross Hotz, was devoted to their sons, Peter Paul and Henry III. Below, Clare as the managing editor of Vanity Fair.

Clare rarely discarded her men. Donald Freeman was an exception. In a letter written at this time, he described himself as being in a state of nervous agitation, so that he often seemed almost hysterical. He felt Clare wore an iron mask and he could not reach her.

From Crotch Island, off the coast of Maine, where she was spending the summer, Clare sent him a long letter saying she wanted their relationship to evolve from love to friendship. Back in New York, on the night of October 2, 1932, Donald Freeman crashed his roadster into a dividing post on the Bronx River Parkway and died without regaining consciousness. The consensus among Freeman's friends was that his death was a suicide.

Clare was shocked, but not shattered. She would always talk warmly about Freeman as her great good friend and "severest critic."

Soon after Freeman's death she inherited his job, his office, and his secretary. As *Vanity Fair's* managing editor, she ruled over a celebrated intellectual circle. It was all very heady. Clare had moved into a new orbit, and it was exactly what she wanted. *Vanity Fair* was a literary stage of quality and distinction, and she was now in charge of that stage. The New York literary world not only accepted her but catered to her. She was welcomed everywhere, wanted everywhere. One moment the Eugene O'Neills were inviting her to dinner, and the next she herself was giving a little soiree for her literary hero, Somerset Maugham.

In 1931 Condé Nast asked Clare to suggest a new magazine idea. Clare and her art staff proposed a large-format magazine with a heavy emphasis on photographs. "I wrote a long memo called 'On Turning *Vanity Fair* into a Picture Magazine Called *Life*,'" recalled Clare. She suggested Nast buy the title *Life* from a defunct magazine. Strong on celebrity, with minimal satire and streamlined, the magazine would be "a sort of *Vanity Fair* for the masses."

Nast instead decided to merge *Vanity Fair* with *Vogue* and make it a weekly as Clare kept fighting to revive and refinance the magazine. Baruch had already invested heavily in it. Clare joined Bernie in London, and he introduced her to Winston Churchill, who, he felt, might be a possible literary contributor. Churchill was charmed enough to ask Baruch to join him for the weekend "and invite that pretty Mrs. Brokaw."

Although the weekend did not convince Churchill to join Clare's contributing writers, he did make a romantic contribution to her life. Churchill tried to serve as a matchmaker between Clare and his son, Randolph. Randolph was going through a tough time with drinking and divorce. Moreover, he was struggling to create a separate identity from his father. Churchill felt that an American woman might revitalize his son.

For an intense, romantic time Clare and Randolph conducted a passionate affair. But Clare would not regard this as a serious match. She had paid her dues with one alcoholic, and didn't want another. Besides, she didn't want to marry the *son* of a great man—she wanted to marry a great man.

"I've never known a man who could resist her spell, once she set her mind to it and had him face-to-face," said Helen Brown. "One after another, she knocked them off like sitting ducks."

Still, she seemed more interested in the conquest than the affair. "I've known men who have slept with Clare, and who said she was just like a dead fish," said a woman. A French artist who dated Clare several times told Clare's friend Helen, "It's a beautiful façade, well-constructed, but without central heating . . . she's not *real*."

To the contrary, when Clare wanted something, she was very real and often quite calculating. She always put her own interests first. When she and writer Dorothy Parker were at a formal affair, both were escorted to the front door to enter the dining room first. Clare stepped aside, graciously commenting, "Age before beauty, dear Dolly." At which dear Dolly swept by with "And pearls before swine, dear Clare." Parker also said, "Clare would be nice to her inferiors— if she could find any."

Clare's hectic social life, the many pressures of her job, and the energy required to juggle so many men left little time for anything or anyone else. Clare's only child got minimal attention. In fact, Clare rarely mentioned Ann and kept her far from the public.

Entitled to possession of daughter Ann for six months a year, she sent her away for some of that time to a camp near Lake Placid, New York. Clare was pleased because Ann seemed to be completely happy with children her age. Superficially, at least, Clare tried to be motherly. Yet she once told a friend that Ann complained that when they were in the same room together, she felt that her mother was hardly aware of her presence. Clare admitted this and said it was the result of trying to live three lives at the same time. There was little question that their time together was minimal enough for Clare to feel guilt, and later remorse, and for Ann to be lonely.

Two years after the divorce Ann's father remarried. But Clare and George continued to have legal fights, particularly over Ann.

By this time Clare's mother and stepfather had separated, but Ann Clare still lived alone at the home in Greenwich. Clare and her mother were in contact, but the contact was no longer close.

CLARE was restless. Always thinking of her next man, her next leap of ambition, she handed Frank Crowninshield her resignation from *Vanity Fair* in February 1934. Her flip excuse was that she didn't like to work in an office anymore. Her real reason was that she had decided she wanted to write plays. Being a playwright not only seemed a romantic thing to do but it would enrich her claim as "the glamour girl of letters" and put her on a new creative level.

While Clare had a large ego, she still lacked the self-confidence needed to write plays. Ardent admirer Paul Gallico, a famed sportswriter, was waiting and willing to collaborate. Their combined effort was *The Sacred Cow*. They needed a producer, and Baruch introduced her to John Golden. After reading the manuscript, Golden told Clare that the play needed a lot of work, but it was fresh and lively. He did not, however, volunteer to produce it.

Clare was disconsolate and retreated to a hotel on a small island called St. Simons, off the Georgia coast. Broadway gossip intimated that Clare was having another affair. It wasn't true; she was not only alone but she insisted to friends that she was very happy being alone. She liked the island, she said, with its dunes and palm trees, and used her time there to begin another play. She hated wasting time.

For Clare this was a thoughtful time. She had done so much and was left with so little. What she had left was a play she harbored in her mind, a play still being shaped, still to come alive. When she returned to New York, producer John Golden asked to see her script.

"I was working for John Golden," said Jean Dalrymple, a vivacious theatrical agent who would become increasingly important in Clare's life. "[Clare] called me up and wanted me to read her play *Abide With Me*. It was about her husband, about Brokaw. He was a terrible drunk. She gave me the script, and I took it home and read it that night. I was horrified that any woman would tell about this terrible man she had been married to. She called me up the next day. I said, 'You must never have this produced. It is an awful thing for people to know.' She didn't like that a bit! I said, 'Please don't let this go around. It's very private, personal information you're giving here.' "

Abide With Me opened that summer at the Beechwood Theater in Scarborough, in Westchester County, New York. It was a shocker. A sadist threatens to kill his child, and his wife kills him. But her mother-in-law persuades the world that it was a suicide, and the wife marries her psychiatrist and lives happily ever after.

The play died quietly. John Golden wrote Clare that it had fine writing in it and that he might still produce it on Broadway. But he did want her to change it to make it right.

Clare was exultant. She now saw everything in a brighter light, and she viewed this as a time of tremendous growth. Yes, she was happy, but she wanted to be much happier. This was her mood when she accepted a dinner party invitation from Laura Hobson.

It would turn out to be a monumental evening.

HENRY Luce had never met a woman like Clare, and he wanted to see her again. He was delighted two months after their first brief encounter when they met again at a dinner party.

During dinner, Clare sat at Luce's right, but he largely ignored her. She was not used to being ignored. After dinner he wandered over to her and suddenly said, "I want to talk to you more about this magazine—the idea you have for a picture magazine."

He then probed with questions, and she supplied pointed replies. Then once again out came the pocket watch, and he mumbled, "Time to go. Good night."

"And here I was, giving my all," Clare remembered.

She had never encountered this kind of man before. She was both angered and attracted. Clare knew that it wouldn't be long before she and Luce met again. And so they did, on December 9, 1934, at a dinner party given by Condé Nast. Among the guests were Mr. and Mrs. Henry Luce. The party was a prelude to a birthday ball at the Waldorf-Astoria in honor of Cole Porter, whose latest musical comedy, *Anything Goes,* had just premiered on Broadway. Nast had persuaded Harry to come with them afterward "just for an hour."

By the time they all arrived at the Starlight Roof of the Waldorf, it was close to midnight. The party was a Turkish ball, attended by four hundred celebrity guests including Hearsts, Harrimans, Rockefellers, Kennedys, Whitneys, Astors, and Ethel Merman.

Clare Boothe was dancing when she saw Henry Luce striding across the floor with a glass of champagne in each hand. As he approached her she excused herself from her dancing partner, hurriedly approached Luce, and said, "Oh, Mr. Luce, is that champagne for me?"

Almost at that moment the lights went out, and they sat down in a far corner of the hall and talked.

The party's hostess, Elsa Maxwell, unveiled a tiny birthday cake for Cole Porter, and he recoiled from it in mock disgust. Maxwell then sounded a trumpet, and curtains parted to reveal another cake, fifteen feet high. Ethel Merman put the evening's entertainment into professional gear by belting "I Get a Kick Out of You."

Clare Boothe and Harry Luce heard none of this. Long after the entertainment was over and the lights came back on, Clare and Harry still seemed oblivious to everyone and everything, both talking intensely.

As he sat with her—absorbing her, admiring her, fantasizing a life with her—suddenly it was as if something within Harry exploded. His conscience was gone, his family was gone, and he wanted this woman more than he had ever wanted anything.

"I could see them at a distance," Lila recalled. "They were just talking. They disagreed and sort of quarreled, and then later went right on talking. This was the second time I had ever seen Clare. Harry came over to me, and he said, 'Would you mind going home? I've been asked to stay here.' That was a bit of a surprise! And of course, I said, 'Fine.' I got in a taxi and went home!"

"At four in the morning, Harry and Clare were still at the same table deeply absorbed in each other," recalled Elsa Maxwell. "When I told them the party was breaking up, they looked around in bewilderment, as though they were coming out of a trance. Still, I didn't think anything of it."

Clare later remembered that Harry asked her then, "Would you come downstairs in the lobby with me? I have something important I must tell you. I can't say it here and I must tell you now."

They went down to the main floor, and he said, "I've just made the most important discovery. How does it feel to be told that you are the one woman, the only woman, in a man's life?"

"Whose life?"

"Mine."

She stood there speechless—a rare condition for her—and then she gasped and said, "Perhaps we've had too much champagne?"

Harry again left Clare abruptly, but not before he asked where she lived and made an appointment for the following afternoon.

If Clare felt bewildered, she also felt bewitched. She was clearly stunned, and so was Harry.

The next morning he called his old Yale friend Archibald MacLeish. Could MacLeish meet him at the Commodore Hotel ballroom? MacLeish later described Harry standing in the semidarkness of the stale-smelling ballroom, "shaken, overwhelmed, infatuated. He was in love with another woman, Harry said, love at first flash. He wanted to marry her and wondered whether I thought he had the *right*, the sheer Christian right, to leave his wife for another woman."

MacLeish listened sympathetically. His own reaction to Clare was that she was a brassy blonde, cold and power hungry. But he understood that Luce felt he and his wife no longer had the same interests.

"And he gave me my answer," Harry said later. "Love is all there is. I haven't any choice. I have to leave Lila because I love Clare."

Harry arrived at Clare's penthouse apartment at the Sherry Netherlands Hotel, on Fifth Avenue. He wasted no time in coming quickly to the point. This was a woman he had never held in his arms. And yet he could say to her, "I think I want to marry you."

This sophisticated woman looked at this highly intense young man, laughed a little nervously, and didn't really know what to say. There was no doubting his seriousness. But it seemed so bizarre, so unreal. She hedged her answer, and he left.

What interested her most in a man, Clare later revealed, was his mind and soul. She regarded sex as the least attractive thing about men. Still, she admitted, the only way to secure a man was to get a physical hold over him.

If Harry knew nothing about flirting or courting or love, Clare now became the challenging faith of his life. "I *will* not fail it!" he told his confidant, Ralph McAllister "Mac" Ingersoll, the managing editor of *Fortune.* "I have faith in love now and I will not lose it! I do not know how I am going to fulfill it, but only that I have to and that if it takes the rest of my life, I will, and to hell with Time Incorporated!"

As Luce pressed his suit Clare was drawn in by the urgent, burning need of this man. If he could not fully sweep her senses, never be a great lover, he could make her mind jump and reel. It was time, too, that her daughter, Ann, now ten years old, had a proper father and a proper home. Luce was also rich, and he did have that craggy look that so much stirred her. And, of course, there was his power, *big* power, strong and almost magnetic.

Still, Clare wanted time to think. She fled to Florida to stay with her mother, and Harry followed her. She moved on to Cuba to be with friends, and he chased her there too.

"It was like breaking open an eggshell," Clare later confided to a friend. The awkward missionary boy disappeared. What he did not know about the techniques of courtship sex, Clare was now happy to teach him. He had never had a sexual experience of that kind. It was a chemistry that worked.

Eventually Clare made up her mind. She finally said yes, she would marry him. Friends insisted that her decision was more "a surrender to sentiment than a victory of tactics."

Laura and Thayer Hobson afterward spent an evening with Harry and Lila Luce, who lived just a block away. Laura told Thayer, "You've been driving yourself too hard, Thayer. You sound tired out. Why don't you take off for a while." That night Lila said the same thing to Harry Luce. "The next night," said Laura afterward, "I got the news from Thayer [that he wanted a divorce in order to marry another woman] and Lila got her [divorce] news from Harry."

Lila was absolutely destroyed. "He was my life," she said. "You see, I never suspected he wasn't happily married. If only he had told me!"

Lila soon went to visit her widowed mother in Chicago, then to Bermuda with her two sons. Harry wrote to her there, called her "Darlingest," and went on to say that one day he would try to tell her of his love and his deep appreciation for all her troubled times caused by his unkindnesses, which he himself could not defend. He still hoped he could be a good father to their sons.

All this revealed a man helplessly caught in the wave of his infatuation, a man who saw clearly what he was losing, but could not stop himself. But Lila was also hoping that Harry would change his mind.

She decided to fight the divorce by insisting on stiff financial terms.

Harry had isolated himself from his family, shocked his parents, bewildered his young sons. He had moved to the Pierre Hotel. At *Time* nobody saw him. He had been going through hell for weeks, he reported, and couldn't work. He kept walking around the block.

At this time Clare was also having problems. George Brokaw had never stopped drinking, and finally drowned in the swimming pool of a nursing home where he had been confined with a nervous breakdown. The legal question was whether the income tax on Clare's alimony should be deducted from her former husband's estate.

Harry, too, was now embroiled with lawyers. While he waited for his divorce, Clare went to Europe. She felt this would give them both more time to be certain of what they were doing. This might have given Harry pause, but it didn't. He thought of his new passion as the great love of all time. Clare toured the Continent, bought clothing and perfume, china, artwork, and books. She and Harry exchanged a flurry of cables, and he kept telling her of his love and his irrepressible joy. Her joy was perhaps more repressible, but it was there.

In their time together she had had a taste of the man, and she was happy about the prospects. Moreover, she was delighted with the idea of being the wife of a celebrated publishing executive, and her imagination worked overtime on the potential of her role. Clare recalled that shortly before her ship sailed, Harry had told her that he didn't want any more babies, and that if she married him, he would start her magazine and she could be coeditor.

The weeks and months progressed, and Clare grew restless. Finally Lila's lawyers agreed upon a settlement of almost $2 million. She also got the country house, and Luce set up trust funds for the children. But he did not give away any Time Inc. stock, nor did he sell a single share of his own. Time stock was his power.

When Clare returned, she went to stay with Baruch at Hobcaw, where her room was always waiting. Baruch rushed to her side. He didn't want any other man to have her, and so his advice was predictable. He counseled against her marriage to Harry and mentioned Luce's reputation for coldness and ruthlessness. When Baruch sensed that she had already decided on the marriage, he openly hoped that it would not end their relationship. It didn't.

Clare's stay at Hobcaw was a turning point. While there, she inter-

Left, two of the outstanding staff members of the Yale Daily News were Henry Luce (front row, second from left) and Briton Hadden (front row, center). They went on to co-found Time in 1923.

Luce's right-hand man in the early days of Time, John Shaw Billings (near right, with Luce), was a courtly southern gentleman who privately disparaged his boss. Luce, below, as head of an enormous publishing empire.

ested Baruch in her new play, *Abide With Me*. Clare was having trouble getting a Broadway production, and as always, Baruch was eager to help. He showed the script to his nephew Donald, a theatrical producer, indicating how much he wanted the play produced. With Baruch's blessing and money Donald mounted a production. Clare was delighted. If only the divorce would come through, all would be well.

In October 1935 the Luce divorce was made final. As impatient as they were for marriage, Clare wanted something more. She didn't want Harry to put her on his pedestal; rather, she wanted to stand on one of her own. Before they married, she wanted to see her play produced so that she could come to him in the flush of success.

Abide With Me was beautifully mounted and acted. Everything seemed right for success, but it was not to be. The critics were devastating. *The New York Times* called it "a gratuitous horror play." The *Herald Tribune* wrote, "Ridiculous action, sheer bad writing."

What would *Time* magazine say? This was Clare's first test case. Everybody knew their boss would soon marry the playwright. Luce insisted on reviewing all drafts of the review, then sent them back for changes. Finally the poor *Time* reviewer assigned this miserable job hesitantly suggested, "Perhaps we should let Mrs. Brokaw see this."

As Clare later recalled, "Harry brought me the original copy of *Time*'s review and said, 'Darling, it was a bad play, and I think this notice is too gentle. See what you can do with it.'" In rewriting it, she used words such as "lousy" and "stinking." On reading her version, Luce said, "No play is that bad!" and modified it. Still, when all the reviews were in, Clare said bitterly, "The play was called *Abide With Me* and abode with no one."

Yet Clare was still uncrushable. It said something about the quality and strength of her character that she could open a play one night, knowing it might be a dismal disaster, and marry the very next day. On November 23, 1935, Harry and Clare wed in a simple, quiet ceremony at the First Congregational Church in Old Greenwich, Connecticut. He was thirty-seven; she was thirty-two.

The elder Luces didn't come to the wedding. They had felt deeply about Lila, and Clare was both flashy and divorced. To them the sophisticated Clare was a cold, designing "other woman." There was also the serious question of the welfare of Harry's two small boys.

But Harry saw this new marriage as the gratification of his life. He thought he had made a big catch and had won the most attractive woman of his time. His devotion to Clare was touching. He would sparkle when she'd walk into a room, his face filled with tremendous pride. To the outside world it was a sort of royal marriage. Clare and Henry were two international celebrities who had joined forces to enrich each other. So they did, for a certain time in a certain way.

CLARE and Harry hurried off on their honeymoon to Cuba, where for six weeks they stayed in a cool, tiled palace on the outskirts of Havana. Mac Ingersoll, now the new general manager of Time Inc., paid the happy couple a visit to clear up some year-end problems. "The hours that I remember best we spent together—the three of us—on the sand, in bathing gear, I at a table under a beach umbrella with sheets of figures from a briefcase and Harry joining me to go over them while Clare made travel poster pictures running along the water's edge, playing with a huge inflated rubber ball, leaping, splashing. She was a pretty sight, and so was Harry, happy at long last, as relaxed as his grim nature could manage."

The honeymooners returned to their new homes in February 1936, both tanned and happy. They had taken a country house in Stamford, Connecticut, and leased a fifteen-room duplex apartment with five bathrooms on East Fifty-second Street, in Manhattan, fronting the East River. Soon after their return they gave a big cocktail party at the Waldorf to introduce Clare to Time Inc. executives and editors. She wore a simple black cocktail dress, but her charm didn't completely enchant the editors. They had a persistent worry that Clare was moving in on the magazines. The real fear was that she would want to run the new picture magazine.

But for the moment Harry seemed to be the creative force behind the new venture. In his prospectus, which he wrote himself, the magazine "would eyewitness great events, watch the faces of the poor and the gestures of the proud, see strange things—machines, armies, multitudes, shadows in the jungle and on the moon . . . see man's work—his paintings, towers and discoveries . . . see things thousands of miles away, things hidden behind walls and within rooms, see and be amazed, see and be instructed."

As he saw the draft of the prospectus he pranced into the office of John Shaw Billings, then *Time*'s managing editor, and cried, "I'm pregnant." Later he amplified. "We are in labor. We are giving birth to a new child."

Clare's comment was telling: "We went off on our honeymoon and a child was conceived—a child later called *Life* magazine."

THE birth of *Life* came at such a perfect time. Harry's wife was everything he wanted her to be—beautiful, scintillating, romantic. He envisioned a life with her of constant adventure and enrichment. No matter how big he became, she would grow with him, as Lila had not. Perhaps Clare could even become a vital part of this magazine.

Luce plunged himself into the new magazine, still nameless. (They would not buy the *Life* title from its original owner until a month before publication.) His excitement was becoming almost feverish. He and Daniel Longwell, who became picture editor of *Life*, worked on two experimental versions and decided that the cover should be a photograph. They often worked in Harry's private office, down on their knees on the plush carpeting, sorting out sample spreads. All the while, said Billings, Luce "was filling me full of *Life*'s principles and purposes." Luce invented the picture essay—one big feature. He also believed that a "word's a word, in small type or in big, just so long as it's readable. But a picture is not."

He believed in big pictures, standing on their own. With *Life*, photographers became the unsung heroes.

Ralph Ingersoll knew that Clare was being considered for the job of managing editor of *Life*. He thought of her as a "fascinating textbook case of arrested development, the arrested emotional development of a precociously bright female child. One cannot truly engage emotionally with such a phenomenon and I never tried." To complicate matters for Ingersoll, he now got the word from Harry: Why not name Clare as the new magazine's managing editor?

"I wasn't about to second Clare's nomination, because a revived *Vanity Fair* wasn't my idea of what my picture magazine was all about," he recalled. "So I thought and I thought and finally I came up with the right way to put it to Harry. It involved telling him the truth."

Ingersoll and Dan Longwell invited Harry and Clare to dinner at a posh restaurant. Over dessert Ingersoll was blunt: "Harry, you have got to make up your mind whether you are going to be a great editor or whether you are going to be on a perpetual honeymoon. You just can't make a success of *Life* with one hand tied behind Clare's back."

Clare broke in quickly. "Harry Luce can publish a better magazine with one hand tied behind his back than you can publish with both of yours free."

Ingersoll then took a brilliant gamble in his argument with Luce. "Look! Clare's a very, very talented woman—but she's your wife. There are only two ways you can use her to forward the success of a magazine that belongs to you: as your full partner—co-boss—or as its star contributor. You can't make her managing editor, because a managing editor is only a hired hand. It wouldn't be fair to her; she's too important for that job and people would wonder why she isn't in your office, in charge with you."

As Ingersoll recalled it, Clare got "whiter and tighter-lipped as the evening wore on. Finally, when she could stand it no longer, she demanded a silence into which she spoke these memorable words: 'Harry, has it ever occurred to you that you have surrounded yourself with incompetents?' She then stood up from the table and left the restaurant, leaving a highly embarrassed husband."

The story quickly circulated at *Time*, and the consensus was this: Harry didn't defend his wife to Ingersoll, because deep down he didn't really want her on the new magazine. "Harry Luce was a very proud man. He wasn't going to be used by her," said Wilfrid Sheed. Luce finally accepted Ingersoll's position.

In many ways Clare had lost the battle without even a fight. Several editors didn't like her long before they met her. They regarded her as phony, and Clare pretended indifference. She relegated the *Time* staff and most of its editors to a level of disdain. More than a bit aloof, Clare wanted them to know that she was their superior and considered them as very inferior indeed. If Harry's staff didn't like her, she didn't like them, she would say in her mocking style. But she resented it all her life.

As for Harry, he quickly figured out how difficult the situation was and struggled to keep Clare at bay. "He'd have had a revolt of the editors if he hadn't," said one *Time* correspondent.

If Clare was a problem for Harry at Time-Life, she was also a source of inspiration. "I can remember no year when he bubbled with so many ideas, when his enthusiasm for well-done stories elicited so much praise," said an editor.

Many felt that Clare's indirect influence on Harry was considerable, that she was always suggesting story ideas. "Clare was a very knowledgeable lady," said Oliver Jensen, who became *Life's* text editor. "She was keenly aware of the world of arts and theater, about which Harry knew little. She knew the notable photographers. They worked together, talked together, and she could explain the meaning and importance of all this. She knew what should be covered by *Life* or *Time*."

"She changed his life as a persona," said Andrew Heiskell, Luce's close *Time* associate. "Before that, he had not been very social; he had not been an important personality in his own right. He and Clare became social lions, political personalities. They lived the full life together. She had a lot to do with making him what he became."

Clare soon turned her attentions away from Time Inc. She persuaded Harry to buy Mepkin, a huge estate in Moncks Corner, South Carolina. Some eyebrows were raised because the new Luce home was only a short drive away from Bernard Baruch's Hobcaw.

Mepkin was situated on 7200 acres, forty miles north of Charleston. The main house was on a bluff overlooking the Cooper River, surrounded by majestic oaks. It had five double master bedrooms. There were stables for horses, kennels, quarters for tenants, and brand-new cabins for the thirty black servants. Landscaped walkways led to the boathouse, and bridle paths threaded through the woods. Clare was delighted with Mepkin, and so was Harry.

Ann came to Mepkin during school vacations and loved it. She was twelve now and had Clare's curiosity, but not her looks. Tall, bright, and rather opinionated, Ann adored her mother, but her mother had not yet bridged the emotional gap.

Harry did. He had always wanted a daughter, and he and Ann formed a tight bond of real affection, with frequent letters between "Annie" and "Dad." He took her with him on vacations to Virginia and southern California. Whatever attention Ann lacked from her mother, she got from her stepfather.

In some measure Harry had an easier relationship with Ann than he did with his own two sons. Lila had full custody of Henry and Peter, and was leery of subjecting them to Clare's presence and influence. But it was something far deeper than divorce and remarriage that affected Harry's relationship with his boys. "I am unaware of the boys playing any part in his life, really," said Allen Grover, a *Fortune* editor and close friend of Luce's. "Harry was never a loving father."

Just as Harry found it easier to reach out to Ann, Clare was often more comfortable with her stepsons than with her own daughter. She invited them to Mepkin and "taught them how to ride, how to shoot, how to play croquet and then, at night, checkers," recalled Harry's sister. "She was awfully good at teaching the kids."

Those who knew Clare well felt that she could do almost anything she set her mind to. Her friend Dorothy Thompson admired Clare's talents. "Her interest gives her vitality. She never stops," Thompson observed. "All the time she did her beautiful intricate needlework, she was talking or planning or giving orders about running the house. To learn Italian, she played records while dressing."

Yet there was a dark side of Clare that was beginning to emerge in the days at Mepkin. Sometimes she would get into an inexplicable black mood and disappear into her bedroom for days. Later in life, as Harry was to discover, Clare's moods would threaten to overwhelm both of them and lead to some very sorrowful times.

6

CLARE was now in her early thirties, and the world was still very much at her bidding. She had a rich, powerful husband and was at the center of an entourage of witty, fawning friends. But something was missing for her. Once again she decided to turn to playwriting.

"I found myself with absolutely nothing to occupy my mind, and decided, with what I sometimes tell myself now was almost a flash of genius, that writing plays was a heavenly way to fill in intellectual gaps," said Clare. A friend described her sitting in her bed in the morning with a bow in her hair, wearing a frilly bed jacket, and dictating to a secretary. "The bed looks like a horror, piled with newspapers, manuscripts, menus, cards, and letters."

Waited on by her four maids and writing with pencil on manuscript paper bound in morocco covers, Clare insisted she wrote the first draft of her play *The Women* in three days. She claimed she got the idea in the ladies' room of the night club El Morocco. "While I was in the loo, I heard two familiar voices at the wash basin," she explained. "They were dishing the dirt about some married friends of ours. It was the most brutal gossip I had ever heard."

She decided to write a play about women, without any men in it. She set a scene she knew well—a hotel in Reno filled with frustrated women waiting for their divorces. There were parts for forty-four women. Clare seemed to be almost mocking herself because the plot featured a heroine losing her husband to a designing blonde. "I not only wrote it," she later said, "I was the leading bitchy character."

The Women quickly stirred controversy in New York. Not everyone agreed with Clare's assessment of the play's origin. "She got the idea from my hairdresser at Saks Fifth Avenue," said theatrical agent Jean Dalrymple. Lila Luce had another version: "Mrs. George Kaufman told a friend of mine that [her husband] George wrote that play."

Whether or not this is true, Mrs. Kaufman had every reason to dislike and disparage Clare. During Clare's Algonquin Round Table days, when she was editor of *Vanity Fair,* she had made Kaufman one of her conquests.

Kaufman and Clare seemed to have continued at least a professional relationship once the play went into production. Bernard Baruch had interceded on Clare's behalf with producer Max Gordon, who agreed to open the show once some revisions were done.

Gordon's story was that he had shown the play to his friend George Kaufman, a recognized play doctor often called in "to fix the unfixable." Gordon told Clare that Kaufman was "just as enthusiastic about the possibilities of the play as I am." (If Kaufman had indeed written the play, Gordon didn't know it or let on to it.)

Harry grew indignant as the rumors spread of Kaufman's involvement. Luce wrote columnist Walter Winchell insisting he had seen the first draft of the play several weeks after Clare outlined it for him. She had been working on it every day and had talked to nobody else during that time. He told Winchell that Kaufman and his partner, Moss Hart, had watched several rehearsals and had discussed the play with Clare, pointing out some weak spots, but that was all. Luce asked Winchell to double-check all these facts and then print the truth.

Clare herself said that Kaufman had made the best comment on the matter when he said, "*The Women* was one of the great hits. If I wrote it, why on earth would I put her name on it?"

Once the controversy of authorship was behind her, Clare faced the jabs of the critics. *The New York Times* called the play a "kettle of venom . . . alleycats scratched and spit with considerable virtuosity. This reviewer did not like it." Neither did columnist Heywood Broun, who said it degraded the whole human race. However, the St. Louis *Globe-Democrat* loved it: "Glorious entertainment. Only women will ever know how deep the truth goes."

In summing up the play later, Clare's friend Margaret Case Harriman wrote, "She tied up her own sex crisply in cellophane and delivered it to the ash can."

Clare rushed to her own defense. "My play is a slice of life; I never said it was the *whole* of life. The play shows what I didn't like—idle parasitical women. The women who inspired this play deserved to be smacked across the head with a meat ax and that, I flatter myself, is exactly what I smacked them with."

At *Time*, critic Louis Kronenberger had not liked the play, and his review was rewritten four times. "Harry sent for the copy of the *Time* review and changed a few lines himself. This was the only time I can ever remember his actually changing a review," recalled Allen Grover. "He softened it quite a lot. The final review talked of 'sharp theatrical impact . . . so clever that few women would willingly miss it . . . packed with cracks.' "

The Women was an enormous commercial success and played to packed houses. It was produced all over the world, twice made into movies, and earned millions. It played in eighteen countries in ten languages. Clare was no longer simply The Great Man's Wife.

THE Great Man himself was now ready at last to launch *Life*.

Volume I, Number 1, published on November 19, 1936, sold out the entire pressrun of 200,000 copies. "*Life* was his wedding present to me," claimed Clare. The opening photograph was a moving photo of an obstetrician holding a newborn baby by its heels. The headline read LIFE BEGINS. Inside were the first aerial pictures of Fort Knox, where the country kept its gold, and of Fort Belevedere, where King Edward VIII entertained Mrs. Wallis Warfield Simpson. There were production shots taken of the current hit play *Victoria Regina*, starring Helen Hayes, and the current hit film *Camille*, with Greta Garbo. In addition, *Life* featured a color portfolio of John Steuart Curry's paintings, and the picture story of a hunting party in honor of the British ambassador to France—complete with a row of dead hares.

As subsequent issues of *Life* rolled off the presses, new paper and inks had to be invented, new presses had to be designed to keep up with the demand. Sales soon reached a million a week. Pollster George Gallup had been proved right: people preferred looking at pictures to reading type. Harry bubbled with delight.

"This is so big!" he told Ralph Ingersoll.

Life was as brassy as it was unpredictable, and everybody wanted part of the action. Movie studios delayed their film release on the promise of a *Life* spread. A Gallup poll discovered that movie studios regarded a two-page layout in *Life* as more important than a one-page newsbreak in any U.S. newspaper. Broadway musicals happily assembled casts in full costume in the hope of a possible *Life* picture. *Life* photographers reported that starlets, even celebrated actresses were ready to do anything, absolutely anything, to get on the cover of *Life*. The aim of his magazine, Luce said, was to present "the good life."

In the midst of this new success and ebullience Luce received a hard slap on the face. On Thanksgiving Day, 1936, *The New Yorker* magazine published a profile of Luce by Wolcott Gibbs, "which everyone in the shop devoured," wrote Billings. An earlier *Fortune* portrait had called *The New Yorker* editor Harold Ross "a madman with a face of rubber, a huge Hapsburg lip to which cigarettes stick." What angered Ross most were *Time*'s inverted sentences and cryptic captions—they "had the same effect on him as a dentist's drill."

When Harry read *The New Yorker* profile of him, he protested, "But goddam it, Ross, this whole goddam piece is ma-ma-malicious!"

"You've put your finger on it, Luce. I believe in malice."

Luce considered the profile a crushing disaster mainly because it was in a magazine of imagination and distinction. "And do you know what the worst of it is?" he asked. "All my friends think it's funny."

Much of it *was* funny. The most quoted line was, "Backward ran sentences until reeled the mind." Ross described Luce as an "ambitious, gimlet-eyed, Baby Tycoon." The article recorded the persistent rumor that Luce had "a wistful eye on the White House. Where it will end, knows God."

For Luce the peaks had come quicker than the valleys. Sixteen years out of Yale, he received a reported income of $963,400 from his editorial ventures. The new offices at the Chrysler Building spread out over 150 rooms on six floors. *The March of Time* radio program reached 8 million people, and *The March of Time* movie appeared thirteen times a year in over 6000 theaters. Luce was on the board of directors of many corporations, including Paramount Pictures.

"Where will he fly?" asked journalist Harford Powel. Another observer reported, "Henry Robinson Luce comes as close to being a Lord of the Press as America can now produce."

Harry's self-confidence then seemed almost supreme. The old, shy, awkward publisher had disappeared. In his place was a Harry Luce who finally had everything he wanted in life. Almost.

What Harry Luce yearned for at this point in his life was to have a moral impact on the world. The glittering prize of the White House was beyond his reach because he was not a glittering man. Yet he wanted to shape the vision of his country. He believed in causes. Through his magazines he would achieve his goals. He articulated this one night in 1937 as seven of his senior editors dined with him at the Waldorf-Astoria. They drank champagne and discussed *Time* policy. Luce posed the questions: "What is the purpose of *Time* besides making money?" and "How well are we using our influence?"

One editor's answer: to amuse, instruct, and inform. Then Luce gave his own credo: "There is such a thing as right and wrong. Liberty and human freedom are to be desired. There is such a thing as progress." Luce later said, "I regard America as a special dispensation under Providence." His basic belief was that as head of Time Inc., he was public defender of the nation.

Time took a stand on virtually everything. The magazine was an early, fervent supporter of civil rights. *Time* bitterly attacked the Ku Klux Klan long before this became a popular stance. A Luce rule was that no one would ever be lynched in America without *Time*'s running a story on it. Discrimination because of color simply went against the grain of Luce's Presbyterianism. Nor did Time Inc. hesitate to interfere in business. Luce ran a series in *Fortune* that was highly critical of U.S. Steel.

The underlying factor in all of *Time*'s crusades was a deep vein of conservative moral values. The average American responded to these values because they were coupled with emotionalism. There was something simplistic and comforting about these values.

Luce tried to infuse his staff with his sense of mission. "You would get memos from him saying, 'Please see me about war' or 'Please see me about peace,' " recalled Richard Clurman, who later became *Time*'s chief of correspondents. "He would be bothered by the thought 'What to do about corruption?' He was constantly trying to get a handle on it for a *Time* story."

"Luce's trouble is he tries to run the world," said one researcher.

In fact, Luce had become the growing giant of journalism, a press lord of enormous, towering stature on the level of Hearst, McCormick, Pulitzer, and Beaverbrook. His close associate Andrew Heiskell pinpointed what set Luce apart from his peers: "He wanted to have it his way as the result of winning the argument, not as the result of giving the orders. He loved anybody who would argue with him. He wouldn't get satisfaction out of having people just obey his orders. It was: 'I made that man change his mind, you know, by sheer logic!' He was fair in an argument." And he would listen to anyone, no matter how young or green, but their facts had to make sense.

Those writers who hedged their opinions to keep them on the *Time* line were seldom successful. Luce was bored by those whose opinions suspiciously echoed his. "I like to see independent thinking," he said. "If it's going the wrong way, I'll straighten them out fast enough."

One of Harry's best writers, Emmet John Hughes, sharply made the point that Luce was not only remarkable in his receptivity to new ideas but even to ideas that were contradictory. He added his judgment that Luce had much more range, much more curiosity, and much less ideology than his magazines.

Part of Luce's problem in the mid-'30s was his persistent support of Laird S. Goldsborough, who came to *Time* as a young Yale man and almost single-handedly wrote all the foreign news for the next thirteen years. Luce relied on Goldsborough's technical expertise and judged him as an eighteenth-century gentleman. Goldsborough's ancestral tree was rooted in Goldsborough, Yorkshire, but he was so self-conscious about having a Jewish-sounding name that he often injected snide anti-Semitic references into *Time*. Goldsborough had interviewed Hitler and Mussolini, liked them both, and said so. Many of the staff felt that Goldsborough was an out-and-out fascist and that Luce defended him for too long.

At *Time* the Spanish Civil War was another source of deep controversy. The conflict soon became a small preview of the coming world war, when Hitler and Mussolini sent troops and planes to support Franco, and the Soviets bolstered the Loyalist government.

Goldsborough promptly sided with Franco, saying the Loyalists were "Red militia, Socialists, Communists and rattle-brained Liberals." Archibald MacLeish protested both to Goldsborough and to Luce that *Time* had presented no factual proof of this charge and that Franco's revolt, in fact, was "an unjustifiable act of aggression by reactionary forces against a popular government."

What made the confrontation more interesting was that Luce permitted both Goldsborough in *Time* and MacLeish in *Fortune* to write their contradictory views. Part of this stance was his delight in keeping his staff slightly "off stride." He also admitted that fostering competition and controversy among his editors made for a livelier magazine.

Periodically Luce would get the editing itch and want to take over a whole issue of *Time*. When Luce edited *Time* for a week, said one staffer, "it was just like a gale-force wind blowing through the office, everyone rushing around, trying to rescue bits of paper and everything. He'd send people off on terrific wild-goose chases. But they all got very much excited." When Luce edited, his staff knew that his instincts for a story were often excellent. Said *Time* editor T. S. Matthews, "I remember pieces of copy when Luce would circle a sentence here and move it up to another place, and it was just absolutely right."

One of Luce's great aims was to reduce redundancy. Instead of tearing out everything and starting fresh, "Harry would just take the banalities out of things with one clean little phrase," said one editor. One of Luce's memorable editorial written comments was, "Make your emphasis come from STRUCTURE not STATEMENT."

Harry also edited *Fortune* on occasion and won praise for his efforts. Editing *Life*, though, was a real challenge for him. "I think Luce came down from the mountain top to edit once every six months, for a week, but it took us weeks to get over it," said Billings, then managing editor of *Life*. "Luce was very impatient with pictures. He'd look at them and say, 'If this picture and that picture were together, I could see it working.' Now, you could put two paragraphs into one, but you couldn't put two photographs into one. He'd suddenly walk off and go upstairs, really depressed. He didn't have the patience for them."

What Luce was best at was brewing ideas for fundamental changes in *Life*. He wanted more narrative pictures, more solid information. He had his own concept of picture essays: "It's like being a Southern preacher. First I tell them what I'm going to tell them; then I tell them; then I tell them what I told them."

HARRY generally slept well, ate anything, chain-smoked, and was always punctual. During the work week, he arrived at his office at nine fifteen a.m. He was a very busy man, and time was a precious word at Time Inc. Luce expected visitors to state their business quickly, and then he let them know when their time was up.

Everything about Luce was intense. Evenings meant little to him because he usually left the office with a load of work. He resented hearing that he had a golden touch or that he was lucky. Luck had as much to do with the shaping of his career "as it has to do with directing the course of an army tank," he liked to say. The proper word was ambition, he carefully pointed out.

Luce's focus was so intense that the mundane parts of life escaped him; coupled with his single-mindedness was his absentmindedness. "Everything had to be in its place," said his secretary. "For example, his briefcase opened at the top. On the right-hand side, you'd put his passport and tickets. If they fell out of that place, he was totally lost. He'd say, 'The tickets aren't there.' Also, when he was going out we'd give him bios on the people he was to meet."

What Luce did *not* go out with was much money. And what he had, he spent very carefully. Correspondents traveling with Luce knew to check his dinner tips so that they, and the magazine, would not be embarrassed. Left to his own devices, Harry might well leave a one-dollar tip for an eighty-dollar dinner.

Harry was so absentminded that he often left his coat somewhere. His secretary had a standing order at Saks Fifth Avenue to replace Luce's coats.

"It was impossible for me to do anything about his clothes," said Clare. "He'd go to the office with one black shoe and one brown shoe. He wore a sort of drab gray kind of clothing. He simply could not match colors. He was indifferent, not color blind. His dress shirts were all frayed. His handkerchiefs were a horror. When I'd protest, he'd get cranky and call it nagging."

Still, Clare tried. She took him to the best tailors, but he couldn't care less. One of the great laughs at Time Inc. was Harry's nomination by the Merchant Tailors and Designers Association as one of the nation's twenty-two best-dressed men, "because he clings to many of the archaic elegancies of the nineteenth century."

Harry *did* receive an award that meant a great deal to him: an honorary degree from Rollins College, in Florida. What made it important was that his parents were in Florida at the time and came to hear him, the first time they had heard their son make a live speech since he was a boy. Harry's father wrote about it to Clare and was ecstatic; he said it was the finest speech he had heard in a decade.

Whatever hurt his parents had over his divorce from Lila was now pushed deeply within themselves. In writing to Clare, Harry's mother expressed warmth and affection, and signed her letters, "Mother." When Ann was ill, Mother Luce offered to come and help. The Luces invited Clare and Harry to Thanksgiving dinner and to a family weekend in Pennsylvania at Christmas. In return, the elder Luces occasionally came to Mepkin. On the surface everything was going extremely well for Harry, personally and professionally.

Luce was now thirty-eight years old. Through his magazines he had carved a place in American life, and the satisfactions were enormous. He saw *Time* in good hands, *Life* safely launched, and *Fortune* progressing nicely. The goals and challenges were met. It was time now to focus more on his personal life.

A THOUSAND days after he wrote his first letter of passionate love to Clare from the Racquet and Tennis Club, in New York, Luce wrote another letter from the same club to his beloved darling. It was a remarkable piece of correspondence from a man sometimes described by his colleagues as a Frigidaire. He talked about how he longed for her lovely body, about his burning memory of their blissful nights, and how much he loved her, loved her, loved her.

Harry had married her because he had admired all of her, not just her body. He desperately needed the constant play of her mind, the glamour and possession of her presence. But the physical was a strong part of his attraction. Yet Harry wanted more than Clare was ready to give. An early feminist, she believed that a liberated woman must renounce being a sex object and admit that the Prince Charming story is a fairy tale. Marriage, she said, "ain't no perpetual honeymoon."

Clare's feelings for Harry were those of admiration and deep affection. She appreciated his voracious intellect and vice versa. But the primal bond seemed to be their common dream of power.

She idealized his power, just as he idealized her glamour. Both were disappointed; neither got everything they wanted. He wanted warmth from her, and never totally received it. She wanted to *share* his power, pull the strings, and he wouldn't let her. The honeymoon was over.

In 1938 the Luces bought a Georgian-style estate in Greenwich, Connecticut, on fifty-nine acres. The property included a main house with twenty-one rooms and eleven baths, a greenhouse, and several farm buildings. Harry and Clare called it The House.

In the reception rotunda the Luces displayed their collection of Chinese art objects, icons, chests, and paintings. A glass circular staircase led to the second floor. In the living room, to the right of the rotunda, countless photographs of the famous people who had touched their lives were arranged on tables. The view from the huge picture windows looked out over a rolling valley, white-fenced horse meadows, a tennis court, a lily pond, and a sparkling swimming pool.

The house was a showcase to which Clare invited a parade of prominent people. The guests were mostly her friends—theatrical people, whom Harry didn't like, and literary people, whom he tolerated.

That same year, the Luces moved from their fifteen-room duplex on Fifty-second Street to a posh suite on the forty-first floor of the Waldorf Towers. There were three bedrooms—one for Harry, one for Clare, and a small one for the maid.

The separate bedrooms were symptomatic of the state of the Luce marriage. They were both aware of the growing distance between them. In so many ways they did not mesh. Harry was so much more ascetic than Clare in his manners and habits. The one vice they shared was heavy smoking. She was a highly sophisticated woman, with the wit and gift for making people open up to her. Before their wedding and in the early months of the marriage, she had succeeded in unleashing Harry's passion. But once he was caught and he was hers, Clare's restlessness urged her on to other places, to other men. Her private papers include folders of love letters from a variety of men.

At first Harry suspected little. He thought that men gravitated toward Clare in social situations only because she was so beautiful.

In the early years of their marriage Clare was often away. She traveled restlessly to Europe to see friends. Harry was a lonely man. When he was at Time Inc., he was home, he was busy, and he was happy. But when the day was done, he would often return to an empty house. He found it difficult to lift a phone and invite somebody over. When he did, he summoned people from Time Inc.

John Hersey, a *Time* writer, was a favorite dinner guest. He was an uncanny copy of Luce. He, too, had grown up in China and gone to Hotchkiss and Yale. Sensitive and talented, Hersey soon found himself absorbed into a kind of father-son relationship with Luce. He saw Luce as a warm, compassionate man, a kind man.

Yet Harry's loneliness increased. He was often withdrawn and taut. Always able to say in letters what he could not verbalize, Harry poured out his loneliness in frequent letters to Clare. Occasionally he turned to Lila for companionship. She confided that Harry told her, years later, that he had wanted a divorce from Clare before he had been married one year and that he wanted one every year after that.

"It's crazy, when you think about it," she said. "One saw pictures in the paper of Clare and Harry holding hands. They were always in the news, lovely pictures. How could I know they weren't happily married? If I had suspected he was unhappily married, I could have said, 'Let's have dinner. Let's go to the opera. Let's *do* something.' But I kept hands off. He later told me that Clare had a love affair with an aviator before they had been married six months," added Lila.

Harry confided to a friend that Clare no longer wanted to sleep with him. Yet Clare later implied that the curtailment of their sex life had more to do with her work habits: "Harry often came home and after we'd had dinner, I'd 'go to bed' and start to write a play. Obviously I didn't know what a *bed* was *for*," she said.

Her recommendation to other women was that they should never let their husbands see them in bed until they are ready to make love.

Clare added a telling footnote that a woman should never marry a man who has walked out on a good wife, because he is as cheerful as someone who has killed his mother.

As THE marriage worsened, Harry sought friendship from Clare's old confidante Laura Hobson, who was working in the promotion department of *Life*. Laura was a dynamo—hard driving, ambitious, and talented—and had no hesitation telling Harry exactly what she thought about anything. Harry liked that. Laura was also extremely attractive. Shortly after he hired her, she became the highest-paid woman on staff and later the only woman to have Time stock.

Harry and Laura spent lunches, dinners, and entire evenings discussing promotion ideas. The setup was perfect for an affair, as Luce's *Time* associate Andrew Heiskell noted. "I don't know whether they ever had one or not," he said. "I suspect, but I don't know. But she had considerable influence on him."

While Harry spent more time with Laura in the late '30s, Clare restlessly sought out a new cause and a new hero. She soon found both in Harry Bridges, a long, lean, hawk-faced labor organizer with the speaking style of a rabid preacher. Brilliant, shrewd, and cocky, Bridges was the founder and president of the International Longshoremen's and Warehousemen's Union. He was also a staunch communist sympathizer, though he did not join the party.

Bridges had the kind of power and magnetism Clare loved. She was mesmerized. "He almost talked me into communism," she said. Clare had been a taster and a wanderer all her life, and suddenly the taste of communism seemed tempting. Bridges also gave her what she no longer received from her husband—the stirring of a physical passion. What finally turned Clare away was when Bridges sent a communist recruiter to persuade her to be an active agent for the party in America. Clare was too individualistic to be an agent for *any* group. The communist credo was too hard and its purpose too cold. It was not the religion she was seeking.

ABOUT this time Clare was rocked out of her political crisis by a personal one. Her mother and a friend were killed in a car collision with a Florida East Coast passenger train. Ann Clare was fifty-two.

Clare and her mother had been very much intertwined. Ann Clare had been her model, and she had been her mother's clay. Her mother had shaped her and pushed her. Clare had absorbed her mother's attitudes toward men and life, and had envied her mother's beauty long before she had developed her own.

Ann Clare's final days had been deeply unhappy. She had suffered a mental breakdown and been hospitalized for extended periods. Then came the terrible accident.

Clare was devastated by her mother's death. Her friends felt that perhaps she would now turn to her own daughter for love and solace, but no. Ann was a timid girl, and not a very pretty one. Clare simply could not reach out to her, despite frequent surges of guilt at spending so little time with her. Ann had been in boarding school for five years and wrote again and again how much she missed her mother, adored her mother, and how she was almost dying of homesickness. She loved her mother very very much, and would do anything she wanted. When was she going to hear from her, see her?

But Clare could not seem to find time for Ann, and when she did plan a visit, she often canceled it. In 1938, however, both Harry and Clare felt it was time to attempt to knit a close family group. They decided to go to Hawaii for six weeks on a second honeymoon. They would take Harry's two sons, ages thirteen and nine, as well as Ann, who was fourteen. Harry also invited his brother, Sheldon, and Sheldon's wife to join them.

The night before Harry was to fly to Hawaii with Clare, Time Inc. employees gave him a farewell black-tie stag dinner at the old Blackstone Hotel, in Chicago. Afterward Harry cornered Ralph Ingersoll and led him to his cluttered hotel bedroom. Ingersoll described Luce as "very tense, tight-lipped, hard-eyed."

"Mac, what I am going to say to you, no one else knows, not even Clare," he said. "There is a time in a man's life when he has to make a decision by himself and I have made mine. I brought you here to tell you that when I go away tomorrow, I may never be back!"

Luce paced the room and stood towering over Ingersoll. "This is my decision, Mac. My love for Clare means more to me than this company. So if I have to choose between them, I will choose Clare."

Ingersoll was astounded and speechless. It was a monologue not meant for rebuttal or response. Harry's marriage had been imperfect, unfulfilled, and perhaps he felt that if it were not purified and made right, then all his life had been for nothing. He was therefore willing to give it his total dedication and prepared to forsake all else, past and present.

IT WAS a happy time, and the children made it happier. When Harry practiced riding a surfboard, his children would yell at him, "Stick with it, Pop." Ann wore her hair in a long bob, and she and Clare rode their surfboards tandem with Hawaiian beachboys. Ann wanted so desperately to show her mother that *she* could do things too.

On the family's return from Hawaii an expectant Ingersoll anxiously searched Harry's face and words for some sort of sign on what he wanted to do with Time Inc. and with his life.

"But there was no communication in Harry's eyes," recalled Ingersoll. "Harry and Clare were just two married people, almost middle-aged, and the night in the Blackstone Hotel had never happened."

Harry returned recharged and ready to be boss again. In a memo to his staff he announced his new title: editorial director of *Time, Life,* and *Fortune.* He wanted to signify loud and clear that he was boss, and that he was available for consultation on any editorial matter, day or night.

In a telling exchange Clare criticized the fact that Harry had all his money tied up in Time Inc. stock. "You know, Harry, that's a terrible mistake, having all your eggs in one basket."

"No," he said, "not as long as it's my basket."

7

I N 1938 *TIME* was fifteen years old. To commemorate the anniversary issue, Luce requested a letter from Franklin Roosevelt, then in the middle of his second term. When FDR complied, Luce offered effusive thanks. But privately Luce was extremely ambivalent about Roosevelt and took it personally when the President granted recognition to the Soviet Union. Luce saw much of worth in the early New Deal and felt sympathetic to many of its issues. He certainly believed in many of Roosevelt's international views—except on Russia.

The White House was *not* amused when *Life* described FDR as "this shrewd, bold, lusty, self-willed man who now truly bestrides the world like a Colossus. His ambition and power are cut to fit . . . President Roosevelt has never shared the majority opinion."

"Roosevelt hated [Luce]," explained T. S. Matthews. "He thought he had an unfavorable, unfair press from Luce. He was right, too, because Luce's theoretical idea was to have *Time* fifty-one percent against the government—no matter who they were. With Roosevelt, instead of fifty-one percent, it was about eighty-nine percent."

Yet when John Shaw Billings wanted to run a picture of the crippled President in a wheelchair, Luce flatly refused. A year later, in a speech at the Ohio Bankers Association, Luce lauded FDR.

Again and again Luce would change his opinion about the President. The relationship was a love-hate one that would last for years. Clare, however, had none of her husband's ambivalence about FDR. She described Roosevelt and his circle as "ramsquaddled, do-gooding New Deal bureaucrats." She never forgot or forgave overhearing the voice of the President, after a White House meeting with her, saying to an aide, "Get that woman out of here!"

In May 1938 Clare and Harry departed on an inspection tour of Europe to assess the growing Nazi threat. The Luces were delighted to be in the thick of things. Though the Nazis had already marched into Austria, London society geared up to give the Luces a reception that was almost royal. They were "feted, dined, wined, complimented, and plastered with praise," observed one British columnist.

While in Great Britain, Harry and Clare renewed their acquaintance with U.S. ambassador Joseph Patrick Kennedy. The two men were friends, but Luce was of two minds about Kennedy. He envied his life-style as a rogue and a pleasure-seeker. What disturbed him about Kennedy was his cynicism and pessimism.

"He was sure the British would be defeated," Luce reported to Billings. "I could only tell him I did not believe that, and so I prayed."

In London, Harry and Clare also touched base with another rogue, William Maxwell Aitken Beaverbrook. The son of a Scottish Presbyterian clergyman, "the Beaver" was a self-made millionaire who owned the *Daily Express,* the *Sunday Express,* and the *Evening Standard.* The author of a book on success and another on power, Beaverbrook usually epitomized both. Yet he occasionally championed causes he regarded as grand and romantic. Those who didn't like Beaverbrook called him Wrong Horse Max and a pompous martinet. His granddaughter would play a pivotal part in Luce's later life.

Clare also had a fond reunion with her adoring Randolph Churchill, who still called her honey child, and vowed to follow her to Paris. Luce knew nothing of this, but he instinctively never liked Randolph.

In Berlin, the Luces hoped for an audience with Hitler. However, they did not meet with the Führer, and moved on to Czechoslovakia, where they met the country's President, Dr. Edvard Beneš. Beneš told Luce that totalitarian systems would collapse and democratic systems triumph within ten years because the dictatorships would go broke. *Time* had scheduled a cover story on Beneš that month, and Luce cabled to make certain the story did full justice to the great leader of a brave people determined to fight and die for country and liberty.

Finally the Luces headed home to New York.

By early 1940 Harry increasingly felt the war in Europe was a U.S. war, and the sooner we got into it the better. Clare said no, we weren't ready for it yet. "Go see for yourself," he told her. After that it was easier for her to persuade him to let her be a *Life* correspondent. The managing editor, Billings, noted, "I had to say yes."

Clare sailed for Naples in February. Shortly after she arrived in Europe, the signs of war grew more ominous. In France, Clare was angered by what she heard. The French did not want to attack Germany, they told her, because that was what Germany wanted them to do. If they bombed Berlin, then the Germans would bomb Paris, and Paris was more beautiful than Berlin. Besides, they were much too busy having fun. What about her? they asked. Was she afraid being in the war zone?

"No," Clare answered. "I've noticed that bombs never make hits—on people who live in the Claridge or Ritz."

Clare was determined to visit the supposedly impregnable French Maginot Line, the massive concrete-and-steel fortifications near the German border. Women were forbidden there. But Clare finally met and charmed the reportedly inflexible General Gamelin, and soon found herself on a rainy hillside in a muddy village in Lorraine called Metzervisse. She had come to visit the men of the 11th Regiment of the Foreign Legion. The legionnaires stared at this attractive woman as she walked by in a smart blue tailored dress that might have been a perfect model uniform for women driving army ambulances. Clare ate with them under an old oak tree in the school yard and listened to the men sing. The colonel gave her a flag of the regiment and kissed her on both cheeks. In a dramatic ceremony the men of the Maginot made Clare their *marraine,* their godmother, and presented her with roses. Clare reciprocated by supplying the 600 men with cigarettes, champagne, and a gold-embroidered flag. The band played "The Star-Spangled Banner," and Clare explained, "I cried a little because I am at heart idealistic, evangelical, and easily stirred by crusader emotions." She felt, too, that she was performing some morale service because "all the officers were quite pleased just to sit and look at me, just because I was a woman, and most of them hadn't seen a woman in months."

The scene was interrupted by a pale-faced radio operator with a message: Germany had occupied Denmark, and was invading Norway. Clare then hurried back to Paris and cabled her husband: COME, THE CURTAIN IS GOING UP. Luce swiftly decided to join Clare in Europe.

The Luces sensed a smugness and complacency in France and Britain. They spent some time with Churchill, who would soon replace Chamberlain as prime minister. In the rising sense of crisis they went to Holland on May 7 for an interview with Queen Wilhelmina. With reported German troop movements on the border, the Queen was too busy to see them. Amid rumors that the Dutch would open the dikes to flood the countryside before the Nazis attacked, Harry and Clare went on to Belgium for a hurriedly arranged interview with King Leopold.

The exhausted Luces went to bed at midnight. At five twenty-five on the morning of May 10, Harry recalled, "a maid rushed in and shook me by the shoulder: 'Les Allemands reviennent [the Germans are returning]!'"

"The show's begun," Harry told Clare, waking her.

It was a beautiful dawn, with sunshine streaming in. Then—*bang!* "The blast knocked me half across the room. I like to say it was the first bomb of the blitz," said Harry. Everybody rushed downstairs in confusion. The square below was now filled with dust from the blast. Clare decided to make some coffee and scrambled eggs. She then filled her purse with an extra supply of powder, lipstick, and cold cream, and put only flat-heeled shoes in her suitcase.

"The next day, I wangled a car," Harry remembered. "That afternoon we started for Paris. We saw the last of the British Army going up to the front."

The Nazi tanks were close and coming closer. Clare recorded seeing the British Queen's Own Westminsters going to the front, and the terror of the refugees streaming the other way, including "half-mad mothers, starving children, the young, the old, the crippled."

Clare was eager to write about the war, and Luce duly sent a cable urging *Life* to use a piece Clare had written as part of its lead story. She sent in a piece on the first day of the war in Brussels. She had written, "Do you know what big guns and incendiary bombs and machine guns are? Do you know what they can do to people and houses and roads? Imagine the worst things you can. They have all happened."

"It was good and I was glad to use it," Billings recorded.

The Luces got to Paris in time for lunch at the Ritz the next day, and they could feel the wave of fear sweeping through the crowd. In another cable home Luce reported that he had talked to half of all the people in the most responsible positions in France, and the most intelligent conversations concentrated on airplanes. He warned that America must go into high gear to build every single military plane it can possibly make in the next six months. He saw it as absolutely essential. No country, he said, must be too fat to fight.

Billings recorded in his diary, "Luce is about ready to declare war! What a guy!"

Was the war inevitable, and what could they do about it? Harry and Clare's time together in Europe that May of 1940 was a heady time in a heady place. They were sharing a great adventure, fraught with danger. Both were part of the making of history; both were part of a great cause in which they intensely believed. If their marriage bond had loosened, here it tightened.

Clare wanted Harry to stay abroad, but he felt his place was with his magazines. He headed home, and Clare stayed on long enough to witness the surrender of Belgium and the dramatic evacuation of 200,000 British troops from Dunkirk. Within days of his return to New York, Luce was on the radio on behalf of the Committee to Defend America by Aiding the Allies, telling the American people, "We can strip off our false cloak of neutrality and announce to the world that we refuse to recognize the Nazi domination of free peoples."

On Clare's return to New York in late June, 1940, she lunched with *Life* editors, and she was on the platform all the time, while the six editors said little. She and Harry were then invited to the White House for a screening of *The March of Time*'s first full-length feature, *The Ramparts We Watch*. It was a propaganda film designed, said Luce, to "make viewers go out and kill Nazis."

At dinner Clare sat next to the President. She described him as a good conversationalist, with a hearty and friendly voice, but she felt that every time she was outspoken and political, Roosevelt seemed to put her down. She felt that FDR didn't think that women should talk politics "unless they were very ugly or agreed with him."

Clare then returned to their house in Greenwich. She had planned to write a report on the war for *Fortune,* but it had been growing into a book. She worked at an enormous table in a pale blue bedroom splattered with enormous pale pink roses. She had almost completed the manuscript when Harry called to invite her to dinner with Wendell Willkie.

Wendell Lewis Willkie was a big bear of a man from Indiana. A Democrat who had voted for Roosevelt, he was now a confirmed Republican, opposed to the New Deal. Only forty-eight, he was called the Barefoot Boy of Wall Street because he was once a poor boy who had become president of a giant utility company. At dinner Willkie suggested that the Republican presidential candidate that year should be a new face, a prominent businessman—"like you, Harry."

Clare quickly protested that it was not politically possible to elect a businessman in this age. Harry reportedly kicked her under the table, and when she persisted, he kicked her again. On the way home "it was one of the few times in our life together when Harry was truly furious with me. He said that until that moment he cherished a foolish notion that I was an intelligent woman." Harry then explained that Willkie didn't want Luce to be President—Willkie wanted Willkie.

So did Harry. He felt that an unprecedented Roosevelt third term spelled danger to the country. He wrote a strong pro-Willkie editorial for *Life,* and *Life*'s lead story reported Willkie's growing bandwagon momentum. Harry also became a key adviser. Willkie would barge into his office about six thirty p.m., and they would talk for hours. Nobody else ever barged into Luce's office.

At the Republican National Convention in 1940 Willkie won the Republican nomination on the sixth ballot.

Politics gave Clare and Harry a fresh shot of adrenaline. They had earlier shared the full adventure and excitement of being center stage at the start of a war. Once again they were exhilarated by a cause, exultant over the use of their power.

Clare made forty speeches for Willkie, and loved it. Luce sent

Willkie a stream of memos, suggestions, and advice, almost on a daily basis. He even wrote drafts of speeches. In addition, he was also on a small key committee to pick Willkie's running mate. But the campaign did not go well. When Willkie lost by a huge margin in November 1940, Luce seemed dazed and dismayed. He felt that the country was going to hell. Clare was so distressed that she told former presidential candidate Al Smith that this was positively the end of politics for her. Smith gave her a wry smile and said that in politics "you just say *au revoir*, you never say good-bye."

THE war and politics had once again pushed Clare's daughter onto the back burner of her life. Ann was now a senior at Foxcroft Academy, in Virginia, and was an excellent student. She asked Clare's secretary, Isabel Hill, to pass along her thanks for the basket of fruit Clare and Harry had sent her for Thanksgiving. She requested a schedule of all of her mother's speeches and radio appearances in case she could hear them. She also wanted a copy of her mother's book about the war, for her school library.

Ann was consistently upbeat and cheerful, but then came a bitter letter in which she said she knew her mother was a busy genius and all that, but all the other mothers had arranged senior parties and dances for their daughters. Why couldn't her mother? But nothing Ann said changed Clare's ways. When the Luces were in Europe, Clare left it to Hill to arrange for the removal of Ann's wisdom tooth, shopping for clothes, and her college admission interviews. Ann finally decided, largely alone, to go to Stanford University.

When it was time for Ann to enter Stanford, Clare and Harry were not there. They had decided on a trip to China. China was never far from Harry's mind; China had helped shape his soul. Both Luces had devoted considerable time to the cause of United China Relief. Harry called the trip "a busman's holiday," and Clare told an interviewer it was "an escape to reality."

Waiting for them in Chungking was *Time* correspondent Theodore H. "Teddy" White, who had come there fresh from graduating summa cum laude from Harvard. John Hersey, Luce's favorite protégé at the time, had hired White in 1939. The forty-three-year-old publisher and the young correspondent struck up an immediate rapport. White was awed by the reception Luce received. "He was

China's single most powerful friend in America," said White. Luce, in turn, was thrilled to be back, particularly since China was at war and there was nothing he relished more than being center stage. As White reported: "The Japanese were bombing the hell out of Chungking. He loved every minute of it—the noise, the passion, the danger."

The Luces met the generalissimo and Madame Chiang Kai-shek. They gave Madame Chiang a bountiful supply of her favorite cigarettes and gave the generalissimo a portfolio of photographs of the Chiangs. Later Luce would describe the "gissimo" as "the greatest ruler Asia has seen since Emperor K'ang-hsi 250 years ago."

The Luces had only one request of Chiang, and it was quickly granted. They wanted to visit the Japanese front on the Yellow River.

They flew in a single-engine Beechcraft, then traveled by train and, finally, by car and Mongolian pony over the Tsinling Mountains. They could see the Chinese shelling the Japanese positions on the cliffs across the river. Though the Japanese already had captured much of the South China coast, Luce was much impressed with the quality of the Chinese soldiers he saw.

Safely back in Chungking, Clare met her match in Madame Chiang, better known as May-ling or the Madame. Educated at Wellesley College, in Massachusetts, more American than Chinese, Madame Chiang had converted her husband to Methodism in a public baptism, which gave Luce his great hope of a Christian China. Madame Chiang was a stunning woman in tight-fitting silk gowns who could change quickly from a coy kitten to a queen. Dark and petite, the Madame could dress down a general with a few well-chosen words, call a quick conference of military leaders, and also give a detailed laundry list of equipment needed for the war. She gave the impression of being a brainy American college girl who had taken over China.

With her usual intentness Clare focused on the Madame. "It was as if she had studied her to see how it was done; and no doubt the Madame was studying her right back. It was one of the great match-ups of the century," said writer Wilfrid Sheed. The Madame gave Clare a pair of silk pajamas and Harry a jade T'ang horse. Harry gave her the full editorial support of *Time, Life,* and *Fortune.*

When the Luces readied to leave after a hectic ten days, Luce decided to take Teddy White, then twenty-six, back with them and make him Far Eastern editor of *Time.* Flying home in a Pan American

Clipper took six days. White described stopping at all the island stepping-stones that were to become famous in military history: Guam, Wake, Midway, and Hawaii. At each stop Luce would send White by car to check how well prepared the island's defenses were for war. They also stopped at the Philippines, where they met General Douglas MacArthur, the commanding general of the American armed forces in the Far East. An imperious man with a giant ego, he told the Luces that he was the one man who could stop Asian world dominance. After meeting him, Harry declared, "He's either a great fraud or a genius. Probably both."

Two months after their return "word came down from Luce that Clare should go to Manila to do text pieces for *Life*," reported John Shaw Billings. "We all think it is a waste of money, but if Luce says so, then she goes and to hell with the budget. Luce is hollering for big names, and Clare Boothe is such a name."

Clare went back to the Philippines to write a profile of General MacArthur. "The introduction as Mrs. Luce was an advantage," she noted. She found him a difficult man to interview. What was incredible to her was that he spoke the same pearl-shaped purple prose both in public and private. She later reminisced that MacArthur's temperament was flawed by an egotism that demanded obedience not only to his orders but to his ideas and his person as well.

Clare admitted to *Life* editors later that she could have said many unpleasant things about MacArthur in her article, but that American prestige in the Far East was tied up with the general. If she had weakened him, she would have hurt America's prestige. He was an ambitious swashbuckler, she felt, but not a phony.

"Clare Luce's piece on MacArthur arrived—seventy-three pages," Billings recorded. "It stunk! It gushed about MacArthur. It told *nothing* about him in the Philippines, just a jumble of words. What a mess! Luce said his wife's piece was 'good stuff' or something, and then began to figure how soon we could get it into print. It shocked me to see Luce standing up for his wife's tripe when in his heart as an editor he must know it was awful. [A writer and I] hedged and fenced around, and finally won a great victory over Luce: postponement of Clare's piece until it could be 'fixed up.' "

On December 7, 1941, the Luces were giving a dinner party for the Chinese ambassador when the butler interrupted, something he was ordered never to do during a meal. He handed Luce a note from the *Time* office. It read, "Pearl Harbor bombed."

Harry jumped up, knocking his chair over and saying, "It's come." Clare said, "We've expected it."

The guests left their desserts and scattered. Cars rushed out of the garage. Harry, too, rushed away. Clare was to give a radio speech and started dictating to her secretary from the bathtub.

Clare's profile of MacArthur had finally gone to press the night before Pearl Harbor, with her own photograph of the general on *Life*'s cover. The article discussed the American showdown with Japan. "The stage was set for war, a distant, dangerous, hard amphibious war for which the American nation was not yet fully prepared."

In his own two-page editorial in *Life*, Luce wrote:

> This is the day of wrath. It is also the day of hope. We accept only two alternatives—either to die in the smoking ruins of a totally destroyed America or else to justify forever the faith of our fathers and the hopes of mankind.

On the day Pearl Harbor was bombed, Luce had called his father at his sister Emmavail's house, in Haverford, Pennsylvania, to share the latest news. "I'm so glad Harry called," Dr. Luce told his wife. "His faith reassures me."

After the call Harry said, "Well, Father will get a good night's sleep."

That same night the elder Luce died in his sleep. The *Time* obituary noted that he was seventy-three and "largely responsible for the establishment of Shantung's first Christian University and Peking's Yenching University. He was a dynamic worker for the political, cultural, and religious education of the Chinese."

The death of Luce's father was the end of an era for Harry, just as Pearl Harbor represented the onset of a new and dark horizon. Both were cataclysmic events for Luce.

CLARE's approach to war was simple: she wanted to be there. It was an excitement that heightened all her senses, put her on a par with any man. She knew she was a good observer, knew how to report sensitively on anything she saw and heard. She wanted to return to the Far East because that's where the action was.

General MacArthur was to go to Australia after the fall of the

Philippines, and Clare wanted to follow him. She mapped a route from Bermuda to Brazil, then across Africa, Egypt, India, Sumatra, and Java—a trip of 75,000 miles. She saw her three months' tour of the war as a time of freedom and adventure. She did have a lingering worry about leaving her husband, sensing the danger of leaving him alone for such an extended period of time. She knew that his power would be an aphrodisiac for other women, just as it was to her.

She felt it necessary to put her concern into a thirty-page memo to Harry, summarizing the bitter, fruitless arguments that had strained their marriage during the past three years. She promised from then on to agree with him as much as she could, and when she didn't, to try to keep her mouth shut.

Clare's journey was at last under way, though many stops were eliminated because of the war. En route to India her fellow passenger on a Pan Am Clipper was brusque-talking Major General Joseph "Vinegar Joe" Stilwell, who was being sent to command the Chinese armies. Clare would soon need his help.

Clare found India complacent but fascinating. Discovering that the air route to Australia was now closed, she settled for Burma, where the war was still fierce. There she again ran into Stilwell. "Burma is no place for a woman," he told her. But then he added with a half snort, "Tomorrow at dawn, I'm driving to Maymyo. If you get up that early, you can join me on the road to Mandalay."

Clare eventually won herself the chance to profile Stilwell for *Life*. She admired this "lean, little, grizzle-haired general who marches with his men, eats with his men, sleeps with his men, speaks fluent Chinese, and understands the Chinese soldiers better than any other living American."

While she was writing about Stilwell his camp was bombed, and Clare shared a slit trench with the others. She wrote about her shaking fear when the shells seemed too close, and she became suddenly more sharply aware of her mortality.

In Burma some 7000 troops had been fighting the oncoming Japanese without relief of air cover or supplies. The British commander, General Harold Rupert L. G. Alexander, admitted to Clare that their campaign was hopeless, but they would hold Burma as long as they could. "We have more than a sporting chance," he told her.

She would meet Alexander many times during the war, and their names were so often romantically linked that Churchill's wife, Clementine, later refused to sit at a table with Clare because of an alleged affair she had "with one of our best generals." Clare's earlier memo to her husband, with its regret and guilt and promises, now seemed part of another life.

After leaving Burma, Clare stopped off at Ku'n-ming, China, the base of the Flying Tigers, under the command of General Claire Lee Chennault. In her *Life* piece Clare told the dramatic story of how these one hundred pilots fought with fifty-four obsolescent P-40 fighter planes and destroyed 500 Japanese planes. She called the pilots "valiant, drunken, disorderly, chivalrous" and gave them full credit for denying the Japanese an easy victory. Afterward one of the pilots said he thought the Flying Tigers name was first used by Clare Luce.

A Chennault staff officer recalled how he was awakened by the noise at the pilot's bar late at night, when pilots were supposed to be resting for the dawn mission. He saw an "attractive blonde in a well-tailored version of Churchill's air raid suit. She was charming everyone, and it was a great party." He announced that the lady must leave.

"But don't you see who she is?"

"I don't care if she's the queen of England—it's time to go."

That same staff officer went to breakfast with General Chennault the next morning and saw him with Clare Luce. When the general introduced her, she replied coldly, "We've met."

The general gave her a farewell present—an automatic pistol, with seven shots. If she stayed near the Japanese front, he warned her, she should save the last shot for herself. If she was caught by the Japanese, he said, she would be good for only one thing when they got through with her, "and that's the taxidermist."

En route home, Clare got stuck in Lagos, Nigeria, for a week waiting for a plane. While there she broke open the seal of the British censors on her notes and started writing a detailed private report of her trip for her husband. The report contained considerable information that would have been valuable to the enemy. Among other things, it described the Libyan campaign, where British officers in Cairo regarded the whole war as a highly social affair.

Clare finally got a seat home on a plane that stopped in Trinidad, where the British customs officers examined her papers, including her report, and promptly put her under house arrest. She was detained for a week and then sent home accompanied by a courier, who took her papers to the British ambassador in Washington.

Clare entered the ambassador's office carefully attempting to hide her nervousness. Lord Halifax looked at her sternly over his glasses, hesitated before speaking, then said, "Good, accurate report, Mrs. Luce. I have forwarded it directly to Prime Minister Churchill."

Shortly afterward Churchill visited the Libyan front, replaced some generals, and put Lieutenant General Bernard Montgomery in command. The headquarters was soon moved out of Cairo.

CLARE was scheduled to write a Burma story for *Life,* using her own photographs. Billings recorded how she dawdled over photographic identifications, telling minor stories as she went along. "What an actress! Every move a gesture," he sighed. "But we don't like each other, perhaps because I won't bow and scrape around her. With the pictures out of the way, we discussed what she could write and she proved difficult and headstrong. Really a horrid woman and not professional." Billings later noted, however, that "the Burma piece— 118 manuscript pages—contained good narrative and observations. Can edit it down and make a notable two-page piece out of it."

He also complained, "On all sides I hear we are running too much 'Clare Boothe' and her pieces are becoming a general joke." Billings observed that one of *The New Yorker*'s fourteen war points was, "Bring Clare Boothe back from the war front and keep her at home."

The ongoing conflicts with her husband's magazines deeply troubled Clare. She constantly questioned her future and her limited role as a power behind the throne. Increasingly she wanted to be her *own* power. For Clare, power was in politics. She had seen the excitement of politics during the start of the Roosevelt era, and she got a small whiff of it again when she visited her stepfather. In 1938 Dr. Albert Elmer Austin had been elected a Representative from Connecticut's Fairfield County. Austin served only one term in Congress and was defeated for reelection. He died a few months later.

Albert P. Morano, a young politician who had served on Austin's congressional campaign, saw Clare as a successor to her stepfather. Morano arranged a meeting with Clare at her home in Greenwich. He reported, "After I had given her all the reasons why I thought she could win, she called for Mr. Luce. She said, 'Harry, Mr. Morano wants me to run for Congress. I want your advice.'"

Luce and Morano walked for an hour in the garden, and Morano later said that Luce was interested and full of questions. What he indicated most strongly was that he didn't want his wife to run unless she could win. Failure would stamp a stigma on the Luce name.

Luce had two critical questions: Would the campaign embarrass him or Time Inc. in any way, and how much would it cost?

When they returned from the walk, Clare gave Morano the strong feeling that she would be a candidate. Later she said, "It was Harry who urged me. Our life together was altogether more agreeable when we did things that interested Harry. Therefore, I chose politics over playwriting."

Clare decided to run. Her potential rival for the Republican nomination was a Westport manufacturer, Vivian Kellems.

Clare's initial hurdle was the Connecticut Republican Convention, where she would be the keynote speaker. Harry asked one of his best editors, Mitch Davenport, to write a speech for her, and she delivered it brilliantly. Suddenly Clare was the center of the biggest stage she had ever imagined. Every flick of her finger seemed to be news, every word an item, every quote a story. She was the most colorful candidate Connecticut had seen in years.

The delegate vote wasn't even close: eighty-four for Clare, only two for Kellems.

Now came the much tougher general election. Clare's Democratic opponent was the incumbent, Congressman Le Roy Downs, publisher of the daily newspaper the Norwalk *Sentinel*.

As the campaign heated up, *Time* staffers worried that it would be very difficult for them to be nonpartisan. Many wondered why Luce wanted her to run. Clare had her own wry explanation for that: "To get me out of the house." Others felt that Luce was simply curious to see what would happen. Clare also said, "I was the chin that Harry led with." The idea was that if elected, she would be the national voice for so many ideas they both believed in. She had no complaints about this.

Clare had another reason. "There could be no legal discrimination against women in Congress, because the law would not permit it. If you are a Congressman, you're going to be paid what any other Congressman is going to be paid. You're going to have just as much chance to talk on the floor of the House. You are in every sense the equal of a man in the eyes of the law. The discrimination that exists against a woman in politics is of a very subtle and complicated kind. But, at least, she has access to the same amount of power as a man has." What made Clare bitter was that for a publisher's wife "I got less support from the publisher than any character in history." Luce did assign *Time* reporter Wesley Bailey to supervise all of her campaign advertising and printing and give strategic advice. Luce also asked other people to help with speeches and even wrote a few himself.

During the campaign, some of Clare's old salvos came back to hurt her. She had blasted Roosevelt in the previous presidential campaign, and FDR neither forgot nor forgave. The President said that he had to hope that there were still enough good solid people in Connecticut who would not elect "a Luce woman."

The great unknown plus and minus of Clare's campaign was the women's issue. Would women vote for a woman? Clare felt that they would if they were convinced she was competent enough. Bernard Baruch suggested she give a big dinner for workingwomen in Bridgeport, and afterward Clare wrote him what a huge success it was.

But the women's issue wouldn't go away. Male reporters often confined their comments to her clothes. "If I wear a dress that is all frilly, they are likely to say, 'Looking far too feminine to be in politics.' If I wear strictly tailored suits: 'Wearing a mannish suit, which ill-disguised her femininity.' The implication is that, regardless of how a woman dresses, her place is not in politics, but in the home."

A big surprise announcement came from Clare's onetime critic Dorothy Thompson, who now said that she was voting for Clare Boothe Luce because "she knows more about world affairs than any other candidate—what she has is brains, freedom, a considerable knowledge of the world. Mrs. Luce is a liberal Republican."

Clare's margin of victory was only 7000 votes out of 120,000 cast. It was the first time in the state's history that a woman had been elected to Congress. In conceding, Clare's opponent said, "I guess I just haven't got glamour."

Harry was exultant. Clare's success was his. He made arrangements to come to Washington almost every weekend. During the week, they would keep the phone lines busy. Whatever help she wanted, he was ready to give. She had made the Luce star a little brighter.

On arriving in Washington, Clare checked into the Wardman Park Hotel. She swiftly let it be known that she had not come to Washington to merge with the woodwork and become one of the boys. She came here to make things happen, especially to make things happen for Clare Boothe Luce. The world was changing, and she would help it change. And, surely, it would change her.

In her maiden speech Clare decided to be provocative. Vice President Henry Wallace had appealed to the world for a good neighbor policy for freedom of the skies. Clare now called it "globaloney." Republican newspapers gleefully headlined her phrase. But the astute Mrs. Roosevelt quickly jumped on Clare. She pointed out to the Vice President that Clare's speech was probably a political payoff. Pan American head Juan Trippe had provided planes for Harry when he was courting Clare in Cuba, and many times since then. He had been a strong supporter during Clare's election. Because open skies meant more competition for Pan Am, Trippe clearly welcomed Clare's stance.

No one wanted to offend Clare for long. Something about her signified power. Reporters observed that she always drew a full house when she spoke. She was a phrasemaker and quick with rejoinders. Representative Knutsen of Minnesota said on the floor of the House that she had a "masculine mind," hoping to give her a compliment.

Clare's response was swift. "I thank the gentleman from Minnesota, but I must refuse the compliment which he has so graciously paid me. Thought has no sex. One either thinks, or one does not think."

Congresswoman Luce found herself creating the impression that she was tackling too many problems at once. She ruefully agreed that in Congress it is optimum to be a piccolo player, stick to one note, and hit it all the time—but she never did it. It just wasn't in her nature.

Clare confounded Republicans by her "soak the rich" tax program and her prolabor votes. She even voted against the appropriation for the Dies Committee on Un-American Activities (the House of Representatives' precursor to McCarthy's Senate committee). *Progressive* magazine called her a certified public liberal.

Clare's congressional office seemed to resemble a Wall Street brokerage house on a big day. While the average Congressman then had a single secretary, Clare had five, and her incoming mail was enormous and national.

Clare and Harry talked about everything she was doing, especially

Right, honeymooning in Cuba, in 1935, Mr. and Mrs. Luce claimed they had never been happier. Below, the Luces during one of their visits to China, where they were escorted by Madame Chiang Kai-shek.

Freshman Congresswoman Luce addresses the House Foreign Affairs Committee in 1943.

on weekends when he came to visit. Harry tried to influence her, but let her run her own shop. He had little alternative, because Clare liked being a force of her own. In fact, the longer she stayed on the job, the more she learned and the more independent she became.

For Clare life in Washington was a cocoon. Once again she pushed everything aside to achieve her goals, and once again she seemed to forget she had a daughter. When a friend of Ann's shocked Clare by writing to suggest that she take time out from her busy life to write her daughter, who adored her, Clare guiltily wrote to Ann thanking her for some anniversary gift and gushing how much she missed her. Ann was then in her sophomore year at Stanford.

If Clare had little time for her family, she did not neglect her romantic life. She was a woman alone in Washington but seldom lonely. Her favorite escorts included handsome army colonel Matthew G. Jones and former movie czar Eric Johnston. Harry was usually there on weekends, and Baruch was a frequent visitor.

Clare was not simply a congressional freshman, she was a national exhibit. It was all going the way she had hoped—the excitement, the brouhaha, the frantic fun. There was no shortage of pending projects, and it was almost as if there were a national searchlight zooming in on her. Everybody seemed to want to know everything about her.

When a columnist questioned the dignity of a national poll selecting Clare's legs as among the most beautiful in America, she replied, "Don't you realize you are falling for the same subtle New Deal propaganda designed to distract attention from the end of me that's really functioning—it's the other end of me, I hope, that's important."

Clare was on a high. She would later tell an interviewer: "[This] is the kind of future I would want for talented girls today who are wondering about choosing a career."

8

ANN had grown up almost without a mother. Clare's shy little girl became a tall, shy young woman. In 1943 Ann was nineteen and a senior at Stanford, scheduled to graduate magna cum laude the following June. Her laugh and voice were like Clare's, and so were the contours of her face. Her hair was brown, her complexion light, her eyes dark. There was a grace about her as well as an obvious interest in people. Friends described her as unspoiled and very simpatico.

More than anything, Ann wanted to be part of her mother's public life. She told Clare that she wanted to take the examinations for diplomatic service and that her ambition was to be "a magazine editor or a diplomat." She kept trying to reach her, to intrigue her.

Ann's despairing letters finally touched Clare deeply enough to cause a sea change. Clare's trickle of letters became a small stream—caring letters full of genuine concern and affection. She seemed to be falling in love with her daughter. With her letters came a steady flow of gifts: valentines, stockings, candy, dresses, jade pins. In return Ann sent her mother a coffee ration coupon that she wasn't using, because she knew how much her mother liked coffee.

As Christmas approached, Clare wrote with real regret that they could not celebrate Christmas together, but promised her daughter that this would be their last Christmas apart and that they would celebrate together every Christmas after that to the end of the world.

The end of their world soon came. Ann had come after Christmas for a short holiday. Clare recalled it as one of their warmest times together. Mother and daughter then traveled on the Sante Fe *Chief* to Los Angeles. "Ann took the upper berth and I took the lower, and I can still see her funny little face sticking out.

" 'Mother, I know the strangest thing. I know, all of a sudden, that I will never be married.'

" 'What a funny idea! You're beautiful—of course you'll be married. Don't you want to be?'

" 'Yes, I do. Of course. But I never will be.' "

They were really mother and daughter again, really sharing. In Los Angeles, Clare gave a speech at the Biltmore Hotel, promising unity in support of the war effort. Harry had joined them for a few days in Palm Springs—a quiet family interval—and had returned to New York. Clare and Ann went to San Francisco, where Clare had scheduled another speech. The two had five days in the area together before Ann had to return to Stanford.

Clare planned to drive Ann back. It was only twenty miles away. The night before, Ann came into Clare's room at the Mark Hopkins hotel and said that her mother didn't have to drive her to school the next morning, because she was getting a ride with a friend. Her mother could join her later for lunch. The two then talked until midnight.

Clare was still asleep early the next day when she was awakened by her hysterical secretary. "Wake up! Your daughter is dead!"

The two girls had been driving in an open convertible. They were only two blocks from campus when a car came down a side road, trying to beat the light, and sideswiped the convertible. Their car spun around, the front door flew open, and Ann was hurled out into a tree. She was crushed between the car and the tree and died immediately. The girl who had been driving was only slightly injured.

Clare felt shattered, in complete shock.

When she called Harry with the news, "I remember the first words he said, 'Not that beautiful girl. Not that beautiful girl. I'll be right out to take care of everything.' " Clare then dressed slowly and walked down the hill to a small Roman Catholic church she and Ann had visited the day before. The only prayer she knew was the Lord's Prayer. Her grief became bitter against a God who had let her daughter be killed.

"When Ann died," Harry said later, "I thought Clare was going out of her mind."

Clare herself admitted, "I had a nervous breakdown."

"Clare's daughter was buried in a small burial ground near a little old church just at the edge of Mepkin," said Clare's friend Dorothy Burns Hallorand. "The funeral was held on one of those beautiful days that touch the South in January. All through the service, the sun was streaming through the windows. Birds were singing. There was consolation in the beauty of the day."

Clare could not stay at Mepkin after Ann's death, so she and Harry moved into Baruch's Hobcaw for the next two months. Harry read aloud a great deal to Clare. They took furious walks, consumed by a terrible restless energy. Clare hardly ate. All her animation seemed gone. She would mostly sit and stare at nothing. It was as if all the past had descended on her, all the guilt of her neglect of Ann. Her health was very poor, and many wondered whether she would survive.

When Luce returned to his offices, Billings was shocked by the way he looked and sounded. "He was in the depths."

It was politics that finally pulled Clare back into reality. It was 1944, time for her to run for reelection. "I'm sure Ann would want me to continue," she told a friend.

In Washington, it was easier for her to recover emotionally. She immersed herself in her work. Although a member of the minority party, she initiated and influenced the passage through committee and the House of considerable constructive legislation, particularly to aid the rights and health of children. She also introduced a draft bill for the military ineligibles to work in war-related industries.

The war was going well on all fronts. U.S. planes were battering Tokyo as well as Berlin. Japan was slowly surrendering the islands it had so bloodily won. A Russian advance had captured 100,000 Germans at Minsk. The Allies prepared for D-day landings in France. Clare petitioned the President to disclose his peace plans, but FDR simply ignored her.

For a time Luce focused his attention on his wife's reelection. Clare was to be a speaker at the Republican National Convention, and Harry was at her side in a white suit. When Clare came to the speakers' stand, he listened, rapt, as she spoke about GI Jim, the brother of GI Joe. She said Joe was the returning war hero, but Jim was the one killed, and buried in an unmarked grave. She mainly blamed GI Jim's death on President Roosevelt, who "lied us into war."

Many felt her speech boomeranged. Many called it cheap demagoguery, and *The New Yorker* commented that her speech "made it difficult to keep anything in our stomach for twenty-four hours." Most Americans didn't want to feel that Roosevelt, who had done so much for the country, was responsible for the death of their sons. A decade later Clare admitted that she wished she could apologize to Roosevelt for that statement "because lying was clearly the only way to get us there."

To run against Clare, the Democrats picked Margaret Connors, a former deputy secretary of state a dozen years younger and also attractive. With Roosevelt as her enemy and with a penchant for angering even her supporters with her tart, often ill-conceived barbs, Clare fought a heated battle. She had serious doubt about winning. In the final tally she squeaked in by 2013 votes. In view of Roosevelt's sweep that night, her victory was considered a political miracle.

With the campaign now over, Clare needed something new to distract her. When the congressional Military Affairs Committee proposed that she visit the Fifth Army in Italy, Clare knew she had found her next diversion.

En route to Italy the committee stopped in France, where Clare met commanding general Dwight D. Eisenhower. She found him a personal challenge. When he offered her a cigarette, she took a firm hold on the package. The general had a reputation for not being generous with his cigarettes, and Clare had made a bet she could scrounge the pack. "The minute he felt the pressure of my fingers on the cigarettes, he withdrew the package, extracted one, and handed it to me. And all the officers laughed, and I said at once, 'General, I've just lost a bet.' Of course, when I got back to my quarters that night, I found six cartons of cigarettes from the general. At any rate, I felt that I had made a warm human contact with him at that point."

Clare spent her Christmas holiday with Fifth Army soldiers in Italy instead of at home without Ann. She traveled by jeep through a blizzard to sing carols with patients and nurses at a hospital. While she was there an Associated Press poll of American newspaper editors selected her as woman of the year.

The war seemed to have given Clare a concentrated purpose. She had made the Fifth Army her urgent cause. She spoke everywhere about these American soldiers fighting a terrible war with heavy casualties and insufficient supplies. She was angry at the American people who had forgotten their fighting sons. One observer in New York remembered, "She was radiant, beautiful . . . completely dominated the scene."

In contrast to Clare, Harry was a far more sober, almost gray presence. The two seemed totally opposite. She liked glamorous people and glittery parties. He gravitated toward what he called "typical" types, such as a small-town manufacturer. Generally he regarded New Yorkers as "smart alecks" and "insular," and preferred the company of those he met on his fact-finding trips around America.

Harry and Clare's intellectual exchange would always be of great value to both Luces. But the rest of their marriage had shifted in the ten years since their wedding. They had become two powerful forces moving in separate orbits. Luce was now an eminence, on a level with Presidents and Kings. His magazines, radio shows, and newsreels reached millions. Politicians and leaders in every segment of society yearned to be on the cover of *Time* as a peak fulfillment, on the cover of *Life* as a celebration, and on the cover of *Fortune* as a special distinction.

Clare was in her own orbit, spinning even faster. More and more polls ranked her next to Eleanor Roosevelt as the most important woman in America and one of the most important in the world. Women marveled at her energy, her brains, her ability to fight her way into the man's world and push to the top. Many Republican leaders now talked of Clare as a candidate for the U.S. Senate or for Vice President.

Despite their power and status, the Luces were privately frustrated, rootless, lonely people. They lacked any central core of love in their lives. The marriage was at a crossroads.

While Clare was away, on a return trip to Italy, Harry moved out of Greenwich and into their apartment at the Waldorf Towers. It was a bare place, with no homey touches. But on the wall there was a portrait of Clare, "looking like an angel," one observer noted.

Once again Luce had to ferret out dinner partners. "I felt sorry for Harry because he had so few friends," noted Allen Grover, who was one of them. "Partly, I suppose, this was because he knew that everybody wanted something from him."

Still, Harry Luce developed a more confident presence than he had had in the early years. He was a man women would look at quickly when he came into a room. "I found him very very attractive physically," said the wife of an associate. "A marvelous specimen of a man—tall, slender, and very handsome."

No man was more hungry for affection, for a sympathetic ear. No man was more ripe for a love affair.

ONE evening in 1943, while Clare was out of town, Luce went to a party Elsa Maxwell was giving at the Waldorf. One of the guests was Jean Dalrymple, an attractive woman with striking eyes, a sensitive face, and a good figure. She had long been an acquaintance of Clare's. Jean was known as one of the most aggressive theatrical agents in town. Still, there was a feminine softness about her, a certain air of quiet mystery. Unlike Clare, she did not need to be center stage all the time. She had the greater gift of knowing when to listen and, therefore, was on everybody's select party list.

"Harry was alone at the party, and Elsa introduced me to him," recalled Dalrymple. "We talked awhile, but I had an appointment, and I had to run. I told him, 'I'm terribly sorry, I have to go.' He was taken aback." The next morning her phone rang. It was Luce.

"He began to call me quite frequently and asked me always to dinner and to the movies," Dalrymple said. "He treated me like any man would who wanted to know me."

But more than wanting to know *her,* Harry wanted her to know *him.* He *needed* somebody to know him—a woman who regarded him not as an icon or as a power, but as a man.

While Luce was courting Dalrymple, Clare was busy with General Lucian Truscott, another one of the generals in the ardent Clare corps. Truscott commanded the 3rd Infantry Division, which had swept through Sicily. Before that, he had organized the Rangers. He was one of the generals Eisenhower relied on most. A strong, dynamic, attractive man, Truscott showed Clare the misery of the war in Sicily. They conducted an affair whenever they could throughout the war.

The Truscott affair was more serious than most. It was so intense, Clare later confided, that she really thought he wanted to go home, divorce his wife, and marry her. But it never happened.

Luce, for once, was enjoying himself while his wife was off with other men. He confided to Jean Dalrymple how very unhappy he was with Clare.

"The marriage was terrible for him," she said. "I don't think it was so bad for her. She just seemed to carry on her own life, and not pay much attention. I said to him once, 'You ought to take a stand with her!' But he never did. He somehow could never face up to her."

On her return Clare quickly learned about Dalrymple. They had many friends in common, and Dalrymple was not pledged to secrecy. She and Harry had dined in restaurants and were the subject of talk.

Clare swiftly called Billings at home and demanded to know everything he knew about Dalrymple. She thought Billings was one of the few to whom Luce confided. But Billings, who *did* know, denied the whole thing.

Clare now made a concerted campaign to regain her husband. From Washington, or anywhere else, she sent a stream of messages, telegrams, and letters full of loving words, telling Harry again and again how much she missed him, how grim it was without him.

But Luce was preoccupied with Dalrymple. She had given him a new contentment. He felt at ease with her. More than once he raised the question of marriage. But Dalrymple regarded this as an exciting interval with a fascinating man, and that was enough for her then.

Thanks to Luce's contentment, those at Time Inc. now found him much more approachable, much less tense. "I really love the boss," Allen Grover told Billings, but expressed the hope that he "doesn't break some vast new concept upon an unsuspecting world without having it thoroughly thought out. You know our sainted boss is not the greatest organization man."

Occasionally Luce reigned from a penthouse office on the thirty-third floor of the Time-Life headquarters, in Rockefeller Center. Harry himself referred to his office as a box, but others called it the cathedral. Billings joked that the office was fit for il Duce and called it il Luce. Certainly it was an impressive expanse, which opened onto a sun deck. Wide windows a story and a half high faced across the East River. On one side of the inner office was a gallery of 100 candid photos of key staff members at Time Inc.

Now and then Luce still went down to the twenty-ninth floor to put out an issue of *Time;* he felt that the weekly needed most of his day-to-day attention. *Life* was on a different wavelength and took more advance planning. He was unhappy with *Fortune.* Its losses coupled with other problems had caused Time Inc.'s income to drop appreciably, but not enough to stop the company from buying two transport planes. Gradually, though, the financial picture improved.

On a more global scale Luce was pleased with events. The war was going well and so was his relationship with the White House. The President still periodically asked Luce to come down and talk.

ON APRIL 12, 1945, President Roosevelt died. For millions FDR had been the only President they had known, their Commander in Chief, the man who had shaped their time and their history.

Luce told his editorial voice, Jack Jessup, that he was afraid Roosevelt "would escape history and be credited with being more interventionist than he really was." But Roosevelt's primary sin, according to Luce, was his final softening toward Soviet Russia.

"Luce had a phobia about freedom," commented Berlin bureau chief John Scott. "His kind of freedom, American freedom. And everything else seems to be dangerous. That's the main policy of his magazine." That anxiety about freedom was at the heart of Luce's violent anti-Soviet feelings. He truly believed that Soviet Russia was an evil, godless empire determined to spread communism all over the world. A communist world to him was a world of slaves—without religion. Communism was one issue on which he and Clare were in complete, enthusiastic agreement.

At the same time, Luce now began focusing his own energies on forging a relationship with FDR's successor, Harry Truman. Both Truman and his wife, Bess, had been victims of Clare's tart tongue in years past. Luce was nervous. Clare had called them Kickback Harry and Overtime Bess. (Truman's wife was on his payroll in the Senate when he was still paying off debts for a failed haberdashery business.) Truman might forgive what you said about him, but not about his wife or daughter. During the Truman presidency, Clare was never admitted to the White House.

Truman did not transfer his ill will to Harry. After the Germans surrendered, in May 1945, he made Luce a very happy man by giving him clearance to tour the Pacific combat zone.

In thirty days Luce and *Time*'s senior editor Roy Alexander traveled 30,000 miles. They stopped in Guam, the Philippines, Iwo Jima, Saipan, Kwajalein, and Hawaii. Luce even visited the destroyer escort *McGinty* to see his ensign son, Hank. For the five-minute chat the navy allowed Luce with his son, he had had to travel by mail plane, destroyer, and packet boat.

On his return to New York, Luce was "bursting with ideas about Pacific coverage," including a special issue of *Life*. He took his ideas to Washington and dined with thirty-three Senators. He detailed his recommendations that the government modify its demand for unconditional surrender and permit a peace that would allow Japan to keep its Emperor on the throne. Otherwise, he warned, it would take a year of bloody fighting and heavy casualties to invade Japan and defeat it. But then the atomic bomb was dropped on Hiroshima and three days later a second one on Nagasaki. Within a week the Japanese unconditionally surrendered.

Japan's defeat still left China facing civil war. From his post in China correspondent Teddy White reported the impending strife and urged *Time* to take a neutral stance for a democratic solution instead of unconditional backing of Chiang Kai-shek. Luce did not question the quality of White's reporting. What Luce soon *did* question was his partisanship. He felt White sympathized too much with the Chinese Communists and ascribed too many virtues to the peasants and too few to the leadership of Chiang Kai-shek.

Luce soon replaced Teddy White with another correspondent, one who regarded Chiang as a "truly great man."

DURING his tours of the Far East and China, Luce had sent cables to Clare, but they lacked his old intimacy and affection. Publicly the couple were still the powerful Mr. and Mrs. Luce. Privately Clare probably assumed she could yet win Harry back from Jean Dalrymple.

Still, a growing malaise affected Clare. Distressed about the state of her marriage, she was also increasingly unhappy in Congress. She felt overworked, trying to perform "the menial and the miraculous," as she called it. The phones were always ringing, the buzzers always buzzing for upcoming votes. There were constant committee meetings to deal with and an unending stream of visitors with requests and demands, as well as mountains of mail—some filled with love, some with hate. One was even addressed simply to "That Woman, Washington D.C."

In her search for something diverting, Clare accepted the title role of Bernard Shaw's *Candida* at a summer playhouse in Stamford, Connecticut. But she was faced with unpleasant publicity about it. She needed a rest. Harry suggested they take a two-week vacation, and Baruch chartered a plane to take them to Hobcaw. They shot quail, rode horses, and retired at ten o'clock. For a time, the marriage seemed back on track. Harry had always been willing to help Clare through rough spots, and this was no exception.

As the second anniversary of Ann's death approached, Clare succumbed to an attack of hysterics; she even talked about suicide. She was clearly suffering. Behind her sharp tongue and willingness to conquer the world was a curious fragility. Moreover, she felt doubts sweeping over her. The idea that she might have petered out as a writer made Clare panicky. Too many people expected too much of her, and now she seemed to be unable to do anything at all. She felt herself a failure.

Clare sat in a darkened room day after day. She later confided to a friend that Harry didn't know how to help her. "He'd come in, sort of pat my hand, and walk out." What she wanted, she said, was for him to put his arms around her and hold her. "But he didn't put his arms around anybody."

She was wrong about that. Harry was putting his arms around a woman who gave him the quiet, loving attention he had never seemed to get from Clare. He had found what she had not.

As HER despair increased, Clare found herself crying and reciting the only prayer she had ever memorized, the Lord's Prayer. Wandering aimlessly around her room, seriously contemplating suicide, she noticed one day an unopened letter on her desk from a Jesuit priest from Cincinnati. He had once written her a fan letter about an article of hers, and when she replied, he had written to her over a period of years. Clare found a telephone book and called Father Wiatrak.

"Father," she said, "I am not in trouble but my mind is in trouble."

Wiatrak replied that he was too simple a priest to counsel her and referred her to Father Fulton J. Sheen, in Washington.

A dinner was arranged, and Father Sheen set the ground rules for Clare: "First, we will consider the existence of God. I will talk for fifteen minutes without interruption and at the end of that time you can talk as you like—two, three, or four hours and ask questions."

Sheen later recalled, "I talked for about five minutes. Then Clare jumped up and shook her finger under my nose and said, 'If God is good, why did he take my daughter?'"

Sheen replied, "Perhaps it was in order that you might become a believer. Maybe Ann's death was the purchase price for your soul."

After that, they met frequently for sessions that lasted up to four hours. Sheen later said that although he had devoted his life to instruction in the church, Clare raised difficulties "the likes of which I never heard before." He described it as a battle of wits.

Clare insisted that Ann's death was not responsible for her conversion, but many thought otherwise. When Clare was received into the church, at St. Patrick's Cathedral on February 16, 1946, only a half-dozen people were present. She explained that she had become a Catholic "to get rid of my sins and start living again, and to find meaning in all this torment." Becoming a Catholic, she said, was "one of the better decisions of my life. It permitted me to love and be loved.

Never having had a father, it was a great joy to discover I had the greatest of them all."

Allen Grover's wife, Bea, felt that Clare had an ambition to be bigger than anybody, and "her happiness in the Roman Catholic Church is partly that it is bigger than even she could hope to be."

There were those who believed Clare's conversion was for a different reason entirely. The rumors of an impending Luce divorce had become persistent. "Clare, being the political operator that she was," said one observer, "figured out how to stop the rumors. And that was to become a Catholic convert. You can't divorce a Catholic." As Harry told Jean Dalrymple, "In her religion, we are no longer married, because in her religion I'm still married to Lila."

Harry was exultant about Clare's conversion. He felt that she had found a home for her soul, and so now she no longer needed him. Now she might let him go.

After Clare's conversion became public, C. D. Jackson, a Time vice president, told Billings that he, Luce, and Luce's attorney had dropped in on Clare at the hospital where she had recently undergone a hysterectomy. There they pressured her for a divorce.

Clare sought Baruch's advice. He told her to ask for fifty-one percent of Time Inc. stock and $4 million.

Clare then told Harry her terms for divorce. Harry refused. He would give her money, yes, but Time stock, no. He would never ever sell control of Time. It was his life.

Harry then presented Clare with some lawyers, who threatened to annul the marriage on the ground that she was frigid.

"Oh, so far am I from being frigid," she said. "Let's go upstairs, Harry, and show these guys!" Luce quickly backed off.

Clare now made a threat of her own: if Harry didn't give her the stock and the money, and if he tried to divorce her in a foreign country, she would give him the most terrible publicity—call him an old lecher and tell about all the different women he'd gone out with.

"I think he was scared of her turning on him—you know, blowing the whole thing—or else afraid that she'd kill herself," said Jean Dalrymple. "That worried him more than anything else, because she tried twice [to kill herself]. She drew a knife across her wrists. He even told me that she had threatened to kill him."

All was now in a kind of legal limbo. However shaky the marriage, this didn't manifest itself to their friends. Harry and Clare were still seen together at public functions and parties.

IN THE midst of his struggles with Clare, and with his heart and mind filled with Jean Dalrymple, Luce headed off for Zurich, en route to Germany. He had been invited by the War Department to view postwar conditions in Germany with a group of V.I.P. journalists.

A young vice-consul, faced with the job of entertaining the visitors, quickly summoned Mary Bancroft, a vivacious American woman living in Switzerland. A former wartime spy, Bancroft, then forty-two, was witty, outspoken, and fiercely intelligent, and the vice-consul felt sure the journalists would like her. Would she come for drinks? At first Bancroft said no. But when she heard that Henry Luce was part of the group, she swiftly changed her mind. Having recently given a talk to a group of French children who had been evacuated to Switzerland, she had discovered that "all the questions without exception were based on something the children had read either in Teem (as they called *Time*) or in Leef (as they called *Life*)," she explained. "I was appalled by the influence of these publications. So I was just lying in wait for him, like a cobra about to strike."

Once they met, she quickly caught his attention. She held it for the next twenty years. Over drinks Bancroft began telling Luce in sharp language all the things she didn't like about his magazines, from the style to the slant. He listened intently, and was alternately angered and intrigued.

"The next day," Mary recalled, "I received an envelope containing a little note that said, 'Thought you might be able to use these.' Enclosed were rationing coupons and meal tickets that Harry, as a foreigner arriving in the country, had been given at the frontier."

When he left Zurich, Harry told Mary that when she came to New York, she must look him up. And so she did.

Mary Bancroft was simply like no woman Luce had ever met. A proper Bostonian by breeding, she grew up in a very privileged household, then attended Smith College. She quit after three months to marry the coxswain of the Harvard crew team. They had two children, were divorced, and Mary moved to Switzerland in 1935, where she married a businessman of Turkish ancestry. She wrote articles, and when Americans entered the war, she became a spy for the Office of Strategic Services.

By the time Mary met Luce, she knew all about men of power and was very skilled as a questioner—and a listener. Luce found himself telling Mary things he had told absolutely no one else. There were few people in the world to whom Luce poured out his heart and soul, and Bancroft was one of them.

After Harry returned to New York, he and Mary began a correspondence. Her letters were long and intense, noted Allen Grover. "It was a marvelous exchange of minds."

Harry kept his new private life a very private secret. Neither Jean nor Clare presumably knew about Mary. Even if Clare had known, it was hardly a matter she could complain about. Clare had been writing intimate letters to men all her life. If she had known about Harry and Mary, it might have raised her estimate of her husband. This was a dimension of him she did not know. A romance with Jean Dalrymple she could understand, but an intellectual affair was something else.

Luce's deep friendship with Mary only heightened his desire for a divorce from Clare. Both Mary and Jean had taught him that a woman could be caring and kind, qualities he no longer saw in Clare. Furthermore, he sensed that Jean Dalrymple would not be there for him forever. Dalrymple was a celebrated woman of the theater and enjoyed her life, but she also relished her relationship with Harry. Now she finally encouraged his idea of a divorce.

But Clare had impressed upon Harry that divorce was rampant in her family and that she considered it a defeat. He was torn. Divorce was a defeat for him too. The guilt and stigma of his first divorce had never left him. Divorce would tumble his life upside down again. Besides, Clare showed no sign of retreating from her impossible demand for Time stock. Privately Harry and Clare hashed out their differences, confiding in almost no one. Whatever their rationale, they finally decided to reconcile. There would be no divorce.

Harry told Dalrymple that he could not divorce Clare, because she needed him. Their affair was over.

CLARE was now forty-three. Once again it was time to run for reelection, and she had grave misgivings. As one of the eleven women among 424 men in Congress, she had made her mark. Most recently she had worked closely with Baruch, proposing international control of atomic energy. She had also proposed a detailed plan for massive aid to postwar Europe, which was a precursor of the Marshall Plan, made effective the following year.

What distressed Clare was the bureaucracy and slow action.

To her friends she claimed that Congress had brutalized and toughened her spirit. To an interviewer she later insisted, "I always regretted that I shifted to politics. You can do nothing truly creative in politics by yourself. You're working with a team all the time."

Of course, Clare was still fiercely ambitious. Republicans still saw her as a political prize, and prominently mentioned her as a candidate for the U.S. Senate. Being Senator was a cherished dream, a national prize, a chance to sit on an equal platform of power with Harry—or without him. Harry Luce hurried to Connecticut governor Raymond Baldwin to talk about it. But Baldwin had his own ideas for the Senate, and Clare was not part of his plans.

When she realized the Senate was impossible, Clare put up her best front, saying that she had refused to run because "I wanted to be with my husband more. It is my firm conviction that a woman's first duty is to her husband and home. In America a full-time federal office is no job for a woman with family obligations." She then added a sharp thrust: "My husband would *never* have had to make such a choice. So the price is still high for a woman."

Harry and Clare decided to start their renewed life together in a new home. In 1947 they bought a red brick Georgian mansion complete with swimming pool and tennis court in Ridgefield, Connecticut. Once again they decorated their home with the Far Eastern furnishings Harry loved. And they maintained a serene public posture.

9

Iᴺ 1948 *Tɪᴍᴇ* celebrated its twenty-fifth anniversary and Luce turned fifty. Several editors wanted to put his picture on *Time*'s cover, but he refused. Luce settled for a birthday cake with five candles on it and a floodgate of reminiscences about the early days, when it was "one hell of a fight."

The anniversary lifted Harry's mood. He seemed more cheerful and optimistic, particularly because his empire was flourishing financially. Time Inc. assets were at their peak, with revenues over $120 million. *Time* and *Life* were thriving, as were *Time*'s four international editions. Only *Fortune* was losing money.

Politically Luce was also feeling optimistic. The mood of the country was more upbeat. People were generally prosperous, and Europe with all its problems seemed far away. Harry Truman had turned out to be a surprisingly good President.

This was also a presidential election year, and once again politics gave the Luces a renewed sense of mission and togetherness. But after Truman beat Dewey, Clare grew despondent. The trauma of shock returned. A few months before, in September, her brother, David, had hired a plane and flown out over the Pacific until the gas ran out. The plane crashed two miles offshore, and his body was never recovered. Although there was no suicide note found, Clare assumed the plane crash was no accident.

Except for David's war years, when he had served as a pilot in seven campaigns, his life had been a frustrated shambles. After the war he seemed deeply troubled. At one point he had wanted to open a gambling casino in Las Vegas, and Clare refused to finance him. She now arranged for a thirty-day vigil light to be placed on the altar at a church in New York in his memory. David was the only one who had truly loved her. It was as if a part of her heart had died.

In the midst of this sorrow Harry's mother died, at age seventy-seven, a few days after the election. She had lived the last years with her daughter Emmavail and Emmy's husband, Leslie Severinghaus, in Pennsylvania. Her stream of letters to Harry had always been adoring, but he never saw her in her final days. His mother had been the central force of the family, and Harry's sister Beth wrote that he was now the family's heart and fountainhead.

Yet Harry found it remarkably difficult to reach his sons. He scribbled occasional notes, mostly apologizing for not writing more often and not coming to visit. To Pete, who was to appear in a school play, Luce asked a curious question: Did he want Dad to come and see the play? When Luce *did* schedule a visit, in a private Time plane, his secretary notified Pete that Luce would stay only for the night, as he was en route somewhere else.

Distanced from Harry's children and filled with sadness, Clare and

Harry decided to take a holiday in Jamaica; this was private time on a private beach. They were now a middle-aged couple wanting to get their marriage back on track. They were tired and drained and ready for peace.

Upon their return, to please Clare, Harry bought Condé Nast's triplex apartment, with a view of the East River. To please her even more, he bought a Picasso and a Manet. The Luces had become public citizens, sponsoring the arts. They contributed heavily to the New York Philharmonic, and Clare was elected a trustee. Harry became a board member of the Metropolitan Museum of Art. Clare now ranked in a Gallup poll as one of the most admired women in the world—after Mrs. Roosevelt and Madame Chiang.

To please Harry, Clare gave big dinner parties for visiting celebrities, including the Duke and Duchess of Windsor, President Gabriel Gonzalez Videla of Chile, and Queen Frederika of Greece.

In April 1949 Harry left for his annual trip to Europe, this time accompanied by Allen Grover. The trip buoyed him. The Marshall Plan had worked. Most of Western Europe had rejected socialism. World leaders were waiting to see Luce, from the pope to Charles de Gaulle. Many of them had been on *Time* covers or soon would be. Beaverbrook's London *Daily Express* treated him to some *Time*-ese enthusiasm, calling him "Vigorous nonstop magnate Luce."

In Zurich, Luce visited Mary Bancroft. But not even she could keep Luce in one place for long. "At the end of the trip," said the harried Grover, "Harry had gained six pounds and I had lost ten."

THAT fall Clare decided to go to Rome, and persuaded her friend Buffy Cobb to go with her. Buffy had also converted to Roman Catholicism under the guidance of Father Fulton Sheen.

"I was sick with fatigue," said Buffy. "Usually I cannot sleep in a plane, but I could have slept on anything. Just as I was conking off, Clare poked me: 'Wake up! Wake up! I have just met the most fascinating man, a wonderful old monsignor. He knows everything and is very wise.' The monsignor was brilliant but I was too shot to enjoy him. Just as I was conking off again, Clare jabbed me: 'Wake up! Wake up! I want you to talk with the pilot. He has a matrimonial problem, and we need your advice. Besides, he's going to let us sit in the control cabin when we land in Rome.' We advised the pilot, and he circled St. Peter's three times. At four o'clock she was shaking me again. 'Wake up! Wake up! We're going to a most interesting dinner.' She had a list of engagements made beforehand.

"On our last day in Rome," continued Buffy, "we got in a car and drove into the humble suburban section of Rome to a school for boys. 'Something I must do,' Clare said. A beautiful blond boy came running out to the car and kissed Clare's hand. She hugged him hard. Then she began to question him about his studies: What was he doing? What did he want? He wanted a watch and a bicycle." (They were sent next day.)

Later Clare talked with the people in the school and spent most of the afternoon with the boy. When they were alone, Buffy asked Clare, "How did you get that child?"

"When I was in Rome during the war," Clare told her, "I found some nuns taking care of a group of lost babies in an old abandoned warehouse. There I saw this baby who was so beautiful and so sick. I took him back to my hotel and got an Army doctor who shot him full of penicillin. I got a nurse for him, and we managed to pull him through."

Rome was so crowded that Clare could not get a room for the child, so he and the nurse slept on her bed while she rested on a couch. Then she got the child into this school, a sort of Boys Town. Ever since then, she had taken care of him. My beautiful American mother, he called her. He was nine years old and named Augusto.

This was a side of Clare few people knew. Somewhere beneath the cool, often brittle exterior was a warm, loving woman. It was rare, however, that these qualities emerged. Most of the time, Clare was her usual driven, self-absorbed self, moving through Europe like a steam-roller, speaking to everyone.

In Paris, Clare and Buffy visited with the Duke of Windsor, who was working on his story for *Life* with writer Charles Murphy. Clare afterward described the Windsor dinner as wonderful, the duchess's clothes perfect, the duke chatty and affable. But she categorized the Windsors as a frail, lost, and unhappy little pair of might-have-beens, with nothing left but golden memories.

And then, recorded Buffy, there was a mysterious visitor. The Grand Duke Otto came to call on Clare, and thrust this note in her hand:

I want to tell you something extremely important concerning our last conversation. There is almost certainly a microphone in this room. So please mention nothing. If you don't mind, we will continue our conversation just walking out in the Jardin de Louvre, because that is safe.

And Buffy added, "Clare disappeared in a cloud of perfume and blue-chiffon scarfs. Grand dukes and mystery!"

While Clare was off in Europe, Harry was forging a deep new bond in New York. This time it was merely friendship with yet another of his younger, liberal protégés. As a successor to White and Hersey he chose Emmet John Hughes.

"Emmet Hughes was a precocious young man," said *Time* correspondent Dave Richardson of Hughes. "He took the liberal point of view that the Roman Catholic Church had to change. On this basis, Luce hired this brilliant young guy and sent him to Rome. He was in his mid-twenties and still wet behind the ears. I always said he had imaginary sources. He was a romantic from the word 'go.' Women melted at the sight of him."

Luce liked this sly approach, this sweeping sense of history he felt Hughes had. And he was willing to forgive Hughes' lack of detail, his lack of hard-nosed reporting. "Emmet had this real dramatic way of writing," Richardson continued. "He'd come out with a story which was half-true, maybe, but boy, it was full of oomph! You'd cry when you read it. Well, Luce loved this."

In his two years overseas in the '40s Hughes had more bylined stories in *Time* than almost any other correspondent before or since. His Catholicism was a major influence on Luce. *Time* began devoting so much space to Roman Catholic news in 1949 that Billings wondered in his diary, "Is Luce flirting with Catholicism?"

The one factor that kept Luce from joining the church was China. The Protestant missionary background was just too deep in him. Religion, then, became another form of competition for the Luces. Clare much admired her Roman Catholicism and rather wore it as a badge of pride. Harry felt equally dedicated to his Presbyterianism.

But Harry needed something new and exciting. The old career had lost its glow. Luce felt so depressed and frustrated that he sent his staff a memo saying he no longer wanted to see any *Time* copy and that he was going away for a while. Harry added that he had to work out a formula as to what he was going to do.

He soon found it. It wasn't a formula; it was a cause.

"HARRY fell in love with Eisenhower as people fall in love with beautiful girls," said Allen Grover. "Here was this marvelous man who came from the heartland of America, the fair-haired boy, the leader of the great armada of World War II, a crusader, honest and straight. Harry idolized Eisenhower as he did almost no one else."

Eisenhower was a man others intuitively liked. He made men smile and had an open warmth. He had been the commanding general for more than 14 million men and women. His name was a household word. With his flashing smile and midwestern manners, Ike was accessible. The American people were ripe for Ike, and he became their hero.

One of Luce's deep wishes was to be a public hero. It seemed insurmountable. His only hope now was a political appointment—possibly Secretary of State. If Luce could make his mark in the Eisenhower Cabinet, he might earn a national respect and an international reputation and come as close as he ever could to being a hero.

Clare visited Ike at Columbia University, where he was president, and urged him to run for President of the United States. But he was evasive. "Just as I was leaving," she recalled, "I asked, 'How many politicians give you advice?'

" 'Nobody can go through that door without giving me advice.'

" 'I'm no exception. If you take my advice you will be President. This is my advice: *Don't take any advice.* Just pursue what you are doing until your own instincts tell you where else and what else you should do.' He gave me one of his great grins and said, 'Now that is the only piece of advice I have received since I've been here that I intend to take. I tell you if I do get to be President, you're going to be one of the people I want on my team.' "

Clare and Harry both went into high gear. In 1951 a *Life* article appeared comparing the presidential potential of General Dwight David Eisenhower, then supreme commander of NATO forces in Europe, with that of Senator Robert A. Taft, the Ohio Senator who was known as Mr. Republican because he seemed supreme in the party. Taft and Luce were in full accord on most issues.

For Luce the Taft issue was a real dilemma. "Harry felt that the man best qualified to become the Republican candidate was Taft," noted Clare. Yet Harry also felt that "Taft simply had no style."

Making his painful choice, Luce said, "I was sure Eisenhower could win. I was not sure that Taft could."

Like Harry, Clare, too, was in a quandary. She said she personally preferred Eisenhower, but that if Eisenhower and MacArthur should both run for President, "it would tear out my heart. I love them both." MacArthur was then commanding an international United Nations force against North Korea.

Harry soon decided upon a trip to Paris to persuade Eisenhower to resign from NATO and come home to campaign. Luce's conversation with Ike helped to clinch his decision that the political time had come for him to run for President.

As the 1952 election grew closer Luce had a long-standing problem with Taft, who had supported the charges of Wisconsin Senator Joseph R. McCarthy. A freshman Senator in 1946, McCarthy received little notice until he hit his real stride in attacking what he called "the communist infiltration of the U.S. government." In one speech he claimed he had the names of eighty-one Communists and party-liners in government, but refused to name any of them.

In a matter of months McCarthy created a national hysteria and managed to destroy many lives and reputations, wreaking particular havoc among creative-minded liberals. *Time* called him "loud mouthed, irresponsible, wretched, a fool or a knave."

In *Life* an editorial deplored Taft's support of McCarthy and noted, "It is right to fight communism; it is wrong, wicked, to smear people indiscriminately, most of whom are good Americans." In this, Time Inc. was far ahead of the American press and of a fearful American people. *Life* called on Taft to repudiate McCarthyism "because truth and decency are at stake."

Luce was personally contemptuous of McCarthy and saw him as a menace. Eisenhower had refused to confront McCarthy during the campaign even though McCarthy had denounced his hero and friend General George Marshall as a traitor. Yet Luce was so enamored of Eisenhower that he did not denounce him for this.

On April 11, 1951, General MacArthur was fired by President

Truman for disobeying orders in trying to widen the war in South Korea. MacArthur, *Time* man of the year, felt he could return as a public hero and sweep the presidency. When he was defeated badly in the Wisconsin primary, Taft became the party favorite. But Luce still felt that only Eisenhower could win in November.

Luce then played a crucial role at a critical moment. At national conventions there are often conflicts between competing sets of delegates claiming voting recognition. The Taft-dominated convention committee approved the slate of Texas delegates favoring Taft instead of the ones for Eisenhower. This was typical and unsurprising. *Time,* however, dramatized the story under the headline THE TEXAS STEAL. Luce did something unprecedented by printing *Time* one day early "because if that story hit the delegates before the crucial ballot at the convention, it would make a great difference." Harry admitted to Clare that it was all his idea and that it was a really dirty trick, "the only thing that weighed heavily on his conscience."

When Eisenhower was finally nominated, both Luces had a right to consider it a personal victory, and so they did.

Truman had decided not to run again, and he privately solicited Illinois governor Adlai E. Stevenson to be the Democratic nominee. *Time,* meanwhile, ran an enthusiastic cover story on the governor. When Stevenson was drafted as the nominee at the 1952 Democratic National Convention, he made a memorable acceptance speech, with the theme "Let's talk sense to the American people." It caught fire all over the country. *Life* called him "the Democrats' best foot."

Luce had met Stevenson and liked him but was adamant about the need to elect Eisenhower. He asked Time Inc. vice president C. D. Jackson to head up Eisenhower's speech-writing staff, with Emmet John Hughes acting as a speechwriter. It was Hughes who wrote Eisenhower's most sensational speech, in which he proclaimed, "I shall go to Korea!" This became a slogan that helped win the election.

During the campaign, *Time* printed twenty-one photographs of Eisenhower, all highly attractive, smiling, and warm. In that same period there were only thirteen pictures of Stevenson, two of them thirty years old and the rest mostly unflattering and frowning. There was the often repeated story at *Time* that photographers going out on assignment asked only one question of their editors, "Good guy or bad guy?"

In the midst of the political heat, Luce often sought the companionship of Mary Bancroft. Now divorced, she had moved to a New York apartment on Eighty-sixth Street, near the mayor's mansion, facing the East River. She lived simply, much as Harry would. For Harry it was a needed retreat, and he visited her often.

Yet Harry once again needed Clare's help in his crusade to elect Eisenhower. A far better speaker than Harry, she made dozens of speeches for Ike.

By October it was time to push even harder. *Time* ran cover stories on the two presidential candidates. The Stevenson cover story carried the blurb "Does he make sense to the American people?" *Time's* answer was no. But the Eisenhower cover story was a glowing tribute.

When Ike won a sweeping victory, Luce went from desk to desk shaking hands with his editors, glowing happily. He had simply assumed they were all for Eisenhower—and most of them were.

Soon afterward Harry asked Clare, "Well, what are you going to ask Ike for? He's certain to offer you something. He *has* to. I mean, he's got to have a woman on his team somewhere."

"Well, you know, Harry, I've decided to leave politics," Clare professed. "But I might ask him if he would make me a representative to the UN, because I can always get home for lunch and dinner."

Luce later confided that Eisenhower once had asked him during the campaign what job he wanted. Luce said, "The only thing I really want, you'd be crazy to give, and that was the Secretary of State."

Any hope of being selected Secretary of State disappeared when Eisenhower picked John Foster Dulles. Eisenhower later said he never offered Luce any spot in his administration, because he never thought Luce was interested.

Clare, too, was waiting. "I rather expected to be offered some job if we won. I never said anything about it. But I never heard a word from Ike. I began to feel hurt. One appointment after another would be announced. I thought, Well, he's just forgotten."

Finally word came: "The boss wants to see you."

As Clare recalled the meeting: "I went in and Ike was very businesslike, very glad to see me. He thanked me for the part I'd played in the campaign, and then he twirled his pencil between his fingers and looked at me and said, 'Now, I would like to ask you what would you think about becoming Secretary of Labor?'"

Clare felt she wasn't qualified, that he needed someone with a far greater knowledge of labor. She said without a smile, "I am not your man."

"All right, now, what would interest you?" countered Eisenhower.

"Well, I was thinking you might put me over there on the UN."

"Nonsense, I'm not going to waste one of my stars on a small job in the UN. What about an embassy?"

London and Paris were not available, he told her. She then eliminated Germany, Mexico, and Spain. Eisenhower mentioned Italy.

In 1940, when Clare was in Europe researching her first book, she had visited the American embassy in Rome and called it "the most beautiful in Europe. How I'd love to be ambassador here."

Clare's account of how Eisenhower offered her the ambassadorship has been disputed. A Luce intimate insisted Harry had told her that he himself was offered the ambassadorship but had suggested that Eisenhower appoint Clare instead. Whatever preceded Ike's offer, Clare told the President that the Rome ambassadorship would be most difficult but agreed to consult with Harry. She wouldn't go without him. She knew that if she did, their marriage would be finished.

Clare wrote Harry—who was traveling in Indonesia—a long letter about it. He cabled back: LETTER FOLLOWING. ACCEPT AT ONCE.

Then he sent what she called an extraordinary letter. "He wrote that it would be an injustice in history if I were not to take the job," said Clare, "and that I owed it to my sex because he knew how I felt about discrimination against career women." He suggested that he could arrange to spend alternate periods of six weeks in Italy. Finally Luce added, Clare "must keep her personal rendezvous with history."

When her appointment was formally announced, Harry's editors noticed that he "even sported a carnation." It was his victory too. An even more remarkable testament to his delight was his decision to leave Time Inc. for six months a year to be with his wife in Rome. This was an extraordinary act for Luce. In his persistent Presbyterian way he was still the optimistic romantic hoping again to make his marriage work. Going to Rome might give it the lift it needed.

CLARE was now fifty years old and had reached a political pinnacle: she was the first woman the United States had ever appointed as an ambassador to a major country. When a reporter asked her what she thought of the possibility of a woman becoming President, she answered, "It makes so much sense that they'll never allow it. That is, in our time."

She was undoubtedly one of the most celebrated, most controversial women of her era, and still quite beautiful. But Clare had a gnawing sense of uneasiness as she sailed for Naples on a cold April day in 1953. Harry had strayed and now was back, yet she sensed a fresh restlessness in him. She would have to keep him close to her, watch him more carefully, cater to him a bit more. He was too good to lose. He must always feel himself a full part of this new adventure. And he must always believe that she needed him.

As the American ambassador to Italy, Clare faced her greatest challenge. Italy was in serious trouble. Poor in natural resources, plagued by unemployment, the country faced bleak economic prospects. With the fall of Mussolini's fascism the 47 million Italians had proclaimed a republic. The Americans had supported the new premier, Alcide de Gasperi, leader of the Christian Democratic Party. But as Clare arrived, the political situation was highly unstable.

Gasperi's government had been distressed by Clare's appointment. A female ambassador was an affront to Italy's male-oriented society. Also, Italy was a Roman Catholic country, and both Luces had previously been divorced. *Candido,* a satirical weekly, highlighted both issues by calling Clare "Mr. Boothe Luce" and running a cartoon showing the American embassy flying a flag of laced-edged panties. To make matters worse, Clare replaced a beloved icon. The departing ambassador, Ellsworth Bunker, an able career diplomat, had been so popular that Italians cried when he left.

But Clare was undaunted and looked for reasons why she would succeed. "A celebrity ambassador," Clare said, "can draw more attention than a diplomat should, but she can also publicize certain national interests better than a faceless functionary." And she promised to make noise only about the few things that mattered.

She had to do all this and more. "Because I am a woman, I must make unusual efforts to succeed. If I fail, no one will say, She doesn't have what it takes. They will say, *Women* don't have what it takes." Clare also liked to point out, "The great trick in diplomacy is to make some unwitting man think your idea is his idea, and women have been doing that all their lives."

The man who would help pave Clare's way agreed. "Actually a woman has advantages," said Elbridge Durbrow, minister counselor of the embassy. "She can often put over a story, make them take a bitter pill better than a man can. If a man talks straight, he is apt to get thrown out before he can finish. But a woman will be listened to out of politeness."

The U.S. ambassador lived in the Villa Taverna, a large sixteenth-century Italian-style country house bought by the U.S. in 1948. "The Villa Taverna was beautiful but terribly run down. It had been terribly neglected, but Harry supplied money to put it in good condition," noted Harry's sister Beth, who had accompanied them at his specific request to oversee the household arrangements.

In the heart of Rome's residential section and set in a parklike seven acres, the villa was a serene enclave filled with sweet-smelling cypress trees, statues, and fountains. Visitors were immediately struck by the lovely winding staircase and the succession of small, elegant rooms. A landscaped terrace led to an expansive classical garden.

When Harry and Clare finally arrived at the Villa Taverna, somebody released white doves. They were the last symbols of peace Clare would see for a while.

Edward C. "Kip" Finch, Harry's sophisticated new assistant, and researcher Margaret Quimby had preceded Luce to Rome to set up his office in an apartment near the Rome bureau of *Time*. Finch felt that Luce would need guidance in Roman society as well as in business and politics. He thought that many people would try to get to the ambassador through Luce. His guest list had to be properly screened. Luce, meanwhile, busied himself with an Italian instructor and tape recordings to learn the language.

It took time to win the approval of the Italian people. Beth said that one of the first things that swayed the hostile staff was the party Clare gave for 300 of them at the villa. They all knew she'd been working until six thirty and figured a beautiful woman needs an hour, at least, to get beautiful. They did not expect her until seven thirty. Instead, she was down in ten minutes, looking perfectly exquisite. "This really gave them a thrill," said Bea Grover, who later replaced Beth as Clare and Harry's household overseer.

Clare quickly got down to business. "A dynamo in a Wedgwood china house" wrote *Newsweek* about her.

Up every morning at seven-thirty (she rarely sleeps more than five hours a night), she goes through half a dozen Rome papers, including the Communist daily *L'Unita*, orders her calendar, plans dinner menus—the things an ambassador's wife normally does—and looks through her private mail. Then, she is rolling along to the embassy in her gray Cadillac. She receives callers, diplomats, Italian politicians, visiting Americans until one-fifteen, when she goes, generally, to an official lunch or takes time out for the hairdresser. Between three and four, she returns and works until six or seven. Then she prepares for dinner or a diplomatic reception.

Clare's days were crammed and unending, so much so that her husband substituted for her on a variety of occasions. And it was a plus to have Harry with her when she dined with the President of Italy.

No sooner had she settled in when the storm broke. Clare arrived only a few weeks before the national election. As she said, "It was a bad break." She saw the masses of underemployed people in Italy—many of them worried about earning their daily bread. She viewed them as a kind of sponge that absorbed communist propaganda and communist ideological promises. Clare felt the need to make a point.

"Diplomatic procedure was for the embassy staff to write your public speeches for you," she noted. "So I was handed this little speech [to give] for Milan. It was delicately expressed, but the effect was that if the Communists took over Italy, we might possibly, perhaps, withdraw our aid programs and our financial help."

The actual phrase read, "If the Italian people should fall unhappy victims to the wiles of totalitarianism of the right or of the left, there would logically follow grave consequences." American aid to Italy then totaled some $650 million, in addition to $300 million more for a NATO procurement program. The speech "was the decision of the entire embassy, and it was a calculated and necessary risk," said Elbridge Durbrow.

De Gasperi lost the election, and an American columnist blamed the defeat on Clare's speech. Italian newspapers resented an American telling them how to vote and threatening them if they voted wrong. Clare saw it as her low point in Italy. And she took the heat at home. At a Democratic dinner, party leader Averell Harriman called her speech a "blunder." Others also denounced it.

Just as she was feeling so unsure of herself, Clare achieved a striking public relations success. A terrible flood engulfed Salerno, and the ambassador rushed to the scene to judge how much food, medicine, and other help might be needed. One newspaper described her as "a porcelain figure of a fairy godmother."

AMBASSADOR Luce soon became one of the sights of Rome. "The Colosseum comes first, of course, and a few other things, but I am generally on the list for tourists," she said. At an embassy reception a flustered American girl actually told Clare, "It's so wonderful to be over here in Rome seeing all these old, romantic ruins and you, too."

When Italy's American hero, baseball star Joe DiMaggio, arrived for a visit, Clare clung to his arm and steered him to a café on Via Veneto to ensure maximum public exposure. Wherever she went, people gathered to see her. Few heads had ever turned for any previous ambassador, but for her, everybody gaped.

An Italian paper, *Il Giorno*, pointed out:

> [The Italians] applauded her and hissed her, raised her up for worship and threw her down in the dust; above all, they chose her as the favorite target for slander: And this, in Italy, is the most certain indication of popularity.

Slowly Clare won applause on both sides of the Atlantic. The Italians realized that Mrs. Luce was a real diplomat, and very powerful because she had the ear of both the President and her husband. They began to appreciate her—not as a woman, but as an ambassador.

One of her tasks was to master Italian. The moment she was appointed, she began to study, using a dictaphone and a verb wheel. "I try to learn a new verb every day," she said, adding, "I could hold a pretty good conversation at a political level, but I couldn't possibly order a dress."

Then she began mastering all the intricacies of protocol.

Virtually every day, Clare faced a social hurdle. "In Rome," she told an interviewer, "there are sixty-nine officials from other countries upon whom I must call. Heads of missions must call me. That makes 138 calls at our offices or theirs. Then I must call—with Henry when he is available—upon each foreign official and his wife, if he has one, at his residence. And he must call on us. That makes 276 more calls.

We also give two or three dinners a week and are invited to an average of fourteen social functions a week—dinners, luncheons, and cocktail parties." Yet Clare claimed to enjoy all this in a certain way. "I've never met a representative of another country who hasn't told me something interesting I didn't know. And information never bores me."

The New York Times correspondent Cyrus Sulzberger had another view. Having dined with her one night, he recalled, "She does not listen to what anybody has to say, because she is talking all the time herself. She is an exceptionally beautiful woman—quite astonishingly so when one considers her age. But this exterior conceals the most arrogant conceit and the most ruthlessly hard-boiled self-assurance it has ever been my privilege to come up against."

Sulzberger also refused to accept Clare's concept that Italy was going to go communist unless the U.S. intervened. "I think she's nuts and merely wants to make a big name for herself as an activist in her first diplomatic job. I mistrust her judgment."

The communist papers referred to her as "the old lady with the evil eye." In posters, pamphlets, and in speeches by Italian Communists, Clare was called all kinds of Kremlin-inspired epithets. One communist poster called her an evil witch. It had a huge photo of her, all distorted to make her look like Madame Frankenstein. When an indignant aide showed it to Clare, she burst out laughing.

Politically Clare's task seemed practically impossible. Whatever she said seemed wrong in some circles. But she persisted. In her first sixteen months she visited every important region of the country and traveled more than 35,000 miles on official business. During her first year in office, she made eighteen speeches on topics such as peaceful applications of atomic energy, the unity of Western nations, the evolution of relations between Europe and America, U.S. overseas private investment, and international cooperation in education. Even if the Italians didn't always agree with her, they got to know her.

At the U.S. embassy there was an enormous lift in staff morale. Elbridge Durbrow summed up the feelings for Clare: "As an old careerist, I could ask for no better boss, for three reasons. One: She is intelligent. Two: She seeks advice and takes it with an open mind. Three: She has a wonderful sense of humor. You could not ask for more. She has won over the staff one hundred percent."

Clare was in her element, at top form. It was going exactly the way she had hoped. When she talked, everybody listened. When she went anywhere, everybody watched. It seemed almost too good to be true.

ONE of the most remarkable things about Ambassador Luce was her husband. When he was with her in Rome, he generally made an effort to stay out of the limelight, but he could talk to political leaders, newspaper editors, and other influential people as they could never talk to his wife. Clare constantly sought his counsel. She was no puppet, but there were discussions, advice, and strong suggestions.

Harry sent his own reports to President Eisenhower, who replied:

> Of course, I never had any doubt that our new Italian ambassador would get started on her work with the good will of everyone who knows her. Likewise, I have no doubt as to the effectiveness of the official performance *you* will turn in.

Luce's unofficial role seemed to give him some of the excitement and power he had hoped to have as Secretary of State. Harry was happy, and this affected his relationship with Clare. They shared a closeness they had seldom felt before.

Clare admittedly was startled at the pleasure with which Harry embraced Roman society. "I took these occasions for granted, but he found them glamorous." Sometimes they presided over several cocktail parties held concurrently in different sectors of the Villa Taverna gardens. "Harry loved the elegant parties," said Clare. "He loved the people, and everyone seemed attracted by him. One of his favorite cracks was, 'I only help Mrs. Luce at social gatherings. I pour tea.' "

Luce said it without resentment. This was a new role, and he was still exploring it. "Harry did have a wonderful time!" said his sister Beth. "It was a vacation for him. He felt he hadn't any free time like this in years. It was a sabbatical, and he knew he needed it."

Luce soon became obsessed with Rome. He knew equally well the decayed as well as the energetic and beautiful parts of the city. He knew all the obscure churches as well as the animals in the zoo. No tourist ever studied more art and travel books with such fervor. His chauffeur had to follow him in case he got lost, as he sometimes did.

Still, it was somehow difficult to imagine Luce sitting at the lower end of a table making small talk, dinner after dinner, party after party. And Harry finally did tire of the entertaining. "I'm so damn sick of this," he told a friend after some months had passed.

Yet Luce did not forget about his magazines. Shuttling between New York and Rome, eager to know what the Rome bureau of *Time* was saying about Clare, he asked the Rome correspondents to file their stories before noon so that he could read them during lunch, which was his freest hour. But he stayed away from the *Time* bureau, lest other news organizations feel he was funneling news directly to Time-Life.

Even if Harry bent over backward to keep a distance between Time Inc. and the embassy, Clare did not. "She periodically would try to throw her weight around, and get the bureau to report things that she wanted us to report, or do stories that she wanted done. That was a kind of pain in the neck," said correspondent Ed Clark. "But Harry was a tower of strength. He just basically said, 'Don't pay any attention to her,' which was a great reassurance."

At the same time, Luce watched "like a hawk" to make certain Clare got all the prerogatives and deference her position deserved. Noted Clare, "Harry really enjoyed it more than I did, because I had the rough end of it and he had the fun end of it. He often spoke of 'my time in Rome' as one of the happiest of his and my life together."

10

ROME had recharged Harry and given him a sense of pleasure he had seldom felt in his lifetime. A staff consensus was that he seemed less combative in his fifties, less rude, and more open-minded. Said a colleague, "He had achieved what he had wanted in life."

Now Harry had something up his sleeve. At a luncheon in 1953 he told his staff, "We are supposed to be magazine publishers. Wouldn't it be a good test if we found out we could bring out another successful magazine?"

He then told them he was considering a sports magazine. "Too much of the world news is dull news," Luce said, and added almost apologetically, "Well, sports is a big thing in the United States."

"But you're not interested in sports," someone said.

"It doesn't matter what I'm interested in," Luce answered.

Indeed, Harry didn't have any knowledge of most sports. He had had to work at school jobs while other boys played baseball or football. He had been a poor boy, and poor boys didn't play tennis and golf, or ride. He learned those later, mostly out of embarrassment and in an effort to be a regular guy. He approached sports the way he did anything he was interested in—questions, questions, questions.

At Time Inc. many people thought Luce was crazy and mockingly referred to the magazine as *Muscles* or *Jockstrap.* Finally it was named *Sports Illustrated.* It would teach people about sports.

Luce launched his new magazine on August 9, 1954, with an initial circulation of 450,000. He needed a strong managing editor, and Mary Bancroft recommended André LaGuerre, a journalist who had been head of the Paris bureau and also had been Charles de Gaulle's public relations man during the war. "André loved sports and understood power," said Bancroft. "Harry could see both things were relevant. The reason I suggested André was that I knew that in order to get the job done, it would have to be someone able to stand up to Harry. If anyone could deal with Charles de Gaulle, well, they could deal with Harry."

When Luce offered LaGuerre the top job at *S.I.,* as it was called, the Frenchman didn't really want it, but said yes. What he really wanted was to be managing editor of *Time,* and this seemed like a foot in the door. It was under LaGuerre that the magazine made money. However, it would take years, and losses of $33 million, to turn *Sports Illustrated* into a profitable magazine.

Clare had her own comment on the magazine: "Ah, yes, the only good things in it are Charles Goren on bridge, which I suggested, and my articles on skin diving."

WHILE Harry absorbed himself in sports, Clare was continuing her endless round of duties in Rome. But she had begun to despair about her lack of real accomplishments in Italy. While she was there, the government lost a new election, and Italy was in a turmoil of internal political friction.

Among Clare's troubles was a conflict between Italy and Yugoslavia. After the war the Allies had divided Trieste and the Istrian peninsula into two zones, one Italian and one Yugoslav. Yugoslavia's Marshal Tito was threatening war if Italians moved into the Yugoslav zone.

Secretary of State John Foster Dulles called a conference of European ambassadors in Luxembourg to discuss the situation. Clare told them, "I think this thing can be settled. It's a pain in the neck to both countries, and there is nothing to be gained by their going to war. If we can find what each of them really wants, besides territory, we can settle it."

Clare wondered how she could get the Trieste issue to the President of the United States. Knowing that Eisenhower liked one-page reports, she sat down at her typewriter and began to try to explain the problem of Trieste on one page. Then she capsulized it in a poem:

> *For want of a Two-Penny Town [called Trieste]*
> *A Prime Minister was lost [de Gasperi]*
> *For the want of a Prime Minister . . .*
> *Italy was lost . . .*
> *For the want of Italy, NATO was lost . . .*
> *For the want of Europe, America was lost . . .*
> *All for the want of a Two-Penny Town [called Trieste].*

"I sent it to Ike through the *Time* correspondent, because I knew he would drop it on his desk," Clare said. "I did not dare send anything so unorthodox through the State Department. And Ike read it aloud to a State Department meeting. They said, 'What does she want?' 'Permission to try to save the two-penny town,' said Ike. And they all said, 'Well, sure.' Boom, we were off. We got the White House's approval to try to settle it."

Under American pressure Italy and Yugoslavia both agreed to secret negotiations in London. A CIA operative told Ambassador Luce privately that Marshal Tito's problem was the failure of the country's wheat crop. Without wheat, there would be famine in Yugoslavia. If he got wheat, he might soften on Trieste. Clare hurried to Washington and met with President Eisenhower. Twelve hours later Tito received a personal letter from Eisenhower offering wheat.

Finally, one and a half years after the partition of Trieste, the issue was settled. Italy got the city of Trieste, and Yugoslavia the surrounding territory. Within three weeks Yugoslavia received 400,000 tons of wheat from the United States. None of these secret negotiations were made public.

Luce sent Clare an exultant letter offering her a 101-gun salute.

Filled with pride about her accomplishments in Rome, he was like a proud parent. Harry added how much he loved her.

Soon after the Trieste triumph Clare developed a severe viral infection in her mouth that affected her teeth. Besides losing her teeth, she began losing her hair. Her alabaster complexion suddenly turned sallow, and she no longer had the energy for her occasional swim. She also claimed a slight motor loss in her right leg.

Clare later claimed that her Italian doctor did a urinalysis and said she was being poisoned by arsenic. Clare further reported that CIA investigators moved in and informed her that she had been absorbing small amounts of arsenic for a long time. They suspected, she said, that somebody might be trying to kill her.

They began checking for Communists in the kitchen. Then they noticed thick gray dust on the phonograph record in Clare's bedroom. Further investigation revealed that every morning, when the washing machine upstairs was being used, the vibrations shook the ceiling. A fine dusting of paint filled with lead arsenate was falling from the stucco roses that decorated the room. The conclusion, as Clare told the story: her physical condition was the result of a daily diet of inhaled arsenic dust.

This, at least, was the account leaked to the press, and Clare emerged as a tragic heroine. However, Richard Clurman, then chief of correspondents for *Time*, has set the story straight: "The whole arsenic story was a fake. She was never poisoned. She had to have massive dental work, and she didn't want to say that."

Frank White, *Time*'s Paris bureau chief, has also confirmed this and amplified the details: "Clare had to be in the States for six months. So the Luces called in Charles Murphy [a *Fortune* editor], and Charlie concocted this story. Clare *did* have some serious viral infection, which presumably caused her visible signs of illness. Of course, Clare was delighted because it was the perfect excuse to get away."

It gave Clare the perfect cover to return to the United States for her dental work—and her resignation. She wanted to quit Rome while she was at the peak. It had been a great experience, but now she was restless and wanted something else.

In Italy the rumor was that Clare took arsenic to clear the skin. But what most intrigued the Italians was the knowledge that the Luces had not slept in the same bedroom, since Harry was not affected.

AFTER SEEING HER DENTIST, CLARE spent some time at a luxurious health spa. When she emerged, she had a long talk with Eisenhower, who persuaded her to stay on until the next year. Publicly she announced, "I want to be where he wants me to be." But privately she told him that she wanted to campaign for him again in 1956.

So Clare returned to Rome, as requested, to complete her duties. Then when Italy's European ally Hungary revolted against Soviet Russia, fully expecting American support, it received none. Clare pleaded with Dulles and Eisenhower to intervene, but to no avail. "An ambassador is just a messenger boy," she complained.

Harry had his own bone of contention with the man he had helped promote for the presidency. "This was the time for American leadership. It was no time for a trumpet with an uncertain sound."

At a farewell dinner for the Luces a *Time* staffer, Dora Jane Hamblin, felt brave enough to announce loudly, "I miss Harry Truman. Truman would have done something."

In the sudden silence Luce said to her, "Do you know what I hope happens to you?"

"No, sir," replied the young woman, now almost paralyzed.

"I hope that when you grow up [long pause] you will get to be editor of a great big magazine and that everybody who works for you is a Republican."

Everybody burst into laughter.

HARRY Luce finally found the woman he loved more than he had once loved Clare, the woman he wanted, the woman who changed his life. When they fell in love, she was twenty-seven and he was fifty-eight, and that seemed to mean nothing to either one. It was the kind of love he had never had—a sweeping, passionate, overpowering love.

Harry first met her in a villa in southern France. She was the granddaughter of a man he considered his friend, Lord William Maxwell Aitken Beaverbrook. Lady Jean Campbell was tall—about five feet ten—with a full, sensuous figure. Her penetrating brown eyes were serious under a shock of dark wavy hair. A lilting, sometimes riotous laugh would reveal her great sense of humor. Jean's regal air was inborn, born to the manor, but nobody could have been less pretentious. She had a marvelous gift of making even the most stuffy, unsure people feel at ease.

Beaverbrook was the Canadian-born tycoon of British journalism. He was a fighting force in the British Conservative Party and had helped engineer the election of David Lloyd George as prime minister. When another friend, Winston Churchill, later became prime minister, Beaverbrook energetically served as minister of aircraft production.

"What a man!" Harry exulted about his friend. "Power, power, power!" They got along marvelously well.

More than his power, Harry envied his reputation as an international rascal. The Beaver was seventy-seven, and a wicked old man. Any attractive woman within his physical reach was considered fair game. Even his granddaughter regarded it as likely that Clare Boothe Luce was one of his early conquests. Clare always made it a point of coming to see Beaverbrook whenever she was in Britain.

Lady Jean Campbell, the daughter of Beaverbrook's daughter and the Duke of Argyll, had been born in a castle in Scotland. Her parents were divorced when she was three, so Jean moved in with her grandfather. She was educated at an English boarding school and then studied Shakespearian acting before moving back in with her grandfather and working as his assistant.

In 1956 Jean came to New York and got a job filing photographs at *Time*. She was in southern France on a two-week holiday with her grandfather when she met Harry Luce. She considered him handsome, but "very, very shy and remote."

Harry, however, thought Jean was fantastic. He couldn't get her out of his mind. One day he simply walked into the *Time* photo department and said to her, "Would you like to come and have dinner tonight?"

"Yes, I'd love to."

"Well, I'll send my car for you."

Jean recalled that when she arrived at the Luce triplex, "I expected it to be a big dinner party. But there were no other guests!" She and Harry then "went in to dinner and talked for a long time.

"The next morning, he called to ask if I would have dinner with him that night. I said yes, though I didn't then find him attractive. But that evening at his apartment, we sat on the balcony and talked about everything in the world. And I saw this man, who had been very cold, very hard, in the morning, suddenly unfold with a flowering of enthusiasm into somebody wonderfully warm and human, with such depth and humanity. And laughter. He loved to laugh. The transformation was so unexpected, so complete, so absolutely fascinating," she reflected. "By the end of the evening I was in love. And I knew, right away, that this was going to be a tremendous love affair."

Jean was then living on the eleventh floor of a small apartment house, with a sitting room and two bedrooms. After spending Christmas with her grandfather in Nassau, she invited Harry to dinner, not quite knowing what would happen. So far there had not been a single romantic word between them. Then after dinner Harry told her, "Of course, you know I've fallen very much in love with you."

"And I said, 'And I've fallen very much in love with *you!*' "

And so it began.

An hour after he left her, Harry called to ask what was the color of the blouse she was wearing that night. It was pink. The next morning he sent her fifteen dozen pink roses.

"Then we saw each other as often as we could," she said.

For Harry it was easy to understand Jean's appeal. She was a free spirit, with her own natural style—the complete opposite of Clare. Jean wasn't trying to impress anyone, had no desire to be center stage, and felt no need to make herself heard. Still, she was never at a loss for words or opinions. Jean not only listened but listened intelligently. She had a broad knowledge of all kinds of things. She found it exciting to keep pace with Harry's mind, and she could.

As their affair progressed, Harry transferred Jean to *Life* magazine as a researcher—a better, more interesting job. Though she distanced herself from the other employees, she was liked and admired. *Life* writer Joseph Kastner remembered her vividly: "She wore a sheath dress, and came out of it in front and behind. It would knock your eyes out. She was gay, effervescent, and bright, and she was so *nice*. She did a certain amount of checking and researching, but she wasn't very good."

Jean's mind was obviously on Harry and little else during her *Life* period. Needing advice, she told her grandfather about the affair. "He thought it was a marvelous match, despite the age difference," she said. He was happy for her and gave the couple his blessing, but it could not be a public blessing. There were too many people in too many positions of power who would not understand.

At first Harry and Jean always met at her apartment. For months they never went to any public place. "My apartment was our private place," Jean said. "In retrospect, what young girl could have put up with that? But then, I adored him so much."

Harry, she said, was completely relaxed and happy. "He talked and talked and told me the whole story of his life. He was just busting with talk. I never got a word in edgeways hardly."

Harry shared his fondest memories with Jean. He also discussed his marriages. "He told me that he and Clare stopped sleeping together after six months, that it was his decision," Jean recalled. Clare "had persuaded him that she wasn't interested in sex. Because of that, I don't think it entered his head for one moment that she was having all those other affairs. He thought that all these men were simply filled with admiration for her. Nothing else would occur to him."

Harry and Jean also talked about Jean Dalrymple, and about Mary Bancroft too. "Harry had talked so much about Mary that I always longed to meet her," said Jean. "Years later, we did meet, and I said, 'Why on earth didn't Harry introduce us? We could have been friends all those years.' "

The marvel of all this, and perhaps a commentary on Harry Luce, was that the two Jeans and Mary really liked one another and became close friends. They were three women sharing someone very special, so special that somehow it did not stir any major jealousy in them. The only woman they resented was Clare, not simply because she was the one married to him but because she was the one hurting him.

WHILE Harry was in New York with Jean, Clare was concluding her tenure in Rome. In December 1956 she threw her silver half-dollar into the green pool of Rome's Trevi Fountain to ensure her safe return, and came home to the United States.

Her health was bad, her ambition low. She went to Phoenix, Arizona, for several weeks to Elizabeth Arden's exclusive Main Chance Spa, where she could be coddled, massaged, and comforted. But she was soon bored by the small talk of moneyed women. Clare wired Harry to come and keep her company at a nearby hotel, and he went. She and Harry took long walks. The winter air in Phoenix was dry, pleasant, and warm. A house there caught their fancy: a tile-roofed Mediterranean villa with a giant olive tree out front. The house had a tremendous living room, a glassed-in porch, and ample servants' quarters. It also faced the fifteenth green of a golf course.

Luce impulsively suggested they buy the house. He felt excited by this idea. Perhaps if Clare could be happy in Phoenix and stay there, he could more easily have an alternative life in New York with Jean Campbell. Perhaps, too, it would make a future divorce easier.

Clare's explanation for Harry's sudden decision was, "Harry's in the midst of male menopause. He likes houses." Of course, Clare enjoyed moving into different houses. She had lived in twenty-eight different places in her lifetime, and seemed to regard each new one as a fresh chance at happiness. And this was a lovely house, light and airy.

Harry, naturally, found it necessary to be in New York and flew back frequently to continue his romance.

By this time Jean had moved to an apartment on Ninety-fourth Street, near Fifth Avenue. It was a pretty place with a bow window in the living room, and Harry was there often. Occasionally they would go out for a beer. But at such times Luce lost his calm. "Who's going to see us?" he constantly asked in a state of nervous guilt.

Even though Jean never talked about her relationship with Harry at *Life,* news of their affair got around. Soon it became a flagrant topic of discussion among the staff. "Harry finally made me quit *Life,* and he was right about that," said Jean. "It became too difficult."

While Harry was off with Jean, Clare was slowly recuperating after her years in Rome. She busied herself with paintings and mosaics, and even taught mosaics to the children of her servants. On trips to Florida she also took up scuba diving. She wrote a three-part series on scuba diving for *Sports Illustrated* and supplied her own photographs.

Luce found it easier to commute from Phoenix to New York than from Mepkin to Connecticut. For a diversion in Phoenix he and Clare frequently invited friends from New York for short stays.

One visitor was Laura Hobson, then working for Luce as a promotion writer for *Sports Illustrated.* She flew to Phoenix on the same plane as Harry, but sat separately en route because she knew he had a fetish about not sitting next to anybody he knew. On the way to the lavatory Laura passed Luce's seat. What she saw startled her. "He seemed slumped sideways in his seat. He was pale and waxy-looking," she remarked. "I knew something was very wrong. I knelt beside him and reached for his wrist to try for his pulse, but he yanked his hand back.

'It's nothing,' he said. 'I'm all right.' But I stayed there; his color began to return. He sat back, straightening himself up. He did look more like himself, but I was glad we were approaching the airport. Harry's chauffeur met us. During the drive to their house, Harry remained silent and so did I. Clare noticed nothing unusual when we arrived, and he told her nothing, at least not then."

Five days later Harry had a chest cold, and Clare called the doctor. As usual Harry minimized everything. But afterward, when Clare brought him some soup, he sat staring and said, "I'm dying."

A doctor and ambulance soon arrived. "I can still vividly remember when the stretcher came out carrying Harry, looking so ill, so unlike the powerful Henry Robinson Luce the whole world knew," Hobson remembered. "Clare went with him in the ambulance, and I followed. When I saw Clare at the hospital, she was talking to a nun. She then came over to me weeping. 'If anything happened to Harry, my whole life would be over,' she told me."

Harry was hospitalized for three weeks. He was told he had suffered a pulmonary embolism followed by a coronary occlusion. For the rest of his life he would be on anticoagulant drugs. "The decision had been made there in the hospital, surely by Clare herself, that the full truth must be kept from the press, from the stockholders, from the stock market, where Time stock might plummet," said Hobson. "As far as the world knew, he had been ill with pneumonia."

Jean Campbell was worried. "He wrote to me from the hospital, saying that he'd had a heart attack and that it was all hushed up."

After some months Harry was back at work in New York. But he now seemed changed. He told his secretary, Corinne Thrasher, "I'll never retire. I'll die at my desk."

"Harry talked about death and age," said Jean. "He felt he was very old. This was just two months before his sixtieth birthday. He certainly didn't look old. He was still a vital man. But he couldn't put death out of his mind."

HARRY's illness had diverted Clare for a time, but now he was better, and so now she began to grow restless. With restlessness came a revival of her fierce ambitions. She told her friend Elsa Maxwell that she might write a new play and that she had definitely had enough of public life.

President Eisenhower's chief of staff, Sherman Adams, knew otherwise. "After she got through being the ambassador to Italy, she made a probe of the possibilities of becoming, if not a roving ambassador, a personal presidential emissary around the world," he reported. That October, Eisenhower sent Clare as his personal representative to attend the funeral of Pope Pius XII. She returned five days later as Eisenhower's emissary to the coronation of Pope John XXIII.

When reporters asked if she would take an ambassadorial job, she replied, "Irvin Cobb was once asked if he planned to attend a big society party. He said, 'No, I'm not, for three reasons. Number one is that I haven't been invited. Which makes the other two academic.' "

Three months later John Foster Dulles asked Harry Luce about his wife's health. The White House then leaked the news that Clare Boothe Luce was slated to be the new ambassador to Brazil.

She had discussed it with Harry, who had said, "It's a great country. You haven't been able to get back on track [with writing] and you enjoyed being an ambassador, and you did well—so sure."

Clare started studying Portuguese and scoured her files for South American contacts. She also ordered 10,000 new calling cards as the ambassador to Brazil. As it turned out, all this was slightly premature.

The Senate usually waived hearings for anyone who had previously been confirmed as an ambassador, but Senator Wayne Morse of Oregon had some scores to settle. *Time* had hit him hard when he switched from the Republican Party to become a Democrat. As a member of the Foreign Relations Committee, his voice had some clout. He made a three-hour speech against Clare, using the theme, "Is she honest? Is she reliable?" He quoted her many diatribes against President Roosevelt. Republican Senator Everett Dirksen protested these references, saying, "Why beat on an old bag of bones?"

Quick with a quip, Democratic Senator Hubert Humphrey stood up with a smile. "I must rise to the defense of the lady."

An embarrassed Dirksen rose to explain that the "old bones" referred to the old references, not to the lady.

In the end, the Senate voted 79–11 to confirm Clare.

But she was now becoming unhappy at the prospect before her. Brazil was attempting to industrialize, but agriculturally it was still a one-crop country, which was crucifying the Brazilians economically. The Eisenhower-Dulles plan was to send Clare Luce down with the message that Brazil wasn't going to get any more American money. "I knew my mission was going to be a hideous failure, sheer disaster," said Clare. "It was the worst can of worms that could have been handed to anyone."

Failure was something Clare never wanted to face. She told her husband, "You got me into this, now help me get out of it."

Luce issued a statement saying that he had asked his wife to resign the appointment because the attacks on her had been too bitter and because they had been aimed at him. For Clare the resignation was a bitter pill—the first time she had ever really quit without fighting.

Clare accepted an offer from *McCall's* magazine for a monthly column and decided to spend more time in Ridgefield, Connecticut. She also spent a great deal of time with her dearest friend Buffy Cobb, who was dying. Buffy's final days were filled with intense suffering, and Clare was there with her at all hours of the day and night. Those who long ago had classified Clare as cold would have marveled at the compassionate woman at her dying friend's bedside in the hospital. Clare could not afford to lose a friend; she had too few.

HARRY's time with Jean Campbell was gloriously happy for him. He laughed more with her, drank more with her, and made love more with her. He also shared poetry with her.

Few at Time Inc. would have recognized this man they thought they knew so well. None of the other women in his life would have believed it. The caterpillar had become a butterfly.

Luce was with Jean almost every night when he was in New York— if Clare was in Phoenix or Ridgefield. Music had long been part of his life, but with Jean it was books and poetry. When they were not making love, they were reading aloud to each other.

Yet Harry was still very much in Clare's grasp. When he was with her, he quietly settled into a routine of walks, bridge, golf, and a small circuit of social dinners.

In the offices of Time Inc., though, Harry was a commanding, assured presence. This was a world he could still control.

By 1960 the total assets of Time Inc. were $230,585,000, and Luce decided it was time for a "reorganization of expectations." His heart attack, still stark in his mind, prompted him to focus on a successor. He picked forty-five-year-old Hedley Donovan, a handsome, serious man with a decisive mind and quick smile, who as managing editor of *Fortune* for six years had transformed it into the magazine Luce always wanted. During one of their many one-on-one dinners in Luce's apartment, Harry asked Donovan if he would be interested "in a few years or so" in having the job of editor in chief of *Time*.

Donovan said he would not be interested in it unless Luce understood how he felt about certain past unfairnesses in *Time*. "I felt *Time* had been quite unfair in several instances to Harry Truman," said Donovan. "[Luce] agreed that this was so. I also felt *Time* had been somewhat unfair in the first Eisenhower-Stevenson campaign." Harry agreed the magazine had been rough on Stevenson, but felt it important that the Democrats not become the permanent governing party.

When Hedley came home, his wife asked, "Did you get fired?"

"No, he wants me to be *him*," said Donovan.

A friend who heard the news later said, "It must be like being elected Moses."

In 1960 Time Inc. had a new home in Rockefeller Center. The new forty-seven-story Time-Life Building had a spectacular view of New York City, the river, and the gardens. Presiding over the new headquarters was a new chairman of the board, Andrew Heiskell, the former publisher of *Life*.

In the new hierarchy James Linen became president of Time Inc. Linen was the grandson of an old family friend; Luce had regarded Linen's family almost as warmly as his own. Roy Larsen, formerly Time Inc. president, became chairman of the board of directors executive committee. C. D. Jackson, a *Time* vice president, was made publisher of *Life*.

Having settled the top management of Time Inc., Luce again turned himself to national affairs. It was the year John F. Kennedy was running for President.

Harry had a complicated concern about the campaign. Part of it was expressed in his reply to his friend Bill Benton, who had asked why he had written an introduction to young John Kennedy's first book, *Why England Slept*, in 1940. Luce simply snapped, "Joe."

Joseph Kennedy, then ambassador to the Court of St. James's, had called Luce from London asking him to write a foreword for his son's book. Luce read the manuscript, liked it, and agreed to do it. He did not remember meeting the young Kennedy before publication.

On another occasion Luce had yielded to the senior Kennedy's persuasive power. In 1956, when JFK had made a run for the Democratic vice-presidential nomination, the Luces were Joe Kennedy's guests on the French Riviera. Luce cabled his editors that they might well devote more space to John Kennedy because he had emerged as a considerable national figure.

The political problem for the Luces was not only the father but the son. As they got to know Jack they both liked him. Clare liked him very much indeed. The result was that she sat quietly on the sidelines during the election and did not allow the Republicans to use her against Jack. Nor did she give him any strong voice of support.

Harry still had mixed feelings about Kennedy. When JFK won the Oregon primary, *Time* correspondent Stanley Karnow recalled Luce's saying, "Well, it looks like we'll have to stop Jack." However, when Kennedy became the front-runner for the Democratic presidential nomination, *Time* did its first cover story for him, which even the highly critical Joe Kennedy considered "a great job."

Joe Kennedy and Harry watched the Democratic National Convention together on TV from Luce's Waldorf apartment, in New York. Luce was not overly impressed with Kennedy's acceptance speech, but did not puncture his guest's glory.

"I want to thank you for all that you've done for Jack," declared Joe Kennedy effusively as he said good-bye to his host.

Time soon did much more. Managing editor Otto Fuerbringer became ill and was replaced for the duration of the campaign by Tom Griffith. The more liberal Griffith quickly announced a policy of absolute fairness, saying the best that could be said of each candidate each week "and the worst." A disgruntled Republican leader was quoted: "This is a heck of a year for *Time* to turn objective!"

During the campaign, Luce gave a dinner at the Waldorf for Vice President Nixon and invited eight of the top Time Inc. editors. Recalled Otto Fuerbringer: "Nixon was his usual stilted self, and he talked in his almost speechlike manner. At one point he said, 'If I weren't a Quaker, I think I'd rather be a Presbyterian more than anything else because it's so easy.'" There followed a terrible moment—absolute silence. "Finally, Luce let it pass."

"I just don't like Nixon. I guess we have to support him, but I don't like him," Luce said. "I don't agree with Kennedy on most things. But I like him." Later Luce expanded on that: "Dammit, why am I so attracted to Jack Kennedy?" He concluded, "He seduces me!"

Yet Hedley Donovan insists that Luce was never seriously tempted by the notion of endorsing Kennedy. The decision was made by a small group that Luce called the College of Cardinals, "leaving it clear who was pope," noted Donovan. They included the editorial director, the managing editors, and John Jessup, the chief editorial writer of *Life*. They were all for Nixon, whom they felt had the edge of experience. Tom Griffith argued for Kennedy, but the *Life* editorial finally came out for Nixon, saying that he had "done more for the nation and the world."

Luce himself privately anticipated a Nixon defeat, but saw a Democratic victory as something journalistically exciting, something that would shake up the country. Moreover, a Democratic President might even sock the idle rich with a tough program of tax reform, which he thought Eisenhower should have done.

After Kennedy's victory Bill Benton reminded the President-elect that Luce treated him very well in his magazines during the campaign and that this may have accounted for the one tenth of one percent that was his margin of victory. Kennedy agreed.

"I like Luce," Kennedy once said. "He reminds me of my father. He's entitled to have his magazine say what he wants because he made it. He's like a cricket chirping away. After all, he made a lot of money through his own individual enterprise, so he naturally thinks that individual enterprise can do anything. I don't mind people like that. They have earned the right to talk that way."

At the inaugural ball the Luces were guests of the Kennedys. On the bus to the gala Lyndon Johnson sat next to Clare. She could not pass up the chance to ask him about something he had told her shortly before the Democratic National Convention, where it seemed certain that he would be the presidential nominee. Clare had asked him then, "Lyndon, what are you going to do if you don't get it? Will you agree to go on Kennedy's ticket?"

"Well, you should have heard him," Clare said later. "He said, 'Clare honey, no *way* will I ever join that sonofabitch.'

"So now here I am on the bus, and here is the vice president and I said, 'Lyndon, come clean.' And he said, 'Clare honey, Bird's been

As one of the most powerful women in Republican politics, Clare gave advice to President Dwight D. Eisenhower, above, and in 1953 served as his ambassador to Italy, left. She was a constant source of curiosity there. Below, President John F. Kennedy paid the Luces special attention at his inaugural.

wanting me something fierce to slow down, and my health ain't been good lately, and, well, I thought this job might suit me a spell.'

"I leaned forward and repeated, 'Come clean, Lyndon.'

"And he leaned close and said, 'Clare, I looked it up; one out of every four presidents has died in office. I'm a gamblin' man, darlin', and this is the only chance I got.' "

11

WITH an exciting young President the world was at a crossroads, and so was Lady Jean Campbell. She loved Harry more than anyone, and always would. But Jean increasingly felt herself living at the end of a long string. Harry could only see her when Clare was away. Jean now wanted predictability. She wanted Harry always. She wanted a home. She wanted children.

She decided to confront Harry to insist that he divorce Clare and marry her.

"His reaction was that I should give him time," said Jean. "He said he had to talk to his lawyers. And that's when he told me about Clare being a manic-depressive and suicidal. He feared what she would do if he again raised the issue of divorce."

During this period, Clare felt that life with Harry was pleasant but dull. He seemed more distant and was less frequently in residence. His power no longer spelled anything important in her future, because politics was dead for her. Perhaps this was now the time to leave him.

Harry had agreed months before to let her build an idyllic house in Hawaii. With that house and all the money she could ever spend, she could explore her writing talent, enjoy her many friends, travel the world. She could also pick and choose among the many men still willing to court her—and do it without fear of publicity.

She confided all this to Shirley Clurman, who had become a kind of substitute daughter. An attractive, bright young woman, Shirley handled Time Inc. promotion and publicity. Talking about Harry with Shirley, Clare remarked sadly, without bitterness, "We never see each other. You know, when I'm here, he's away; and when I'm away, he's here. There's really no sense going on."

Harry carefully made his move. As his personal adviser he chose

Roswell Gilpatric, a young lawyer with the firm Cravath, Swaine, and Moore. Gilpatric had a reputation for brains and great sophistication, and had been one of Kennedy's ardent supporters. Later he would serve in his administration as assistant secretary of defense.

When Harry initially approached Clare for a divorce, things went smoothly. She got a tough divorce lawyer. Luce's attorney intimated that there really wasn't any dispute about money. Clare was to get some $200,000 a year plus the new Hawaiian house and the house in Ridgefield.

Of course, when she read an item in a New York gossip column that suggested an impending Luce divorce and mentioned Lady Jean Campbell, Clare was enraged.

"I got a telephone call in the office," said Shirley Clurman. "Clare screamed at me, 'How could you not tell me? I thought you were my friend. All you care about is your loyalty to Harry!' I was so shocked. I hadn't even seen the story yet! I told her, 'I swear to you. I knew absolutely nothing.' Then Harry called up. If any press calls come through, he told me, I was to issue a denial. And that was that."

Harry's sister Beth Moore told Jean she thought it would be wiser if she went back to Scotland for a while until everything calmed down. So Jean returned to Scotland. She then went to London to stay with her grandfather. "It was a very difficult time," Jean said sadly. Luce wrote to her every day, sometimes twice a day. "And he telephoned every night," she recalled. "And he'd talk for an hour or two."

Then on June 4, 1960, Jean received a letter from Harry that in essence said good-bye forever.

Clare had written him a long letter on May 16, 1960. She was trying to put him more at ease with his decision to break with Jean. Clare noted that Jean had prepared herself psychologically for the end of the affair when she insisted on a marriage she knew could not happen. It could not happen, because, as Jean knew, Clare had refused to agree to a divorce. Clare pointed out the frustrating problem of any affair between an unmarried woman and a married man. This, of course, was something about which Clare knew much. She made a great point in saying that Jean was young and that the young always adjust and survive. The most important thing of all, Clare asserted, was that now they could both wipe the affair out of their minds and concentrate on the survival of their own marriage. What was extraordinary about the letter was how objective Clare appeared, as if she were watching the whole scene from a distance.

The reason Luce was so harsh to a woman whom he called the love of his life was Clare. She had made a serious suicide attempt in Phoenix by taking an overdose of pills. Luce could not bear the thought that he was the cause of a possible loss of life.

Harry was overwrought. He had so few people he could turn to. One evening he even visited his former wife, Lila, who was staying at her mother's apartment, on Park Avenue, and talked with her.

Harry could not let Jean go. He was desperately trying to restructure his life, to combine reality with fantasy. Completely ignoring the good-bye letter he had written earlier, he met Jean in England and asked her to buy a house in Jamaica for the two of them. If he couldn't divorce Clare, why not let Clare stay in Hawaii while he once again commuted on their six months' plan?

Back in New York, he urged his lawyers to get busy again about the divorce. He told them to check into getting a "fugitive divorce" in Tijuana or the Dominican Republic. He said he didn't care whether Clare attacked the decree.

Clare seemed to be seesawing in the divorce discussions, as if she herself was no longer certain what she wanted. Jean's impatience with matters increased, and she and Harry had some stormy scenes. "I was getting fed up. We had been together four years. It was very hard to listen to someone saying how much he loved you and still be in the same situation," she remembered.

And then the world crashed in on them. Leonard Lyons, in his national column, "The Lyons Den," printed the item that Luce would marry Lady Jean Campbell.

Now it was a national story, with headlines everywhere. When the columnist Cholly Knickerbocker, who had been the one to first print the rumor months before, reached Luce on the phone at his Ridgefield home, Harry would only say, "Clare and I are here together. It is all very premature to say the least." The key word was "premature."

Clare, too, denied any separation rumors. She had been hospitalized in Phoenix with pneumonia when the news broke, and said, "So help me heaven, there's nothing to it." Privately she was more venomous. "Clare again let it be known that she would not go quietly. She would raise a national scandal," said George Harris, a *Life* editor. She reportedly told Harry, "I will sue you in every court in America. I'm not going to have this little British trollop make a fool of me."

As the scandal worsened, attorney Gilpatric struggled to come up with a solution. But Clare was hitting where she knew it would hurt Harry most. "She wanted control of Time Inc.—*active* control," said Gilpatric. "She wanted a say in the editorial policy, too."

Clare had asked for the impossible. The trigger was the national publicity on the story. If there had been no publicity, the divorce might still have happened quietly. But the publicity was a hard slap in the face, and nobody did that to Clare Boothe Luce.

Why didn't Harry proceed with an alternative divorce someplace? For the same reason he didn't do it when he wanted to marry Dalrymple. The surrender of editorial control of Time Inc. was unthinkable. National scandal was degrading. His love for Jean was overwhelming, but Time Inc. was his whole life. In the final analysis he chose propriety over love.

Harry was so distraught that he failed to call Jean one day. Sensing the affair was over, she accepted an invitation to a party at Gore Vidal's house. There she met author Norman Mailer.

"I threw myself at Norman," she later admitted. "It was a very wrong thing to do. I was on the rebound. I did it for survival."

Campbell and Mailer soon married in a quiet ceremony, and produced a daughter. But the marriage would be short and fiery, and Harry was always in her mind. "I loved him as he was," she said.

FOR their twenty-fifth wedding anniversary Harry bought Clare a silver gilt cactus plant from Tiffany. In many ways it was symbolic of their marriage. The cactus is a prickly plant that survives with minimal nourishment. Some cacti even have succulent fruit and a lovely flower. Once, Harry might have likened Clare to that species of cactus. But now the lovely flower was fading, the fruit no longer sweet. Only the prickly needles remained.

Whatever Harry intended with the gift, he was miserable. He and Clare were tied together by circumstance, pretension, and power. Their lost loves were sharp aches, and their future resembled a cold fog. Harry again retreated to his inner self.

Clare would live all her life filled with guilt about her daughter, but she felt no such guilt about holding Harry from his true love. For one thing, she knew he had a certain salvation in his work. Time Inc. gave him a peace with himself, a wider horizon, a soul healing.

Clare had no such form of therapy. Whenever she was bored, she sought a new home. This time she persuaded Harry to sell their triplex apartment and move to a smaller but still elegant apartment on Fifth Avenue, near Seventy-fourth Street, facing Central Park.

For at least half the year they lived in Phoenix. Though they had been competing with each other all their lives, there now seemed nothing more to compete about. There were no more grand prizes. Clare and Harry had reached a silent accord: they would live their lives together with as little rancor as possible.

Every morning the maid set up a folding table in Clare's bedroom and Luce would trundle in barefoot, in his crimson dressing gown, to join her for breakfast. She would talk and he would read his paper. Their pet cockatoo would sing "Stars and Stripes Forever."

They regularly watched *Perry Mason* on TV, each trying to guess who committed the crime. They both read voraciously. And every night he would read to her, "sometimes detective stories, sometimes more serious stuff," she told friends. "There's nothing I enjoyed more, and he never got tired of it." While Harry read, Clare made Christmas tree ornaments. She bought synthetic foam balls in all sizes and decorated them with jewels and velvet. Harry called them "imperial baubles," even though Clare sold them for charity.

They discussed anything and everything, including whether or not Mao Tse-tung was America's greatest ally because he was the prime force in preventing the Soviet takeover of Asia. "We both had strong views," said Clare. "Usually we'd agree. Rarely we'd disagree. Then we might argue the question intellectually for days."

Clare liked Harry's response when she broke in on him. "For God's sake, dear, will you stop talking when I'm interrupting."

She once complained to him, "You have time for everything but me."

Very seriously he quietly replied, "Do you realize that I have given you more time and thought and concern than all the other people of my life put together?"

Another time Clare said to her husband, "Harry, you're married to an old woman."

It was one of the few times Harry was ever graceful. He said, "Yes, but such a beautiful old woman."

Throughout this period Harry exhibited a more subdued, conservative presence at Time Inc. There was a collective feeling that Harry suddenly seemed closer to all those boring people who would have bored him in earlier years. He now seemed to want the respectability that came with awards and titles and positions. His editors felt he didn't really know how powerful he had become and didn't realize that most people needed him more than he needed them.

The proof of his power was always in evidence when Luce was called upon to speak at a Senate committee hearing. Testifying against communism, he said he did not consider peaceful coexistence possible with Russia and Red China. The shy young man in his badly shaped Chinese-made suit who had stammered when he waited on tables was also the honored guest at the forty-fifth reunion of his class at Hotchkiss. He now had a pretax income of $1 million and occasionally lunched with the President of the United States.

Few Presidents took *Time* as seriously as JFK. He got early copies of *Time* and *Life* hand-delivered to his office a day ahead of publication. They were airlifted from the Chicago printer to the White House. When someone borrowed his copy, he was furious. Luce once complained that Kennedy saw a copy of *Time* before he did. JFK's interest in it was almost fanatic. *Time* went to press by Saturday afternoon; if Kennedy was making an important speech on a Monday, he'd make sure *Time* saw an advance copy of the speech to get it into that issue.

JFK was so obsessed with *Time* that he even enlisted the help of an old friend of Clare's, Letitia Baldrige, who worked as a White House aide. Tish, as everybody called her, phoned Clare to say the President was unhappy with some of the things written about his family in *Time* and wanted to see her. It was a time of national tension. The Eisenhower administration had trained an exile force of Cubans for possible use against communist dictator Fidel Castro, and the Kennedy administration further organized this exile brigade to invade Cuba. Rumors of this invasion filled the press.

It seemed unlikely that the President could be concerned at this time with *Time*'s treatment of a family incident. He wasn't. He felt Clare was privy to her husband's views—views that Luce as head of Time Inc. could not express, but that Clare could. Furthermore, he respected the quality of her mind.

Clare agreed to meet Kennedy at the White House. There was no small talk that day. Clare told him one of her favorite phrases, that "a great man is one sentence, with an active verb in it, describing a unique action, and you don't have to know the man's name." She then illustrated her point. "He died on the cross to save us" or "He sought a new way to the old world and discovered a new world."

She wondered aloud what sentences would be written about Kennedy after he left office. "You're talking about Cuba," he replied.

"No, I wasn't, but I can imagine such a sentence. 'He broke the power of the Soviet Union in the Western world' or 'He failed to break the power of the Soviet Union in the Western world.' "

"Well, what you're talking about is my using force in Cuba."

Clare said she didn't think he could resolve the crisis without force.

They walked to the balcony, with its lovely view. "Well," he said, "I'll have to go to work on that last sentence."

The Cuban invasion of April 1961 was a fiasco. It took Castro only three days to crush the rebels and capture them. The President accepted full responsibility. Khrushchev promptly reassessed his strategies and considered Kennedy an easier target.

Shortly after the disastrous invasion Harry Luce lunched with the President. "He came down [in] the elevator and asked me what he should do now," recalled Luce, "and I said, 'Well, in my mind the answer is very simple, namely that a strong application of the Monroe Doctrine should be reapplied, reasserted.' "

Kennedy then asked Luce to undertake a special mission of advice and counsel to the President—the only time Luce was ever asked to do this. The President wanted him to review the question of the admission of communist China into the United Nations. Ten days later Luce returned his verdict: "No."

Kennedy's overture to Luce didn't deter the preparation of an article in *Fortune* blaming Kennedy for the Bay of Pigs defeat in Cuba because he had refused to provide critical air power.

THE women in his life saw Harry more clearly than anyone. Jean Dalrymple sensed a change of mood. Mary Bancroft, who saw Luce whenever he came to New York, felt an inner struggle.

Harry was almost sixty-five, and he was depressed. He seemed to be spending an inordinate amount of time reading his Bible, even before cocktails, as if he were somehow trying to find answers there.

Harry talked to Mary much more about death. With Jean Campbell out of his life it was as if his last hope of real living was also gone. Mary emphasized all the awesome power he held and how much good he could do with it.

In October 1962 Luce finally understood his power when Kennedy summoned him to discuss a crisis that could have meant the end of the world.

Kennedy asked Luce and Fuerbringer, then *Time*'s managing editor, to the White House for a conference. Kennedy's practice was to probe the best brains in the nation for their judgments on crucial situations before making his own decisions. Luce recalled how tired the President looked, how deep was his emotion. Harry expressed his thanks for being consulted, and Kennedy said with a smile, "Well, you've been very interested in Cuba for a long time." Harry replied, "Not just Cuba, the global situation."

The Russians had put nuclear missiles in Cuba, within easy range of the southern United States. Kennedy was concerned that the Russians might take advantage of the missile crisis to overrun Berlin. He feared a nuclear war. He kept asking Luce, "Are you for or against invasion?"

Luce said he was not for an immediate invasion, but he did endorse a naval blockade, searching incoming Soviet ships for more missiles.

"Then we went over to the Pentagon and were shown this extraordinary display of reconnaissance photographs," Luce recalled. Some of these photographs were made exclusively available to Time Inc.

Time Inc. supported the President in his final showdown until the Russians took out their missiles and the crisis was over.

IF THIS were not enough to convince Luce of his power, the fortieth anniversary of *Time*, in the spring of 1963, did the trick. This was a jolt of jubilation for him at a time when he needed it most.

"People don't celebrate anniversaries except the twenty-fifth or fiftieth—why the fortieth, Harry?" Clare asked him.

"Because I won't be here for the fiftieth."

So for the event he invited 650 people who had been on the covers of *Time*. Almost half of them accepted.

Luce extended a personal invitation to President Kennedy, but the President hedged. When he eventually sent regrets, Vice President

Lyndon Johnson came as a substitute. It was an evening of glitter and elegance, a champagne reception in the Waldorf-Astoria ballroom for everybody to meet Luce and his editors. Among the 284 cover subjects who had accepted was a range of celebrities from baseball manager Casey Stengel to General Douglas MacArthur. A succession of toastmasters included Bob Hope. "This is what the UN would look like if it had Mr. Luce's circulation," quipped Hope.

Kennedy sent a message praising Luce as "one of the creative editors of our age." He said of *Time* that it "had instructed, entertained, confused, and infuriated its readers for nearly half a century. I do not always agree with *Time*, but I nearly always read it."

In his reply that night, Luce said, "I hope that *Time*'s number one subscriber will always be the President of the United States."

One of the most poignant moments of the evening was when Luce introduced his wife, who was decked with emeralds and diamonds. Clare, he said, was "one who has never been on the cover of *Time* for a very poor reason—she married the editor in chief."

This was Luce's night, and it was a celebration of success. "Never in our experience have so many titans and titanesses of industry, sports, music, theater, philanthropy, politics, publishing, finance, science, medicine, government, advertising, and religion taken spotlighted bows in one place," said a writer for *The New Yorker*.

Luce had a new hearing aid and may have missed many of the anniversary speeches that night. But his pleasure was evident. After all the sorrows of recent years he basked in a moment of pure glory.

At five o'clock in the morning Hubert Humphrey was still dancing with Gina Lollabrigida. It was the party Luce had yearned for.

THE glow was short lived. Soon Luce—and the nation—were embroiled in another controversy. The voice of *Time* was not speaking softly on the emerging war in Vietnam.

With Chiang's China overrun by communism, the Luces were loud and fearful that it must not happen in Southeast Asia. Luce told his editorial voice, Jack Jessup, "Some liberals who would not want to see Europe overcome by communism may actually think communism is a good thing for China—and perhaps for the rest of Asia. The same liberals who want to be color-blinded in the U.S. seem to be quite color-conscious when it comes to world affairs."

Clare and Harry both felt that the inevitable outcome of Vietnam would be a negotiated peace and that the area then would be controlled by Chinese Communists. Hedley Donovan felt that Luce was more open-minded and less militant about Vietnam than people thought he was.

Controversy at *Time* over coverage of the growing war suddenly stilled with the news that an assassin had shot and killed the President.

At Time Inc. on November 23, 1963, there was chaos. Harry Luce was too busy to grieve, and Clare Luce grieved too much to be busy. The next issue of *Life* had already closed, and 300,000 copies were in railroad cars at printing plants in Chicago. A crew flew out to Chicago to do new layouts and replace the cover. With the slaying of Oswald the issue had to be changed again.

The new President was now that "gamblin' man," Lyndon Baines Johnson. LBJ started touching important bases and quickly called Luce in Phoenix. As Luce's son Hank remembered, "He just wanted to say hello and tell Henry Robinson Luce he was President." During the call, Clare whispered, "Tell Lyndon hello for me." Johnson replied, "She's the sweetest little woman I ever served with in Congress."

Clare and Harry had the highest regard for the power and presence of Lyndon Johnson. Clare remembered his force in Congress, his skill at manipulation, and the impact of his poor childhood, with which she empathized. This was a man of strength and determination.

Eliot Janeway, a consultant, who had introduced Clare to Johnson when she first came to Congress, said afterward, "I'm sure she had an affair with him, although I wasn't there."

It is surely not inconceivable. Johnson was a raunchy man, with the reputation for reaching quickly for any pretty woman. And Clare was often sexually attracted to a man of power. The awesome power of the leader of the Senate might have been irresistible.

But now Johnson was President, and Harry was the one impressed by Johnson's power. "Harry never lost his sense of awe of the presidency," said Clare, "be it FDR, Ike, or LBJ."

Like Kennedy, Johnson was an avid reader of *Time*. When he had been Senate majority leader, he would set aside Thursday night for *Time* magazine. "At six o'clock every Thursday he'd call me up," said Hugh Sidey, *Time*'s Washington correspondent. "He knew my dead-

Above, President Lyndon B. Johnson demanded advance copies of Time *each week and often conferred with its editor in chief (left). Theatrical agent Jean Dalrymple, right, was the first woman to nearly break up the Luce marriage. Below, Lady Jean Campbell became the love of Harry's life.*

lines and he'd brief me. He'd say he'd rather have one story in *Time* magazine or *The New York Times* than three or four everywhere else."

At this time of recognition, Harry was preparing formally to step down into a valley of greater personal peace. He would no longer be "Owner/Editor, Big Boy of the Works," as he once put it. The time had come for Luce to leave his magazines—and the world—alone and to turn inward, to his own soul and his own private life.

WHEN Luce turned sixty-six, he decided the time had come to pass the scepter to forty-nine-year-old Hedley Donovan. Observing this extraordinary change of command, Teddy White issued a ripe remark: "When the tree begins to fall, for the first time you see how tall it is. Harry's the biggest timber in American journalism."

Observers quickly pointed out that Luce was not stepping down, but sideways. "I will contribute, criticize, and suggest, but my advice does not have to be taken," he said. Still, the succession had begun.

In officially taking over, in April 1964, Hedley Donovan told the assembled Time Inc. staff, "We do not claim to be neutral; we do claim to be fair." Then came his declaration of independence: "The vote of Time Inc. should never be considered in the pocket of any particular political leader or party. It is an independent vote."

The 1964 presidential campaign was soon under way. Senator Barry Goldwater was a Phoenix neighbor of the Luces and an occasional bridge partner. As Clare got to know him, she decided that he best represented her own views on the extreme right. He asked Clare to make a seconding speech for him at the convention, and she agreed. Luce edited the speech but otherwise stayed politically aloof.

In her speech Clare called Goldwater "a prophet of a free and fearless America." Her stepson Hank sent her a telegram congratulating her on her eloquence, even though he disagreed with her choice of candidate. At sixty-one, her hair now white-gold, Clare looked deceptively fragile until she started speaking. Her name was mentioned as a possible vice-presidential running mate for Goldwater, but most political observers regarded Clare's prospects as dim.

As the election neared, the Time Inc. magazines were not by any stretch in the Goldwater camp. "How can we expect to win when even your magazines say such things about Senator Goldwater?" one of the Senator's aides asked Clare. Her reply: "Well, in the first place, they're not my magazines." She knew Harry didn't like Goldwater.

Life magazine finally endorsed Lyndon Johnson. Commenting on it, Clare said, "I don't disagree with them. They disagree with me." Luce avoided the political flak of the *Life* endorsement by going to the Far East and staying away for five weeks.

After Johnson won the election, Luce visited him often in the White House. He was particularly pleased with LBJ's inaugural speech, on the Great Society, which Luce called "the best speech of the decade."

He had been similarly pleased when Johnson got his civil rights bill passed. "Well, thank God, *that* problem is solved," said Luce. "Now we can go on to something else."

MOST of the other men in Clare's life were now gone, notably Bernard Baruch. He died in June 1965 at the age of ninety-four. For his birthday Clare had sent him a telegram with the word love repeated ninety-four times. Shortly before his death he had phoned to say how ecstatic he had been over their recent evening together, that she looked more beautiful than ever and reminded him of when she was a very young girl. Clare had replied that she could not imagine her world without him. He had been one of the rocks of strength in her life. In the last years he had complained of some neglect from her, but never for long. His death was a hole in her heart.

As for Harry, he still mourned the emotional loss of Jean Campbell.

SOME months after turning the top editorial job over to Donovan, Luce was asked by an associate how he liked retirement. Luce's reply was curt: "It ain't good."

But he refused to let retirement slow him down. He still dropped in at *Time* bureaus, still made speeches all over the country on his favorite subjects of American morality, justice, the responsibility of journalism, and the future of the Far East. He still wrote most of his own speeches. He involved himself in an international convocation of statesmen and scholars to discuss world peace, and even spent time at Yale in seminars with students, defending or explaining *Time*.

Harry had not changed much physically. His red-gray brows were as imposing as always. There was perhaps more gray in his thinning hair, more of a stoop in his shoulders.

Luce seemed more aware now of people's feelings. Family relationships, however, would never be easy for him. He saw his brother, Sheldon, several times a year, and they played golf. He also enjoyed being with his grandchildren, nieces, and nephews. With smaller children Harry was at his best, his most relaxed, his warmest.

With his sons the relationship was more strained. Perhaps he expected too much from them. His younger son, Peter Paul, was a very outgoing young man—tall and good-looking. He attended M.I.T. for three years and then worked at Grumann Aircraft for a while. He wanted nothing to do with Time Inc.

Harry was amused and baffled by Peter, who eventually went to live in Denver with his wife. There they raised four daughters, and Peter worked as a consultant.

Henry, or Hank, as everybody but his father called him, had joined the London bureau of *Time*. Luce had a father's pride whenever Hank did well in any of his Time Inc. jobs; earlier Luce had put Hank in charge of the construction of the new Time-Life Building. But in London, Hank wanted to learn and do on his own.

CLARE was still planning her million-dollar home in Hawaii, and spent much of her time at a rented house nearby. She wrote Harry that she found life without him like being in an Italian palazzo in the winter without heat. Very simply, she needed him at her side.

When Harry did go to Hawaii, he felt very isolated there. He would pad around barefoot, in shorts, looking ill at ease. Clare spent her time in a billowing muumuu, painting at an easel beside the swimming pool. An interviewer suggested he couldn't imagine her "undertaking anything at which you expected to be a failure."

"I'm already better than Churchill was," Clare said.

Meantime, Luce tried to continually broaden his experience. He eagerly accepted an invitation to speak to students at Yale, even though the overture came from John Hersey. After they had had a break, in 1945, the two lost contact. But Hersey was now master of Pierson College, at Yale, and wrote Luce a friendly letter saying he wanted to see him again.

When Luce arrived, said Hersey, eighteen students came to meet him. Luce recommended to them the experience of being a cub reporter "whether or not you're going to be a poet or a banker. Being a cub reporter," he said, "enables you to see life in the raw."

Joseph P. Kennedy (far right) entertained the Luces at his villa on the Riviera. Below, Clare always kept in touch with her old friend Bernard Baruch.

Below, near the end of their lives, the Luces reached an accord with one another.

Luce felt too many of the students had lost their faith in God and country. Some, afterward, admitted being impressed by his dynamism and his candidness, even though they could not share his faith.

Said Hersey, "These sixties kids were a little bit hostile in the way they dealt with him. After they'd left, he had a scotch, and said, 'Oh, John, I've been experimenting with LSD, and it's the most wonderful thing! You look at that glass on the table, and see shimmering colors on either side of it.' This was at a time when LSD was ruining lives at Yale," added Hersey. "I thanked my stars that he didn't say that when the kids were there!"

Harry was not so reticent at the Hunt Ball, a traditional formal annual dinner for the staff of *Life* held at the Waldorf. In a brief speech Luce told about how he and Clare had experimented, under controlled conditions, with LSD.

"I remember there was absolute silence," recalled Time chairman Andrew Heiskell. "Not a person could think of a proper response to this declaration! I guess [Harry] had to prove that at past sixty-five, he was still young, still one of the boys."

Luce's public admission about LSD did not affect his status as journalism's elder statesman. Yale gave Luce an honorary doctorate of law and so did Williams College. Syracuse University School of Journalism also gave him its Distinguished Service Medal. *Der Spiegel,* the German magazine, summed up Luce's status by saying, "Luce printed products are the intellectual supplement of Coca-Cola, Marilyn Monroe, and dollar diplomacy."

Pleased with his grand stature, Luce was nevertheless plagued by the advanced age that went with it.

Perhaps sensing his mortality, he once again wanted to see Jean Campbell. He missed her deeply. He asked Jean Dalrymple to try to find her. "I was in Washington, when she called and gave me Harry's message," said Campbell. "I got back to New York and was so excited. And then she called again, and said, 'No, he just can't do it.' " Harry simply could not summon the courage for an emotional confrontation.

It was far easier for him to do Clare's bidding and not risk any unwanted inner turmoil. So when the Commonwealth Club in San Francisco asked Clare to speak about the United Nations, Harry went with her and even helped write the speech.

That Saturday, after their return to Phoenix, Harry played nine holes of golf, had drinks and lunch with friends, and joined a dinner party at the Arizona Biltmore.

On Sunday morning Luce was uncharacteristically still in bed when the cook brought him his breakfast. He couldn't eat it, and later he vomited. Too restless to stay in bed, he wandered over to Clare's studio to watch her paint. She took his temperature, which was 102 degrees. Clare called a doctor. By the time he arrived, Harry had a nosebleed and was coughing up blood. His blood pressure and pulse were both normal, and the doctor decided to let him rest. Harry stayed with Clare in her room, tried eating some soup and again vomited. The doctor ordered a nurse to stay with Luce. The next morning Harry again vomited, and the doctor ordered an ambulance.

When he was settled in at St. Joseph's Hospital, he admitted to the doctor, "I seem to be unusually sleepy." For the rest of the day he underwent medical tests. Luce persuaded Clare to keep a dinner date. "Should I come over afterwards?" she asked. He said no.

That night he slept poorly, and kept getting out of bed and pacing the floor, despite the nurse's protests. About three a.m. he went to the bathroom, and the nurse heard him yell, "Oh, Jesus!" Hearing him fall, she rushed to find Luce on the floor, already unconscious from a coronary occlusion. A hospital emergency team applied shock treatment and heart massage. The mother superior of the hospital told Clare to hurry over. But by the time she arrived, Harry was dead, five weeks short of his sixty-ninth birthday. The date was February 28, 1967. On this day, exactly forty-four years before, the first printed copy of *Time* had been delivered to his door.

THE memorial service for Luce, at the Madison Avenue Presbyterian Church on March 3, 1967, was packed with some 800 prominent people. A private hookup transmitted the service to the auditorium and reception lounge of the Time-Life Building for some 1200 employees, who sang the hymns in unison with those in church.

Luce had wanted to be buried at Mepkin. He had loved the peace of their South Carolina estate, and went back there even after Clare had sold it to the Trappist monks. He would be buried near his stepdaughter, Ann, whom he truly loved. Those close to Luce knew of another fitting reason for his being buried in South Carolina: it was on a moonlit night at Camp Jackson that young Luce and Briton

Hadden had made their final decision about starting *Time* magazine.

Harry's grave, marked by a simple four-foot marble stone carved with the abstract motif of an old live-oak tree, was on a hilltop. The Mepkin monks would care for the gravesite.

THE company Luce started with a loan of $86,000 in 1923 now had a market value of $690 million. His personal holdings in Time stock totaled 1,012,575 shares, worth about $109 million. Most of it was set aside for the Henry Luce Foundation, created in honor of his father, to promote Christian education and intellectual exchange between the United States and Far Eastern countries. The foundation became the largest single stockholder in Time Inc., and Henry Luce III was made president. Clare received various properties plus stock shares worth $19 million. She was not included on the board of the foundation. Even in his death Harry would not leave her any editorial control over Time Inc.

All his life Luce had been an outsider craving to become an insider. Perhaps being an outsider gave him a special unclouded vision. It enabled him to bring to *Time* a simplicity and idealism that attracted the general public. His magazines, especially *Life,* gave people the image of an America they *wished* they knew.

The sorrow of Luce's life was that he never got what he truly wanted—the lifetime love and laughter of a tender woman. For that he deserved compassion. He remained a man of frustrated hopes, banked fires, and deep passions. Yet his soul was always his own, and he was never truly defeated. He had discovered the great gift of life: to wake in the morning filled with the excitement of what he would do that day. It is a gift given to few. It was a gift he had earned.

12

NOBODY saw Clare cry when Harry died. There was grief, but no tears. Those who knew her well wondered if the grief was for Harry or for herself. She was alone now, with all the houses and money she would ever need. But she was sixty-four years old, and she felt empty and confused.

Clare had lost her throne, but not her royalty. She was still on the lists as one of the most important, most admired, best-dressed women in the world. She still received invitations, requests for articles, and solicitations for political support. Her name on a committee board was considered a coup, her presence at a party regarded as a special event.

Clare soon started to sort out her life. She gradually felt a sense of freedom and space. She hurried to complete her house in Hawaii, which sat on a beautiful beach, with sweeping views of the sea, and settled easily into its soft, slow pace. The oils she painted hung from her walls and so did her colorful mosaics. The sofas were covered with her needlepoint pillows. Scattered throughout the house were tiny Chinese vases, each holding a single orchid.

When guests arrived at the house, which was called Halenai'a—the House of the Golden Dolphin—she kissed them on both cheeks and draped them with leis of ginger, tuberoses, and pikake blossoms. Her guests understood that she worked in the morning, dictating in bed to her two secretaries. She swam in the afternoon and talked in the evening. Punctuality was almost religious—lunch at twelve, supper at seven. Promptly. "My cook gets noivous," she explained with a staged Brooklyn accent.

Clare was the queen of Honolulu, the focal point for every visiting celebrity. She had a rapid succession of big dinner parties. Everybody loved her, wanted her. And she kept her sense of humor.

When *Harper's* magazine headlined an article CLARE BOOTHE LUCE, FROM COURTESAN TO CAREER WOMAN, Clare commented, "If only it had read, 'Clare Boothe Luce, from Career Woman to Courtesan.' At my age, *that* would have made me sound more interesting."

With time Clare felt more keenly the problems of a single woman. "I would enjoy a good friend and companion I could go to the movies with, sit and yap with, count on as an escort," she said. "But most of the intelligent men who would interest me are married. I do miss very much some one person I can really be close with."

Clare still made her trips abroad, mostly to see friends. Her health was "exceptionally good." Time passed in a smooth, uneventful flow, without many bumps. But once again Clare became restless. Playing the role of a pampered rich woman was not for her. Life's stage was too big, and Clare was an actress in need of a big part.

Politics had always been an integral part of her life, and as the 1968 presidential campaign neared, Clare found a new calling. Positioning herself as "the Conservative," she took a prowar stance on Vietnam, siding with those who espoused the domino theory—that Vietnam's fall would mean the fall of many nearby nations. Vietnam had become to Clare what China had been for Harry.

Feeling that Henry Kissinger would in some measure share her views, she introduced presidential candidate Richard Nixon to him three weeks before the election. The two men had met casually before, but Clare felt they belonged together. "I knew that Henry was not a Nixon man, but I thought they would hit it off. I told Nixon, I think you'll admire Henry. I knew that if Henry spent an hour talking to Nixon, the two men would get along famously."

Several weeks after the election Nixon gave Kissinger the second most powerful job (presidential assistant for National Security Affairs) in foreign policy in the world. Clare once again delighted in her role as political manipulator.

Nixon later appointed Clare to the President's Foreign Intelligence Advisory Board, designed to assess American foreign intelligence efforts. The board consisted of a small group of similarly bright people with inquisitive minds. For Clare the job was a pure treat. She saw it as being in a highly charged environment—just what she loved.

It meant reading and discussing a lot of secret documents that might influence national policy, a task that greatly suited her. She would later say that her life spanned twenty administrations of fifteen Chief Executives, eight of whom she had known personally, and some of them much more intimately. When her latest presidential friend faced impeachment, Clare wrote him a long letter of advice and encouragement. She told Nixon that history would always regard him as a great President—no matter what had happened.

Clare tried to help Nixon. When she learned that her stepson Hank was writing the *Time* editorial urging Nixon to resign, she tried to stop it. But Hank rebuffed her efforts to intercede at *Time*.

Later she wrote a letter to *Time* attacking the magazine "for its editorial over-investment in the destruction of the president." Clare blamed the press for savaging Nixon and applauded him as a gutsy fighter. If Nixon lost, she said, the country would lose.

Harry would probably have disagreed. He had never liked Nixon. But he might have smiled at the fact that the only way Clare could get into *Time* was by writing a letter to the editor.

After Nixon resigned, in 1974, Clare once again retired to her Hawaiian home. Now, almost ten years after Harry's death, the sun seemed dreary, the beach forlorn. Life had lost its tang. Clare's guests became more occasional. Finally Clare sold her Honolulu house and moved back to Washington, where she bought an elegant five-room apartment in the Watergate complex, with views of the Potomac River, Key Bridge, and the spires of Georgetown University.

Clare now described Washington as "a city of human proportions." Here her friends always eagerly awaited her. In 1980 one of her friends, Ronald Reagan, became President of the United States. He reappointed Clare to the reconstituted President's Foreign Intelligence Advisory Board, which had been disbanded by President Carter.

As awards and medals streamed in, including the Distinguished Service Award from Congress and the highest honor bestowed by West Point, one of Clare's admirers called her "a national resource." If she was, she was more often a sad and lonely one. She had proposed marriage to her old friend Stan Swinton, an international editor of The Associated Press. She had known him well in Rome; he had been her bachelor escort before he married. He was a talented, handsome man, with a wonderful mind and an easy manner. But Swinton had no intention of giving up his lovely wife and family. His refusal did not stop Clare from calling up the Swintons to ask if she could join them if they were going to the same party.

When Sandra Day O'Connor was named to the Supreme Court, in 1981, Clare admitted that she was envious. "I would just like to have had that kind of chance," she said. What she really wanted, said a critic, was the life of an actress without going to the trouble of acting.

As Clare approached eighty she grew more and more autocratic. At parties she often talked throughout an entire meal. Shirley Clurman once told her gently, " 'The dinner party I can't stand is when some bore starts talking at the beginning and doesn't stop till the end!' That did it. It sunk in, and she didn't do that again."

In the end, too, Clare dramatized the many men in her life, claiming some affairs that never happened. She invented more and more stories, and was upset when she was caught in a flat lie. "Nothing about Clare looked or sounded right, at that point," said a friend. "She was so frail."

Clare confided to a reporter that if she didn't fill her remaining years with intellectual relationships and work, she would wither away. The reporter then asked whether she still believed in love.

"It has always appeared to me that love makes the world go round, but money greases the axle. Life without love is satisfactory to no one. Love, children, family—I think you simply cannot live without them and remain, or become, a whole person," she reflected.

At Clare's eighty-third birthday party, when asked what a woman should do to be successful, she answered with a straight face, "Get herself elected to Congress, become an ambassador, and marry a rich man—all of this." Then as an aside she added, "It would have been awful if I had fallen in love with a man who had no money."

At another time Clare was asked if she had any regrets. "Yes, I should have been a better person, kinder, more tolerant," she said.

What *did* please Clare was that she had lived to see women's roles change, so that she was no longer "ahead of her time." She had always predicted change, and was delighted when her visions came true.

As she moved through her eighties there were larger intervals of loneliness for Clare and fewer friends to call. "I don't go to beauty parlors anymore," she complained. "My hair's so thin and my nails won't grow." Her voice became tremulous.

Then doctors discovered Clare had a brain tumor. When she realized the end was near, she refused to stay in a hospital. Instead, she orchestrated a series of gatherings to say good-bye to her friends. At one party a guest described her as making "a painful slow entrance, supported by two attendants. We were shocked at her skeletal appearance, made more macabre by a silver wig. Clare held court on a low couch, munching popcorn and drinking Perrier."

The evening was a living wake. Everybody knew they would never again see her alive. But she was going out in style, grace, and dignity.

That evening was her final performance. Clare died a week later, on October 9, 1987. She was eighty-four.

At Mepkin she was laid to rest close to her husband, closer than they had been for most of their lifetime. Nearby was her mother, whom she had loved early, but not late, and her daughter, Ann, whom she had loved too late.

As Clare's gleaming pine coffin was placed in the ground one of the

Mepkin monks said softly, "There is no distance between them now."

Clare's farewell advice to her friends had been, "Do not defend me!" She had also quoted Mencken, saying, "He told me once that he answered all his mail, pleasant and unpleasant, with just one line: 'You may be right.' That's the way I feel now. It is the realm of possibility, just barely, that I could be the one who's wrong."

WHEN Henry Robinson Luce married Clare Boothe, some called it a mating of eagles, and perhaps it was. He surely was an eagle, soaring high above his peers. But she was more of a peregrine falcon, who could soar as high as he—only if she followed in his current.

He did not put her on a pedestal; she built her own. She had made herself into an international celebrity, carved out her own careers in theater, magazines, and politics, and she raised herself up to be one of the most admired women in the world. But in the end, the power was his, and she knew it, and he would not let it go.

Their relationship was fascinating to watch, sad to see. He found a field, exploited it to the hilt, and built an empire. He had a clear vision, a strong faith, and a great mind. To the watching world the Luces represented the peak of power, the ultimate American dream. Their words could reach millions of people, shape ideas, and help elect Presidents. Popes, Kings, and prime ministers were always eager to see them and listen to their views. Celebrities of every kind groveled before them. Their names opened every door.

But without Harry, Clare was tolerated and smiled at, but rarely listened to. She wanted people to pay attention to her, as they did to him. Her final frustration was that she wanted all the perks, kudos, and trappings to continue. She was more emotionally bound to him and his position than she knew. At her death she must have known that he had given her more than she had given him.

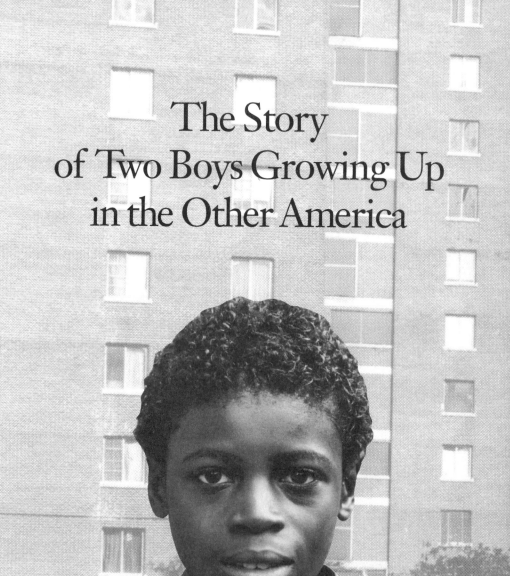

The Story
of Two Boys Growing Up
in the Other America

ALEX KOTLOWITZ

There Are No Children Here

. . . LaJoe knew that Lafeyette and
Pharoah were like millions of
other children living in the nation's
inner cities. She knew that she was
not alone in her struggles, that other
women in other cities were watching
their children grow old quickly, too.

It wouldn't happen to Lafeyette and
Pharoah, she vowed to herself. They
would have a childhood. They would
have a chance to enjoy the innocence
and playfulness of youth and to
appreciate the rewards of school and
family. They would bring home
high school diplomas. They would
move out of the neighborhood.

—*There Are No Children Here*

Preface

I FIRST met Lafeyette and Pharoah Rivers during the summer of 1985. Lafeyette was then ten. Pharoah was seven. I was working as a free-lance journalist at the time and had been asked by a friend to write the text for a photo essay he was doing on children in poverty for *Chicago* magazine. He'd met the two boys and their mother through a local social-service agency and had spent a number of days taking photographs of them at the Henry Horner Homes, a public housing complex.

Before I ever met Lafeyette and Pharoah, I had seen their likenesses. One photograph in particular struck me. Lafeyette stood in a dark hallway of his building. He was wearing a striped tank top, baggy jeans, and a Kangol cap that was too big for him; his high tops were untied. In his hands was what appeared to be a baseball. And yet, despite the youthful attire, he looked like an old man. There seemed bottled up inside him a lifetime's worth of horrors. His face revealed a restless loneliness.

When I went to meet him and his family, the interview didn't last long—maybe a few hours—because I was writing only a short essay to accompany my friend's photographs. But even during my short stay with Lafeyette, I was unnerved by the relentless neighborhood violence he talked about. In fact, I had trouble believing it all. And then I asked Lafeyette what he wanted to be. "If I grow up, I'd like to be a bus driver," he told me. *If,* not *when.* At the age of ten, Lafeyette wasn't sure he'd make it to adulthood.

Two years later I returned to the Henry Horner Homes to write a story for *The Wall Street Journal* on the toll inner-city violence takes of the children who live there. I spent the summer at Horner, playing basketball with the kids, going to lunch with them, talking with their parents, and just hanging out. Over those weeks I became good friends with Lafeyette and Pharoah, and our friendship lasted after the *Journal* story appeared and, I'm sure, will continue well beyond the publication of this book. We have spent time together nearly every weekend. We visit museums, play video games, take walks in the country, go to the movies. Each summer we take a fishing trip to northern Michigan. And we keep talking. I've been encouraged by their resilience, inspired by their laughter, and angered by their stories.

In 1988 I suggested to their mother, LaJoe, that I write a book about Lafeyette, Pharoah, and the other children of the neighborhood. She liked the idea, though she hesitated, saying, "But, you know, there are no children here. They've seen too much to be children."

One of every five children in the United States lives in poverty—an estimated twelve million children. In cities like Chicago the rate is considerably higher—one of every three children. Many grow up in neighborhoods similar to Lafeyette and Pharoah's. By the time they enter adolescence, they have contended with more terror than most of us confront in a lifetime. They have had to make choices that most experienced and educated adults would find difficult. They have lived with fear and witnessed death. Some of them have lashed out. They have joined gangs, sold drugs, and, in some cases, inflicted pain on others. But they have also played baseball and gone on dates and kept diaries. For despite all they have seen and done, they are—and we must constantly remind ourselves of this—still children.

LaJoe was not only agreeable to the project, she felt it important that their stories be told. She once said to me that she occasionally wished she were deaf. The shooting. The screaming. Babies crying. Children shrieking. Sometimes she thought it would all drive her insane. So maybe it would be best if she couldn't hear at all. Her hope—and mine—was that a book about the children would make us all hear, that it would make us all stop and listen.

All dates, place-names, titles, and events in this story are factual. However, the names of certain individuals have been changed in order to afford them a measure of privacy.

This book follows Lafeyette and Pharoah over a two-year period as they struggle with school, attempt to resist the lure of the gangs, and mourn the death of friends—all the while searching for some inner peace. During this time both boys undergo profound changes. They are at an age when through discovery of themselves and their world, they begin to form their unique identities. Consequently, it is a story that doesn't have a tidy ending. It is, instead, about a beginning, the dawning of two lives. Most of all, it is a story about two friends.

SUMMER 1987
One

NINE-YEAR-OLD Pharoah Rivers stumbled to his knees. "Give me your hand," ordered his brother Lafeyette, who was almost twelve. Pharoah grabbed hold of his brother's slender fingers, which guided him up a slippery narrow trail of dirt and brush.

"C'mon, man." Lafeyette's stick-thin body whirled around with a sense of urgency. "Let's go." He paused to watch Pharoah struggle through a thicket of vines. "Man, you slow." He had little patience for the smaller boy's clumsiness. Their friends had already reached the top of the railroad overpass.

It was a warm Saturday afternoon in early June, and to reach the railroad tracks, the children had to scale a steep mound of earth shoved against the aging concrete viaduct. Bushes and small trees grew alongside the tracks; in some places the brush was ten feet thick. Pharoah clambered to the top, moving quickly to please his brother— so quickly that he scraped his knee on the crumbling cement. As he stood to test his bruised leg, his head turned from west to east, his wide eyes and his buckteeth making him seem in awe of the world.

Looking east, Pharoah marveled at the skyline. With the late afternoon sun reflecting off the glass-and-steel skyscrapers, downtown Chicago glowed in the distance. As he looked south a few blocks, he glimpsed the top floors of his home, a red brick seven-story building. It appeared dull and dirty even in the brilliant sun. Farther south he could just make out his elementary school and the First Congregational Baptist Church. The view, he thought, was pretty great.

But he soon was distracted by more immediate matters. A black-and-yellow butterfly weaved effortlessly through the wind. Fixed on its dance, Pharoah stared silently for minutes until a rising breeze carried it away. The abundant white and lavender wildflowers along the rails soon won his attention, so he bent to touch the soft petals.

Lafeyette jostled his brother from behind. "Stop it," Pharoah screeched, swatting at him, as if he were an annoying pest. Lafeyette laughed. He could be rough in his play, which annoyed Pharoah. Sometimes their mother called Lafeyette "Aggravatin'," as in "Aggravatin', get over here" or "Aggravatin', stop aggravatin' your brother." Lafeyette took the ribbing good-naturedly.

He thrust a crowbar into Pharoah's hands, one of four they and their six friends had dragged to the top of the viaduct. The boys split into pairs, trying to be soft afoot, but their whispers quickly turned to muffled shouts as their arms hacked away at the high weeds.

Pharoah glued himself to his cousin Leonard Anderson, whom everyone called Porkchop. A couple of years younger than Pharoah, Porkchop was unusually quiet and shy, though filled with nervous energy. He grinned rather than talked. The cousins were inseparable. When they met after school—each attended a different one—they frequently greeted each other with a warm embrace.

Lafeyette wandered off with James Howard, a close friend. They had grown up together, and lived in the same building. A wiry, athletic boy, James was more easygoing than Lafeyette; his mischievous grin spanned the width of his face.

Lafeyette and James found what they thought might be a good spot—a small bare patch in the brown dirt. Lafeyette plunged the crowbar into the ground again and again. The soil gave way only a couple of inches with each plunge of the makeshift shovel. James' small hands unearthed a few more inches. Nothing.

"Daaag," muttered James, clearly disappointed. "There ain't nothing up here." Again they noisily plowed through the weeds.

The boys were looking for snakes. For an hour they dug holes in the hard soil, determined not to go home empty-handed. They had gotten the idea for this urban safari last year, when an older friend named William had nabbed a garter snake and showed it off to all the kids. William let them touch it and hold it and watch it slither across their building's breezeway. William died a few months later, when a friend, fooling with a revolver he thought was unloaded, shot him in the head. Lafeyette never learned what happened to the snake.

The boys' search turned up little, though that might have been expected—they had never seen a snake in the wild and didn't really know where to look. James spotted the only animal of the afternoon: a foot-long rat sniffing along the tracks for a treasure of its own.

Bored by the fruitless search, Pharoah and Porkchop wandered to a ten-foot-high stack of worn automobile tires and scrambled in and out of the shallow rubber tunnels. James, who had also given up the hunt, hoisted himself into an empty boxcar on a sidetrack. A friend sighted a commuter train approaching from downtown. "There's a train!" he yelled. James frantically helped Lafeyette into the boxcar, where they found refuge in a dark corner. Others hid behind its huge wheels. Pharoah and Porkchop threw themselves headlong into the weeds and lay motionless on their bellies. "Keep quiet" came a voice from the thick bushes. "Shut up," another barked.

The youngsters had heard that the suburb-bound commuters, from behind the tinted train windows, would shoot at them for trespassing on the tracks. One of the boys, certain that the commuters were crack shots, burst into tears as the train whisked by. Some of the commuters had heard similar rumors about the neighborhood children; indeed, some sat away from the windows as the train passed through Chicago's blighted core. For both the boys and the commuters the unknown was the enemy.

The train passed without incident, and soon most of the boys joined James and Lafeyette in the boxcar, sitting in the doorway, their rangy legs dangling over the side. Lafeyette and James giggled at a private joke, their thin bodies shivering with laughter.

Pharoah was too small to climb into the car, so he crouched in the weeds nearby, his legs tucked under him. He was lost in his thoughts, thoughts so private and fanciful that he would have had trouble articulating them to others. He didn't want to leave this place and the sweet smell of the wildflowers. There was a certain tranquillity here that extended into the horizon, like the straight silvery rails. In later months, with memory made that much gentler by the passage of time, Pharoah would come to savor this sanctuary even more.

None of the boys was quite ready to call it a day, but the sun had descended in the sky, and nighttime here was dangerous. Reluctantly they slid down the embankment, and as Lafeyette took Pharoah's hand to cross the street, they began the short trek home.

THE CHILDREN CALLED HOME THE projects, or simply the jects (pronounced "jets"). Pharoah called it the graveyard. But they never referred to it by its full name: the Governor Henry Horner Homes.

Nothing here, the children would tell you, was as it should be. Lafeyette and Pharoah lived at 1920 West Washington Boulevard, even though their high rise sat on Lake Street. Their building had no enclosed lobby; a dark tunnel cut through the middle of the building, and the wind and strangers passed freely along it. Those tenants who received public aid had their checks sent to the local currency exchange, since the building's first-floor mailboxes had all been broken into. And since darkness engulfed the building's corridors even in the daytime, the residents always carried flashlights, some of which had been handed out by a local politician during her campaign.

Summer, too, was never as it should be. It had become a season of duplicity.

On June 13 Lafeyette celebrated his twelfth birthday. Under the gentle afternoon sun, yellow daisies poked through the cracks in the sidewalk as children's bright faces peered from their windows. Green leaves clothed the cottonwoods. Like the fresh buds on the crab-apple trees, the children's spirits blossomed with the onset of summer.

Lafeyette and his nine-year-old cousin Dede danced across the worn lawn outside their building, singing the lyrics of an L. L. Cool J rap. They were on their way to a nearby shopping strip, where Lafeyette planned to buy radio headphones with $8 he had received as a birthday gift.

Suddenly gunfire erupted. The frightened children fell to the ground. "Hold your head down!" Lafeyette snapped, covering Dede's head with her pink nylon jacket. If he hadn't restrained her, she might have sprinted for home—a dangerous action when the gangs started warring. "Stay down," he ordered the trembling girl.

The two lay pressed to the beaten grass until the shooting subsided. Then Lafeyette held Dede's hand as they cautiously crawled through the dirt toward home. When they finally made it inside, all but fifty cents of Lafeyette's birthday money had trickled from his pockets.

LAFEYETTE'S summer opened the way it would close—with gunshots. For Lafeyette and Pharoah these few months were to be a rickety bridge to adolescence. If the brothers had one guidepost in their young lives, though, it was their mother, LaJoe. They depended on her; she depended on them. The boys would do anything for her.

A shy, soft-spoken woman, LaJoe Rivers was known for her warmth and generosity. Though she received Aid to Families with Dependent Children, neighbors frequently knocked on her door to borrow a can of soup or a cup of flour, and she always obliged. LaJoe had often mothered children who needed advice or comforting. Many young men and women still called her Mom.

But the neighborhood, which hungrily devoured its children, had taken its toll of LaJoe as well. In recent years she had become more tired as she questioned her ability to raise her children here. Many of the adults had aged with the neighborhood, looking as worn and empty as the abandoned stores that lined the once thriving Madison Street. By their mid-thirties many women had become grandmothers; by their mid-forties, great-grandmothers. They nurtured and cared for their boyfriends and former boyfriends and sons and grandsons and great-grandsons.

LaJoe had been stunning in her twenties, her smooth, light brown complexion highlighted by an open smile, her almond-shaped eyes gazing out from a heart-shaped face. Now she was thirty-five, and men still whistled and smiled at her on the street. She hadn't put on much weight, and her high-cheekboned face still had a sculptured look. But the confidence of her youth had left her. Her shoulders were often hunched, and her smile was less frequent now.

LaJoe had watched and held on as the neighborhood had slowly decayed, as had many urban communities like Horner over the past two decades. First the middle-class whites fled to the suburbs. Then the middle-class blacks left for safer neighborhoods. Then businesses moved—some to the suburbs, others to the South. Over the past ten years the city had lost a third of its manufacturing, and there were few jobs left for those in Horner. Unemployment, officially estimated at 19 percent, was probably much higher. There were neighborhoods in Chicago worse off than Horner, but the demise of this one was often noted because it had once been among the city's wealthiest areas.

Ashland Avenue, a six-lane boulevard near Henry Horner, was named for the Kentucky estate of Henry Clay. By the mid-nineteenth century it had become one of the city's smartest thoroughfares, lined with Attic marble dwellings, fashionable churches, and exclusive clubs. But as immigrants from Europe settled on the West Side, the city's glitter moved eastward, to the lake, to a strip just north of downtown now known as the Magnificent Mile and the Gold Coast.

The Ashland Avenue area quickly lost its luster. Its mansions were transformed into rooming houses for transients. By 1906 tuberculosis had claimed 5 percent of the West Side's population. The blight has continued, and is particularly evident today west of Horner, a section of the city that, along with the South Side during the 1930s, 1940s, and 1950s, became home to over a half-million blacks who migrated from the South, displacing the earlier immigrants. Western Avenue, now a strip of fast-food outlets, car washes, and family-run stores, borders Henry Horner to the west. On its other side the rubble continues. The two- and three-family tenements sag, and many are vacant, their contents lying on the sidewalk.

To LaJoe the neighborhood had become a black hole. There were no banks—only currency exchanges, which charged customers up to $8 for every welfare check cashed. There were no public libraries, movie theaters, skating rinks, or bowling alleys to entertain the neighborhood's children. For the infirm there were two neighborhood clinics, yet the death rate of newborn babies exceeded infant mortality rates in a number of Third World countries. And there was no rehabilitation center, though drug abuse was rampant.

According to a 1980 profile of the Twenty-seventh Ward—which includes both Henry Horner and Rockwell Gardens, a smaller, but no less forbidding, public housing complex—60,110 people lived here, 88 percent of them black, 46 percent of them below the poverty level. Yet where there used to be thirteen social-service agencies, there were now only three: Missionaries of Charity, set up by Mother Teresa; the Boys Club; and the Chicago Commons Association.

Despite Horner's proximity—one mile—to the city's booming downtown, LaJoe and her neighbors felt abandoned. Horner sat so close to the city's business district that from the Sears Tower observation deck, tourists could have watched Lafeyette duck gunfire on his birthday. But city residents never had reason to pass the housing complex unless they attended a basketball or hockey game at the Chicago Stadium, just a block away.

Though the isolation and the physical ruin of the area's stores and homes had discouraged LaJoe, it was her family that had most let her down. Her three oldest children, to whom she felt she'd given every-thing she could, had all disappointed her. All had dropped out of school. All had been in jail at least once. All had been involved with drugs. The oldest, LaShawn, a slender twenty-year-old, was so deli-cately featured some called her China Doll. She worked as a prosti-tute from time to time to support her drug habit. Nineteen-year-old Paul, whom everyone called Weasel, had served time for burglary. Terence, now seventeen, had been the most troublesome problem for LaJoe and, because of their extraordinary closeness, her biggest dis-appointment. He had begun selling drugs at the age of eleven and had been in and out of trouble with the law ever since.

LaJoe also had four-year-old triplets: Timothy, Tiffany, and Tam-mie. All eight children had the same father, Paul, to whom LaJoe had been married for seventeen years. But the two had long ago fallen out of love. He lived at home only sporadically.

LaJoe wanted it to be different for Lafeyette and Pharoah, differ-ent from the way it had been for her three oldest children and different from the way it had been for her.

In her husband's absence Lafeyette had become LaJoe's confidant. She relied on him. So did the younger children. Lafeyette watched af-ter Pharoah and the triplets. He wouldn't let anything happen to them. He'd been a carefree child, a bit of a ham, in fact—for a photo-graph taken when he was about four, he had shoved a big cigar in his mouth and plopped a blue floppy hat on his small head. When he got to be eight or nine, he'd hop on the Madison Street bus by himself to visit his grandmother. And he loved to draw—mostly pictures of superheroes. He was a boy bubbling with energy and verve.

But over the past year Lafeyette had begun to change. The past spring he'd been caught stealing candy from a Walgreen's downtown. It was the first time he'd gotten into trouble. He had been hanging out with a youngster, Keith, who was known among the neighborhood kids for his ability to swipe expensive bottles of cologne from down-town department stores. Lafeyette was placed in a six-month Chicago Commons counseling program. Keith moved out of town, and Lafe-yette made friends with Chicago Commons staff members, whom he'd periodically visit after the program's completion.

Lafeyette still laughed and played with Pharoah and friends, but he could be bossy, ordering around his younger brother and the triplets with cockiness and the fury of a temperamental adult. He had inherited his mother's temper and could turn on them in an instant. It wasn't that he and they didn't get along; it was that he worried about them, like a father worrying about his children. He admonished them for hanging out with the wrong people or straying from sight. He cared almost too much about everything and everybody. Sometimes the strain showed in his thin, handsome face—it would tighten, like a fist, and his deep-set, heavy-lidded eyes would stare straight ahead. His face revealed so little, his mother thought, and yet so much.

Pharoah was different, not only from Lafeyette but from the other children, too. He didn't have many friends, except for Porkchop, who was always by his side. LaJoe had given him his name but, like his brother's name, spelled it in an unusual way. At the time, LaJoe hadn't known the story of Moses and the pharaoh, but in later years, when she found out, she laughed. Pharoah was anything but a king.

Pharoah clutched his childhood with the vigor of a tiger gripping his meat. He wouldn't let go. Nobody, nothing would take it away from him. When he was two, Pharoah would run around the apartment naked; sometimes he'd be wearing just small white shoes. When he was four or five, he told LaJoe he wanted to live on a lake so he could always feel the wind on his back. Frequently he got so lost in his daydreams that LaJoe had to shake him to bring him back. His flights of fancy seemed to help him fend off the ugliness around him.

Now, at the age of nine, he giggled at the slightest joke; he cried at the smallest of tragedies. He had recently developed a slight stutter, which made him seem even more vulnerable. And he listened to classical music on the radio because, he said, it relaxed him. He sensed that his playfulness delighted the adults, so he would tease them and they him. They adored him.

Pharoah liked to tell people he was big-boned, "like my mama," though she was, in fact, a small woman. He had LaJoe's open and generous smile, and like his mother, who was only five feet two, he was short, so LaJoe could pass him off as a five-year-old to get him on the bus without paying fare.

LaJoe knew that Lafeyette and Pharoah were like millions of other children living in the nation's inner cities. She knew that she was not alone in her struggles, that other women in other cities were watching their children grow old quickly, too. It wouldn't happen to Lafeyette and Pharoah, she vowed to herself. It just wouldn't happen. They would have a childhood. They would have a chance to enjoy the innocence and playfulness of youth and to appreciate the rewards of school and family. They would bring home high school diplomas. They would move out of the neighborhood. They would get jobs and raise families. She had made mistakes with the older children that she was determined not to repeat with her younger ones.

But during the summer of 1987, when drugs and the accompanying violence swept through the neighborhood, she lived in daily fear that something might happen to her young ones. Already that year fifty-seven children had been killed in the city. Lafeyette and Pharoah knew of more funerals than weddings. So that summer LaJoe wanted to be prepared for the worst—she started paying $80 a month for burial insurance for Lafeyette, Pharoah, and the triplets.

LAFEYETTE had promised his mother he wouldn't let anything happen to Pharoah. But for a brief moment he thought he had lost him.

Three days after Lafeyette's birthday, gunfire once again filled the air. It was two thirty in the afternoon; school had just let out. As Lafeyette and his mother hustled the triplets onto the floor of the apartment's narrow hallway, they caught glimpses through the first-floor windows of young gunmen waving their pistols about. One youth toted a submachine gun.

The dispute had started when two rival drug gangs fired at each other from one high rise to another.

From his apartment Lafeyette, who had left his fifth-grade class early that day, watched hopefully for Pharoah as the children poured out of the Henry Suder Elementary School, just a block away. Panicking, many of the youngsters ran directly toward the gunfire. Lafeyette and his mother screamed at them to turn back. But they kept coming, clamoring for the shelter of their homes.

Lafeyette finally spotted his brother, first walking, then running, taking cover behind trees and fences. Then he lost sight of him. "Mama, lemme go get him," Lafeyette begged. He was afraid that Pharoah would run straight through the gunfire. LaJoe refused. She couldn't even go herself. The guns kept crackling.

Lafeyette's friend James, who was cowering behind a nearby tree, sprinted for the Riverses' apartment. Pharoah saw him and ran, too.

The two pounded frantically on the metal door. "Let us in! Let us in! It's James and Pharoah!" But with all the noise no one heard their frenzied pleas, and the two ran to a friend's apartment upstairs.

Meanwhile, the police, who at first thought they were the targets of the shooting, had taken cover in their cars and in the building's breezeway. Passersby lay motionless on the ground, protected by parked vehicles. Then, as suddenly as it began, the battle ended. No one, amazingly, had been hurt.

The police made no arrests. A reporter called police headquarters the next day and was told there was no record of the shoot-out.

But Lafeyette knew. So did Pharoah.

Two

THOUGH only four years old at the time, LaJoe forever remembered the day she and her family had moved into the Henry Horner Homes. It was October 15, 1956, a Monday.

The eight-block-long complex was so new that some of the high rises had yet to be completed. But to LaJoe it all looked dazzling. The brand-new bricks were a deep, luscious red, and the clean windows reflected the day's movements with an almost magical clarity.

It was quiet and peaceful; there were not even any passersby. On this unusually warm fall day LaJoe could even hear the shrill songs of the sparrows. The building, 1920 West Washington, stood empty. They were the first family to occupy one of its sixty-five apartments.

LaJoe's parents had both come from the shacks and the shanties of the South. Her mother, Lelia Mae, left Charleston, West Virginia, for Chicago at the age of twenty, in 1937. Once there, Lelia Mae, already divorced and with one child, met her second husband, Roy Anderson, who worked in one of the city's steel mills. Roy hailed from Camden, Arkansas, where his father had been a Baptist deacon.

Roy and Lelia Mae had been eagerly awaiting this move. They had been living with their thirteen children in an apartment above a Baptist church, but their home was to be demolished to make way for the new Illinois Institute of Technology. They were given the opportunity to move into public housing, the grand castles being built for the nation's urban poor.

In the 1950s publicly financed high-rise complexes sprang up across the country, like dandelions in a rainy spring. To address a postwar housing crisis, Congress had authorized loans and subsidies for 810,000 units of low-rent housing nationwide. At the time it was viewed as an impressive effort to provide shelter for the less fortunate.

But white politicians wanted neither poor nor black families in their communities. In Chicago the public housing complexes were built on the edges of the city's black ghettos. Rather than providing alternatives to decrepit living conditions, public housing became anchors for existing slums. And because there were few sites available, the Chicago Housing Authority had no alternative but to build up rather than out. So the ghettos grew toward the heavens, and public housing became a bulwark of urban segregation.

On the city's Near West Side was built the Henry Horner Homes. The complex of sixteen high rises, seven to fifteen stories high, was constructed on the cheap. The apartment walls were of cinder block. There were no lobbies to speak of—only the open breezeways, with no communication system to the tenants. During the city's harsh winters elevator cables froze; in one year alone the CHA needed to make over 1500 elevator repairs. And that was in just one development.

The trash chutes within each building were too narrow to handle the garbage. The boiler systems continually broke down. Each bathroom medicine cabinet was not only easily removed but was connected to the medicine chest in the adjoining apartment. Over the years residents had been robbed, assaulted, and even murdered by people crawling through the medicine cabinets.

But on this day in 1956, LaJoe and her siblings were bubbling over with joy at the sight of their new home. They counted off the five bedrooms in delighted giggles. The freshly painted walls shone a glistening white; even the brown linoleum floors had a luster to them.

In those early years the children of Horner thrived. LaJoe and her sister LaGreta joined the Girl Scouts. They attended dances and roller-skating parties in their building's basement. They delighted in the new playground, and their brothers frequented the project's grass baseball diamond. All of them spent time at the spanking new Boys Club, which had a gym and, in later years, an indoor Olympic-size swimming pool. On Friday nights the family attended fish fries. LaJoe joined the popular drum and bugle corps.

The Anderson children were also exposed to politics. Their mother was active in the local Democratic Party, and politicians visited the complex and paid attention to the people's concerns. They had to—people were well organized. In the 1960s, area residents formed the Miles Square Federation, which vigorously fought for better schools and health clinics. The Black Panthers' city headquarters was only a few blocks from Horner. Martin Luther King, Jr., on his visits to the city, would preach at the First Congregational Baptist Church.

LaJoe held on tightly to those early memories because so much had since gone sour. By the 1970s the housing authority had run out of money to paint the apartments. The cinder-block walls became permanently smudged and dirty. The building's bricks faded. The windows collected grime. In 1975 someone, to this day unknown, strangled one of LaJoe's grown sisters in her bathtub. The oldest brother, home on leave from the marines, died of a heart attack that day on hearing the news. LaJoe's parents moved out of Horner because of the murder. Roy, the father, died of bone cancer in 1982.

LaJoe hadn't moved far since that fall day in 1956. She was just down the hall, where she now lived with Lafeyette, Pharoah, her two oldest sons—Weasel and Terence—and the triplets.

"When I got my apartment, I thought this is what it was meant to be," she said thirty-one years later. "It wasn't like it is now. The grass was greener. We had light poles on the front of the building. We had little yellow flowers. We had it all. I really thought this was it. And I never knew, until I lost it all, that it wasn't."

LAFEYETTE and Pharoah huddled on the apartment's hallway floor, sweating in the early July heat. Pharoah shook with each gun pop, his big eyes darting nervously from one end of the hall to the other, his small body curled up against the security of the cool concrete wall.

The muscles in Lafeyette's face tensed. He had his hands full watching over Pharoah and the triplets. The young ones chattered and fought until Tiffany, too restless to sit still for long, stood up. Lafeyette shoved her back down.

"We wanna go," whined Tiffany.

"Be quiet," admonished her brother. "You crazy?"

The narrow hall of their four-bedroom apartment had become their fallout shelter. Stray bullets had zipped through their apartment before, once leaving holes the size of nickels in the living-room curtains.

Another time a bullet found its way into the hallway; it had traveled through a bedroom window and door, missing Terence by inches. The children now knew enough to sit away from the doorways.

The five children squatted on the musty floor long after the shooting subsided. LaJoe, who huddled with them, could sit still no longer. She walked into the kitchen and began to sweep the floors. Cleaning house was the only way she could clear her mind, to avoid thinking about what might happen or what might have been. The kids knew to stay out of her way, except for Lafeyette, who, like his mother, also found cleaning a useful distraction.

"Lemme help you," he begged, still sitting by the wall. "You figuring to clean 'cause you upset." LaJoe didn't hear him. "Mama, let me help you. Ain't nobody gonna get killed out there today."

"Stay there, Lafie," LaJoe said. "Someone's gotta watch the triplets."

For LaJoe, cleaning the apartment seemed nearly hopeless. Eight people lived there—nine if the children's father stayed over. Food-caked dishes often filled the kitchen sink, or the garbage container overflowed. Roaches were everywhere. Maggots nested in the building by the undersized incinerator, which overflowed with garbage.

Even had LaJoe been able to catch up with the dishes and garbage, the apartment itself defied cleanliness. Housing-authority maintenance was a bare minimum. With the smudged walls, the encrusted, worn brown linoleum, and the heating pipes snaking through the apartment, the home at night resembled a dark, dank cave. The bedrooms were particularly drab. Only ten by eleven feet, they got little sunlight. The kitchen and living room were essentially one room partly divided by a cinder-block wall halfway down the middle.

The thirty-year-old kitchen cabinets, constructed of thin sheet metal, had rusted through. They were pockmarked with holes. LaJoe piled her dishes in the corners of the cupboards to avoid having them fall through the ragged openings.

But the apartment's two bathrooms were in the worst shape of all. Neither had a window. In the first bathroom a horrible stench, suggesting raw, spoiled meat, periodically rose from the toilet. The second bathroom housed the family's one bathtub. It doubled as a clothes washer, since the building's laundry was abandoned long ago, and the closest one was now a mile away. The tub's faucet couldn't be turned off. Scalding hot water cascaded day and night.

In the winter the building's heating system stormed out of control. The apartment could get like a furnace, hotter than in the warmest days of summer. These summer months were a welcome relief.

LaJoe had done what she could to spruce up the place. By the television, which she left on nearly twenty-four hours a day to discourage prowlers, she had placed artificial logs. On the living-room wall she had hung two identical drawings of a red rose, a portrait of Jesus, and a rendering of a waterfall and a country home on black velvet.

"Mama, lemme help," Lafeyette now pleaded again. His words were lost in the roar of the elevated train, which passed just a hundred feet from their building. Lafeyette waited for it to pass. "Mama. Mama. I'm gonna take out the garbage."

"No, you ain't." LaJoe looked at him and the others. They had had enough sitting. "Okay, Lafie, just tie up the garbage. Don't take it out."

Lafeyette jumped to his feet and walked quickly into the kitchen. The triplets wandered into the living room, continuing their chatter, beseeching their mother to let them go outside. Pharoah lazily strolled to the couch, where he balled up, lost in his private thoughts. He, too, wanted to go outside. But there wasn't much to do out there.

The Riverses' building and three other high rises were laid out roughly in the shape of a diamond, so that they all opened up onto a concrete park. The two swing sets, which boasted only one swing between them, and the three sliding boards were, as far as anyone could tell, the original equipment, installed thirty-one years before. Across the street sat the baseball diamond, long since paved over for reasons residents couldn't recall. Nearby, a rusted basketball rim was shoved and twisted against a leaning backboard.

On this early summer day children arced jump shots into the opening created by the crossbars of a faded yellow-and-blue jungle gym. Lafeyette could dunk on this makeshift rim; Pharoah, not quite yet.

"Hey, Laf, let's play," James urged his friend.

"I don't wanna play ball with them," Lafeyette said, referring to the children by the jungle gym. "They might try to make me join a gang."

About a week earlier, members of one of the local gangs had asked Lafeyette to stand security, and it had made him skittish. His mother told the teenagers she would call the police if they kept after him. "I'd die first before I let them take one of my sons," she said.

Gangs often recruit young children to do their dirty work. Lafe-

Pharoah and Lafeyette at the
Henry Horner complex.
Nothing here was as it should be.

yette and James constantly worried
that they might be pulled in. Lafeyette
knew what might happen. "When you
first join, you think it's good—they'll
buy you what you want. You have to
do anything they tell you to do. If they
tell you to kill somebody, you have to
do that."

So while a group of young boys
shrieked in delight as the basketball
ricocheted through the jungle gym's
opening, Lafeyette, James, and a few
other boys perched idly on metal
benches in front of the building. Like
the swing sets, the benches resembled
an ancient archaeological find. They were missing most of their metal
slats. Not far away, Pharoah and Porkchop pitched pennies.

"I'm gonna have my own condominium in Calumet Park," James
told the others, referring to a Chicago suburb. "It's nice out there.
You could sit outside all night and nothing would happen."

"They have flowers this tall," said Lafeyette, holding his hand four
feet off the ground.

James laughed, and hurled an empty Canadian Mist bottle onto the
concrete, where it shattered, adding to the hundreds of shards of glass
on the ground. "If I had one wish, I'd wish to separate all the good
from the bad and send them to another planet so they could battle it
out and no innocent people would get hurt," he mused.

"That's two wishes," asserted Lafeyette. "I wish to go to heaven."

"I'd wish there be no gangbangers," piped up Pharoah, wishing out
of existence those who fought for the gangs.

"Wherever you go, there be gangbangers," replied Lafeyette.

"Not in Mississippi," Pharoah assured him. An argument ensued as
to whether there was, in fact, any state or city or neighborhood that
didn't have gangs. It was on their minds a lot these days.

By season's end the police would record that one person every three
days had been beaten, shot at, or stabbed at Horner. In just one week
they confiscated twenty-two guns and 330 grams of cocaine. Most of
the violence here that summer was related to drugs.

On a warm day in mid-July three cars pulled up to the sidewalk at the two high rises across the street from the Riverses'. Two young body-guards stepped out of the first and last sedans. Then from the middle emerged thirty-eight-year-old Jimmie Lee, a barrel-chested, square-jawed man no more than five feet seven. He held his cellular phone at his side as a band of worshipping teenagers mobbed him.

A commotion caught Lee's attention. In the entranceway of one of the buildings a drunken man was berating his young daughter. "You bitch. What did I tell you?" the father screamed at the cowering girl. Lee walked over and, with a suddenness that left the father defense-less, slugged him in the jaw, knocking him to the ground.

"You don't give no kid disrespect," he told the man.

"But that's my daughter," the fallen man explained.

"I don't care. She's thirteen years old, and you're calling her a bitch. Don't do it again." Lee walked into the building, where he had a meeting with some of his workers.

Lafeyette, Pharoah, and the other children knew to keep their distance from Jimmie Lee. But they also knew that he and no one else—not the mayor, the police, or the housing authority—ruled Henry Horner. When he pulled up in his caravan, they knew enough to go inside. When nighttime fell and Lee's business swung into action, they knew enough to stay away. And when something hap-pened to Lee or one of his workers, they knew enough not to talk about it. Jimmie Lee, it was said, was everywhere. He knew who was talking about him, who was finking, who was flipping to the other side. And when he knew, someone would pay.

Jimmie Lee headed a drug gang called the Conservative Vice Lords. Its members controlled Henry Horner. No one could sell drugs without their approval. Their arsenal included pistols, Uzis, and grenades. Lee even had an "enforcer," whose job it was to maim and kill and who kept a two-shot derringer for such a purpose.

Residents so feared and respected the gang's control that they refused to call 911. Snitching could get you killed. The police installed a hot-line number and promised confidentiality, but in all of 1986, public housing residents called the number twenty-one times.

By 1987 Lee's photo, taken with five other high-ranking Vice Lords, hung on the walls of every police station on the city's West Side. The text warned: "They are known to be involved in drug traffic, home invasions of dope flats, extortion, and other crimes. They have been known to employ fully automatic weapons."

But Lee ruled by more than fear. To neighborhood residents he could sometimes be a positive force. He reportedly didn't take drugs himself. He occasionally bought food for families who needed it. He refused to let "peewees"—those around thirteen or fourteen—gang-bang for the Conservative Vice Lords. On occasion Lee gave children dollar bills or, if their shoes were torn, bought them new ones.

Lee's efforts paid off. To the residents of Horner he became a fig-ure of contradictions. To some he was a model. In a neighborhood of runaway fathers Lee had been married to the same woman for nearly twenty years. And adults and children alike pointed to his generosity.

The police speculate that Lee, who grew up in Horner, had been associated with the Vice Lords, which has more than twenty factions, for as long as twenty years. When Lee was nineteen, he and some buddies had robbed three men at gunpoint, and Lee served four years in one of the Illinois prisons, notorious for their strong gang populations. After his release, in 1974, he was in and out of trouble with the law. In 1986 the police caught him with fifty-six grams of heroin. He met the $50,000 bond and continued about his business. To Horner's residents he seemed to operate with impunity.

The city's black street gangs, of which there are three main ones—the Vice Lords, the Disciples, and the El Rukns—originated in the early 1960s, mostly as kids duking it out over turf rights. At Henry Horner the Vice Lords and the Disciples fought fist to fist with white gangs, whose turf lay just north of the complex. As the whites moved out, the Vice Lords and the Disciples fought among themselves.

By the late 1960s the gangs had won some standing among the Establishment, particularly with liberals, who felt that these young hoodlums, given proper guidance, might turn their energies to better-ing their neighborhoods. Jeff Fort, the El Rukns' head, managed to pull in over $300,000 in funds from federal agencies for job-training programs. During the riots following the death of Martin Luther King, Jr., the El Rukns took to the streets to calm the neighborhoods. The gang won such legitimacy that Fort was invited, at the behest of a United States Senator, to President Nixon's inauguration.

At Henry Horner the Vice Lords gained a similar standing when a local hospital bequeathed a former Catholic boys' school it owned, coupled with a grant of over $20,000, to local gang leaders in the hope that they would open a neighborhood center. This effort, though, failed miserably. Within months the gang had gutted the school and misused much of the grant money.

The El Rukns' good intentions unraveled, too, though not as quickly. In the early 1970s a judge sentenced Jeff Fort to five years in Leavenworth for conspiring to misapply federal funds.

By the late 1970s the city's gangs had turned to big business: the marketing of narcotics. The gangs became so powerful in Chicago that they managed to do what no big-city police force has done—they kept crack out of the city. Not until 1988, long after the crack scourge had devoured entire neighborhoods in New York and Washington, D.C., were there any crack-related arrests in Chicago. Even then, crack made up only 5 percent of all drugs. If crack found its way to Chicago, the inexpensive, highly addictive drug would open up the market to small entrepreneurs and possibly break the gangs' oligopoly over the drug trade.

The city's top gang leaders and drug lords have such standing in the community that every summer they throw a huge bash for friends at the Dan Ryan Woods, on the South Side. One summer, fliers in many of the city's poor black neighborhoods promised free food and drink, softball for the children, and a car show and a wet T-shirt contest for the adults. About 2000 Chicagoans danced to the funk rock of a live band, and grilled hot dogs and ribs. Cars were so backed up going into the park that the police assigned extra traffic details.

IN 1985, AT the age of ten, Lafeyette had his first encounter with death—he saw someone killed. It was the beginning of Henry Horner's brutal drug wars, when the Conservative Vice Lords made their move to take control. They pushed to oust the Disciples from the complex's east end, the more populated section and thus the more lucrative. The first victim was a young Disciple nicknamed Baby Al, who was shot with a .357 Magnum not far from the Riverses' building. Wounded, he ran into the high rise, where while trying to climb the stairs, he lost consciousness. Lafeyette came running out of his apartment to see what all the commotion was about. He watched as Baby Al bled to death. Two years later his blood still stained the stairwell.

By late 1986 the Conservative Vice Lords occupied the two high rises across the street from the Riverses'. Lee's soldiers used the buildings' four stairwells to escape from the police. They found refuge in several of the vacant apartments, some of which were connected by large holes knocked in the walls, through which they could make their getaways. The gang also rented out rooms in three apartments to store drugs, guns, and money.

The bulk of the gang's business was with outsiders, who parked their cars in front of the two buildings. Usually they didn't have to get out; young runners took their orders. The soldiers sold the cocaine and heroin, then returned a percentage of the proceeds to the bosses and kept the rest. Both the police and former gang members estimated that Lee's business grossed $50,000 to $100,000 a week.

On December 13, 1986, a frenzy began that would last the summer. Four top Vice Lords chose to show their force against a rival drug gang—the Gangster Stones—that was encroaching on their turf. They had already successfully moved the Disciples farther west.

The four waited until midnight, when the tough plainclothes cops of the city's gang-crimes and public housing units went off duty. They strolled into the breezeway of a nearby building, carrying with them an Uzi, two sawed-off shotguns, and a .25-caliber automatic handgun. The first rival gang member they came on in the dark lobby was Larry Wallace. The gunfire lasted maybe thirty seconds. Wallace was shot five times. One bullet pierced his chest; another entered through the back and lodged in his cheek. Buckshot pellets littered his buttocks. Even at Horner the viciousness of this slaying unnerved people. By summer's end, as the Vice Lords established their dominance, the war had touched the lives of almost everyone living there. Lafeyette and Pharoah, as well as the adults, began talking of the "death train" that drove smack through their community.

Three

B IRD Leg loved dogs. And for that reason Lafeyette loved Bird Leg. His real name was Calvin Robinson, and though, at fifteen, he was three years older than Lafeyette, he let the younger boy tag along with him, in part because he had few friends. The older boys made fun of his obsession with dogs; the younger ones seemed to understand it.

Bird Leg and Lafeyette hunted for German shepherds, mutts, and even pit bulls in the small, fenced-in backyards of the Hispanic and white neighborhoods just north of the housing project. Ordinarily, the dogs growled and fought with strangers, but Bird Leg could communicate with them in ways Lafeyette found uncanny. As he climbed into the backyards Bird Leg talked to them, consoled them, cajoled them, lured them, until they sidled up to him, drooling on their newfound friend. Then he unchained them and brought them home.

With Lafeyette's assistance Bird Leg kept his assortment of canines—some stolen, some strays, some raised from birth—in an abandoned garage catty-corner from Lafeyette's building. Bird Leg often got down on his hands and knees to speak to his companions, and sometimes he kissed them on their sloppy chops. A few nights a week he scrounged through the trash bins behind the nearby Kentucky Fried Chicken and collected half-finished meals to feed them. Lafeyette often helped.

As Bird Leg got older he became involved with the Vice Lords, and he and Lafeyette grew apart. Lafeyette was too young and too wary to join the gangs, but he cherished all that Bird Leg had taught him about dogs. And he missed him.

Bird Leg, his mother suspects, sought protection with the gang in the same way he sought love from his dogs. Jimmie Lee had become like a big brother, though Bird Leg didn't run drugs for him. Also, a close relative was a Vice Lord, which meant that Bird Leg, who lived on the western edge of Horner—Disciple territory—frequently had to withstand a beating just to enter his building.

As a teenager, Bird Leg became increasingly reckless and hardheaded. By the age of fourteen he had, for all intents and purposes, dropped out of school. Friends say he would sometimes borrow a shotgun and randomly shoot at Disciples, a practice not uncommon among the very young gang members. He also started raising his pit bulls to fight, and used one to threaten a police officer.

In the summer of 1986, while shooting dice with some friends, Bird Leg was approached by a man with a shotgun, demanding his money, and he ran. The man emptied a cartridge of buckshot into Bird Leg's shoulder. That incident caused his mother to move her family to the city's Far North Side. But as is often the case when families move, Bird Leg kept returning to Horner to visit friends.

SOMETIMES AT HENRY HORNER you can almost smell the arrival of death. It is the odor of foot-deep pools of water that, formed from draining fire hydrants, become fetid in the summer sun. It is the stink of urine in the stairwell corners. It is the stench of a maggot-infested cat carcass lying in a vacant apartment and of rotting food in the overturned trash bins. It is, in short, the collected scents of summer.

By mid-August of 1987 the police had increased their presence at Horner because of the summer's violence. The gangs knew that more police would only disrupt their drug transactions, so they agreed among themselves to stop, in their own word, "clowning." But for young members like Bird Leg, such business acumen seemed at odds with what had become almost instinctual: Vice Lords got along with neither Gangster Stones nor Disciples—truce or no truce.

On a Thursday night late in August, a rival gang member shot Bird Leg in the arm with buckshot. After being treated at the hospital, he joked with his older brother and cousin that if he were to die, he wanted to be buried in his white jogging suit. They laughed and told him they would oblige him.

The next evening, August 21, Bird Leg visited friends at Horner. As he sat and watched them play basketball a group of young Disciples started taunting him, tossing bricks and bottles at his feet. His thirteen-year-old sister, who also was visiting Horner, pleaded with Bird Leg to come inside the building to their cousins' apartment.

"Get your ass upstairs," Bird Leg ordered her. "I'm gonna kill some of these punks today, or they're gonna kill me." It was tough talk for a fifteen-year-old; his sister ran inside crying. By the time she climbed the six floors to her cousins' apartment, a single pistol shot had echoed from below.

Twenty-four-year-old Willie Elliott had stepped from between two parked cars and aimed a pistol at Bird Leg, only two feet away. The bullet tore through Bird Leg's chest. He clutched his wound and ran, hollering in disbelief, "Man, I've been shot!" He appeared to be heading for the safety of a busy street. He didn't make it. Struggling to breathe, he collapsed beneath an old cottonwood and died.

Word of death spreads fast in Henry Horner. From a friend's second-floor window Lafeyette heard the news. He did not join the children who ran across Damen Avenue to the crime scene. "I just didn't want to go," he said later. He had already seen enough.

James, however, more adventurous, sprinted across Damen and snaked through the crowd that had already gathered around Bird Leg. He later told Lafeyette what he saw. On the grass, only ten feet from a small playground filled with young children, lay Bird Leg, his white jogging suit stained with blood. Wrapped around one of his closed fists was his only weapon—his belt.

Within minutes after Bird Leg died, Jimmie Lee stepped through the crowd. People moved back to let him by. He looked down at Bird Leg's limp body, said nothing, and then walked back through the crowd, where he assembled a band of thirty teenagers. With Lee at their flank the young militia marched west, looking for revenge.

Charlie Toussas, a plainclothes officer who knew Lee well, confronted Lee and his army. "Jimmie, this isn't a good time for this." Lee silently turned to his followers, lifted his hand, and pointed to the other side of Damen; the contingent marched back to their own turf.

In the weeks to come, Disciples were the targets of gunfire.

BIRD Leg's swollen face made him look twice his age. But the new red-trimmed white jogging suit, which his mother had bought to honor his wishes, and a small gold friendship pin bearing his initials were reminders that Bird Leg had been only fifteen.

Lafeyette, Pharoah, and James were the first to file up to the open casket at the Zion Grove Baptist Church. Lafeyette ran his fingers along Bird Leg's jogging suit. At first hesitantly and then with great affection Lafeyette caressed the boy's puffy face. James also gently touched the body, pulling back before his fingers reached his friend's rounded cheeks. Pharoah kept his hands to his side.

"It looks like he's breathing," James whispered to Lafeyette, desperately wanting to be told he was wrong.

"He ain't breathing," Lafeyette assured him.

James glanced at Bird Leg, and to no one in particular muttered, "I'm figuring to cry." He wiped his tears with the back of his hand.

The three boys found seats. In the late August heat Bird Leg's friends, relatives, and fellow gang members shifted uncomfortably in the red-cushioned pews. To the deep, sorrowful spirituals played on the church's organ, the Reverend C. H. Stimage climbed to the lectern. "God needs some young soldiers among the old soldiers," he consoled the gathered mourners, about 150 in all. When young gang members die, other youngsters attend church; it was, reasoned the minister, the only time he could preach to them about the love of God.

Carla Palmore, a friend of Bird Leg's, followed the minister to the lectern. Carla wanted to be upbeat, to be hopeful, but despite her efforts, her speech underlined the general feeling among her peers that many of them, like Bird Leg, might not make it to adulthood. Lafeyette and James and the others in the church nodded in assent.

Another family friend led the congregation in a spirited rendition of "Lean on Me," a pop song that always stirred Pharoah's emotions. Here, in the company of other sobbing children and adults, large tears slid down his plump cheeks. He clutched his rolled-up sweatshirt to his chest for security, and as often happened to him in tense situations, he found himself battling a piercing headache.

James cried, too. It looked to some as if he might be doubled over in pain, but he hid his teary face in his black felt hat, which he held between his legs so that others wouldn't see him cry. Lafeyette stared hard at the whirling blades of the electric fan behind the lectern, his eyes sad and vacant, his right arm slung over the pew in front of him so that he could hold the hand of his two-year-old nephew, Snuggles, Terence's child. "I cried on the inside," Lafeyette said later. "I didn't have enough in me to cry."

As the service closed and the mourners moved forward for one last look at the body, Pharoah, still gripping his balled-up sweatshirt, asked, "What's up in heaven? Do they have stores?"

"Shut up," Lafeyette said. "You don't know what you talking 'bout."

Passing the casket for the last time, gang members flashed the hand signal of the Conservative Vice Lords. Lafeyette and James and Pharoah didn't speak until they were outside the church.

"We're gonna die one way or the other, by killing or plain out," James said to Lafeyette. "I just wanna die plain out."

Lafeyette nodded. "Me, too."

LAFEYETTE froze, then stabbed at a fly resting on the stove. "Got it." He shook his fist a couple of times and threw the startled insect into the hot, stagnant air.

"C-c-c-c'mon, Lafie, let's . . . let's . . . let's go," Pharoah pleaded.

Lafeyette reached out again, this time swatting the back of his brother's head. "Shut up, punk. I ain't going."

Lafeyette. *His face revealed so little, his mother thought, and yet so much.*

Pharoah begged his brother to take him back to the railroad tracks. He wanted to get away from his suffocating home, from Horner, from the Vice Lords, from the summer. It was the only place that offered him a respite, some momentary peace of mind.

The summer's violence had woefully unnerved Pharoah, and his stutter, which only a few months before had been nearly imperceptible, had become a real impediment to communicating. Words tangled in his throat. Sometimes he struggled so hard to get a sentence out that his neck muscles constricted, as if he were trying to physically push the words out. Embarrassed by his stammer, he kept to himself, hanging out mostly with Porkchop.

Pharoah now trembled at any loud noise. A few weeks before, while bullets tore past the living-room window, Pharoah had pleaded with LaJoe, "M-m-m-mama, make 'em . . . make 'em stop!" As the gunfire continued, he fainted.

Earlier in the summer Lafeyette, along with James, had given in to Pharoah's pleadings and agreed to go back to the tracks. But then they heard that someone had gotten trapped under a train and lost his legs while hunting for snakes. Rumor here is often taken for truth. Given the brutality of Horner, almost everything is believable. The boys decided not to take any chances with their own limbs.

"Man, you . . . you lied," Pharoah whined, ducking yet another blow.

"I ain't lied. Don't tell no stories," Lafeyette countered.

"Let's . . . let's . . ."

Lafeyette, impatient, walked away without letting Pharoah finish his thought. He just wasn't going. That was it. It wasn't safe.

The summer had begun to change Lafeyette. LaJoe couldn't remember the last time she'd seen him cry. She scolded him for being too hard on Pharoah, but she knew it was only because he felt protective of the younger boy. For a twelve-year-old he felt too responsible. She remembered one afternoon when Lafeyette, braving gunfire, tried to get a young friend to take cover. The friend remained glued to the swing, repeating over and over, "I wanna die. I wanna die." Lafeyette wouldn't leave him there alone.

Bird Leg's funeral haunted him. But he confided to LaJoe, who tried vainly to get him to verbalize his grief, that talking wasn't going to help him, that everything that "goes wrong keeps going on, and everything that's right doesn't stay right."

His face masked his troubles. It was a face without affect, without emotion. Even in its emptiness it was an unforgiving face. Lafeyette was an unforgiving child. "I don't have friends," he told his mother. "Just associates. Friends you trust."

To look into Lafeyette's rust-colored eyes that summer was to look into a chasm of loneliness and fear. Yet those darting eyes missed little. And so, despite Pharoah's repeated requests, he refused to return to the railroad tracks. It would, he believed, only invite trouble.

FALL 1987–SPRING 1988
Four

A NARROW parking lot cut between the back of the Riverses' building and a paint factory. LaJoe and her closest friend, Rochelle, leaned against a rusted sedan, its windows and front tires long gone. Though it was a few weeks into September, summer still lingered. A warm breeze swirled through the development, cutting through the breezeways and the parking lot.

Rochelle was six years younger than LaJoe. They'd met as children and eventually became best of friends—the only real friends, they would say, each one had. Rochelle had no children of her own, though LaJoe would say that she had become "like a second mother" to Lafeyette, Pharoah, and the others; Rochelle occasionally bought them clothes or toys, or gave them a dollar for candy. Though she no longer had a job, Rochelle ran a card game, which sometimes netted her as much as $700 a month. She and her parents lived a couple of blocks from LaJoe, in Horner; LaJoe often visited them. And Rochelle, as on this day, often came by to see LaJoe.

Whenever the gangs entered into a peace treaty, the parking lot became a meeting ground for neighbors. This was such a day, and the children took advantage of the reprieve. While the adults watched, they pursued each other from one end of the lot to the other. Pharoah stood by himself on the building's back stoop, leaning on the black metal banister and staring into space.

"He's daydreaming lots," LaJoe said to Rochelle. "He's getting more forgetful. Pharoah!" she called. "Pharoah, come here."

The boy's head jerked up. He smiled and ran over to his mother, and she ran her fingers through his hair. Rochelle gave him a smile.

"What you thinking?" LaJoe asked. Pharoah looked up at her.

"Mama, w-w-when . . . when . . . w-w-when . . ." The words tangled in his throat as he strained to answer her.

She didn't let him finish. "Soon, Pharoah. Once they get off strike."

The city's teachers were into the second week of their fourth strike in five years. As in the other walkouts, the main dispute centered on money. The teachers wanted a pay raise. The school board, on the other hand, proposed trimming the school year by three days to save money, which would result in an effective 1.7 percent pay cut.

Pharoah loved school. Unlike the streets, where his stammer and small size made him the object of ridicule, he stood tall in school. Although he read two months below grade level, he was near the top of his upcoming fourth-grade class.

When school was in session, Pharoah was the first to leave home each morning. During all of third grade he had been late only four times. At night he frequently read until his eyes hurt. Because he had no lamp or working overhead light in his bedroom, he would lie on his belly on the brown floor, with his head poking out the door to take advantage of the naked sixty-watt hallway light.

When he got bored or had nothing better to do, Pharoah practiced his penmanship. His teachers noted that he had an unusually neat and delicate handwriting for someone so young, and this summer he had had a lot of time to practice it. But for him the strike-extended vacation dragged on far too long. During the long summer another friend of the family's was shot and killed. When school finally did open, on October 4, Pharoah approached it with fervor.

THE HENRY SUDER ELEMENTARY School is a horseshoe-shaped two-story red brick building whose architecture is more utilitarian than aesthetic. Its courtyard butts up against Horner, separated only by a waist-high fence.

Suder is somewhat unusual for an inner-city school. While its children test below grade level, its halls are well monitored, its children, for the most part, well behaved. Moreover, the reading and math scores of its students show steady improvement by the time they graduate from eighth grade. Much of the good record is due to Brenda Daigre, who has been the school's principal since 1975. Ms. Daigre won't tolerate hats or earrings, both of which signify affiliation with a gang. The school is free of graffiti and violence.

But there are elements beyond Ms. Daigre's control. Like other big-city schools, Suder has experienced financial constraints. Its art and music classes were cut in 1980. Its one counselor's administrative duties leave little time for counseling the school's 700 students. Also, Suder must share a nurse and a psychologist with three other schools. And it has another problem: of its thirty-eight teachers, only a handful are men. In a community where positive male role models are scarce (an estimated 85 percent of the households at Horner are headed by women), the lack of male teachers is felt acutely.

It was the first day back at school after the strike, and Diana F. Barone, forty, strode into her fourth-grade classroom. Her students fluttered around her, like baby robins angling for a worm.

"Where you been?"

"D'you get your money?"

"Sure happy you back."

The questions and comments came at her fast and furious. They made her feel good. Students and teachers alike were glad the strike was finally over. (The teachers had won a 4 percent pay boost.)

Ms. Barone had begun teaching at Suder sixteen years earlier, and while she hadn't lost her enthusiasm, she had become a bit leery of investing as much energy and time as she once had. She tired of the large classes, which at one point had swelled to as many as thirty-four students, and of the funding cutbacks. And she worried so much about her students—many of whom came in tired or sad or distracted—that she developed an ulcerated colon.

The relentless violence of the neighborhood also wore her down.

The parking lot behind the school had been the site of numerous gang battles. When the powerful sounds of .357 Magnums and sawed-off shotguns echoed off the school walls, the streetwise students huddled under their desks. Ms. Barone placed the back of her chair against a pillar, a solid object between herself and the window.

She dreaded the walk from and to her car. She no longer wore jewelry. She carried a cheap plastic purse and regularly slipped her paycheck into her bra before making the short trek to her car.

But none of this had depleted Ms. Barone's tremendous energy. A short, spunky woman, she turned to her military training in the marines and the air force reserve to help maintain order. Her students had to follow a set procedure for getting to their desks, marching single file to the back of the room and then down the appropriate aisle. A student who took home a book placed it the next morning on the upper-right-hand corner of the desk. Children could go to the bathroom no more than twice a day and could dispose of garbage only on the way out of the classroom.

"The kids want this orderliness," Ms. Barone reasoned. "It gives them a sense of being in an environment that is safe and comfortable."

On the first day of school Ms. Barone had the students introduce themselves. When it was Pharoah's turn, she noticed his stammering. "M-m-my . . . my name . . . m-m-my name is Pharoah Rivers," he told the class. She was struck by his determination. The words came hard sometimes, but that didn't stop him. Ms. Barone urged Pharoah to slow down, to take his time talking. But Pharoah's stutter that year, as his family ran into a series of problems, would only worsen.

Pharoah flourished under Ms. Barone's rigid discipline and high energy. And despite his stuttering, he liked to talk in class. Sometimes he'd answer questions out of turn; other times he'd simply start up conversations, often in the middle of a lesson. In all likelihood Pharoah talked and livened up at school because he felt protected there.

Because of his size, Pharoah was picked on by other children. Once, in the middle of a test, a girl next to him hit him on the neck with a spitball. Pharoah screeched, then hollered, "Old girl be hitting me! Old girl, stop it." Everyone laughed. Pharoah was always referring to others as old girl and old boy, even the adults, and it never failed, though he couldn't fathom why, to tickle everyone who heard him.

But Pharoah most endeared himself to his teacher and his classmates by his imagination and writing. He loved words. He'd remember names of places, like Ontonagon River and Agate Falls, because he liked the way they sounded. When he could, he'd play Scrabble with friends, spelling out words like motel and quake. He was so proficient that later in the year Ms. Barone would choose him to compete in the annual spelling bee, one of the school's biggest honors.

PHAROAH first met Rickey at school, where they were classmates. Rickey asked Pharoah for a favor. Rickey had developed a crush on Pharoah's cousin Dede. "Pharoah," he said, "ask Dede if she'd go out with me." Pharoah giggled, delighted to be entrusted with such a task. When he delivered the message, Dede told him, "No way."

"Ask her again," Rickey implored. Pharoah did, and this time Dede said she would give it a try. Before too long, graffiti began appearing in Pharoah's building: RICKEY LS [LOVES] DEDE. Rickey and Pharoah became friends after that.

Rickey lived in Henry Horner, just two buildings west of Pharoah's, but his house was on the other side of Damen Avenue, the dividing line between the Vice Lords' and the Disciples' turfs. So for starters, it seemed strange that a boy from west of Damen would befriend a boy from the other side. But more surprising was that Rickey and Pharoah would find some bond despite the startling differences between them. Where Pharoah was slight, Rickey, a year and a half older, was, in the words of one local policeman, "built like a pit bull." Where Pharoah adored school, Rickey shunned it. He could barely read, and had already been held back a year. Moreover, he had been written up so many times for bad behavior that the compilation was nearly the thickness of a phone book.

And where Pharoah tried to keep a distance from the neighborhood's violence, Rickey was in the thick of it. Rickey had been with Bird Leg when he died. The two were second cousins. Rickey was one of the younger children whom Bird Leg had befriended, and like Lafeyette, he had loved being around Bird Leg's dogs. On the day of the shooting, Rickey had joined the battle, hurling bricks at Bird Leg's assailants. He heard the lone gunshot and watched his cousin fall by the cottonwood and die. He then sat on a nearby bench and wept. For the next two days he stayed in his apartment, refusing to talk or eat.

"I felt like I lost a big brother," Rickey said later. "Seem like I don't care no more. I don't feel sorry for people no more, 'cause when they killed Bird Leg, the peoples who shot him mustn't of felt sorry for him." Often when Rickey became embroiled in a fight, he began to relive Bird Leg's last minutes, and his anger turned to rage.

Pharoah was unaware of the effect of Bird Leg's death on Rickey. Beneath the raw exterior lay a tender child who took the hands of younger children to help them cross the street. LaJoe thought Rickey's eyes were filled with sweetness. But it was a guarded softness. When he smiled, he seemed uncomfortable, as if he might be judged a sissy. There were times later on, after numerous entanglements with the law and flirtations with the gangs, that Rickey would act distant and tough. But at eleven, he didn't try to hide his kindness.

What cemented Pharoah and Rickey's friendship was an incident that took place during gym class one day, shortly after Rickey started dating Dede. Another boy, Cortez, snatched a basketball from Pharoah's hands. Pharoah was furious. "Give . . . give . . . give it to me!" he demanded. Cortez smiled, and dribbled the basketball, taunting Pharoah. Pharoah, who didn't like to fight, did nothing. Rickey grabbed the ball and gave it to Pharoah. A few minutes later Cortez went over and threw Pharoah to the ground.

"Cortez, man, why you do that?" Rickey demanded. He put Cortez in a headlock, then pummeled him. "Poom! Poom! Poom! Then I stopped," he later recalled. "Everybody picks on Pharoah 'cause he's so short and he doesn't like to fight. It just feel like he's a little brother to me." Cortez left Pharoah alone after that.

To the adults Rickey's friendship with Pharoah seemed odd. But from Pharoah's perspective it was easy to understand. Rickey offered Pharoah protection; he was a trusted friend. When Rickey had money, he would give some to Pharoah. Though he never said as much, it was understood that he wouldn't let anything happen to him.

LAFEYETTE was wary of his brother's new friend. "I worry about Pharoah a lot," Lafeyette explained. "I don't want anything to happen to him, because he's my little brother. I'm supposed to watch after him. He makes me mad at times, but I still love him."

He was proud of how well Pharoah did at school. A smart child himself, Lafeyette never took school as seriously as Pharoah did. He had already been held back a year. His attendance record at times was woeful—in 1986 he missed thirty-five days and received a D average. The excuses varied: flu, stomachache, no clean clothes to wear. Sometimes he was suspended because of fights in school. He secretly wished his mother would push him more, make him go to sleep early, make him do his homework. LaJoe conceded that she could be too soft on her children, though she wanted nothing more than to see Lafeyette and Pharoah graduate from high school.

Despite his poor attendance record, however, Lafeyette tested particularly well in his favorite subject—math. When he did attend school with some regularity, as in fourth grade, he earned a B minus average. His teacher this fall, in sixth grade, liked him. She found that when he came to school, he wanted to learn and was earnest about his work. Lafeyette on occasion would skip gym class to talk with her about problems at home or in the neighborhood. He told her he sometimes found himself daydreaming in class, worrying about his brothers and sisters.

It especially frustrated Lafeyette that his younger brother refused to fight. He believed he had an obligation to toughen Pharoah up. He'd badger him—sometimes calling him fag and punk—and slap him until Pharoah could take it no longer and would flail back.

"You gotta fight," Lafeyette would tell him. "I ain't gonna be there all the time to fight for you. C'mon, c'mon, hit me."

Pharoah would beg his brother to let him be. "It ain't right," he said to Lafeyette. "Why's people fighting people?"

"That's stupid," Lafeyette countered.

Lafeyette talked to his mother. Wasn't there something she could do to keep Pharoah away from Rickey, who undoubtedly would get him into trouble? It was, to be sure, a peculiar match—the bully and the bookworm. And so it came as no surprise to Pharoah that his brother would disapprove of his friendship with Rickey.

"Hey, man, he only gonna get you in trouble," Lafeyette warned Pharoah.

"You . . . you . . . you ain't my father," Pharoah retorted, walking away from his brother.

"He too old for you to be with," Lafeyette yelled after him.

But the friendship persisted despite Lafeyette's efforts. And ironically, in the end it was Lafeyette who would be more influenced by Rickey than Pharoah was.

Five

THE apartment was too crowded, but LaJoe didn't have the heart to kick anyone out. Her children had no place to go.

Shortly before Christmas, LaShawn, the oldest, had moved back home. She brought with her a small entourage: her boyfriend, her boyfriend's brother, and her two children—Tyisha, who was seven, and Darrell, who was one. Everyone called him Baldheaded except Pharoah, who insisted on calling him Sir Baldheaded.

LaShawn and her children had been renting a room in a tenement with friends, but they ended up not getting along. LaJoe worried that LaShawn might be harmed when her boyfriend, Brian, went to work. Brian sold fake gold jewelry to unsuspecting tourists at O'Hare Airport, where he worked every day. LaJoe had also been concerned about her daughter's ability to take care of her two children, given her drug habit. She smoked Karachi, a potent mixture of amphetamines and Pakistani heroin particularly popular on the West Side.

Like many other public housing apartments, the Riverses' overflowed with people—as many as fourteen if the children's father, Paul, stayed over. LaShawn, Brian, and Baldheaded slept in one room, Terence and Weasel in another. The triplets and Tyisha bedded down in the front bedroom. Lafeyette and Pharoah shared the back room with Brian's teenage brother, Larry. Pharoah had trouble adjusting to the crowded apartment, but he conceded that having all those people made him feel safer: "If someone snatch you, you'll have a witness." LaJoe usually slept on the couch or with the triplets.

LaJoe felt pressured that winter. On occasion she would explode in anger, ordering her young ones to shut up or telling Lafeyette and Pharoah to clean their room. She battled persistent colds and headaches. She rarely felt that she could sail through a day and enjoy such simple moments as the coming of spring or Pharoah's smile or Lafeyette's playful teasing. There was no time to reflect on the past or to plan for the future. If it wasn't the shooting outside, it was Lafeyette's troubles at school or Pharoah's stammer. She felt, she said, as if her insides were being shredded. LaJoe once said that had she known all that her younger children, from Lafeyette on down, would have to endure, she would have returned them to the womb.

THE PROBLEMS HAD STARTED WITH Terence. He had been LaJoe's closest child, and his failure was her biggest disappointment. For LaJoe,
Terence became a measuring stick for Lafeyette and Pharoah. She
worried that they, like him, might let her down.

Born on January 31, 1970, Terence grew up during a difficult time
for LaJoe and Paul. The two had met four years earlier at Swingville,
a local dance hall. They still dispute who first asked the other to
dance. But there's a lot now they disagree about.

Paul, then seventeen, was—and still is—a handsome man. Like
LaJoe, he was shy and small in stature, but because he boxed as an
amateur bantamweight, he had a rugged, wiry build. Despite his
pugilistic hobby, Paul was of a gentle nature and quick mind. He read
a lot—magazines and newspapers mostly. He was a connoisseur of
jazz and loved to debate politics. He became involved peripherally
with the Black Panthers, whose city headquarters was just two blocks
from Horner, and then with the local Democratic Party ·machine.
Major Adams, the leader of the Boys Club Drum and Bugle Corps
and a kind of father figure for the neighborhood's youth, thought
Paul one of the smartest young men he'd ever met at Horner.

Paul and LaJoe wasted little time. Within a year of their meeting,
LaJoe, only fourteen, gave birth to LaShawn, and then, a year later,
to Weasel. Soon after, they decided to get married. But on the day of
the wedding Paul backed out and got stone drunk. Furious, LaJoe's
mother barred him from visiting LaJoe. The two continued to date
surreptitiously and eventually moved in together. A third child, Terence, soon arrived, and that's when the dream began to fall apart.

Paul had already fathered a boy by another woman—a child born
within a few days of Terence. LaJoe never quite forgave Paul his
philandering, though in her youthful determination to make things
right, she got him to marry her. LaJoe wanted her children to have
a father. Paul, too, wanted the children to grow up with a man around
the house. On August 22, almost seven months after Terence was
born, they took the bus down to city hall, where they were wed.

In a neighborhood where men fathered children and then disappeared, Terence and his siblings had an unusual family situation—
their mother remained married to the same man, and he fathered all
eight children. They began to fall out of love, though, when LaJoe
learned of Paul's drug habit.

Paul, unbeknownst to LaJoe, began to dabble with drugs in the early 1970s, shortly after they were married. By the age of twenty-two Paul started shooting up heroin; the habit, which he has bucked at times, has stayed with him for the better part of twenty years.

LaJoe first learned for certain of Paul's habit—she had earlier suspected it—around 1978, when Terence was eight. She was sitting in the front bedroom when she heard Paul collapse in the bathroom. He lay there unconscious; blood filled the syringe bulging from his forearm. LaJoe yanked the needle out and called for an ambulance. After he had been taken to the hospital, she cried for hours.

Paul survived and a couple of years later made it through yet another overdose. LaJoe hated him for it. Most of his heroin was financed by his good-paying jobs with the city—in the sewer department, as a garbage collector, and more recently as a bus driver.

LaJoe wanted to kick him out for good. But she also strongly wanted her children to have a father. So she let him come around and even allowed him to stay over, though they rarely slept together. Having gone back to school to earn her high school equivalency, LaJoe worked off and on for five years as a clerk for the Miles Square Health Center. She had also flirted briefly with a modeling career, which quickly foundered. The disappointment lingered, and it was one of the few things LaJoe refused to discuss with anyone. During the times she was unemployed, she received welfare.

In Paul's absence LaJoe found comfort in her children, particularly Terence. As a young boy, Terence, rail-thin and gangly, wasn't a gifted athlete, nor was he much of a fighter. An anxious child, always by LaJoe's side, he seemed to some a mama's boy. LaJoe did pamper him. "Anything I asked my mama for, I got it," Terence later recalled. LaJoe so adored Terence that she even promised him she would have no more children, that he would be the last.

When she later gave birth to Lafeyette, then Pharoah, and then the triplets, Terence became jealous of the new arrivals. His mother had let him down. LaJoe grew impatient with Terence's clinging.

"Terence was the one maybe I should have paid more attention to. He always wanted to be under me," LaJoe recalls. "Terence never wanted to turn me loose. As the other kids came, he used to tell me all the time, 'You should of just had me.' But Terence just left one day. He was about nine. No. He was about ten. I couldn't find him.

The police were looking for Terence. When I saw him, it was three months later. I couldn't do nothing, 'cause I didn't know."

What LaJoe didn't know was that a local drug dealer, Charles, had taken Terence under his wing. Charles used the youngster, who had not yet entered sixth grade, to sell T's and blues—a mixture of Talwin and antihistamines—at the time a popular substitute for heroin.

It was 1981, about the time drug prices began to drop, and the trade blossomed. Terence would stand on Madison Street among the liquor stores and pawnshops, just two blocks south of the projects. He hid his wares in the steel pillars that supported the el tracks. Using juveniles to sell is popular among drug dealers, since children tend to be treated less harshly than adults by the courts. What's more, once found guilty, they are rarely held beyond twenty days.

Terence was not only earning as much as $200 a day but Charles virtually adopted him, setting him up with his own room, complete with bed and television. Sometimes Charles entrusted Terence with as much as $10,000 in cash, knowing that neither the police nor extortionists would suspect an eleven-year-old of carrying that kind of money. Charles also taught Terence to shoot a .45-caliber revolver. Terence was so small that he had to hold the gun with both hands. He had little need for school; he dropped out in the seventh grade.

By the time LaJoe learned what had become of Terence, she couldn't win him back. Once, she confronted Charles.

"I want my son," she told him.

"Terence is my son. He belongs to me," Charles replied.

She tried everything. She even went to the police. If they brought him home, he stayed a few weeks, then took off again. Paul also tried, confronting Charles at a diner where he was known to hang out. But people appeared out of nowhere, surrounding Paul, and he had to back off.

LaJoe and Paul lost Terence to the neighborhood. It is not unusual for parents to lose out to the lure of the gangs and drug dealers. And the reasons aren't always clear. In one Horner family a son has become a big drug dealer, a daughter a social worker. In another, one boy is in jail on a gang-related murder, another has set up a neighborhood youth program. Some parents simply won't let their children leave the apartment. A common expression among mothers at Horner is "He ain't my child no more."

Lafeyette, who was six at the time, knew only that his brother sold T's and blues, though he didn't understand until later years what that meant. Lafeyette considered Terence his favorite brother. He would see Terence in the street and, in full run, throw his arms around him.

"C'mon, Terry, let's go home."

"Naw, man. I gotta take care of my business," Terence would reply.

"C'mon, brother."

"Here's five dollars. Now go on. Tell Mama and them I say hi."

"Okay. You gonna come home tomorrow?"

"Yeah, I'm gonna come."

Terence eventually grew tired of belonging to Charles. What finally brought him home was an incident with LaJoe.

"My mom, she give me anything I want," he recalled. "She wasn't doing that no more. She stopped giving me anything. She just got fed up. There was one particular day—I didn't have no money, and I told her to give me ten dollars. She told me no. She was real aggravated, real angry at me. She said, 'You don't listen to me no more.' And that hurted me. That was the first time she ever turned me down."

Terence returned to his family, but the troubles didn't end. He ran with a fast crowd. He and his friends shoplifted and broke into video games. He started dabbling first with marijuana, then Karachi.

He briefly joined the Disciples, who at that point oversaw his end of Horner. And like many of his teenage friends, he became a father: he had three children—two girls and a boy. Like his mother, he had his first child at fourteen. As tradition dictated, the child was named after his dad, Terence, though everyone called him Snuggles.

There were times when Terence tried to slow down, and for a while he shined shoes at the airport or just hung around at home. But by the time he turned eighteen, he had been arrested forty-six times for crimes ranging from disorderly conduct to purse snatching.

FOR six months, from the summer of 1987 through January of 1988, fifteen taverns in the Nineteenth Police District, on the city's mostly white North Side, reported robberies, sometimes as many as two a month. Two to four black males would pry open video poker games and run off with the change. In one instance it amounted to $1500 from one machine.

The robbers almost always worked the same way. Two teenagers would find a working-class neighborhood tavern, where early in the day the clientele would be older and less likely to resist. One youth would dance and shout in false excitement, playing the game, while his cohort would use a long screwdriver to jimmy open the coin box. The police considered these nuisance crimes, but North Side barkeepers had been complaining regularly. The police said to alert them if any suspicious people came into the taverns.

On January 15 the police received such a call from Lawry's Tavern. Two young black males had come in, one of whom ordered a Coca-Cola. Three plainclothesmen hurriedly drove to Lawry's, entering separately so as not to arouse suspicion. As they watched from different ends of the bar, the boys walked over to the video poker machine and began to play it. Then, suspecting that the three new customers might be police, they surreptitiously stashed their screwdriver behind a radiator. As they started to leave, the police placed them under arrest. From one of the boys they recovered a set of keys to other video machines; they also found the screwdriver. The police charged them with a misdemeanor and took pictures of them in the hope that if they continued their robberies, bartenders would be able to identify them. The younger of the two, Terence Rivers, was the more easily identifiable—he wore his long hair combed back and down to his shoulders. Moreover, Terence was slightly built, rangy and short.

Two weeks later four black males robbed Ann's Longhorn Saloon, allegedly at knife point. When one of the accomplices was identified as Terence, it was reasonable to conclude that, in fact, he had broken into yet another video poker game. Only now he was an adult, which meant that the penalty would be much stiffer than a month or two in the juvenile home.

Three days later the police knocked on LaJoe's door. "We're looking for a Bobby Anderson. He here?" one of the officers asked. Terence used an alias; Anderson was LaJoe's maiden name.

Terence sauntered out of a back room. He told LaJoe he hadn't done anything. She asked the officers not to handcuff her son in front of Lafeyette and Pharoah, but they did so anyway.

"They ain't gonna bring you back," Lafeyette muttered. Pharoah said nothing.

The charge was armed robbery. The owner of Ann's Longhorn Saloon had identified Terence from the earlier Polaroid photograph.

Six

WELFARE recipients call it the interrogation room. It is tucked away on the second floor of the local welfare office, an expansive brick building directly across Western Avenue from Henry Horner. In 1987 this Department of Public Aid office paid $31,720,194 in benefits to 23,247 West Side recipients of such grants as Aid to Families with Dependent Children and Medicaid.

On this windy April day, when it alternately snowed and rained, the welfare-office waiting area was half filled. LaJoe, dressed neatly in jeans and a blue denim coat, waited nervously.

"LaJoe Rivers," a caseworker finally called. LaJoe got up to follow the caseworker through a tangled maze of desks and dividers to the interrogation room.

LaJoe had received notice from the Department of Public Aid that it had launched an investigation into her eligibility. She knew nothing more than that. The $931 she received each month, a combination of both welfare and food stamps, was her only income. She spent most of the money within three days of receiving it: nearly $400 for groceries, which she bought in one shopping trip; $80 for burial insurance; $122 for rent; and $8 to cash the check at the currency exchange. She used the remaining $300 or so to purchase small items, as well as clothes for the children, most of which had been placed on layaway.

The room where LaJoe was led was small. Four strategically placed metal chairs—one facing the other three—and a metal desk devoid of papers gave it the appearance of a place meant for interrogation.

LaJoe sat in the chair clearly intended for her—the one standing apart. She folded her hands and waited. Someone brought in one more chair and lined it up with the others. Ten minutes later three women and a man filed in. They did not introduce themselves.

One of the women explained that LaJoe was here for a preappeal hearing, in which she would get a chance to hear the charges against her and, if she desired, to respond to them. Another woman then took over. Citing Chapter 320 of the Public Aid statutes, she said, "We have found substantial information that your husband has claimed your residence as his home. Do you have anything to dispute that?"

LaJoe nervously fingered her gold-colored loop earrings. She spoke so softly that the four inquisitors had to lean forward to hear her. "He's at his mother's and sister's. Here, there." She went on to explain that she gave Paul his mail when he came around.

"Was there a place you could always find him?" the woman asked.

"He was always on the corner of Lake and Woods," said LaJoe, referring to a local liquor store where men of Paul's age hung out.

The woman continued to rattle off the proof that the department had compiled, placing Paul at LaJoe's. It was damning. She cited joint income tax returns. She noted Paul had received unemployment benefits and a court summons at LaJoe's apartment. Four single-spaced pages outlined the charges. A fifth page listed the benefits LaJoe had received since 1974; they totaled $109,373 in financial assistance and food stamps.

"You have to prove to us that our findings are false," the woman concluded. "We have substantial evidence placing him in your home."

"Is that it?" LaJoe asked, referring not to the evidence, but to the meeting itself.

"Yes," the woman replied.

Confused and upset, LaJoe walked silently out of the room. She slammed the door behind her. She would later apologize to her inquisitors for her impoliteness, but she wouldn't offer much defense against the department's charges. She didn't ask whether she was entitled to legal counsel. She didn't ask where she would get money to feed her children. She didn't ask for a caseworker to come look at her home. Now, as she made her way through the labyrinth of desks, she wondered how to break the news to the kids.

Lafeyette knew his mother had gone for a hearing and that the department was considering cutting her benefits, so when she came home, he was by the door to greet her. As she walked into the apartment his eyes locked with hers. His long fingers cupped her face.

"What'd they say?" he asked.

"Off," LaJoe replied in a voice that barely approached a whisper. Lafeyette's shoulders sank. LaJoe hugged him.

She chose not to tell Pharoah, at least not yet. He had lately responded to nearly every instance of violence and family trouble with the same refrain—"I'm too little to understand." She was convinced that his attitude gave him some peace of mind and the strength to push on, so she avoided burdening him with stories of hardship.

She wished, in fact, that she hadn't told Lafeyette, but he was the only person she felt she could talk to about it. It was as if he were as much a husband as he was a son. He was her confidant.

Lafeyette believed that the only person he could depend on was his mother, and he would do anything to protect her. A year before, when two teenagers robbed her and Rochelle, one of the assailants severed the nerves in the middle and ring fingers of LaJoe's right hand with a butcher knife. The fingers now often swelled and were painful. Lafeyette told her, "If I was around and I had a gun or something, I'd of shot him. I don't play that about my mother."

Later he said, "Sometimes I be in my bed crying so God can hear me so my mama's fingers get well. She can't hardly do nothing with them. If she has to open up a can, I'll help her." He would scrub the family's dirty clothes because the work hurt his mother's hand.

The night of the hearing, after the other children had gone to sleep, Lafeyette got out of bed and joined his mother on the living-room couch. "What you worrying about?" he asked.

"I ain't worried," LaJoe lied.

"Yes, you is. Don't worry 'bout nothing. I be worrying for you. I'm gonna help you." Lafeyette drew closer to his mother, placing his arm awkwardly around her shoulders.

"Lafie, I'm not worried about nothing. We're gonna be all right." LaJoe then explained that the reason she had gotten into trouble was that she had let Paul use their address.

"You ought to put them out, all of them," Lafeyette said of his father and his older sister.

"If I put them in the street—they live their lives in the street—they'll look like the street. I can't put them out."

"If they ain't helping me the way you helped us, I wouldn't help them. I wouldn't care 'bout them."

"It ain't them. They not even theyself," she said, referring to their drug problems.

"You should stop being so weakhearted." Lafeyette could see his mother's pained expression. That remark hurt LaJoe because she knew there to be some truth in it. She *was* weakhearted. She didn't have the resolve to kick her older children out of the apartment or, for that matter, to put her foot down and not allow Paul to stay over on occasion. She sometimes seemed passive, unable to act on what she knew was right. But her strength was also her weakness. She gave and gave and gave—and then didn't get it back. The problem was that she didn't know when to stop giving.

"No, I don't mean weakhearted," Lafeyette corrected himself. "But you don't like it here. You don't like nothing that be going on at this time. I would leave. One day I might just walk up and find a whole bag of money and bring it home, Mama, and then we can move out of the projects. When I grow up, I don't know where I be headed, but I'm gonna have a white house. It'd be made of wood, and Pharoah and all them—they're gonna be my kids."

Lafeyette talked frequently of getting out of Horner, and sometimes would feel such urgency about it that he would get angry at his mother for not trying harder. He once demanded that she wait on line to apply for one of 285 rehabilitated apartments that were federally subsidized. She did, but there were over 1000 people on line ahead of her, some of whom had been camped out since the previous morning. Another time Lafeyette insisted that she inquire about some new rental units in one of the few restored brownstones in the neighborhood. She did that, too, but they cost far too much.

Lafeyette now suggested that he quit school and find work to help feed and clothe the family. LaJoe told him that was nonsense; they would manage, and he should stay in school. The two talked until about two in the morning. Now and then they fell silent, and Lafeyette rested his head on his mother's shoulder. During their talk he confessed, "Mama, one time I had said to myself I wasn't gonna talk no more. I got tired of peoples talking to me. What I try to say ain't worth saying to nobody anyways. Nothing happens."

Lafeyette had become more and more reticent, keeping to himself. He relied on as few people as possible: his mother, maybe his brother Pharoah, and himself. These were the only ones he knew for certain wouldn't cross him, who wouldn't desert him.

James Howard, one of Lafeyette's closest "associates," had moved out of Horner earlier in April. So many friends and acquaintances passed through Lafeyette's life that he didn't seem to give James' absence much thought. He was used to being disappointed. No one else, it seemed, ever held up his end of a bargain. Lafeyette was certain that a neighbor or friend had called Public Aid about Paul.

"The things I should of been talking to Paul about I was talking to

Lafie," LaJoe later said. "I put him in a bad place. But I didn't have anyone to talk to. Lafie," she said regretfully, "became a twelve-year-old man that day."

PHAROAH didn't find out about Public Aid's decision until a couple of weeks later, when LaJoe didn't go to do her usual monthly shopping. Pharoah loved to help his mother carry in the groceries and then organize them in the cabinets and refrigerator. When it became apparent that his mother wouldn't be shopping, Pharoah asked what had happened. His mother explained their situation.

"Old girl, we're really poor now," Pharoah said.

LaJoe laughed and thought to herself, As if we weren't poor already.

Pharoah surprised her. He seemed to take it all in stride. One afternoon he asked her for a quarter but, before she could refuse him, covered his mouth in embarrassment. "Oops, I forgot," he apologized, and went on about his business.

LaJoe leaned on friends and family. One of her sisters gave her $65 worth of food stamps. Rochelle supplied her with some food. But her family and neighbors were limited in what they could give her. So LaJoe played cards for money.

Like housecleaning, it got her mind off her problems. A friend's mother ran an all-night card game for women, and LaJoe now played almost nightly, winning $35 one time, $20 another. She'd leave after putting the children to sleep, and not come home until morning, usually early enough to help prepare the kids for school.

LaJoe also looked for work. She applied for jobs at three local hospitals, but couldn't get any interviews. She spent a day checking with stores in the Loop, the city's downtown area, but could find nothing. Part of LaJoe's difficulty was her timidity. It sometimes made her seem unusually tense, even aloof. She lacked the ability to combine her humility and self-assuredness—two powerful traits that alternately dominated her personality—in her interviews. Also, after staying home with her children for seven years, she was unprepared to reenter the job market. She had no skills to offer. And there were few jobs to be had.

LAJOE still had an appeal hearing in which an administrative law judge would hear first Public Aid's case and then her response. It didn't go well.

Paul felt guilty and responsible for the family's predicament, so he visited a caseworker before the appeal to tell of his history with drugs and his separation from his wife. He asked that the conversation be kept confidential from his employer. The caseworker understood that to mean confidential from everyone. She didn't mention his visit at the appeal hearing.

But what upset LaJoe was knowing that any caseworker who visited her apartment would have realized that she could not be double-dipping. Lafeyette and Pharoah slept on lumpy, torn mattresses. The triplets and LaShawn's daughter, Tyisha, were crowded into one bed. LaJoe's living-room couch had cost $45 at the local Goodwill; the matching chairs, $20. The family had no kitchen table; they ate their meals seated in the living room. Many of the children's clothes were secondhand. Besides, LaJoe thought, if she had had the benefit of Paul's full income, they would have long ago moved from Henry Horner.

Also—and this LaJoe failed to make clear to Public Aid—Paul had been suspended from his job in January, four months earlier, for drinking. The transit authority sent him to a rehabilitation center, but Paul started drinking and taking drugs again. In effect, he had been permanently suspended. He now had no income.

LaJoe felt so defeated that she barely put up a fight. At the hearing she mentioned only in passing that Paul had been suspended. She didn't refer to his drug problem, perhaps to protect him. Not surprisingly, the judge ruled against her. Public Aid would strip her of her benefits. If she wanted, however, she could reapply.

LITTLE else changed. As the summer approached, the shooting picked up. Twice in May, LaJoe herded the children into the hall to avoid stray bullets. Pharoah's stutter worsened. He continued to shake whenever he heard a loud noise. Lafeyette told his mother, "Mama, if we don't get away, someone's gonna end up dead. I feel it."

On May 22 a nine-year-old friend of the boys' was shot in the back of the head. Alonzo Campbell had been walking into his building, just across the street, when he was hit by a bullet meant for someone else. The shooting might have gone unnoticed outside Horner had it not offered a stark contrast to what had taken place two days earlier in Winnetka, an affluent northern suburb.

Laurie Dann, a thirty-year-old emotionally disturbed woman, had walked into a second-grade elementary school classroom and shot six children, killing eight-year-old Nicholas Corwin and wounding the others. Later that same day Dann killed herself.

The murder-suicide made national news. Winnetka's citizens brought in a crisis team of psychologists and social workers to deal with the trauma. Governor Jim Thompson called for increased school security. Others demanded tighter gun-control laws and a tougher examination for mental illness.

To many at Horner, the two shootings served to highlight everything they didn't have. Alonzo's shooting received extensive coverage in a local newspaper, but only because its aftermath so sharply contrasted with the response to the Winnetka shooting. No one counseled Alonzo, who survived, or his friends. Lafeyette and Pharoah talked to no one about the incident, though they prayed for their schoolmate. In Winnetka the shooting was an aberration; in Horner it was part of normal life.

I've got to keep smiling to keep from crying, LaJoe counseled herself. If I ever slow down, I'll lose it.

LaJoe, Lafeyette, Pharoah, and the triplets walked through the guarded fence, through the revolving door, and into the visitors' waiting room of Division Four of the Cook County Jail, a fifty-four-acre complex on the city's South Side. Built to house 1200 prisoners, it now holds 7000, a thousand of whom sleep on mattresses on the floor. Nearly all the people here are awaiting trial. They stay an average of 138 days, though the jail authorities may release any inmate who has committed a crime against property. In 1988 alone, the jail set free 25,000 accused criminals because it didn't have room for them.

After a twenty-minute wait a guard pointed LaJoe and the children to a room on the right. They could meet Terence there, he told them. The children eagerly followed LaJoe. They hadn't seen their brother since he was arrested several months earlier.

The rectangular visiting room has a countertop running its full length. It could pass for a small diner if it weren't for the pane of inch-thick bulletproof glass extending up to the ceiling, cutting the room in two. Six stools face each side of the glass. To hear a person on the other side, you must place your ear flat against a circular metal grate, while the other talks in a loud voice to compete with the other visitors and inmates in the room.

As LaJoe and the children crowded around the one free stool, Terence walked into the room on his side of the glass. He spotted his family and broke into a huge grin. So did Lafeyette, Pharoah, and the triplets. Terence sat down, beaming.

Tiffany pulled herself onto the countertop and pressed her lips against the metal grate. "I love you," she told her brother. "I love you, too," he replied. Then they all, in turn, told Terence they loved him. Lafeyette shared the stool with LaJoe, trying to catch Terence's every word. Pharoah fought to restrain the triplets, who in their excitement clamored for space on the countertop. He could hear little of what Terence had to say that morning.

As the joy of seeing his family wore off, Terence's smile disappeared. "I'm hurting," he told LaJoe, his clenched left fist drumming the countertop. "I wanna be outta here." He insisted repeatedly that he hadn't robbed the Longhorn Saloon. LaJoe believed him. Only once before in his over three dozen arrests had Terence professed his innocence. And that time he had, indeed, been wrongly accused.

"Don't give up hope. Be a man," LaJoe told him. She couldn't think of anything else encouraging to say.

Lafeyette leaned his full weight on the countertop; he pressed his lips against the dirty cold metal. "Hi, Terence," he said meekly.

Terence smiled, shaking his head and pointing. "Hey, homey, you look good." He launched into a ten-minute lecture, urging Lafeyette to stay in school and to keep to himself. Lafeyette listened raptly as his brother, who seemed eager to impart these guidelines, rambled on. "Lafie, I don't want you to follow my footprints. I want you to be better than me."

"Time to go," a guard called to Terence.

"Watch out for Mama," Terence urged Lafeyette in a rush. He then gave LaJoe lengthy instructions to say hello to his children and their mothers.

"Time to go," the guard said again.

"Okay, man!" Terence yelled.

He stood up from his stool and blew kisses to Lafeyette, Pharoah, and the triplets. "Send me some pictures," he hollered.

A COUPLE OF WEEKS LATER LAFEYETTE and Pharoah were curled up on the sofa watching Saturday morning cartoons. LaJoe sat on a nearby chair talking with Rochelle. "When's Terence getting out of jail?" Lafeyette interrupted his mother.

"I don't know," she replied.

"Guess," he demanded. "By the summer?"

"Lafie, I don't know," she said.

"Could he come home tomorrow?" he persisted.

"I don't think so, Lafie. I just don't know. Stop asking."

Lafeyette let out a low grunt of dissatisfaction and went back to watching cartoons. Ever since the arrest, Lafeyette asked about Terence regularly. He had even been having dreams about Terence, dreams that woke him, dreams he refused to share with anyone.

Pharoah, too, thought a lot about Terence. It especially upset him that Terence might be serving time for something he didn't do. Pharoah's sense of justice, of right and wrong, was so powerful that it sometimes took the form of righteousness. No one could get away with anything, including himself. At school he sometimes raised his hand to tell on himself if Ms. Barone asked who'd been chattering. And this past Christmas he had awakened early, stolen a look at the presents piled in the back room, and run in tears to his mother, complaining that she had forgotten him. Of course she hadn't; his gifts had been squirreled away in the front closet. For weeks afterward Pharoah apologized to his mother for questioning her love for him. "It bothered my conscience," he explained.

Pharoah knew that Terence had once before been locked up for something he hadn't done. Two years earlier nineteen-year-old Maggie Atlas told the police that Terence had shot her in the stomach. He spent five months in the county jail awaiting trial on charges of attempted murder before Atlas said she had lied—a friend who was a Vice Lord had tried to kill her and then told her to finger Terence. The friend had since been killed, so Atlas came forward. It was a harrowing experience for the family.

"What would you do if someone said you did something and you didn't?" Pharoah asked a friend. "What would you do if they still said you did? If the judge said you did? If they didn't believe you?" The incident so unsettled him that he cried whenever he recounted it.

Terence's new arrest had shaken Lafeyette and Pharoah. In a

neighborhood of losses it was yet another family member or friend gone: their neighbor William shot accidentally, their friend Bird Leg killed, and now Terence. LaJoe tried to reassure them. Maybe, she told them, Terence was better off in jail. He's off the streets and can't get in more trouble, she told them. But they wanted him home.

Pharoah sent Terence a black-and-white photo of himself. He was wearing a button-down shirt, standing in front of the building, smiling, his head cocked to one side, like a puppy's. On the back he wrote in clear, crisp block letters: "Terence I'm to little to understand what is happing. But I want to tell you I miss and love you. Pharoah."

PHAROAH would have liked Rickey to root him on at the spelling bee, but his friend spent the period in the principal's office, where he sat out most assemblies. Ms. Barone sent him there as a precaution—if he felt moved to, he could have disrupted the entire proceedings.

Pharoah prepared diligently for the annual spring event, which pitted the school's top third, fourth, and fifth graders against one another. A dozen students competed, two from each classroom. To do well, Pharoah knew that he'd have to control his stammer, which had worsened with his family's troubles. He established a routine in which he'd sound the word out in his head, pause a moment, and then spell it, drawing out each letter slowly. For over three weeks he studied fourteen mimeographed sheets of words.

On the day of the competition Pharoah and the other contestants lined up on the small wooden stage in the school's gymnasium. Pharoah looked handsome in his freshly pressed turquoise cotton shirt, buttoned at the collar. The bright yellow name tag with huge block letters looked weighty on his tiny frame.

Pharoah was much more nervous than anyone knew. He was praying that he wouldn't stutter. Not in front of all these people. He started wringing his hands in apprehension. The

Pharoah. *"Mama, I'm just too young to understand how life really is."*

head judge explained the rules. There was a stool for those who, like Pharoah, couldn't reach the microphone. If a student misspelled a word, a buzzer would sound, and he or she had to leave the stage.

Pharoah was so focused on controlling his speech that the first few rounds were a blur. All he remembers were words like Catholic and abandonment, adjust, and Appalachian. He knew how to spell them all. As student after student walked off the stage in defeat, Pharoah realized he was getting closer and closer to winning. Then, as the contestants were whittled down to five, his nerves began catching up with him. He could feel himself losing the self-control he'd fought so hard to retain. His next turn came around quickly.

"Endurance," the teacher announced. "Endurance."

Pharoah felt his heart pumping fast and loud. He knew how to spell the word. He couldn't restrain his joy, and abandoning his usual routine, he spoke in a rush. His eyes darted around excitedly.

He repeated the word. "Endurance," he said, spitting out the three syllables as if they were one. He started to spell it: "E-n-d-u . . ." He couldn't hear a thing. Nothing came out of his mouth. Nothing. He tried again. Nothing. His stutter devoured him. The veins in his neck strained as he tried to get the letters out. The buzzer sounded. Pharoah's lips quivered in disappointment. He did all he could to keep from crying in front of his friends.

When Pharoah got home from school that day, he walked straight back to his room. LaJoe knew something must be wrong; he always greeted her. She went back to see him. He was lying on his bed.

"How'd you do today, Pharoah?" she asked. He told her. LaJoe assured him there was nothing to be ashamed of. "It's going to be all right. You okay in my book." She tried to soothe him, stroking his head. "I love you. You can spell for me whenever you get ready to." He had tried his hardest.

"Pharoah is Pharoah. He's going to be something," LaJoe would tell friends. "When he was a baby, I held him up and asked if he'd be the one. I've always wanted to see one of my kids graduate from high school. I asked him if he'd be the one to get me a diploma."

But for Pharoah that wasn't good enough. He should have won or at least placed second. He was just going to have to work harder. Pharoah promised his mother he'd do better next year. Pharoah was not one to break his word.

SUMMER 1988
Seven

IN HINDSIGHT it was a summer of disappointment and, ultimately, of tragedy. At the time, though, LaJoe thought it a season of hope, a respite from the family's recent troubles. It was a dramatic change from what she now referred to as "the war-zone summer" of last year.

On this blistering, humid May afternoon the plaintive falsetto of pop singer Keith Sweat floated from outside the building:

> *"Let me hear ya tell me you want me*
> *Let me hear you say you'll never leave me baby*
> *Until the morning light*
> *Just make it last forever and ever."*

Please, LaJoe thought to herself, make this moment last forever. Over fifty adults and children had gathered by the front entrance of 1920 West Washington, their bodies pulsating to Sweat's hit tune. It was an unusual sight at Henry Horner—a large crowd of people mingling and laughing together. Even Lafeyette, who stood to the side, his back and shoulders rattling rhythmically, smiled at the scene.

The young man responsible for this musical gathering was Craig Davis, a good-natured eighteen-year-old who didn't even live at Horner, but at another public housing complex—the ABLA Homes. (ABLA, a mile and a half southeast of Horner, is a complex of four developments: the Jane Addams Homes, the Robert Brooks Homes, Loomis Courts, and the Abbott Homes.) Craig's girlfriend lived on the second floor of Lafeyette's building, and Craig visited her regularly after school. Though it took a few weeks before the Vice Lords were assured he didn't belong to a rival gang, he quickly won the hearts of the younger children. When he walked the distance from Horner to ABLA, he usually stopped to shoot baskets on the jungle gym with Lafeyette and others.

Craig was currently enrolled at Cregier High School. Though slowed down by a slight learning disability, he had managed to make it to his senior year, something three fourths of his freshman class had failed to do. He particularly impressed his teachers with his creative writing. But Craig lived for his music. Whenever he had a spare moment, he wrote raps. He shared some of them with Lafeyette and would often ask for his opinion. He was planning to apply to a broadcasting school, where he could learn to be a radio deejay.

Craig was different from all the other teenage boys Lafeyette knew. Here was an older boy who not only paid attention to him but took him seriously. What's more, Craig had thought about the future. He had the grandest of dreams: a home in a safe, neat neighborhood, and a family. He warned Lafeyette to stay away from the gangs.

Lafeyette idolized Craig, whom he considered a friend, not an associate. "I liked how he thought," Lafeyette later said. "He used to talk about a lot of good things."

On this particular afternoon, as Craig would do numerous times through the summer, he had set up two turntables and a speaker in front of Lafeyette's building, on the "porch," a ten-foot-deep slab of concrete leading into the breezeway. An overhang had the acoustical effect of directing the music out into the playground. People in the three surrounding buildings drifted to 1920 West Washington, lured by the blasting beat of pop stars, rap groups, and soul singers.

As the evening wore on and the crowd swelled, Craig persuaded even the shyest of friends to start dancing. "Mama," Pharoah yelled over the rowdy raps of the group El Jabbar, "w-w-watch . . . w-w-watch me. It's the w-w-wop." His shoulders and arms began to move in military syncopation as his legs propelled his body up and down.

LaJoe poked Rochelle. "Will you look at the old boy," she said, laughing with a freedom she hadn't felt in a long while.

Next to LaJoe and Rochelle stood Rickey and Lafeyette. Rickey seemed to revel in the joy and energy of the dancers. A self-conscious child, he buried his hands deep in his pockets and smiled nervously. "Hey, Lafie, man, look at Pharoah," he said, pointing to the writhing youngster.

Lafeyette laughed. "Man, he don't know what he doing." He launched into an exaggerated imitation of his brother's rendition of the wop.

As Rickey came to spend more time with Pharoah, Lafeyette began to accept him. The three boys played tag or basketball, and Lafeyette enjoyed having Rickey around. He could be generous if he had any money and would occasionally buy a hot dog or a soda pop for

Lafeyette or Pharoah. If Pharoah trusted Rickey, Lafeyette now figured, so could he.

"C'mon out here. Let's dance," Rochelle urged Lafeyette. She grabbed his hand, dragging him into the group of dancers.

"I don't wanna. I just wanna look," he protested. But children and adults alike began a quiet chant: "Dance, Lafie, dance." He did. His long arms moved tentatively and awkwardly as his upper body moved back and forth in time with the music. Then for just a moment he let loose, his legs and torso moving with surprising grace.

For those few minutes he was at peace with himself, his facial muscles relaxed into a full, unencumbered smile. The dancers continued to gyrate and whirl through the hot, humid night.

WHEN Audrey Natcone, a public defender, first met Terence, she was struck by how young he seemed. A skinny boy, painfully shy among strangers, Terence seemed much younger than eighteen. Audrey felt sorry for him, as she did for many of her clients. But with more cases than she could properly handle, Audrey couldn't spend enough time on Terence's. Moreover, Terence rarely challenged her about his case, and he didn't have a phone, which made it impossible for her to get quick answers to questions that came up. The only time they could meet was at each court date, before his case was called.

In May a friend helped bail Terence out of jail. Terence spent most of the summer in the apartment, sequestered in a back room. On occasion he and a friend took the el to O'Hare Airport, where they shined shoes at a dollar a polish. Frequently, though, the airport police booted them out for not having a vendor's license.

What most impressed Audrey about Terence was his close family ties. Usually parents and siblings didn't visit her clients or show up on court dates. With Terence it was different. Each time he had a court date, LaJoe was sure to join him. Because of LaJoe's unbending loyalty, Audrey paid closer attention to the case.

LaJoe strongly believed that Terence hadn't robbed Ann's Longhorn Saloon. And as Audrey spoke to Terence about it she, too, began to believe that he may have been wrongly accused. It wasn't that Terence wasn't capable of participating in the caper at the bar. It was just that the evidence didn't point unwaveringly to his presence there.

For months the police delayed providing photographs of the lineup from which Terence had been identified. This raised Audrey's suspicions that all was not right. Was there something about the lineup that would have made it particularly easy to pick out Terence? Had the police shown Ann Mitchell, the owner of the saloon, snapshots of Terence before she picked him out? If that was the case, Audrey planned to argue that that had prejudiced Ann.

What Audrey didn't know was that Johnny Adams, the young man who had orchestrated the robbery, could have testified that Terence was not with him the night he robbed the saloon. But Johnny didn't come forward, because in doing so, he would have incriminated himself. It wasn't until an interview a year later, after he'd been convicted for his part in the robbery, that Johnny Adams talked openly about the crime and said Terence had not been with him.

Even without such testimony, though, Audrey was confident that she could win the case.

It was a Friday afternoon in late June, and a swirl of adults and children filled LaJoe's apartment. The kitchen table, a recent hand-me-down from a friend, was loaded with platters of food. Baked ham. Macaroni and cheese. Collard greens. Corn bread. Sweet-potato pies. "It was," LaJoe later said, "the happiest moment in my house."

There was much to celebrate.

Terence, it appeared, would beat his case. That particularly relieved Lafeyette and Pharoah, who knew, as did most of the children, that prison consumed and mangled its inhabitants quicker than the neighborhood. They were also glad to have him home, out on bond. Their family was whole again.

Also, LaJoe had reapplied for welfare, and a caseworker told her she would soon have her benefits restored. Public Aid could no longer claim that Paul supported the family. He was still out of work, and as the months passed, his chances of returning seemed slimmer and slimmer, as he continued to drink and take drugs. With the family's income restored, LaJoe promised her five youngest children new bunk beds. "I'll get them on layaway," she assured them. "You'll have them by Christmas."

But the reason for the feast had nothing to do with Terence or Public Aid's decision. Dawn Anderson, LaJoe's niece and Porkchop's older sister, was to graduate from Richard T. Crane High School, the second of Lafeyette and Pharoah's generation in the Anderson family to graduate. Nine children had already dropped out.

LaJoe was very close to Dawn. The girl, whose name everyone pronounced "D'won," leaned on her aunt for advice and support. A feisty, scrappy girl who was quite pretty, Dawn backed down from no one—and had had her share of fights in the neighborhood. But it was that determination and fearlessness that had gotten her this far and, everyone hoped, would carry her even further.

Dawn's accomplishment was made even more notable by the fact that she had, at the age of eighteen, four children—ages four, two, one, and three months. She raised the kids with the help of her boyfriend—the children's father, Demetrius Nance—in a third-floor apartment in LaJoe's building. They lived there illegally, since the rightful tenant had moved out and had let Dawn pay the rent. (Such illicit arrangements are frequently made in Chicago public housing because the waiting list for units is so long.) LaJoe helped Dawn get through her senior year by baby-sitting the children on occasion.

Lafeyette and Pharoah revered Dawn. Lafeyette told her he would do twice as many years of college as she. "I have to do a lot of studying to bring up my grades," he said. "I wanna be like my cousin D'won." Pharoah told her he'd beat her reading scores. But however proud they were of their older cousin, both boys were emphatic about one thing: they didn't want to attend Crane.

Crane, a quarter mile south of Horner, is one of the city's worst high schools. About half the entering freshmen never graduate. In 1985 the seniors' reading tests were in the eighteenth percentile nationwide. Security is a problem. In Dawn's yearbook two full pages were devoted to photos of the school's eleven security guards. Students were prohibited from wearing jackets in the lunchroom because they might use them to conceal weapons. Some children went to live with relatives in other neighborhoods and even other states to avoid attending Crane and the area's other high schools.

Dawn was in a special honors program at Crane and, as a result, was resented by some of the other students. She had thought of dropping out numerous times. But LaJoe pushed her. "You got too far, girl," LaJoe would tell her. "Whenever you don't want to go to school, just go, 'cause it's going to pay off. You're going to live like the people on the South Side, like in Beverly [a South suburb]." Dawn's persistence culminated in her graduation—and the party thrown by LaJoe.

Cousins, aunts, and friends piled into the apartment, where they drank beer and wine coolers, and filled their stomachs with LaJoe's homemade dishes. Everyone seemed almost giddy at Dawn's accomplishment. Toasts were made to Dawn's future and her health.

"She got to make it," LaJoe said. "She got to. She got to get a job. If they don't see her life take her nowhere after finishing school, it will be the truth. Only thing out here left is to sell drugs. D'won got to be the one to prove it's not true."

Eight

JIMMIE Lee stood and faced Judge Robert Boharic in the courtroom. Lee looked impassive, as he had throughout his two-day trial. Nothing seemed to unsettle him.

Boharic, a former prosecutor known for his toughness as a judge, had decided early on that if he found Lee guilty, he would give him a long sentence. He would set an example with him. Lee, Lee's wife, and another woman had been charged with possession of sixty-nine grams of heroin—enough to incur a thirty-year sentence. Lee had also been charged with unlawfully possessing an automatic weapon.

The police officers in the city's gang-crimes unit are some of the most streetwise and savviest among the city's cops. Michael Cronin, a seventeen-year veteran, probably knew the Vice Lords organization as well as its members did, if not better. He knew in great detail of Lee's operations—and he knew Lee. But even Cronin hadn't been able to catch him with any weapons or drugs. Lee never carried guns or drugs. He always had intermediaries do the dirty work.

Because of the police department's own internal workings, the gang-crimes cops couldn't launch extensive narcotics investigations. But Cronin had obtained a warrant to search Lee's apartment on the tip that he kept an automatic weapon there. When he and five other officers forced open the door with a sledgehammer, they discovered more than they had bargained for. On the bedroom and kitchen floors and in the toilet were hundreds of packets of heroin. At the bottom of an air shaft lay a 9-mm assault rifle with a banana clip holding twenty-eight live rounds.

At the trial Lee's attorneys raised doubts that the weapon belonged to him. His wife and the other woman were acquitted of all charges. Judge Boharic, however, found Lee guilty of possession of a controlled substance with intent to deliver.

In a presentencing report Lee stated that he had been working as a manager of a car wash. But in the presentencing hearing, in front of Judge Boharic, the prosecution attempted to establish Lee's high ranking in the Vice Lords. Charlie Toussas, the plainclothes officer, told about the time Bird Leg had been shot and Lee led a band of his soldiers over to the Disciples' turf. Another officer estimated that the Conservative Vice Lords, the faction controlled by Lee, sold "thousands of dollars a day in both heroin and cocaine."

Judge Boharic now gave Lee the maximum: thirty years. "If I could give him more years under the law, I would," he said.

Word of Lee's extraordinarily long sentence traveled fast. A neighbor delivered the news to LaJoe.

"What?" Lafeyette asked, overhearing the hushed conversation.

"Shut up," LaJoe told him. "You don't talk about them peoples. They still got peoples out here. They could get the family hurt."

A few days later the Chicago *Tribune* ran a story about Lee's sentence. In the accompanying picture a teenage boy had his arms raised. He didn't want to answer a reporter's question, so he shrugged his shoulders and thrust his arms into the air. The Vice Lords thought he was celebrating Lee's sentencing. The next day they beat him up badly. Even without their leader, there was discipline among the ranks. Jimmie Lee, it was clear, wouldn't be missed long.

THE white gypsy cab pulled up to the back of 1920 West Washington, its back seat and trunk loaded down with groceries. It was July, and LaJoe had resumed her monthly trip to stores that charged less than the hiked-up prices of the closer markets.

Lafeyette and the triplets raced out to help their mother carry in the bags of food. Where was Pharoah? LaJoe wondered. He always showed up to help. She had told him she was going shopping. That was just like Pharoah to forget, she thought. Daydreaming again.

Three blocks south of Horner sits a condominium complex called Damen Courts, with manicured lawns and graffiti-free walls. When Pharoah discovered this small paradise, he retreated regularly to the comfort of its lush lawns. He was there when his mother returned from shopping. The grass carpet offered a quiet resting place; it was like going to the beach. Pharoah found a shady place on the lawn and shot marbles or read a *Captain America* or *Superman* comic. Or, if the mood fit him, he just sat and daydreamed. He thought about school and next year's spelling bee. He urged on the Chicago Cubs and imagined himself a professional wrestler.

Pharoah had long sought such a refuge. For a few months last spring, he attended Bible classes at the First Congregational Baptist Church, but grew bored with them and began to question whether there was indeed a God. He often prayed to Him, asking that He let them move from the projects. But "I be praying, but He don't do nothing," Pharoah would say. "Maybe there ain't no God." It was as much a question as it was a statement.

At Damen Courts, Pharoah found some respite. No one knew of his discovery. He wanted it that way. He wanted a place that he could escape to, where nothing interrupted his daydreams, where no one tried to fight him, where he didn't have to worry about gunshots.

In the weeks immediately following Jimmie Lee's conviction, the drug dealing slowed down. With fewer shootings and a reprieve from some of the family's troubles, Pharoah's stutter became less noticeable. In later months it would recur, but never would it immobilize him as it had during the past year.

With the uneasy calm, Pharoah and Lafeyette found several distractions. They frequented the large outdoor swimming pool in Union Park and learned to swim. They visited the Boys Club to play basketball or shoot pool. Pharoah badgered Lafeyette and Rickey to take him to the railroad tracks, but the stories of lost legs were still fresh in their minds. So Pharoah spent more time at his private sanctuary.

On this particular afternoon, after his mother had put away the groceries, Pharoah wandered through the front door, his head cocked slightly to one side. "Where you been, Pharoah?" LaJoe asked.

"Nowheres," he said, turning away. It was hard for him to lie, especially to his mother.

"Pharoah?"

Pharoah thought about telling her, but didn't. "I been playing video games with Porkchop," he said, and walked back to his room.

In later weeks he finally confided in his mother about his discovery. "My mind be cleared of everything there," he told her.

FALL 1988–WINTER 1989
Nine

IN THE intervening months Lafeyette and Rickey had become friends or, in Lafeyette's word, associates. Closer in age, they seemed a more likely pair than Pharoah and Rickey. LaJoe speculated that Lafeyette first started hanging out with Rickey because he wanted to keep a close eye on Pharoah. But Rickey and Lafeyette took a liking to each other.

Rickey introduced Lafeyette to some of his friends, many of whom had been in trouble with the law. A group of them, including Rickey, had been arrested regularly for what was known as smash and grabs. They smashed the windows of cars stopped at the traffic light on the corner of Damen Avenue and Lake Street and then grabbed jewelry from the motorist or snatched a purse or valise from the passenger seat. Rickey was known by all thirty officers in the Thirteenth District's tactical unit. "By the time he's eighteen, he'll be dead or in the penitentiary," one cop prophesied.

Because of Rickey's problems at Henry Suder, he had been sent to the Moses Montefiore School, a school for troubled boys. He still watched after Pharoah, but he moved with a crowd that was too old and brazen for the younger boy. Lafeyette was torn. He liked Rickey and, unlike Pharoah, could hold his own among Rickey's friends.

On a Saturday two weeks before Christmas, Pharoah, Rickey, Lafeyette, and several other friends went window-shopping. They walked more than a half mile north to a videocassette store on bustling Milwaukee Avenue. Lafeyette desperately wanted a VCR, but he knew his mother couldn't afford one. Still, he thought, nothing wrong with make-believe.

"Let's go see what we could be buying when we get some money," Lafeyette said to his friends. The six of them straggled into Erol's Video Club, a spacious, well-lit store with row upon row of videotapes. Pharoah wandered through the stacks to the Wrestle Mania movies. An avid sports fan, he regularly watched professional wrestling on television. It was one way he could, albeit vicariously, fight.

Nearby, Lafeyette and Rickey looked at new releases. "Hey, Lafie," Rickey whispered, "let's take us some." Pharoah overheard him.

"Lafie, let's go leave them," he pleaded, sidling up to his brother.

"I'm still looking 'round, man. If you wanna go, go!" Lafeyette said in a loud whisper.

Pharoah and the others left. Pharoah was disappointed in Rickey but even more so in Lafeyette, who seemed to bow to the pressure of his friend. Maybe they wouldn't get caught, he hoped. "I'm never going to jail," he had said more than once.

Rickey grabbed a ninja movie and slid it under his coat. He nudged Lafeyette, who pushed a tape under his jacket. The two boys walked quickly toward the exit.

Mario Vera, the assistant manager, had been watching them on a video camera from the back of the store. When he saw the children bunching up together and whispering, he knew that they were thinking of shoplifting, so before they could leave, he grabbed them.

"What you doing?" Rickey boldly asked.

Vera smiled. "Now, come on, just give us the tape."

"What tape?" Rickey said.

"The tape you have there." Vera pointed to the bulge in his coat.

"Man, you don't leave me alone, my big brother, he be burning this place down." Rickey didn't have a big brother.

Another store employee, who held Rickey from behind, began to pat him down. The tape slipped out from under his jacket. Lafeyette then produced his.

"What's your name?" Vera asked Rickey.

"Joe Styro." Rickey evidently had gotten the idea from a nearby Styrofoam cup stand.

While Rickey stood there, unflustered if not somewhat cocky, Lafeyette looked worried. "Since you got the tape, mister, why don't you lemme go?" he asked Vera. "I'm sorry. I won't come back."

"Sorry?" Vera replied. "It doesn't work that way." Vera, though, felt bad for Lafeyette, who seemed genuinely apologetic. Privately he wanted to let the two boys go. But he couldn't. Store policy demanded he report to the police any incidents recorded on the camera.

While they waited for the police, Vera took the two boys to the back of the store, where he seated them in folding metal chairs. "Is this the first time you've done this?" Vera asked Lafeyette.

"Unh-unh," Lafeyette mumbled.

"Like what?"

"Twinkies, cupcakes, potato chips."

Lafeyette sat with his arms tightly crossed against his chest, his face revealing little. Rickey leaned back in his chair as if he had nothing better to do than pass the time. Vera sensed that beneath Rickey's tough demeanor he was scared.

"You guys want something to drink?" Vera asked.

Lafeyette nodded. Rickey looked at Vera defiantly. Vera brought Lafeyette a root beer. Lafeyette was surprised at Vera's friendliness and later expressed a desire to apologize to him for his actions.

When the police arrived, Vera didn't press charges. Instead, the cop gave the boys a short lecture and dropped them near home.

LaJoe might not have found out about the shoplifting had a neighbor's daughter not told her. She began to think of how quickly she had lost Terence to the neighborhood. She knew that Lafeyette, who would turn fourteen next June, would have to make some choices soon. It would be easy for him to get caught up with boys who were more daring. She made him stay in the house for a week and a half. Lafeyette didn't seem to mind. He knew what he had done was wrong.

WHAT happened wasn't clear then—and probably never will be. But by the time it was over, Lafeyette was wet and hurting and unusually angry at the police. And Pharoah was confused and disappointed with himself for not doing more to help his brother.

The late afternoon rain had warmed the December air ever so slightly—enough for Lafeyette and Pharoah to decide to work the Chicago Black Hawks game that night. Lafeyette wore his nylon Black Hawks warm-up jacket. Pharoah refused to wear what the kids called starter jackets, the nylon jackets with sports-team logos that had become so popular that teens were stealing them off the backs of others. Pharoah, instead, had a black polyester coat that looked like leather. He also had a fancy new hairdo that made him look older.

For decades children of the West Side viewed "stadium nights" as a way to make a few dollars' spending money. When the Chicago Bulls or Black Hawks played, thousands of well-dressed, mostly white sports fans poured into the neighborhood. The children would offer to watch people's cars if they parked on the side streets instead of the parking lots. If the driver refused to pay to have his car watched, the children might smash a window and steal the radio or a jacket or anything else left behind. But mostly the children had no intention of breaking in; they just wanted to earn some spending money.

Pharoah took the job seriously. He and Porkchop were partners. If someone paid them to watch a car, they would stay by it at least fifteen minutes past game time and then retreat to Pharoah's apartment, where they would watch the game on television. They would check on the car three or four times during the evening. When asked his name by stadium patrons, Pharoah always told them, "Jimmy." Everybody had an alias, even the young children.

That night Lafeyette, Pharoah, and Porkchop joined some friends as they got to Washington Boulevard, which runs along the southern edge of the complex. "The police told us to get away, not to watch no cars," one boy told the others. A disjointed conversation ensued. Should they turn back, or should they try to avoid the police? Pharoah and Porkchop turned back, choosing instead to play basketball on the jungle gym. Lafeyette went on to the stadium with his friends.

Lafeyette helped a parking lot attendant. The boys could make $5 to $10 flagging cars into the lots. A policeman approached and told Lafeyette and a few of his friends, who were waiting for cars to pull into the side streets, to go home. Lafeyette may have talked back to him or he may have been slow in moving, but two other boys have separately recounted what happened next. The policeman grabbed Lafeyette and heaved him into a puddle of water. He then kicked Lafeyette in the rear. "What you doing here?" he demanded. "Little punk, you ain't supposed to be working here. These white people don't have no money to give no niggers."

One of Lafeyette's friends ran to the safety of Horner, where he told Pharoah what had happened. Pharoah panicked. He didn't want to go to Lafeyette, because he was afraid the policeman might kick him, too. He didn't want to summon their mother, because he worried that "she probably would of gotten involved, and they would of taken her to jail for keeping her kids out late." He was paralyzed with fear.

Meanwhile, two boys had sprinted to get LaJoe, who bolted from her apartment without her coat. By the time she reached Washington Boulevard, Lafeyette was in the back seat of the squad car. She started arguing with the policeman. Two other officers then showed up and released Lafeyette. No charges were filed.

Lafeyette later recalled that one policeman had warned him he could get hurt out there at night. "I've been living here all my life, and I ain't got hurt so far," he said. "Only the police have hurt me."

For several weeks neither Lafeyette nor Pharoah worked the stadium. LaJoe told the two never to go back, but eventually they went. Working the stadium was the only way to earn spending money.

For the first time Pharoah, now ten, began to wonder aloud about being black. "Do all black people live in projects?" he asked his mother. "Do all black people be poor?" He was upset that Michael Dukakis hadn't chosen Jesse Jackson as his running mate. "Why don't people elect black people?" The incident at the stadium had unnerved him. He felt that "the white polices don't like the black children." It was the first time he acknowledged any bitterness toward anybody.

The incident brought back unsettling memories for LaJoe. Like other longtime Henry Horner residents, she had mixed feelings about the police. On the one hand, LaJoe and others felt sympathy. What young cop, after all, would want to be stuck alone in a neighborhood like Horner after dark? The residents knew it wasn't safe for them. Why would it be safe for anyone else? Most officers wouldn't venture into Horner by themselves even during the daytime. Who could blame them?

Still, the residents didn't fully trust the cops. For one thing, they felt stuck in the middle between the drug gangs and the police. The cops came and went, but the gang members were there twenty-four hours a day. It was a question of common sense. But much of their wariness was rooted in the past. Horner, like so many other inner-city black communities, had been a victim of the police's overzealousness or brutality, depending on the way you looked at it.

In the late 1960s the nation's black ghettos were filled with rage and fury, a stark contrast to the resignation and personal excesses of the late 1980s. It was a period when people felt that they could find allies in the system to help make it work for them. During those years the residents of Henry Horner, like many others, organized. Pressuring the federal government, they were able to get funds for the founding of a neighborhood health clinic—the Miles Square Health Center. They put pressure on schools to bring in more sympathetic principals. They helped get a swimming pool built at the Boys Club. And then in the fall of 1969 they demanded a traffic light.

It didn't, at the time, seem an extravagant request. Washington

Boulevard had become a virtual expressway for commuters driving from the Loop to the western suburbs, and since the opening of school, two children had been hit by motorists. But the city refused. A traffic light would impede the flow of traffic, officials said.

Parents and children turned out in protest. They formed a never-ending picket line, moving back and forth across the boulevard. Police arrived in full riot gear and stood ready to make mass arrests. Twenty-one-year-old Michael Soto, on leave from Vietnam, got into a shoving match with a policeman and was arrested for obstructing traffic and resisting arrest, charges that were eventually dropped.

On October 5, nineteen days later, Michael's younger brother, sixteen-year-old John, berated two white policemen who were arresting two of his friends. One of the officers shot and killed John Soto. The police said it happened when the boy started to scuffle with the officer; witnesses said it happened without provocation.

On October 10 Michael Soto, while standing on a landing between the first and second floors of the Horner high rise where his family lived, was also killed. Also by a policeman. The police said he had just robbed someone. Within minutes the residents of Horner rose in indignation and waged furious combat with the police. Snipers shot from windows. Residents brandished revolvers and shotguns. The police took cover behind their squad cars and under the el tracks. When the shooting subsided, ten policemen and a twelve-year-old girl had been wounded.

The city installed a traffic light. But there was trouble again only two months later. Two more blacks were killed when policemen stormed the home of several Black Panthers. The police at first contended that the Panthers had opened fire on them as they tried to serve a search warrant. A later FBI investigation found that the Panthers had fired one shot to between eighty-three and ninety-nine shots by the police. The Panthers lived only a few blocks from Horner; they had started a breakfast program for the children and had helped with the traffic-light protest. In the subsequent trial the police officers were all acquitted.

The four killings left an indelible scar on the people of Henry Horner. "What you thought would protect you, you found out that you couldn't trust," said LaJoe, who was seventeen at the time. "How can people kill a person like that? And lie? And cover it up?"

The police weren't all bad. It was just that when something tragic happened, LaJoe couldn't understand why they didn't just admit they had made a mistake. And now Lafeyette had been roughed up by a policeman. The incident itself wasn't that big a deal, she thought. There were no serious injuries. What worried her was that Lafeyette's cynicism had begun to define his person. People had let him down so many times, and now he was losing faith in the police. That wariness would only grow in coming months.

THE apartment bulged with people that winter. Weasel, the boys' oldest brother, had a girlfriend, who moved in. LaJoe's mother, Lelia Mae, who was recovering from a stroke that had paralyzed one side, moved in, too.

Lafeyette was particularly glad to have Lelia Mae there. He liked to take care of old people. It made him feel needed. At McDonald's he would help older people with their trays. He ran errands for his grandmother. They'd always been close. Now he helped his mother bathe her and would rub her feet with alcohol.

The apartment seemed to collapse under the weight of all these people. The oven stopped working, and for most of eight months LaJoe couldn't bake. The pipes leading to the kitchen sink sprang a leak. For two weeks, while she waited for them to be repaired, LaJoe had to wash dishes in the bathtub, which still ran day and night.

In all this activity both Lafeyette and Pharoah were most troubled by their father's depression. It didn't look as if Paul would get his job back. He still drank and occasionally took heroin. He had become so desperate for money that he stole a small black-and-white television LaJoe's mother had given the boys, and pawned it for $15. But he felt so guilty that he pulled the money together and got the television out of hock and returned it without their knowing who had taken it.

Lafeyette deeply resented his father. He didn't feel he had lived up to his promises. When he was younger, Paul had told Lafeyette he would move the family out of Horner. "One of these days, son," he had promised, "you'll have your own backyard to play in, have some room for a dog." Nothing had seemed impossible. He and LaJoe were working at the time, and though the two had their problems, money wasn't one of them. Until Paul's habit overtook him.

Paul had not only welshed on his promises, he was too dejected to be of much support for the kids. "I remember times when I would come to the house drunk or high, and the kids would seem to detect it," he said. "Everybody would be sitting in the living room, and when I came in, one by one they would leave and head to the back. At times they just totally disregard me. If I want to go in any part of the house, I have to knock on the doors. That's rough."

LaJoe didn't talk much to Paul either. She had never forgiven him for taking drugs. She was restrained, though, in the way she spoke of him. "I can't be angry with him," she said, " 'cause he doesn't understand himself. If he can't help himself, how's he going to help me?"

Paul respectfully called LaJoe a conscientious objector, since she didn't drink or get high. Even though LaJoe virtually ignored Paul, he still had strong feelings toward her. "I love that woman," he would say. "I'm the one that care, but I can't show how much I care."

Paul continued to come around because he wanted his children to know their father. And at least he had Pharoah. Pharoah felt sorry for his father and often tried to cheer him up. If there was a basketball game on television, Pharoah would try to get his father involved. He'd make a gentleman's bet on one team; his father would take the other. Anything to keep his father from becoming too pensive.

One balmy December afternoon Paul sat at the edge of the double bed in the front bedroom, his eyes staring at the brown floor. Pharoah lay on his belly, his chin in his hand.

"Let's go outside," Pharoah urged.

Paul shook his head. "I'm all right here. Why don't you go on?"

"Is you going back to work?" Pharoah asked.

"I'm off temporarily. It's a suspension," explained a sullen Paul.

"Daddy, if you ain't working, how you gonna keep your promises to us?" Paul had promised to buy the children bicycles and snowsuits.

"Don't worry about it. Sooner or later I'm going to get back to work, and I'm going to try and hold them promises." The two sat in silence for a few minutes. Pharoah looked at his dad, who stared at the floor.

"Why you drink? What you get out of it?"

The question stunned Paul. Pharoah would rarely have the courage to ask his father about his drinking. He would always say that what his father did was his father's business. But it bothered everyone.

"Why you don't want me to drink?"

"It stinks, and you don't look right. You act funny," Pharoah said.

Paul said nothing. He knew Pharoah was right. He should stop drinking. He had slowed down in taking drugs, but he should stop. He desperately wanted to return to work, but hadn't had any success in getting rehired at the transit authority. More than anything, he felt that he had let his children down.

Pharoah got up and sat behind his father, tenderly placing a hand on his shoulder. He made a point of looking cheerful.

"You gonna get your job back, Daddy. If not that one, then another one. Remember you used to pick up them big old garbage cans? You want that job back?"

Porkchop's grinning face poked through the door. Pharoah looked at his father and stood up to leave. "Daddy, bye. I'm going." He hopped out of the room. Paul couldn't help cracking a smile.

Ten

As it did every winter, the temperature in the apartment approached a dry, crackling eighty-five degrees. Stripping down to their underwear was of no relief to Lafeyette and Pharoah; it was like being inside an oven. If they opened a window, they had to put up with a frigid draft. Pharoah had developed a blistering cough. The scorching heat tired the boys and put everyone on edge.

LaJoe wanted to find some excuse to get them out of the apartment. As Christmas approached, she wanted to do something special for herself and the children. She had already promised them they would be getting bunk beds for the holidays, but after buying their presents, she didn't have the money. They'd have to wait until spring.

LaJoe decided to take the younger ones to see the Christmas windows downtown, something she had done with her mother as a child. The triplets had never before been in the Loop; Pharoah, only a couple of times. So on a Thursday, after school, LaJoe gathered them up, with Tyisha, Baldheaded, Snuggles, and a friend of the triplets', whom everyone called Esther B. LaJoe walked the young battalion to Madison Street, where they hopped the bus.

"Why's that window so clean?"

"Where them lights come from?"

"Ooooh, look at them tall buildings."

"Them's glass."

"No, they ain't."

So the banter went as the bus was swallowed by the city's downtown. The skyscrapers seemed to rise forever into the darkening sky. The children pressed their faces against the windows, their warm breath clouding the glass. Frantically they rubbed off the mist to glimpse the high rises that dared tower over their own. LaJoe began to share their excitement, began to feel a part of an ordinary family, a family without problems.

When the bus driver pulled up to State Street, the children pushed and tumbled off the bus. "Ain't no one going anywhere," LaJoe shouted. "Pharoah, take Tammie's and Tiffany's hands."

Pharoah gripped the bare hands of the two five-year-olds. Tyisha grabbed Timothy and Snuggles. LaJoe picked up Baldheaded in one arm and held Esther B. with the other. Like paper chains, the eight of them floated down State Street toward the elaborate windows of the major department stores.

The children screamed in delight at the sight of the mechanical children in the windows, some singing carols, two celebrating Christmas in a spaceship. "Are they real little kids?" Timothy asked.

"No," LaJoe told him. "They make them move by battery."

"I wish I could go in there and live with them," Timothy said.

Pharoah guided LaJoe and the others from window to window, block to block. He'd fly ahead of the pack, with Tammie and Tiffany as his wings. "Mama, come see this!" he'd scream. At one window Pharoah read for the little ones: " 'Singing carols on the steps of the Art Institute has a way of making even Scrooge look cute. . . . There's Tiny Tim and Bob Cratchit from Dickens' past.' "

"Perfect," said a young couple who had stopped to listen. Pharoah smiled proudly.

LaJoe led the children to McDonald's, where they ate and talked feverishly. "Where we going next?" they asked. "Mama, where?"

"One more stop: the big Christmas tree," she told them.

They hiked one more block, then oohed and aahed at the huge city tree. "Is that God's tree?" Tiffany asked. "It's almost in the sky."

"No. That's everybody's tree. But God probably be around here somewhere," LaJoe told them.

Finally, she brought them to Garrett's, a popcorn emporium, where she bought them two huge bags—one of cheese-flavored and the other of caramel popcorn. She popped a kernel of each kind in each of their mouths as they giggled and chewed and asked for more. It was, they told LaJoe, the best popcorn they'd ever had.

On the bus ride home LaJoe sat back in the seat, her head against the cold window. She was physically exhausted but, in an odd sort of way, had more energy than she'd had in a long time. It felt good to see the children giddy with excitement, seeming so unencumbered.

Pharoah, too, was exhausted. It had been an extraordinary day. He got to help his mother take care of the kids and to read to them from one of the windows. "I'd like to go again, Mama," he told LaJoe.

"Me, too." LaJoe smiled, and patted Pharoah's head.

When they got home, Lafeyette was seated on the couch.

"Why didn't you take me, too?" he demanded.

"I didn't think you'd want to see a Christmas tree and the windows with all those dolls in it," she said.

"I wanted to go."

Next time, LaJoe promised herself. She had to remind herself that Lafeyette, despite his adult worries, was still a thirteen-year-old boy.

LAFEYETTE got angry when he heard the news. There was no way their brother could go to prison for ten years. No way. He wasn't *that* bad. When LaJoe had told Lafeyette, he disappeared into the bathroom for nearly half an hour. His stomach tied up into knots when he got anxious, and he had terrible bouts of diarrhea.

When Pharoah heard that his brother might be sent away for ten years, his face dropped. "I be thinking," he told his mother, "why they be locking people up and taking them away from their parents?" LaJoe tried to explain why it happened. She was concerned about Pharoah. His teacher had called and said he had been daydreaming a lot in his class. LaJoe suspected he was troubled about Terence.

"Terence is gonna be a man about what they give him," LaJoe assured Pharoah. "And you have to be a man for him also, no matter what they do. Your brother's gonna be all right, so don't worry."

"Mama," Pharoah interrupted, "I'm just too young to understand how life really is."

The prosecution had offered Terence ten years if he would agree to plead guilty. That may have seemed an outrageous offer, particularly since he adamantly proclaimed his innocence. But Terence had been arrested again. Another armed robbery. Only this time the police had substantial incriminating evidence.

Over the summer Terence, while out on bond, had been determined to stay out of trouble. He felt good about his public defender, Audrey Natcone. She cared, and she believed him. Nonetheless, Terence didn't share her optimism about his getting off. Hadn't he once spent five months in detention for a crime he hadn't done? No one came to his rescue then, he thought. He just didn't trust the system. *They* didn't listen. *They* didn't understand. So if *they* wanted him to be a bad guy, then he'd be a bad guy. It was his own confused method of seeking justice. And so he told a friend, perhaps somewhat presciently, "Man, they ain't gonna convict me with something I ain't do like that. I'm gonna give them something to convict me for."

On September 5 Terence and an acquaintance held up Mazury Tavern, on the city's North Side. As the police reported it, Terence's friend held the bartender at bay with a pistol while Terence jimmied open a video game and the cash register. The police said that they found Terence's fingerprints and that Terence gave them an oral confession, though he refused to sign it. In the statement he said that for his role in the robbery he had received two bags of heroin.

His arrest upset Audrey, but it didn't come as a surprise. Many of her clients committed crimes while out on bond. She had hoped it would be different with Terence. She also felt they had had a strong case. She believed he hadn't committed the first armed robbery. The police still hadn't provided the lineup photos, which made her think something was amiss. But now it didn't matter. The prosecutors could try the second case first—and Terence didn't seem to have a chance.

The prosecution, though, was already overburdened with cases. It didn't want to go to trial. The prosecutors told Audrey they would offer Terence ten years in exchange for a guilty plea. She believed she could negotiate a shorter term.

IN EARLY February, Pharoah returned from watching cars at a Black Hawks game. He shuffled to his room, folded the $2 he'd made, and stuffed them into a jacket pocket. Pharoah always saved his money, but this time he had a purpose: the Boys Club's annual talent show, in which local children and teens put together singing, dancing, and comedy acts. He and Lafeyette never missed going.

The Boys Club's one-story building was as old as Henry Horner. The club was an oasis for the neighborhood's children, though it served mainly those who lived east of Damen Avenue. The children on the other side, who couldn't cross the boundary for fear of being attacked by rival gangs, frequented Chicago Commons. For the talent show, however, the gangs' geographic boundaries temporarily disappeared. It was one of the few community gatherings.

On the evening of the show the club's gym filled up quickly. Pharoah, Porkchop, and Lafeyette found a place in the top row of the bleachers, where they could have a clear view of the stage. Children, teenagers, and young mothers filled the folding chairs. The Vice Lords cocked their hats to the left, the Disciples to the right.

"How you doing out there?" the show's master of ceremonies, a club staff member, shouted into the microphone.

"Fine!" Pharoah and Lafeyette yelled back with the crowd.

In preparation for the singing of the national anthem, the emcee yelled, "Don't you love this country?"

"Nooooooo," the crowd roared, drowning out Pharoah's meekly spoken yes. Only a few in the crowd, including Pharoah, placed their hands on their hearts during the anthem.

For the first act five teenage boys from Rockwell Gardens put together a highly choreographed routine. They called themselves the Awesome Force. The girls in the gym yelled and screamed and nearly fainted. Pharoah bounced to the music as he tried to keep from getting pushed off the bleachers. The gym was getting crowded.

Lafeyette wandered away with a companion. They swiped some straws from the concession stand and snaked through the crowd, blowing spitballs at girls. *Swwwooosh.* One smacked a girl in the back of her neck. She turned around. "Get your hormones together!" she screamed. Lafeyette and the other boy guffawed, repeating the retort to one another with obvious adolescent satisfaction: "Get your hormones together. Maaan, get your hormones together."

Everyone was in good spirits. Even an overweight girl who sang Keith Sweat's "Make It Last Forever" off key and was booed off the stage managed a smile. It upset Pharoah, though, who commented to Porkchop, "They booing her. They shouldn't be doing that."

"Hey, Pharoah." Rickey had spotted his young friend in the bleachers. "Hey, Pharoah." Pharoah clambered down to greet him.

"Wanna hot dog?" Rickey asked.

"Sure," Pharoah replied. He followed Rickey, who bought him a hot dog and pop and also gave Pharoah $2.

"Thanks, Rickey."

"You straight, Pharoah." Pharoah rejoined Porkchop and shared the food with him. Rickey returned to his friends.

As the show wound down toward midnight, a rumor floated through the crowd that a teenage girl named Alice had been shot in the head four times somewhere farther west. Some had her already dead; others had her holding on for her life. Lafeyette and Pharoah just listened to the talk. They both knew her, though not well. They prayed for her and asked about her for weeks after.

LAFEYETTE had looked for Craig Davis at the talent show, but couldn't find him. Craig had turned Lafeyette on to music, and Lafeyette now often brought the older boy new rap tapes to hear. A few evenings after the show he heard that Craig was visiting his girlfriend, so he went upstairs to see him. Craig was sitting on the couch writing a poem, a music tape blaring in the background.

"What it is, Laf," Craig said.

"Hey, Craig." Lafeyette sat down next to the older boy and watched him scribble. He needled Craig a bit about his girlfriend.

"She gonna be my girlfriend," he told him.

"You can have her."

"I can have her?" Lafeyette chuckled. Craig continued to write.

The brothers inside their building. *"I worry about Pharoah a lot,"* Lafeyette explained. *"I don't want anything to happen to him."*

"What you think?" Craig asked, showing Lafeyette the poem. It was entitled "Children of the Future," and though its grammar and spelling were rough, Lafeyette understood it was an ode to learning. Craig was always telling Lafeyette how important school was.

"Straight out," said Lafeyette, who was tickled that someone older than he would ask for his opinion. Lafeyette so admired Craig. There was something soothing about just being around him. Craig told Lafeyette he was going to deejay a party at the Boys Club in a couple of weeks, on March 3. He told Lafeyette to stop by.

It was late February, and in the dreariness of a Chicago winter afternoon Pharoah could be found locked in his bedroom. On his bed he had spread about him mimeographed sheets of hundreds of words.

One of the triplets, Timothy, banged on the door.

"What you want?" Pharoah hollered.

"Let me in," Timothy pleaded.

Pharoah opened the door slightly. "I'm studying, Timothy. Now get on outta here." When Timothy took a step into the room, Pharoah swatted his younger brother on the back of his head, hard enough so that Timothy started to cry. It was out of character for Pharoah, but he wasn't messing around. He was going to do okay in the upcoming spelling bee. Nothing was going to distract him. Almost every day after school, Pharoah headed directly for his bedroom. Sometimes he'd have his mother bring him his dinner so that he didn't have to interrupt his studying. On occasion Lafeyette joined Pharoah on the bed and, as if he were a marine drill sergeant, flung words at his brother, hoping to find particularly difficult ones to stump him with.

This year Clarise Gates, one of the school's brightest, was chosen as the other class representative for the bee. She and Pharoah liked each other. On Tuesdays and Thursdays they got to school half an hour early to test each other. There were some words Pharoah had trouble pronouncing because of his stutter. "I can't say this right," he'd cry in frustration. "No such thing as can't," Clarise would remind him. And the two would work at sounding out the word, syllable by syllable.

The week before the spelling bee was a disturbing time for the family. First there was a shoot-out in the house between Willie, who sold fake jewelry with LaShawn's boyfriend, and a neighbor upstairs.

No one was hurt, but Lelia Mae moved out—the violence was too much for her. Five days later LaShawn went into labor with her third child. LaShawn, who had stopped smoking Karachi, gave birth to a five-pound fourteen-ounce boy, whom she named DeShaun.

Despite this flurry of activity, Pharoah remained remarkably focused on the spelling bee. Perhaps in anticipation of it he began having pleasant dreams, one of which he particularly liked to recall. In it he was a grown man looking for employment, and people were calling him because they thought they might have a job. He remembered the smallest of details, like the blossoming white roses he could see from his office window, and his new clothes—a starched white shirt and blue tie, with matching vest and pants, and spanking new black shoes. He had indeed gotten the job, and at work, people started calling him the Brain. He can't recall what kind of work the job entailed. He does, however, remember how good the dream made him feel. "I started thinking about if I do be a lawyer or something, then I'd make a better living and my mama be outta the projects."

SPRING 1989
Eleven

On Thursday, March 2, winter seemed intent on unleashing some of its final fury. The day began with a soft snowfall, but by midafternoon the swirling snowflakes had turned to hard-driving droplets of frozen rain. It made for an icy and slippery turf. Had Craig Davis been able to foresee the ugly intersecting of forces that night—the wretched weather, official duty, and lonely fear—he might have stayed inside. But Craig wasn't one to sit still.

He left work that afternoon and headed directly to Henry Horner to visit his girlfriend. He had graduated from high school two months earlier and quickly landed a job as a stock boy at a stationery store downtown. Craig so impressed the manager there that he was thinking of training Craig in sales.

That evening Craig visited briefly with his girlfriend and then took the bus to the ABLA row house where he lived with his uncle and his uncle's girlfriend. There he grabbed a turntable needle and two cassette tapes of rap and pop music he had assembled. "I'm going right out. To a friend's. Be back real soon," he yelled to his uncle.

Craig was on his way to pick up two turntables and speakers from a friend's. Tomorrow night was his debut as a deejay at the Boys Club. His uncle, who knew Craig went to bed by eleven every night, left the door unlocked.

FRANCIS Higgins and Richard Marianos cruised the streets of ABLA in their unmarked sedan. Higgins, thirty-four, was a Chicago police officer assigned to a new gun task force investigating the illegal shipment of arms. Marianos, twenty-three, was an agent for the Bureau of Alcohol, Tobacco, and Firearms (ATF), a division of the U.S. Treasury Department. Both officers were looking for someone they knew only as Craig, who they'd heard had recently purchased a sawed-off shotgun.

While driving, the two officers came on three teenage boys, including Craig Davis. The boys were on their way to pick up the stereo equipment. It wasn't clear why the police thought they looked suspicious, or had any cause to stop them. It was only eight at night. On seeing the two white officers, Craig turned to one of his friends. "I ain't going to no jail again," he said.

Five months earlier Craig was arrested with four others for allegedly stealing cookies from a delivery truck. It was his first arrest and was such an upsetting experience that he cried. He had been recording music tapes at a friend's when the police came in on another matter and saw boxes of chocolate chip cookies in the living room. The police arrested all five boys in the apartment. Now Craig feared the police, so on this cold night he ran.

Marianos gave chase. Higgins questioned the remaining two youths. (Later, in a police report, he said they told him the boy who had run was named Craig. They say, however, that they refused to give the police Craig's name.) Higgins let the boys go and caught up with his winded partner a couple of blocks away. Craig had eluded Marianos.

The boys saw Craig one more time. Having outmaneuvered Marianos, Craig was intent on picking up the stereo equipment. From about a half block away Craig spotted his friends and hollered at them, "Let's get them turntables!" At that point the squad car turned the corner. Marianos got out of the car and resumed the chase.

They ran down one street and up another, then through a darkened breezeway. Marianos lost sight of Craig for a "split second," according to a later police investigation, and so unholstered his service revolver, a .357 Smith & Wesson. Craig turned left to get back to the safety of his uncle's house. Marianos caught up with him there, grabbed him from behind, and shoved him up against the wall.

Marianos had his revolver near Craig's head. He later told homicide detectives that Craig had struggled, that he "reached over his shoulder and made contact" with Marianos' right hand. But the medical examiner's report cited evidence of "soot staining within the wound," which indicated that the gun may have been pressed up against Craig's skull when it discharged. Whatever the case, it appeared that Marianos slipped and fell backward onto a fresh sheet of ice, and when he did, the Smith & Wesson accidentally discharged.

The pop of the pistol echoed off the brick row houses. But few paid much attention to it. Even Daniel Davis, Craig's uncle, thought nothing of the noise. "When we heard the shot, we just figured it was more shooting," he later said. "They got a lot of shooting around here." Ten minutes later, when it was clear from the commotion that someone had been wounded outside his apartment, he opened the door.

There lay Craig, face down in a pool of blood. The police had strung yellow tape from tree to tree to keep angry spectators at a distance. Anonymous threats rose from the growing crowd.

"You shouldn't done that!" someone yelled.

"We see you 'round here, man, we're gonna kill you!"

"Them sons of bitches shot him in cold blood," one resident said to another. "They ain't got no reason to have done that."

"Man, who care? They don't. It's just another nigger to them."

By the time an ambulance got Craig to a hospital, he had no blood pressure, pulse, or respiration. Four doctors administered cardiac massage. They injected adrenaline and atropine, then tried shocking the heart. Craig was pronounced dead at eight forty-eight p.m.

An ATF spokesman told reporters Craig was a Disciple and suspected gunrunner. Two days later a one-paragraph account of the shooting appeared in the Chicago Sun-Times.

ON FRIDAY, March 3, the day of the spelling bee, Pharoah looked his best. The night before, he had washed his good clothes in the bathtub and then dried them with a fan. This morning he ironed his evergreen-colored sweater and a pair of new jeans, and shined his Fila high tops. After he was dressed, he sneaked into his brother Weasel's room to use some of his cologne. Then he appraised himself in the mirror, fidgeting with his sweater. He looked okay.

When he got to school, he and Clarise led their fifth-grade class into the gymnasium. Pharoah seemed surprisingly calm. He felt confident he could spell well enough to win, but he kept reminding himself to take his time and to speak slowly.

The judge ran through the rules, though Pharoah and Clarise hardly listened. Pharoah was too busy thinking about not stuttering. When his turn came, he stood poised and ready.

"Acceptable," the judge said. "Acceptable." Pharoah drew a deep breath and took his time.

"Acceptable." Pharoah pulled the microphone down toward him. "A-c-c-e-p-t-a-b-l-e. Acceptable." He went to the back of the line.

Clarise was given the word abdicate.

"Abdicate," she repeated in a forceful voice that carried through the gym. She almost shouted the individual letters. "Abdicate."

By the third round four students had missed words. It was Pharoah's turn again. As the contest progressed, he felt more self-assured. Nary a stutter, and the competition was nearly half over.

"Aerial," the judge said. "Aerial." Pharoah wasn't sure how to spell it. He wasn't even sure what it meant. He paused, then guessed.

"A . . ." he said tentatively, almost asking. No buzzer. Fifteen seconds elapsed. ". . . e-r-i-a-l." He thought he'd gotten it wrong and, his head bowed, started to head for the steps off the stage.

"Come back. That was right," the judge yelled out to him.

"It was?" Pharoah said in disbelief. Students giggled. Pharoah put his hands over his eyes in embarrassment.

The words kept coming, round after round, until there were only three contestants left: Pharoah, Clarise, and a boy named William.

"Amendment," the judge said to William. "Amendment."

"Amendment," William repeated. "A-m-e-n-d-m-a-n-t. Amendment." The buzzer sounded, and William walked off the stage. Pharoah broke into a big grin and threw a fist into the air. He quickly caught himself and pulled his hand down. But he didn't stop smiling. He was guaranteed at least second place.

Clarise got the word catbird.

"Catbird." She enunciated each letter with precision. "Catbird."

The judge gave Pharoah cellblock.

"Cellblock. S-a-l-e-b-l-o-c-k. Cellblock." The buzzer sounded. Clarise now had to spell it right to win. She stepped up to the microphone and twisted it so that she didn't have to bend over.

"Cellblock. S-a-i-l-b-l-o-c-k. Cellblock." The buzzer sounded again. They would get one more word. Otherwise it would be a tie.

"Darken," the judge said. "Darken." Clarise looked at her partner. She knew how to spell it. Pharoah wasn't so sure. But he proceeded as if he knew. He couldn't or wouldn't lose it now.

"Darken," he repeated. "D-a-r-k"—he hesitated for a moment—"i-n. Darken." The buzzer sounded. He'd gotten it wrong. Clarise stepped confidently to the microphone.

"Darken," she repeated. "D-a-r-k-e-n. Darken." Her classmates erupted in wild applause. Pharoah might have been upset, except that he was happy for his friend and satisfied with second place. The two children embraced each other, their faces radiant in victory.

Pharoah felt good. He'd accomplished what he'd set out to do. He hadn't stuttered. Not once. Pharoah thrust his fist into the air, waving it back and forth. This time he didn't bring it back down.

In his joy Pharoah alternately skipped and ran home from school, his red ribbon flapping in his hand. He couldn't wait to tell his mother of his triumph and show her his award.

Pharoah pushed open the apartment door, which his mother left unlocked when school let out. Everything was eerily quiet. The television was turned down. The triplets were in their room. Pharoah could even hear the running bathtub through the bathroom door. Lafeyette sat by the window straining to hear the conversation at the kitchen table between LaJoe, Rochelle, and a neighbor, Clementine, whom everyone called Dutt; it was conducted in hollow whispers.

Pharoah first stood at the entranceway. "That little round pie of a face," his mother later recalled, "it looked like the pie had just got cut all up and ate up. He was so happy." Pharoah went to his mother's side, thrusting the ribbon in her lap. "I . . . I . . . I c-c-came in second place." In his excitement his stutter had returned.

LaJoe smiled. "Second place. That's still good."

"Mama, if . . . if . . . if I hadn't m-m-missed a word . . ." For a moment, flustered by the silence, he lost his train of thought. "I . . .

I . . . I knew right away it was wrong. My . . . my . . . my— You know, my heart . . . my heart was beating so fast . . ."

Pharoah realized that something was terribly wrong. No one seemed to care about his triumph. Dutt was weeping. Lafeyette stared vacantly out the window. The family had just minutes earlier learned of Craig Davis' death the night before.

LaJoe turned from Pharoah to Dutt, whose daughter had been Craig's girlfriend. For much of the afternoon the three women remained at the table, sometimes talking, sometimes sitting in silence. Lafeyette huddled still as a statue, listening. During one long pause in the conversation he spoke, his voice flat and tired.

"He didn't have to die like that." His stare was directed at his mother. "He had to die the way that he lived, God's way. You die the way that you live, and Craig wasn't bad, so why him?" Lafeyette returned to looking out the window, his face taut.

In the meantime Pharoah had shuffled out the door, unnoticed. This was not the time or the place to celebrate his spelling victory. He went to play with Porkchop in the second-floor hallway. "I don't like to see nobody sad," he said later.

CRAIG's funeral was conducted at the A. R. Leak Funeral Home, one of the city's oldest and most esteemed black-owned funeral homes. It was clear from the size of the crowd that Craig had many admirers. Six former teachers attended. Children from both ABLA and Henry Horner were there, as were colleagues from work, including Craig's boss. Flowers—an entire garden, it seemed—surrounded the casket.

LaJoe came with Lafeyette. She knew Craig only from the dances in front of the building, but she understood how much he had meant to Lafeyette, so she wanted to be here with him.

The preacher's voice reverberated among the mourners, but his protestations seemed empty at such a tragic occasion. "Craig was no gang member," he bellowed. "There is drugs, lots of dope out there, but Craig would have none of that. He knew enough to walk away from trouble." His voice reached a crescendo; it was the only moment of untamed anger. *"He knew enough to walk away from trouble,"* he repeated. "Amen," some muttered to themselves.

Lafeyette hadn't stayed for the service. When he had first arrived and viewed Craig's body, he pictured the summer evenings spent dancing by the porch—a laughing and joking Craig spinning records, his body swaying to the music. Lafeyette couldn't get those snapshots of memory off his mind. So he shuffled out of the chapel into the hallway, where he slumped into a plush gold armchair, his chest pulled down to his knees. His face tightened; his expression became flat and vacant. He was unwilling, perhaps unable, to cry. Only his rust-colored eyes offered any hint of his anguish. He spoke to no one.

Craig's death, LaJoe believed, broke Lafeyette. From that day on, she said, he started thinking, "I ain't doing nothing. I could get killed, or if not get killed, I might go to jail for something I didn't do. I could die any minute, so I ain't going to be scared of nothing."

For weeks afterward LaJoe felt Lafeyette personally carrying the burden of Craig's death, as if there were something he might have done to help his friend. He rarely mentioned Craig. "I don't want nothing on my mind," he would say. Shutting out the past was perhaps the only way he could go forward or at least manage the present. Besides, he knew, nothing could bring Craig back.

He fell into a deep depression, collapsing in bed immediately after school and sleeping long hours. And when the outward grief diminished, his distrust of others built. He soon affected a long, jerky gait, his eyes locked on the ground. He no longer looked thirteen; his bobbing, cocky walk made him look older.

Many weeks after the funeral, in a rare moment, Lafeyette talked about Craig with a controlled anger that unnerved those around him. "He wasn't no gangbanger. They lied. If I was Craig's mama or daddy, I would of walked up to that police and shot him in the head the same way he did Craig. I hope the policeman dies."

The younger children quickly learned it was best to leave Lafeyette alone; he had become irritable and, on occasion, violent, like the time he punched Pharoah in the eye all because Pharoah had tried to finesse a seat by the window in a friend's car. "I'm gonna tell Mama," Pharoah threatened through his tears. "When we get outta here, nothing's gonna stop me from hitting you with a rock."

Lafeyette, despite his orneriness, shrugged and laughed nervously; he had not meant to hit his brother with such force. It was a period during which Lafeyette didn't seem in touch with himself; his anger and sorrow were tangled inside him, his moods shifting wildly.

Pharoah hadn't been as strongly affected by Craig's death. He figured the cop had just been doing his duty and had gotten the wrong guy. When tragedy struck, Pharoah didn't want to know. He continued to tell his mother he was too young to comprehend it all, as if he were trying to prolong his childhood. But he, too, worried about his brother. " 'Cause he's getting older, they'll probably try to use him in the gangs," he would say.

One evening Lafeyette, who hadn't talked much since the funeral, told LaJoe, "Mama, I'm real tired. I could go outside and don't have to come back. Anytime I go out, I ain't guaranteed to come back."

LaJoe felt Lafeyette had begun to recognize his own mortality, to come to terms with death. Once, he asked a friend whether he'd ever considered taking his own life—just walking in front of a car and ending it.

"Lafeyette be telling me how tired he is, and I always ask him this because I made a mistake with Terence once," LaJoe said. "Terence used to tell me he was tired, but I used to think he was tired from just being tired, and I'd say, 'Go lay down.' But Terence meant he was just tired with what was going on. So that made me in the habit of asking now when they say they're tired, 'What you mean?' "

A month later, amid a round of semiautomatic gunfire outside the apartment's window, LaJoe shepherded the triplets and Pharoah into the hallway for safety. She couldn't, though, get Lafeyette to join them. He continued to watch television on the small black-and-white set in his sister's room.

Twelve

THE six boys posed for the camera. Like royalty, Rickey sat slumped in a broad-backed wicker chair, his legs spread wide. His subjects surrounded him. Two knelt at his side. The other three stood behind him. All displayed four fingers, the sign of the Four Corner Hustlers. All looked cocky and defiant. Except for one. Dressed like the others—in jeans, starter jacket, and high tops— he had an expression of consternation. He looked like a wounded animal seeking help. He looked as if he didn't really want to be there. It was Lafeyette.

Rickey and Lafeyette hung out together a lot now, and that didn't bode well for Lafeyette. For $5 they had had this photo taken at the

Factory, a nightclub that catered to teenagers. The boys had begun attending the Factory on Friday and Saturday nights; it was a place to be among friends and dance and meet girls.

Rickey and his buddies formed the Four Corner Hustlers. They had commandeered a vacant apartment as a clubhouse and padlocked the door. Each boy wore an earring in his left ear. They weren't a real gang, as they didn't run drugs. For the most part they were young boys—only thirteen or fourteen years old. But they controlled their turf. They were like a training brigade for the real thing.

LaJoe felt the distance growing between herself and Lafeyette. He had, for one thing, become interested in girls. He'd been dating a girl named Red, and LaJoe warned him that he should use a condom when he was ready to have sex. He didn't want to be a father yet, she told him. Lafeyette said that he didn't want to have children, not for a long while, "not till I turn twenty-eight." It was to be the only time Lafeyette would talk openly with his mother about girls.

But it wasn't his interest in the opposite sex that worried LaJoe. She fretted, instead, about his friendship with Rickey. It wasn't that she still didn't find Rickey sweet and good-natured. Yet one afternoon she had watched from a street corner as he smashed the window of a stopped car and snatched the driver's necklace. She couldn't believe how brazen he'd been, and she told Lafeyette not to hang out with him. But Lafeyette didn't listen. And LaJoe didn't persist. When Lafeyette got sent home for wearing his earring and the school officials tagged him as a gang member, she felt him slipping away.

Rickey had grown more troubled. He and his friends had begun drinking cheap red wine and smoking marijuana. They also played with guns. Although Lafeyette spent time with Rickey, he didn't like hanging out with Rickey's friends and thought them too ready to fight. Lafeyette felt he could keep Rickey out of trouble. Maybe he could be a good influence.

A few weeks after Craig's death Lafeyette went to the stadium to park cars with Rickey. The two boys strolled by a new Hyundai that had a detachable radio. "You wanna get it?" Rickey asked. "No," replied Lafeyette, and kept on walking. Rickey followed. Even Rickey recognized Lafeyette's good influence. "Lafie's the best friend I have. He don't like getting in trouble. You have to con him. He tell me, 'You shouldn't do that, man. There ain't no cause for that.' "

Lafeyette denied belonging to a gang, and there was some truth in his denial. A group like the Four Corners only imitated their older counterparts. Had it been in another community, perhaps the gang would have been just a band of friends who occasionally got into mischief. But this was Horner. Such affiliation marked children. Lafeyette resisted, partly at the insistence of his mother. Yeah, he would concede, he hung out with the Four Corners, "but just 'cause I be with them don't mean I be in the gang. The people you thinking be nice, them the ones that gonna be in the gang."

Lafeyette had grown increasingly cynical. And in a child who has not experienced enough to root his beliefs, such an attitude can create a vast emptiness. He had little to believe in. Everyone and everything was failing him. School. The Public Aid Department. His father. His older brother. The police. And now, in a sense, himself.

JUDGE Francis Mahan's courtroom in the Skokie branch of the Cook County courts is clean and well lit—a stark contrast to the musty courtrooms in the main Criminal Courts Building in Chicago. The courts are so overburdened that the county has transferred many of its Chicago cases to Skokie. The prisoners are bused daily from the county jail, twenty miles away.

Judge Mahan's court was late getting started this morning of March 21. It gave Audrey Natcone some time to discuss Terence's case with the prosecution. She approached Casey Bartnik, the state's attorney who was handling Terence's charges. The two began to negotiate the terms of the plea bargain.

"What did we offer last time?" Casey asked innocently.

"Ten," replied Audrey.

"That sounds reasonable to me for two armed robberies."

"I haven't even seen the photos," Audrey said. "I'd like to see them before we make any decisions." She was still angry that the police had not honored her request for the lineup photos.

The state's attorney pulled from his briefcase a set of Polaroid shots of Terence, as well as two lineup photos. Ann Mitchell, the owner of the Longhorn Saloon, had identified Terence from the lineup pictures after first viewing the Polaroids. Audrey looked at the lineup photos, shaking her head. Terence stood at the end of the row of men, all of whom towered over him.

"Look at this!" Audrey said. "He's the tiny shrimp at the end. Will you look at this? Of course she picked him out."

"I'll tell you what. I'll give you eight," Casey conceded.

"Can't you give me six?" Audrey asked.

"Go to trial."

Audrey reminded Casey that these were Terence's first offenses as an adult and that he had a supportive home life. But the conversation ended there. Casey wouldn't come down from eight years.

TERENCE had asked LaJoe not to come this day. He didn't want to put his mother through any more pain. He saw how worried she was each time she came to court.

A deputy sheriff led Terence and the two other defendants into the courtroom. Terence glanced at neither the spectators nor the attorneys. The three stood shoulder to shoulder, facing Judge Mahan, their hands clasped behind their backs, as if they were still in handcuffs. The silver-haired judge talked in a low whisper to the two attorneys. At their request he consented to a private conference.

In the conference Judge Mahan agreed to the plea-bargain arrangements. If Terence pleaded guilty, the judge would sentence him to eight years. The prosecution would avoid a trial, and Terence would eliminate the possibility of getting more time. Audrey now had to convince Terence.

The two met for fifteen minutes in a back room. Terence remained silent through much of Audrey's explanation.

"Why don't you try to get me seven years," he muttered.

"I don't think I can, Terence. The best they're offering is eight."

"I can't bear with eight years. Maaan." He turned his head away.

"What's six months extra?" Audrey asked. Many prisoners in Illinois serve only half their sentence, since they're given one day off for each day of good behavior. Audrey noticed that Terence's eyes were red. She thought he was about to cry.

Audrey wished that Terence were older, a little more seasoned, so that he could see that it was in his best interest to take the eight years. She told him to talk with LaJoe about the offer. She felt his mother might give some sound advice. He agreed.

The judge granted Terence a two-week continuance so that he could talk to his mother.

ON TUESDAY, APRIL 4, TERENCE was sentenced, and Richard M. Daley was elected mayor. LaJoe would remember the date. The two had absolutely nothing to do with each other, and that's what bothered her. Maybe if the politicians cared, some of the neighborhood's lost children might be saved. The politicians' silence upset LaJoe greatly.

LaJoe had gone to the county jail a couple of weeks earlier to talk with Terence. She encouraged him to take the eight years. She couldn't endure a trial and the possibility that he might be sent away for a longer time. Terence listened to his mother.

Three days before his sentencing, Lafeyette and Pharoah, along with Tammie, Tiffany, Snuggles, Baldheaded, and Paul, visited Terence to say their good-byes. LaJoe went later in the day. Lafeyette donned a dapper blue silk suit that Terence had had made for himself when he was making money selling drugs. He wanted to show Terence that he was older, that he could take care of the family, particularly their mother.

It tickled Terence to see his brother so grown. The suit made him look like a young man. "It looks sharp, Laf," he mouthed through the thick glass. All Lafeyette could bring himself to say was, "I'm straight." He sat and listened to Terence for the rest of the visit, his eyes fixed on his brother behind the glass. Pharoah told Terence, "I love you." The visit, which was filled with awkward pauses, lasted half an hour.

LaJoe couldn't stop thinking of Terence. She tried to rationalize his imprisonment. It would be good for him to get off the streets, to get away from the drugs and the shootings. But she knew in her heart of hearts that prison wasn't much of an option. It would change Terence. He would lose his softness, his gentleness.

LaJoe had once described her three oldest children as red roses whose petals had wilted and fallen off. She wished she could give new life to those flowers. But she was tired of trying. And now she worried that her younger buds might never bloom.

LaJoe kept her grief to herself. She had no one, except Rochelle, to share it with. She didn't talk to her husband. And she no longer wanted to burden Lafeyette with her worries. Her insides, she said, "don't be nothing but threads. My children are my strength. They're my love. They're what I didn't have, and I had them to get it. And when they go away, it's like taking a part of me. My heart broke 'cause of what happened to Terence. It ain't too much more I could take."

PHAROAH WARNED FRIENDS OF THE human-headed cats in his building's basement. It didn't take much, given all that was found down there, to make that leap of imagination. When Gwen Anderson, the newly appointed housing manager of Horner, ventured into Horner's basements, she vomited. On April 20 Ms. Anderson wrote a memo to her superiors at the Chicago Housing Authority:

> During inspection of basements of buildings (6) in Henry Horner Homes Project, the following was found:
>
> An estimated two thousand (2000) appliances: Refrigerators—some new, some standing in pools of water and rusting away. Ranges—some stacked wall to wall, parts missing, standing in the water and rusting away. These appliances were heavily infested with roaches, fleas. Dead rodents and animals were lying in the storage areas, [and] stench abounded.
>
> Kitchen cabinets—some still in cartons—were sitting in pools of water, rusted beyond use, amidst dead animals, excrement and junk.
>
> According to one of the long-time employed resident janitors, most of the aforementioned have been in basements in Henry Horner Homes at least 15 years.

It was anybody's worst nightmare. For fifteen years people had been living over this mess, and the CHA had only now discovered it. These were the basements where LaJoe and her sisters had attended dances and roller-skating parties. Politicians had visited with residents here to listen to their complaints and to get their votes. Now these were the last places on earth anyone would want to spend time in.

The rotting carcasses explained the putrid odor rising from the Riverses' toilet. The pools of water explained LaJoe's backed-up kitchen sink—sewage had risen up through the pipes. But what most infuriated LaJoe were the brand-new ranges wasting away just a floor below her while for nearly a year her oven and broiler rarely worked.

It all was the perfect metaphor, LaJoe thought, for what was happening to her spirit.

Henry Horner now had 699 vacancies—188 more than last year—fueling speculation that the city had plans to tear down the complex to make way for a new stadium. In the high rises west of Damen the CHA discovered that heating coils were missing in every single building; none of the apartments could be heated come the cold weather.

And the early spring wading pool formed by a hydrant in front of LaJoe's building became a bottomless gulch. A boy waded into the muddy water and disappeared into an uncovered sewer opening. Luckily, some young friends pulled him out. The CHA called the city for a new manhole cover. It took three months.

PHAROAH and Porkchop ran up the three flights of stairs. Out of breath, they banged on Dawn's door.

"Who is it?" Dawn hollered.

"Pharoah and Porkchop," Pharoah hollered back.

She let in her cousin and brother. The two boys often came to visit Dawn, who had continued to live illegally in the building. In recent weeks, though, Dawn had been so depressed that she'd pretend she wasn't home. So the boys were glad when she came to the door.

"You got any quarters, D'won?" Pharoah asked, hoping for some change to play video games. Dawn shook her head. Pharoah and Porkchop lingered.

Pharoah admired and respected Dawn, but he couldn't understand why she still lived at Horner. After all, she had graduated from high school, and now she was attending a two-year college. Why was she still hanging around the projects? "That don't make sense," Pharoah would tell his mother. Lafeyette, too, was puzzled. "She should move," he'd urge. Dawn, who had placed her name on the housing authority's lengthy waiting list—public housing was all she could afford with four children—began to feel she was failing her family.

Since her graduation from Crane and the party at LaJoe's, it had been a struggle. She still lived with her boyfriend, Demetrius, but neither had a job, so they couldn't afford the money for a wedding. Dawn had hoped to find a retail job and had filled out applications at numerous clothing stores. She had also applied for a job with the county. But nothing materialized, so she remained on public aid.

Dawn's apartment was sparsely furnished. The living room was bare except for a battered stereo. She and Demetrius shared a mattress on the floor, with a color television at one end. They were saving up for the box spring. The four children shared two beds.

Despite these difficult times, Dawn continued to maintain a close-knit family. Demetrius was an attentive and loyal dad. As a teenager, he had been a member of the Disciples, but having children had slowed him down. He baby-sat while Dawn took classes in business administration at college, and he repaired cars to help supplement Dawn's income. Dawn and Demetrius never let their children out of their sight. Dawn read to them in the evenings or, when she could afford to, bought them Mother Goose tapes.

Pharoah and Porkchop glanced at the cartoons on TV. Dawn's four children were gathered on the mattress, entranced by the animation.

"What you do at college?" Pharoah asked his cousin.

"You pick your own days to go to school, your own credit hours."

"What are credit hours?" Pharoah asked.

"Each class is three credits."

"What if you pick four classes?"

"You get twelve credits," Dawn patiently explained.

Pharoah pondered that for a moment, then beckoned to Porkchop. "Let's go," he said. The two walked to the front door. It made Pharoah sad that Dawn hadn't gotten very far. It worried him to think that even if he made it through high school, he'd still be stuck in the projects. It worried him a lot.

"When you gonna get a job?" Pharoah asked.

"I'm trying," Dawn replied.

As Pharoah walked out the door he turned around, as if he'd forgotten to tell Dawn something. "Have a nice day," he called out. It had become one of his favorite expressions. "Have a nice day."

SUMMER 1989
Thirteen

ON FRIDAY, May 19, LaJoe and Rochelle taped the last of the streamers to the walls. Balloons hung from the ceiling, and party hats and party favors lay on the table. A gold paper crown sat to the side for the birthday boy. Eleven candles circled the strawberry shortcake, which read I LOVE YOU. FROM MAMA AND ROCHELLE.

A few weeks earlier, after Pharoah had attended a birthday celebration for a friend, he mentioned to his mother that he'd never had a party. So she decided to throw him one—and to keep it a surprise.

With summer fast approaching, LaJoe wanted to lift her spirits and her children's. She had finally made the last down payment on the bunk beds, and bought a handsome wooden table and chairs from the same used-furniture dealer. Pharoah particularly loved the wooden table; he told his mother it was the kind they had in mansions.

The triplets and Lafeyette traipsed home from school, wet from the spring downpour. Other youngsters, mostly the triplets' age, arrived. They awaited the birthday boy. Someone knocked on the locked door. The children, giggling, put their fingers to their lips. "Shh. Shh." Lafeyette moved to the side of the door and undid its lock.

"Surprise!" Pharoah shuffled into the living room, surprised and embarrassed by the attention. The children, about ten in all, quickly scattered. Pharoah's toothy smile lit his face. He didn't say anything. Instead, he walked back to his room and sat on the new bed, trying to take it all in. Lafeyette sat with him.

"I thought you forgot it," Pharoah told his mother, who had poked her head in the door. She rubbed the back of his head and gave him his present—a green shorts set. Pharoah put it on. With the suspenders and knee-length shorts, he looked quite handsome. He silently readied himself for the party: he found a new pair of white socks and scrubbed his face and hands; he ran gel through his hair and then secured the gold paper crown on his head.

"You look proper," Lafeyette told his brother. Rickey, who had been invited to the party by Lafeyette, wandered into the bedroom. "You look straight, Pharoah," he assured him. "Happy birthday."

"Thanks," Pharoah said. He didn't say much that afternoon. He mostly grinned and giggled. In Polaroid photos of the day his smile seems to cover his face. In one photo he stands behind his seated grandmother, who had come over for the party, with his arm affectionately around her neck. In another LaJoe steadies Pharoah's small hands as he cuts the cake with a big kitchen knife.

Once Pharoah had made his entrance into the party amid the screaming gaggle of kids, Lafeyette and Rickey sneaked out the door. Lafeyette told his mother he didn't want to hang around "no children's party." It was LaJoe's one disappointment. All the guests were much younger than Pharoah; no one his age came. He didn't have many good friends, except for his cousin Porkchop. But even he wasn't there. Throughout the festivities Pharoah asked, "Where's Porkchop?" Porkchop showed up two hours after the party had begun—he'd forgotten all about it. The two, as usual, embraced. "Happy birthday," Porkchop mumbled through his soft giggles.

The children danced to the rap music of L. L. Cool J, while Pharoah sat with his mother and grandmother as they admired his new outfit.

"Keep the kids inside," a panicky voice hollered to LaJoe. "Keep them here. Someone's figuring to get killed at four trey." Dawn had come by with her four kids. Four trey was how everyone referred to the building next door—1943 West Lake. LaJoe locked the door.

"Y'all stay inside, you hear," she told the children, who had momentarily stopped their dancing. Apparently there had been an altercation between drug dealers in the next building, but nothing more happened. The children resumed dancing. Dawn gave Pharoah a hug.

Just as Pharoah blew out the candles—after an off-key, half-shouted rendition of "Happy Birthday"—something heavy fell in the living room. The crash startled everyone. A relative of LaJoe's, who had passed out on the couch and had been there throughout the noisy party, had tried to get up to go to the bathroom. He didn't make it. He lay face down, urine seeping onto the linoleum floor.

Pharoah took Porkchop's hand, and the two went outside to get away from their drunken relative and the screaming kids. As they walked out the building's back door, they stopped. A teenage girl stood there vomiting. The two boys quietly walked around her. Pharoah hadn't stopped smiling.

At Suder's year-end assembly, Pharoah received two certificates: one for placing second in the school's spelling bee, the other for special effort in math and reading. His brother Timothy got three, Tammie received two, and Tiffany got one. Along with the certificates came ribbons. LaJoe was so proud of her children's accomplishments that she pinned all eight of the ribbons to her sweatshirt.

After the assembly Pharoah and his mother attended a meeting at which it was announced that Pharoah was one of twenty-five Suder students chosen for Project Upward Bound, a summer school at the University of Illinois designed to assist minority students in bringing up their math and reading scores. The Upward Bound staff described the program, then asked the assembled children what they wanted to be when they grew up. Pharoah knew—a Congressman.

"I want to change a lot of rules," he told the others. "I want to change them, and everybody move out of the projects. I'll pay people to build housing. Any gang member who has their hat turned, they'd go directly to jail. Stop stealing and stuff. A little kid got to come into a store with their parent or guardian, or they can't come in. They'd probably steal." He paused, then added, "If you be a Congressman, there be people guarding me so you won't get hurt. I like that."

LaJoe and the children got caught up in the warmth and beauty of those first few days of summer. Pharoah's and the triplets' awards at school had brightened the family's outlook. They offered promise of a better tomorrow. And everyone was thrilled with Pharoah for being picked for the summer program. He would come back with tales of the university campus that delighted LaJoe—of the students who seemed to be everywhere, carrying books. But it wasn't long before LaJoe was rudely reminded of summer's true character at Horner.

One afternoon, as she and Rochelle were walking down Washington Boulevard, two teenage boys she knew were walking on the other side of the street. Both wore red, the Vice Lords' color, in Disciples' territory. Two children—one no bigger than Pharoah—and a young man were tailing the teens. They'd duck into alleys and behind porches. LaJoe yelled to the teens that they were being followed, then watched in horror as the man handed a pistol to the little boy.

"Go kill the motherf_____," LaJoe heard him say. The boy aimed the pistol, his entire body straining just to hold it straight, and opened fire on the two teens. *Pow. Pow.* LaJoe and Rochelle ducked into a corner store for cover. The teens ran and escaped unharmed.

The incident angered and frightened LaJoe. How did that little boy even know whom he was shooting at? All he saw was a couple of people wearing red and their hats turned to the left. Later that day LaJoe ripped the red Louisville cap off Lafeyette's head and told him he couldn't wear any hats. No earrings either. She was putting her foot down. That could have been Lafeyette the boy was shooting at.

On July 13 the housing authority's new chairman, a black developer named Vincent Lane, met with the neighborhood's leaders. Twenty residents, most of them women, packed the apartment at 1900 West Washington that had been converted into an office for Horner's tenants' association. It had been many years since the group was a real force in the neighborhood, but its leader, Mamie Bone, could, when she wanted, make lots of noise and force a swift response.

The women sat on folding metal chairs fanning themselves to push away the still and heavy heat. They bristled with anger. It had taken them weeks to get a full account of the mess in their basements. They'd heard rumors, all right. Finally, though, when they couldn't get answers from the bureaucrats at the housing authority, Ms. Bone went to see Lane personally. She told him what she'd heard, and he began to ask around. He had heard nothing about the basements.

Gwen Anderson's April 20 memo had never reached him. Those who had received the memo held on to it, afraid they would get fired if Lane found out about the 2000 rusted ranges and refrigerators. When Lane learned of all this, he was outraged. And when he got hold of the memo, he got sick to his stomach. Nobody ever thought of the tenants, he fumed. Now he'd have to explain why everything had been so hush-hush and why nothing had been done.

The eighth head of the troubled agency in five years, Lane came to his job with few illusions. As early as 1965 the Chicago *Daily News* ran an extensive series on the Robert Taylor Homes, the city's largest development, detailing regular shootings and rapes, broken elevators, and apartments so overheated that children got nosebleeds. A steady stream of investigations of the CHA followed. Lane knew about all the exposés. Nonetheless, he was in for some startling surprises.

The most horrific surprise was the gangs' virtual control of public housing's high rises. Lane decided to reclaim some buildings. The first one he raided was in Rockwell Gardens, a few blocks west of Horner. With the help of sixty policemen, housing officials went from apartment to apartment looking for weapons and drugs. They confiscated only one gun and made no arrests. Lane learned later that someone in the CHA had tipped off the gangs the night before.

In subsequent months Lane got word from a drug dealer that if he wanted to take back the high rises at Rockwell Gardens, he could have them. The dealers would just move to the low rises at ABLA and other complexes—these didn't have a single entrance only, which could be enclosed and guarded. Lane heard about threats on his life. He was assigned two bodyguards. The CHA received a bomb threat. During one of the raids, which came to be known as sweeps, the police found two pounds of C-4 explosives and two electrical detonators—enough to blow up a considerable section of a high rise. This summer of 1989 Lane vowed to sweep all eight buildings at Rockwell and reclaim the entire complex. Then came Henry Horner.

At the meeting Lane told the women it would cost as much as $500,000 to clean the basements. But that wasn't all the money Horner would need. It would cost upwards of $400,000 to replace the stolen heating coils. Moreover, because the CHA didn't have the money to fix up apartments as tenants left, 85 percent of the units in some buildings sat empty. Sinks and toilets had been stolen, as had window frames—249 in all—which addicts sold for scrap.

"Now, I'll tell you, I can't wave no wands or anything, but we're going to make a difference," Lane said. "The gangbangers and drug dealers are eating this development alive. We've got to make these buildings manageable. I have the faith and belief that people in public housing are no different than anyone else."

Lane told the tenants he'd get the basements cleaned up. He'd fix the heating coils. He'd get the money. But what he couldn't tell them was that he wasn't sure what he'd do about the gangs and drugs.

JIMMIE Lee may have been gone, but as the residents knew all too well, there were many people waiting to fill in for him. No one stepped forward with the power and authority Lee had, but the drug trafficking continued, and the gangs battled for retail turf. Standing in their way was a new and determined CHA, led by Lane, so the gangs sent a message to him.

In late June the local management staff at Horner came under attack. The assistant manager had to fend off two teenagers with a camera he was carrying. The manager's 1989 Hyundai was vandalized. Two female maintenance employees were badly beaten by a group of teenage girls, and Gwen Anderson was shot at while escorting a group of U.S. Census workers through the development.

The shooting continued. Pharoah told his mother he hoped Lane would sweep their building. But it was only one of 125 Lane felt needed to be swept. To do all of them, he needed $30 million—money the CHA didn't have.

One night in July, amid the rat-a-tat of a semiautomatic weapon, LaJoe heard a noise in the hall. She turned to see what it was. In his sleep Pharoah was crawling in the hallway to escape the gunfire.

A few days later Pharoah told a friend, "I worry about dying—dying at a young age, while you're little. I'll be thinking about I want to get out of the jects. I want to get out. It ain't no joke when you die."

Fourteen

LAFEYETTE sat on the edge of his bed as he quietly folded his shirts and his slacks, and stuffed them into a cardboard box. His whole wardrobe fit without much fuss. Pharoah lay in bed and watched. LaJoe poked her head in the door.

"Come on, Laf, we got to get going," she said. She looked at the box next to Lafeyette and realized how scared he must be.

On June 2 Lafeyette had been arrested, along with four other boys, for allegedly breaking into a small Toyota truck parked by the stadium. Taken from the truck were two speakers, a radar detector, twenty music tapes, and a box of shotgun shells. Lafeyette insisted to his mother that he hadn't done it, that he was passing by when a boy he knew slightly smashed the truck window. He told her that he ran for fear of getting blamed. The police caught him and four others racing toward the safety of Horner. Today was their first date in court.

"They're not going to keep you locked up," LaJoe assured him. "They're just going to hear the case." But though she knew better, LaJoe got to worrying, too. What if they did lock Lafeyette up? What would she do? Could she last through another child's going to jail? LaJoe gathered herself before her fears overran her.

"Take that stuff out of that box, Laf. You ain't going nowhere. Now come on, I'll meet you outside." LaJoe walked out of the room.

Lafeyette didn't take his clothes from the box. Instead, he placed the box on the highest shelf in the closet.

"Don't you go wearing none of these," he instructed Pharoah, who remained tucked beneath the covers. "You hear me?"

"See you," Pharoah said softly. "Good luck." He, too, wasn't sure that Lafeyette was coming back.

EVER since the altercation at the stadium last December, Lafeyette hadn't been in any trouble with the police. LaJoe had watched him closely. As she had requested, he no longer wore a baseball cap or his earring. He stopped going to the Four Corners' building. He hung out with a fast crowd but excused himself when it looked as if things might get out of hand.

If anything, Lafeyette seemed to be spending more time in the house. He didn't trust going outside. Too much going on, he'd say. Too many wrongheaded people. But being cooped up inside the sweaty, noisy apartment wasn't without its tensions. LaShawn often left in the mornings and didn't return until nightfall. "I'll be back in five minutes," she'd tell Lafeyette or their mother. Then she wouldn't come back until evening. Lafeyette yelled at her for leaving Baldheaded and DeShaun behind. Though LaShawn denied taking drugs since the baby's birth, four months earlier, Lafeyette suspected her of still dabbling, and like his mother, he'd have none of it.

Late in the afternoon of June 2, Lafeyette went to the stadium with a boy named Curtis to watch the Chicago Bulls go in early for a play-off game. At the same time, Michael Berger, who worked for a catering service, pulled up to the stadium in his white Toyota four-wheel drive. A young boy, no older than fourteen, asked Berger whether he could watch his vehicle. Berger told him no. "I'd sure hate for something to happen to your truck, mister," the boy said. Berger locked the doors and pretended to set a burglar alarm.

Forty-five minutes later Berger came out to find police surrounding the truck, and the right window smashed. Whoever had broken in couldn't get the radio out, but had ripped the dash apart in trying. A few minutes later a police officer spotted five black teens running toward Horner. They started dropping things from their pockets: a screwdriver, a pair of pliers, and five of Berger's tapes. Though he didn't know who dropped what, the officer arrested all five boys, including Lafeyette.

THE Juvenile Temporary Detention Center, a five-story building a mile and a half south of Horner, takes up an entire block. Any child seventeen and under who has committed a crime is tried here unless the violation is heinous and violent, like murder or rape.

There are 250 probation officers and 137 state's attorneys, public guardians, and public defenders operating in Illinois's juvenile court system. The attorneys and judges are overworked. Public defenders frequently have only a few minutes to prepare for a case. Judges handle seventy-five to eighty cases a day.

The fourteen courtrooms line both sides of the first floor. The juvenile jail occupies the other four floors, housing up to 500 children. Some children have been sent here as many as fourteen or fifteen times. On the day Lafeyette went to court, Rickey was just completing a two-week stay here for a smash and grab.

LaJoe pushed her way through the center's revolving door. A quiet and despondent Lafeyette followed. All LaJoe could think about was how often she had walked through these doors with Terence straggling behind her. Now she thought, Here we go all over again.

The hearing was set for one thirty. They had gotten there fifteen minutes early. It was to be a long, anxiety-ridden day.

After they walked through the metal detectors, LaJoe and Lafeyette joined the four other accused boys and their mothers on a marble bench in the lobby. Two of the boys were called into a nearby office. A few minutes later Lafeyette was called. Each child who comes to juvenile court goes through an initial screening interview. It is a way to weed out cases that do not have to go to trial.

Lafeyette and LaJoe sat across a desk from Mr. Smith, a court official. Lafeyette told his version of the story, his voice barely audible. Mr. Smith didn't even seem to listen. He handed LaJoe a copy of the complaint and directed them to their courtroom—Calendar 7.

In a waiting room outside the sealed-off courtroom, LaJoe gave her name to the deputy sheriff in charge. He told her he'd call them when their name came up. That was at two thirty. Lafeyette and LaJoe sat on a bench, next to Curtis. Curtis' name was called around three thirty, and he left with his mother. Lafeyette waited.

At five thirty, four cases remained to be heard. The deputy sheriff asked LaJoe her name again. "Rivers," she replied, holding back her exasperation. Finally at six o'clock Lafeyette's case was called.

The courtroom held only the judge, the court reporter, the state's attorney, the public defender, and the deputy sheriff. Judge Robert E. Woolridge had his head buried in papers. He never so much as glanced at Lafeyette. The questions started coming faster than Lafeyette could think: "What's your name?" "When were you born?" "What's your address?" "Where does your father live?" "When did you last see him?" Lafeyette became so flustered that LaJoe had to answer. The judge handed out the trial date—September 8.

As LaJoe and Lafeyette left the courtroom LaJoe realized that the judge had given them a different court date from that of the other four boys. Had he made a mistake? She told the deputy sheriff, who told them to go back into the courtroom. When they did, LaJoe explained the situation to the judge. Judge Woolridge looked up from his papers. "What's the name again?" he asked Lafeyette.

"Lafeyette Rivers."

The judge looked bewildered. "Did we have a case by that name?"

LaJoe felt as if no one cared. It was as if they were invisible. No one saw them or heard them or treated them like human beings.

Lafeyette, though, was relieved. At least he was going home.

EARLIER in the summer Weasel brought home two pit bull puppies for Pharoah and Lafeyette. The boys kept them locked up in one of the bathrooms. Pharoah lost interest in his and gave it away. But Lafeyette took a liking to his dog. Ever since his time with Bird Leg, he relished the thought of owning his own. He called his Blondie.

One July afternoon Lafeyette came inside after hanging out on the porch with some friends. He went straight to the bathroom to say hi to Blondie and to take her out for a walk. The puppy wasn't there. "Anybody seen my dog?" Lafeyette yelled out to no one in particular. He walked up and down the hallway, poking his head into each of the bedrooms, calling, "Blondie, Blondie." He whistled for her, too, but got no response. "If my dog don't show up, I'm gonna snap," he muttered, loud enough for his mother and father to hear. His father was sitting on the couch watching a show on public television; his mother was at the kitchen table. "Somebody took my dog."

"Laf, there's nobody in here but me and your father. Who you talking to?" LaJoe asked.

"Mama, I ain't talking to you," Lafeyette said politely.

Paul knew what was going through his son's mind: Lafeyette suspected him of selling the puppy for drug money. He got to his feet.

"Son, if you continue to talk like that, to suspect me, I'm going to put you in your place." Lafeyette sat down at the kitchen table. He ignored his father's protestations. It was a familiar scene. Lafeyette just pretended his father wasn't there.

"Your dog's here somewhere," Paul said. "You have to look for it."

"You probably got it and sold it," Lafeyette accused.

"If I had, ain't nothing you could do about it," Paul challenged.

"I wish you'd stay out of our house. I don't know what you be coming back for. You be on the corner with all those dope fiends, embarrassing us."

"What'd you call me?" Paul walked over to Lafeyette, placed a firm grip on his shoulder, and shook him. "What'd you say?"

Lafeyette jumped up from his chair and backed up against the window. Paul reached for him again. "What'd you call me?"

Lafeyette's right fist came smashing into his father's temple. Paul reeled back, as much out of shock as pain, and then assumed the fighter's stance, his fists moving, circling his son.

"You're fourteen. You're of age. You want to be a man. Okay, you got a chance to be a man," Paul told his son. Lafeyette could hold his own, but certainly not with his dad. The jabs hit him sharply. In the shoulder. The chest. Open-palmed slaps got Lafeyette across the head. He didn't try to fight. He just tried to soften the blows. His eyes glared menacingly at his father, never losing contact.

"Y'all stop that!" LaJoe tried to break up the fracas. "Y'all stop it." She restrained Paul for a moment—enough time for Lafeyette to run for the front door. LaJoe and Paul said nothing to each other.

Minutes later Lafeyette appeared at the door. He held a steel chain in his right hand. "C'mon outside. C'mon outside," he yelled at his father. "I'm gonna kick your ass."

Paul jumped up from the couch and headed toward his son.

"No, Paul!" LaJoe screamed. "Don't go out there."

Paul hesitated. So did Lafeyette. "Boy, you don't know what you're up against." Paul pointed his finger at Lafeyette, who looked more scared than anything else. The last thing he wants is for me to come out there, Paul thought. He realized then he had made a big mistake. He felt ashamed for putting Lafeyette in such a squeeze.

"LaJoe, talk to your son, 'cause I'm having problems getting anything across to him." Paul shrugged and sat back down. Lafeyette took a step into the apartment.

"You dope fiend," Lafeyette muttered. "That's the reason why you ain't working now, because you're a dope fiend."

Paul's shoulders shrank. He knew no son would hit his father over a lost dog. It was the drugs. They had destroyed his relationship with LaJoe and now with his son. He had never hit Lafeyette before, except for occasional spankings when he was younger. It wasn't his nature. Now his own children were turning on him. He sank into the couch and didn't say a thing. Nor did Lafeyette, who continued to look for Blondie. He found her hiding under the stove.

Every morning Pharoah went off to summer school with energy and anticipation. He liked being on a college campus. He also liked being considered a scholar. But his brother was tired. The long summer days dragged, and Lafeyette talked a lot about getting out of Horner. He and his father, who came around even less now, ignored each other. Lafeyette kept to himself. He told his mother he'd stop hanging out with the wrong people. But he seemed on edge. He stopped confiding in his mother. He stopped confiding in anybody.

One early July evening, under a cool drizzle, a group of teenagers on Damen Avenue surrounded a fourteen-year-old boy. LaJoe happened to be walking by and could hear the taunts and then the sound of fists smacking. Then she heard a familiar voice. It was Lafeyette's. "Stop. Don't hit him. Stop." Lafeyette was in the middle of the fracas, trying to keep the others from beating his friend.

LaJoe ran to the circle and started making her way through. Lafeyette's friend was doubled over, gripping his stomach.

LaJoe was furious. "What y'all doing? Get off of him. What you beating on him for?" The teenagers seemed to listen only momentarily. One took a plank of wood and smacked the boy across the back. It looked as if they might take on her and Lafeyette next.

A voice rang out. "Don't hit my mama. Now y'all, don't hit my mama." It was a friend of Weasel's, a boy who, like others, LaJoe had nurtured as a child. "Let 'em go. Ya hear me. They're straight." The other boys listened. They dispersed. LaJoe sent the beaten boy home. She and Lafeyette walked back to their building.

LaJoe wiped Lafeyette's forehead where he'd been nicked with a broken bottle. His face was without emotion; the eyes stared straight ahead. He never cried. LaJoe would say, "When he laugh, you caught him off guard." His face seemed incapable of expression.

This evening, as they neared the porch, Lafeyette dropped to his knees. LaJoe wasn't sure whether he had slipped or whether his legs had just given out. "I'm tired, Mama," he said. She helped him to his feet. She wondered what he meant by tired. She remembered what Terence had once told her. She believed he was just tired of being.

The raindrops appeared incandescent in the midafternoon sun, like crystals falling from a chandelier. Pharoah stood by his bedroom window, mesmerized by them.

"Pharoah, let's get us some fries," Lafeyette said. Pharoah didn't hear. As was often the case, he was daydreaming. "Pharoah!" Lafeyette yelled, his adolescent voice rising. "Maaaan, Pharoah, you hear me?" In order to get Pharoah's attention, he started across his bed to smack him. But Pharoah heard him and turned around.

"It be raining," he said.

Lafeyette stuck his hand out the open window. "It ain't raining. Maan, you lying." Pharoah looked back outside. The rain, indeed, had let up. Bright rays of sunlight tore through the clouds like powerful spotlights; even the muddiest puddle seemed to sparkle.

"Come on, you going?" Lafeyette asked.

"Yeah," Pharoah replied.

On the way to a take-out hot dog stand on the corner of Damen and Madison, the two boys ran into Rickey, who asked whether he could join them. They hadn't seen much of him in recent weeks, especially after he had been arrested. They'd heard rumors that Rickey was running drugs for the older boys, making as much as $600 a week. Nonetheless, being fond of him, they invited him along.

At the hot dog stand, Rickey bought Pharoah a bag of cheese-coated french fries. Lafeyette bought his own. They stood in the parking lot in front of the stand relishing the cool, crisp summer air. Suddenly Pharoah got excited. He couldn't quite get the words out. His neck strained; his mouth worked hard. Finally he just pointed. A brilliant rainbow seemed to emerge out of Lake Michigan and arc over the Sears Tower, setting down just a mile or so south of Horner. It was the first rainbow the boys had ever seen.

All three—Pharoah, Rickey, and Lafeyette—stood in the parking lot munching on their fries, admiring the arc of colors.

"Daaag," Lafeyette muttered. "I thought it wasn't any real rainbow."

"L-l-l . . ." Pharoah tried again. "Let's . . . let's . . . let's . . . letsgochaseit." He spat the words out. "Letsgochasetherainbow."

"Maaan, I ain't gonna chase no rainbow," Lafeyette said, deriding his brother's loony scheme. "That's kiddie stuff."

"It . . . it . . . it . . . pro-pro-probably be some gold there," Pharoah said. "Maybe there be leprechauns."

"Shut up," Lafeyette said. "Ain't nothing there."

Rickey laughed heartily at Pharoah's imagination. He, too, thought there might be something there, but he didn't dare say so out loud.

Lafeyette might think him foolish. He'd heard, when he was younger, that if you got to the end of such a thing, you could dig and find some treasure. At thirteen, he held on, however tenuously, to that hope.

"I'll go, Pharoah. C'mon," Rickey said curtly.

"Go if you want. Don't make no sense," Lafeyette scoffed.

Pharoah and Rickey trotted south on Damen, their eyes following the rainbow's arc. It looked as if it might come down right around Cook County Hospital, about a half mile away. They alternately ran and walked. As they approached Crane High School, Pharoah noticed that clouds had begun to hide part of the rainbow. Then he realized it was beginning to fade. "The rainbow's leaving," he said to Rickey.

"Sure is," Rickey said. Pharoah ran faster. He hoped to get there before it disappeared altogether.

"I ain't chasing it no more, Pharoah. It's going," Rickey said.

Pharoah kept racing—ten, twenty, then thirty yards in front of Rickey, who was shaking his head, smiling, not letting his little friend get out of his sight. The rainbow vanished, its colors melting back into the sky. Pharoah craned his neck. Nothing. Dejected and exhausted, he walked slowly back to Rickey.

"Man, we could of seen what was there," he insisted. Rickey was too out of breath to argue. They walked back in silence.

Lafeyette was still in the parking lot, eating his fries, the setting sun warm on his back. He, too, had watched their treasure fade. "You was psyched out," he needled Pharoah and Rickey. "I told you so. Man, it stupid—chasing rainbows." Rickey laughed.

Eleven-year-old Pharoah said nothing. He couldn't believe how

Pharoah and
Lafeyette
on their
playground's
jungle gym.
*Despite all they
have seen and
done, they are
still children.*

close they'd come. He knew there might not have been anything at the rainbow's end, but he had wanted the chance to find out for himself. At the least, he figured, he could have made a wish. He had turned it over in his mind as he was running. Not until weeks later did he disclose what his request to the heavens would have been.

"I was gonna make a wish," he said. "Hope for our family, like get Terence out of jail, get out of the projects." When he disclosed his appeal, he had to stop talking momentarily to keep himself from crying. It hurt to think of all that could have been.

Lafeyette, too, conceded that he'd wondered about what they might have found at the rainbow's end. He had pooh-poohed the chase as kid stuff. But maybe Pharoah was right. Maybe they could have found something there. Heaped with disappointments, fourteen-year-old Lafeyette wanted to believe.

Maybe, he said later, "there be some little peoples, not more than just an inch." He held apart his skinny index finger and thumb. "I wish I could of found some real little peoples, and they'd of been my friends, went home with me. I wouldn't of told nobody."

SEPTEMBER 29, 1989

LaJOE grabbed Lafeyette's hand before they walked into the Juvenile Temporary Detention Center. She could see the fear in his tightly wound face. Last night he had asked, "Mama, what you think's gonna happen?" "They're gonna let you go," she had told him, only half believing it herself. As she caressed her son's thin hand this morning, she assured him that "everything's gonna be all right. You hear me?" Lafeyette looked away.

The two slowly pushed through the revolving door. Lafeyette hobbled along on crutches. The previous week he'd tripped over loose metal stripping on the stairwell in a friend's building, fallen down a full flight of steps, and torn a ligament.

In the waiting room at Calendar 14, LaJoe and Lafeyette met up with the four other accused boys and their relatives. The five boys barely spoke to one another. With the exception of two, who were cousins, they didn't know each other well. Lafeyette sat on a wooden bench, next to Curtis. The cousins sat on another bench. The fifth boy, Derrick, who Lafeyette said had broken into the car, sat by himself.

After a short wait their public defender, Anne Rhodes, called the five boys and the adults into a small room to explain their options. On first encounter, Anne Rhodes appeared hard boiled and curt, almost as if she didn't care. And because her caseload was so large, she had little time to befriend her clients. But Anne Rhodes' appearance and demeanor were deceiving. Unlike many public defenders, she chose to work here. What could be more redeeming, she thought, than defending troubled children from impoverished neighborhoods? Her two years here had been difficult and tiring. The children could be brash and unnerving. But there were moments—like the time a fifteen-year-old boy, on trial for mugging people with a fake gun, burst into tears in his mother's arms—when Anne was reminded that, whatever their misdeeds, they were still just children.

The adults stood against the room's white walls as the five boys huddled around the circular table. Anne began with her usual lecture. "There's going to be a trial. The person making a complaint against you will testify. Then you will. Just tell the truth. If you don't remember, don't be afraid to say you don't remember."

Curtis spoke up. "If I didn't do it, how come I have to sit up here with them?" he asked indignantly, nodding at his codefendants.

"Shut up," Anne shot back. She then chastised herself for her impatience. The irony in this instance was that she believed most of the five boys were innocent.

Anne continued to explain procedure for another ten minutes; then Lafeyette and the others returned to the waiting room. About half an hour later Anne again approached the group, explaining that the man whose car had been broken into, Michael Berger, was willing to make a deal. If each boy's family would pay him $100 in restitution, they wouldn't go to trial. Instead, the boys would be placed on supervision, which is essentially probation without a finding of guilt.

The boys and their parents had stopped listening. After hearing the amount $100, they had begun shaking their heads. "We're gonna go to trial," one mother said. "Where am I gonna get that kind of money?" another asked rhetorically. Anne had expected this response. It happened all the time. The victim comes to court figuring he might get reimbursed for his losses, but the families can't afford it.

Anne next met with the five boys without the adults. She had only five minutes to prepare for trial. She asked them what happened. She needed to figure out who should testify, who would be the most articulate. It was clear from seeing them together that they weren't all friends. That made it seem unlikely to her that they had all broken into this truck as an organized gang of kids. Moreover, they all seemed to have credible alibis—except Derrick, who conceded that he had asked the man whether he wanted his car watched.

Even with adequate time, trial preparation was difficult with children, Anne thought. They could rarely remember where they were on a particular day. Each day seemed like the next to them. And they often got flustered. In the end, she felt, children just wanted to please adults, so they would do what they could to that end. Anne chose the three most verbal boys to testify. Lafeyette was not one of them.

The deputy sheriff called the case. The five youngsters nervously lined up in front of Judge Julia Dempsey. Lafeyette pushed up his thin body on the crutches. As the judge determined the identity of each child, the boys stood erect, almost automatically placing their arms behind their backs. All LaJoe could think was that it looked as if they were handcuffed. Her stomach churned with anxiety. A court officer asked them if they swore to tell the truth. In unison they muttered, "I do."

The trial lasted about twenty minutes. Michael Berger testified as to what happened and what he had lost. He pointed out Derrick as the boy who had asked if he could watch the truck. "He told me he sure would hate for something to happen to my truck," Berger said.

Two police officers testified next. The first, Bill Freeman, was stationed at the Boys Club and knew the neighborhood children well.

"What happened when you arrived in the area?" the prosecutor asked Freeman.

"I observed five male black teens running northbound." Freeman pointed to the five boys, describing what each was wearing.

"What happened after you saw the minor respondents?"

"I ordered them to stop, and at that time they began dropping stuff from their pockets."

"Could you describe what stuff that was?"

"Screwdrivers, pliers. I couldn't tell which one dropped what."

"Did you recover any of this stuff?"

"Yes." Freeman said he also found five cassette tapes.

The next officer who testified had arrived on the scene after Freeman had apprehended the five boys. He testified that he had found part of the truck's radio on Derrick and, contrary to Freeman's testimony, that he had recovered the screwdriver and pliers from Curtis. In cross-examination Anne Rhodes tried to establish that the officer couldn't remember whether Curtis was wearing sweatpants or shorts. In later testimony Curtis said he was wearing shorts without pockets.

Anne called Derrick, Curtis, and one of the cousins to testify. Their alibis, filled with gaps and pauses, seemed unconvincing in the courtroom. When the state's attorney asked Curtis what store he was coming from, he replied that he didn't know the name of it.

"What did you buy at the store?" she asked the youngster.

"I can't recall that either. We just going up there," Curtis answered.

Anne argued that the evidence was "purely circumstantial." She also tried to point out some apparent contradictions in the police testimony. "Further, Your Honor," Anne continued, "there has been no eyewitness testimony as to anyone seeing these minors breaking into the truck. We believe the evidence falls woefully short of proof beyond a reasonable doubt. We ask for a finding of no delinquency."

Judge Dempsey, though, felt differently. She had seen many cases like this. Cars by the stadium got broken into all the time. The kids always denied they were involved.

"I have no doubt whatsoever that these minors broke in and took all those things," she told the attorneys. "I am going to enter a finding of delinquency against all five. Do any of them have any background?"

"No," the state's attorney replied.

"If they had background, I would have taken them into custody," the judge said. "I think they are really a big threat to the public . . . out there breaking into cars that are parked. The disposition [sentencing] date on all five is October eighteen."

Both Anne Rhodes and the state's attorney were surprised by the verdict. Anne truly believed that at least four of the boys were innocent. The prosecutor felt certain that the judge would find one guilty, but not all five. She, like Anne, was saddened by the huge volume of cases and the little time she had to prepare for them.

Lafeyette had thought the judge would lock them up, and his immediate reaction was relief. His face didn't show it, though. It looked angry. Angry that Derrick had not confessed his crime. Angry that he didn't have a chance to say he hadn't broken into the truck.

Angry that the judge said he had done something he adamantly denied doing. Though on crutches, Lafeyette was the first one out the courtroom door. He didn't linger. He hobbled ten feet in front of his mother until he left the building through the revolving door. There he waited, muttering something unintelligible.

"What'd you say?" LaJoe asked.

"Mama, I didn't do it," he insisted.

"They found everybody guilty."

"Ain't nothing you can do?" he pleaded.

"No."

Lafeyette raced ahead.

ONCE home, Lafeyette went straight to his room. He hadn't said anything since leaving the courthouse. An hour later Pharoah came home from school, his heavy book bag slung over his shoulder.

"Where's Lafie?" he anxiously asked his mother.

"He's in the back," LaJoe said.

Pharoah ran to his bedroom. LaJoe could see he was happy that his brother hadn't been locked up. He had been worried. The two brothers looked out for each other. Pharoah, in particular, now worried about Lafeyette.

As LaJoe sat on the couch braiding the hair of one of the triplets, she heard shouts from one of the back bedrooms. Lafeyette had lent Pharoah's Bulls T-shirt to Tyisha without asking.

"You better get it back!" Pharoah shrieked.

"I ain't gonna get nothing," Lafeyette huffed.

"Yes, you is!"

"No, I ain't!"

As LaJoe walked back to break up the fight she smiled. At least, she thought, I still have them both. At least they're still mine. She never thought it could be such a comfort to hear her sons arguing.

Epilogue

IT HAS been nearly a year since Lafeyette was found guilty of breaking into the truck. He was given a year's probation and was required to perform a hundred hours of community service at the Boys Club. After school he taught small children how to catch, and played games with them. Lafeyette loved being a big brother to small children. But his troubles didn't end with probation.

I helped get both boys into a private school a couple of miles west of Horner: Providence–St. Mel. All 500 students there are black; three quarters are from the surrounding neighborhood. The principal, Paul Adams, runs a strict school. No gangs. No drugs. No excessive absences or tardinesses. Over 90 percent of each graduating class goes on to college. Funding is a constant struggle, though. Half the school's annual $2 million budget comes from private sources.

Pharoah is thriving there. He likes being challenged and being given two hours of homework every night. But it hasn't all been easy for him. Behind in reading and math before he entered, he hasn't completely caught up. His one consistently good subject is, not surprisingly, spelling. His daydreaming and forgetfulness have sometimes interfered with school. There were times, for instance, when he forgot to complete assignments. Now he writes down upcoming events in a small notepad he calls his memo. Through the school he was awarded a full scholarship to a summer camp in Indiana.

For Lafeyette, Providence–St. Mel was more of a struggle. He was unable to keep up with the work, and returned to public school with two months left in the year. The year wasn't by any means a waste, however. Lafeyette discovered what it meant to be a student. And despite his poor grades, he learned a lot. He also learned to ask for help, something that is extraordinarily difficult for him.

But after just two months back in public school, Lafeyette was wrestling again with the lures of the neighborhood. He was caught smoking marijuana one morning before school, and on occasion he played hooky. After his mother was called to the school, Lafeyette promised to straighten up. LaJoe has kept a close eye on her son.

On June 19, 1989, Lafeyette, who had just turned fifteen, graduated from eighth grade. It was one of the few times he seemed truly at ease. He laughed and smiled and embraced his mother and friends with such warmth and spirit that everyone was filled with pride and hope for him. He plans to enter a parochial school that offers special assistance to children who have learning problems.

Rickey began running drugs for one of the local gangs, though he insists that he has since stopped. The Four Corner Hustlers slowly evolved into a gang that sold drugs, rivaling the Conservative Vice

Lords and the Disciples. A man in his early twenties, fresh out of prison, became the group's leader. Rickey and his friends continued to belong to the Four Corner Hustlers.

Last February the police caught Rickey with a long butcher knife. Since he was on probation for breaking into a car, they put him back in the Juvenile Temporary Detention Center for six weeks. His mother now checks Rickey's room every few days to make sure he isn't storing any guns. Rickey rarely attends school and spends many nights away from home. "I feel someone's gonna hurt him or he's gonna hurt someone if he doesn't get out of here," his mother says.

Lafeyette doesn't hang out with Rickey anymore, though they run into each other all the time. Lafeyette still worries about his friend.

If there is one constant at Henry Horner, it is the violence. In one two-week period in the spring, six people were shot, including a plainclothes detective. The proprietor of the hot dog stand where the boys first saw the rainbow was also shot. Pharoah and Lafeyette saw his body wheeled away on a stretcher. They presumed he was dead, but later, much to their relief, learned that he had survived.

Weeks later Lafeyette saw a friend run out of a building clutching his stomach and hollering, "I've been shot! I've been shot!" Lafeyette thought he was joking until the friend moved his hand, revealing a circle of blood. Lafeyette ran to the corner store to call an ambulance. None of these shootings made the newspapers.

Both Lafeyette and Pharoah want to move to a safer and quieter neighborhood. Lafeyette talks about it on occasion. So does Pharoah, who sat on his bed one day and cried because he worried that he might never get out of the projects.

LaJoe had told both boys she was going to try to move before Terence came back to Horner. In the spring it seemed as if she'd found a way. Through friends she contacted a man named Robert Curry, who told her that for $80 he could get her name on the top of a waiting list for subsidized housing. She gave Curry the money and met with him regularly. But it wasn't to be. As the promises flowed and the time dragged, LaJoe became suspicious. Finally she went to check out the building where she was promised an apartment. It didn't exist. That same day Curry was arrested. His was the second housing scam uncovered that year. Humiliated and depressed, LaJoe planned to testify at Curry's trial.

Some things have improved. Chicago Housing Authority employees, wearing moon suits and gas masks, cleaned the basements at Henry Horner. In the Riverses' apartment the bathtub faucet no longer runs day and night. Also, LaJoe got a new stove, as well as paint, which she and Lafeyette used to put a fresh coat on the walls in the kitchen and in two bedrooms.

Vincent Lane, the CHA's director, reclaimed all eight buildings at Rockwell Gardens. Each high rise now has round-the-clock security guards. The complex has new playground equipment, and in the spring the area is awash in pink and red begonias, and white and pink rosebushes. CHA employees there wear buttons that read I'M PART OF THE SOLUTION. Lane would still like to sweep Henry Horner and the other nineteen complexes, but money from the Department of Housing and Urban Development has not been forthcoming.

Dawn and Demetrius, who had been evicted from Horner and had moved back to her mother's, finally got an apartment—in the ABLA Homes. They're doing everything they can to get by. Dawn got pregnant again and now has a new son, named Demone. Although she hasn't found permanent work, she spent six weeks, while pregnant, going door to door for the U.S. Census. Demetrius continues to watch the kids and lands an occasional job repairing cars. They rarely visit Horner.

Terence expected to get out of prison sometime in 1991. He has earned his high school equivalency and writes regularly to his family. LaShawn, Brian, and their three children live with LaJoe. Paul—Weasel—the boys' oldest brother, moved out of the apartment with his girlfriend. They got their own apartment elsewhere in Horner. Paul, the boys' father, found a part-time job with a moving company. After his first few days on the job he was able to give LaJoe money to buy Tammie and Tiffany sandals for the July Fourth holiday.

About the Authors

BOB WOODWARD's name is synonymous with the best in investigative journalism. An assistant managing editor of the Washington *Post,* he is the author of five books about the workings of our nation's capital, including the Watergate classic, *All the President's Men* (written with Carl Bernstein); *Veil: The Secret Wars of the CIA 1981–1987;* and *The Brethren* (written with Scott Armstrong), about the Supreme Court. Like his previous books, *The Commanders* is a national best seller. Woodward lives in Washington, D.C., with his wife, Elsa Marsh.

DENNIS B. LEVINE (left) maintains a connection with Wall Street as president of the ADASAR Group, the financial advisory firm he launched after his release from federal prison. *Inside Out* represents the first time he has told the story of the experiences that brought him national attention. He and his family still live in their Park Avenue co-op in New York City. **WILLIAM HOFFER** has co-authored a number of other nonfiction books, including *Midnight Express, Not Without My Daughter,* and *Adams v. Texas.*

RALPH G. MARTIN, a noted biographer and journalist, has spent the last three decades chronicling the lives of a number of celebrated figures, among them Eleanor and Franklin Roosevelt, the Windsors, Golda Meir, and Charles and Diana. His two-part biography, *Jennie: The Life of Lady Randolph Churchill*, spent months on best-seller lists and was made into an acclaimed public television series. Martin has written for many national magazines and newspapers. A native of Chicago, he lives in Westport, Connecticut.

ALEX KOTLOWITZ, a *Wall Street Journal* reporter, won the Robert F. Kennedy Journalism Award for the articles on which *There Are No Children Here* is based. To write the book, Kotlowitz took a leave of absence from the *Journal*'s Chicago bureau and spent nearly every day of seven months at the Henry Horner Homes with Lafeyette and Pharoah. LaJoe Rivers has now succeeded in moving her family out of the projects. All proceeds from the sales of this book are going into a trust fund the author has established for the two boys' education.

CREDITS